THE BRITISH CINEMA BOOK

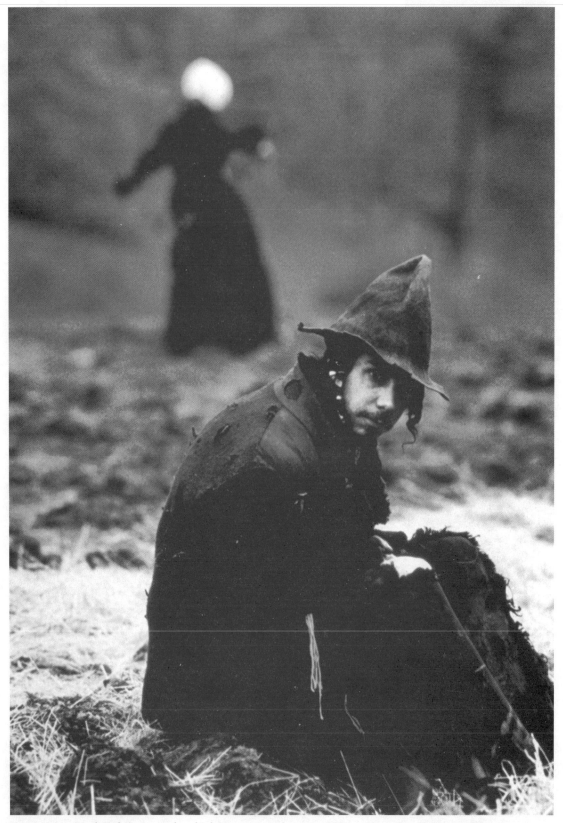

Simon Magus (Noah Taylor) contemplates his lot as outcast and scapegoat (*Simon Magus*, Ben Hopkins, 1999)

THE BRITISH CINEMA BOOK

3rd Edition

Edited by Robert Murphy

A BFI book published by Palgrave Macmillan

For Rosie, Urs and Zora Feurer

First published in 2008 by
PALGRAVE MACMILLAN

on behalf of the

BRITISH FILM INSTITUTE
21 Stephen Street, London W1T 1LN
<www.bfi.org.uk>

There's more to discover about film and television through the BFI.
Our world-renowned archive, cinemas, festivals, films, publications and learning resources are here to inspire you.

Palgrave Macmillan in the UK is an imprint of Macmillan Publishers Limited, registered in England, company number 785998, of Houndmills, Basingstoke, Hampshire RG21 6XS. Palgrave Macmillan in the US is a division of St Martin's Press LLC, 175 Fifth Avenue, New York, NY 10010. Palgrave Macmillan is the global academic imprint of the above companies and has companies and representatives throughout the world. Palgrave® and Macmillan® are registered trademarks in the United States, the United Kingdom, Europe and other countries.

Cover design: couch
Cover image: *This Is England* (Shane Meadows, 2007 © Warp Films/© FilmFour/© UK Film Council/© EM Media/© Screen Yorkshire
Text design: couch
Set by Cambrian Typesetters, Camberley, Surrey
Printed in China

This book is printed on paper suitable for recycling and made from fully managed and sustained forest sources. Logging, pulping and manufacturing processes are expected to conform to the environmental regulations of the country of origin.

British Library Cataloguing-in-Publication Data
A catalogue record for this book is available from the British Library

ISBN 978–1–84457–275–5 (pb)
ISBN 978–1–84457–276–2 (hb)

Contents

Acknowledgments

I would like to thank Sophie and Edward Noel, Richard Dacre, Anne and Jerry Eardley, Jo Mills, Jill Nelmes, Chris Goldie, Steve Chibnall, Geoff Brown, Tim O'Sullivan, Andrew Spicer, Ewa Mazierska, Tracy Scoffield, Emily O'Toole, Honey Salvadori, Pius Hume, Helen Gray, Sean and Tessie O'Mahoney, Dave Walley, Michael Wilson, Nicholas O'Sullivan, and the ever-helpful staff of the BFI Library. Also, Chantal Latchford for her diligent editing and, of course, my forty-four contributors who have responded to my badgering with intelligence and good humour. I am also particularly grateful to Markku Salmi, Richard Chatten, Richard Dacre and Jim Robertson, for their zealous eradication of wrong dates, misspelt titles and dubious facts.

Notes on Contributors

Ian Aitken is Associate Professor of Film Studies at Hong Kong Baptist University. He is author of *Film and Reform: John Grierson and the Documentary Film Movement* (1990), *European Film Theory and Cinema* (2001), *Alberto Cavalcanti: Realism, Surrealism and National Cinema* (2001), *Realist Film Theory and Cinema: The Nineteenth-Century Lukácsian and Intuitionist Realist Traditions* (2006), and editor of *The Documentary Film Movement: An Anthology* (1998) and *Encyclopedia of the Documentary Film* (2006).

Charles Barr's writings on British cinema include *Ealing Studios* (3rd edn, 1999) and *English Hitchcock* (1999), and he had a joint script credit with Stephen Frears for *Typically British*, the centenary history of British cinema broadcast on Channel 4 in 1995. After working for many years at the University of East Anglia in Norwich, he is now Visiting Professor at University College Dublin.

Geoff Brown writes film and music criticism for *The Times*. Studies of British cinema include *Walter Forde* (1977), *Launder and Gilliat* (1977), *The Common Touch: The Films of John Baxter* (1989) and contributions to *The Unknown 1930s* (1998) and *British Cinema of the 90s* (2000). He was associate editor of *Directors in British and Irish Cinema* (2006).

William Brown is currently Lecturer in Film Studies at the University of St Andrews. He recently completed a doctoral thesis at the University of Oxford on the use of digital special effects technology in contemporary cinema. His interests and research also include French cinema and questions of British national identity.

Stella Bruzzi is Professor of Film and Television Studies at the University of Warwick. Her books include *Undressing Cinema: Clothing and Identity in the Movies* (1997), *New Documentary* (2000 and 2006), *Bringing Up Daddy: Fatherhood and Masculinity in Postwar Hollywood* (2005) and *Seven Up* (2007).

Jon Burrows is an Associate Professor in the Department of Film and Television Studies, University of Warwick. He is the author of numerous essays and articles on different aspects of silent British cinema and also the book *Legitimate Cinema: Theatre Stars in Silent British Films, 1908–1918* (2003).

James Chapman is Professor of Film Studies at Leicester University. His books include *Licence to Thrill: A Cultural History of the James Bond Films* (1999; 2007), *Past and Present: National Identity and the British Historical Film* (2005), *Inside the Tardis: The Worlds of 'Doctor Who' – A Cultural History* (2006) and *War and Film* (2008). He is also the co-editor of *The New Film History: Sources, Methods, Approaches* (2007). He is a council member of the International Association of Media and History and is book reviews editor for the *Journal of British Cinema and Television*.

Steve Chibnall is Professor of British Cinema at De Montfort University, Leicester. He has written numerous articles on British cinema and is author of *Law-and-Order News* (1977), *Making Mischief: The Cult Films of*

Pete Walker (1998), J. Lee Thompson (2000), Get Carter (2003), Brighton Rock (2004); and co-editor of British Crime Cinema and British Horror Cinema. His latest book is Quota Quickies: The Birth of the British 'B' Film (2007).

Pamela Church Gibson is Reader in Cultural and Historical Studies at the London College of Fashion, within the University of the Arts, London. She has published extensively on film, fashion, fandom, heritage and history, and has co-edited three collections of essays including The Oxford Guide to Film Studies (1998). Her current project is a monograph on cinema, cities and consumption. Her most recent anthology More Dirty Looks: Gender, Pornography and Power, was published in 2003.

Ian Conrich is Director of the Centre for New Zealand Studies, Birkbeck, University of London. He has written for Sight and Sound and the BBC, and is the author of Contemporary New Zealand Cinema: From New Wave to Blockbusters (2008). He has edited or co-edited eleven books, including The Technique of Terror: The Cinema of John Carpenter (2004), and the forthcoming Horror Zone: The Cultural Experience of Contemporary Horror Cinema.

Richard Dacre has written and lectured widely on British cinema and is the author of Trouble in Store: Norman Wisdom – A Career in Comedy (1991). He was a member of the Other Cinema Collective and managed the Scala Cinema before becoming the proprietor of Flashbacks Movie Poster mail-order business and archive. He also runs the distribution company Respectable Films.

Raymond Durgnat was Visiting Professor at East London University after a Cloister-and-the-Hearth alternation between the film industry and the groves of academe, having been Visiting Professor at UCLA, UC Berkeley and Columbia University, and sometime Staff Writer at the Associated-British Picture Corporation, Literary Adviser for MGM-British, Iris TV, Elstree Distributors, etc. His writings on British cinema include A Mirror for England: British Cinema from Austerity to Affluence (1970) and The Strange Case of Alfred Hitchcock (1974). He died in May 2002.

Allen Eyles is a film historian who edits the Cinema Theatre Association magazine Picture House and formerly edited Focus on Film and Films and Filming. He has written numerous career studies, including Humphrey

Bogart (1990) and The Complete Films of the Marx Brothers (1992), as well as many books on cinemas, including ABC: The First Name in Entertainment (1993), Gaumont British Cinemas (1996), The Granada Theatres (1998), Odeon Cinemas 1: Oscar Deutsch Entertains Our Nation (2002) and Odeon Cinemas 2: From J. Arthur Rank to the Multiplex (2005).

Christine Geraghty is Professor of Film and Television Studies, University of Glasgow. She has written extensively on film and television with a particular emphasis on gender and genre. Her publications include British Cinema in the Fifties (2000) and Now a Major Motion Picture: Film Adaptations of Literature and Drama (2008). Her study of My Beautiful Laundrette was published in 2004.

Christine Gledhill is Professor of Cinema Studies, University of Sunderland. She has written extensively on feminist film criticism, melodrama and British cinema. Her most recent publications include her co-edited anthology with Linda Williams, Reinventing Film Studies (2000), Reframing British Cinema 1918–1928: Between Restraint and Passion (2003) and various essays on British cinema, genre and Irish cinema, and the screen actress from silence to sound.

Kevin Gough-Yates has done all sorts of things including teaching at the University of Westminster, working for Channel 4, and being Visiting Reader at Southampton.

Sheldon Hall is a Senior Lecturer in Film Studies at Sheffield Hallam University. He is the author of Zulu: With Some Guts behind It – The Making of the Epic Film (2005), co-author with Steve Neale of Epics, Spectacles and Blockbusters: A Hollywood History (forthcoming), has contributed articles on various aspects of cinema to books and journals including Film History, and provided audio commentaries on the Paramount Home Entertainment DVDs of Zulu and Once Upon a Time in the West.

Benjamin Halligan is a Senior Lecturer in the School of Media, Music and Performance, University of Salford. He is the author of a critical biography of Michael Reeves (2004) and is currently preparing studies on Aleksandr Sokurov and film and globalisation.

Sue Harper is Professor of Film History at Portsmouth. She is the author of Picturing the Past: The

Rise and Fall of the British Costume Film (1994), *Women in British Cinema: Mad, Bad and Dangerous to Know* (2000), and with Vincent Porter, *British Cinema of the 1950s. The Decline of Deference* (2003 and 2007). She is also co-editor, with James Chapman and Mark Glancy, of *The New Film History* (2007), and is heading up a major AHRC Research Project on 1970s British cinema.

Erik Hedling is Professor of Comparative Literature at Lund University, Sweden. He is the author of *Lindsay Anderson: Maverick Film-Maker* (1998), *Filmanalys* (1999), and *Brittiska fiktioner: Intermediala studier i film, TV, dramatik prosa och poesi* (2001). He is the editor of *Blågult flimmer: svenska filmanalyser* (1998) and the co-editor of *Filmteori 1 and 2* (1995), *Interart Poetics: Essays on the Interrelations of the Arts and Media* (1997), and *Cultural Functions of Intermedial Exploration* (2002), *Solskenslandet: svensk film på 2000-talet* (2006) and *Välfärdsbilder: svensk film utanför biografen* (2007).

Andrew Hill is Research Fellow in Visual Culture in the Centre for Research in Socio-Cultural Change at the Open University. He has published on several aspects of culture and politics and is the author of *Re-imagining the War on Terror* (2009).

John Hill is Professor of Media at Royal Holloway, University of London. His publications include *Sex, Class and Realism: British Cinema 1956–63* (1986); *Cinema and Ireland* (co-author, 1987); *The Oxford Guide to Film Studies* (co-editor, 1998); *British Cinema in the 1980s* (1999) and *Cinema and Northern Ireland* (2006).

Peter Hutchings is Professor of Film Studies at the University of Northumbria. His books include *Hammer and Beyond* (1993), *Terence Fisher* (2002), *Dracula* (2003) and *The Horror Film* (2004), and he has also written numerous articles on British cinema.

Nick James is the editor of *Sight and Sound*. A former rock musician, he found a second career in film journalism at the London listings magazine *City Limits*, where he became film editor in 1991. He joined *Sight and Sound* as deputy editor in 1995 and has been editor since 1997. His book on Michael Mann's *Heat* was published in the BFI's Modern Classics series in 2002. He was the presenter of the BBC documentary *British Cinema: The End of the Affair* that same year.

Barbara Korte is Professor of English Literature at the University of Freiburg, Germany. Recent publications include work on the British short story, English travel writing, Black and Asian British culture and the cultural reception of World War I. She is editor of the *Penguin Book of First World War Stories*.

Marcia Landy is Distinguished Professor of English and Film Studies at the University of Pittsburgh. Her publications include *Fascism in Film: The Italian Commercial Cinema, 1930–1943* (1986); *British Genres, 1930–1960* (1991); *Imitations of Life: A Reader on Film and Television Melodrama* (1991); *Film, Politics, and Gramsci* (1994); *Queen Christina* (with Amy Villarejo, 1996); *Cinematic Uses of the Past* (1996); *The Folklore of Consensus: Theatricality in Italian Cinema, 1930–1943* (1998); *Italian Film* (2000); *The Historical Film: History and Memory in Media* (with Lucy Fischer, 2003); *Monty Python's Flying Circus* (2005); and *Stardom Italian Style: Screen Performance and Personality in Italian Cinema* (2008).

Alan Lovell taught Film at Staffordshire University until his retirement. He has written widely on British cinema and television topics, including books and articles on the documentary film, Lindsay Anderson, Karel Reisz, British television drama and the contemporary independent film and television movement. He has also worked in the independent film and television sector.

Brian McFarlane is Honorary Associate Professor in the English Department at Monash University, Melbourne and Visiting Professor, Film Studies, University of Hull. His books include *Novel to Film: An Introduction to the Theory of Adaptation* (1996), *An Autobiography of British Cinema* (1997), *Lance Comfort* (1999) and *The Encyclopedia of British Film* (2003, 3rd edn, 2008).

Martin McLoone is Professor of Media Studies at the University of Ulster. He is the author of *Film, Media and Popular Culture in Ireland: Landscapes, Cityscapes, Soundscapes* (2007) and *Irish Film: The Emergence of a Contemporary Cinema* (2000). He has also edited *Broadcasting in a Divided Society: 70 Years of the BBC in Northern Ireland* (1996) and *Culture, Identity and Broadcasting in Ireland: Local Issues, Global Perspectives* (1991), and co-edited *Irish Films, Global Cinema* (with Kevin Rockett, 2007), *Big Picture, Small Screen: The Relations between Film and Television* (with John Hill, 1996), *Border Crossing: Film in Ireland, Britain and Europe* (with John Hill and Paul Hainsworth, 1994) and *Television and Irish Society* (with John MacMahon, 1984).

Andrew Moor is Reader in Film History & Theory at Manchester Metropolitan University. He is the author of *Powell and Pressburger: A Cinema of Magic Spaces* (2005) and the co-editor (with Ian Christie) of *The Cinema of Michael Powell: International Perspectives on an English Film-maker* (2005). He has written on various aspects of British and queer cinema.

Robert Murphy is Professor in Film Studies at De Montfort University and the author of *British Cinema and the Second World War* (2000) and other books on British cinema. He edited *Directors in British and Irish Cinema* (2006).

Lawrence Napper gained his PhD from the University of East Anglia in 2001. He currently teaches at King's College (London) and at the University of Greenwich. His book on *British Cinema and Middlebrow Culture* is due to be published by the University of Exeter Press in 2008.

Michael O'Pray is a Professor in the School of Art and Design, University of East London. He edited *Andy Warhol: Film Factory* (1989), *The British Avant-Garde Film 1926–1995: An Anthology of Writings* (1996) and (with Jayne Pilling) *In the Pleasure Dome: The Films of Kenneth Anger* (1989). He is the author of *Derek Jarman: Dreams of England* (1996) and numerous articles on avant-garde cinema.

Jim Pines teaches Media Arts at the University of Bedfordshire. He is editor of *Black and White in Colour* (1992) and co-editor with Paul Willemen of *Questions of Third Cinema* (1989).

Vincent Porter is Emeritus Professor of Mass Communications at the University of Westminster and Visiting Research Professor in Film History at the University of Portsmouth. He is co-author, with Sue Harper, of *British Cinema of the 1950s. The Decline of Deference* (2003 and 2007), author of *On Cinema* (1985) and co-editor of *British Cinema History* (1983). He has written many journal articles, including 'All Change at Elstree: Warner Bros., ABPC and British Film Policy 1945–1961', for which he was awarded the Carfax-IAMHIST prize for the best article to appear in the

Historical Journal of Film, Radio and Television during 2001.

Tim Pulleine is on the editorial staff of the *Guardian* and has written extensively on the cinema for that newspaper and for various publications, including *Sight and Sound*, *Monthly Film Bulletin* and *Films and Filming*.

Jeffrey Richards is Professor of Cultural History at Lancaster University, author of *Films and British National Identity* (1997) and co-author of *Britain Can Take It* (3rd edn, 2007).

James C. Robertson, a retired teacher, is the author of *The British Board of Film Censors: Film Censorship in Britain, 1896–1950* (1985), *The Hidden Cinema: British Film Censorship in Action, 1913–1972* (1989), *The Casablanca Man: The Cinema of Michael Curtiz* (1993) and (with Anthony Aldgate) *Censorship in Theatre and Cinema* (2005). He has also written a number of articles on cinema history and interwar international affairs.

Tom Ryall is Emeritus Professor of Film History at Sheffield Hallam University. His books include *Alfred Hitchcock and the British Cinema* (1986 and 1996), *Britain and the American Cinema* (2001) and *Anthony Asquith* (2005).

Justin Smith is Principal Lecturer in Film Studies at the University of Portsmouth. Recent publications include a chapter on web ethnography in *The New Film History* (2007). He is currently writing a book based on his PhD entitled *Cult Films and Film Cults in British Cinema, 1968–86*.

Andrew Spicer is Reader in Cultural History at the University of the West of England. He is the author of *Typical Men: The Representation of Masculinity in Popular British Cinema* (2001), *Film Noir* (2002), *Sydney Box* (2006) and the editor of *European Film Noir* (2007), as well as numerous articles on British cinema.

Claudia Sternberg is Lecturer in Cultural Studies at the University of Leeds. She is author of *Written for the Screen: The American Motion-Picture Screenplay as Text* (1997) and co-author with Barbara Korte of *Bidding for the Mainstream? Black and Asian British Film since the 1990s* (2004).

Sarah Street is Professor of Film at the University of Bristol. Her books include: *British National Cinema*

(1997), *British Cinema in Documents* (2000), *Transatlantic Crossings: British Feature Films in the USA* (2002), *Black Narcissus* (2005) and *Film Architecture and the Transnational Imagination: Set Design in 1930s European Cinema* (with Tim Bergfelder and Sue Harris, 2007).

Melanie Williams is Lecturer in Film Studies at the University of Hull. Her work on British cinema has appeared in *Screen*, *Cinema Journal*, *Sight and Sound*, *Journal of British Cinema and Television*, *Film Quarterly* and the *Independent*, as well as the edited collections

British Cinema of the 1950s: A Celebration (2003) and *24 Frames: The Cinema of Britain and Ireland* (2005). She is currently working on a book about the films of David Lean and co-editing a collection of essays on the British women's film.

Linda Wood is a freelance writer and researcher whose publications include *Maurice Elvey and British Films 1927–1939* (1987); she has edited the London Film Festival Official programme, and is co-ordinating an oral history on Elstree Studios.

Introduction

Robert Murphy

It is over ten years since the first edition of *The British Cinema Book* was published. It was deemed necessary because the teaching of British cinema was becoming widespread and the two collections of essays on the subject, Charles Barr's *All Our Yesterdays* (1986) and Vincent Porter and James Curran's *British Cinema History* (1983), though full of interesting and original essays made no attempt to provide anything like comprehensive coverage of the subject. The last general histories of British cinema, George Perry's *The Great British Picture Show* (1974) and Roy Armes's *A Critical History of British Cinema* (1978) had become dated, and though Sarah Street's *British National Cinema* (1997), and subsequently Amy Sargeant's *British Cinema: A Critical and Interpretive History* (2005), offer useful insights, neither attempt the task of providing a comprehensive history. This is probably impossible now in a single volume; what *The British Cinema Book* attempts to do is to provide introductory essays on a rich variety of topics that together offer an overview of the major issues, history and debates about British cinema.

The choice of essays for the first edition was to some extent determined by who and what was available; back in 1997 British cinema was still a minority interest. By 2001 there had been an upsurge, reflected in the twelve new pieces, which ranged from Jon Burrows's examination of the Stoll Film Company in the 1920s to Steve Chibnall's assessment of the wave of crime films that hit British cinema at the end of the 20th century. In 1997 it would have been difficult to interest more than a very small core of enthusiasts in studio production in the 1920s, or to imagine that British cinema was ever again to attempt to storm the box office with popular genre films. Now the early history of British cinema is celebrated annually at the increasingly popular and prestigious Nottingham Silent Cinema Festival; and the production of low-budget genre films has continued, with Mike Hodges's *I'll Sleep When I'm Dead* (2003), Shane Meadows's *Dead Man's Shoes* (2004) and Paul Andrew Williams's *London to Brighton* (2006) taking the crime film into more interesting areas and horror enjoying an unexpectedly successful revival.

British cinema seems to be an ever-expanding field and it would have been possible to publish a third edition double the size of the second. New pieces were suggested on Scottish, Irish and Welsh cinema; on films set in London and films set in provincial cities; on actors, directors, art directors, cinematographers, editors, scriptwriters and producers; on music and musicals; on animation; on cinemagoing and audiences. Those that actually materialised concern the rich flowering of British silent films at the end of the 1920s and the surprisingly interesting films of the late 1960s; the representation of women in 1950s cinema and of gay men in mainstream British films; the upsurge of British Asian cinema which began in the 1990s; the phenomenon of British cult cinema and of post-British cinema; and a survey of the new generation of British films and filmmakers that has emerged since the mid-1990s. In several of the existing essays, contributors have inserted 500-word case studies on individual films that exemplify the concerns of their essay. Most of these films are available on DVD (though a few which are not have been included in the hope that they will soon become so).[1]

Enthusiasm for British cinema spilt out into the mainstream in 2007, when the BBC and the Film

Council organised a 'Summer of British Film', the high point of which was a seven-part series, 'British Film Forever'. Ill-informed and dull, it probably prejudiced a generation too young to remember cringing with embarrassment during the 'British Film Year' of 1985. Alex Cox argues that:

> Ten seconds' thought leads you to realise that the BBC and the UK Film Council aren't necessarily interested in British cinema *per se*. As quangos funded by the government, they are obliged to come up with a war-friendly – and essentially mid-Atlantic – version of British film history that suits their paymasters.[2]

Cox might be seeing conspiracy where there is only incompetence, but a worrying decline in standards was very clearly exposed when BBC4 replayed the well-researched 1993 series *Hollywood-UK: British Cinema in the 60s*, where directors, writers and actors rather than B-list celebrities talk about films. It is not as if the knowledge and expertise isn't there: Stuart Maconie's *Cinema Show* (2005–6), tucked away on BBC4, manages to find aspects of British cinema which are unusual and entertaining; and to show how things might have been done, *Arena* showcased *Flames of Passion*, a cogently argued ninety-minute polemic which took Raymond Durgnat's *A Mirror for England* as inspiration and argued that mainstream cinema between 1939 and the early 1960s was visually flamboyant, socially relevant, highly professional and immensely revealing of the society which supported it. The intelligent script, the selection of extracts from rarely seen films, the willingness to develop an argument showed producers John Wyver and Michael Jackson and director Mick Confrey to possess a knowledge of British cinema balefully lacking in most of the contributors to 'British Film Forever'.

Cox's criticisms of the UK Film Council might stem from its lack of enthusiasm for his own projects but that hardly makes them invalid. Unlike the British Film Institute, where troubles – which have multiplied in recent years – are publicly aired, it is not an easy institution to penetrate. Typical New Labour diseases – a fatal confusion of intentions and achievements, of presentation over substance – appear to be at least incipiently present. But skilled public relations have kept at bay the sort of hostile criticism the Arts Council suffered when it handled Lottery funding for film production. Only a brief scurry of indignation over the Film Council's involvement in *Sex Lives of the Potato Men* (2004) has caused any serious embarrassment. Bureaucracies are very good at protecting their backs, but come the next recession when some rising Treasury minister realises how much can be saved by pulling the plug on this seemingly safe little sinecure, the artificial edifice of New British Cinema might well collapse. Hopefully before that happens, a film culture will have been established which will be capable of sustaining a viable industry.

Notes

1. DVDs are best bought new or second-hand from the Amazon 'marketplace', though ebay is also an option. For *Joanna* (1968) and *Deep End* (1971) (and other obscure British films with cultish credentials) go to ZDD (www.zddvisualmedia.com). *The Love Test* (1935), *Dance Hall* (1950) and *Woman in a Dressing Gown* (1957) have not been released on DVD, though they do crop up on television.

2. Alex Cox, 'A Very British Cop-out', *Guardian*, 15 August 2007.

PART ONE

Debates and Controversies

1

The British Cinema: The Known Cinema?

ALAN LOVELL

The great French film-maker, François Truffaut, once famously said that there was a certain incompatibility between the words British and Cinema. Well, bollocks to Truffaut.

Stephen Frears

In the late 1960s I presented a paper, 'The British Cinema: The Unknown Cinema', to a British Film Institute seminar group. Its starting point was a suggestion that scholarly neglect of the British cinema was so great that it was effectively an unknown cinema. A lot has changed since then. Today, British film scholars can hardly be accused of neglecting their national cinema. In the space of thirty-five years we moved from scarcity to abundance. There are now available solid histories of the British cinema; detailed explorations of British genre film-making; analyses of important historical 'moments'; critical examinations of influential film-makers; wide-ranging anthologies; informed discussions of the economic and cultural context of current British film-making; informative accounts of Welsh and Scottish film-making.

Inevitably, there are still gaps. My priorities for further investigation would be: the contribution of cameramen, editors, sound recordists, set and costume designers, special effects – and of their union, ACT (later ACTT, now BECTU); British film acting, especially the rich late 1940s and early 50s tradition of female acting represented by Kathleen Byron, Googie Withers, Joan Greenwood, Pamela Brown, Jean Simmons and Deborah Kerr; and the historical development of British film audiences, including a detailed account of film exhibition.[1]

Despite these gaps, increasing critical interest has meant that the British cinema now exists as an object for study. Its contours, at least, are visible. Undoubtedly this is a substantial achievement. But what are the consequences of this work? How is the British cinema now perceived?

It is certainly perceived more positively. If you engage in a substantial act of critical recovery/discovery, you need some belief in the value of what you are doing. When I wrote this chapter, British film criticism showed strong signs of that built-in antipathy to 'things British' which George Orwell complained of.[2] The basic perspective was Marxist, with modern capitalism portrayed as being heavily dependent on the effects of ideology for maintaining its dominance. Cinema was seen as a major ideological institution and realism the form through which it sought to 'naturalise' capitalism.

But as Raymond Williams points out in *Keywords*, realism has a variety of meanings, some of which are contradictory.[3] It's a particularly difficult term to pin down in the context of the British cinema because definitions tend to be casual and operational rather than sustained and reflective. To encourage a more sympathetic and detailed interest in realism, I'll offer a sketch of its historical development.

In what sense were the documentary film-makers of the 1930s realists? They were realists because they believed it was the purpose of art to provide a true understanding of the world. Art had therefore to be socially responsible, it had to have a serious relationship with society. This general belief was given a more specific character by a belief in the 'heroism of modern life', a heroism which was principally located in the activities of working people.[4] Art could best provide a 'true understanding' if it focused on those activities.

Artistically, this second belief is important because it pushes artists towards naturalism, which I take to be a commitment to the importance of describing surface appearances.

The belief in social responsibility has been enormously influential on the British cinema. It is most often articulated in terms of the cinema having a serious relationship with society. As such its acceptance runs pretty much without challenge through the history of the British cinema from the 1930s to the 1990s. Its power can be seen in its acceptance by the film-makers and critics of the *Screen* generation, despite their claim to be 'anti-realists'.

The belief that cinema ought to have a serious relationship with society was one of the clearest motivations for strengthening the presence of realism in feature film-making in the early 1940s. The commitment to describing the heroism of everyday life was made easy by the war, but revealing the underlying forces of social change hardly seemed relevant when what mattered was winning the war.

In pre-war documentaries like *Coal Face* (1935), heroism was expressed through a formalist concern with visual composition and the use of sound. Increasingly, the documentarists came to think that this formalism was inappropriate. They felt it made the films remote, cutting them off from desired audiences. A preference for naturalistic description began to shape films. *Night Mail* (1936), with its awkward mixture of naturalism and formalism, marks this change very well.

A successful naturalistic representation depends heavily on the ability to convince audiences that what is being represented has been accurately observed. Because of the demands of manual work and the nature of the cinema, the documentarists found it easy to represent manual work convincingly. They didn't find it so easy to represent informal, personal relationships. *Night Mail* is again a good example. The representation is convincing when the men are deftly sorting the letters because they are sufficiently absorbed to ignore the film-makers. But when they are chatting and joking, they are clearly aware of the presence of the film-makers and their banter is awkwardly self-conscious.

Realist feature films faced similar problems. *In Which We Serve* (1942) is impressively convincing when it represents the ordinary seamen in action. When it represents their personal life, the conviction disappears. The problems are most evident in the dialogue, which is constructed around ungrammatical forms and catch-phrases giving the characters a 'quaint' quality. The

actors add to the problems. In speaking the dialogue, they make frequent shifts between working-class and middle-class articulations. The overall effect is to patronise characters and/or make them comic.

Whatever the problems, realism clearly was a creative force in wartime feature film-making. In particular, *In Which We Serve* and *'Fires Were Started –'* (1943) seem to me to be films any national cinema could be proud of. But the creative impact of realism was closely tied to the war. In the post-war British cinema, its creative impact diminished. The belief that films should have a serious relationship with society was increasingly reduced to the exploration of topical subjects from within a conventional moral/social perspective. Naturalistic description became limited to scripts based on the lives of 'ordinary' people plus location shooting.

As a strong, creative presence, realism was not revived until the second half of the 1950s, when the Free Cinema writers and film-makers (Lindsay Anderson, Karel Reisz, Tony Richardson) reaffirmed realist beliefs. In his essay 'Get Out and Push!', Anderson incisively criticised liberal critics and artists for their irresponsibility and frivolity. He also argued for the urgency and importance of providing convincing representations of working-class life.[5]

Anderson's arguments were influential and played an important part in re-energising British film-making. His work was supported by the emergence of new writers (Alan Sillitoe, David Storey, Shelagh Delaney) and new actors (Rachel Roberts, Albert Finney, Richard Harris, Rita Tushingham) who, for a variety of reasons, were better able to cope with the demands of representing working-class life.[6]

For all its energy, this 'kitchen sink' realism was a short-lived and limited phenomenon. If we date its beginning to the production of *Room at the Top* in 1958, it was pretty much over by 1965. In fact, the dominance of realism was even more attenuated than this suggests. After *Saturday Night and Sunday Morning* (1960), Karel Reisz directed *Night Must Fall* (1964), an adaptation of a 1930s stage thriller/melodrama. He followed this with an adaptation of David Mercer's surrealistic fantasy, *Morgan, A Suitable Case for Treatment* (1966). Lindsay Anderson's first feature, *This Sporting Life* (1963), has obvious Expressionist elements. Tony Richardson's first three films, *Look Back in Anger* (1959), *The Entertainer* (1960) and *A Taste of Honey* (1961), showed realist impulses, particularly through location-shooting, but all three were based on successful stage plays.

However, realism was not abandoned. Rather, it changed its form. In the late 1950s Brecht's work increasingly had an impact on British artistic culture. Crucially Brecht was a realist without being a naturalist – he believed that it was art's job to provide a 'true understanding' but he didn't believe this could be achieved through a description of the surfaces of life. The encouragement his work gave to a move from naturalism was supported by the influence of surrealism, which was also prevalent at that time.[7]

Lindsay Anderson's work clearly reveals both these forces at work – surrealism in *If . . . .* (1968), Brecht in *O Lucky Man!* (1973). The same processes can be seen at work in television drama. Dennis Potter's 'Nigel Barton' plays (1965) are strongly marked by the influence of Brecht. David Mercer moved from the naturalistic drama of the *Where the Difference Begins* trilogy (1961–3) to the surrealist-influenced *A Suitable Case for Treatment* (1962).

It can be argued that realism with a strong naturalistic dimension survived in series and serial television forms, from *Z Cars* (1962–78) and *Coronation Street* (1960–) to *Between the Lines* (1992–4) and *Brookside* (1982–2003). In terms of the British cinema, Ken Loach has been a distinctive figure because of his commitment to maintaining realism as a viable artistic form by modernising it. To achieve this, he used the advances in camerawork and sound made possible by the cinéma-vérité movement. He also addressed the problems posed by acting for naturalistic realism in a radical way, using little-known or non-professional actors and only giving them pages of the script on a day-by-day basis in order to keep them fresh. But perhaps his greatest commitment has been the reaffirmation of the critical dimension of realism by giving it a Marxist perspective.[8]

The strongest positive thrust from the new scholarship has been an attempt to validate 'anti-realist' filmmaking. Contemporary scholars have explored areas of film-making represented by Hammer horror films, Gainsborough melodramas and the *Carry On* comedies. Julian Petley outlines this position very clearly in his essay 'The Lost Continent':

> Of course, the vaunting and valorising of certain
> British films on account of their 'realism' entails as
> its corollary, as the other side of the coin, the
> dismissal and denigration of those films deemed
> un- or non-realist . . . These form another, repressed
> side of British cinema, a dark, disdained thread

Dilute surrealism?: Dawn Archibald as the witch woman in Neil Jordan's *The Company of Wolves* (1984)

> weaving the length and breadth of that cinema,
> crossing authorial and generic boundaries,
> sometimes almost entirely invisible, sometimes
> erupting explosively, always received critically with
> fear and disapproval.[9]

The work that has been done in this area has been invaluable in calling attention to films and film-makers which have languished for too long without proper critical attention. If the claims made for them were persuasive, then a new and interesting account of the British cinema would have been constructed. Unfortunately the case for the anti-realist genres has been much weakened by its dependence for its sense of value on a 'dilute Surrealism'. Effectively, surrealism has operated as a form of easy genre-valuing, privileging the 'excess' of horror films, melodrama and low comedy as against the oppressiveness of realism.

The treatment of melodrama first alerted me to the weakness of the case. I remember preparing for a course on British cinema by reading the plot summaries of all the films made in 1946–7. What appeared to be a melodramatic current stood out. Many films seemed to be marked by extravagant plotting and characterisation. The dramatic forces which shaped the dramas were emotional and large-scale, the fictional worlds marked by erotic cruelty, violence and perverse relationships. I thought I had uncovered an extraordinary and disturbing area of British cinema.

Seeing the films proved a huge disappointment. I quickly become aware of how the elements which had interested me were downplayed and made safe by the writing, camerawork, acting and direction. I shouldn't have been surprised. As contemporary scholars are fond of pointing out, British cinema has been heavily marked by qualities like good taste, restraint, reticence. Why should melodramas (or horror films or comedies) be free of these characteristics? Gavin Lambert sensibly remarked that he found it difficult to take *The Wicked Lady* (1945) seriously because its notion of wickedness was so suburban!

I think contemporary scholarship has fallen into a trap by posing excess and restraint against each other. British cinema is often most exciting when restraint and excess interact with each other. *Brief Encounter* (1945) provides a classic example of what can be achieved when the interaction takes place, and of the problems created when one dominates the other. The film is structured around Laura's monologue, which dramatically explores a struggle to use language to contain powerful, disruptive emotion. That may seem a simple operation, so it is easy to miss the art involved in making it work. Noël Coward's language appears simple, almost banal. But, through the use of varying sentence rhythms, it supports and encourages a performer to capture both restraint and excess. Similarly the railway station evokes both the 'ordinariness' of a branch-line station and the 'adventure' of train journeys.

In other parts of the film, the film-makers aren't able to create a successful interaction between restraint

---

It Always Rains on Sunday (Robert Hamer, 1947)

It Always Rains on Sunday provides some excellent examples of the strengths of the British cinema of the late 1940s and early 1950s. Acting was a particular strength of that era. *It Always Rains on Sunday* is graced with a number of fine performances. Googie Withers, in the central role, works within the restrained style that was dominant in the period. She gives the central character of the wife hiding an escaped convict an intense presence with a disciplined and consistent performance. It's all the more impressive in that the script doesn't always help her – some of the exchanges with her daughters are clumsily written. Working within the same style, Betty Ann Davies gives a similar intensity to the character of the betrayed wife. There are also some strong male performances. Those of John Slater and Sydney Tafler, as the 'spiv' and the errant husband, use a broad, expressive style – one that has roots in popular entertainment – to give their characters vivid and engaging presences.

Realism is usually cited as a central strength of the British cinema and *It Always Rains on Sunday* is frequently discussed within this context. With the benefit of hindsight, this seems misleading. There is, in fact, a creative tension between realism and Expressionism in the film. On location the night streets are uncannily empty with dark shadows and pools of soft, diffused light disguising their everydayness. The final sequences, which were filmed on location, are shot expressively rather than realistically; and in the climactic scene in the railway yard the geography of the setting is sacrificed in order to heighten the dramatic action.

Apart from the final chase sequences, a limited number of scenes are set in actual locations, and these are often incidental. The central action, the hiding of the fugitive, takes place in a set, the Sandigates' house. The design of this set (and other interiors), rather than realistic backgrounds, is one of the strengths of the film. There's an excellent use of compressed space with the smallness and proximity of the rooms emphasised. Privacy is difficult to find, which makes the hiding of the fugitive much more fraught. The credit for this obviously belongs to the art director, Duncan Sutherland; his achievement highlights production design as another of the strengths of the post-war British cinema, with the work of Alfred Junge, Vincent Korda and John Bryan being some of the best-known examples.

Robert Hamer undoubtedly brought a distinctive sensibility to *It Always Rains on Sunday*, but the tendency to see Hamer (along with a few others like Alexander Mackendrick and Michael Powell) as exceptions to a general mediocrity and detach the films he directed from the main body of British cinema is mistaken. As is evident from the acting, art direction, cinematography and other aspects of *It Always Rains on Sunday*, the quality of these films depends on effective collaboration and is more the result of an industry ethos than an individual talent.

FURTHER READING

John W. Collier, *A Film in the Making* (London: World Film Publications, 1947).

Christine Geraghty, *British Cinema in the Fifties: Gender, Genre and the 'New Look'* (London: Routledge 2000).

and excess. Alec, the other central character, is weak because his emotional situation is poorly defined. Little information is given about his relationship with his wife and he doesn't have the resources of interior monologue to express his feelings. As far as locations are concerned, David Lean and Robert Krasker are unable to generate images of either the countryside or small-town life which have the dramatic power of the railway station.

The creative interaction between excess and restraint can often be seen in films directed by Michael Powell. In *The Small Back Room* (1949) the hero, Sammy Rice, has an artificial leg that gives him great pain, which he tries to ignore. As he sits in an underground train with his girlfriend Susan, the pain is so great that he stands up to be more comfortable. Standing in a crowded train, Susan and Sammy are forced to become more physically intimate. Responding to his pain, she embraces him. The scene now gains an extra charge as the experience of pain produces a physical expression of sympathy with an erotic undertone. This charged feeling is carried over

British cinema is often most exciting when restraint and excess interact: Kathleen Byron and David Farrar, *The Small Back Room* (Michael Powell and Emeric Pressburger, 1949)

by a dissolve to the entrance to Sammy's flat, where the couple's physical intimacy is heightened by big close-ups of their faces in soft light with deep shadows as they embrace and kiss. The erotic feeling heightens as Susan takes off her coat and they embrace on the sofa. The erotic intensity that has been slowly built up is dispersed by a phone call asking Sammy to investigate a bomb explosion.

I have deliberately introduced Michael Powell into my discussion because he has been a key figure in the critical attempt to construct a British anti-realist cinema. Undoubtedly the renewed interest in Powell has revealed a substantial film-maker. However, I believe his work has been treated in an uncritical way which hasn't helped the anti-realist case. For example, film criticism which has been otherwise alert to questions of national identity has been indulgent of the complacent and reactionary version of English identity dramatised in *The Life and Death of Colonel Blimp* (1943) and *A Matter of Life and Death* (1946). Film criticism which has been alert to questions of class and gender has been indulgent of the snobbery and misogyny present in *Peeping Tom* (1960). The Powell/Pressburger partnership has never been critically scrutinised. The scripts of their films often have obvious weaknesses. Narrative development is uncertain, central characters thinly drawn, the comedy insubstantial and the whimsy irritating. Can we blame Emeric Pressburger for these faults or is the responsibility a collective one?

One of the most interesting areas of new scholarship has been the attempt to construct a case against a Thatcherite free-market approach to film production. It draws heavily on the way British films are thought to have constructed national identity, and has been put most sympathetically and intelligently by John Hill. Recognising the difficult economics of British film production, Hill argues that the case for government support has to be based on cultural grounds. It is necessary to establish that films play a valuable role in British society. For Hill, that value can be established through attention to the way films construct national identity. He points out that most of the scholarship which has explored this issue has been unsympathetic to the way films have done this. It has seen the identity they have produced as 'narrowly nationalist or else in hock to a restricted homogenising view . . .'.[10] He goes on to argue that this doesn't have to be so; a positive case for the British cinema can be made on its potential for constructing national identity:

. . . it is quite possible to conceive of a national cinema, in the sense of one which works with or addresses nationally specific materials, which is none the less critical of inherited notions of national identity, which does not assume the existence of a unique, unchanging 'national culture', and which is capable of dealing with social divisions and differences.[11]

Hill's support for this possibility depends on a rather guarded affirmation of 1980s independent cinema, as represented by films like *My Beautiful Laundrette* (1985) and *The Passion of Remembrance* (1986). He suggests that films like these provide a more acceptable construction of national identity. Why they should be able to do this isn't explained. I suspect that beneath a sophisticated

Vera Drake (Mike Leigh, 2004)

In the fifty years between the making of *Vera Drake* and that of *It Always Rains on Sunday* the character of British film-making changed dramatically. That change is usually seen in terms of decline – fewer films, tiny budgets, limited audiences. However, these changes did have some positive consequences. Crucially, an interesting production area emerged, created out of a mix of television companies, state funding bodies and the film industry proper. The support they provided made it possible for some film-makers to work consistently and with a great degree of creative freedom. Mike Leigh is one of those film-makers.

The advantages for Leigh are most obvious because of the way it allows him to work with actors. Influenced by the work of John Cassavetes and Peter Brook in cinema and theatre, Leigh tries to make the gap between the actor and the script as small as possible. His actors are substantially involved in the creation of the script. As is well known, before the script is written Leigh works with the actors and, through a combination of research and improvisation, characters are developed. At the end of the process, Leigh uses this work to write the script.

Vera Drake is a stark, gripping drama of how unwanted pregnancies were dealt with in a society with strong class divisions – Britain in the early 1950s. It's a fine demonstration of what can be achieved in the new production structure. As might be expected, the acting is at the core of the film's achievement. In both major and minor parts it's of a consistently high quality. The basic style is low-key naturalism. Actors establish their characters by lightly emphasising the aspects of everyday behaviour – facial expression, posture, movement, tone of voice – they think appropriate. Because of their knowledge of the characters they can make these choices with confidence and sensitivity. The way Imelda Staunton establishes Vera through quick, busy movements, frequent smiles and a sympathetic tone of voice, is a perfect example of this.

Large demands are made on the actors because of the way *Vera Drake* is structured. The narrative is made up of a series of vignettes. By using this form Leigh is able to create a detailed and varied social world. But if the vignette form is to work every detail has to be significant. And since most of the vignettes consist of simple interactions between a few characters, the actors carry the burden of making a scene significant. (They do receive excellent support, especially from Jacqueline Durran's costumes and John Bush's set decoration).

Vera Drake is particularly powerful because it is free from the unevenness often present in Mike Leigh's work. In other films, characters who are conceived and acted naturalistically combine uneasily with characters who are conceived and played with comic exaggeration. There are hints of comic exaggeration in *Vera Drake* (the daughter, Ethel, and some of the middle-class characters), but overall the writing and acting are impressively disciplined and consistent.

FURTHER READING

Michael Coveney, *The World According to Mike Leigh* (London: HarperCollins, 1997).

Mike Leigh, 'The *Vera Drake* Interview', *Sight and Sound*, January 2005, pp. 12–15.

Happy family life: Imelda Staunton and Daniel Mays in *Vera Drake*

surface, a simple critical position is evident – good films are ideologically sympathetic, bad films are ideologically unsympathetic. Since good (ideologically sympathetic) films can't be made within a market framework, there needs to be government intervention. I don't think this is a strong case either intellectually or politically.

The problems generated by this kind of discussion and possible ways out of them have been illuminated by a critical exchange in *Sight and Sound*. In a review of *Braveheart* (1995), Colin McArthur attacked the film for its reactionary account of Scottish national identity. The attack was based on an intelligently detailed account of the way 'regressive discourses' shaped the film. For McArthur these discourses are of an ideological kind – he talks about the film's 'ideological project' and in a reply to critics says that *Braveheart* has to deliver 'an ideological framework conducive to a mass audience'. He doesn't try to explain *Braveheart*'s success with audiences.

McArthur's critics, Sheldon Hall and Martin Price, both point out that a proper understanding of the relationship between *Braveheart* and its audiences can be better achieved through a discussion of artistic issues like genre and identification rather than political ones of national identity.[12] I am sympathetic to their position because I think they open up ways of dealing with a film's popularity with audiences.

Colin McArthur's and John Hill's position is fundamentally a realist one. Films should be judged by the way they provide 'true understanding' – for Hill, an expanded version of Britishness through a sensitivity to social difference; for McArthur, a historically accurate account of Scottish history. I don't think a satisfactory account of how films interact with their audiences can be developed from such an assumption. It's much too limiting and blocks off a proper discussion of entertainment in the cinema.[13]

This persistent linking of British film production with the question of national identity is odd. It has run through discussion of the British cinema for much of its history. That such a link exists is, at one level, a truism – any activity engaged in by British citizens can be seen as a way of constructing national identity. In discussions of British cinema it is taken for granted both that the link exists and that it is a politically important one – it often seems as if the cinema is the key tool for the construction of British national identity. At present, the belief in the importance of the link seems to depend heavily on the unacknowledged acceptance of the old view of the cinema as having magical powers of expression.

A few years ago, a teaching experience encouraged me to reflect on my attitudes to the British cinema. I saw *Saturday Night and Sunday Morning* along with *Rebel without a Cause* (1955) and *Breathless* (1959) as part of a day school for students. Most of those students hadn't been born when any of the films were made and knew little about them. *Saturday Night and Sunday Morning* was the one they most enjoyed. It had a simplicity and directness which was very attractive. In comparison *Rebel without a Cause* seemed sentimental and over-wrought and *Breathless* clever-clever.

The students' response made me think how much British cinema had been underrated. My view was strengthened by Stephen Frears's robust affirmation of British cinema in his television documentary 'Typically British'.[14]

Frears's enthusiasm is surely justified. At the very least, a cinema which can produce films as varied as *The 39 Steps* (1935), '*Fires Were Started* –', *Black Narcissus* (1947), *Henry V* (1944), *It Always Rains on Sunday*, *The Ladykillers* (1955), *Saturday Night and Sunday Morning*, *If . . . .*, *Kes* (1969), *Withnail and I* (1986), *Distant Voices, Still Lives* (1988), *Trainspotting* (1996), and *Vera Drake* deserves celebration. Arguments can be made that comparable cinemas like the French or Italian have, over their whole history, been superior to the British cinema but the differences are only relative ones. British cinema isn't a special case. There isn't some fundamental British cinematic deficiency which needs to be accounted for. Bollocks to Truffaut indeed!

Notes

1. A start has been made with Duncan Petrie's *The British Cinematographer* (London: BFI, 1995); Roy Perkins and Martin Stollery, *British Film Editors: 'The Heart of the Movie'* (London: BFI, 2004); and the BECTU Oral History Project.

2. See, for example, Victor Perkins, 'The British Cinema', *Movie* no. 1, 1962; Tom Nairn, 'Deceased at the Paramount Cinema Piccadilly – The British Cinema', *Cinema* vol. 3, June 1969; Thomas Elsaesser, 'Between Style and Ideology', *Monogram* vol. 3, 1972.

3. Raymond Williams, *Keywords* (London: Flamingo, 1976), pp. 257–62. See also Eric Auerbach's *Mimesis* (Princeton, NJ: Princeton University Press, 1953).

4. The phrase is Baudelaire's but I've taken it from Linda Nochlin's book *Realism* (Harmondsworth: Penguin, 1971).

5. 'Get Out and Push!' was published in the Angry Young Man anthology: Tom Maschler (ed.), *Declaration* (London: MacGibbon & Kee, 1957).

6. A comparison between Googie Withers in *It Always Rains on Sunday* and Rachel Roberts in *This Sporting Life* is instructive. Both actresses give their characters a hard edge by limiting their expressiveness. The combination of the characters' hardness and the actresses' erotic physical presence makes the characters vivid and distinctive. In contrast to Rachel Roberts, Googie Withers's performance is partially undermined by her delivery of dialogue, which consistently has middle-class articulations.

7. Surrealism influenced British pop music of the period, especially in the work of the Beatles. Its principal conduit was the art schools. David Mercer was originally an art student.

8. It is a mark of the political limitations of much contemporary film scholarship that a book about the contemporary British cinema – *British Cinema and Thatcherism: Fires Were Started* (1993) – had substantial discussions of Peter Greenaway's work and none of Ken Loach's. The new edition of the book (London: Wallflower Press, 2006) does include a chapter on Loach's work.

9. Julian Petley, 'The Lost Continent', in Charles Barr (ed.), *All Our Yesterdays: 90 Years of British Cinema* (London: BFI, 1986).

10. John Hill, 'The Issue of National Cinema and British Film Production', in Duncan Petrie (ed.), *New Questions of British Cinema* (London: BFI, 1992), p. 15.

11. Ibid., p. 16.

12. Colin McArthur's review of *Braveheart* is in *Sight and Sound*, September 1995. Sheldon Hall's letter is in *Sight and Sound*, October 1995. Martin Price's letter with Colin McArthur's reply to both critics is in *Sight and Sound*, February 1996.

13. Film criticism has relied for too long on Richard Dyer's discussion of the issue in 'Entertainment and Utopia', in Bill Nichols (ed.), *Movies and Methods* (Berkeley and Los Angeles: University of California Press, 1985). This was a brave attempt but its flaws are now obvious, particularly its failure to confront the art/entertainment distinction.

14. 'Typically British' (BFI TV) was first broadcast on Channel 4 on 2 September 1995. Frears could not have made his case without the benefit of our new knowledge of the British cinema. It is no accident that one of the writers of the programme was Charles Barr, who has probably done most to develop the new study of British cinema.

Bibliography

Anderson, Lindsay and Ryan, Paul, *Never Apologise: The Collected Writings of Lindsay Anderson* (London: Plexus, 2004).

Barr, Charles, *Ealing Studios* (London: David & Charles, 1977).

Barr, Charles (ed.), *All Our Yesterdays: 90 Years of British Cinema* (London: BFI, 1986).

Berry, David, *Wales and Cinema* (Cardiff: University of Wales, 1994).

Christie, Ian, *Arrows of Desire: The Films of Michael Powell and Emeric Pressburger* (London: Waterstone, 1985).

Christie, Ian and Moor, Andrew (eds), *Michael Powell: International Perspectives on an English Film-maker* (London: BFI, 2005).

Curran, James and Porter, Vincent (eds), *British Cinema History* (London: Weidenfeld and Nicolson, 1983).

Harper, Sue, *Picturing the Past: The Rise and Fall of the British Costume Film* (London: BFI, 1994).

Harper, Sue, *Women in British Cinema: Mad, Bad and Dangerous to Know* (London and New York: Continuum, 2000).

Higson, Andrew, *Waving the Flag: Constructing a National Cinema in Britain* (Oxford: Clarendon Press, 1995).

Hill, John, *Sex, Class and Realism* (London: BFI, 1986).

Kemp, Philip, *Lethal Innocence: The Cinema of Alexander Mackendrick* (London: Methuen, 1991).

Landy, Marcia, *British Genres: Cinema and Society 1930–1960* (Princeton, NJ: Princeton University Press, 1991).

Leigh, Jacob, *The Cinema of Ken Loach: Art in the Service of the People* (London: Wallflower Press, 2002).

Lovell, Alan, *British Cinema: The Unknown Cinema*, BFI Education Seminar Paper, March 1969.

McArthur, Colin (ed.), *Scotch Reels: Scotland in Cinema and Television* (London: BFI, 1982).

Moor, Andrew, *Powell and Pressburger: A Cinema of Magic Spaces* (London: I. B. Tauris, 2005).

Murphy, Robert, *Realism and Tinsel: Cinema and Society in Britain 1939–49* (London: Routledge, 1989).

Petrie, Duncan (ed.), *New Questions of British Cinema* (London: BFI, 1992).

Richards, Jeffrey, *The Age of the Dream Palace: Cinema and Society in Britain 1930–39* (London: Routledge, 1984).

Ryall, Tom, *Alfred Hitchcock and the British Cinema* (London: Athlone Press, 1996).

Street, Sarah, *British National Cinema* (London: Routledge 1997).

2

British Cinema as National Cinema: Production, Audience and Representation

John Hill

Following the Oscar-winning success of *Chariots of Fire* (1981) on 23 March 1982, the film was re-released and showed successfully across Britain in the weeks that followed. On 2 April, the Argentinians invaded the Falklands/Malvinas and, three days later, the Thatcher government despatched a naval task force from Portsmouth which successfully retook the islands in June. In a sense, the coincidence of Oscar-winning success in Los Angeles and subsequent military victory in the Falklands seemed to link the two events, and the idea of a national resurgence in both cinema ('the British are coming') and national life became intertwined. Indeed, Hugo Young reports that David Puttnam, the producer of *Chariots of Fire*, was a subsequent guest of the Prime Minister's at Chequers and that there was 'much talk in the Thatcher circle about the desirability of something similar being put on to celluloid to celebrate the Falklands victory'.[1]

There are, however, two factors which complicate this story. Despite its reputation, *Chariots of Fire* is a more complex work than is commonly suggested. Indeed, a film which is reputedly so nationalist is surprisingly conscious of the complexities of national allegiance, focusing as it does on the running careers of two 'outsiders': Harold Abrahams, a Jew of Lithuanian background, and Eric Liddell, a Scotsman born in China. If *Chariots of Fire* did become identified with renascent national sentiment, then this was probably not so much the result of the ideological outlook that the film itself manifests as of the moment at which its success was achieved. The other complicating factor is that when the film was re-released it was as a part of a

double bill with *Gregory's Girl* (1980). While this double bill was undoubtedly intended to showcase the range of new British cinema, there is also something a touch subversive in the way these films were coupled. For while both are British, they also represent rather different kinds of British cinema.

Chariots of Fire, at a cost of £3 million, was a comparatively expensive film for British cinema in 1980. And although it was strongly identified with 'Britishness' it was actually funded from foreign sources, including Hollywood. *Gregory's Girl*, by contrast, cost only about £200,000 and was financed from domestic sources, including the National Film Finance Corporation and Scottish Television. A clear contrast in formal approach is also apparent. Despite some play with temporal relations, *Chariots of Fire* employs a relatively straightforward narrative structure, organised around goal-oriented action and positive heroes. *Gregory's Girl* opts for a much looser, more episodic form in which surface realism, comedy and domesticated surrealism are combined in a way which successfully fuses British comic traditions with a modernist sensibility. These differences also extend to content. While *Chariots of Fire* is focused on the past, *Gregory's Girl* is resolutely of the present. The version of the past which *Chariots of Fire* constructs, moreover, is strongly identified with the English upper classes and male achievement, while *Gregory's Girl* is set among the suburban middle and working classes and gently subverts conventional stereotypes of male and female roles. And if both films are 'British', *Chariots* is very much an 'English' film whereas *Gregory's Girl* is clearly 'Scottish'.

Chariots of Fire (Hugh Hudson, 1981) focused on the past and strongly identified with the English upper classes

While both films are, at least partly, set in Scotland, there is a significant difference in the representations of Scotland which they provide. *Chariots of Fire* tends to look at Scotland from the outside (or rather from the metropolitan English centre), associating it with the 'natural' and the 'primitive'. *Gregory's Girl*, on the other hand, uses the 'new town' of Cumbernauld to avoid the conventional signifiers of 'Scottishness' and, in doing so, suggests an altogether more complex sense of contemporary Scottish identity. This, in turn, has links to what might be characterised as the films' different modes of cultural address. *Chariots*, with its enthusiasm for the past and links with conventional notions of English 'national heritage', offers an image of Britain that generally conforms to the expectations of an international, and especially American, audience. *Gregory's Girl* is a much more obviously local and idiomatic film. It too has an international appeal, but for an audience more likely to be European than American. And while *Chariots of Fire* is conventionally taken to be the landmark in the revival of British cinema, it may in fact be *Gregory's Girl* which provided the more reliable indicator of the way in which British film-making was developing.

Production

In the 1980s British cinema returned to the position in which it found itself in the 1920s when the government first introduced a quota for British films. In 1925 some 10 per cent of films exhibited in British cinemas were British; by 1926 this had dropped to 5 per cent.[2] The bulk of films shown were, of course, from the US. Following the abolition of the quota in 1983, the percentage of British films on British screens dwindled to similar proportions. Thus in 1992 the US had a 92.5 per cent share of the British exhibition market while British films accounted for only 4 per cent.[3]

The responses to US domination that have been available to the production sector of the British film industry in the 1980s and 90s are, however, different from those of the 1920s. In his essay on the conceptualisation of national cinemas, Stephen Crofts identifies a number of strategies available to national cinema production. For the British cinema the most important are what he describes as the imitation of Hollywood, competition with Hollywood in domestic markets, and differentiation from Hollywood.[4] The imitation of Hollywood involves the attempt to beat Hollywood at its own game, a strategy which has been tried at various junctures in the history of British cinema: by Alexander Korda in the 1930s, by Rank in the 1940s, by EMI in the 1970s and by Goldcrest in the 1980s. Given the competitive advantage which Hollywood enjoys over other national industries by virtue of its scale of production, size of domestic market and international distribution and exhibition network (among other factors), this has proved an economically unviable strategy and, despite some success with individual films, all such attempts have resulted in financial disaster. It is therefore the second, competitive strategy that has constituted the mainstay of British cinema.

As a result of the quota (and, later, some additional forms of state support), the existence of a commercial British cinema which did not compete with Hollywood internationally but only in the domestic market proved possible from the 1930s to – just about – the 1970s. The basis of this cinema, however, was a size of audience sufficient to sustain a domestic film industry. As cinema audiences began to decline, especially from the 1950s, the commercial viability of a cinema aimed primarily at British audiences came under threat. As a result, regular British film production (characteristically popular genre film-making) aimed at the domestic market came to a virtual halt after the 1970s when Hammer horror, the *Carry On*s and the

Confessions films all ceased to be produced. While it had previously been possible for British films to recoup their costs on the home market, this became an exception from the 1970s onwards. Only a minority of British films achieved a domestic gross of over £1 million during the 1980s, and even an apparently popular success such as *Buster*, which grossed £3.7 million in 1988, failed to recover its production cost of £3.2 million from British box-office revenues (given that only a fraction of these actually returns to the producer).

In consequence, the place of British cinema within the international film economy has had to change. Writing in 1969, Alan Lovell argued that, unlike its European counterparts, the British cinema had failed to develop an art cinema (or at any rate that the documentary film had served in its place).[5] During the 1980s, however, it was art cinema which was to become the predominant model of British film-making. The category of 'art cinema' is not, of course, a precise one and it is used here in a relatively generous sense. David Bordwell, for example, has attempted to define 'art cinema' as a distinctive 'mode of film practice' characterised by realism, authorial expressivity and ambiguity.[6] His definition, however, is too tied to the 1960s and fails to do justice to the range of textual strategies employed by art cinema in the 1980s and 90s. Thus, in the case of Britain, the category of art cinema may be seen to include not only the 'realism' of Ken Loach and Mike Leigh and the post-modern aesthetic experiments of Derek Jarman and Peter Greenaway, but also the aesthetically conservative 'heritage' cinema of Merchant Ivory. In this last case, the 'art' of 'art cinema' derives not so much from the authorial presence of the director or the distance from classical narrational and stylistic techniques which such films display, as from the cachet of 'high art' which such films borrow from literary or theatrical sources.

For Crofts, art cinema is the prime example of a national cinema avoiding direct competition with Hollywood by targeting a distinct market sector. This model, he argues, aims 'to differentiate itself textually from Hollywood, to assert explicitly or implicitly an indigenous product, and to reach domestic and export markets through those specialist distribution channels and exhibition venues usually called arthouse'.[7] In this respect, the adoption of aesthetic strategies and cultural referents different from Hollywood also involves a certain foregrounding of 'national' credentials. The oft-noted irony of this, however, is that art cinema then achieves much of its status as national cinema by

circulating internationally rather than nationally. While this means that art cinema (as in the case of Greenaway) may be as economically viable as ostensibly more commercial projects aimed at the 'popular' audience, it is also the case that successful British films have often done better outside Britain than within. A notorious example of this was Ken Loach's *Riff-Raff* which, at the time it won the European Film Award for Best Film in 1991, had been seen by more people in France than in the UK. Even in the case of the heritage film, it is international audiences, especially American, which have become a key source of revenues as well as prestige. As a result, it has become an attractive option to open such films in the United States before a release in Britain, as was the case, for example, with both *The Madness of King George* (1994) and *Sense and Sensibility* (1995).

In both these cases – the cinéma d'auteur which circulates in Europe and the heritage film which appeals to the US – it can be argued that the changed economic circumstances of the British film industry have led to a certain decline of 'national' cinema, insofar as the national address which earlier commercial British cinema appeared to have is no longer so evident. In this respect, much of the lamenting of the current state of the British film industry registers a sense of loss of the connection which it is assumed the British cinema once had with a national popular audience. There is a further twist to this argument, however. For, if the decline in domestic cinema audiences has made British film production increasingly dependent upon international revenues, it has also increased its reliance on television for revenues and production finance as well. The

Gregory's Girl (Bill Forsyth, 1980): gently subverting stereotypes of male and female roles

increasing interrelationship between film and television which has resulted has had consequences for how film is consumed, and for the way it may be judged to be 'national'.

Audience

The changing character of British cinema in the 1980s may be explained, then, in terms of the new production strategies that emerged in the wake of declining cinema audiences. In 1946, annual cinema admissions reached an all-time high of 1,635 million, but then fell steadily until 1984, when they plummeted to 58 million. There has been a subsequent increase – admissions reached over 123 million in 1994, but this is still less than for any year before 1974. It is these figures that provide the backdrop to perceptions of cinema's declining national role. For if the British cinema of World War II is still regarded as a watershed in national cinema, it is not only as a result of the films which were then made but because of the size of the cinema audience which attended them. In 1940, admissions topped 1,000 million for the first time when, partly because of a lack of alternatives, films were the most popular form of entertainment. In this respect, wartime cinema is regarded as pre-eminently 'national', because of the size and range of its audience.

Even at its peak, however, the cinema audience was never fully representative of the nation. A survey of the British cinema audience in 1943, for example, revealed that 30 per cent of the population didn't go to the cinema at all, and that certain social groups were more likely to attend the cinema than others.[8] Women went to the cinema more than men, the manual working class and lower middle class went more frequently than managerial and professional groups, town-dwellers more than country-dwellers. Most strikingly of all, the cinema audience was characteristically made up of the young rather than the old: the under-45s accounted for 85 per cent of the cinema audience but only 68 per cent of the overall population. Cinemagoing declined significantly with age, and 60 per cent of the over-65s are reported as never going to the cinema at all. The 'national' audience for British films, even during the 'golden age' of British cinema, was neither as homogeneous nor as socially representative of the nation as is sometimes assumed.

Audience factors are also relevant when considering the subsequent decline of the cinema. If the cinema audience has become a smaller proportion of the overall population and cinemagoing no longer occupies the

central place in leisure activities it once did, the social character of the audience and its cinema-watching habits have also changed.[9] Cinemagoing has become even more heavily concentrated among the young, particularly the 15–34 age group, which accounted for 78 per cent of cinema attendances in 1990 (but represented only 37 per cent of the population). By comparison, only 11 per cent of the over-45s attended the cinema despite representing 46 per cent of the population. The class basis of cinemagoing has also altered. Cinemagoing is no longer a predominantly working-class activity, and in 1990 social classes ABC1 accounted for 59 per cent of cinemagoers (while representing 42 per cent of the population).[10] One explanation for this is the growth of multiplexes, which since 1985 have been responsible for reviving the cinemagoing habit, especially among car-owners.[11] Multiplexes have also made the cinema more attractive to women, who, following a decline in attendance in the 1950s, have accounted for about 50 per cent of the cinema audience in the 1990s. From the 1950s onwards, the working-class cinema audience has been in decline and has been replaced by an increasingly young and more affluent audience; this reflects more general trends in cinemagoing which have seen an increase in the importance of the 15–24 age group (estimated to be as much as 80 per cent of the worldwide cinema audience for English-language films).[12] This audience demography is clearly significant for national cinema: what is most popular at the cinemas is not necessarily popular with a fully representative section of the 'nation', but only with a relatively narrow segment of it.

A further complication is that, while these trends are fairly clear with regard to cinemagoing, cinemas themselves are no longer the primary site for viewing films. Despite the global decline in cinema attendances, Douglas Gomery has argued that watching films is more popular than ever.[13] People may no longer watch films in the cinemas but they do watch in increasing numbers on television and video, especially in the UK where TV and video penetration is very high by world standards. Some comparisons are appropriate. In 1994, for example, total cinema admissions in Britain were 123 million; in the same year, video rentals (which were dominated by feature films) amounted to 194 million (a considerable drop, in fact, from 328 million the previous year) and there were 66 million video-retail transactions.[14] In the case of television, the contrast is even more striking. There were considerably more films on TV than in the cinemas: in 1994, 299 features were released in UK cinemas, of which thirty-five were 'wholly' British,[15] but in the same year 1,910 films were screened on terrestrial TV, of which 413 were British productions.[16] Films on TV were also watched by considerably more people. In 1994 the viewing figures for the top ten films on TV alone matched the total audience for all 299 films shown in the cinemas. This also meant that individual films, including British films, were seen by significantly more people on television than in the cinemas. The most popular 'wholly' British film of 1992, *Peter's Friends*, was seen by approximately four times as many people when it was shown on television in 1994 than in the cinema.[17] A commercially unsuccessful film such as *Waterland* was seen by nearly thirty-four times as many people when it was shown on television in 1994; if its television viewing audience of 3.3 million had been converted into cinema attendances, this would have put it in the box-office top ten for 1992.

Clearly, people watch more films on television and video than they do in the cinema; and the television/video audience is more representative of the 'nation' as a whole. The group which is over-represented in the cinemas – the 16–24-year-olds – is under-represented in the television audience, and those groups which are infrequent cinemagoers – the over-45s, social groups DE, country-dwellers – are much more likely to see films on TV.[18] While there are no precise figures, it does seem that many contemporary British films which are not regarded as especially 'popular' are nonetheless seen on television by as many people as 'popular' British films of the past. To put it provocatively, it may be that a British cinema that is generally regarded as being in decline is nonetheless producing films that are often seen by as many, and sometimes more, people as films made during the 'golden age' of British cinema.

There are provisos, of course. As has often been argued, the cinema experience and the television viewing experience are dissimilar: watching films on TV or video is characteristically less concentrated than in the cinema.[19] But it is also worth noting how habitual cinemagoing was in its heyday. Browning and Sorrell report that in 1946 nearly three-quarters of those who went to the cinema more than once a month did so whatever films were being shown and without choosing between cinemas.[20] Cinemagoing was only exceptionally an 'event' and, in a number of respects, television has taken over the cinema's former function of catering to the 'regular cinemagoer'. While this is true of most television scheduling of films, however,

television can also use film as an 'event', breaking up the televisual flow and offering a 'special' experience. This commonly happens with the first screening of a Hollywood blockbuster but would also be true, for example, of Channel 4's heavily trailered first screening of *Four Weddings and a Funeral* (1994) in 1996, which attracted an audience of 12.38 million.[21]

Although films can achieve very high audience figures on television, other forms of drama (especially serial drama) achieve even higher figures. In this respect, the national reach of film is generally less than that of television drama. Indeed, John Caughie has expressed an anxiety that the growth in involvement of television in film production has led to an increased investment in drama on film aimed at the international market at the expense of more local forms of television drama. He contrasts the work of Ken Loach in the 1960s and the 1990s. '*Ladybird, Ladybird*,' he argues, 'circulates within an aesthetic and a cultural sphere which is given cultural prestige (and an economic viability) by international critics' awards, whereas *Cathy Come Home* circulated as a national event and functioned as documentary evidence within the political sphere'.[22] The point is well made but it sets up too stark an opposition. For if television drama circulates less as a 'national event' in the 1990s than it did in the 1960s, this is not simply the consequence of television involvement in cinema. It has more to do with the transformations which broadcasting as a whole has undergone, especially the increase in channels (both terrestrial and non-terrestrial), the rise of video (and its opportunities for alternative viewing and time-shifting), and the fragmentation of the national audience which has resulted. If the capacity of both television drama and film to function as a national event has lessened, this is partly because the national audience for television does not exist in the same way as it did in the 1960s and partly because neither individual television programmes nor films can lay claim to the same cultural dominance within the entertainment sphere that they once could. The national audience is in fact a series of audiences, which are often addressed in different ways. At the same time, the representations which British cinema then makes available to them have themselves become much more complex and varied.

Representation

There is a scene in David Hare's *Strapless* (1988) that is suggestive in this regard. A doctor, working for the NHS, addresses a group of assembled hospital workers and speaks up on behalf of 'English values'. It is a scene with loose echoes of wartime movies such as *In Which We Serve* (1942) or *Henry V* (1944) in which morale-boosting speeches upholding traditional English virtues are delivered to an assembled group (in these instances, sailors and soldiers). There are, however, significant differences. In *Strapless*, the speech is delivered not by an Englishman but by an American woman, and the group she speaks to is not the homogeneous white male group of the earlier films but one which is differentiated by gender and ethnicity. By having an American defend the 'idea of Englishness', the film acknowledges the difficulty that such a speech presents for a contemporary British film and attempts to sidestep the irony which would, almost inevitably, have had to accompany its delivery by an English character (even so, there is still a hint of pastiche in the way the scene is realised). The difficulty of speaking for England is indicated, however, not only by the nationality of the speaker, but by the composition of the group she is addressing. Unlike in the earlier films, there is no confident assumption of who represents 'Englishness'.

Important works on British cinema by Jeffrey Richards on the 1930s, Charles Barr on Ealing and Raymond Durgnat on the post-war period have all uncovered in British films an effort to tell stories which invite audiences to interpret them in terms of ideas about the 'nation' and 'national identity'.[23] More recently, Andrew Higson has identified what he regards as a characteristic way of 'imagining the nation' as a 'knowable, organic community' in British films, which he links to a typically 'national style' characterised by episodic narratives involving multiple characters, a distanced observational viewpoint and a non-narrative use of space.[24] Clearly, there is a danger that such arguments underestimate the variety of British cinema and are too ready to make pronouncements about all British cinema on the basis of a selective sample of films (Higson's book deals with only five films in any detail). Nonetheless, it is equally evident that, if not all British cinema, then at least significant strands (such as wartime cinema and Ealing comedies) have evolved an aesthetic and a way of telling stories which clearly display a national-allegorical import.[25]

If this is so, then it is also apparent that the certainties concerning the nation upon which such films relied have, since the 1960s, increasingly dissolved. The strategy of national allegory, in this respect, has not so much been abandoned as refashioned to express a new sense of difference and even conflict. Films such as *My*

Beautiful Laundrette (1985) and *Sammy and Rosie Get Laid* (1987) continue to employ, with a few post-modern embellishments, the stylistic features of British national cinema which Higson identifies, clearly inviting the individual stories of its characters to be read in terms of an 'allegory' of the 'state of the nation'. They do so, however, to project a much more fluid, hybrid and plural sense of 'Britishness' than was seen in earlier British cinema. Such films are responding to the more complex sense of national identity that has been characteristic of modern Britain. In this respect, the interests of the art film (which are often individual and subjective) may be seen to have merged with the pre-occupations of public-service television (which are characteristically more social and 'national' in scope). As a result, the alliance between film and television, which Caughie sees as lessening the local dimensions of television, may also be read as a strengthening of the local aspects of cinema.

Since the 1980s, it can be argued that not only has British cinema articulated a much more inclusive sense of Englishness than previously but that it has also accorded a much greater recognition to the differing nationalities and identities within Britain (including, for example, the emergence of a distinctive black British cinema). In this respect, British national cinema now clearly implies Scottish and Welsh cinema as well as just English cinema. Indeed, two of the most successful British films of the mid-1990s – *Shallow Grave* (1994) and *Trainspotting* (1996) – were very clearly Scottish. This has implications, not only for the inclusiveness of the representations of Britain which British cinema provides but also, as the example of *Gregory's Girl* indicates, for the way in which issues of national identity are then addressed.

Graeme Turner, writing of Australian cinema in the 1990s, has noted the suspicion that often accompanies discussion of both the nation and national cinema because of the socially conservative versions of national identity which these tend to imply. He argues that the post-colonial status of Australia means that its discourses of the nation are much less settled, and that it is possible for Australian films to provide 'a critical . . . body of representations within mainstream Western cinema'.[26] In the same way, the peculiar historical circumstances of Scotland and Wales – which may have gained economically from the British colonial enterprise but which, culturally, encountered subordination – provide an opening for a more complex negotiation of the discourses around the 'nation' than English/British cinema has traditionally provided. *Trainspotting* is an interesting example in this regard. The most commercially successful British film of 1996, it was fully financed by the public-service broadcaster Channel 4, and combines an interest in social issues (drug-taking, AIDS, poverty) with a determinedly self-conscious aesthetic style reminiscent of the French and British 'new waves'. In experimenting with cinematic style, however, it also plays with the inherited imagery of England and Scotland. Thus when the film's main character, Mark Renton (Ewan McGregor), arrives in London, the film cheerfully invokes the most clichéd images of London in an ironic inversion of the touristic imagery which commonly accompanies the arrival of an English character in Scotland.[27] In a similarly iconoclastic manner, the film escorts its main characters to the Scottish countryside, not to invoke the 'romantic' beauty of the Scottish landscape but to provide Renton with the occasion for a swingeing attack on 'being Scottish' ('We're the lowest of the fucking low . . . . It's a shite state of affairs and all the fresh air in the world will not make any fucking difference'). So while *Trainspotting* may speak with a voice that is decidedly Scottish, it also does so in a way which avoids simple pieties concerning Scottish, or 'British', identity.

Conclusion

I have argued elsewhere that the idea of British national cinema has often been linked, virtually by definition, to discourses of nationalism and myths of national unity.[28] However, this formulation of a national cinema underestimates the possibilities for a national cinema to re-imagine the nation, or rather nations within Britain, and also to address the specificities of a national culture in a way which does not presume a homogeneous or 'pure' national identity. Indeed, as Paul Willemen has argued, the national cinema which genuinely addresses national specificity will actually be at odds with the 'homogenising project' of nationalism insofar as this entails a critical engagement with 'the complex, multidimensional and multidirectional tensions that characterise and shape a social formation's cultural configurations'.[29] In a sense, this is one of the apparent paradoxes that this chapter has been addressing: that while British cinema may depend upon international finance and audiences for its viability, this may actually strengthen its ability to probe national questions; that while cinema has apparently lost its 'national' audience in the cinemas, it may have gained a more fully 'national' audience via television; and that while the British cinema may no longer assert the myths of 'nation' with its earlier confidence, it may nonetheless be a cinema which is more fully representative of national complexities than ever before.

Notes

1. Hugo Young, *One of Us* (London: Pan, 1990), p. 277.
2. Cinematograph Films Act, 1927: Report of a Committee Appointed by the Board of Trade (London: HMSO, 1936), p. 5.
3. *Screen Digest*, December 1993, p. 280.
4. Stephen Crofts 'Reconceptualizing National Cinema/s', p. 50.
5. Alan Lovell, *The British Cinema: The Unknown Cinema*, BFI Education Seminar Paper, March 1969, p. 2.
6. David Bordwell, 'The Art Cinema as a Mode of Film Practice', *Film Criticism* vol. 4 no. 1, Fall 1979.
7. Crofts, 'Reconceptualizing National Cinema/s', p. 51.
8. Louis Moss and Kathleen Box, *The Cinema Audience: An Inquiry Made by the Wartime Social Survey for the Ministry of Information* (London: Ministry of Information, 1943).
9. In 'Cinemas and Cinema-Going in Great Britain', *Journal of the Royal Statistical Society* vol. CXVII no. 11, 1954, p. 135, Browning and Sorrell indicate that in the years 1950–2 the cinema accounted for over 83 per cent of all taxable admissions on entertainment (including theatre, sport and other activities). In 1992, by comparison, spending on cinema admissions accounted for less than 6 per cent of household expenditure on entertainment. See Monopolies and Mergers Commission, *Films: A Report on the Supply of Films for Exhibition in Cinemas in the UK* (London: HMSO, 1994), p. 90.
10. Karsten-Peter Grummitt, *Cinemagoing 4* (Leicester: Dodona Research, 1995), p. 1.
11. Between 1985, when the first multiplex was opened, and 1994 the number of multiplexes grew to seventy-one sites (incorporating 638 screens). By the end of 1993, about 40 per cent of all visits to the cinema were to multiplexes. See Monopolies and Mergers Commission, *Films: A Report on the Supply of Films for Exhibition in Cinemas in the UK*, p. 96.
12. See the figures used by media consultant James Lee in *Movie Makars: Drama for Film and Television* (Glasgow: Scottish Film Council, 1993), p. 44.
13. Douglas Gomery, *Shared Pleasures: A History of Movie Presentation* (London: BFI, 1992), p. 276.
14. These figures are taken from the *BFI Film and Television Handbook 1996* (London: BFI, 1995), pp. 34 and 47.
15. *Screen Finance*, 11 January 1995, p. 13. *Screen Finance* defines films as 'wholly' British when they were made solely by British production companies.

16. *Screen Finance*, 8 February 1995, p. 12.

17. Figures for box-office revenue come from *Screen Finance*, 24 February 1993, p. 9. I have estimated admissions for individual films by dividing 1992 box-office revenues by the average realised seat prices for that year, as identified in Monopolies and Mergers Commission, *Films: A Report on the Supply of Films for Exhibition in Cinemas in the UK*, p. 102. Television viewing figures may be found in the *BFI Film and Television Handbook 1996*, p. 57.

18. Patrick Barwise and Andrew Ehrenberg, *Television and Its Audience* (London: Sage, 1988), p. 29. The renting and buying of pre-recorded videos is also highest among the 'lower' social grades, especially the C2s. See BMRB International Report: *CAVIAR* 10, vol. 3, *Report of Findings* (February 1993), p. 21.

19. As in the cinema the bulk of films watched by British audiences on television and video are American. But it is worth noting that television not only shows more British films than the cinemas but that, as the films it shows are from different periods, the circulation of British cinema for the modern audience also involves a sense of both its past and present. Thus in 1995, to take just one example, almost as many people watched Ken Loach's *Kes* (1969) as the same director's *Raining Stones* (1993). See *Screen Finance*, 24 January 1996, pp. 16–17.

20. 'Cinemas and Cinema-Going in Great Britain', p. 146.

21. These viewing figures made *Four Weddings and a Funeral* Channel 4's third most-watched broadcast ever. See *Broadcast*, 8 December 1995, p. 24.

22. John Caughie, 'The Logic of Convergence', p. 219.

23. See Jeffrey Richards, *The Age of the Dream Palace: Cinema and Society 1930–39* (London: Routledge & Kegan Paul, 1984); Charles Barr, *Ealing Studios* (London: Cameron and Tayleur, 1977); and Raymond Durgnat, *A Mirror for England* (London: Faber and Faber, 1970).

24. Andrew Higson, *Waving the Flag: Constructing a National Cinema in Britain*.

25. The idea of 'national allegory' has been employed, somewhat controversially, by Fredric Jameson in relation to 'Third-World' literature. See 'Third-World Literature in the Era of Multinational Capitalism', *Social Text* no. 15, Fall 1986.

26. Graeme Turner, 'The End of the National Project? Australian Cinema in the 1990s', in Wimal Dissanayake (ed.), *Colonialism and Nationalism in Asian Cinema* (Bloomington: Indiana University Press, 1994), p. 203.

27. The script refers to this interlude as a 'contemporary retake of all those "Swinging London" montages'. See John Hodge, *Trainspotting* and *Shallow Grave* (London: Faber and Faber, 1996), p. 76.

28. John Hill, 'The Issue of National Cinema and British Film Production'.

29. Paul Willemen, 'The National', p. 212.

Bibliography

Caughie, John, 'The Logic of Convergence', in John Hill and Martin McLoone (eds), *Big Picture, Small Screen: The Relations between Film and Television* (Luton: John Libbey/University of Luton Press, 1996).

Crofts, Stephen, 'Reconceptualizing National Cinema/s', *Quarterly Review of Film and Video* vol. 14 no. 3, 1993.

Higson, Andrew, 'The Concept of National Cinema', *Screen* vol. 30 no. 4, 1989.

Higson, Andrew, *Waving the Flag: Constructing a National Cinema in Britain* (Oxford: Clarendon Press, 1995).

Hill, John, 'The Issue of National Cinema and British Film Production', in Duncan Petrie (ed.), *New Questions of British Cinema* (London: BFI, 1992).

Hill, John, *British Cinema in the 1980s* (Oxford: Clarendon Press, 1999).

Hill, John, McLoone, Martin and Hainsworth, Paul (eds), *Border Crossing: Film in Ireland, Britain and Europe* (Belfast: Institute of Irish Studies/London: BFI, 1994).

McArthur, Colin (ed.), *Scotch Reels: Scotland in Cinema and Television* (London: BFI, 1982).

Richards, Jeffrey, 'National Identity in British Wartime Films', in Philip M. Taylor (ed.), *Britain and the Cinema in the Second World War* (Basingstoke: Macmillan, 1989).

Richards, Jeffrey, *Films and British National Identity: From Dickens to Dad's Army* (Manchester: Manchester University Press, 1997).

Willemen, Paul, 'The National', in Paul Willemen (ed.), *Looks and Frictions: Essays in Cultural Studies and Film Theory* (London: BFI, 1994).

3
British Cinema's US Surrender – A View from 2001

NICK JAMES

A sanctioned derision towards British cinema now exists that only partly derives from the failure of so many Lottery-funded films. It comes as much from a widespread recognition that psychologically the British film industry already 'leaves it to the Americans' and has done so ever since the collapse of the Goldcrest company in the late 1980s. Complaints about the American dominance of British cinema are as plentiful as the dollars that flow through Pinewood and Shepperton whenever big US films are made there. Yet this recent press attitude seems to go beyond the ingrained deference towards American cinema prevalent in British film-reviewing since the 60s. It represents a qualitative shift towards abjection: the acceptance of a future in which the British film industry can never be more than a handmaiden to the global – i.e. Hollywood-dominated – film industry.

Hollywood Rules the World
To accept Hollywood's methods of film-making as superior, without recourse to US-scale resources and without thought for the long-term consequences for film-making in Britain, is now a reflex action within the British film world. In making this claim I'm trying neither to rattle the rusty tambourine for national cinema – though any film critic wants to live in a country with a thriving film-making culture – nor to sling stones at the American Goliath. I simply want to look at the ways in which the continuing globalisation of the world's film industries compromises British cinema's attempts to define itself not only against a US mainstream which it otherwise cannot emulate, but in any coherent way at all.

By the global film industry I mean that predominantly controlled by Americans through vertically and horizontally integrated distribution and exhibition structures and whose centre is Hollywood.[1] By Hollywood I mean that industry town whose studios are bought and sold by multinational corporations (such as Japan's Sony, Australia's News International and France's Vivendi), and which employs talent from all over the world. This paradox tends to be read either as the perfect cover for the US industry's ruthless pursuit of global trade dominance, or as a genuine rapprochement that recognises and makes best use of the strengths of various national resources around the world. In my view, both readings are true and the latter is a response to the former.

The public is encouraged to see British film-making almost entirely in the context of a competition with the Americans. Winning an Oscar is the only universally acknowledged marker of success; by comparison a BAFTA award, like the press-sponsored awards or the film festival prizes, is a negligible achievement. The press can behave like this in part because talented Brits do win so many Oscars, especially in comparison with film-makers from other countries. Of course, this success comes from our sharing the same language with the Americans. Yet what the press now assumes is that film language is exclusively American, that global domination is a done deal and British films can now only be seen on US terms.

New Labour, New Cinema
In 1998–9 the British film industry, suddenly awash with Lottery cash, seemed for a moment like the British

pop music industry of the 60s: a place for making catchy youth anthems that could be knocked out at great speed using the talents of advertising and music promo directors. This brief combination of cash and *Zeitgeist* coincided with the last gasp of the mid-90s idea of Cool Britannia – the aura of success around Britpop and British fashion that the new Labour government exploited when it was elected in 1997. But it was also a response to a new interest among film-goers in home-grown films inspired by the likes of Danny Boyle's *Trainspotting* (1996). Until *Trainspotting* came along, internationally successful British films tended to fall under the loose category of the 'heritage' movie – ranging from tasteful costume dramas directed by James Ivory such as *A Room with a View* (1985) to the upper-middle-class comedy of *Four Weddings and a Funeral* (1994). But after the success of Boyle's aggressively youthful film about heroin addicts in Scotland, some fresh and vigorous new film-makers were given the chance to make features. The apotheosis of this brief burst of energy might be considered the international success of Guy Ritchie's *Lock, Stock and Two Smoking Barrels* in 1998–9. But what happened in the wake of *Lock, Stock . . .* proved disastrous.

Cool Britannia was a marketing concept thoroughly complicit with the unashamed media populism that first drew accusations of Britain 'dumbing down'. It was as if making a film with a properly developed screenplay was suddenly against the spirit of the times. Two films of the soon-to-be lamented new British gangster genre are typical. The BBC-backed *Love, Honour and Obey* (2000) exploited the celebrity of Jude Law and his friends – Sadie Frost, Ray Winstone, Jonny Lee Miller and Rhys Ifans – and was shot in the crude home-movie fashion developed by the same collaborators in the execrable *Final Cut* (1998). *Honest* (2000) was directed by pop producer-songwriter Dave Stewart and starred non-actors Nicole Appleton, Natalie Appleton and Melanie Blatt from All Saints. These films were so gloriously and publicly inept (*Honest* was pulled from Britain's screens with phenomenal speed) that the industry tried to distance itself from them and to shrink back under the shelter of Hollywood competence and bigger budgets.

One indication of the extent to which the British film industry instinctively defers to America is the versions of Britishness it presents to the global market-place. In the multiplex and blockbuster boom years of the 1980s and 90s, when British film fortunes were at their lowest, we became used to British actors being cast as evil masterminds in big-budget Hollywood films. More recently, in British movies, a new kind of character and class system has been created, mostly for export. In the wake of the US success of *Lock, Stock . . .* and the revival of Mike Hodges's classic British gangster movie *Get Carter* (1971), a violent and vicious caricature of young working-class criminality was given full rein in a rash of British gangster films such as *Rancid Aluminium* (2000), *Circus* (2000), *You're Dead* (1999), *Fast Food* (1999), *Gangster No. 1* (2000), as well as *Love, Honour and Obey* and *Honest*.[2] The alacrity with which British producers jumped on the gangster movie van, believing that here was one exportable genre they could exploit in a hurry, said much about the way Britain's production industry operates – that is, blindly, as a series of small competing teams trying to outdo each other in their craving for the Yankee dollar.

Alongside these denizens of disenfranchised youth, we were presented with a comic vision of middle-class English mediocrity stemming initially from the success of *Four Weddings and a Funeral* but coming to fruition in *Notting Hill* (1999), *Bridget Jones's Diary* (2001), *Love Actually* (2003), and *Bridget Jones: The Edge of Reason* (2004), whose worldviews are virtually identical. They take the comedy of incompetence, visible in such Ealing antecedents as *The Lavender Hill Mob* (1951), and make it into a defining middle-class trait. Like the friends of Hugh Grant's bookseller in *Notting Hill*, Bridget Jones and her pals are under-achievers convinced of their utter worthlessness, doing jobs badly as if by right. Even when he's Prime Minister (in *Love Actually*) Grant is nondescript, until his love for the slightly overweight tea-lady inspires him to stand up to the bullying US President. There's a strong undercurrent of self-hatred in these films, one that goes beyond traditional British self-deprecation. It seems accepting of, or actually defeatist about, the general 'dumbing down' of British culture. Of course these were mid-Atlantic co-productions, so the suspicion that this is a view of the British that meets with approval in Hollywood is a reasonable one.

It's tempting to see the 'gangster' and 'failure' caricatures of Britishness as mimicking the media's own postures. There's the thug jingoism that overrates any Brit Oscar victory as triumph, the shrugging middle-class defeatism that expects every British film to be a disaster, and even perhaps the occasional lone megalo-maniac who thinks that we could do Hollywood better than they do. Indeed Richard Curtis is brilliant enough to have built British film industry defeatism into the plot of *Notting Hill*, his romance between an insignificant British bookseller and a world-famous Hollywood movie star.

Culture Wars

Anyone writing about British cinema old and new will be struck by the contrast brought about by social change. Actors in films of the 1930s, 40s and 50s sound comically 'posh' today. This is not only because Received Pronunciation has been killed off but also because so many of the offspring of the 60s middle classes have adopted downshifting 'Estuary' accents. In those days of cut-glass accents it was easier for Americans to characterise British films as unwatchable (although harder to ignore the booming British cinema market). British films had some limited pre-war success in the US, notably with Alexander Korda's *The Private Life of Henry VIII* (1933). But when J. Arthur Rank was hoping to take a serious crack at the US market in the mid-40s, he was told that American audiences had several basic objections to British films.

1. The action was too slow.
2. There was too much dialogue.
3. The actors talked too fast and their accents and slang words were difficult to understand.
4. The actresses looked dowdy and the actors seemed effeminate.
5. The physical quality of the films often looked inferior to American productions.[3]

Many of these complaints still seem relevant today. In the immediate aftermath of World War II when Rank was operating, British audiences, as well as the left-wing critics of *Tribune* and the *Penguin Film Review*, thought that British films (particularly war films) were better than US films. One of the marked differences between then and now is that a critical caucus in favour of a national cinema no longer exists. Now, neither the film reviewers nor the industry really believe in national cinema. As Benedict Anderson and Colin McArthur have both argued, national identity is a cultural process of constant formation, and it's no accident that a suddenly fragile sense of identity has struck British film at a time when the United Kingdom itself seems to be fragmenting through

political devolution. It's doubtful in the globalised future that we will talk about British cinema reflecting national concerns. We will continue to have heritage films supported by US finance – and gangster films and Richard Curtis comedies (though these can be seen as heritage concoctions along with the Jane Austen, E. M. Forster and other literary adaptations). But the likelihood of any widely distributed cinema that relates to the multicultural, digital-age, North/South-East divide experiences of today's English population seems remote.

International audiences remain hungry for British subject matter. James Bond, Harry Potter, the denizens of Tolkien's Middle Earth, even Mr Bean, have huge box-office appeal. But is it possible to imagine these films being 'all-British' productions? In the past Alexander Korda might have made them here, perhaps using Powell and Pressburger as his film-making team. Today such fantasy cinema is only conceivable under US control because of the scale of expectations raised by the US blockbuster special-effects movies of the 1980s and 90s. The films might have an all-British cast (as the Harry Potter films do), but most of the profit will find its way back to the American backers. What's at question here is not how high a national identity quotient it takes to make a film British but whether the idiosyncrasy of British literary work is recognised and backed in the UK. Despite the enormous strength of tradition of fantasy literature and film-making in Britain, film companies shy away from imaginative subject matter, and the strong impression gathered from the films they do make is that caution is ever the unconfident watchword.

British Films, American Rules

In May 2000 the Film Council complained that:

> the lack of support for script development is the single biggest problem affecting the ability of the UK industry to deliver a consistent flow of high-quality films. All sectors of the industry agree that . . . this results in finished films which are too often sub-standard and subsequently wholly or partially rejected by the distribution sectors.[4]

The three main potential sources of funding – FilmFour, the BBC and the Film Council's own Premiere Production Fund – quickly adapted to the new development/management culture. All these entities now have the same main aim in mind: to make substantially profitable films with high production values. Such values necessitate big budgets and a determination to control risk factors as much as possible. Scripts have to be able to attract (US and UK) star casting, and work according to the precepts laid down by such American script gurus as Robert McKee, Syd Field and Linda Seger. Stories of British production heads returning from LA with evangelical fervour and wanting everyone to do everything the US way are as sadly routine as is their inevitable, eventual failure. If one looks at the films made via the development process (*Billy Elliot*, 2000, for instance) one might legitimately fear that all idiosyncrasies of structure and texture are routinely ironed out. In that context it is hard to imagine a Michael Powell or a Nic Roeg project ever having been commissioned.

A big budget is the clearest sign that you are making a film that matters. Nothing produces more excitement in the trade press than the bandying about of big figures. But big budgets have unfortunate connotations in Britain. They remind us of Lew Grade's comment about his 70s flop *Raise the Titanic*, that it 'would have been cheaper to lower the Atlantic'. And the $27 million failure of Goldcrest's Al Pacino vehicle *Revolution* (1985) casts its shadow long.[5] A couple of flops of such magnitude can send the whole British industry back into its shell. After Goldcrest collapsed, production had to rely on the television companies fostering a modest British realism from the likes of Ken Loach, Mike Leigh and Stephen Frears.[6] British film-makers wanting to work with bigger budgets usually went to Hollywood.

The approach now is more 'global'. In 2001 FilmFour made *Charlotte Gray* with Warners for more than £12 million. The previous year there was *Bridget Jones's Diary* (Miramax-backed) at £13 million, *Enigma* (a Mick Jagger consortium) at £18.5 million, *Captain Corelli's Mandolin* (Miramax-backed) at £13 million and *Kingdom Come* (Pathé/UA-backed) at £12.5 million.[7] Budgets are creeping up in answer to the complaint that British production values are too inferior for the multiplex age, but with higher budgets tends to come a co-production blandness. Big-budget films can be packaged and made here but only with US 'fire-control'. British producers access big budgets through a controlling US partner (typically Miramax, a company whose yen for British-originated subject matter is very pronounced), because even if the British could raise the finance they don't trust themselves to control the numbers.

British films are very often scolded for looking too much like television, and during the low-budget late 1980s and 90s, this was usually a matter of cleaving to close-ups because it's a cheaper mode of film-making. Many of our directors were trained in shooting television drama, and they do sometimes seem unduly shy of wider shots, but as British directors and cinematographers work regularly on large-scale Hollywood films, such reticence is clearly not endemic to British cinema. In any case some films require an intimate form of cinematography and the lighting style of, for instance, Barry Ackroyd (who shoots Ken Loach's films), is widely imitated across Europe. The push now is for films made for the international market to look 'cinematic', even when it may not be appropriate. It's hard, for instance, to see how the domestic love traumas of *Bridget Jones's Diary* required the same size budget as the epic *Captain Corelli's Mandolin*, though the former's huge success presumably is its own justification.

When a film is entirely funded and shot in Britain and mainly for British consumption, however, the deferential mindset kicks in. The emphasis is always on how little money it can be done for, not on how much it needs to fully achieve its ambitions. For interesting recent British movies, such as Jamie Thraves's *The Low Down* (2000), the low budget (£1 million) is meant somehow to be a funky virtue, but the money was stretched too thin to help its fragile, subtle, tale of slacker lovers. On the other hand, in Saul Metzstein's *Late Night Shopping* (2001), another slacker love story pushed in a more American direction, the script seems skimpily underdeveloped for the opulence of its big-screen approach.

Nothing brings one up colder to the stark realities of the new global film industry than learning how few

Kate Ashfield, Aidan Gillen in *The Low Down* (Jamie Thraves, 2000)

British actors can 'open' a film budgeted above, say, £4 million. To be sure of your cash on the bigger-budgeted films you'd need some A-list movie stars and that has nearly always meant Americans (or Americanised foreigners such as Cary Grant, Sean Connery or Mel Gibson). British producer Herbert Wilcox recognised this in the silent period when he boosted international sales by importing D. W. Griffith starlet Mae Marsh for his *Flames of Passion* (1922), just as Working Title did by casting Texan actress Renée Zellweger as Bridget Jones. When the British film industry does manage to build up its own stars, it then has to compete with Hollywood for the actor's services – Keira Knightley, Jude Law, Daniel Craig, Kate Winslet – are certainly big, after their exposure in Hollywood or Hollywood-backed films, but they are also expensive.

It's worth noting, though, that many of today's international movie stars were 'discovered' in indie or art-house films, not big popular hits. This is true of Russell Crowe (*Proof*, 1991), Antonio Banderas (*Tie Me Up! Tie Me Down!*, 1989), Juliette Binoche (*Mauvais Sang*, 1986), Brad Pitt (*Johnny Suede*, 1991) and Leonardo DiCaprio (*What's Eating Gilbert Grape?*, 1993) as well as Knightley (*Bend It Like Beckham*, 2002), Law (*Shopping*, 1994), Craig (*Love Is the Devil*, 1998) and Winslet (*Heavenly Creatures*, 1994). Perhaps Britain would be better at creating its own movie stars if it wasn't so desperate for a popular audience, or if British television were not such a sinecure for good actors who then find themselves passed over when big screen parts come along.

British Genres

In the 80s it was fairly easy to categorise the kinds of films the British were making. To the fore were Goldcrest-style epics (*Cry Freedom*, 1987, *The Mission*, 1986), heritage films (*A Passage to India*, 1984, *A Room with a View*, 1985) and historic moment films (*Dance with a Stranger*, 1984, *Hope and Glory*, 1987, *White Mischief*, 1987). Supporting these were television-backed social dramas (*My Beautiful Laundrette*, 1985, *Letter to Brezhnev*, 1985), comedies (*Withnail and I*, 1986, *Personal Services*, 1987, *Rita, Sue and Bob Too*, 1986) and political films (*Defence of the Realm*, 1985, *A World Apart*, 1987, *Handsworth Songs*, 1986, *Comrades*, 1986). A visionary sector might also be constructed for the maverick talents of Terry Gilliam (*Brazil*, 1985), Ken Russell (*Gothic*, 1986), Nic Roeg (*Eureka*, 1982), Derek Jarman (*Caravaggio*, 1986), Terence Davies (*Distant Voices, Still Lives*, 1988) and Peter Greenaway (*The Belly of an Architect*, 1987).

The 90s saw much of this fall away, especially in terms of quality, and a greater generic confusion of low-budget films rise up in its place. The epics more or less disappeared (until Miramax brought them back with *The English Patient*, 1996). Heritage films began to lose their lustre (for every *The Madness of King George*, 1994 there was a regrettable *Tom and Viv*, 1994). Social comedies (*Riff-Raff*, 1991, *Bhaji on the Beach*, 1993, *Secrets and Lies*, 1996, *Brassed Off*, 1996, *The Full Monty*, 1997) flourished, and there was a curious trend for producing American independent films (*Trust*, 1990, *Naked Lunch*, 1991, *Walking and Talking*, 1996) from London. But there were fewer political films and historic moment dramas and the wave of gangster films which followed in the wake of *Lock, Stock . . .* , proved even less successful than such films as *Shopping* and *Young Americans* (1993), which had at least proved effective calling cards for their ambitious, Hollywood-bound directors Paul Anderson and Danny Cannon.

In the twenty-first century there has, ironically, been a return to World War II, with big-budget adaptations of *Enigma*, *Captain Corelli's Mandolin* and *Charlotte Gray*. The success of *The English Patient* and *Saving Private Ryan* (1998) might have sparked off this interest but it is the popularity of novels set in the period which has been the most significant factor. The one thing that is predictable about current international film genres is that they follow literary success. History and heritage will thus continue to provide most of Britain's exportable film stories, and nostalgia remains a better bet than any aspect of today's Britain.

Audiences

One disadvantage for any British film set in the present is how difficult it is to seem as universal to international audiences as any ordinary US film about, say, family life. By the careful knitting of recognisable heritage locations and US movie stars into their films, the production company Working Title has managed to conquer this problem. Somehow, for an international audience, the Notting Hill of *Notting Hill* seems as comfortably familiar a place as, say, the Seattle of *Sleepless in Seattle* (1993). One could also argue that the Sheffield of *The Full Monty* is recognisable to anyone living in an industrial town in the post-industrial era; and even that the decorative use of the 1980s miners' strike and an authentic North of England setting were contributing factors to the success of *Billy Elliot*. But this necessitates a compromise, smoothing away the specifically British aspects of the subject.

Since UK audiences mostly show such a pronounced preference for Hollywood cinema, it is often assumed that they should be treated no differently from US audiences. If you want to succeed with the smaller UK demographic, it is argued, then simply aim for the larger US one and kill two birds with one stone. But British producers seem curiously slow to recognise audience trends. The genuine stirrings of national interest aroused by *Trainspotting* were carelessly dissipated. And while Hollywood shifted from its reliance on a predominantly young male audience to cultivate neglected sectors such as children, girls, women and adults (i.e. those over twenty-four), British producers were still trying to please the legendary Des Moines teenage boy with gangster movies. The first crop of Lottery-franchise films – apart from the sumptuous *fin-de-siècle* concoction *An Ideal Husband* (1999) – made few concessions to audience preferences. Lynn Ramsay's *Ratcatcher* (1999), a tale of love and survival on a grim 70s Glasgow estate, Gillies MacKinnon's *Hideous Kinky* (1998), centred upon a feckless mother in hippy-era Morocco, Simon Beaufoy and Billie Eltringham's *The Darkest Light* (1999), a prescient warning about foot-and-mouth disease and social tensions in a Yorkshire farming community, and *The Lost Son* (1999), Chris Menges's sombre story of the smashing of a paedophile ring by a world-weary French detective, are all worthwhile projects, but they seem very distant from the commercial films that the Film Council argues are required to create 'a sustainable British film industry'. The remainder of the bunch – *Janice Beard 45 WPM* (1999), *Fanny and Elvis* (1999), *Love's Labour's Lost* (1999), *Hold Back the Night* (1999), *It Was an Accident* (2000) and *There's Only One Jimmy Grimble* (2000) – are the inevitable

The good mother: Kate Winslet and Carrie Mullan in *Hideous Kinky* (Gillies MacKinnon, 1998)

misfires which might have been excused had the better films enjoyed any commercial success.

Given the traditional antipathy to British films, there is a limit to the number that UK audiences can reasonably be expected to support. During the wartime heyday of British cinema, when critics and the public both (briefly) preferred British films to the US variety, production was at a low of less than fifty films a year. The current glut of production churns out on average at least two new British films a week. In an era when competing demands on leisure time – from the internet to club culture – are more urgent and plentiful than ever, it seems absurd to expect all these films to attract an audience. The problem of wanting 'a sustainable British film industry' is that the domestic market alone may never be hungry enough to support it. The industry is therefore obliged to have a global outlook, but without the resources or the advantage of the huge domestic market enjoyed by Hollywood.

Why Bother?

In terms of being the best European base for studio work, talent scouting, sales agencies and facilities houses, Britain continues to thrive – money earned in these ways has long outstripped any income from film production. But Britain's film companies now shy away from the idea of trying to take on the rest of the world out of any nationalistic impulse. We have been burned every time we do this, as the histories of Korda, Rank, the Grade brothers and Goldcrest confirm.

Now deference is built into every stage of the production process and the US way and the US market are seen as the only game in town. Britain's film industry can't afford to acquire the country's best subject matter. Its film companies want to make substantially budgeted films but generally have to draw in a US partner before they can raise the money. Attempts to please the American market lead to the ironing out of British idiosyncrasies and the reliance on settings and subjects that feel 'universal'. British producers need stars to open these films but only US films can make British actors into stars. Government support has boosted production levels, but few of the films appeal to a mass audience accustomed to big-budget Hollywood fare. US financial acumen and marketing muscle call the shots.

Implicit in the policies of the Film Council's New Cinema Fund is the assumption that cheaper digital 'film'-making will take the place of low-budget and independent film, and that its mode of distribution will not necessarily be through cinemas, but through any number of alternative digital venues. For experimental film-makers the new technology might be seen as a liberating force. John Ellis, for example, argues that, 'The demand from critics that film-makers should create something called "British cinema" is one of the greatest psychic constraints on film-making in this country.'[8] The advent of the sort of artistically adventurous cinema Ellis proposes must surely be welcomed. But its appeal would almost inevitably be limited to a minority audience, and there would be worrying cultural implications if the creation of a subsidised cinema for intellectuals sanctioned the abandonment of popular cinema to Hollywood.

One might hope that the bigger-budget co-productions planned by FilmFour, the BBC and the Film Council will carve for Britain a larger niche of the international film-making market. But the US industry would only welcome such a state of affairs as long as the majority profits continued to leak back to the motherland. If Britain started to self-fund and claim that larger chunk for itself, the full historic force of US protectionism would again be weighed against British cinema.

So the sensible target for the Film Council is a much higher level of co-production that could keep everyone happy without the Americans feeling too threatened. The depressing consequence of this though, is more of the Natopudding – more films in the mould of *Chocolat* (2001) and *Captain Corelli's Mandolin*. When one of the characters in Wim Wenders's *Kings of the Road* (1976) claimed that 'the Americans have colonised our subconscious', it was viewed as a controversial – if perceptive – insight. Now American cultural and economic dominance is accepted as a fact of life. It has its advantages (big-budget Hollywood cinema can sometimes be a joy to behold), but with such cultural homogenisation comes the danger that the stories told within this Americanised global subconscious will be vapid ghosts of what they might have been had cultural diversity survived. That's why we still need British movies.

Notes

1. According to David Puttnam, the crucial change came in the 1980s and 90s when the film industry's 'move towards international financing reflected the globalisation of capital which resulted from the deregulation of financial markets around the world'. David Puttnam, *The Undeclared War*, p. 324. For an explanation of vertical and horizontal integration see 'Vertical Hold', *Sight and Sound*, October 1994, p. 3.
2. See Chapter 41 by Steve Chibnall in the present volume for a more positive assessment of the gangster cycle.
3. Geoffrey Macnab, *J. Arthur Rank and the British Film Industry*, p. 73.
4. Film Council, 'Towards a Sustainable UK Film Industry', 2 May 2000, p. 14.
5. Figure from SIFT, the BFI's database.
6. For Goldcrest's rise and fall see Jake Eberts and Terry Ilott, *My Indecision Is Final*.
7. Figures from *Screen Finance*, 5 July 2000.
8. John Ellis, 'British Made', *Sight and Sound*, December 1991, pp. 33–4.

Bibliography

Barr, Charles, *Ealing Studios*, 2nd edn (London: Studio Vista, 1993).

Eberts, Jake and Ilott, Terry, *My Indecision Is Final* (London: Faber and Faber, 1990).

Hill, John, *British Cinema in the 1980s* (Oxford: Clarendon Press, 1999).

Macnab, Geoffrey, *J. Arthur Rank and the British Film Industry* (London: Routledge, 1993).

Puttnam, David, with Neil Watson, *The Undeclared War* (London: HarperCollins, 1997).

Roddick, Nick, 'Show Me the Culture', *Sight and Sound*, December 1998.

Romney, Jonathan, 'On New Trends and Emerging Talents in Current British Cinema', *Film Comment* vol. 37 no. 1, January/February 2001.

Rosenbaum, Jonathan, *Movie Wars* (Chicago, IL: A Capella, 2000).

Ryall, Tom, *Britain and the American Cinema* (London: Sage, 2001).

4

Paradise Found and Lost: The Course of British Realism

GEOFF BROWN

The cinema, it seemed for a moment, was about to fulfil its natural destiny of discovering mankind. It had everything for the task. It could get about, it could view reality with a new intimacy; and what more natural than the recording of the real world should become its principal inspiration?
John Grierson, 'The Course of Realism'

Grierson and the Establishment of the Realist Aesthetic

The particular moment John Grierson writes about in his famous essay about cinema realism was the end of the 19th century, when Louis Lumière aimed his Cinématographe at workers leaving the Lumière factory in Lyons, at the train puffing into La Ciotat station, or his brother Auguste and his wife feeding their baby. In Grierson's eyes the moment of bliss did not last long. The Lumière workmen were scarcely out of the factory, he wrote, than cinema

> was taking a trip to the moon and, only a year or two later, a trip in full colour to the devil. The scarlet women were in, and the high falsehood of trickwork and artifice was in, and reality and the first fine careless rapture were out.[1]

Grierson writes about the onset of Georges Méliès and his films of fantasy almost as though Méliès were Satan himself, hurling a wrecking ball at the Garden of Eden. There is a reason for this. Grierson's childhood upbringing was among Presbyterians, who took the strong Calvinist view that play-acting was a sinful activity. Imagine the shudder, then, when instead of documenting places, people and their workaday lives, cinema took off to visit the devil's lair itself.

In Britain, cinema began in the same way as in France. It observed the world. In 1895 Birt Acres used his camera to record actual sporting events, the Oxford and Cambridge Boat Race on 30 March, the Derby on 29 May, or natural spectacles like *Rough Sea at Dover*. Once again the devil's work – trick shots and fantasy – soon appeared. Robert Paul, who collaborated on the camera used in Acres's early films, proved particularly adept at exploring slow-motion, superimpositions, and other simple ways of moving beyond what Grierson called 'the recording of the real world'.

Grierson's commitment to the realist cause did not blind him to other aesthetics: this was the man who had a passion for marionettes, and supervised some film shorts in 1928 featuring puppet burlesques of Hollywood stars. But through word and deed he proselytised so hard for what he termed 'the documentary idea' that when serious film criticism developed in Britain (from the late 20s onwards) realism quickly became accepted as our cinema's worthiest goal and greatest strength. The talents drawn into the Empire Marketing Board Film Unit, the GPO Film Unit and other documentary outfits of the 1930s were also the country's brightest critics: in articles and reviews for *Cinema Quarterly*, *World Film News* and other organs, Grierson himself, Paul Rotha, Basil Wright and Edgar Anstey proved passionate champions of realist films and skilled debunkers of whatever pap poured from Hollywood or Denham.

'The British film lacks honest conception,' Paul Rotha thundered in his seminal book *The Film till Now*, first published in 1930. In Rotha's eyes it also lacked a British nationality: we were either aping American models or groping vaguely for the stylistic and psychological habits of the German school. The world beyond the studio doors was being ignored: 'Our railways, our industries, our towns, and our countryside,' he wrote, 'are waiting for incorporation into narrative films.'[2]

At the time, Rotha only had Grierson's own herring-fleet epic *Drifters*, completed in 1929, to place on a pedestal as 'a suggestion of that which waits to be accomplished'. As the 1930s developed, there were occasional film documents for the realist propagandists to praise – like Flaherty's *Man of Aran* (1934), or Wright's *Song of Ceylon* (1934) – but they found slim pickings in a fictional cinema dominated by the extravaganzas of Korda or the vocal twirlings and high kicks of Jessie Matthews. The railways, the industries, the whole realist aesthetic, were waiting still. Only in World War II, when Britain's feature film-makers received new blood from the documentary field, did mainstream cinema begin to win critical favour for reflecting life beyond the studio gates.

The success of the British wartime product, from *'Fires Were Started –'* (1943) to *Millions Like Us* (1943) and *The Way Ahead* (1944), further cemented the realist aesthetic as the critics' preferred mode for British films. Few later writers quite shared Grierson's preacher's zeal, but you can certainly feel an echo of the Calvinist distaste for fiction coursing through the influential pages of the *Penguin Film Review* in the 1940s. To Roger Manvell and the other earnest evangelicals of the *Review*, it was far better to stare soberly at fishermen's nets or Bren guns than to gaze in delight at Betty Grable. From their perspective, the national ideal remained *In Which We Serve* (1942) or some other wartime epic of quiet heroism, shot in various shades of battleship grey. The national disgrace was the dingy sensationalism of *No Orchids for Miss Blandish* (1948), or *They Made Me a Fugitive* (1947) and its fellow spiv dramas.[3]

The British cinema revival of the late 1950s only strengthened the critical orthodoxy that enthroned the realist aesthetic. The British New Wave of Richardson, Anderson, Reisz and Schlesinger was greeted with fanfares because the films faced people's emotions head-on and swept away what had grown to be regarded as dull studio artifice. Cameras went out and about, especially up North, far from the Rank Organisation's domain in Pinewood, where Dirk Bogarde preened in pretty pullovers, or the theatre's stronghold in Shaftesbury Avenue, which had stocked our cinema with so many actors and so much material. Characters were not cosy couples in Mayfair or the shires, but working-class people, tart and passionate. The same value was found in Ken Loach's focus on social problems and the underprivileged in *Poor Cow* (1967) and *Kes* (1969); though for some the suspicion was growing that in abandoning the drawing room for the kitchen sink, British cinema had substituted one easy formula for another. Reviewing *Poor Cow* appreciatively in the *Sunday Times*, Dilys Powell still observed that 'the cinema, in fact is as class-ridden as ever, and a new snobbery has been substituted for the old'.[4]

Only in the 70s and 80s did the pendulum decisively swing the other way, against realism. Critical and popular appreciation grew for what you might almost term Satan's cinema: the adventurous work of Derek Jarman or Peter Greenaway, or, reclaimed from the past, the films of Powell and Pressburger, Hammer horrors and Gainsborough melodramas. At the same time, in the journal *Screen* and numerous academic havens the very mechanics of cinema were being investigated; films and their meanings were deconstructed into codes, signifiers and modes of representation. This put the entire notion of realism under threat in a different way: if what we saw on the screen is a mere chimera, an illusion manufactured through symbols, and audience expectations, how could we ever believe again in the reality of Grierson's herrings, Humphrey Jennings's firemen, or the other touchstones of British realism?

The increasing technical sophistication of the films audiences see has brought its own damage to the realist aesthetic. Our gaze now is not so trusting or innocent. But the history of British screen realism remains: a persistent, convoluted history stretching from the fishermen of *Drifters* and the down-and-outs of John Baxter's *Doss House* (1933) to the flyers, gunners and factory workers of World War II, the Northern lads of *Room at the Top* (1959) and its New Wave successors, right up to the urban flotsam of Andrea Arnold's *Red Road* (2006) or Shane Meadows's *This Is England* (2006). The history includes an iconography, too. Think British realism, and you think inevitably of kitchen sinks, tall chimneys, cobblestones, railway arches, bleak stretches of moor or beach, graffiti-lined council estates, people and landscapes placed in spare and striking juxtaposition. You also tend to think black-and-white: the perfect colour scheme for gloomy skies, smokestacks and poetic melancholy.

The same history teaches us that one decade's notion of what constitutes realism rarely matches another's. Eyes that have become used to the raw dialogue exchanges and lurching camerawork of contemporary fly-on-the-wall TV and the voyeurs' paradise of *Big Brother* will always find fault with most vintage films that carry the realist label. Looking now at Laurence Harvey's portrayal of Joe Lampton in *Room at the Top*, we tend to see Harvey the glamorous and pushy film star, strutting about with his porcupine brush of hair, self-assurance and carefully applied Northern accent, rather than John Braine's original character of the vulgar opportunist desperate to escape the mean streets of his small Yorkshire town. In some ways Harvey's characterisation is not much of an advance on the Yorkshire fisherfolk depicted in J. Arthur Rank's first venture into feature film-making, *Turn of the Tide* (1935), an important realist milestone in its day, but now rendered quaint by, among other things, the number of times that Irish-born actor Niall MacGinnis keeps trying to prove his new nationality by saying 'Champion'. Similarly, in *San Demetrio London* (1943), one of Ealing's main contributions to realist cinema, admiration for the script's expression of homely heroics as the crew of a burnt-out tanker struggle home across the Atlantic is compromised, however slightly, by the knowledge that their life-and-death battle with the elements takes place in the studio tank.

Film history also demonstrates that realism in British cinema has marked class boundaries. The notion that realist films could embrace characters of the upper middle-class and beyond has rarely been considered. Realistic characters in British films wear cloth caps, not top hats, though most of the top industry personnel would have been far more at home in the Mayfair night clubs and hotels that haunt British films, of the 30s and 50s especially, than any eel-and-pie shop. Should the accepted iconography of British realism be extended, then, to include the padded armchairs of gentlemen's clubs, complete with monocled twit slumbering over *The Times*, or a butler holding out cocktails on a silver tray, or the marbled halls that were home to Anna Neagle and Michael Wilding in escapist frolics like *Spring in Park Lane* (1948)? It is worth a thought.

Communist, zoologist and intermittent film-maker Ivor Montagu certainly realised the camera's ability to record the aristocracy, follies and all. Entrusted by Gaumont-British with filming linking sequences for *Wings over Everest*, an account of a 1933 flying expedition financed by the flamboyantly patriotic Lady

Houston and led in the air by the Marquess of Clydesdale, he found he had inadvertently made what he later described as 'the most perfect picture of the English governing class that has ever been seen'.[5] There is realism of a sort, too, in the parade of stilted officers who appear as themselves in propaganda shorts of World War II, answering phone calls from Whitehall, briefing pilots, pointing at targets on maps, sometimes venturing to speak words of uplift straight to the camera. Vowels, moustaches, body language: all now belong to a vanished world, preserved by the camera like a fly in amber.

Realism versus Artifice: Feature Films in the 1930s

During the 30s, boom years alike for British commercial production and the documentary movement, you can clearly see the tussle in films between the gospels of realism and artifice. It was not only Grierson, Rotha and their colleagues who proselytised for a greater reflection of real life in British films; film-company executives, mindful of the prevailing critical temper, also emerged with ringing declarations of patriotic intent. Here is Michael Balcon, two years before he established himself at Ealing, writing in the London *Evening News* in October 1936:

> We see the dramatic entertainment in the life of the
> farmer on the fells of the North, of the industrial
> worker in the Midlands, of the factory girls of
> London's new industrial areas, of the quiet shepherds
> of Sussex. I believe that the sweep of the Sussex
> Downs against the sky makes as fine a background to
> a film as the hills of California; that Kentish and
> Worcestershire orchards and farms are as picturesque
> as the farmlands of Virginia; that the slow talk of
> labourers round an English village pub fire makes as
> good dialogue as the wise-cracks of 'City Slickers' in
> New York.[6]

Balcon, however, was writing after five years as head of production at the Gaumont-British studios of Shepherd's Bush, where you would more likely find Ruritanian royalty, American gangsters or music-hall Cockneys than slow-talking farm labourers supping pints. Only once had Gaumont-British allowed something approaching the realism that Grierson favoured through its portals; and that was Flaherty's *Man of Aran*, a somewhat romantic account of the Aran islanders' daily battles with sea and seaweed, potatoes and sharks, off the Galway coast, for which Flaherty began preliminary investigations in 1931.

For Gaumont-British the project meant cultural prestige, and a way of fending off increasing criticism that British films, theirs included, neglected real life. With *Man of Aran* finally completed in 1934, every possible publicity angle was utilised to bring home the film's exotic appeal. Maggie Dirrane, the islander who played the wife of the nameless Aran man whose travails provided the slender story, was paraded in Selfridges by the *Daily Express* and asked for her opinion of silk stockings. A stuffed basking shark was put on display in the window of Gaumont-British's Wardour Street offices. Since the shark was too large for the available space, a chunk was removed from its middle, to Flaherty's fury: a choice symbol for the way market forces squeezed realism out of mainstream British cinema.[7]

Ballyhoo and the lure of Flaherty's images made the film a modest commercial success. But it scarcely paved the way for regular doses of realism, even of Flaherty's highly scented variety. Like *Man of Aran*, Rank's *Turn of the Tide*, directed by Norman Walker, won a prize for Britain at the Venice Film Festival, but no ballyhoo was whipped up by the distributors – Gaumont-British again – and lack of promotion ensured a quiet death at the box office.

Up until the months before World War II, when two adaptations of novels by A. J. Cronin, *The Citadel* (1938) and *The Stars Look Down* (1939), caught some aspects of working-class conditions, realism had led an almost subterranean life in British feature films. Efforts to reach down into society were relegated to low-budget,

The Common Touch (John Baxter, 1941): a keen eye for the detail of working-class life

second-feature ventures like John Baxter's *Doss House*, a brave excursion into the lower depths of a London lodging-house, an exercise repeated in several later Baxter films like *Hearts of Humanity* (1936), *The Common Touch* (1941) and *Judgment Deferred* (1951). From today's perspective it is easy to smile at the sentimental colouring Baxter gives to his down-and-outs, and his naive belief that kindness alone will make the world a better place. Easy, too, to grate the teeth at the amount of cap-doffing and the acquiescent talk about 'people like us'. But Baxter still showed a keen eye and ear for the detail of working-class life. Even John Grierson recognised the value of Baxter's approach: his films, Grierson, wrote, were 'sentimental to the point of embarrassment; but at least about real people's sentimentalities'.[8]

Realism Goes to War

With the onset of war, Baxter contributed much simple, morale-boosting entertainment. He also made a film from Walter Greenwood's novel about a Lancashire family in the teeth of the Depression, *Love on the Dole* (1941), a project that had only recently emerged from the British Board of Film Censors' ban on prospective film versions. The BBFC had objected to bad language, the conflict between unemployed workers and the police, and the fate of the heroine, Sally Hardcastle, who escapes from poverty only by becoming a bookmaker's mistress. War changed the climate; and the film duly arrived, hampered occasionally by studio artifice and the theatrical poise of Deborah Kerr (Sally) and Clifford Evans (her agitator fiancé), but carried through to victory by pungent dialogue and depth of feeling.

Not everyone was gratified. 'Why *Love on the Dole* now when *Love in a Shelter* would perhaps be more apt?', Paul Rotha commented in November 1940 when Baxter's film was in production.[9] In time British cinema got to grips with shelters, dug-outs, cockpits, factory canteens and the other arenas of war on the home front and abroad. Only now did expectant talk about 'putting the real Britain on the screen' produce concrete results: after years of uncertainty and a good deal of trailing in America's shadow, the war finally gave British films a distinctive subject to pursue, and a moral reason for doing so. For their escapist entertainment, audiences would now turn mostly to America: aside from our comedies and thrillers, where some old habits still persisted, British films began to be peopled by men in uniform, women at the work bench, girls in the ATS or the old faithfuls in the Home Guard.

Wartime realism did not arrive overnight. When Balcon mounted *Convoy*, his first fictional war feature, in the spring of 1940, the extensive location material shot in the North Sea had to fight it out with Clive Brook festooned with gold braid and decorations viewing the war through binoculars, a dull romantic triangle, and a U-boat crew who talk about firing 'torpedo number Zwei'. Even though Balcon's ranks at Ealing were swelled with recruits from the documentary field, like the cinema virtuoso Cavalcanti and Harry Watt, the director of *London Can Take It* (1940) and *Target for Tonight* (1941), artifice ran rampant one year later through *Ships with Wings* (1941), a drama about the Fleet Air Arm containing puppet characters and unusually bad model work. Asked for his opinion after a private screening, Noël Coward, appalled at its artificiality, uttered only one word, 'Gamages', the name of the London toy store.[10]

At the time Coward, helped by co-director David Lean, was preparing his own naval war drama, *In Which We Serve*, one of the films that established the parameters for feature-film realism not just during the war but throughout the 50s, when British cinema fought the war all over again with Kenneth More or Jack Hawkins. In this drama inspired by the fortunes of Mountbatten's ship, HMS *Kelly*, the classes were clearly defined: working, middle and upper; the dialogue crisp, a touch theatrical, especially when Coward himself (as the Mountbatten surrogate, Captain Kinross) was talking. Once talk stopped, however, and action took over, sharply paced editing and sober, documentary-style photography lifted the film away from theatre to present a convincing cinema reflection of the prevailing mood of all classes pulling together for Britain.

Post-war: The Fall from Paradise and the British New Wave

The success of *In Which We Serve* and others enthroned realism as the preferred national style. It 'set a new standard in the English cinema', Dilys Powell wrote in 1947.[11] Without the urgent necessity of war, however, British cinema began slipping from paradise. The post-war years saw the Technicolor follies of Powell and Pressburger, the Expressionist angles and dark shadows of *Odd Man Out* (1947) and *They Made Me a Fugitive*. The realistic approach persisted but atrophied as the range of fresh material tackled by British movies shrunk, and location material was wrapped around dim, anodyne family comedies or dramas.

Searching for moments of piercing realism or contemporary relevance in British films of the early and middle 50s is a doleful task. Surveying the scene from 1945 onwards in his 1957 essay 'Get Out and Push!', Lindsay Anderson penned a litany echoing the lists of British cinema's missing ingredients drawn up by Rotha and others decades earlier:

> The nationalisation of the coal fields; the Health Service; nationalised railways; compulsory secondary education – events like these, which cry out to be interpreted in human terms, have produced no films. Nor have many of the problems which have bothered us in the last ten years: strikes; Teddy Boys; nuclear tests; the loyalties of scientists; the insolence of bureaucracy . . .[12]

Though staring at much British cinema in the 50s is indeed like staring into a void, the realistic surface of the films never entirely disappears. A negative brand of realism exists in the *Scotland Yard* series of low-budget crime shorts hosted by Edgar Lustgarten, where inspectors sit in dingy offices surrounded by Eastlight box files and track down criminals at 30 mph in their Wolseley cars. Livelier examples bubble to the surface in a stage comedy on film like *Sailor Beware!* (1956), directed by Gordon Parry, which taps into the humorous vernacular that sustained British music-hall, and demonstrates a sharp nose for lowly detail. In the home of Ma Hornett, the dragon whose daughter is getting married, the camera cuts to a teapot stain on a newly polished sideboard. Cigarette ash is tapped, perforce, into a cast-off shoe. A seedy church organist pedals away in his socks. Such details may not be what Grierson had in mind when he wrote in 'The Course of Realism' about the cinema being able to 'view reality with a new intimacy', but they linger in the mind and their force should be not denied.

Ironically, it was the producers of *Sailor Beware*, Jack Clayton, James Woolf and the Romulus–Remus outfit, who proceeded to *Room at the Top*, one of the films that gave British cinema its much needed kick in the pants in the late 50s. Laurence Harvey's impersonation of a Northerner may have been a sop to the old star system, just as Simone Signoret's casting in a role conceived in John Braine's novel as a local character reinforced the old-fashioned notion that loose, dangerous women were usually foreign, and generally French. But future films called on the services of a new breed of actors, mostly from the North, trained in the theatre, whose faces, accents and rebellious spirit helped immeasurably in strengthening the new brand of realism. There was Albert Finney in *Saturday Night and Sunday Morning* (1960); Tom Courtenay in *The Loneliness of the Long Distance Runner* (1962) and *Billy Liar* (1963); Richard Harris in *This Sporting Life* (1963); Rita Tushingham in *A Taste of Honey* (1961).

To many British audiences and film-makers, the industrial landscapes and bleak Northern skies shown in these films had an almost exotic lure. 'Directors certainly were enchanted with the North,' Keith Waterhouse, the co-author of *Billy Liar*, recalled in 1993; 'At one time you couldn't walk around the slag heaps without tripping over a light cable. They were roaming all over the place.'[13] Slag heaps, smoking chimneys, canals: the black-and-white photography of Denys Coop and Walter Lassally revelled in them all.

However, the new urge to rush out on location and probe neglected areas of Britain did not derive directly from the realist tradition of Grierson. The impetus to look and think afresh came partly from the spate of new writing and theatre in the mid-50s: the era of the Angry Young Man, personified most memorably by John Osborne's creation Jimmy Porter, who sprawled among Sunday newspapers in a dingy Midlands flat in *Look Back in Anger*, spewing out vitriol. Encouragement also came from the films of the French *nouvelle vague*: those of Godard and Truffaut gloried especially in the handheld camera's giddy freedom as it sped along streets catching passers-by unaware.

Any documentary allegiances that the new breed of British directors claimed were rather to the brief phenomenon of Free Cinema, a label originally attached to six programmes of shorts and documentaries presented at the National Film Theatre between 1956 and 1959, including Lindsay Anderson's portrait of the Covent Garden market, *Every Day except Christmas* (1957) and Karel Reisz's *We Are the Lambeth Boys* (1959). Their surrounding publicity emphasised the importance of artistic freedom and a commitment to portraying contemporary society; the films' styles combined documentary reportage with the cinema tools of montage and the poetic image.

In the event the British New Wave proved more of a ripple. As the 60s advanced and naturalism's novelty waned, so did the cinema audience's taste for the bleaker side of life. Directors like Anderson, Richardson and Schlesinger shifted their ground, back to theatre, or forwards to Hollywood. Anderson's *This Sporting Life*, the most uncompromising of all the New Wave features, fared badly at the box office in 1963; *Billy Liar*, where realism and fantasy jostled in the hero's larkish mind, was more to the public taste. At the end of the film Billy was supposed to flee the parochial North and take a train to London. At the last minute he ducks the challenge, leaving his girlfriend (Julie Christie) to go alone. British cinema duly followed, discovering – indeed, half-inventing – Swinging London. Realism was edged out; caricature and parody moved in.

Realist Television and Ken Loach

By the mid-60s, images of direct social observation were far more likely to be found on television, not in the cinemas. No British cinema film of 1966 had a fraction of the force of *Cathy Come Home*, Jeremy Sandford's play about a homeless mother, filmed by Ken Loach for the *Wednesday Play* slot on BBC2. The camerawork was unadorned, the tone unrelenting, almost belligerent. *Wednesday Play* dramas ripped stories from headlines, and made television seem the natural place for the airing of social issues.

The situation continued for much of the intervening forty years, for all the tension between broadcasters and government that developed during the Thatcher years. Film-makers will follow the funding, and for many with a naturalistic bent this led them to the BBC, and, after 1982, to Channel 4. Even now, when economic, commercial and technological considerations have diluted and diminished serious TV programming, the continuing history of British cinema realism remains linked to the box in the living-room corner.

The continuing history of British realism is also inextricably linked to Ken Loach, who has shown remarkable steadfastness to socialist beliefs and a realistic aesthetic during years of upheaval among unsympathetic governments and the changing priorities of film and television executives. All the concern Loach shows for Sandford's homeless mother in *Cathy Come Home* is lavished almost three decades later on the prickly heroine of *Ladybird, Ladybird* (1994), a single mother with a violent streak who runs foul of the social services.

Not that Loach's brand of realism has been set in concrete. *Poor Cow*, his first cinema feature, adopts a naturalistic mode for the acting, but punctuates and cradles scenes with title cards and other distancing devices. The later Loach forgoes embellishments and stylistic disruption. He appreciates the telling image, like the rat caught in the opening shots of *Riff-Raff* (1991) scurrying by a crumpled NHS prescription form; but his message is mostly conveyed by an unfussy camera usually

Poor Cow (Ken Loach, 1967)

'On the muddy grass a blue plastic comb and a sweet paper.' This descriptive sentence from Nell Dunn's 1967 novel *Poor Cow* might almost have been lifted from a shooting script. In fact, Ken Loach's adaptation, made the same year, passes the comb and paper by; it's the heroine and her situation that grips the camera. His adaptation slims but does not distort Dunn's plot – her first long-form creation after the interlinked stories of *Up the Junction*, filmed by Loach for TV two years earlier.

Our heroine, named with ironic intent, is Joy (Carol White): in her early twenties, living in London's dowdy Fulham with a young child and her husband (John Bindon), a petty thief with a violent streak. Robbery booty briefly whisks them to the suburbs, but after Tom is sent to jail Joy falls for the more tender care of Dave (Terence Stamp), another criminal. When he too goes to jail, Joy drifts into compromise and promiscuity, but never shakes off the vague dream that love with Dave will find a way.

Where is the realist tradition here? You're hit with it in the opening birth scene, deliberately placed as a slap in the face. You find it reflected in Brian Probyn's Eastmancolor photography, darting hand-held with Carol White against the background of passers-by, soaking up the grim housing, or the windswept beach. No leading player consistently manages to give words a natural, improvised flow; but the dialogue's salt is real enough.

Yet repeatedly, the realist surface becomes disrupted by shifts in register and tone. Title cards interrupt scenes with brusque clarity, like refugees from a Godard film or a dramatic narrative by Brecht. The realism is complicated further by soundtrack stretches of Joy's musings (indulgent, sentimental); readings from Joy's letters to Dave; and her climactic monologue to camera, delivered to an off-screen interviewer. *Poor Cow* was Loach's first cinema film, and it's tempting to regard these distancing tricks as outdated flourishes. But Dunn's novel rotates its viewpoints in similar ways, with the chaotic perspectives of Joy's monologues and letters spliced into a spare narration. Dunn's text inspired these visual jolts, not artistic fashion.

Another disruption arrives with Joy and Dave's trip to Wales, when Joy is enthralled by a waterfall. Probyn's camera follows suit: its glistening jets form

Sixties realism: Carol White in *Poor Cow*

the backdrop to an extended lovers' kiss. Does this cliché show the hand of a producer (Joseph Janni), insistent upon a marketable shot? Possibly. But it also chimes with the romantic perspective threaded through the film. Joy herself burbles with clichéd phrases – "It was terrific . . . it was fantastic" – and White's warmly felt performance contributes its own softening, smoothing the edges of a character often devious, always naive. No moral judgments are passed on these people; any finger-pointing is directed at circumstances and environment.

There is no equivocation about Loach's ending. Filmed cinéma-vérité-style, Joy talks about her right to happiness with Dave; but the framing and her awkward angle tell us that, poor cow, she's chasing a phantom.

FURTHER READING

Jan Dawson, '*Poor Cow*', *Monthly Film Bulletin*, February 1968, p. 23.

Nell Dunn, *Poor Cow* (London: Virago Press, 1988).

directed at non-professional actors, and a microphone happy even with the fearfully strong local accent of the Glaswegian teenager in *Sweet Sixteen* (2002).

Any variations in tone between Loach's films stem rather from the writers. Bill Jesse, in *Riff-Raff*, provides salty comedy and always makes his building-site crew of Geordies, Scots, blacks, whites, dreamers and activists people rather than political mouthpieces. Jim Allen, whose collaborations range from the four-part TV series *Days of Hope* (1975) to *Land and Freedom* (1995), has a keen eye and ear for life at the bottom of society's ladder, but tends to mount his soapbox. At best Paul Laverty, Loach's regular writer since *Carla's Song* (1996), can bring real heart and anger to a project, as in *Sweet Sixteen*. At less than his best, in the mixed-race drama of *Ae Fond Kiss . . .* (2004), naturalism can be compromised by the sense of a formula grinding away.

Mike Leigh

Loach's realism is realism with a cause, and few other current directors share his passionate commitment. Mike Leigh, who also in his early days alternated between television and film, works in an ostensibly realistic mode, but has often treated ordinary life as the subject for cruel satire, not compassion. He came into film through theatre, continuing his stage practice of hammering out characterisations and action with his cast through weeks of intense improvisation. *Bleak Moments* (1971), his first film, assembled a string of uncomfortable social encounters between London suburban types, twisting the silences and halting words into a painfully comic portrait of repressed, wasted lives. Subsequent work, largely for television or theatre until the late 80s, swiftly revealed that for all the use of group improvisation to ward off the cadences learned in acting schools, Leigh's brand of realism came perilously close to caricature.

From *Bleak Moments* through to *Abigail's Party* (1977), *Life Is Sweet* (1991) and *Career Girls* (1997), the class and character of Leigh's creations are constantly pinned down through verbal or physical tics: a tradition some might trace back to Ben Jonson's comedies of humours or even the *commedia dell'arte*. In *Bleak Moments* characters are defined through their nervous gasps of breath, the grimaces of their mouths, the way they finger a nose. Even when Leigh raised his ambitions with *Naked* (1993) the tactic still held. For all the compassion spread among his unfortunate and woebegone characters, traces remain in later films, especially *All or Nothing* (2002). The thickness of gloom in Leigh's

films can also be a problem. One doesn't wish the 1950s abortionist heroine of *Vera Drake* (2004) to fall into the song and dance of *Topsy-Turvy* (2000), Leigh's amiable Gilbert and Sullivan biography, but the film's concentrated austerity of mood and setting eventually suggests miserabilism rather than realism.

Paradise Lost – or at Least Mislaid

Yet for all their patterned behaviour and chiselled misery, Leigh's strongest films, *Naked* among them, still reverberate as realist documents in post-1980s cinema. For these are hard times for the realist aesthetic, and they have been for some years. True, the arrival of Channel 4 generated an explosion of small-scale television films with a realist surface; there were tales of adolescent love, of illness and urban disillusionment. The impoverished London of Stephen Frears's *My Beautiful Laundrette* (1985), written by Hanif Kureishi, struck a chord, but too much of the product plumbed no depths and hurt no one.

Aside from realism in fictional form, however diluted, television in the 80s increasingly played host to fly-on-the-wall documentary series such as Roger Graef's *Police* (1982), where the cameras spied on a Reading division of the Thames Valley police as they went about their daily business. Saturated at home with real-life dramas, whether authentic or feigned, audiences found less need to seek them out in the cinema; and film-makers, financiers and distributors felt less need to provide them. The late 70s had seen the rebirth of the Hollywood escapist spectacle, with *Jaws* (1975), *Star Wars* (1977) and their successors. Such films pulled a new, younger audience into the cinemas, an audience keyed to American tastes. You went to the cinema to be amazed, showered with special effects and the unreal. If you really wanted two British people arguing round a kitchen sink, you stayed at home and watched your parents, or switched on the box.

Britain made its own contribution to Hollywood's new cinema of wonder: in many cases we supplied the studios and technicians. Our indigenous product followed the fashion, too, though at a distance. Aside from Loach, Mike Leigh, the Amber Collective's dramas of life in north-east England, or the intense and poetic biographical excavations of Terence Davies, British cinema in the 80s was weighted towards fantasy, the surreal, and period nostalgia. Peter Greenaway built a cult audience for the eccentric artifice of *The Draughtsman's Contract* (1982) and its successors. With films like *Caravaggio* (1986) and *The Garden* (1990)

Naked (Mike Leigh, 1993)

Mike Leigh's abrasive *Naked* advertises its dominant tone in the very first sequence. A hand-held camera hones in on a rape in a grim alley; the scene is violent and uncomfortable. The male perpetrator (David Thewlis) runs off to a car and drives through the night, from Manchester to London. But he only escapes to another urban nightmare. Moving between his ex-girlfriend's rented flat and the unfriendly streets, Thewlis's Johnny – scruffy, misogynist, a motormouth spokesman of millennial doom – continues to spew aggression. Even so, he's trumped in violence by the invasions of the yuppie Jeremy (perhaps the flat's landlord, perhaps not), who rapes with a preening cruelty made nastier still by the character's cartoon depiction.

In his Director's Statement written for the Cannes Festival première, Leigh hoped that he'd made a film 'as funny as it is sad, as beautiful as it is irksome and as responsible as it is anarchic'. Female viewers, especially, might struggle to find an equable balance among these contradictions. The film's stylistics offer their own battleground. In its broad material, *Naked* approaches the social topics that have come to mark the modern British realist film: the unemployed, the drifting homeless, the drugged, the sharpened social divide left by Thatcher's Britain. But his approach to image and character always shades in enough artifice to leave the film's realism smudged and compromised.

Operating his own camera, Director of Photography Dick Pope lights and frames with a formal regard displayed in no previous Mike Leigh film, and few indeed that have come after. The editing is proactive, too, tightening the scenes' conflicts through swift cuts and juxtapositions. The characters maintain their own distance from reality through Leigh's tendency to caricature through language and behavioural tics. Lesley Sharp's ex-girlfriend Louise, bruised but pliable, seems the most normal, truthful creation. The most artificial are Greg Cruttwell's Jeremy, a cardboard cut-out yuppie monster, and Claire Skinner's Sandra – a late arrival in the plot who greets

Millennial doom: David Thewlis in *Naked*

the flat's chaos with unfinished sentences and much chopping of hands. Thewlis's Johnny, grating but compelling, and Katrin Cartlidge's Sophie, the forlorn Goth dopehead who talks through her teeth, belong in the middle range: recognisable characters at their core, but pushed to excess.

The script takes its own detours from realist expectations. Out on the streets, Johnny is saved from a cold doorstep by Brian (Peter Wight), security guard for an unoccupied City office block. Their existential debate, roping in Nostradamus and the Book of the Apocalypse, might not be that believable; but it pleasurably allows Leigh's bleak despair about urban living to emerge with wry humour, not rage.

And despite the violence, there is compassion of sorts inside the film's startling mosaic. Not compassion for the homeless: as a social document *Naked* never progresses far, though there's a genuine and affecting concern, as usual with Leigh, for the lost and insecure. "Will you give me a cuddle, Johnny?" Louise asks near the end: a moment of tenderness in the flat's toilet. But there's still no happy ending.

FURTHER READING

Michael Coveney, *The World According to Mike Leigh* (London: HarperCollins, 1997).

Howie Movshovitz (ed.), *Mike Leigh Interviews* (Jackson: University Press of Mississippi, 2000).

Derek Jarman achieved his own following for his exuberantly personal work, combining avant-garde stylistics with a strongly romantic sensibility.

Helped by the novels of E. M. Forster, the Merchant Ivory production team consolidated their position as chief purveyors of 'heritage cinema', producing films that coalesce in the mind into a dream picture of Edwardian bliss, of country houses, parasols, ormolu clocks, pretty ladies and willowy young men. Films such as *Howards End* (1992), perhaps the most accomplished of the breed, offer an escape into an imaginary paradise. Like the BBC's adaptations of novels by Jane Austen, George Eliot or lesser mortals, they are comfort blankets for a hostile age.

Out in British cinema's commercial sector, 110 years after the medium's birth, Grierson's concern for 'recording . . . the real world' finds scant reflection. The 1990s brought a rush of films with no time for patient observation, least of all Paul Anderson's *Shopping* (1994) and Danny Cannon's *Young Americans* (1993): slam-bang multiplex fodder with an American beat. The black comedy thriller *Shallow Grave* (1994) and the comedy of heroin addiction *Trainspotting* (1996), from the team of director Danny Boyle, producer Andrew Macdonald and writer John Hodge, had higher ambitions and paid careful attention to their urban settings (chiefly Edinburgh). But they shared the same urge to connect with young audiences whose natural film language was American, not British, and whose God was Quentin Tarantino. Their kinetic force, use of stylised studio décor, subjective camerawork and driving pop music carried both films far from the dictates of social realism, which was seen by Britain's young film-makers as yesterday's cinema. 'We made a very early decision . . . that it wasn't realism and we didn't want to do it like that,' Andrew Macdonald recalled about *Trainspotting*. 'Real cinema,' he declared elsewhere, 'is about the imagination, about fantasy': sentiments which his grandfather, Powell's collaborator Emeric Pressburger, would have heartily approved.[14]

Since then, subject to the usual fluctuating funding, British film-makers have sought to grab audiences' attention by chasing a multitude of styles and habits, old and new. The northern landscapes beloved of the 60s realist boom collided with the late 90s 'feelgood' factor in *Brassed Off* (1996), *The Full Monty* (1997) and *Billy Elliot* (2000), films that swing at a moment's notice from spry satire to soggy sentiment, their realistic details jostling with easy stereotypes. *Trainspotting* and the Tarantino factor generated a rash of rough-and-ready dramas about gangsters, lads on the town, and the chemically enhanced, most notably *Lock, Stock and Two Smoking Barrels* (1998) and *Human Traffic* (1999). In *Ratcatcher* (1999) Lynne Ramsay viewed her seedy Glasgow council-estate setting through the eyes of a poet, bold colours and off-centre camera angles taking us far from the realist aesthetic and the grey shades previously enthroned as the national style. Other feminist

variations on the style emerged in Carine Adler's *Under the Skin* (1997), a story of a disintegration filmed with a markedly European eye, and Andrea Arnold's *Red Road* – conventional in its working-class setting, but not in its focus on female sexuality. Among recent films only Saul Dibb's *Bullet Boy* (2004) plunged back into the old unadorned TV realism, pitching non-professionals into a blunt and powerful East End ghetto drama of inarticulate black youths, strutting machismo and the tattered remains of family life. With such diverse films and film-makers the Griersonian paradise may remain a conscious memory, and may even be glimpsed from afar; but it is unlikely ever to be regained.

Notes

1. John Grierson in 'The Course of Realism', p. 132.
2. Paul Rotha, *The Film till Now*, p. 315.
3. For a wider discussion of the *Penguin Film Review* and its reflection of post-war attitudes, see Geoff Brown, 'Which Way to the Way Ahead?: Britain's Years of Reconstruction', pp. 242–7.
4. Dilys Powell, *Sunday Times*, December 1967, collected in Christopher Cook (ed.), *The Dilys Powell Film Reader*, pp. 26–7.
5. Geoff Brown, 'Table Tennis over Everest', *Sight and Sound*, Spring 1984, p. 98.
6. Michael Balcon, 'Putting the Real Britain on Screen', London *Evening News*, 1 October 1936.
7. Details of *Man of Aran*'s promotion from Arthur Calder-Marshall, *The Innocent Eye: The Life of Robert J. Flaherty* (London, W. H. Allen, 1963), p. 164; and John Grierson, 'Summary and Survey: 1935', p. 110.
8. John Grierson, 'The Course of Realism', p. 143. For more on John Baxter see Geoff Brown and Anthony Aldgate, *The Common Touch: The Films of John Baxter*.
9. Paul Rotha, 'The British Case (1)', in *Rotha on the Film*, p. 217.
10. Information from Sidney Gilliat.
11. Dilys Powell, *Film since 1939*, excerpted in *The Dilys Powell Film Reader*, p. 5.
12. Lindsay Anderson, 'Get Out and Push!', p. 160.
13. Interview in 'Northern Lights', the first programme of *Hollywood-UK*, produced by Charles Chabot and Rosemary Wilton, BBC Television, 1993.
14. 'The Boys Are Back in Town', *Sight and Sound*, February 1996, p. 10; 'The Hit Squad', *The Times Magazine*, 20 January 1996, p. 21.

Bibliography

Anderson, Lindsay, 'Get Out and Push!', in Tom Maschler (ed.), *Declaration* (London: MacGibbon and Kee, 1957).

Brown, Geoff, 'Which Way to the Way Ahead?: Britain's Years of Reconstruction', *Sight and Sound*, Autumn 1978.

Brown, Geoff and Aldgate, Anthony, *The Common Touch: The Films of John Baxter* (London: BFI, 1989).

Gillett, Philip, *The British Working Class in Postwar Film* (Manchester: Manchester University Press, 2003).

Grierson, John 'The Course of Realism', in Forsyth Hardy (ed.), *Grierson on Documentary* (London: Collins, 1946), p. 132; originally included in Charles Davy (ed.), *Footnotes to the Film* (London: Lovat Dickson, 1938).

Grierson, John, 'Summary and Survey', in Forsyth Hardy (ed.), *Grierson on Documentary* (London: Collins, 1946).

Hill, John, *Sex, Class and Realism: British Cinema 1956–63* (London: BFI, 1986)

Powell, Dilys, *Film since 1939* (London: Longmans Green, 1947), excerpted in Christopher Cook (ed.), *The Dilys Powell Film Reader* (London: Carcanet Press, 1991).

Rotha, Paul, 'The British Case (1)', in *Rotha on the Film* (London: Faber and Faber, 1958).

Rotha, Paul, *The Film till Now*, revised and enlarged edition (London: Spring Books, 1967).

Sussex, Elizabeth, *The Rise and Fall of British Documentary* (London, Berkeley, Los Angeles: University of California Press, 1975).

5

Lindsay Anderson and the Development of British Art Cinema

Erik Hedling

Very little scholarly work has been done on the British art cinema, on its aesthetics and its auteurs. Until the 1990s British cinema as a whole tended to be overlooked by film scholars; and the general critical bias inspired by the Althusserian–Lacanian paradigm of contemporary film theory of the late 1970s and 80s has emphasised popular film genres or historical overviews of specific periods. In terms of British cinema history, the concept of art cinema has mostly been used in connection with the documentary-realist tradition, or as a term that describes how the intellectual film culture of the 1940s understood British 'quality cinema' of the period.[1]

Art cinema as a specific, historically determined mode of narration in post-war European cinema has been clearly defined by David Bordwell, and it is in this sense that the term is used here. Bordwell writes:

> The art film is nonclassical in that it creates permanent narrational gaps and calls attention to processes of fabula construction. But these very deviations are placed within new extrinsic norms, resituated as realism or authorial commentary. Eventually, the art-film narration solicits not only denotative comprehension but connotative reading, a higher-level interpretation.[2]

Art cinema was mainly targeted at an educated, middle-class audience, and was heavily influenced by modernist literature. The art cinema tried to achieve higher levels of realism, objectively – as in the spatial and temporal verisimilitude of Italian neo-realist works like Vittorio De Sica's *Bicycle Thieves* (1948) – and subjectively, for example in the symbolic uses of cinematic style in Ingmar Bergman's *Wild Strawberries* (1957). The works of art cinema were often 'open works', in Umberto Eco's sense, relying on narrative ambiguity: the beginning and the end of the story difficult to discern in traditional terms, the plot episodic, and often concerning some kind of individual psychological crisis.[3] The film could be highly self-conscious, and attention was drawn to the process of cinematic narration. Art cinema films were often marketed as personal visions, with a strong emphasis on the director, the creative artist. In terms of thematic content, art cinema films tended towards a leftist bias. And as Steve Neale has pointed out, art cinema challenged the dominant norms of film-making, as well as sustaining itself financially by a tendency towards sexual explicitness.[4]

Britain did not have an internationally well-known art cinema in this sense until Peter Greenaway, Derek Jarman and other film-makers emerged in the 1980s. There were, nevertheless, critical and cinematic practices which connected British film culture to the development of the European art cinema in the post-war period, most clearly in the journal *Sequence*, published between 1947 and 1952, and the film movement which came out of it.

Anderson as Critic

Although a small specialist magazine, edited by a few cinema enthusiasts from Oxford University, *Sequence* became a force behind a British art cinema aesthetic and an intellectual venture to be reckoned with.[5] Influenced by romanticism and the new literary criticism, the writers of *Sequence* spurned most contemporary British cinema, especially the documentary doctrines of John Grierson and his beliefs in the utilitarian aspects of film. Lindsay Anderson, one of the editors summed up his argument for a creative, non-industrially based cinema: 'What is required is a cinema in which people can make films with as much freedom as if they were writing poems, painting pictures or composing string quartets.'[6] Cinema, then, was an art, and not a Griersonian institution of public education. The key notions in the Andersonian discourse were 'poetry' and 'poet', metaphorically used to describe film art and the cinematic artist.

Anderson discussed at length the question of cinematic authorship, presenting a strong argument for the director in articles like 'Creative Elements' and 'The Director's Cinema?'.[7] Although he expressed his deep admiration for European film-makers like the Italian neo-realists and the French surrealist Jean Vigo, his preferred auteur was John Ford. In his writings on Ford, Anderson stressed the aspects of Ford's film-making which could be connected to what were later identified as formal properties of the European art cinema. Accordingly, in a close reading of Ford's *They Were Expendable* (1945), Anderson found that the film deconstructed traditional narrative, and that it was also an expression of a deep personal vision.[8] Close-ups were spontaneous, silent pauses were inserted and the long takes were often allowed to transcend their narrative motivation, being there for their own sake or as a kind of pure 'artistic' matter. The cult of Ford among the writers of *Sequence* also had political implications, besides the struggle for a more personal kind of cinema. The films they championed – like *She Wore a Yellow Ribbon* (1949) – were the ones that celebrated

This Sporting Life (Lindsay Anderson, 1963): Richard Harris and Lindsay Anderson

specifically American values, thus representing a counter-cultural challenge to the class-ridden, chauvinistic and traditionalist British heritage.

The critical paradigm introduced by *Sequence* at the end of the 1940s – objective realism, cinema as an art, the harmonic relationship between form and substance, the director as author – became the general trend of British film criticism in the 50s, as interest grew in the European art cinema. But in his writings in *Sight and Sound* – the flagship of British film culture – during the 50s, Anderson altered his critical approach, and began to incorporate some of the Griersonian doctrines that he had earlier rebelled against. These ideas were articulated in pieces on Elia Kazan's *On the Waterfront* (1954) and the critical manifesto 'Stand Up! Stand Up!' in 1956, where Anderson, now associated with the New Left, called for a more socially conscious and responsible British cinema as well as for personal vision.[9] Anderson's stress on personal style and leftist politics points forward to the development of a British art cinema based upon radicalism in form as well as in substance.

Free Cinema

In 1956 Anderson and others organised a series of screenings at the National Film Theatre under the label 'Free Cinema', with films by Anderson, Karel Reisz and Tony Richardson, and Lorenza Mazzetti; other Free Cinema programmes included films by Truffaut, Chabrol, Polanski, Tanner and Goretta. Anderson's first contribution was his twelve-minute documentary *O Dreamland* (1953), a film that can be regarded as paradigmatic for his later practice as an auteur.[10] In the spirit of Richard Hoggart, the film attacks the leisure habits of the masses at 'Dreamland', an amusement park at Margate. Anderson's worldview is expressed by constant manipulations of cinematic style, like the self-conscious and ironic juxtaposition of Frankie Laine's song 'I Believe' against images of vulgar popular pleasures.

As important for the development of art cinema as the influence of the 'poetic' realism of Free Cinema was the theatrically inspired stylisation which came out of the Royal Court Theatre in the late 1950s and early 60s. Both Anderson and Tony Richardson directed at the Royal Court, where they utilised Brechtian devices which later became part of the standard repertoire of art cinema.[11] Anderson, Reisz and Richardson soon made the transition from low-budget documentaries to feature films, largely through Richardson's connection with the theatre. Richardson had directed the phenomenally successful stage production of John Osborne's *Look*

Back in Anger, and Osborne was able to insist that he should direct the film as well. Richardson then invited Reisz to direct *Saturday Night and Sunday Morning* (1960), and Reisz, in his turn, supported Anderson in making *This Sporting Life* (1963).[12]

The Brechtian influence on the Free Cinema directors was not immediately apparent in their first feature films: Anderson's adaptation of David Storey's *This Sporting Life*, with its carefully constructed flashback pattern and naturalistic acting, conformed to a classical model in terms of narrative progression and *mise en scène*, in spite of its ambitious 'artiness'.

The art cinema aesthetic, in the sense elaborated by Bordwell, is much more obvious in later works, Anderson's rarely shown *The White Bus* (1966), for example. It was based on a short story by Shelagh Delaney and filmed as part of a cinematic triptych, *Red, White and Zero*, that was never released as such. In this film, Anderson employs the ingredients that came to be typical of the European art cinema of the period: surrealist devices (in the shape of recurring instances of narration representing thought rather than spoken word), manipulations of time and space (continuous soundtrack over ellipses in the imagery), unclear relation between plot and story (moments of stasis in the diegesis), arbitrary colour alterations (the image suddenly bursts into colour without codified meanings), recurring allusions and quotations (for instance the live replications of paintings by Manet, Fragonard and Goya), separation of elements (the sudden foregrounding of weird diegetic sounds), anti-establishment rhetoric (the sexual hypocrisy of the mayor, who condemns contemporary literature for its perversion but later tries to feel the heroine's leg in the bus), avant-garde music (Misha Donat's unpredictable synthesizer sounds), irony (the distance created between the mayor's bragging and the visual depiction of the drab life in Salford) and self-reflexivity (Anderson's allusions to Humphrey Jennings, whose 1939 film *Spare Time* clearly lingers in the background). Anderson also explicitly quotes Brecht by inserting a performance where Anthony Hopkins sings Brecht and Eisler's song 'Resolution' from *Die Tage der Commune*. In a typical art cinema strategy, the song operates metaphorically, commenting on the failure of liberalism to deal with oppression both in the days of the Paris Commune and in modern society.

Anderson's Trilogy

If . . . . (1968), Anderson's second feature, echoes some of the formal devices of *The White Bus* – arbitrary colour alterations, surrealism, allusions, authorial self-reflexivity, the open ending and the Brechtian device of chapter headings – but in a more commercial and recognisable genre, the public-school film. The narrative refers back to Vigo's surrealist classic *Zéro de conduite* (1933), a film about boys revolting against their masters which Anderson had praised as a critic. There is a general strategy of quotation and allusion at work in *If . . . .*, which deconstructs traditional narratives in a typical art cinema fashion: Kipling's poem 'If' as the title, the references to Byron, Wordsworth, Tennyson, Blake, Kleist and Plato, the cinematic allusions to Hitchcock, Lean, Ford, Jennings and even to Anthony Pélissier's *The History of Mr Polly* (1949), a film that Anderson, in spite of his otherwise general dismissal of 40s British cinema, had reviewed favourably in *Sequence*.[13] The allusions were conceived as a kind of Brechtian *Verfremdungseffekt*, constantly drawing attention to the artificial nature of narrative by crossing the fictional borders of the diegesis.

Writing in 1973, Thomas Elsaesser characterised the new European art films – by Herzog, Chabrol, Tanner – in terms of their irony: 'In almost all cases the stance is one of ironic "as-if".'[14] Elsaesser unaccountably rejects *If . . . .*, although it fits very well his description of Brechtian art films during the period. The 'as-if' dimension can be seen in surreal moments, as for instance when the headmaster pulls out the chaplain from the locker in his office, a scene of stylised theatricalisation staged within what is otherwise perceived as a 'real' scene. The device is shocking because it is so sudden and ostensibly out of style, but the film constantly challenges stable notions of fantasy and reality.[15]

If . . . . received enthusiastic reviews in the British press, did well at the box office and even won the prestigious Palme d'Or at the Cannes Film Festival in 1969, at a time when the European art cinema was at its height (its main competitors were Costa-Gavras's *Z* and Bo Widerberg's *Ådalen 31*). It also played a decisive role in crossing the 60s sex barrier with its scenes of full-frontal female nudity. Alan Lovell stresses Anderson's importance for the British cinema at the time, in particular his attempt 'to grapple with the problem of the British cinema's relationship with the American cinema and the art cinema by positively combining elements from both'.[16]

The art cinema aesthetic was by no means limited to the films of Lindsay Anderson, although his work is crucially important. In his book on 60s British cinema, Robert Murphy claims that at the end of the decade new dimensions had entered British films:

Fantasy sequences (in which everything becomes possible), slapstick (in which the world collapses into chaos), outrageous visual jokes, distancing devices such as the use of a narrator, inter-titles or direct address to camera spread across films as different as *The Bliss of Mrs Blossom* and *Poor Cow*, *Here We Go round the Mulberry Bush* and *If . . . .*[17]

Apart from the inspiration from *Sequence*, Free Cinema and the Brechtian practices at the Royal Court, the incorporation of art cinema practices into British cinema was also influenced by foreign directors at work in Britain during the 60s, such as Joseph Losey, Roman Polanski and Michelangelo Antonioni. In an essay on Nicolas Roeg and Donald Cammell's *Performance* (1970), a film which represents the ethos of 1968 and the British film industry's flirtations with a counter-culture, Peter Wollen claims that it is the 'British film which comes closest to a modernist art film in the New Wave mould', and that 'its direct predecessors were *The Servant* (1963), *Repulsion* (1965) and *Blowup* (1967), all London films made by foreigners – Losey, Polanski, Antonioni'.[18]

Many other examples of art cinema practices can be seen throughout the 60s: the Brechtian narrative of Richardson's *Tom Jones* (1963), the *Kammerspiel* aesthetics of Jack Clayton's *The Pumpkin Eater* (1964), the bold deconstruction of classical narrative in Richard Lester's *A Hard Day's Night* (1964), the modernist montage of John Schlesinger's *Darling* (1965), the radical uses of style to present psychological crisis in Karel Reisz's *Morgan* (1966), the use of ironic cartoons in Richardson's *The Charge of the Light Brigade* (1968) and the sexually explicit imagery of Ken Russell's *Women in Love* (1969). The art cinema, then, had a considerable impact on British cinema during this period.

Because of the decline of British cinema in the 1970s, directors like Karel Reisz, Tony Richardson, John Schlesinger and Jack Clayton went to America. Anderson was marginalised after failing at the box office with his grand epic *O Lucky Man!* (1973), an explicitly Brechtian film which failed to sustain his reputation as a significant auteur. The rejection of the film for its supposedly reactionary aesthetics by the film journal *Screen* pointed to the generation gap between Anderson's 1950s New Left liberalism and the explicitly Marxist approach of much academic critical discourse of the 70s.[19]

O Lucky Man! was really an extension of the story and narrative strategy of *If . . . .*, following the progress

O Lucky Man! (Lindsay Anderson, 1973): Alan Price, Lindsay Anderson and Miroslav Ondrícek

of Michael Travis (played by Malcolm McDowell) from heroic rebel to capitalist errand boy and finally to actor. The film is a road movie, with echoes of Preston Sturges's *Sullivan's Travels* (1941). It is also self-consciously constructed as a cinematic labyrinth in the style of Fellini's *8½* (1963). The film ends where it really started with Travis applying for the role in the movie *O Lucky Man!* (this scene, where McDowell is photographed with a gun and books, and with a cameo appearance by Anderson himself, was, according to scriptwriter David Sherwin, based on McDowell's audition for his role in *If . . . .*).

One of the more radical aspects of the film was the use of rock musician Alan Price's songs, which were interweaved with the narrative, with brief glimpses of Price and his band in the studio providing an ironic contrast to Travis's follies, much like the Street Singer in Brecht's *Threepenny Opera*.[20]

The actors, most of them belonging to Anderson's stock company, play multiple roles which often refer back to their parts in previous Anderson films. They are Brechtian 'social types', or 'humours' as Anderson himself preferred to call them.[21] The style is caricature rather than psychological realism. Peter Jeffrey's director and prison warden are clearly reminiscent of his headmaster in *If . . . .*, and Mary McLeod's lovesick landlady is similarly based on the matron in that film. Geoffrey Chater as the priest and Anthony Nicholls as the General play the same parts in both films. Patricia Healy's brief guest appearance brings *The White Bus* to mind, while Rachel Roberts once again portrays the poverty-stricken working-class widow from *This Sporting Life*. In contrast, McDowell's identity as Travis is constantly undermined by the difference from the character in *If . . . .*, by references to his role as Alexander de Large in Kubrick's *A Clockwork Orange* (1971), and by the allusions to McDowell's well-publicised personal life. The film also contains the other art cinema devices which Anderson championed: intertextual allusions (Browning, Coleridge, Gorky, Eisenstein, John Ford, etc.), inter-titles and authorial self-consciousness.

In Anderson's third story about Michael Travis, his last British feature film *Britannia Hospital* (1982), the hero, once again played by McDowell, dies at the hands of modern science gone berserk. This film is formally more traditional, but it conforms to the theatrical stylisation and Brechtian 'lessons' established in *If . . . .* and *O Lucky Man!* A lively intertextuality informs the film, most famously at the end when Professor Millar (Graham Crowden, who was also Millar in *O Lucky Man!*) has his monstrous creation quote Hamlet's 'What a piece of work is man'. There are, surprisingly in view of Anderson's reputation as an auteur in the European art cinema tradition, several positively charged allusions to the 'low' genres of the 60s, particularly the hospital comedies (the hospital as metaphor for society), the *Carry On* series (literally when the nurse tells Travis, 'Your work will carry on') and the Hammer horror films (the professor as Frankenstein, Travis as the monster). Anderson mobilises the ironic potential of popular genres in order to create something of the carnivalesque, in Bakhtin's sense – a counter-cultural, self-conscious vulgarity used for a fiercely satirical attack on contemporary attitudes and policies.[22]

If . . . ., O Lucky Man! and *Britannia Hospital* form a cinematic trilogy. This is another aspect that binds Anderson closer to the European art cinema, for as Thomas Elsaesser points out, 'A look at the filmographies of Godard, Antonioni, Truffaut, Wenders, Herzog, Kieślowski shows how important a prop the idea of the trilogy is for the self-identity of the European auteur.'[23]

The Art Cinema Legacy
Many writers have argued that the 1980s represented a renaissance in British cinema. James Park, for example, claimed in 1984 that the British cinema had finally learnt to 'dream' by incorporating new and more radical forms.[24] And Thomas Elsaesser writes of

> a relatively new and perhaps overdue phenomenon in British cinema (*pace* Nicolas Roeg), which has had the effect of opening out film narrative towards more adventurous forms of fiction. A heightened, emblematic or dream-like realism has appeared, for which the

implements, objects, customs, the visual (and often musical) remnants of a bygone popular culture have become the icons of subjectivity.[25]

What had happened was that art cinema had finally established itself as a prominent and critically acknowledged mode in British cinema. Elsaesser's words are an apt description of the art cinema aesthetics of works like Peter Greenaway's *Drowning by Numbers* (1988), Terence Davies's *Distant Voices, Still Lives* (1988) or Dennis Potter's television drama *The Singing Detective* (1986). They could also describe *If . . . .* and *O Lucky Man!*, which, it could be claimed, prefigure the British art cinema of the 80s.

The connection between the art cinema of the 1960s and the new cinema of the 1980s is most evident in the films of Peter Greenaway and Derek Jarman. Greenaway's *The Draughtsman's Contract* (1981) explores a similar theatrical stylisation to that in *If . . . .* and *O Lucky Man!*, in the use of multiple symbolic layers, the acting within 'quotation marks', the self-conscious artificiality, the intertextuality and the labyrinthine storyline. Jarman's *Caravaggio* (1986) uses theatrical space, a complex pattern of allusion (like the reference to Waldo Lydecker typing in his bath in Otto Preminger's *Laura*, 1944), and art cinema devices such as the anachronistic appearance of a typewriter in a film set in the 17th century. Jarman explicitly quotes Anderson's *mise en scène* of riot police in *Britannia Hospital* in his bold adaptation of Marlowe's *Edward II* (1991).

In an article on the films of Greenaway and Jarman, Peter Wollen explores their common backgrounds as artists in the 60s, and describes their films in terms of a late cinematic modernism in Britain.[26] Wollen denies the 60s British 'new wave' the status of art cinema, because of the lack of auteurs in the established sense and because the films were based on literary material. He claims that these films fall into the category of traditional 'good realism' rather than art cinema. But he does admit that 'A good case can be made for Lindsay Anderson as a bilious but authentic "auteur" '.[27]

I have tried to make that case. In response to Wollen, one could claim that Lindsay Anderson was an auteur in the established European sense. Films like *If . . . ., O Lucky Man!* and *Britannia Hospital* were not based on literary texts but were original scripts, written by Anderson's friend David Sherwin. Anderson himself never explained his films in terms of traditional notions of realism; indeed, he repeatedly challenged these notions in order to stress the 'poetic' aspects of film, which in his own words meant that 'you should operate suggestively on people so that you let their imagination run free'.[28] This is, of course, exactly the opposite of the traditional notion of realism.

Anderson's position within a tradition of British art cinema has been noted by the new auteurs themselves. Greenaway says that he found Anderson's *If . . . .* 'painfully accurate', and Derek Jarman repeatedly expressed his admiration for Anderson, insisting that *Britannia Hospital* is one of the masterpieces of British cinema.[29]

The internationally acclaimed British art cinema of the 1980s and early 90s could, then, be seen as having its roots in aspects of 60s film culture, which in turn could be referred back to the 40s and in particular to Powell and Pressburger and Humphrey Jennings. Ironically as British commercial film production dwindled to an insignificant trickle, British directors – Jarman, Greenaway, Davies, Loach, Leigh – were at last welcomed into the pantheon of European art cinema.

Notes

1. See Andrew Higson, *Waving the Flag*, pp. 262–71.
2. David Bordwell, *Narration in the Fiction Film* (London: Methuen, 1985), p. 212.
3. Umberto Eco, 'The Poetics of the Open Work', in *The Role of the Reader: Explorations in the Semiotics of Texts* (London: Hutchinson, 1979), p. 63.
4. Steve Neale, 'Art Cinema as Institution', *Screen* vol. 22 no.1, 1981, pp. 11–39.
5. 'Across the intervening decades, one found tantalizing references to it in the writing about cinema, suggesting how influential it had been among those who took cinema seriously', writes Brian McFarlane in '*Sequence*: Saying Exactly What We Liked', p. 31.
6. Lindsay Anderson, 'A Possible Solution', p. 9.
7. Lindsay Anderson, 'Creative Elements', pp. 8–12, and 'The Director's Cinema', *Sequence* no. 12, Autumn 1950, pp. 6–11, 37.
8. Lindsay Anderson, 'John Ford and *They Were Expendable*', *Sequence* no. 11, Summer 1950, pp. 18–31.
9. Lindsay Anderson, 'The Last Sequence of *On the Waterfront*', *Sight and Sound*, Spring 1955, pp. 127–30, and 'Stand Up! Stand Up!', *Sight and Sound*, Autumn 1956, pp. 63–9.
10. For conflicting views of *O Dreamland* see John Hill, *Sex, Class and Realism: British Cinema 1956–63*, p. 152; and Paul K. Cornelius, 'Images of Social Dysfunction in Films of Lindsay Anderson', pp. 26–40.
11. Thus Anderson's productions of Harry Cookson's *The Lily White Boys* (1960) and Keith Waterhouse and Willis Hall's *Billy Liar* (1960) were noticed for their Brechtian aesthetics. See Peter Mathers, 'Brecht in Britain: From Theatre to Television', p. 81.
12. See the interview with Anderson in Eva Orbanz, *Journey to a Legend and Back: The British Realist Film*, p. 48.
13. Lindsay Anderson, 'The History of Mr Polly', pp. 41–2. The allusion occurs when Mick Travis looks towards the Archangel Michael, who is painted on the chapel window. The subjective image corresponds exactly to the similarly romantic and dreamy Mr Polly focusing on the church windows when entering what proves to be a disastrous marriage.
14. Thomas Elsaesser, 'The Cinema of Irony', *Monogram* no. 5, 1973, p. 1.
15. Harold Pinter thought the device 'very out of style'. See Elizabeth Sussex, *Lindsay Anderson*, p. 86.
16. Alan Lovell, *British Cinema: The Unknown Cinema*, BFI Education Seminar Paper, March 1969.
17. Robert Murphy, *Sixties British Cinema*, p. 3.
18. Peter Wollen, 'Possession', p. 23.
19. See Colin MacCabe, 'Realism and the Cinema: Notes on Some Brechtian Theses', *Screen* vol. 15 no. 2, Summer 1974, p. 26, and Alan Lovell, 'Brecht in Britain – Lindsay Anderson' (on *If . . . .* and *O Lucky Man!*), pp. 62–80.
20. 'The use of the chorus as an instructive device is particularly Brechtian, especially due to the fact that Alan Price's presence in the film is not hidden or masked or used in a conventional "musical film" sense', writes Carl David Ferraro. See 'Toward a Brechtian Film Aesthetic, with an Investigation into the Films of Lindsay Anderson, Rainer Werner Fassbinder and Luis Buñuel', p. 164.
21. See David Robinson, 'Stripping the Veils Away', *The Times*, 21 April 1973.
22. Many critics noticed the *Frankenstein/Carry On* connection, without making too much of it. A good description of the film was the heading of Michael Wood's review, 'Carry On Hamlet', in *New Society*, 3 June 1982, p. 392.
23. Thomas Elsaesser, 'Putting on a Show: The European Art Movie', *Sight and Sound*, April 1994, p. 26.
24. James Park, *Learning to Dream: The New British Cinema* (London: Faber and Faber, 1984), p. 13.
25. Thomas Elsaesser, 'Games of Love and Death, or an Englishman's Guide to the Galaxy', p. 291.
26. Peter Wollen, 'The Last New Wave: Modernism in the British Films of the Thatcher Era', pp. 35–51.
27. Ibid., p. 37.

28. Quoted from the interview in Joseph Gelmis, *The Film Director as Superstar* (Garden City, NY: Doubleday, 1970), p. 106.
29. Jonathan Hacker and David Price, *Take Ten: Contemporary British Film Directors*, pp. 208 and 259.

Bibliography

Aldgate, Anthony, *Censorship and the Permissive Society: British Cinema and Theatre 1955–65* (Oxford: Clarendon Press, 1995).

Anderson, Lindsay, 'A Possible Solution', *Sequence* no. 3, Spring 1948.

Anderson, Lindsay, 'Creative Elements', *Sequence* no. 5, Autumn 1948.

Anderson, Lindsay, 'The History of Mr Polly', *Sequence* no. 7, Spring 1949.

Anderson, Lindsay, 'Stand Up! Stand Up!', *Sight and Sound*, Autumn 1956.

Cornelius, Paul K., 'Images of Social Dysfunction in Films of Lindsay Anderson' (Thesis, University of Texas at Dallas, 1987).

Elsaesser, Thomas, 'Games of Love and Death, or an Englishman's Guide to the Galaxy', *Monthly Film Bulletin*, October 1988.

Ferraro, Carl David, 'Toward a Brechtian Film Aesthetic, with an Investigation into the Films of Lindsay Anderson, Rainer Werner Fassbinder and Luis Buñuel' (Dissertation, Wayne State University, Detroit, IL, 1988).

Hacker, Jonathan and Price, David, *Take Ten: Contemporary British Film Directors* (Oxford: Clarendon Press, 1991).

Hedling, Erik, *Lindsay Anderson: Maverick Film-Maker* (London and Washington: Cassell, 1998).

Higson, Andrew, *Waving the Flag: Constructing a National Cinema in Britain* (Oxford: Clarendon Press, 1995).

Hill, John, Sex, *Class and Realism: British Cinema 1956–63* (London: BFI, 1986).

Lovell, Alan, 'Brecht in Britain – Lindsay Anderson' (on *If . . . .* and *O Lucky Man!*), *Screen* vol. 16 no. 4, Winter 1975–6.

Mathers, Peter, 'Brecht in Britain: From Theatre to Television', *Screen* vol. 16 no. 4, Winter 1975–6.

McFarlane, Brian, '*Sequence*: Saying Exactly What We Liked', *Filmviews*, Autumn 1988.

Murphy, Robert, *Sixties British Cinema* (London: BFI, 1992).

Orbanz, Eva, *Journey to a Legend and Back: The British Realist Film* (Berlin: Volker Spiess, 1977).

Sussex, Elizabeth, *Lindsay Anderson* (London: Studio Vista, 1969).

Wollen, Peter, 'The Last New Wave: Modernism in the British Films of the Thatcher Era', in Lester Friedman (ed.), *British Cinema and Thatcherism: Fires Were Started* (London: University of Central London Press, 1993).

Wollen, Peter, 'Possession', *Sight and Sound*, Autumn 1995.

6

The Wrong Sort of Cinema:
Refashioning the Heritage Film Debate

SHELDON HALL

Henry V is the culmination of a wartime series, almost a genre in itself, of 'heritage' films, which include – among many others – *This England*, *The Young Mr Pitt*, and the Nelson film of this war, Churchill's own favourite, *Lady Hamilton*; also, incorporating literature as well as history, *A Canterbury Tale*, short films like Jennings' *Words for Battle*, and even Carol Reed's film of the H. G. Wells novel *Kipps*. Whatever their merits, and they are an uneven lot, none of these was simply recreating a bit of heritage in an inert, Trooping-the-Colour manner, and *Henry V* achieved a very superior status as a high-quality British product. It made an encouraging impact abroad as well as at home, most importantly in America.[1]

This passage, from Charles Barr's Introduction to his 1986 edited collection *All Our Yesterdays: 90 Years of British Cinema*, contains the first use of which I'm aware of a phrase which has now passed into the everyday language of film studies: 'heritage films'. It has come to signal not just a particular group, or cluster of interrelated groups, of films, but a particular *attitude* to those films, and indeed to the audiences presumed to enjoy them. Heritage cinema is very largely a critical construct, but its currency in academic debates concerning the cultural and ideological significance of certain trends in recent British (and latterly European) cinema has subsequently been extended through its diffusion into journalistic and even popular usage – though not, presumably, among the films' target audience.[2]

Barr's own discussion of the heritage film (henceforth my use of the term will be without inverted commas) involves a number of key points that have

tended to recur in subsequent debates. They include: the linkage of a loose body of films through their common invocation of British history, literature and/or an 'approved' cultural tradition; the suggestion that, diverse as this body of films is, it has some of the characteristics of a genre (albeit with a problematic relationship to notions of 'the popular'); the prestige attached to these films as quality products, evidenced in certain features of their marketing campaigns, and in their frequent appearance in the lists of nominations for Oscars, BAFTAs and other film-industry awards; and their desirability as goods for export, especially to America, an attribute often leading to the suspicion that such films are designed as much for foreign as for domestic consumption. There are, however, significant emphases in Barr's discussion which have tended to become marginalised, or ignored entirely, in later academic accounts of heritage cinema. This chapter is mainly concerned with problems that I see with these more recent discussions and the debates they have engendered.

The passage from Barr quoted above occurs in the context of a discussion of a particular phase of British cinematic and politico-cultural history – World War II – which has not usually been the focus of heritage criticism since. Indeed, most such work has concentrated on the period in which Barr himself was writing: the 1980s, and the cultural and political ethos of Thatcherism which produced the 'heritage industry', of which, it has been claimed, these films are a prime instance.[3] Hence, the film usually seen as initiating the recent heritage cycle, the Oscar-winning *Chariots of Fire* (Hugh Hudson, 1981), has most often been

Stiff upper lips: Anthony Hopkins and Emma Thompson in *The Remains of the Day* (James Ivory, 1993)

construed as the embodiment of Thatcherite patriotic rhetoric. Though patriotism is rendered ambivalently in the film itself, its commercial and critical success led to its being seen, by defenders and detractors alike, as a model of creative and economic 'enterprise'. One of the other key films to figure in heritage cinema debates, *A Room with a View*, was released in *All Our Yesterdays*' year of publication, 1986. Thereafter, that film's production team of producer Ismail Merchant and director James Ivory (Indian- and American-born, respectively) became closely identified with heritage cinema. Though they had specialised in adaptations of literary source material for more than two decades – including two films of Henry James novels, *The Europeans* (1979) and *The Bostonians* (1984) – it was not until then that 'the brand label "Merchant Ivory" [became] virtually a synonym for "heritage"'.[4]

The responsibility for the subsequent widespread adoption of heritage film as a legitimate descriptive term – its institutionalisation within academic film studies – largely belongs to Andrew Higson, who first

used it in his influential article 'Re-presenting the National Past: Nostalgia and Pastiche in the Heritage Film', published in 1993. The heritage film, as Higson and others have defined it, incorporates a number of generic sub-categories and cycles (the definition is also usually extended to encompass serials and single dramas made on film for television). Roughly in order of centrality to the heritage debates, they include:

1. Adaptations from works of classic literature: centrally those of Austen, Dickens, Eliot, Forster, James, Waugh; tangentially, the Brontës, Hardy, Lawrence, Orwell, Rattigan, Wilde and Woolf. The core texts include *A Room with a View*, *Maurice* (James Ivory, 1987), *A Handful of Dust* (Charles Sturridge, 1987), *Little Dorrit* (Christine Edzard, 1987), *Howards End* (Ivory, 1991), *Where Angels Fear to Tread* (Sturridge, 1991), *The Browning Version* (Mike Figgis, 1994), *Emma* (Douglas McGrath, 1996), *Keep the Aspidistra Flying* (Robert Bierman, 1997), *An Ideal Husband* (Oliver Parker, 1999), *The Winslow Boy* (David Mamet, 1999), *The*

Golden Bowl (Ivory, 2000) and, foremost among many television 'classic serials', Brideshead Revisited (Granada, 1981), Middlemarch (BBC, 1994) and Pride and Prejudice (BBC, 1995).

2. Costume dramas adapted from modern literary works and theatrical properties, or written directly for the screen, set primarily in the late Victorian, Edwardian and interwar eras, and preferably among the aristocracy and upper middle classes. Examples include: Chariots of Fire, Another Country (Marek Kanievska, 1984), A Month in the Country (Pat O'Connor, 1987), A Summer Story (Piers Haggard, 1987), The Dawning (Robert Knights, 1988), The Bridge (Sydney MacCartney, 1990), The Fool (Christine Edzard, 1990), Fools of Fortune (O'Connor, 1990), Enchanted April (Mike Newell, 1991), The Remains of the Day (James Ivory, 1993) and Shadowlands (Richard Attenborough, 1993).

3. The 'Raj revival': films set in colonial India, mostly during the dying days of the British Raj, notably Gandhi (Attenborough, 1982), Heat and Dust (Ivory, 1982), the Forster adaptation A Passage to India (David Lean, 1984), and the ITV television series The Far Pavilions (1984) and The Jewel in the Crown (1985). The Kenyan-set White Mischief (Michael Radford, 1987) and the Merchant Ivory-produced Raj adventure The Deceivers (Nicholas Meyer, 1988), adapted from a John Masters novel, are arguably close relations.

4. Historical dramas: reconstructions and representations of real events and figures from documented history, rather than purely fictional inventions. These include dramatised portraits of kings, queens and other figures of officially recognised historical importance: Gandhi, Lady Jane (Trevor Nunn, 1985), The Madness of King George (Nicholas Hytner, 1994), Mrs Brown (John Madden, 1997); as well as biopics of literary or artistic figures, including Shadowlands (about children's author C. S. Lewis) and Wilde (Brian Gilbert, 1997) – the latter described by one reviewer as '"heritage" soap opera with a muck-raking spin'.[5]

5. Shakespeare adaptations, albeit mostly those set 'in period' (not necessarily Elizabethan): the key texts are Kenneth Branagh's Henry V (1989), Much Ado about Nothing (1993) and Hamlet (1996), as well as Othello (Oliver Parker, 1995), in which Branagh appeared as Iago, A Midsummer Night's Dream (Adrian Noble, 1996) and Twelfth Night (Nunn, 1996). Modernised updates, such as As You Like It (Christine Edzard, 1992), Richard III (Richard Loncraine, 1995)

and Branagh's disastrous 1930s musical version of Love's Labour's Lost (2000), are somewhat marginal cases.

Within a couple of years of Higson's 1993 article, heritage cinema had achieved sufficient formal recognition to merit an entry in the British Film Institute's Encyclopedia of European Cinema, which identified the heritage film as a pan-European, rather than exclusively British, phenomenon, partly to be accounted for in terms of an industrial strategy of product differentiation from current Hollywood models.[6] 1993 is also the year cited by Claire Monk as seeing the emergence of a new 'strand of period/literary films with a deep consciousness about how the past is represented' which she suggests be termed 'post-heritage'.[7] Monk names as the standard-bearer of this revisionist trend Sally Potter's film of Virginia Woolf's novel Orlando (1992), as well as Tom and Viv (Brian Gilbert, 1993), Century (Stephen Poliakoff, 1994) and Carrington (Christopher Hampton, 1995). To these could be added The Portrait of a Lady (Jane Campion, 1996), Mrs Dalloway (Marleen Gorris, 1997), Washington Square (Agnieszka Holland, 1998), Mansfield Park (Patricia Rozema, 1999) and The House of Mirth (Terence Davies, 2000).

Other contributions to the discussion of 'post-heritage' cinema have taken as their examples films which appear to represent further developments in the heritage film's standard mode of operation, or those which seem anomalous in relation to received notions of it. Hence, Pamela Church Gibson discusses Sense and Sensibility (Ang Lee, 1995), Persuasion (Roger Michell, 1995), Jude (Michael Winterbottom, 1996), The Wings of the Dove (Iain Softley, 1997), Elizabeth (Shekhar Kapur, 1998) and Shakespeare in Love (John Madden, 1998) in terms of post-modernism and generic hybridity and sees 'a fissuring and fracturing in the monolith of heritage'.[8] The film industry has itself given heritage the ultimate sanction with the appearance of Stiff Upper Lips (Gary Sinyor, 1996), a spoof in the mould of Mel Brooks's and the Zucker brothers' genre parodies.

The concentration by most academic critics on films of the 1980s and 1990s has tended to inhibit the historicisation of heritage films within broader cinematic traditions of costume drama, period reconstruction and literary adaptation. Of the major contributors to the heritage cinema debates, only Higson has gone

Judgment day: *A Man for All Seasons* (Fred Zinnemann, 1966)

to any lengths to locate the more recent examples within an industry trend extending back into the silent era: a point also anticipated by Charles Barr, who cites *Nelson* (Maurice Elvey, 1918) as an early instance.[9] Barr makes the crucial point that the heritage film tradition tends to (re)surface at those historical moments when it has a valid (i.e. widely recognised and welcomed) cultural and economic role to play: hence, the war years saw the development of 'a national cinema able to exploit effectively those two distinctive objects of pride, British understatement and the rich British heritage, which had previously appeared rather intractable material for films'.[10] However, most period costume films of the 1930s and 1940s have been discussed in terms of the traditions and conventions of popular melodrama or historical adventure rather than as heritage texts, so that the opportunities for direct comparisons of similar works from different cinematic periods, and discussion of the cyclical development of patterns of generic production, has generally been neglected.[11]

The films of the 1960s, in particular, are conspicuous by their absence from all the critical discussions of heritage cinema. There are 60s (and indeed 70s) equivalents for most, if not all, of the heritage subcycles described above: period literary adaptations, from both 'classic' and modern authors such as *The Innocents* (Jack Clayton, 1961), *Tom Jones* (Tony Richardson, 1963), *Lord Jim* (Richard Brooks, 1965), *Far from the Madding Crowd* (John Schlesinger, 1967), *The Prime of Miss Jean Brodie* (Ronald Neame, 1969), *Women in Love* (Ken Russell, 1969), *The Go-Between* (Joseph Losey, 1971); Imperial epics like *Zulu* (Cy Endfield, 1964), *Khartoum* (Basil Dearden, 1966), *The*

Long Duel (Ken Annakin, 1967), *The Charge of the Light Brigade* (Richardson, 1968); biopics: *The Trials of Oscar Wilde* (Ken Hughes, 1960), *Lawrence of Arabia* (David Lean, 1962), *Isadora* (Karel Reisz, 1968), *Young Winston* (Richard Attenborough, 1972); and Shakespeare films: *Othello* (Stuart Burge, 1965), *William Shakespeare's Romeo and Juliet* (Franco Zeffirelli, 1968), *Hamlet* (Richardson, 1969), *Julius Caesar* (Burge, 1970), *King Lear* (Peter Brook, 1970) and *Macbeth* (Roman Polanski, 1971). Particularly notable, for their considerable box-office and prestige success, was a cycle of 'monarchic' films, which included *Becket* (Peter Glenville, 1964), *A Man for All Seasons* (Fred Zinnemann, 1966), *The Lion in Winter* (Anthony Harvey, 1968), *Anne of the Thousand Days* (Charles Jarrott, 1969) and *Mary, Queen of Scots* (Jarrott, 1971), as well as the commercially less successful *Alfred the Great* (Clive Donner, 1969) and *Cromwell* (Hughes, 1970). Both *Mary, Queen of Scots* and the British-funded *Henry VIII and His Six Wives* (Waris Hussein, 1972) bore close relation to recent BBC classic serials, including the casting of their respective stars, Glenda Jackson and Keith Michell. Yet despite their 'culturally British' subject matter, this cycle and most others of the films mentioned above are specifically excluded from detailed consideration in Robert Murphy's history of *Sixties British Cinema* because their American funding relegates them to the category of 'an international, Hollywood-dominated cinema'.[12]

Such marginalisation can largely be accounted for in terms of the currency of particular critical constructions of British cinema with respect to particular periods: social realist dramas, 'swinging' sex comedies, trenchant satires, pop musicals, crime, horror and comedy films have all been seen as characteristic of Britain in the 1960s, projecting an image of modernity for that decade which sits ill with the more backward-looking heritage films of the same period. A similar critical (and ideological) imperative has presented (a particular version of) heritage cinema as *representative* of the 1980s and (to a lesser extent) the 1990s. Within this period, certain historical dramas and literary adaptations have been characterised as heritage texts while others have been excluded. No place has been found in discussions of recent heritage cinema for such contemporaneous and arguably relevant films as *The French Lieutenant's Woman* (Karel Reisz, 1981), *The Wicked Lady* (Michael Winner, 1983), Alan Bridges's *The Return of the Soldier* (1982) and *The Shooting Party* (1984), Ken Russell's *Gothic* (1986), *Salome's Last Dance* (1987) and *The Rainbow* (1989), *Angels and Insects*

Anne of the Thousand Days (Charles Jarrott, 1969)

In the last decade of his long and distinguished career, the independent Hollywood producer Hal B. Wallis made four films in Britain that share a number of common themes and motifs. *Becket* (1964), *Anne of the Thousand Days* (1969), *Mary, Queen of Scots* (1971) and *A Bequest to the Nation* (US title: *The Nelson Affair*, 1973) all dramatise stormy relationships representing in microcosm some of the key national issues of the period in which they are set. Like several other major contemporary costume dramas – notably *A Man for All Seasons* (1966), *The Lion in Winter* (1968) and *Cromwell* (1970) – each of these films focuses on the causes and repercussions of a titanic battle of wills, from which can be inferred the interplay of historical forces as well as a clash of individual egos.

Adapted from a 1947 Broadway play by Maxwell Anderson (author also of *Elizabeth the Queen*, on which Wallis's 1939 production *The Private Lives of Elizabeth and Essex* was based), *Anne of the Thousand Days* was the first feature film of British television director Charles Jarrott, who went on to collaborate with Wallis and co-screenwriter John Hale on *Mary, Queen of Scots*. As well

Anne of the Thousand Days: Geneviève Bujold prepared for heavy weather

as its nine Oscar nominations, *Anne* – like *Mary* – enjoyed the prestige of a Royal Command première in London, a risky accolade given its potentially troubling subject matter: the conflict between the carnal desires of King Henry VIII (Richard Burton, in full ranting mode), who chooses to rid himself of his ageing, barren first wife Catherine of Aragon in favour of the more nubile and fertile Anne Boleyn (beautifully played by the French-Canadian actress Geneviève Bujold), and Anne's equally powerful desire for marital and political legitimacy.

The film's first half concerns Anne's resistance to Henry's sexual importuning (already successfully directed towards her older sister, by whom he has a bastard child) until he has guaranteed her a lawful marriage, which ultimately entails Henry's excommunication from the Catholic Church and a rift with his close friend Sir Thomas More (history which this film shares with *A Man for All Seasons*). Its latter portion, following the birth of Anne and Henry's daughter, deals with the king's attempts to replace Anne with another wife who can give him a male heir, while Anne strives to hold on to the lineage she has won for their child, who will later reign as Elizabeth I.

While Shekhar Kapur's *Elizabeth* (1998) is often cited by critics as an iconoclastic take on British regal history, *Anne* is, like its contemporaries, regularly overlooked in feminist accounts of 'heritage' cinema. Perhaps its rather theatrical, declamatory acting style – wittily parodied by Peter Cook and Dudley Moore in an episode of *Not Only . . . But Also . . .* (1965–70) – and handsome but conservative *mise en scène* are partly to blame, but the neglect is undeserved. Whereas *A Man for All Seasons* dwells on the religious and moral principles leading to Thomas More's martyrdom (principles which ultimately die with him), *Anne* sees its heroine's struggle in more overtly political terms: Anne's execution, necessitated by Henry's desire for a son to ensure patriarchal succession, has a positive, pragmatic outcome in allowing her daughter ultimately to take the throne and undertake the transformation of the nation.

FURTHER READING

Margaret Hinxman, 'Old Friends at Court', *Sunday Telegraph*, 1 March 1970.

Pauline Kael, 'Blessed Profanity', *Deeper into Movies* (London: Calder and Boyars, 1975), pp. 95–7.

(Philip Haas, 1995), *Amy Foster* (Beeban Kidron, 1997), or for Peter Greenaway and Derek Jarman's costume forays such as *The Draughtsman's Contract* (1982), *The Baby of Mâcon* (1993), *Caravaggio* (1986) and *Edward II* (1991). Examination of any of these diversely anomalous (and highly variable) works in relation to the 'mainstream' of heritage might have revealed the concept of heritage cinema and its academic usage to be overly narrow and monolithic.

Evidence of the continuing distinction between period/literary films which are considered heritage cinema and those which are not can be found starkly laid out in the November 2000 issue of *Sight and Sound*. Reviews on facing pages of *The Golden Bowl* (source: Henry James) and *The House of Mirth* (source: Edith Wharton) introduce the former as 'the latest in a long line of heritage productions' made by Merchant Ivory, and discuss the latter without a mention of heritage except to note that Terence Davies's film (evidently to be regarded primarily as *un film d'auteur*) is 'different' from the kind of 'period film [which] doesn't at least fall half in love with its fancy frocks and immaculate crockery' (i.e. the conventional notion of the heritage film).[13]

Andrew Higson makes the point that:

> As critics, we should not try to regulate the genre or cycle too closely or too loosely . . . . The definition of the heritage film is only as good as the critic makes it . . . the most we can really do is to say that, as critics, we have identified a cycle of films which *tend* to operate in this way rather than that. But there are no hard and fast rules to be adhered to or broken. After all, it is we critics who make up the rules as we write.[14]

The slippage from the notion of the critic *identifying* the conventions of a genre, discovering and describing them as an attentive observer, to one of the critic *creating* a genre according to his or her own priorities is revealing. It implicitly grants the critic much greater power over definitions than is healthy and helps explain the construction of heritage cinema as a category defined more by *critical* attitudes and priorities than by aesthetic, cultural or economic practices.

There is a further telling difference between Barr's account of heritage films and later writings. Though Barr refers to the overall unevenness of the wartime films he mentions, it is in the context of a positive appraisal of their varied merits. There is no irony in the description of Laurence Olivier's *Henry V* (1944) as achieving 'a very superior status as a high-quality British product' nor any scorn in the reference to its American success. This contrasts markedly with the standard academic line on heritage films of the 1980s and 90s, which, taking its cue from the critics' antipathy to Thatcherism generally, views the films as virtual extensions of that ideology, and attacks them accordingly.[15]

Thus, the direct or indirect relationships which can be seen to exist between heritage films and their contemporary cultural context, and which can be used to account for the resurgence of the genre in the 80s and 90s as well as the wartime 40s, have tended to be seen in the case of the more recent cycles as an index of their ideological perniciousness. Indeed, the very term heritage film may itself be seen as 'overwhelmingly pejorative and censorious' in its typical academic usage, tending to imply that the films are 'vessels of a complacently bourgeois (and literary) notion of quality and of a triumphalist English cultural imperialism'.[16] In the term's linkage of the films to Thatcherite heritage culture (whose characteristic mode of operation has been described by Higson as 'the commodification of the past', typified by nostalgia for a vanished and fantasised past and its elite bourgeois culture), there is thus already built into the designation heritage cinema a hostility towards such films, and beyond that towards the audience which would pay to see them.

As Claire Monk has noted, detailed empirical research into this audience, its habits, interests and desires, is almost non-existent compared to generalised assumptions and imputations about it. This is in the context of a new interest in academic film circles in 'reception studies', which seek to complement or supplant critical assumptions about audience behaviour with research in the form of recorded interviews with, and statistical documentation of, actual audience members.[17] It seems reasonable to assume that the distaste felt by left-wing critics for the presumed conservatism (or Conservatism) and middle-class origins of the heritage audience underlies not only their reluctance to consider this audience directly, but also their aversion to the films themselves.

It is rare for heritage critics to acknowledge their own (personal and/or political) stake in discussing and evaluating heritage films. When they have done so, it has largely been justified by reference to theories of cultural discourse, spectatorship and broader ideological imperatives. In an article which is part recapitulation of his earlier writings on the subject, part auto-critique,

The Remains of the Day (James Ivory, 1993)

Duty, order and propriety are the values by which Mr Stevens lives, just as they are the dominant themes of the novel and film of *The Remains of the Day*. The model of an English butler, Stevens (played in James Ivory's screen adaptation by Anthony Hopkins) obeys a strict professional code of self-effacement bordering on self-abnegation. To be in service is for him to be discreet to the point of invisibility; above all, to know his place in overseeing the efficient organisation and maintenance of a great country house which plays host both to social gatherings (the local hunt, formal dinners) and to top-level discussions of international affairs.

The political counterparts of Stevens's professional stance are shown to be class deference and appeasement. In at least two respects both he and his employer, Lord Darlington (James Fox), are guilty of passive complicity with 1930s fascism: in failing to give permanent domestic employment to two Jewish refugees from Nazi Germany, thus enforcing their return to Europe and probable deaths; and in entertaining a secret meeting between Prime Minister Chamberlain and representatives of the German government, misguidedly intended to ensure 'peace in our time'. Book and film pay due attention to this subject, but they are also centrally concerned with Stevens's sexual and emotional stultification, equally entailed by his obsessive regard for tradition and the 'done thing'. Unable to declare his feelings for the housekeeper, Miss Kenton (Emma Thompson), Stevens stands by stolidly as she accepts an offer of marriage from a rival, and on meeting her again years later sadly recognises the impossibility of turning back time and regaining what he had lost.

Ruth Prawer Jhabvala's screenplay is characteristically respectful of the tone and the substance of Kazuo Ishiguro's fine Booker Prize-winning novel (written in the first person from Stevens's point-of-view), though it subtly alters the balance from the political to the personal and gives more space to the flashback narrative than to the framing scenes set in the 1950s. Where the film adds most to its source material is in the superb performances Ivory draws from his cast, never patronising characters whom less sensitive directors might have reduced to caricature. Hopkins's stiff postures, fixed expressions and hollow stares mutely convey deep reservoirs of pain and regret, only once spilling over into an out-loud cry of frustration.

Ivory's skill also extends to the eloquently expressive use he makes of the spaces and ornaments of the fictional Darlington Hall (a composite of several actual houses). A dustpan mistakenly left by an open panel on an otherwise immaculate staircase; the shocking disturbance of a dropped tea tray or a smashed wine bottle; the meticulous *mise en place* of a dinner table, threatened by a droplet of mucus precariously suspended from an ageing nostril; the constricting frame of a window pane and the darkened sanctity of a private pantry. These are among the visual and dramatic highlights of a melodrama in which intense emotion, ever present, is movingly signalled by symbols of its repression.

FURTHER READING

John Baxendale and Chris Pawling, *Narrating the Thirties: A Decade in the Making: 1930 to the Present* (London: Palgrave Macmillan, 1995), pp. 188–212.

Brian McFarlane, '*The Remains of the Day*', *Cinema Papers* nos 97–8, April 1994, pp. 51–2.

and part self-defence against the criticism of others, Higson hints at what might be entailed in such an acknowledgment when he explains that, despite his attempt to perform an 'ideological critique' on heritage cinema,

> I had to take on board the fact that I also rather
> enjoyed these films, although I'm not sure I felt that I
> could admit as much, since this would reveal my own
> class formation, my own cultural inheritance, my
> attachment to the wrong sort of cinema for a Film
> Studies lecturer.[18]

Higson accounts for his own criticism of heritage cinema in terms of the academic imperative to question the conservatism (political and aesthetic) of traditional literary culture and its favoured canonical works, and to embrace both 'the central texts of political modernism' and popular culture, into which neither (arguably incompatible) categories can heritage films be easily fitted. This, unfortunately, is as far as the discussion of such intimate matters gets before Higson moves on to the 'more important' issue of the heritage films' own 'ambivalence' towards the nostalgia which – it is argued – constitutes their principal source of appeal.

Much of Higson's critique (echoed by other writers) centres on his analysis of what he sees as the characteristic narrative form and *mise en scène* of heritage films, and especially their organisation of spectacle – the spectacle of the past and its contents – in an 'aesthetic of display', a 'museum aesthetic', which 'fetishises' objects as consumable properties and images as surface simulacra, rather than producing a critical (political) interrogation of the past. From this aesthetic (itself a highly arguable construct, which tends to homogenise a varied cycle of films into a unitary group style and ignores the distinctions between and diversity among them and their makers) can be extrapolated a typical heritage spectator: *uncritical, undiscriminating,* a passive and complacent consumer of images.

The sort of spectator-consumers Higson posits certainly exist. I recall having to shush a pair of old ladies seated behind me at a revival screening of *The Go-Between* when they loudly remarked on the quality of the silverware displayed in the lavish country house where most of the film's action is set. This may not be what Richard Dyer had in mind when he referred to the heritage film's 'attention to fixtures and fittings . . . typically requiring the skilled reading of a female spectator', but it does seem likely to be a common 'reading strategy' adopted by many spectators, and might therefore appear to confirm Higson's argument.[19] But one could argue that such enjoyment (vocalised or otherwise) is not confined to heritage or women's films, but is basic to the appeal of the cinema itself. It is in the nature of cinema's representational 'realism' (a term here to be understood in its broadest sense: the photographic reproduction of real places and things) that the richness of film images of locations, sets, costumes, objects, even actors, almost always exceeds their assigned dramatic or narrational functions. As André Bazin argued, the 'thinginess' of filmic representations is the very essence of cinema:

> The aesthetic qualities of photography are to be
> sought in its power to lay bare the realities. It is not
> for me to separate off, in the complex fabric of the
> objective world, here a reflection on a damp sidewalk,
> there the gesture of a child. Only the impassive lens,
> stripping its object of all those ways of seeing it, those
> piled up preconceptions, that spiritual dust and grime
> with which my eyes have covered it, is able to present
> it in all its virginal purity to my attention and conse-
> quently to my love.[20]

An active enjoyment of place, space, people and objects for their own sakes is one of the pleasures which we find in the cinema, and for which many spectators go in anticipation.[21] The expressiveness of these features as *mise en scène* neither contradicts nor excludes such other uses of them by spectators. They can only *be* expressive because they are present and plausible first as objects and places existing semi-autonomously within the films' diegetic world, and thus function only secondarily as narrational devices or vehicles for authorial comment.

Claire Monk has argued against the notion of the reactionary audience by discussing her own enjoyment of heritage films, and by describing them as 'feminine' texts offering 'feminine narrative pleasures'. In her reading of heritage films, their typically slow-moving, digressive narratives, multiple characters offering multiple points of identification, and 'concern for character, place, atmosphere, and milieu rather than for dramatic, goal-oriented action', all construct and address a 'feminine subject position' as the ideal spectatorial mode (the analogies with notions of differently constituted masculine and feminine sexual pleasure are far from incidental to Monk's argument).[22] Monk, like Richard Dyer, Mark Finch and Richard Kwietniowski, sees heritage films as contemporary developments of the traditional 'woman's film', typified by melodramatic plot devices, narratives revolving around romance, emotion and desire, and a floridly expressive *mise en scène* (comparatively subdued in the British heritage version).[23]

Intriguing as these latter readings are, it seems to me unfortunate that a critical defence of heritage films should depend upon an elaborate theoretical construct – the feminine subject position – rather than textuality in its own right. It is especially dismaying, for heterosexual male spectators such as myself, to find offered as the sole alternative a version of masculinity constructed in terms of the short attention span and hyperactivity of an immature adolescent (admittedly the target demographic of most contemporary Hollywood movies). Despite her professed wish to avoid collapsing discussion of heritage films' meaning and value into an either/or 'binarism' (conservative/progressive, spectacle/history, etc.), Monk inevitably reinstates it by adding a further, equally dubious, pair of oppositions (masculinity/femininity). Her defence also smacks of a dubious kind of special pleading (heritage films must be interesting because women and gay men like them).

It is a central failing of almost all heritage criticism that it has not been able to deal adequately with the films' *mise en scène* as such. Higson responds to criticisms of his position by Richard Dyer and Ginette Vincendeau by suggesting that alternative readings 'are all in the end no more than readings. How do we decide to validate one reading over another?'[24] One of the ways, I would suggest, in which some readings are (and can be seen to be) more valid than others is in the degree of their attentiveness to the particularities of actual texts, and the degree to which claims about them can be verified by close reference to those texts. Projecting discussion of films onto theoretical 'subject positions' is another means of evading that attentiveness – the kind of evasion which is characteristic of most British cinema scholarship. Study after study which claims to take textuality as a major concern turns out to offer no more than a superficial engagement with the detail of particular films.[25]

This may be a weakness endemic to generic and historical approaches to film studies – approaches which have come to be the preferred modes for the study of British cinema – which tend to favour broad generalisations over close analysis of particulars. However, when heritage critics do turn to the analysis of shots, scenes and sequences from individual films, their observational and analytic skills are often questionable. Andrew Higson's discussion of two short sequences from *Howards End* manages to get the order (and therefore the significance) of shots in one of these wrong, and to use the other merely as the vehicle for restating a polemical point which already seems tautologically obvious (that the scene 'makes the most of the opportunity to display some fine authentic period properties, which are of course the properties of a very privileged class').[26] Argument which rests on so slender and unreliable a base of empirical evidence does not instil much confidence in its more wide-ranging pronouncements. No amount of attention to 'reading formations', cultural 'determinations', discourses of tourism, consumption, publicity or marketing, can substitute for detailed first-hand engagement with the films themselves.[27]

I want to conclude with some further observations on the future prospects of 'heritage' as a useful critical category (and here I must reinstate inverted commas and reassert my own critical distance from the term). If its continued presence in academic film studies is to be at all productive and it is not simply to be dispensed with (as I have often had cause to wish), several changes must be made in its definition and use. First, it needs to be purged of its pejorative connotations and its attachment to the Thatcherite phase of cultural history. If not,

its only value can be as the designation of a particular critical attitude towards a narrowly defined, and parodically described, group of films made during and shortly after that period. This is not, of course, to demand a wholesale positive revaluation of all the 80s and 90s heritage films, or to deny that many of them were as bland, staid, stolid and dull as has often been supposed.[28] But a generic label can hardly expect any longevity if its connotations are entirely negative.

Second, if the term is to have wider utility and less partisan implications, it needs to be extended to encompass other periods of British film history in which significant forms of heritage cinema have been produced, especially those – like the 1960s – which ideological and institutional imperatives have thus far led to be neglected; and beyond that, following Richard Dyer and Ginette Vincendeau's example, to other countries' versions of heritage films, including European, Australasian, and indeed American variants and equivalents.[29]

Third, greater attention needs to be paid to textual, as well as contextual, analysis, and through that to engagement with the particularities of individual films rather than loose generic groupings. Heritage critics (hostile and favourable alike) could benefit from a consideration of the subtlety, precision, passion, sensitivity and intimate, sympathetic understanding of a film text (and its literary source) shown by Robin Wood in his BFI Modern Classics monograph on *The Wings of the Dove*, which in its ninety-odd pages never once mentions heritage.

Notes

1. Charles Barr, 'Introduction: Amnesia and Schizophrenia', in Charles Barr (ed.), *All Our Yesterdays: 90 Years of British Cinema* (London: BFI, 1986), p. 12.

2. For a concise summary of recent critical debates over heritage cinema, see Chapter 4 of John Hill, *British Cinema in the 1980s*.

3. See, for example, Tana Wollen, 'Over Our Shoulders: Nostalgic Screen Fictions for the 1980s', and the other essays included in John Corner and Sylvia Harvey (eds), *Enterprise and Heritage: Crosscurrents of National Culture*.

4. Claire Monk, 'The Heritage Film and Gendered Spectatorship', p. 6.

5. Tony Rayns, '*Wilde*', *Sight and Sound*, October 1997, p. 65.

6. Richard Dyer, 'Heritage Cinema in Europe', in Ginette Vincendeau (ed.), *Encyclopedia of European Cinema* (London: Cassell/BFI, 1995). See also Vincendeau, 'Unsettling Memories', *Sight and Sound*, July 1995; and Vincendeau, 'Issues in European Cinema', in John Hill and

Pamela Church Gibson (eds), *The Oxford Guide to Film Studies* (Oxford: Oxford University Press, 1998), for further discussion of heritage cinema in the European context. It should be noted that Dyer's and Vincendeau's own uses of the term heritage cinema tend, atypically, to be neutrally descriptive rather than judgmental in tone.

7. Claire Monk, 'Sexuality and the Heritage', p. 33.

8. Pamela Church Gibson, 'Fewer Weddings and More Funerals: Changes in the Heritage Film'. As Church Gibson's title indicates, the contemporary-set *Four Weddings and a Funeral* (Mike Newell, 1994) has also been annexed by some critics to the heritage film, largely on the basis of its upper-middle-class characters and heritagey locations, and its export-friendly representation of Britishness. *Notting Hill* (Roger Michell, 1999) and *Bridget Jones's Diary* (Sharon Maguire, 2001) presumably also qualify for inclusion on the same, questionable basis.

9. See Andrew Higson, *Waving the Flag: Constructing a National Cinema in Britain*, especially Chapter 3 (mainly on Cecil Hepworth's 1924 version of *Comin' thro' the Rye*). Higson has also discussed *Nelson*, in 'The Victorious Recycling of National History: *Nelson*', in Karel Dibbets and Bert Hogenkamp (eds), *Film and the First World War* (Amsterdam: Amsterdam University Press, 1995).

10. Barr, 'Introduction: Amnesia and Schizophrenia', p. 12.

11. For an account of the production and popular reception of costume films and historical dramas in the 1930s and 40s, see Sue Harper, *Picturing the Past: The Rise and Fall of the British Costume Film* and H. Mark Glancy, *When Hollywood Loved Britain: The Hollywood 'British' Film 1939–45* (Manchester and New York: Manchester University Press, 1999). For adventure films and melodramas of these periods, see Jeffrey Richards, *Films and British National Identity: From Dickens to Dad's Army* (Manchester: Manchester University Press, 1997); and Richards (ed.), *The Unknown 1930s: An Alternative History of British Cinema 1929–1939* (London: I. B. Tauris, 1998). For the 1950s see Sue Harper, 'Bonnie Prince Charlie Revisited: British Costume Films in the 1950s', Chapter 30 in the present volume. For American views of the 1980s and 90s heritage cycle, see Harlan Kennedy, 'The Brits Have Gone Nuts', *Film Comment* vol. 21 no. 4, July–August 1985; Martin A. Hipsky, 'Anglophil(m)ia: Why Does America Watch Merchant-Ivory Movies?', *Journal of Popular Film and Television* vol. 22 no. 3, Fall 1994; and Donald Lyons, 'Traditions of Quality', *Film Comment* vol. 28 no. 3, May–June 1992, which compares several of the recent films to 'Hollywood British' literary adaptations of the 30s and 40s.

12. Robert Murphy, *Sixties British Cinema* (London: BFI, 1992), p. 6.

13. Ginette Vincendeau, '*The Golden Bowl*', *Sight and Sound*, November 2000, p. 52; Kevin Jackson, '*The House of Mirth*', ibid., p. 54. Despite its unpromising introduction, Vincendeau's review is generally favourable and makes some interesting remarks on the film's *mise en scène*. For further discussion of *The House of Mirth* in the context of Terence Davies's *oeuvre*, see Philip Horne, 'Beauty's Slow Fade', *Sight and Sound*, October 2000.

14. Andrew Higson, 'The Heritage Film and British Cinema', p. 235.

15. The most virulent critiques of the heritage films of this period are probably Tana Wollen's in the *Enterprise and Heritage* chapter already cited, and Cairns Craig's startlingly snide 'Rooms without a View', *Sight and Sound*, June 1991.

16. Monk, 'The Heritage Film and Gendered Spectatorship', Part 1, pp. 2–3.

17. See Claire Monk, 'Heritage Films and the British Cinema Audience in the 1990s', for an attempt to initiate such audience research. Stout opponents of heritage cinema would doubtless have had their prejudices confirmed by the audience with which I saw Branagh's *Hamlet* (1996) at a regular weekday matinée at the Curzon Mayfair in London (the standard première venue for such films), among which were a number of patrons accoutred in dress suits, fur coats and jewellery.

18. Higson, 'The Heritage Film and British Cinema', p. 238.

19. Dyer, 'Heritage Cinema in Europe', p. 204.

20. 'The Ontology of the Photographic Image', in André Bazin, *What Is Cinema? Volume 1*. Essays selected and translated by Hugh Gray (Berkeley, Los Angeles and London: University of California Press, 1974), p. 15.

21. Richard Dyer, in 'Feeling English', makes similar observations in passing.

22. Monk, 'The Heritage Film and Gendered Spectatorship', Part 2, pp. 3–4.

23. See Dyer, 'Feeling English'; and Mark Finch and Richard Kwietniowski, 'Melodrama and *Maurice*: Homo Is Where the Het Is'.

24. Higson, 'The Heritage Film and British Cinema', p. 246.

25. A prime offender among those works already cited is Sue Harper's *Picturing the Past*.

26. Higson, 'The Heritage Film and British Cinema', pp. 240–2.

27. In addition to Higson and Wollen's work, I am thinking of Amy Sargeant, 'Making and Selling Heritage Culture: Style and Authenticity in Historical Fictions on Film and Television', in Justine Ashby and Andrew Higson (eds), *British Cinema Past and Present* (London and New York: Routledge, 2000), which has much to say about marketing and very little about style.

28. For the record, I regard *The Remains of the Day* as the finest (and generally most underrated) of the recent cycle, and *Little Dorrit* as by far the worst.

29. Graeme Turner, 'Art Directing History: The Period Film', in Albert Moran and Tom O'Regan (eds), *The Australian Screen* (Harmondsworth: Penguin, 1989), and Jonathan Rayner, in *Contemporary Australian Cinema* (Manchester: Manchester University Press, 2001), discuss the cycle of Australian period films (mainly made between 1974 and 1981), which preceded the British heritage revival of the 80s and 90s, and which led Pauline Kael to describe *Chariots of Fire* as 'probably the best Australian film ever made in England' ('Three Pairs', *New Yorker*, 26 October 1981; reprinted in Kael, *Taking It All In*, London and New York: Marion Boyars, 1986, p. 247).

Bibliography

Church Gibson, Pamela, 'Fewer Weddings and More Funerals: Changes in the Heritage Film', in Robert Murphy (ed.), *British Cinema of the 90s* (London: BFI, 2000).

Corner, John and Harvey, Sylvia (eds), *Enterprise and Heritage: Crosscurrents of National Culture* (London and New York: Routledge, 1991).

Craig, Cairns, 'Rooms without a View', *Sight and Sound*, June 1991.

Dyer, Richard, 'Feeling English', *Sight and Sound*, March 1994.

Finch, Mark and Kwietniowski, Richard, 'Melodrama and *Maurice*: Homo Is Where the Het Is', *Screen* vol. 29 no. 3, Summer 1988.

Harper, Sue, *Picturing the Past: The Rise and Fall of the British Costume Film* (London: BFI, 1994).

Higson, Andrew, 'Re-presenting the National Past: Nostalgia and Pastiche in the Heritage Film', in Lester Friedman (ed.), *British Cinema and Thatcherism: Fires Were Started* (London: University of Central London Press, 1993).

Higson, Andrew, *Waving the Flag: Constructing a National Cinema in Britain* (Oxford: Clarendon Press, 1995).

Higson, Andrew, 'The Heritage Film and British Cinema', in Higson (ed.), *Dissolving Views: Key Writings on British Cinema* (London: Cassell, 1996).

Higson, Andrew, *English Heritage, English Cinema* (Oxford: Oxford University Press, 2003).

Hill, John, *British Cinema in the 1980s* (Oxford: Clarendon Press, 1999).

Monk, Claire, 'The British "Heritage Film" and Its Critics', *Critical Survey* vol. 7 no. 2, 1995.

Monk, Claire, 'Sexuality and the Heritage', *Sight and Sound*, October 1995.

Monk, Claire, 'The Heritage Film and Gendered Spectatorship', *CloseUp: The Electronic Journal of British Cinema* vol. 1 no. 1, 1997 (www.shu.ac.uk/services/lc/closeup/title.htm).

Monk, Claire, 'Heritage Films and the British Cinema Audience in the 1990s', *Journal of Popular British Cinema* no. 2, 1999.

Monk, Claire, and Sargeant, Amy (eds), *British Historical Films* (London and New York: Routledge, 2001).

Pidduck, Julianne, *Contemporary Costume Film: Space, Place and the Past* (London: BFI, 2004).

Wood, Robin, *The Wings of the Dove: Henry James in the 1990s* (London: BFI, 1999).

7
British Cult Cinema

JUSTIN SMITH

The rise of the cult film in British cinema may be explained by an examination of four related factors: a survey of economic determinants; an overview of cultural changes; some observations about key film texts; and a consideration of fan reception. First, however, it is important to explore the critical context of the term cult cinema.

Critical Context

The term 'cult' in its modern sense came out of the popular youth culture of the 1950s. One of the earliest identified print references in Britain was an entry in the *TV Times* advertising 'The James Dean Legend', an Associated-Rediffusion documentary broadcast on 1 November 1957, which proclaimed that 'James Dean has become a legend and a cult for many of his generation'.[1] Cult was also a key concept in the critical vocabulary of the new American film critics of the period (themselves much influenced by the writers and film-makers of the French *nouvelle vague*): Parker Tyler, Manny Farber and later Andrew Sarris.[2] Sarris employed the term with almost all the associations that it has since come to assume: an obsessive devotion to a personal canon of films which require continual and expert critical appraisal and support, sometimes in spite (or because) of their lowly, neglected or disparaged official status.[3] This was an attempt to critique and classify popular texts in a new way, while also taking a modishly perverse delight in championing works with debased cultural origins that had previously been ignored or maligned. This critical attitude both drew on, and in turn influenced, the prevalent attitudes of youth culture, forging a breach between its own diverse cultural

practices and those of the established order. It was at once a cry for recognition and a retreat into obscurity. This dynamic remains at the heart of cult fandom today.

Economic Determinants

The British New Wave films of the late 1950s and early 60s were serious and realist. But by the mid-1960s they had been superseded by a cinematic populism that cashed in on the international popularity of British pop music and fashion. These 'Swinging London' films, along with the internationally successful James Bond films, were in large measure financed by American studios. All the Hollywood majors established production offices in London and by 1968 US investment reached an all-time high of £31.3 million.[4] Briefly, London became the epicentre for the production of films whose paymasters remained conveniently distant. Despite this boom in production, cinemagoing continued to decline. The highly regulated and inflexible distribution market prompted smaller circuits and independents 'to break away from the standard release pattern and programme their cinemas with popular classics, foreign sex and art films, and the 'X' films which the circuits were reluctant to show'.[5] This marked the beginnings of a fragmentation of cinema at the exhibition level and the formation of niche markets in the general context of its continuing decline.

Into this curiously permeable film world of strange alliances, speculative investments and creative innovation, other kinds of entrepreneur entered, from backgrounds as varied as television and fine art, the theatre and fashion, public relations and popular music. Film is by its nature a collaborative medium that draws in any number of specialist creative and technical skills as well as various sorts of venture capitalist. But unique circumstances arose in Britain in the second half of the 1960s, whereby generous Hollywood companies were willing to back loose associations of diverse (sometimes untried) talent without the overarching control of conventional production regimes.

Cultural Changes

1968 has been widely acknowledged as a cultural turning point. But in Britain the impact of that moment had perhaps less to do with violence on the streets of Paris and more to do with the passing, the previous year, of progressive legislation legalising abortion and homosexuality, making the contraceptive pill available and (the following year) reforming the divorce laws. As important to the counter-culture was the delayed effect of the 1944 Education Act, whose grammar-school beneficiaries were emerging from the rapidly built new universities of the 1960s.

Whatever the wider implications of the claims for 1968 as a revolutionary moment, it was the year with which a surprising number of British cult films have a connection.[6] The young British director Michael Reeves released his third and final feature *Witchfinder General*. The fledgeling partnership of Donald Cammell, Nicolas Roeg and Sanford Lieberson began work on *Performance* (which was destined to remain unreleased until 1970). The Who's Pete Townshend began a creative journey that would result, seven years later, in Ken Russell's film of his rock opera *Tommy* (1975). And, cold and penniless in a dismal flat in Camden Town, a struggling actor named Bruce Robinson embarked on a comic autobiography which would become a nostalgic lament for late-60s romanticism: *Withnail & I* (1986).

In several respects, *Performance* offers a useful case study of the interrelations between capital and culture at this time.[7] At its core is the mercurial figure of Donald Cammell, artist and dilettante turned screenwriter, who drew his inspiration for the project largely from personal acquaintances in the Chelsea set of the mid-1960s. The whole enterprise captures the unprecedented manner in which establishment figures of the day rubbed shoulders with London's criminal fraternity at parties thrown by artists, fashion designers and pop stars on budgets provided by television executives, advertising agents, record moguls and pornographers. In this rarefied milieu, class boundaries, at least temporarily,

were forgotten. New money was the great leveller, hedonism the common cultural currency. It was a vibrant, brash, unstable scene from which some, like Rolling Stone Brian Jones, the model for Mick Jagger's jaded, reclusive rock star Turner, ultimately dropped out.

The film's achievement is remarkable not least as a measure of the faith which major Hollywood studios were prepared to invest in ramshackle alliances of variously inexperienced talent. Sandy Lieberson, a Hollywood agent based in London, approached his friend Ken Hyman who had just been appointed head of production for Warner Bros. (then under the control of Hyman senior's Seven Arts media corporation). Warners were very keen to back a project starring Mick Jagger, though he was untried as a screen performer.[8] Lieberson had never produced a film any more than Cammell had directed one; key to the project, therefore, was securing experienced actor James Fox and respected cinematographer, Nicolas Roeg. A budget of £400,000 was agreed for an eleven-week shoot, entirely on location, beginning in July 1968. Although the production was allowed almost complete freedom by its backers, once studio executives actually saw what they had paid for they were appalled at the film's cocktail of sex, drugs and impenetrable narrative structure, and delayed its completion and release.

Performance shows how Hollywood was prepared to risk investing in what was essentially counter-cultural British production. The unstable film market of the period also encouraged the influx of investment from the pornography industry, sometimes with extraordinary results.[9] Here again, we see how diverse, radical and marginal tastes at this time, were allowed to take centre-stage: in the films of Roman Polanski and Michael Reeves, for example. According to J. Hoberman, *Witchfinder General* 'has long been a cult item – in part because its talented 25-year-old director, Michael Reeves, died of a drug overdose before the film's release, but mainly because it is an extraordinarily bleak story of political evil'.[10] Peter Hutchings argues that although Reeves 'exhibited both a sensitivity to strains and tensions within British society at this time and an awareness of the challenge these presented for a type of filmmaking to which he was artistically committed', the resulting film ultimately fails 'to pull these elements together into a coherent whole'.[11] But what is remarkable about *Witchfinder General* is its radical conjunction of mainstream, populist appeal (as a horror/exploitation film) with a transgressive, cult force. A common trait of the cult film is its very inability to 'pull these elements together into a coherent whole'. There is always another stratum of intense feeling breaking through the surface of the imagined narrative world.

Witchfinder General's accomplished and disturbing concoction of sexual violence and profoundly ambivalent gender and generational relationships, attempts to articulate a response to the cultural politics of a complex historical moment. If *Performance* follows Antonioni's *Blow-Up* (1966) in casting dark clouds over the happy land of Swinging London, it is simultaneously the harbinger of those British films of the early 70s – *The Devils* (Ken Russell, 1971), *Get Carter* (Mike Hodges, 1971), *A Clockwork Orange* (Stanley Kubrick, 1971), *Straw Dogs* (Sam Peckinpah, 1971), *Don't Look Now* (Nicolas Roeg, 1973) – which typify a search for understanding and identity in an amoral world of tragedy, violence and excess.

One of the ways in which historical upheavals are negotiated across society is by applying new knowledge, or by revitalising naive or debased systems of thought, to expose objects of traditional taboo: sexual difference, cleanliness, the body. An element of the emerging counter-cultural discourse was a fascination with paganism and the occult, from the Stones' 'Their Satanic Majesties Request' (1967) to hippy environmentalism and back-to-nature rhetoric, from fascination with Aleister Crowley to the avant-garde films of Kenneth Anger. For Leon Hunt this 'growing interest in paganism was partly bound up with uncovering a more "authentic" national identity and culture'.[12] For Steve Chibnall the horror film was 'the most important site for the allegorical exploration of the struggle between the emergent discourses of radical change . . . and the beleaguered discourses of reaction'.[13]

Witchfinder General and *The Wicker Man* (Robin Hardy, 1973), both work as allegorical displacements of anxieties about social disturbance. Both films demonstrate the seductive power – and repellent violence – of alternative systems of belief presided over by symbolic 'bad fathers'.[14] But their perspectives are very different. Amid the turbulence of the English Civil War, self-appointed 'witchfinder general' Matthew Hopkins carries out his own campaign of sadistic violence. His elaborate, pseudo-scientific system of detection and punishment is a means of ensnaring the innocent. He is cruel and evil, and though Vincent Price's charismatic performance gives him a mesmeric appeal, the

'witchcraft' he exposes is a chimera. Christopher Lee's Lord Summerisle in *The Wicker Man* is a sincere believer in the pagan system over which he presides, and calmly rationalises its need for human sacrifice. His Christian opponent Sergeant Howie (Edward Woodward), is equally sincere, but he is bumptious and blinkered. In contrast to Hopkins, who sees witchcraft where there is none; Howie is forced to recognise that the disappearance he has come to investigate is consequential on an organised system of paganism. But he proves no match for the sly, sexy pagans. He is too repressed to heed the siren charms of the seductive Willow (Britt Ekland) and is shocked and repelled by his other erotic encounters: couples copulating on the village green, a sex-education lesson at the local school, a woman breast-feeding in the ruined churchyard, Ingrid Pitt in her bath. But his refusal to countenance the pagan procreation creed blinds him to the dangers of their death rituals. His final sacrifice, in the cage of the Wicker Man's abdomen, symbolises a return to the womb for this man who has, on religious principle, thwarted his own entry into the phallic community. The symbolic androgyny of this defining moment is plain: fatal incarceration within a male womb. It marks both the culmination of the profound anxiety about earthly sexual difference which is conspicuous throughout the film, and the spiritual transcendence (in Christian orthodoxy) to a realm in which sexual difference doesn't matter. To this extent, the film's dynamic of sexual permission and repression rehearses a familiar adolescent rites-of-passage initiation, just as, at another level, it exposes the political and generational divide between the policeman's authority and the counter-culture's liberation of the late 1960s.

Alexander Walker remarked, of David Puttnam and Ray Connolly's David Essex double-bill *That'll Be the Day* (1973) and *Stardust* (1974), that the early 70s heralded 'the start of a revisionist view of the Sixties'.[15] However, these films presented a jaundiced, social realist view of young, male ambition. Other kinds of responses indulged the glamorous excesses of kitsch and camp, in a celebration of the permissiveness the 60s had ushered in and the early 70s pushed to new extremes or parodied with ironic detachment in, for example, *A Clockwork Orange*, *The Rocky Horror Picture Show* (Jim Sharman, 1975) and *Tommy*. Economic determinants remain the driving force behind such cultural innovation. With the rapid withdrawal of American funding from British film production at the beginning of the new decade, a fragmented domestic industry necessitated investment from new quarters, sometimes with innovative results.

Ken Russell's film of *Tommy* was produced by Robert Stigwood, the Australian music entrepreneur who was keen to reach a wider audience with products that would transcend discrete media, in this case a triptych of rock album/stage show/feature film. *Tommy* was a combination of composer Pete Townshend's desire to develop the format of the popular song beyond the commercial strictures of the single and the album

Tommy (Ken Russell, 1975)

The enduring success of *Tommy* reflects several combined factors. It was a film pre-sold on its musical credentials. It worked as a cross-over project. It gained solid, if limited, backing from its independent producers. It had both the creative potential and the formal boundaries Ken Russell requires in order to achieve his best film work. And, it combined a pop-synthetic retrospective of the 60s generation with state-of-the-art sound reproduction and forward-looking, MTV-style visuals that set a trend in pop music films for the next ten years.

Scenes shot in the Lake District as a narrative framing device for the film's beginning and ending, and the use of the Gaiety Theatre on Southsea Pier (together with other locations in and around Portsmouth) marry the Romantic and elemental with a seaside-postcard, post-war, cartoon-realism. Russell's location hunting is often a triumph of the pop artist's sensitivity to the found object: a naval scrapyard piled with discarded mooring buoys is transformed with silver paint into a nightmarish pinball park.

The film's flat, televisual quality lends immediacy to physical action, while the garish colour palette and high contrast anticipate the pop video. Furthermore, the cumulative effect of a concentration on spherical objects (from giant pinballs to silver eyeballs) against flat, geometric surfaces renders this world curiously impermeable, yet endlessly symbolic. Smooth surfaces without openings resist penetration. They become visual playgrounds: safe, sterile, asexual places.

Tommy is not a musical film, but a filmed performance of a song cycle. The cast were required to perform for the camera to the playback of their pre-recorded soundtrack: a feat which is especially accomplished in the case of Oscar-nominated Ann-Margret as Tommy's mother. But what it achieves consistently, above all else, is an immense, visceral, emotional charge.

The effect of casting stars from the world of popular music to charismatic screen roles invites identification and mistrust in equal measure. Roger Daltrey in all his stiff, awkward vulnerability both is and isn't Tommy.

'We're not gonna take it': the pop cult of *Tommy* rebels

The film pities its protagonist and draws our sympathy. Then, it cynically transforms him into the money-grabbing shaman of a fake religious cult. He remains untouchable, sealed in his private (rock star's) world, autistic, out of reach.

The central relationship is that of Tommy and his mother; the rest are cartoon caricatures, albeit nicely drawn (Oliver Reed's Uncle Frank, Keith Moon's Uncle Ernie, Paul Nicholas's Cousin Kevin, Tina Turner's Acid Queen). But what gives shape, dramatic contrast and some emotional depth to the narrative is the juxtaposition of Nora Walker's guilt-ridden yearning with Tommy's mute impassivity. And plainly the underlying framework (in Russell's augmentation of Pete Townshend's tale) is an Oedipal archetype.

Narratively, *Tommy* works as a rite-of-passage journey from childhood, through adolescence to manhood; our hero's mute, alienated, insentient condition operates as a hyperbolic metaphor for the universal problems of maturation and socialisation. *Tommy* problematises masculinity itself and ultimately transcends it. It offers stimulation and consolation in equal measure.

FURTHER READING

Richard Barnes and Pete Townshend, *The Story of Tommy* (Twickenham: Eel Pie Publishing, 1977).

Gene D. Phillips, *Ken Russell* (Boston, MA: Twayne, 1979).

towards a unifying thematic concept, and a personal expression of a spiritual route from the watershed of 1968 (via the teachings of Indian mystic Meher Baba):

> I realised that there was a parallel in the shape of the autistic child . . . I decided that the hero had to be deaf, dumb and blind, so that, seen from our already limited point of view, his limitations would be symbolic of our own.[16]

Spiritual doctrine aside, this idea of sensory alienation points to the adolescent's concern with being in the world but not of it, which is analogous to the achievement of socio-sexual identity. Pop culture and fandom play a crucial role for many teenagers in negotiating this formative transition. It is a trend that continues in British youth films of the 1970s, for example, *Quadrophenia* (Franc Roddam, 1979) and *Jubilee* (Derek Jarman, 1978), and also in those which, like *Performance* and *Tommy*, exploit the cult appeal of iconic figures from the world of popular music. Consider also David Bowie's charismatic performance as the alien visitor Thomas Jerome Newton in Nicolas Roeg's 1976 sci-fi fantasy *The Man Who Fell to Earth*, wherein alienation is the dominant theme explored visually through the viewing experience.

Contemporary critics pointed to the time-lag between the moment of *Tommy* (the album) and its filmic incarnation. Even the most enthusiastic of reviewers asserted: 'It is a film that *should* have been made around 1970 . . . when it was immediate'.[17] Such attitudes are illustrative of the lukewarm reception accorded many subsequent cult films on their first release (for example, *The Wicker Man*). The distance between the Who's *Tommy* (1969) and Ken Russell's film of 1975 incorporates a nostalgic, sometimes parodic, and frequently hyperbolic, rendition of the source material. We might characterise this *post hoc* situation in terms of patterns of cultural slippage. The space this opens up within the film text is a playground for cultish sensibilities.

Textual Analysis

In analysing a range of films that fans and critics have come to consider cult what quickly becomes apparent is that textual characteristics of excess and incongruity are paramount. Frequently, such films display both a Baroque sensibility and a Romantic nostalgia. Their pastiche of certain low-budget genres is both eclectic and lacking in irony. Yet their iconic tributes are too

diverse to adhere to established generic categories, and their narrative disjuncture often confounds conventional readings. Better clues as to their peculiarity may be found elsewhere in the *mise en scène*.

Performance, as its title suggests, focuses our attention on visual style and music. The casting of amateur actors and pop-music icons brings to the fore acting technique, physical deportment and the voice. Here, as elsewhere in *Tommy* and *The Man Who Fell to Earth*, iconic stars from the world of rock music bring to screen roles both the signifying practices of their established media personae and the quality of redundancy which is a feature of their untrained screen performance. But such conspicuous allure is not the preserve solely of pop stars. Established actors when cast against type often produce performances of sublime charismatic attraction: for example, Vincent Price's Matthew Hopkins, Edward Woodward's Sergeant Howie and Christopher Lee's Lord Summerisle, Malcolm McDowell's Alex de Large and Richard E. Grant's Withnail. Sometimes this is the result of a combination of narrative power with physical vulnerability. Frequently the timbre of voice, patterns of gaze and physical deportment are constituent factors in this appeal. Finally these elements of performance in cult films often create an iconic mask that draws attention to its own charismatic artifice and reveals the hollowness behind it. But in cult films the mask is never a perfect fit.

These charismatic performances often depend on an imbalance between performance and other aspects of the *mise en scène*. Cult films do not produce orderly fictional worlds. Their codes of excess frequently include violence and the breaking of other taboos. They manifest an oblique, sometimes surreal attitude to the world of objects, without resorting to complete fantasy. This has not only to do with the objects themselves, but also their physical arrangement within the frame. Take for example the grotesque pop-art objects at the cat lady's house in *A Clockwork Orange*, or the Magritte-influenced giant silver balls in *Tommy* – impenetrable spheres without fissure. In each case physical disproportion is accentuated by a deliberated flattened or distorted picture plane. We are denied the reassurance of depth of field and the balance of classical perspective. Sometimes such disorientation is produced by the inexplicable close-up and fast, analytical editing (in *Performance* and *The Man Who Fell to Earth*, for example). Elsewhere, locations are equally unsettling. The East-Anglian landscape of *Witchfinder General*, the malevolent Lake District of *Withnail & I*, the mythical

Scottish Summerisle and the New Mexican 'land of enchantment' in *The Man Who Fell to Earth*, are each disquieting in their own way.

The breaching of social taboos is a common feature of cult films. Some are extremely violent (*Performance, Witchfinder General, A Clockwork Orange*, ultimately *The Wicker Man* too). Often this is the more disturbing for treating the subject in a detached, sometimes picaresque or analytical manner – presenting violence as spectacle. A similar attitude towards the body is offered in such films' approach to sex too. Once again voyeuristic tendencies are complicated by anxiety and unease.

For all their challenge to codes of permission, however, few cult films descend into anarchy. Rather, they display an unusual respect for rules and rituals. Consider Sergeant Howie's methodical police inquiry pitted against the alternative religious practices of Summerisle. Or Matthew Hopkins's systematic reign of terror. The need for codes of practice is manifest in cult films, though often these are alternative in character. Sometimes they are playful inversions of normal social conventions that present a carnivalesque irreverence for the traditional sites of power. Elsewhere they govern extremely antisocial behaviour. Frequently they traverse the hinterland of primary taboos concerning dirt, mess, bodily hygiene and matter out of place. Everywhere they stand as a reminder of the necessity for, but ultimate contingency of, rule-based systems. And they speak of the desire for a framework in which to formulate belief. This leads us to a consideration of audience reception and the nature of cult fandom itself.

Cult Fandom

Certain kinds of cultural texts – ones whose unfinished structure allows remarkable creative agency and psychic investment on the part of the viewer – can be used to displace shared subjective anxieties. These examples may exist on an individual basis of course, as Lacan posits in the case of an unresolved Oedipal crisis, but are often culturally inscribed at what Kaja Silverman terms moments of 'historical trauma'. Her own case study relates to the figuring of male anxiety as a form of war neurosis in Hollywood films in the years immediately after World War II. Sue Harper's work on Gainsborough melodramas of the same period encourages those films to be read as another kind of female cultural response to a similar crisis of belief in the 'dominant fiction'.[18] Interestingly, however, Silverman also acknowledges: 'It

has only been very recently that yet another threat has come into play in a politically organized way – that constituted through the representational and sexual practices of feminism and gay liberation.'[19]

It seems to me that the specific crisis of masculinity to which she refers emanated from the cultural revolution of the late 1960s and the rise of feminism and gay liberation, which gathered political momentum during the 1970s and 1980s. The impact of debates about gender politics and sexual orientation during this period was also exacerbated by what might be termed a crisis of faith in the family as a symbolic institution. Each of these matters is explicitly addressed, though never resolved, in cult films of the same period. Cult films may be viewed as one kind of textual response to this crisis of masculinity. But why? What psychic needs do they fulfil?

I suggest that such texts work for fans, both male and female, to both stimulate and console. There is ample evidence that fans have profound affective attachments to the films I have mentioned here. Psychic disposition, as well as general cultural factors, draw certain individuals to cult films as 'transitional objects', in the process of subjective self-recognition with which we are all engaged.[20] Fans use these films as resources through which to rehearse subjective identities and demonstrate cultural competence. The strategies and processes involved are various, just as individual needs must be diverse. Yet if cultural texts can be viewed, like religious icons, as objects through which we structure our desires in the constitution of our own subjective identities, then cult films are the repositories of fears and longings in the negotiation of sexual difference and subjectivity. This is how *Withnail & I* rekindles late-60s rebellion with such nostalgic allure. Such texts endorse cultural marginality, reassuring their devotees that not 'fitting-in' is fine, maybe even heroic. They offer alternative systems of order, symbolic rituals and rites of passage. They provide frameworks for alternative forms of belief.

In fan interactions, these texts promote remarkable candour and rancour; they enable fans to demonstrate canniness about films that are frequently obscure and profess devotion to the debased. At the same time, internet identities allow for the orchestrated projection of a subjective self which cannot be exposed as incomplete, unfinished or socially inept. They enable amateurism to be taken seriously. Newsgroup communications can be a way of producing a symbolic self that is a misrecognition of subjective identity – a mask of disavowal. Finally, the symbolic work which cult fandom enables allows

Withnail & I (Bruce Robinson, 1986)

Withnail & I has inspired more oft-quoted lines and drinking games in student bars than any other film. While it is small scale, it is also exceptionally well crafted: Robinson's sharp script and the accomplished ensemble acting (Richard E. Grant, Paul McGann, Richard Griffiths, Ralph Brown) are key to its iconic status.

Withnail (Grant) is a tragicomic hero, a man whose delusions of his own greatness are limited only by his frustration at the refusal of a decaying, tawdry, hostile and trivialised world to recognise his genius. Together with flatmate and fellow thespian Marwood (McGann), he struggles to rise above the detritus of his own personal and domestic squalor, through drink, drugs and any other substance that might temporarily enhance the reality of his own circumstances. They flee to a Lake District cottage owned by his wealthy homosexual uncle, Monty (Griffiths) but find the rigours of an unaccustomed country life (not to mention the advances of the reptilian Monty) intolerable, and return to London. Withnail is arrested for drink-driving while the more pragmatic Marwood receives an offer of work. Histrionic to the last, a bereft Withnail winds up intoning a soliloquy from *Hamlet* across Regents Park. His invective and hyperbole are at once a smoke-screen and defence mechanism to keep the world at bay; a means of ordering things so as to engage with reality obliquely.

Withnail and Marwood live in conditions of squalor that are as much the product of their own lifestyle as of the circumstances of their penury. That they are overwhelmed, disgusted and terrified by the horror of their own filth marks a childlike psychological recognition of their humanity. Similarly, fear of physical grossness is represented in the obese pulchritude of Uncle Monty. An adolescent fear of sex, and especially gay sex, is repeated throughout. Indeed, sex is totally repressed. The film (like their lives) is without female interest.

Reviewing the publication of the screenplay in 1995, novelist Will Self pinpoints the story's appeal:

'We're at the end of an age. We live in a land of weather forecasts': Richard E. Grant and Paul McGann are entertained at Uncle Monty's Lakeland retreat in *Withnail & I*

> In Marwood and Withnail, Robinson has created an apotheosis of the idea of romantic artistic youth as countercultural rebel. I feel sure that part of the reason for the film's enduring popularity is the sense contemporary youth have that the 60s were the last time when rebellion like this was valid.

Withnail & I had the audacity to recall an era that had become deeply unfashionable, and to make a virtue of that enduring sense of alienation one feels at being out of step with the age. These maverick traits, beautifully observed, lend it special cult appeal. The psychic and emotional schisms manifest in Withnail's declamatory physical histrionics can be seen as reflecting the struggle between the iteration of the 'authentic' self and its self-conscious performance. Performance is a means of both presenting and hiding oneself. The adornment of the body, its physical deportment, and linguistic repertoire, are all devices for achieving this paradox. Thus the film utilises late-60s Romanticism as a dynamic bridging device: articulating the space between the psychic and the physical, the personal and the material, the charismatic hero and the cult fan.

FURTHER READING

Kevin Jackson, *Withnail & I* (London: BFI, 2004).

Will Self, 'Play Things', *Sight and Sound*, November 1995, p. 35.

for the fashioning of a text in one's own image. It also fosters the ability to confer order, significance and meaning, and ignore the established categories of critical value. One contextual reason for the cult fan's focus on textual marginalia is precisely its lack of critical provenance: it is neither highly acclaimed nor widely popular, but it is imaginatively accommodating. However, as cult criticism and market awareness converge upon the phenomenon, it may already be under threat. The notion of setting out to make a cult film would have been unthinkable thirty years ago. Today, thanks to its critical prominence across a range of reception arenas (fandom, marketing, media journalism and academia), all the now-familiar ingredients are ready to hand. Are cultists, one wonders, running out of safe places to hide?

Notes

1. <www.tvtip.bufvc.ac.uk>. Accessed 24 November 2005.
2. See Greg Taylor, *Artists in the Audience* and Parker Tyler, *The Three Faces of the Film*.
3. Andrew Sarris, *Confessions of a Cultist*, p. 13.
4. Bill Baillieu and John Goodchild, *The British Film Business*, p. 84.
5. Robert Murphy, *Sixties British Cinema*, p. 105.
6. See Arthur Marwick, *The Sixties*.
7. See Colin MacCabe, *Performance*.
8. Alexander Walker, *Hollywood, England*, pp. 415–16.
9. See John Hamilton, *Beasts in the Cellar*. The key figure, Tony Tenser, was executive producer on Polanski's *Repulsion* (1965) and *Cul de Sac* (1966) as well as many of the most interesting non-Hammer horror films of the period.
10. <www.villagevoice.com/film/0522,closeup, 64493,20.html>. Accessed 31 May 2005.
11. Peter Hutchings, *Hammer and Beyond*, p. 151.
12. Leon Hunt in Steve Chibnall and Julian Petley (eds), *British Horror Cinema*, pp. 92–3.
13. Steve Chibnall in Chibnall and Petley (eds), *British Horror Cinema*, p. 159.
14. Other macabre evocations of paganism in the horror film include *Taste the Blood of Dracula* (Peter Sasdy, 1970) and *Blood on Satan's Claw* (Piers Haggard, 1970).
15. Alexander Walker, *National Heroes*, p. 71.
16. Richard Barnes and Pete Townshend, *The Story of Tommy*, p. 30.
17. Robin Bean, *Films and Filming*, May 1975, p. 35.
18. See Sue Harper, *Picturing the Past*.
19. Kaja Silverman, *Male Subjectivity at the Margins*, p. 52.
20. An idea derived from D. W. Winnicott, *Playing and Reality*. For a more detailed application of this theory to a reading of *Withnail & I*, see J. Smith, 'Withnail's Coat: Andrea Galer's Cult Costumes', *Fashion Theory* vol. 9 no. 3, 2005, pp. 305–22.

Bibliography

Baillieu, Bill and Goodchild, John, *The British Film Business* (Chichester: John Wiley & Sons Ltd, 2002).

Barnes, Richard and Townshend, Pete, *The Story of Tommy* (Twickenham: Eel Pie Publishing, 1977).

Bean, Robin, 'Tommy', *Films and Filming*, May 1975, pp. 35–6.

Chibnall, Steve, 'Pete Walker and Gothic Revisionism', in Steve Chibnall and Julian Petley (eds), *British Horror Cinema* (London: Routledge, 2002).

Hamilton, John, *Beasts in the Cellar: The Exploitation Film Career of Tony Tenser* (Godalming: FAB Press, 2005).

Harper, Sue, *Picturing the Past: The Rise and Fall of the British Costume Film* (London: BFI, 1994).

Hunt, Leon, 'Necromancy in the UK: Witchcraft and the Occult in British Horror', in Steve Chibnall and Julian Petley (eds), *British Horror Cinema* (London: Routledge, 2002).

Hutchings, Peter, *Hammer and Beyond: The British Horror Film* (Manchester: Manchester University Press, 1993).

MacCabe, Colin, *Performance* (London: BFI, 1998).

Marwick, Arthur, *The Sixties: Cultural Revolution in Britain, France, Italy and the United States, c. 1958–1974* (Oxford: Oxford University Press, 1998).

Murphy, Robert, *Sixties British Cinema* (London: BFI, 1992).

Sarris, Andrew, *Confessions of a Cultist: On the Cinema, 1955–1969* (New York: Simon & Schuster, 1970).

Silverman, Kaja, *Male Subjectivity at the Margins* (London: Routledge, 1992).

Taylor, Greg, *Artists in the Audience: Cults, Camp, and American Film Criticism* (Princeton, NJ: Princeton University Press, 1999).

Tyler, Parker, *The Three Faces of the Film: The Art, the Dream, the Cult* (South Brunswick, NJ: A. S. Barnes, 1967).

Walker, Alexander, *National Heroes: British Cinema in the Seventies and Eighties* (London: Harrap, 1985).

Walker, Alexander, *Hollywood, England: The British Film Industry in the Sixties* (London: Harrap, 1986).

Winnicott, D. W., *Playing and Reality* (London: Tavistock, 1971).

PART TWO

Industry, Genre, Representation

8

British Film Censorship

JEFFREY RICHARDS AND JAMES C. ROBERTSON

It is impossible to understand the development and nature of the British cinema without a full appreciation of the work and influence of the censors. They provided the framework within which cinema operated. They dictated the limits of what was permissible on the screen.

Early Years

When cinema first appeared in Britain, it was totally unregulated, but from the outset society's moralists were expressing concern about the influence of films. The charge that cinemagoing among the young led directly to juvenile delinquency was made early and has continued to be made ever since, although nowadays less frequently. Teachers, clergymen, magistrates, public-morality bodies and influential middle-class organisations like the Mothers' Union demanded control of the new art form, which had from its first appearance derived its greatest support from the working classes and the young.

It was concern about fire hazards that prompted the 1909 Cinematograph Act. This act gave local authorities the right to license cinemas but its wording also allowed them to act as censors of film content. Local councils began banning and censoring films. The London County Council (LCC) was the first, in 1910 banning a film of the recently staged fight for the heavyweight championship of the world in which a black man, Jack Johnson, had beaten a white man, James J. Jeffries.

The prospect of 688 local authorities all taking different views on whether individual films could be shown so terrified the film industry that in 1912 it voluntarily set up the British Board of Film Censors (BBFC). The Board was financed by fees paid by the producers to the censors for viewing the films. Its decisions were to be final and the industry committed itself to abide by those decisions. The Board took its lead from the Lord Chamberlain's office, which censored stage plays. Indeed, it appointed as its first president George A. Redford, a retired play reader in the Lord Chamberlain's office. He was given four assistants, all anonymous, and they classified films as 'U' (suitable for universal viewing) and 'A' (for adults only, i.e. those over sixteen). In its first year the Board banned twenty-two films.

On the Home Office's recommendation, most local authorities accepted the Board's rulings. But they retained and indeed still retain the right to censor, and this has led to periodic episodes when that right has been systematically exercised. In 1932, for instance, Beckenham Council briefly set up its own film censorship board and began cutting, banning and reclassifying films already certificated by the BBFC, until forced to abandon its operations by mounting opposition both from the picture houses which saw audiences falling drastically and from the audiences, forced to travel to neighbouring boroughs to see the current popular films.

Brooke Wilkinson, O'Connor and Shortt

Although Redford was president of the Board from 1912 until his death in 1916, he was in ill health for much of his tenure and the key figure in the day-to-day running of the Board from its inception in 1912 until his death in 1948 was Joseph Brooke Wilkinson. A former minor journalist and then secretary of the Kinematograph Manufacturers' Association, Wilkinson became arguably the most influential figure in the British film industry during his thirty-six years of office. A man of Victorian principle and stern moral rectitude, he established for more than three decades the moral tone of British films. In its obituary of him, *Kinematograph Weekly* characterised him as 'highly respected for his personal charm, integrity of character and unfailing tact'.[1] Veteran documentarist John Grierson was rather more caustic:

> Poor dear censor Wilkinson, with his Blake's poetry
> and his beloved Pre-Raphaelites, has, in the jungle of
> Wardour St, the strength of ten. Great figure he is, for
> on his charming old shoulders, he carries the burden
> of our servility and our shame. Created by the trade
> as an image of gratuitous fright, it is not surprising
> that his slogan of No Controversy is abjectly obeyed.[2]

The control exercised over the content of films was far tighter on paper than that exercised over stage productions by the Lord Chamberlain, precisely because the cinema was the mass medium, regularly patronised by the working classes, and the working classes were deemed to be all too easily influenced. The pamphlet *Censorship in Britain*, issued by the BBFC to explain its policies, confirms that this idea was central to its thinking. It was guided, it said, by

> the broad general principle that nothing will be passed
> which is calculated to demoralize the public . . . .
> Consideration has to be given to the impression
> made on the average audience which includes a not
> inconsiderable proportion of people of immature
> judgement.[3]

It is evident that moral censorship was the Board's primary aim. T. P. O'Connor, the Board's second president, said in 1919 that the Board was concerned to ensure that nothing was passed 'that can teach methods of or extenuate crime, that can undermine the teachings of morality, that tends to bring the institution of marriage in contempt or lower the sacredness of family ties'.[4] His successor, Edward Shortt, put it more succinctly when he said in 1934: 'My job in life is to try and prevent our morals being made worse than they naturally are.'[5] Initially the Board had only two rules – no nudity and no depictions of the figure of Christ. But these were

rapidly expanded and were outlined by O'Connor in his evidence to the 1917 National Council of Public Morals inquiry into cinema. They became known as 'O'Connor's 43'.[6] Thirty-three of these rules concerned matters that may properly be called moral: banning the depiction of prostitution, premarital and extramarital sex, sexual perversion, incest, seduction, nudity, venereal disease, orgies, swearing, abortion, brothels, white slavery and so on.

The other area of concern for the censors was essentially to maintain the political status quo. So no criticism was permitted of the monarchy, government, church, police, judiciary or friendly foreign countries. There should also be no depiction of current controversial issues (strikes, pacifism, the rise of fascism, for instance). 'No controversy' was the rule, and 'harmless' was the censors' favourite term of approval for film projects. From its inception to the early 1970s the Board banned some 500 films completely for breaching its rules.[7] Many more were subjected to cuts.

It was extremely convenient for the Home Office that the BBFC should be independent. For whenever film censorship was debated in parliament, the Home Secretary could declare that the Board operated by its own rules free of government interference. But this was being economical with the truth. The presidents of the Board were always appointed after consultation with the Home Secretary, and after the death of the first president, Redford, they were always prominent political figures well versed in the moulding of public opinion until the appointment of Lord Harewood in 1985. T. P. O'Connor, president from 1916 until his death in 1929, was a veteran Liberal MP, journalist, author and editor, and Father of the House of Commons in the 1920s. His successor, Edward Shortt, president from 1929 until his death in 1935, had been a Liberal MP and served both as Chief Secretary for Ireland and Home Secretary, in which posts he had achieved considerable success in countering Sinn Fein and Communist agitation. He was succeeded by Lord Tyrrell of Avon, president from 1935 until his death in 1947, and formerly head of the news department of the Foreign Office, chairman of the British Council and ambassador to Paris. All three were privy councillors.[8] Shortt certainly made no bones about his desire to use the cinema to shape public opinion: 'There is in our hands as citizens, an instrument to mould the minds of the young, to mould the mind of the adolescent and create great and good and noble citizens for the future.'[9] Not only were the BBFC presidents senior public figures but all controversial subjects were regularly referred to the appropriate government department for comment. So in 1938 the BBFC banned production of *The Relief of Lucknow*, a film about the Indian Mutiny, because the India Office felt that it was inexpedient to remind the Indian population of past conflict when they were attempting to find a peaceful constitutional settlement to current Indian unrest.[10]

So satisfied with the operation of film censorship was the government that there was only one serious attempt to take it over. A plan was published by Home Secretary Sir Herbert Samuel to set up a state censorship board on 1 January 1917. But before it could be put into effect there was a change of government and the new Home Secretary abandoned the plan. Criticism of the existing system was further deflected by publication in 1917 of the report of the National Council of Public Morals' inquiry into the state of the cinema, which, although it recommended the institution of state censorship, admitted that the BBFC was doing its work well. The appointment of the respected O'Connor to succeed Redford as chief censor clinched the Board's survival. Thereafter the attitude of the government towards the BBFC was summed up by the Labour Home Secretary, J. R. Clynes, when he told the Commons in 1930 that he had 'no reason to believe that any alternative system so far proposed would produce better results or command general support, or that the standard of censorship in this country was not at least as high as that in any other'.[11]

The successful co-operation between the BBFC, government departments and the government's press censorship apparatus during World War I further convinced the Home Office that the Board could be relied upon. Initially the government banned film of military operations at the front and the BBFC faithfully implemented its wishes. But later the Ministry of Information became a convert to film propaganda, and towards the end of the war documentary films of the conflict were permitted.

Controversial Films

Although by 1918 the system was well and truly entrenched, there were throughout the interwar years successive controversies and disputes about individual films. Immediately after the war there was censorial concern about social problem films, which were both controversial and in breach of the Board's morality code. A succession of such films was banned: the anti-abortion

film *Where Are My Children?* (1916); the white slavery exposé *White Slave Traffic* (1919); a film on the effects of venereal disease, *Damaged Goods* (Alexander Butler, 1919); and the anti-drugs film *Human Wreckage* (1923). But Dr Marie Stopes fought hard to get a film version of her birth-control book *Married Love* made and passed. It emerged in 1923 as *Maisie's Marriage* (Alexander Butler), a romantic drama with an underlying birth-control message, which O'Connor wanted to ban but the LCC were willing to pass. In the end there was a compromise: the film was released but only after cuts.[12]

In the early 1930s the vogue for horror films caused the censors great unease. The president said of them in the Board's 1935 Annual Report: 'I cannot believe that such films are wholesome, pandering as they do to the love of the morbid and the horrible.'[13] So Rouben Mamoulian's *Dr Jekyll and Mr Hyde* (1931) was heavily cut, and both Tod Browning's *Freaks* (featuring real-life circus freaks) and Erle C. Kenton's *Island of Lost Souls* (1932, from H. G. Wells's *The Island of Doctor Moreau*), which included vivisection, were banned. But horror films were popular with audiences and continued to be produced by Hollywood. A compromise was reached in 1933 that led to the introduction of the 'H' (for horrific) certificate, which remained in force until 1951 when it was replaced by the 'X' certificate. Thirty-one films between 1933 and 1939 received an H certificate. *Island of Lost Souls* remained banned until 1958 and *Freaks* until 1963.[14]

Individual *causes célèbres* included Cecil B. DeMille's epic film version of the life of Christ, *The King of Kings* (1927). This was not shown to the BBFC because it offended against the prime directive banning depictions of the materialised figure of Christ. But it was shown to churchmen, gained their approval and was subsequently licensed by local authorities and widely shown. The Foreign Office pressed the BBFC to ban Herbert Wilcox's *Dawn* (1928), about the life and death of Nurse Edith Cavell, because it would offend the Germans. But Wilcox mounted a major publicity campaign, whipped up patriotic outrage against the authorities for seeking to denigrate a British heroine, and got the film widely licensed by local councils.[15]

The primary duty of the censors was to examine all films and classify them for exhibition. But the censors' control over the production of films tightened in the 1930s with the introduction of the practice of script-vetting to eliminate unacceptable material before shooting began. The process was voluntary but was regularly encouraged in the Board's annual reports. It was pointed out that producers would save money by submitting scripts for vetting because they would then not run the risk of having to reshoot offending scenes. The evidence suggests that about a third of all films produced in Britain in the 1930s were approved at script stage, including all the prospective productions of Gaumont-British.[16] A study of the scenario reports reveals an overwhelming desire to preserve propriety and decorum.[17] So there are endless requests for the toning down of language and systematic deletions of such words as 'nuts', 'bum', 'lousy', 'gigolo', 'belly', 'bawdy', 'nappy', 'prostitute' and 'nymphomaniac'. There were many requests to tone down or eliminate undressing scenes. 'O'Connor's 43' were widely but not always rigidly enforced. A proposal to film D. H. Lawrence's *Lady Chatterley's Lover* was summarily rejected, for instance. Pre-production scenarios based on Walter Greenwood's influential novel *Love on the Dole* were rejected because they contained swearing, perceived sexual immorality and scenes of the police charging unarmed hunger marchers. A filmed life of the notorious seventeenth-century 'Hanging Judge', Lord Jeffreys, was rejected as likely to bring the legal system into disrepute.

There was clearly a double standard when it came to crime films. British films critical of prisons and police were regularly rejected, but the American crime drama *Each Dawn I Die* (1939) was passed with a foreword stating: 'Prison conditions revealed here could never exist in Great Britain but they are tragically true of many penal establishments where corruption defeats justice and the voices of men who fight for justice are lost in the solitary cells.' This suggests that at bottom the censors were more concerned with the political effects of films attacking the prison system in Britain than the moral effects of prison dramas *per se*.[18]

Politics in films was frowned upon. In 1936 Lord Tyrrell, who had become president of the Board the previous year, told a conference of exhibitors: 'Nothing would be more calculated to arouse the passion of the British public than the introduction on the screen of subjects dealing with religious or political controversy.' He added, 'So far we have had no film dealing with current burning political questions.'[19] The kind of film the censors liked was *The Last Barricade* (Alex Bryce, 1938), set during the Spanish Civil War, of whose script the censor wrote: 'Quite harmless love story. The setting though purporting to be Spain might just as well be Ruritania for all the political significance it possesses.'[20] It tended to be left-wing politics that produced bans.

A three-minute pacifist film, *The Peace of Britain*, was banned in 1936, causing an outcry in the press and the rescinding of the ban. The Russian classics *Battleship Potemkin* (1925), *Mother* (1926) and *Storm over Asia* (1928) were banned as likely to provoke revolutionary outbursts. But when in 1937 anti-war activists demonstrated at showings of a patriotic naval film, *Our Fighting Navy* (Norman Walker), the censors took no action against the film.

The censors followed a policy of appeasement when it came to overseas governments. Scripts which involved 'friendly foreign countries' were regularly referred to the relevant embassies. Thus Alexander Korda's long-cherished plans for an epic film on the life of Lawrence of Arabia never came to fruition because of objections from the Turks at being portrayed as the villains and pressure on Korda from the Foreign Office.[21] In 1933 a number of proposals for films denouncing Nazi persecution of the Jews were all rejected, with comments like those on the proposed *The Mad Dogs of Europe*: 'This is pure anti-Hitler propaganda and as such I think unsuitable for production as a film.' The film-makers sought to get round the censors' prohibitions by using a fictitious or a historical setting. In Hitchcock's *The Lady Vanishes* (1938) and Walter Forde's *The Four Just Men* (1939), the enemy is the Gestapo but it is never named as such. A drama about anti-Jewish persecution in eighteenth-century Wurttemberg, *Jew Süss* (Lothar Mendes, 1934), contains the line '1730, 1830, 1930 – they will always persecute us'.[22] Nevertheless script-vetting and strict censorial enforcement of the rules led to the tightening

'1730, 1830, 1930 – they will always persecute us': anti-Hitler propaganda missed by the BBFC in *Jew Süss* (Lothar Mendes, 1934)

of studio control over film production. In 1933 the BBFC banned twenty-one films; by 1936 they found it necessary to ban only six.

Opposition to the activities of the BBFC came from two directions. The liberal and left-wing intelligentsia, described by *The Film in National Life* (1932) as 'numerically negligible but culturally important', were concerned about political censorship and campaigned for greater freedom for film-makers to tackle the subjects they wanted to.[23] But there was even more pressure from religious groups, teachers' unions, morality councils and middle-class pressure groups for tighter censorship. The complaint was that films were teaching sex, criminality and bad values to the youth of Britain.[24] The BBFC, steering a course between the two currents, aimed to maintain the status quo politically, socially and morally – and did so successfully. The practical effect was to limit film producers to a diet of

'harmless' comedies, musicals and thrillers; but judging by surveys such as that undertaken by Mass-Observation, this is what people wanted.[25]

Wartime Censorship

During World War II, the BBFC continued to function but its scope was restricted because much censorship activity was transferred to the Ministry of Information and the armed services, each of which had its own censor. The BBFC was now chiefly concerned with moral matters. Four minor American horror films were banned during the war. But the pre-war ban on criticism of Germany and Japan was lifted and the Boulting brothers' *Pastor Hall*, a grim drama based on the persecution of Pastor Niemöller by the Nazis, rejected in July 1939 by the censors, was rushed into production as soon as war broke out and became a valuable tool of British film propaganda.[26]

Love on the Dole (John Baxter, 1941)

Walter Greenwood's novel *Love on the Dole* vividly portrays working-class life in an industrial area of northern England amid the great depression and swiftly rising unemployment of the early 1930s. The tale centres upon the poverty of the Hardcastle family – husband, wife, son and daughter – and from a censorship viewpoint the dangerous material included much swearing, a strikers' demonstration leading to a violent clash with the police, and the decision of Sally Hardcastle to become the mistress of a well-to-do local bookmaker in order to obtain jobs for her father and brother.

Published in 1933, shortly after British unemployment had reached its peak, the novel soon became a best-seller and was adapted into a drama by Ronald Gow, which was sufficiently popular to be staged in London, although the demonstration clash was described rather than shown and the only cuts imposed by the Lord Chamberlain involved bad language. Yet the story was not converted into a film until 1941, by which time Britain was at war and unemployment had been reduced to a relatively minor problem. The *Sunday Pictorial* review of 1 June 1941 suspected that censorship lay behind this delay, but hard evidence was lacking until 1981 when Jeffrey Richards published the adverse comments by the British Board of Film Censors on two pre-production scenarios for projected films during 1936. These revealed that the BBFC

opposed *Love on the Dole* as 'undesirable' on the grounds of profanity, perceived immorality on Sally's part and the violence between strikers and the police. Neither film was made, although it remains unclear whether the BBFC was solely responsible.

In 1984 Ronald Gow disclosed that during the war Joseph Brooke Wilkinson, the BBFC's secretary, had in effect summoned him and Greenwood together to tell them they had to resolve their differences, whatever these were, for on the orders of an unspecified 'higher authority', later revealed as the Ministry of Information, the film had to be made. The fact that the Ministry had selected Wilkinson to take this initiative presumably was intended to inform both the BBFC and the writers that henceforth censorship would be no obstacle. This explains why Greenwood scripted an undiluted version of his novel for British National with an optimistic note absent from the book tacked on at the end, and why the BBFC passed the film uncut on 3 April 1941 even though it contravened the BBFC's pre-war rules on several counts. As the *Sunday Pictorial* review already mentioned rightly exclaimed, 'What a difference a war makes!'

FURTHER READING

Jeffrey Richards, 'The British Board of Film Censors and Content Control in the 1930s: Images of Britain', *Historical Journal of Film, Radio and Television*, October 1981, *Guardian*, 14 March 1984, p. 12.

The Ministry of Information co-ordinated the use of film propaganda, took over censorship of newsreels, and controlled the allocation of raw film stock and the licensing of club showings of non-certificated films. In the circumstances of war, a certain relaxation was allowed by the censors. The hitherto banned words 'bloody' and 'bastard' were permitted in wartime films like *In Which We Serve* (David Lean/Noël Coward, 1942) and *Western Approaches* (Pat Jackson, 1944) as long as they were applied to the Germans. The sensitive subject of labour relations was allowed to be treated in films like *The Stars Look Down* (Carol Reed, 1939) and *The Proud Valley* (Pen Tennyson, 1940). *Love on the Dole*, banned throughout the 1930s, was filmed and released in 1941 as an illustration of the kind of world Britain was not going back to after the war. Winston Churchill, a great film fan, sought to interfere in censorship, usually unsuccessfully. The most celebrated case was his attempt to ban *The Life and Death of Colonel Blimp* (Powell and Pressburger, 1943), which criticised the mindset of the old-style officer and gentleman. His bid failed, merely serving to give publicity to the film, which was billed as 'the film they tried to ban'.[27]

The Post-war Period

At the end of the war, the old guard which had been in charge of film censorship for two decades or more stood down. Colonel J. C. Hanna, deputy chief censor since 1930, retired in 1946. Lord Tyrrell died in 1947, aged eighty-three. J. Brooke Wilkinson died in 1948. A new generation of censors prepared to face new problems. Sir Sidney Harris, the new president, and Arthur Watkins, the new secretary, were both former civil servants from the Children's Department of the Home Office. They had to deal with an upsurge of violence and sexuality in British films, which can be traced directly to the social dislocation of the war. The Gainsborough costume melodramas and a cycle of British spiv and gangster films cleaned up at the box office but outraged those critics who were committed to documentary realism, literary respectability and moral uplift as dominant values. They excoriated the new film genres with a venom which did nothing to dent their box-office popularity. The storm finally broke in 1948 over a British imitation of American gangster films, *No Orchids for Miss Blandish* (St John Legh Clowes), which to the film critics symbolised the unacceptable level of sex and violence in post-war British cinema. Although much toned down from James Hadley Chase's lurid original novel, and vetted by

Nauseating and disgusting: Jack La Rue, Linden Travers, Walter Crisham in *No Orchids for Miss Blandish* (St John L. Clowes, 1948)

the censors through several different scripts before the finished film received a certificate, it was denounced by parliamentarians, film critics and the press in general as nauseating and disgusting, and London County Council demanded further cuts.[28] Sir Sidney Harris apologised for 'failing to protect the public'. But as memories of the war receded, so the vogue for sex and violence for the moment passed and audiences settled for blander film fare.

A new subtlety entered the censors' considerations during Watkins's regime. Artistic considerations became more important than they had been under Wilkinson. The quality of the film and the intentions of the director began to count for something, and on these grounds foreign films such as *Rashomon* (1950) and *La Ronde* (1950), which otherwise transgressed the Board's moral rules, were allowed to pass. The 'X' certificate was introduced in 1951 to allow the licensing of films for viewing by adults. This applied in the main initially to foreign films, which often contained more sex and violence than was permitted in British films and were unlikely to receive a wide British distribution, but also increasingly to British films as the 1950s progressed.

The principal social concern of the early 1950s was juvenile delinquency. It was the theme of films such as *The Blue Lamp* (Basil Dearden, 1950) and *Cosh Boy* (Lewis Gilbert, 1953). But concern about British youth imitating the exploits of American juvenile delinquents led to six minutes of cuts in *Blackboard Jungle* (1955) and the complete banning in 1954 of *The Wild One*, in which a gang of bikers led by Marlon Brando terrify a Californian town. It was only finally certificated in 1967, by which time it looked distinctly tame.

Despite the relaxation in attitudes towards foreign films, Watkins still believed that the Board was

> performing a service both to the public and to the film industry if it removed offensive and distasteful material which cannot be regarded as entertainment and which if not excluded would in the long run do harm to the kinema's claim to that universal patronage on which its economy rests.[29]

In 1956 Arthur Watkins resigned and was replaced by John Nichols, who had a fondness for both Japanese films and the works of Ingmar Bergman, which he passed uncut. Watkins's concept of artistic criteria was still being pursued in regard to foreign films. Elsewhere the usual strict rules largely applied. Director J. Lee Thompson was so outraged at the demand for cuts in the script of his World War II drama *Ice Cold in Alex* (1958) that he organised a meeting between the British Film Producers' Association and the BBFC to discuss the possibility of 'a more enlightened and adult approach to censorship'.

The Trevelyan Years

In 1958 Nichols resigned and was replaced as secretary by John Trevelyan, a former teacher and educational administrator who was to preside over what Anthony Aldgate has called 'the slow, complex and fraught process of liberalisation'.[30] Trevelyan was the guiding spirit of the BBFC during the 1960s, a time of rapid and far-reaching social and cultural change. He had to endeavour to keep up with changing public taste while fighting lengthy battles with writers and directors who resented having to make any changes in their films, and at the same time deflecting criticism from vocal forces in society bitterly opposed to any relaxation of censorship.

Trevelyan began the process by allowing adult films to deal with adult themes in a responsible fashion. He wrote in his autobiography:

> In my time at the Board we worked on a general policy of treating with as much tolerance and generosity as possible any film that seemed to us to have both quality and integrity, and of being much less tolerant of films which appeared to us to have neither of these qualifications.[31]

The landmark film in this process was Jack Clayton's adaptation of John Braine's controversial best-seller

Room at the Top (1959). Although advertised as 'a savage story of lust and ambition', it was in fact a serious-minded, non-exploitative social-realist film. Trevelyan judged that the public was ready for a film that discussed issues of sex and class seriously, and the popular reaction persuaded him to grant an 'X' certificate to responsible films on serious adult subjects.

In retrospect, the changes in the censorship system appear startling and speedy. Nudity had been banned from films until 1951. Thereafter some discreet nudity was allowed in the naturist films that began to appear in the 1950s. But the first full-frontal female nude was allowed in the Swedish film *Hugs and Kisses* (1967). Full-frontal male nudity was specifically forbidden in the 1963 film *This Sporting Life* (Lindsay Anderson) but allowed for the first time in *Women in Love* (Ken Russell, 1969). Homosexuals were shown sympathetically in *Victim* (Basil Dearden, 1961) and *A Taste of Honey* (Tony Richardson, 1961). The depiction of an abortion was banned in *Saturday Night and Sunday Morning* (Karel Reisz, 1960) but allowed in *Up the Junction* (Peter Collinson, 1968). Drug-taking was banned as a central theme in *The Trip* (1967) but permitted as an incidental event in *Easy Rider* (1969). The prohibition on swearing was steadily relaxed, with 'bloody' heard regularly from 1963, 'bugger' from 1967 and 'fuck' from 1970. By 1970 the old moral prohibitions of the BBFC had been almost totally abandoned.

However, sensationalism in dealing with sex, violence, drugs and madness still elicited bans for films, and the Hollywood productions *Lady in a Cage* (1964), *The Naked Kiss* (1964), *Shock Corridor* (1963), *The Wild Angels* (1966) and *The Trip* were all banned in the 1960s. With public opinion changing rapidly, Trevelyan abandoned the explicitly moralistic stance the Board had adopted since its inception and redefined its role:

> The British Board of Film Censors cannot assume responsibility for the guardianship of morality. It cannot refuse for exhibition to adults, films that show behaviour which contravenes the accepted moral code, and it does not demand that 'the wicked' should always be punished. It cannot legitimately refuse to pass films which criticise 'the Establishment' and films which express minority opinions.[32]

Henceforth the censors were to see their work as limiting excessive displays of sex, violence and antisocial behaviour.

Censorship Debates

As censorship relaxed, films became more and more explicit in the areas of sex and violence. The 1960s also saw the development of private cinema clubs showing uncertificated soft-core pornographic films. In the mainstream commercial cinema, the censors showed an increasingly relaxed attitude towards sex and violence. In the early 1970s, they certificated *The Devils* (Ken Russell, 1971), *A Clockwork Orange* (Stanley Kubrick, 1971), *Straw Dogs* (Sam Peckinpah, 1971), *Deliverance* (John Boorman, 1972) and *Last Tango in Paris* (1972). This provoked a backlash from critics and moralists. Moral campaigners like Mary Whitehouse, a small minority of politicians and elements of the popular press now combined to blame the cinema for moral decline and the measurable increase of violence in society. Stephen Murphy, who had succeeded Trevelyan in 1971, came under extreme pressure as he vigorously defended the BBFC's position. He resigned for family reasons in 1974 and was replaced in the following year by the American James Ferman, who had been resident in Britain since the early 1950s, and was thoroughly anglicised as a result; unusually, he also had practical experience as a television director and documentary film-maker.

Since 1960 executive power within the BBFC had resided with the secretary rather than the president, though the liberalising measures of Trevelyan and Murphy were wholeheartedly backed by Lord Harlech, the president since 1965. Towards the end of Murphy's secretaryship, the supporters of Mary Whitehouse had resorted to the courts to restrict the release of films passed by the BBFC, most notably *Last Tango in Paris*. In consequence the film industry sought to have films brought within the 'deprave and corrupt, when taken as a whole' obscenity test of statutory legislation as a defence against private prosecutions. Murphy had opposed this policy, as at first did Ferman, but when in mid-1976 a jury found obscene *More about the Language of Love*, a Swedish sex-instruction film already certificated by the BBFC, Ferman changed his mind. Henceforth he spearheaded the film industry's pressure on the Home Office, with the outcome that the Obscene Publications Act was amended to include film with effect from 1 December 1977.

This was intended to be an interim measure pending the findings of a commission on media obscenity established in mid-1977 and headed by Professor Bernard Williams. Towards the end of 1979 the commission recommended the abolition of local-authority censorship and the creation of a statutory body in place of the BBFC, although it accepted that the ability of films to 'deprave and corrupt' remained unproven. However, the recently elected government of Margaret Thatcher rejected the report in January 1981, and consequently films have become permanently subject to the 'deprave and corrupt' obscenity test. As no BBFC-certificated film or video has since been successfully prosecuted, the law effectively served as a bulwark for existing BBFC practice.[33]

The controversies surrounding films during Murphy's secretaryship had encouraged some local authorities occasionally to disregard the BBFC, but during his first five years Ferman gradually brought this situation under control. His approach was generally liberal, utilising his skill as an editor to produce acceptable versions of films that might otherwise have had to be rejected or unnecessarily cut. He resisted pressure to reject *Monty Python's Life of Brian* (Terry Jones, 1979) over alleged blasphemy, but took a firm line against the sado-masochistic *Histoire d'O* (1975) and against sadistic violence, especially against women, in other films.

In 1970 the BBFC's certification structure had been extended and brought more into line with the American rating system, a development updated again in 1982 when the old 'U', 'A', 'X' system of certificates was replaced by a new system: 'U' (universal), 'PG' (parental guidance), '15' and '18', with an 'R18' rating for licensed sex cinemas only. However, the most significant development of the 1980s was the emergence on the open market of the video cassette and thereafter a flood of extreme horror films, which the moralists soon labelled 'video nasties'. A media-induced moral panic set in during 1982–3, producing the 1984 Video Recordings Act (VRA), the first state censorship of a visual medium in British history. Ferman had been vainly warning the Home Office about the perceived need for pre-censorship of videos since 1976, arguing that greater stringency from the censors was required because videos were designed for home viewing. By 1981 he had set in motion moves towards a voluntary system through the BBFC similar to that in place for film. However, he was overtaken by political events, and could do little more than negotiate with the Home Office to ameliorate the VRA's more draconian restrictions and ensure that when the Act came into force on 1 September 1985 the BBFC served as the government's designated agency.

Ferman had never favoured the VRA, and his resolute stand against it in private was probably responsible

The Devils (Ken Russell, 1971)

Ken Russell's *The Devils*, based loosely on John Whiting's dramatisation of Aldous Huxley's novel *The Devils of Loudun* (1952), was filmed in Britain for Warner Bros. during the last months of 1970. Set in seventeenth-century France, it deals with a liberal but womanising priest (Oliver Reed), who for political reasons is accused of being satanically possessed and of using his evil powers to stimulate nuns' sexual desire for him. Despite torture and death by burning, he never acknowledges his guilt.

The return of a Conservative government in the June 1970 general election had encouraged those intent on attacking a perceived over-liberal trend in the arts. Russell, already notorious for *Women in Love* and *The Music Lovers* (1970) was regarded as one of the worst offenders. Sensational press reports of the director revelling in the sex and horror of his new production further incited hostile critics.

Warners had slashed five minutes from the film, a climactic scene of a blasphemous orgy, before its American release. The BBFC by this time had long abandoned its pre-production scenario system, but in January 1971 Russell arranged a private viewing of his film for John Trevelyan, the secretary, and Lord Harlech, the president, with the American cuts restored. Trevelyan was adamant that the orgy would have to go, and it had been deleted when the film was officially submitted to the BBFC on 9 February 1971. Amid much concern on both sexual and horror grounds from within the BBFC, Trevelyan eventually allowed *The Devils* an 'X' certificate in May 1971, cut by approximately ninety seconds' running time. It was released in Britain in July, by which time the opponents of the so-called 'permissive society' had mobilised themselves into the Festival of Light. *The Devils*, which encountered a flood of press criticism

Master magician: Ken Russell prays that all will go well in *The Devils*

upon its release, presented a blatant target. Stephen Murphy, Trevelyan's successor in mid-1971, saw the film only after its release but agreed with Trevelyan's decision, standing firm against acute pressure from the Festival and some local authorities.

Ultimately only seventeen out of some 200 local authorities banned the film, but the uproar has had a lasting impact, for the full version has never been seen publicly and is probably no longer extant. The video version passed by the BBFC was cut by a further six minutes, while mainstream television versions have to date been the BBFC-authorised one of 1971. In 2007 an internet campaign was launched to persuade Warner Bros. to release an official DVD version to replace the less-than-perfect bootleg DVD in circulation.

FURTHER READING

Much of the information here is derived from the BBFC file on *The Devils*. See also Anthony Aldgate and James C. Robertson, *Censorship in Theatre and Cinema* (Edinburgh: Edinburgh University Press, 2005), pp. 172–80.

---

in 1985 for the Home Office's attempt to install Sir Ian Trethowan, a known Thatcher sympathiser, as BBFC president following Harlech's death in a car accident. Ferman, together with the BBFC's Council of Management, successfully resisted the Home Office; Lord Harewood, a noted opera-lover and cousin of the Queen, was appointed in his stead. The BBFC was retitled the British Board of Film Classification, the secretary became the director, and the Board expanded its

premises and staff so that more than twenty censors were now employed.[34]

The second half of Ferman's period at the BBFC was overshadowed by three horrendous events: the Hungerford killings of 1987, the murder of two-year-old James Bulger in 1993 and the Dunblane massacre of schoolchildren in 1996. Partly as a result, Ferman officially banned more than fifty videos between 1985 and 1998, but in addition the submission of videos likely to be banned, such as *The Exorcist*, was discouraged and a list by the Director of Public Prosecutions (until 1992) of videos already found obscene in the courts or awaiting trial swelled the number still further. Video killed off the specialist sex cinemas, but the amount of violent video material continued unabated. Towards the end of 1993 the James Bulger murder was erroneously linked at the trial of his murderers with the video *Child's Play III* (1991), which the BBFC had allowed, and Ferman and the BBFC were constantly pilloried in parts of the press, particularly the *Daily Mail*.

Controversy also surrounded the release of Oliver Stone's *Natural Born Killers* (1994), Larry Clark's *Kids* (1995), Neil Jordan's *Michael Collins* (1996) and, above all, David Cronenburg's *Crash* (1996), all passed uncut despite a clause in the 1994 Criminal Justice Act requiring the BBFC to pay special attention to the manner in which videos dealt with violence, criminality, horror and drugs. In March–April 1996, in the immediate aftermath of the Dunblane horrors, a House of Commons motion declaring that the video of *Natural Born Killers* contravened this clause attracted the signatures of some 200 MPs from all parties, while its sponsor, the Catholic Liberal Democrat MP David Alton, also called for Ferman's resignation.

Ferman survived this acute pressure, but, after Harewood's retirement as president in 1996 and Labour's general election triumph of May 1997, Home Secretary Jack Straw appointed newspaper editor Andreas Whittam Smith as Harewood's replacement despite BBFC resistance, and increased the executive power of the president. Ferman retired in 1998, to be succeeded by Robin Duval, but, surprisingly to some, under the Whittam Smith/Duval regime liberalisation proceeded apace, as it has done since under their successors, Sir Quentin Thomas (2003) and David Cooke (2004). Government responsibility for the BBFC was transferred from the Home Office to the new Department of Culture, Media and Sport after the 2001 general election. Material that Ferman rejected or banned, such as *Histoire d'O* and the video of *The Exorcist*, was passed in 2001 without arousing public commotion, while earlier rejections like Roger Corman's *The Trip* have also been reversed. Furthermore, the 'R18' category now includes (in licensed sex shops) hard-core pornography, including material such as bondage and sado-masochism, although sexual violence by men against women remains taboo. In 2002 a new '12A' certificate was created to allow for parental guidance to twelve-year olds.

Conclusions

The arguments for censorship (social control, moral concern, protection of the innocent) and against it (artistic liberty, freedom of expression, consumer choice) have remained the same since films first arrived in Britain. Local-authority film censorship remains in place, as the Westminster City Council ban on *Crash* in 1996–7 demonstrated. And the blasphemy law effectively prohibits the video release of films like Nigel Wingrove's *Visions of Ecstasy* (1989). Public concern has risen and fallen in cycles, but by 2006 the inevitable compromise between the two had swung heavily towards the latter. Video/DVD bans and film rejections had become few and far between and cuts were demanded in only ten of the 555 films submitted to the BBFC.[35] On the other hand, the large, powerful, official censorship body which the BBFC has become is a constant reminder to film-makers that should they dare to cross the line of what is currently acceptable there will be a high price to pay.

Notes

1. *Kinematograph Weekly*, 27 July 1948.
2. Quoted in Charles Davy (ed.), *Footnotes to the Film* (London: Lovat Dickson, 1938), p. 141.
3. Ibid., p. 267.
4. BBFC Annual Report for 1919, p. 3.
5. *Kinematograph Weekly*, 1 March 1934.
6. They are reprinted in Neville March Hunnings, *Film Censors and the Law*, pp. 408–9.
7. James C. Robertson, *The Hidden Cinema: British Film Censorship in Action 1913–1972*, p. 2.
8. Nicholas Pronay, 'The First Reality: Film Censorship in Liberal England', in K. R. M. Short (ed.), *Feature Films as History* (London: Croom Helm, 1981), p. 122.
9. Conference on 'The Influence of Cinema', 29 May 1933, BBFC, Verbatim Reports 1932–5, pp. 13–14.
10. Jeffrey Richards, *The Age of the Dream Palace: Cinema and Society in Britain 1930–39*, pp. 144–5.
11. House of Commons Debates, vol. 342, p. 127.
12. Annette Kuhn, *Cinema, Censorship and Sexuality 1909–1925*.
13. BBFC Annual Report for 1935, p. 8.
14. James C. Robertson, *The British Board of Film Censors*, pp. 56–9, 183–4.
15. James C. Robertson, '*Dawn* (1928): Edith Cavell and Anglo-German Relations', pp. 15–28.
16. Richards, *The Age of the Dream Palace*, p. 108.
17. BBFC Scenario Reports, 1930–47, are held in the British Film Institute National Library.

18. Richards, *The Age of the Dream Palace*, pp. 112–20.

19. BBFC Annual Report for 1936, p. 6.

20. Richards, *The Age of the Dream Palace*, p. 122.

21. Jeffrey Richards and Jeffrey Hulbert, 'Censorship in Action: The Case of Lawrence of Arabia', pp. 153–70.

22. Richards, *The Age of the Dream Palace*, pp. 126–8.

23. Commission on Educational and Cultural Films, *The Film in National Life* (London, 1932), p. 34.

24. Richards, *The Age of the Dream Palace*, pp. 48–85.

25. Jeffrey Richards and Dorothy Sheridan (eds), *Mass-Observation at the Movies* (London: Routledge, 1987).

26. James C. Robertson, 'British Film Censorship Goes to War', pp. 49–64.

27. James Chapman, '*The Life and Death of Colonel Blimp* (1943) Reconsidered', *Historical Journal of Film, Radio and Television* no. 15 (1995), pp. 19–54.

28. Robert Murphy, *Realism and Tinsel: Cinema and Society in Britain 1939–49* (London: Routledge, 1989), pp. 187–90.

29. Tom Dewe Mathews, *Censored*, p. 135.

30. Anthony Aldgate, *Censorship and the Permissive Society: British Cinema and Theatre 1955–1965*, p. 152.

31. John Trevelyan, *What the Censor Saw*, pp. 66–7.

32. Mathews, *Censored*, p. 174.

33. As Dewe Mathews pointed out, ibid., p. 222.

34. A number subsequently expanded to over seventy to cope with the huge numbers of films and video games the BBFC now has to process.

35. Cuts were required in 589 videos, but this represented only 3.9 per cent of the 15,122 submitted. www.bbfc.co.uk/statistics/index.php.

Bibliography

Aldgate, Anthony, *Censorship and the Permissive Society: British Cinema and Theatre 1955–1965* (Oxford: Clarendon Press, 1995).

Hunnings, Neville March, *Film Censors and the Law* (London: George Allen & Unwin, 1967).

Knowles, Dorothy, *The Censor, the Drama and the Film* (London: George Allen & Unwin, 1934).

Kuhn, Annette, *Cinema, Censorship and Sexuality 1909–1925* (London: Routledge, 1988).

Mathews, Tom Dewe, *Censored* (London: Chatto & Windus, 1994).

Phelps, Guy, *Film Censorship* (London: Gollancz, 1975).

Pronay, Nicholas, 'The First Reality: Film Censorship in Liberal England', in K. R. M. Short (ed.), *Feature Films as History* (London: Croom Helm, 1981).

Richards, Jeffrey, *The Age of the Dream Palace: Cinema and Society in Britain, 1930–39* (London: Routledge and Kegan Paul, 1984).

Richards, Jeffrey and Hulbert, Jeffrey, 'Censorship in Action: The Case of Lawrence of Arabia', *Journal of Contemporary History* no. 19 (1984).

Robertson, James C., 'British Film Censorship Goes to War', *Historical Journal of Film, Radio and Television* no. 2 (1982).

Robertson, James C., *The British Board of Film Censors: Film Censorship in Britain 1896–1950* (London: Croom Helm, 1985).

Robertson, James C., '*Dawn* (1928): Edith Cavell and Anglo-German Relations', *Historical Journal of Film, Radio and Television* no. 4 (1984), pp. 15–28.

Robertson, James C., *The Hidden Cinema: British Film Censorship in Action 1913–1972* (London: Routledge, 1989).

Robertson, James C., *James Ferman and Screen Censorship, 1975–1998* (Unpublished manuscript at the BFI National Library, 2006).

Robertson, James C., 'The Home Office and the BBFC Presidency 1985–98', *Journal of British Cinema and Television* vol. 3 no. 2 (2006).

Trevelyan, John, *What the Censor Saw* (London: Michael Joseph, 1973).

9

Exhibition and the Cinemagoing Experience

ALLEN EYLES

Getting Started

In cinema's early years, from 1896 to 1909, the exhibition of films took place in three contrasting types of venue. Music halls drew especially large audiences when newsreels of topical events were presented. Shops and spaces like railway arches were converted into cinemas with little more than brown paper over the windows and benches on the floor. Public halls and specially constructed fairground booths were used by travelling showmen, and sometimes had capacities of up to 1,000.

Licensing came into effect in 1910 to ensure that premises showing inflammable film were suitable for the purpose (with a separate projection box and more than one exit in case of fire). This encouraged the construction of purpose-built cinemas with seating on raked floors to give better sightlines. Many cinemas had separate entrances down a side passage for the cheaper seats nearest the screen: this avoided disturbance to the patrons seated further back, as well as saving them from the odours associated with the 'great unwashed' – 'a very real problem to the public entertainer', noted the 1912 book *How to Run a Picture Theatre*. Attendants used hand-sprays between and during performances to prevent disease and provide a sweet scent. The advent of feature-length films led to larger cinemas with better facilities, although major films were initially presented as special events and often shown in theatres with separate performances at high prices. The Italian epic *Quo Vadis* (1913) was presented at the Albert Hall, and seen by the King and Queen.

Rare examples of early purpose-built cinemas that have been restored and still show films are the Duke of York's, Brighton (1910), Brixton Pavilion (1911, now the Ritzy), and the Electric, Harwich (1911). These early cinemas were usually rectangular in form, with seating on a single floor beneath barrel-vault ceilings, payboxes open to the street and minimal foyer space. Pianists or small orchestras were employed to accompany the silent films, while many cinemas employed an effects artist to provide sound effects such as galloping horses, rolling waves on the seashore, or the shutting of a door. With much lower overheads than the music hall, cinemas were able to charge very low prices and attract whole families.

From 1908 numerous companies began building chains of cinemas, some dispersed over a wide area, others concentrated in particular towns or regions. The most significant of these companies was Provincial Cinematograph Theatres (PCT), formed in 1909 with capital of £100,000 to open fifteen cinemas in cities and towns outside London with a population of at least a quarter of a million. PCT provided a standard of luxury and elegance – restaurants, cloakrooms, lounges for reading and writing – designed to attract affluent middle- and upper-class patrons who would not have stooped to enter the average early picture house.

The outbreak of war in 1914 led to difficulties for most cinema operators. Feature films had made programmes longer and more costly to hire, while reducing the number of performances; war newsreels were very expensive to hire; box-office takings were down because servicemen paid only half price; and cinemas were less efficiently run because skilled management and staff were called up. In addition, a hastily conceived 'temporary' Entertainments Tax was introduced in May

1916, which most affected the cheaper prices of admission. Many cinemas closed for good.

The film business had its opponents, particularly the National Council of Public Morals. The most serious charges levelled against the cinema were an increase in juvenile crime and indecent conduct among the audience. It was suggested that children were influenced by crime on the screen to steal the money for admission: that they were liable to catch diseases like ringworm; and that they were at risk of being molested in the darkness. However, it was conceded in favour of the cinema that it countered the attraction of the public house.

There was considerable opposition to cinemas opening on Sundays, prompted mostly by the threat to church attendances. Cinemas were permitted to open in certain areas, sometimes with restrictions (in Hartlepool, only after the church services; in Southport, only admitting those over sixteen years of age), but Sunday opening did not become universal until the 1950s.

In 1920, attendances surged to their highest level yet, and exhibitors regained their confidence. The first super-cinemas, inspired by American examples, arrived in 1921, including PCT's widely acclaimed Regent in Brighton, the Capitol in Cardiff and the Rivoli at Whitechapel in London. These were followed by such giants as the Piccadilly, Manchester, the Majestic, Leeds, and the Pavilion at Shepherd's Bush, West London.

Start of the Combines

Until 1926, exhibition was essentially independent of production and distribution. But vertical integration of these branches of the industry had flourished in the United States and new combines soon appeared in Britain. In 1927, merchant banker Isidore Ostrer created the Gaumont-British Picture Corporation, and in 1928 GBPC succeeded in acquiring PCT and became the largest film combine in the country. It was rivalled by British International Pictures, which formed a subsidiary, Associated British Cinemas (ABC), combining three existing cinema circuits. This expanded rapidly by acquiring and building cinemas.

The 1930s was the great decade for the construction of new cinemas in Britain (whereas American movie palaces were largely built in the 20s). Cries of 'saturation', 'surfeit' and 'over-building' were commonplace as existing cinema owners attempted to block newcomers, almost always in vain. Comparatively few older cinemas were forced to close, but most of them had to accept an inferior position as newer, larger buildings

opened up in direct opposition. Prices in the West End and provincial centres were much higher than in the suburbs and small towns. In 1934, audiences paid from one shilling and sixpence (7½p) to eight shillings and sixpence (42½p) at the première-run Tivoli in London's Strand, but would be asked for only seven pence (3p) to two shillings (10p) at a local super-cinema such as the Broadway at Stratford, East London, when films arrived there many weeks later. Lesser cinemas would have even lower prices. A cinemagoer always paid more to sit in the best seats, usually in the front circle and usually paying three or four times as much as those who sat in the front stalls. Queues formed for particular seat prices, and the cheapest seats usually sold out first.

A specialised form of programming suited to smaller existing cinemas or small new spaces was the newsreel theatre, showing approximately an hour of newsreel material and shorts. Originated in the United States in 1929, this policy was successfully introduced at some struggling cinemas in Britain and, later in the 30s, purpose-built newsreel cinemas appeared in most major cities. These newsreel cinemas were often placed in or near terminal stations to take advantage of the many people with time on their hands waiting for trains to arrive or depart. Other uses for small cinemas were as art houses (beginning with the Academy in London's Oxford Street from the early 1930s) or as repertory cinemas (notably the Classic chain, which built a flagship cinema in London's Baker Street).

In the 30s, the Gaumont chain added fifty-one purpose-built cinemas, while the ABC circuit erected ninety-eight. Many smaller chains also competed: Granada built seventeen cinemas, including huge Gothic-style properties at Tooting and Woolwich in the London suburbs. The Union circuit was a particularly aggressive competitor until its financial collapse in 1937, after which it was taken over by the ABC chain. The Hollywood majors in general restricted themselves to operating West End flagships to launch their product: Metro-Goldwyn-Mayer had the Empire, Leicester Square; Warner Bros. built the Warner a few doors away. Paramount was more aggressive: it had the Plaza and Carlton in the West End, acquired a suburban chain of four large Astorias at Brixton, Finsbury Park, Streatham and Old Kent Road, and built large city-centre cinemas in Birmingham, Glasgow, Leeds, Liverpool, Manchester and Newcastle.

The most striking newcomer of the 30s was the Odeon circuit, the brainchild of Birmingham businessman Oscar Deutsch, who had promoted some cinemas

Odeon, Kingstanding, Birmingham

in the late 20s and opened one Odeon at Perry Barr in 1930. Deutsch drew up plans for a circuit in 1932 and began opening cinemas the following year. By the end of the decade, 136 Odeons had been inaugurated, including the flagship Odeon in Leicester Square. Deutsch gave his circuit a distinctive image, in particular through a stylised, straight-edged name sign that is used to this day. He also encouraged his architects (principally the Harry Weedon, George Coles and Andrew Mather practices) to create eyecatching streamlined exteriors with curved corners, slab towers and much use of yellow faience tiles (the Leicester Square cinema was faced in black to provide a deliberate contrast). Whereas the new cinemas of other chains often included variety acts, elaborate stage facilities, organs, vast restaurants and even dance halls, Deutsch wanted more economical buildings dedicated to showing films.

Deutsch built Odeon into a national circuit which rivalled Gaumont and ABC by the end of the 30s. In order to obtain quality British films and to meet quota obligations, he went into partnership with United Artists, which distributed Alexander Korda's productions. Odeon's numerical strength was increased by a number of acquisitions, including the County chain and the Scottish Singleton circuit, and capped by the takeover (outside the West End) of the small but powerful Paramount circuit, which gave it large properties in the major city centres.

Deutsch had his eye set on taking over Gaumont-British, which was in an unhealthy financial state because of losses on production and distribution. However, the entrepreneur's own poor health took a turn for the worse after he was injured in a bomb blast, and he died in December 1941 at the age of forty-eight. By this time J. Arthur Rank had become closely

involved in both Odeon and Gaumont and his companies took control of the two circuits, although the Board of Trade required them to be run as separate, competing entities.

World War II

When war was declared in September 1939, cinemas and other places of public entertainment were closed for a week as a safety precaution until it was realised that people needed them as a refuge – literally so, when bombs eventually rained from the sky. Although messages would be flashed on the screen warning of imminent air raids, most cinemagoers preferred to stay put, realising that they were safer in a massive, well-constructed building than out on the street or in their own homes. World War II put a freeze on cinema construction, and it was not until 1955 that building restrictions were relaxed to enable cinemas only half-completed to be finished, and those severely damaged by bombing to be reconstructed and reopened.

Helped by a shortage of alternative entertainments, picturegoing boomed in the war years, except when areas were subjected to intense bombing during the London Blitz. South-coast cinemas also suffered because of population decline through evacuation and restricted access to the area. But in 1941, attendances rose by an amazing 30 per cent over the preceding year, and they continued to climb to an all-time peak of 1,635 million admissions in 1946. After this, attendances fell year by year, but it was not until 1957 that they reached pre-war levels of under 1,000 million.

In 1947, the Labour government, in an attempt to stem the flow of sterling across the Atlantic, imposed a 75 per cent *ad valorem* levy which resulted in the American companies refusing to import any new films. Their backlog of new titles already in Britain was eked out with reissues from the autumn of 1947 until May 1948, when the tax was suddenly withdrawn. British film production had been stepped up to fill the screen time, and suddenly a number of hastily conceived, cheaply made British productions were forced to compete with a huge influx of Hollywood pictures. The American product had, however, to fit in around a legal quota requirement that 45 per cent of main features and 25 per cent of supporting features should be British. This latter figure could include a number of reissues of older films, often abridged. Patrons were frequently hostile to new British 'B' features, and resented watching films they had seen before. But many British main features were successful, and the top attractions for the years 1947–9 were British: *The Courtneys of Curzon Street* (1947), *Spring in Park Lane* (1948) and *The Third Man* (1949). The main feature quota was eased to 40 per cent in 1949 and to 30 per cent from 1950.

By 1948, the ABC circuit totalled 442 cinemas, Odeon had 317, and Gaumont 304. Although the circuits controlled a minority of the 4,700 cinemas in Britain, they had a disproportionate power because they were virtually guaranteed the first showing of the best films. For a film to be widely exhibited it had to be given a circuit release by one of these majors (in places where a chain was unrepresented another cinema would step in to take its release).

Extended runs were confined to London's West End cinemas and, occasionally, other city-centre cinemas. Fixed well in advance, West End runs were often inflexible since a film's general release had already been scheduled and the next attraction fixed. There were one-week pre-release presentations at seaside resorts in the holiday season, concurrent with the West End showings. Films began their general release with the London suburbs. There had been a simple north London–south London split, but in order to reduce the number of prints in wartime the London suburbs were divided into three regions: north and west, north and east, and south. Films played from Monday for six days, with Sunday (when part of the takings went to charity) being devoted to revivals. Normally, there was no question of a film being held over for a second week: this would have dented the business of other cinemas waiting to play the film. The weekly change of programme was also favoured because many patrons went to the same cinema virtually every week, regardless of what was showing.

Normally, two feature-length films were shown with a newsreel and trailers. Occasionally long, spectacular productions played with a 'full supporting programme' of shorts and cartoons rather than a supporting feature. After touring London, films played the rest of the country, taking as long as six months on their first run. Many older, smaller cinemas, and some newer independent ones that did not have the booking power of the major circuits, survived by showing films that had not obtained a circuit release, either because they were comparatively unappealing or because they were handled by a minor distributor; these cinemas also revived the most attractive films that had played the major circuits.

The Big Decline

In the United States, movie attendances slumped dramatically after 1947, and in the early 50s Hollywood attempted to combat television by making more films in colour, 3-D and CinemaScope.

In Britain, the slow decline in attendances almost halted in 1954, the year in which CinemaScope and stereophonic sound were introduced. The process was owned by 20th Century-Fox, which fell out with Rank's Odeon and Gaumont circuits over their refusal to give extended playing time to Fox pictures and install full stereophonic sound. Consequently, Fox created a new circuit to show its films, consisting mainly of Essoldo and Granada theatres, and the Odeon and Gaumont circuits lost the often popular Fox product.

Between 1956 and 1960 British cinema attendances more than halved, from 1,101 million to 501 million. During this period over 1,000 cinemas shut down. Apart from reducing admissions, since not all patrons switched to other cinemas, these closures also made cinemagoing seem unfashionable – they prompted newspaper headlines and the unwanted buildings often became derelict eyesores. The broad reason for the cinema's decline was, as in the United States a few years earlier, rising standards of living. Whereas some patrons in the 1930s had never stepped on carpet until they went into a super-cinema, in the post-war period comfort in the home often outstripped that of cinemas.

In the late 1930s British cinemas had experimented with the new medium of television, offering large-screen presentations of live events such as the 1938 Derby. Television closed down during the war, but the BBC resumed transmissions in 1945 and gained a huge boost from the 1953 Coronation of Queen Elizabeth II. But it was the coming of ITV that particularly hurt cinemas as the regional commercial TV companies aimed to appeal to a mass audience; they also acquired libraries of still attractive, old Hollywood films, some of which they showed on Saturday evenings.

Another significant problem faced by cinemas was the decline in the number of new major Hollywood features. Cinemas were struggling to find enough attractive features to maintain the four-circuit system – many reissues and second-rate programmes went out just to fill the screens. The circuits even played some subtitled foreign-language films, including *Le Salaire de la peur* (*The Wages of Fear*, 1953) and *Rififi* (1955), which had been major hits in the West End. Rank initially resisted showing 'X'-certificate films on the Odeon and Gaumont circuits because they prevented families from attending, but they gradually relented. Independent cinemas without access to one of the circuit releases had even fewer films to choose from, and the survivors turned increasingly to exploitation material: cheap horror and science-fiction pictures, nudist features and 'sexy' Continental titles.

Audiences were losing the habit of attending cinemas regularly, only going in large numbers to a few hit films each year. Ancillary sales (ice-creams, soft drinks) became increasingly important, as did the revenue from screen advertising. Larger cinemas also developed evenings of live shows with pop stars.

In 1958, the problem of product shortage was finally addressed. Fox began to wind down its separate release programme and Rank regrouped its best Odeon and Gaumont cinemas into a new weekly Rank release. Redundant cinemas were converted to dance halls, bowling alleys and bingo clubs or pulled down to make way for supermarkets and office blocks.

In the 1960s, major mainstream films were released to either the ABC or Rank (Odeon) circuits. For a while, Rank was tied to a disproportionate number of Hollywood majors, dating from the time when it operated two circuits, but first Paramount and then Universal switched from Rank to ABC, which retained its connection with MGM and Warner Bros. Besides its own and other British productions, Rank was left with Disney, Columbia, United Artists and 20th Century-Fox pictures.

In the 1960s it became apparent that most cinemas were too large: it was uneconomic to maintain them, and depressing for audiences to be scattered in handfuls around a vast auditorium. Initially, many buildings were split horizontally into two halves. Sometimes, the downstairs half became a dance hall or bingo club; sometimes both halves functioned as cinemas, often making a cinema elsewhere redundant. The first mini-cinema opened in former restaurant space at the Odeon, Preston in 1970 with 105 seats, the old auditorium having already been divided into a ground-floor dance hall and upstairs cinema. However, the fall in cinema attendances continued, annual admissions dropping from 501 million in 1960 to 193 million in 1970. The number of cinemas fell from 3,034 to 1,529.

In the 1970s most profitable Odeons and ABCs were converted into three-screen film centres. New equipment had been devised, requiring only one projector that could basically run itself, with the programme on large reels on a tower or horizontally placed on a platter. ABC favoured closing sites for several months to create two cinemas in the former stalls and one in the circle, each with new screens and curtains, and attempted to relaunch these film centres as a new creation. Rank preferred to spend less money with 'drop-wall' conversions whereby the space beneath a balcony was closed off and divided down the middle to create two mini-cinemas while the circle functioned as the largest cinema, using the existing screen, and stayed open for all or most of the conversion period to maintain some income and keep the cinemagoing habit alive.

Picturegoers found themselves with a greater choice of films since in many suburbs and towns there were competing ABCs and Odeons, each with three screens. Hit films like *Women in Love* (1969) and *Percy* (1971) were now being given standard two-week runs, but in three-screen centres they could stay even longer on a smaller screen. A smash hit, like *Jaws* (1975), played at some local cinemas for as long as six months.

Cinemagoers became increasingly selective, partly because admission prices were no longer cheap. Only the main feature mattered now, so double bills, shorts and supporting features vanished: a single feature, and advertising, was shown with separate performances replacing the time-honoured continuous show. Regular children's Saturday shows declined in the face of television's alternative appeal, then ceased altogether.

Apart from a sharp rise in 1978, fuelled by a raft of box-office successes led by *Star Wars* (1977), attendances continued to decline, and the relative cheapness and flexibility of video seemed to pose a real threat to cinemagoing. The future of cinemas had never looked bleaker. More cinemas closed, even some of those converted to three screens. Press and display advertising was cut back. Small-print advertisements for cinemas in local papers created a poor impression, as did the fronts of some cinemas, which now permanently displayed a large sign – 'You can't beat a good film' – rather than naming the actual picture showing. By 1984, annual attendances were down to 58 million, Odeon had only 75 cinemas with 194 screens, while ABC (now part of the Thorn-EMI conglomerate) had 107 sites and 287 screens.

Return of the Audience

In 1985, attendances went up to 71 million, and recovery was sustained by the arrival of the multiplex. British exhibitors and leisure operators were well aware that the multiplex cinema had revitalised film exhibition in North America, but doubted if the idea would work in Britain because of the high cost of land. However, Bass Leisure, in developing the Point leisure complex at Milton Keynes, wanted a multiplex and linked up with a leading US chain, American Multi-Cinema (AMC), to obtain one. AMC decided to import its operating practices wholesale rather than adapt to local conventions. It was rewarded when the ten-screen cinema at the Point, opened in October 1985, achieved 1 million admissions within its first year of operation.

Even before the opening of the Point, the ABC circuit had laid plans for multiplexes, but the parent company decided to dispose of the circuit to an American company, Cannon, which applied its name to the cinemas, including Britain's second multiplex, the eight-screen Cannon at Salford Quays, Manchester, opened at the end of 1986. (Cannon renamed its multiplexes and some older properties MGM Cinemas after its parent company acquired the MGM studio.)

AMC led the way by opening seven more multiplexes before it was taken over by another American operator, CIC (a partnership of Paramount and Universal), the combined chain soon being rebranded UCI. Other American concerns burst onto the British exhibition scene, National Amusements opening Showcase cinemas with as many as fourteen screens. Warner Bros. spread beyond its long-standing Leicester Square launch-pad to open multiplexes, beginning with a twelve-screen cinema at Bury in Lancashire that seated 3,996 (just short of the biggest single-screen cinema of the past) and cost £9 million. Multiplexes, with their soft drinks and popcorn, out-of-town sites close to motorways, and computerised box offices, succeeded in attracting young people with cars and disposable income.

Most early British multiplexes were built in the Midlands and the North where land was cheaper and

sites more readily available, but the South soon caught up. New chains, like Cineworld and Apollo, began exploring smaller markets where rents were lower, and Cineworld in particular added Bollywood to the multiplex 'offer', Indian cinema accounting for the exceptional success of its Feltham site (along with the absence of a multiplex in nearby Hounslow).

Many old-fashioned cinemas, including some in nearby town centres, were forced to close by multiplex competition. Odeon made most of its older cinemas more competitive by introducing extra screens and belatedly joined the multiplex revolution, developing a new look without entirely losing its old identity. But in 2000 the Rank Organisation made its final exit from the film industry, selling off Odeon to an overseas-based private equity group.

In early 1996, Warner Bros. opened several multiplexes in the outer London area and started a partnership with Australia's Village Roadshow to operate in Europe and Asia, resulting in Warners' British chain being renamed Warner Village. By this time, Richard Branson had added the MGM chain to his Virgin empire. His emphasis on branding forced rival chains to sharpen their images, but Virgin soon sold out to the French UGC concern.

By 1997 new planning regulations favouring city centres over out-of-town sites led to a rash of inner-city multiplexes within leisure and retail developments that killed off almost every traditional high street venue. A new generation of multiplexes featuring stadium seating and ever larger foyers led to the demise of some of the early ones. The increasing number of multiplexes was largely responsible for the rise in attendances, which reached 176 million in 2002, exactly the same as in 1971.

Five major chains – Cineworld, Odeon, UCI, UGC and Warner Village – emerged, and in the art-house sector, City Screen established a strong presence. In 2003, Warner Village was put up for sale and acquired by a fledgeling group and renamed Vue. The UCI circuit was sold and absorbed into Odeon, and the UGC chain likewise became part of a much larger Cineworld. This resulted in three major circuits, as in the heyday of cinemagoing, though now they were all showing the same new films. However, the new circuits were forced to sell off several multiplexes to satisfy the competition regulators, and these were formed into the new Empire chain. Some independent cinemas gained a new lease of life by going upmarket and installing luxury seating and bar service.

Competition between three major circuits in 1952

Since 2002, the number of admissions has fallen back slightly. Foreign-language and small, independent films lost ground as multiplexes increasingly showed several prints of new blockbusters at staggered starting times rather than expanding choice. The UK Film Council launched an initiative to supply both multiplex and traditional cinemas with digital projectors in return for an agreement to devote more showing time to more specialised titles (foreign as well as small British works). Digital copies are far cheaper and quicker to produce than a conventional print, but the scheme was handicapped by the dislike audiences for more mature films feel for the multiplex environment. There is also the problem that the reduction of the 'window' between cinema and DVD release (partly to combat piracy), has shortened the life of films in the cinemas.

American ownership of multiplexes and the absence of a quota system compelling cinemas to show British or European films mean that domestic productions rarely make an impact at the box office. Occasional exceptions like *The Full Monty* (1997), *Calendar Girls* (2003) and *The Queen* (2006) have succeeded in breaking through, but the more usual British presence at the multiplex is as junior partner in big-budget Hollywood films like *Casino Royale* (2006) and *Flushed Away* (2006) which draw on an array of British talent.

Bibliography

Atwell, David, *Cathedrals of the Movies* (London: Architectural Press, 1980).

BFI Film and Television Handbook (London: BFI, 1983 to 2005). Statistics of cinemas, screens, admissions.

The Cinema: Its Present Position and Future Possibilities, Being the Report of and Chief Evidence Taken by the Cinema Commission of Inquiry Instituted by the National Council of Public Morals (London: Williams and Norgate, 1917).

Docherty, David, Morrison, David and Tracey, Michael, *The Last Picture Show? Britain's Changing Film Audience* (London: BFI, 1987).

Eyles, Allen, *ABC, The First Name in Entertainment* (Burgess Hill: Cinema Theatre Association/London: BFI, 1993).

Eyles, Allen, *Gaumont British Cinemas* (Burgess Hill: Cinema Theatre Association/London: BFI, 1996).

Eyles, Allen, *The Granada Theatres* (London, BFI, 1998).

Eyles, Allen, *Odeon Cinemas 1: Oscar Deutsch Entertains Our Nation* (London: Cinema Theatre Association/BFI, 2002).

Eyles, Allen, *Odeon Cinemas 2: From J. Arthur Rank to the Multiplex* (London: Cinema Theatre Association/BFI, 2005).

Halliwell, Leslie, *Seats in All Parts* (London: Granada, 1985). Reminiscences of Bolton's cinemas.

Hanson, Stuart, *From Silent Screen to Multi-screen: A History of Cinema Exhibition in Britain since 1896* (Manchester: Manchester University Press, 2007).

How to Run a Picture Theatre (London: E. T. Heron, 1912).

Kelly, Terence, with Norton, Graham and Perry, George, *A Competitive Cinema* (London: Institute of Economic Affairs, 1966).

Kinematograph Year Book, 1914 to 1959; *Kinematograph and Television Year Book*, 1961 to 1969 (London: various publishers). Listings of cinemas, circuits, etc.

McBain, Janet, *Pictures Past: Recollections of Scottish Cinemas and Cinema-going* (Edinburgh: Moorfoot, 1985).

Manders, Frank, *Cinemas of Newcastle* (Newcastle upon Tyne: City Libraries & Arts, 1991).

O'Brien, Margaret and Eyles, Allen (eds), *Enter the Dream-House* (London: Museum of the Moving Image/BFI, 1993). Interviews about going to the cinema and working in the cinema.

Picture House (Cinema Theatre Association). Magazine started in 1982 containing articles and interviews about cinema design and operation, circuit histories, programming, etc.

10

Action, Spectacle and the *Boy's Own* Tradition in British Cinema

JAMES CHAPMAN

As Marcia Landy observes: 'Films that celebrate patriotism and myths of national identity are a staple of most national cinemas.'[1] This is especially true of British cinema, which has a rich heritage of adventure films in which stories of heroism, patriotism and duty have been prominent motifs. From the Khyber Pass to the battlefields of Europe, from the deserts of the Sudan to the depths of the North Sea, British adventure heroes have fought to protect nation and Empire from a myriad array of invaders, warmongers, rebels, terrorists and spies. Between the mid-1930s and the late 1960s, films of adventure, war and Empire were regularly among the most popular films with British cinemagoers, if not necessarily with critics. And yet, despite the prominence of these films in the generic profile of British cinema over a substantial period of its history, the British adventure film has received scant attention from film critics and historians.[2] This chapter seeks to explore the reasons for that neglect and to suggest some avenues of approach to writing the history of the British adventure film.

Parameters and Contexts

It is necessary in the first instance, however, to establish certain parameters. As a generic classification, the label 'adventure film' is less clearly defined than most: indeed, this might be one reason why film historians have left it pretty much alone. In a literal sense, the adventure film would include any narrative in which a protagonist or group of protagonists undertake 'adventures' outside normal everyday experiences. More commonly, it tends to be used in reference to those narratives where action and visual spectacle are fore-grounded: the swashbuckler, the war film, the Empire film, the sensational spy thriller, the mythological fantasy and perhaps the historical epic. The adventure film is best understood not as a discrete genre in its own right but as a flexible overarching category that encompasses a range of different, though related, narrative forms. In the British context, three particular traditions or lineages can be identified, all with their own particular generic regimes and conventions, but all inhabiting similar cultural and ideological terrain: the British Empire film, the war adventure film and the sensational spy thriller.[3]

For the purposes of this chapter the adventure film is defined as a fictional narrative – thus excluding films based on actual historical events (*Zulu*, 1963, *Khartoum*, 1966) or personages (*Scott of the Antarctic*, 1948, *Lawrence of Arabia*, 1962) or those war films which reconstruct particular wartime incidents (*The Dam Busters*, 1955, *Dunkirk*, 1958). While this distinction is open to debate, it has two advantages. First, in narrowing the scope to fictional representations of adventure and heroism, the cultural antecedents of the adventure film can more easily be identified. Second, it avoids confusion between the adventure film and other types of narrative, such as the historical film and the war film, which have traditionally been classified as such in British cinema historiography.

In an influential article, Alan Williams suggests that 'genre studies with real historical integrity' involve three aspects:

1. Starting with a genre's "pre-history", its roots in other media.

2. Studying all films, regardless of perceived quality.

3. Going beyond film content to study advertising, the star system, studio policy, and so on in relation to the production of films.[4]

While such a thorough-going history of the British adventure film is beyond the scope of an exploratory essay such as this, it is possible, nevertheless, to make some general observations which fulfil Williams's schemata.

The 'pre-history' of the adventure film is to be found in a tradition of popular fiction that pre-dates the cinema. This is what is referred to as 'the *Boy's Own* tradition': those tales of heroism, derring-do and muscular Christianity that became popular reading matter in the mass-circulation boys' story papers during the late 19th century. The *Boy's Own Paper*, founded in 1879 by the Religious Tract Society, was the most enduring of these papers, whose ranks also included *Union Jack, Chums, Young England, Marvel, Pluck, Boy's Friend* and *Boy's Realm*. In his masterful study of the representation of war and heroism in British popular culture, Michael Paris demonstrates how 'the boys' papers created powerful myths about the nature of war and the British soldier'.[5] With their combination of words and pictures, Victorian boys' papers provided a ready source of inspiration for the cinema, which adopted wholesale their images of heroism and their ideologies of patriotism and duty. Throughout its history, indeed, the adventure film has frequently drawn on popular literature: the stories of Edgar Wallace and John Buchan were adapted by Alexander Korda and Alfred Hitchcock in the 1930s, while in the 1960s the best-sellers of Ian Fleming and Alistair MacLean were turned into very popular British films. Each of the different lineages of the adventure film has its origins in an already extant lineage of popular literature.

With a handful of exceptions, the adventure film has not won much favour with film critics. In traditional film criticism there are few 'good' adventure films; those that have won critical acclaim have usually done so on grounds other than their status as genre films. The celebrated British thrillers of Alfred Hitchcock, for example (*The Man Who Knew Too Much*, 1934, *The 39 Steps*, 1935, *Secret Agent*, 1936, *The Lady Vanishes*, 1938), have generally been placed within an auteurist context (as 'Hitchcockian' films) rather than analysed in terms of their generic characteristics (as imperialist spy thrillers).[6] There are, however, plenty of 'bad' adventure films. Critical reaction to the early James Bond films

exemplifies the tendency either to denigrate popular culture as being harmful and pernicious or to dismiss it as mere entertainment of no social import, while the reception afforded later films in the series reinforces the notion that popular genres are formulaic, repetitive and predictable.[7]

Why, at a time when other aspects of popular British cinema have begun to receive long-overdue critical rehabilitation, does the adventure film continue to be marginalised? I would suggest there are two principal reasons. On the one hand, the adventure film, with its heroic narratives and foregrounding of action and spectacle, does not fit the criteria of realism and quality that for so long have dominated critical discourse around film in Britain. On the other hand, the patriotic and nationalist agendas of the adventure film are such that it does not offer the possibility for the sort of transgressive pleasures that some commentators have identified in nonrealist genres such as the costume melodrama and the Gothic horror film. The 'cinema of the Right' – and most adventure films are ideologically somewhere to the right – still remains the 'relatively unexplored and unfashionable area' that it was when Jeffrey Richards made the first tentative steps into this territory in the 1970s.[8]

The British Empire Film

Various commentators have suggested parallels between the British Empire film and the Hollywood Western: themes such as the expansion of the frontier, the taming of a wilderness and the triumph of white culture over barbarism are common to both. The parallels extend further. Just as the Western film had its literary origins in the novels of Owen Wister and Zane Grey, and owed much of its iconography to the paintings of Frederic S. Remington and Theodor R. Davis, so too the British Empire film follows on from a literary heritage that includes the adventure stories of Henry Rider Haggard, Rudyard Kipling and A. E. W. Mason, and borrows many of its visual conventions from paintings by the likes of W. B. Wollen and George Joy. It might be argued, furthermore, that a point of convergence can be found between the Western and the British Empire film in the form of the 'pre-Revolutionary' or 'colonial' adventure – narratives set on the North American continent before the War of Independence, such as James Fenimore Cooper's Leatherstocking Tales (*The Last of the Mohicans* being the most famous and oft-filmed by Hollywood) – though it is more generally accepted that the historical period of both the Western and the Imperial adventure film falls in the late 19th century.

The heyday of the Imperial adventure film in British cinema was the 1930s, a period when the British Empire had reached its fullest geographical extent and when the ideology of Imperialism was disseminated widely through popular culture (books, postcards, stamps, cigarette cards) and propaganda (the Empire Marketing Board, its successor the Colonial Empire Marketing Board and the BBC's Empire Service). Screen adaptations of Imperial fiction included films based on the stories of Rider Haggard (*King Solomon's Mines*), Edgar Wallace (*Sanders of the River*), Kipling (*Elephant Boy*) and Mason (*The Drum*, *The Four Feathers*). Significantly, Hollywood studios also showed an interest in Imperial adventure films during the mid- and late 1930s (*Lives of a Bengal Lancer, Wee Willie Winkie, Gunga Din*), which shared with their British counterparts a pro-Imperialist, pro-British ideological stance. 'The basic assumption is that British rule is a jolly good thing,' Richards observes. 'Its aim is consistently declared to be the preservation of peace and law and the protection of its subject peoples.'[9]

The ideology of Imperialism was most fully embraced in a cycle of films produced by Alexander Korda. Korda's 'Imperial trilogy' – *Sanders of the River* (1935), *The Drum* (1938) and *The Four Feathers* (1939), all directed by his brother Zoltan – represent between them most of the narrative variations and geographical locations possible within the British Empire film. Although invariably grouped together, the differences between the films are instructive. *Sanders of the River*, whose primary concern is to justify British colonial administration in West Africa, is quite sober in style and refrains from excessive displays of jingoism. The British are personified in the character of the benevolent commissioner (Leslie Banks) who governs in the interest of the native population. Sanders's relationship with loyal native chief Bosambo (Paul Robeson) represents a consensus between the British and the Africans that brings about peace and progress. *The Drum*, while also concerned to support the principle of British rule in India, eschews the somewhat pious moralising of *Sanders* in favour of a more straightforward tale of adventure and intrigue on the Northwest Frontier. It is, effectively, a tale of the 'Great Game' of Empire described by Kipling in *Kim*: Captain Carruthers (Roger Livesey) is the soldier-diplomat who defeats a palace *coup* and brings peace and justice to the province. The visual possibilities of the Imperial adventure are opened up by the use of Technicolor, while the prominent role accorded to the newly discovered 'elephant boy' Sabu provides a point of narrative identification for younger audiences and reinforces the genre's links with popular juvenile fiction.

It was with *The Four Feathers*, however, that the Imperial adventure film found its definitive form. With a literate script by R. C. Sherriff and stunning Technicolor photography by Georges Périnal, Osmond Borrodaile and Jack Cardiff, *The Four Feathers* represents the British Empire (in this case the Sudan) as a mythical space for the enactment of a drama of personal courage and redemption. It is no longer deemed necessary to justify the Imperial mission: it is taken for granted that the campaign to avenge the death of General Gordon at Khartoum is morally justified. The emphasis, instead, is on visual spectacle, with lavishly staged battle sequences and panoramic desert landscapes that are the equal of any Hollywood epic of the time in their visual impact. The importance of visual style is exemplified in Korda's anecdotal response to a technical adviser when he insisted on red uniforms rather than the correct dark blue for the sequence of the regimental ball: 'This is Technicolor!'[10]

The Imperial adventure film was absent from British screens during the 1940s when first World War II and then the partition of India following independence in 1947 made the subject matter politically too contentious. When it returned in the 1950s, the Empire film was more concerned with the policing of the African colonies than with spectacular tales of derring-do, exemplified in the contemporary rather than period narratives of *Where No Vultures Fly* (Harry Watt, 1951), *West of Zanzibar* (Harry Watt, 1954) and *Simba* (Brian Desmond Hurst, 1955), the latter set against the background of the Mau Mau war in Kenya. *Storm over the Nile* (Zoltan Korda and Terence Young, 1955) was a carbon-copy remake of *The Four Feathers*, using the earlier film's action footage stretched out to fit the CinemaScope ratio. A belated entry in the cycle, *Death Drums along the River* (Lawrence Huntington, 1963), was a lacklustre and pointless remake of *Sanders of the River* made at a time when the British were winding up their colonial Empire and withdrawing from Africa.

There was, however, to be one last, glorious flowering of the old-fashioned Imperial adventure film before the genre became a relic of the past. *North West Frontier* (J. Lee Thompson, 1959) was, on one level, a *Boy's Own*-style adventure yarn in which the heroic Captain Scott (played by Kenneth More in his best 'good chap' persona) leads a disparate group of people to safety during an uprising in 1905. The film employs the familiar

Reluctantly taking up arms: Lauren Bacall and Kenneth More in *North West Frontier* (J. Lee Thompson, 1959)

device of a hazardous journey through dangerous territory – critics compared it to John Ford's Western *Stagecoach* (1939) – that has been a staple of adventure fiction since Maupassant's classic short story *Boule de suif*. Made twelve years after Indian independence and three years after the débâcle of Suez had demonstrated the fragility of Britain's continued Imperial pretensions, however, *North West Frontier* incorporates a partial critique of Imperialism into its narrative. The bloody legacy of partition is implicit in the opening voice-over narration: 'Men find many reasons for killing each other – greed, revenge, jealousy, or perhaps because they worship God by a different name.' Captain Scott distances himself from the gung-ho attitude of the British warrior caste imagined in Imperial fiction ('A soldier's job, Mr Peters, is not primarily to kill,' he tells an arms salesman who is one of the party. 'We have to keep order, to prevent your customers from tearing each other to pieces'), while traditional British character and customs are mocked by Lauren Bacall's forthright American governess ('The British never seem to do anything until they've had a cup of tea, and by that time it's too late'). In response to Scott's paternalistic statement that the rebels are 'only children', the villain Van Leyden (Herbert Lom) points out that they are 'fighting for freedom – for the freedom of their country'. The British presence is justified, however, insofar as the rebels seek to kill a six-year-old prince and the boy's father, a maharajah, has requested the British to help, thus making Scott's actions laudable and just. The supremacy of British culture is assured, moreover, through the inspired use of the 'Eton Boating Song' on the soundtrack as the party are

carried to safety by an old train symbolically named 'Empress of India'.

The War Adventure Film

Like the Imperial adventure film, the war adventure film has its origins in the late-nineteenth- and early- twentieth-century fictions of writers such as G. A. Henty – the popular novelist who 'perhaps more than any other individual, was instrumental in making war an acceptable literary subject'.[11] The war adventure story was almost indistinguishable from the Imperial adventure story when dealing with the 'little wars of Empire' in the late 19th century, but followed a more distinct path of its own following World War I. It is instructive, given that all the best-known literary accounts of World War I adopt a defiantly anti-war stance – exemplified by the war poetry of Wilfred Owen and Siegfried Sassoon, by Erich Maria Remarque's novel *All Quiet on the Western Front* and by Robert Graves's memoir *Goodbye to All That* – to note that popular fiction in the 1920s and 1930s still portrayed war as an exciting adventure and a test of true manhood. The most popular juvenile reading matter of the 1930s, for example, included the Biggles stories of 'Captain' W. E. Johns (tales of aerial warfare set during World War I) and the Hornblower novels of C. S. Forester (seafaring adventure yarns set during the Napoleonic Wars).

Although war narratives were relatively sparse in British cinema of the early 1930s, they became more numerous in the second half of the decade as the government stepped up its rearmament programme. The Gaumont-British Picture Corporation made two films promoting the armed services. *Forever England* (Walter Forde, 1935) was based on C. S. Forester's World War I adventure *Brown on Resolution* and starred a young John Mills – later to become an iconic presence in the British war films of the 1950s – as a naval rating who, wounded, alone and armed with only a rifle, pins down the crew of a damaged German battlecruiser until the arrival of the Royal Navy. The overtly patriotic intent of the film was evident in the trailer which described it as 'a sea drama to stir the blood of everyone of British stock'.[12] *O.H.M.S.* (Raoul Walsh, 1936) did a similar job for the British army: a small-time American racketeer, on the run from the police, enlists in the 1st Wessex Regiment under an assumed name and finds redemption when he dies a hero's death in a battle against Chinese bandits. The film was well received by critics, according to *World Film News*: 'Propaganda is usually of doubtful box-office value, but in this case the trade considers that propaganda and entertainment have been admirably blended and looks forward with confidence to a financial success.'[13]

World War II provided a new arena of conflict for the adventure film. The war against Hitler's Germany could be represented unproblematically as just and necessary, while Nazi-occupied Europe provided a dangerous environment for fictional secret missions. While the realistic, semi-documentary war narratives of World War II have won most plaudits (*In Which We Serve, San Demetrio London, Nine Men, The Way Ahead*), they need to be seen within the context of a film culture that also included cloak-and-dagger melodramatics in the occupied countries (*Secret Mission, Escape to Danger, The Flemish Farm, The Adventures of Tartu*). When the war film returned to prominence in the 1950s and early 1960s the trend was for factually based special mission narratives (*Odette, The Cockleshell Heroes, Carve Her Name with Pride*) which, along with their fictional counterparts (*Orders to Kill, Circle of Deception*), represented a move back towards psychological realism. The prisoner-of-war cycle (*The Wooden Horse, Albert R.N., The Colditz Story, Danger Within, The Password Is Courage*), however, presented the experience of captivity as a game in which British officers and gentlemen outfoxed their dim-witted captors, poking fun at the enemy through the ritual of 'goon-baiting' when they were not actually escaping.

They Who Dare (Lewis Milestone, 1954) exemplifies the tension within the 1950s war film between the adventure story on the one hand and the discourse of psychological realism on the other. Dirk Bogarde is the leader of a Special Air Service raiding party on a mission to destroy German airfields on Rhodes. Bogarde plays much the same sort of 'amateur' soldier as he did in the factually based *Ill Met by Moonlight* (1957); his character here is nicknamed 'Boy' and regards war as a game of adventure and chance. His attitude is contrasted with that of Sergeant Corcoran (Denholm Elliott) who is clearly affected by the unpleasant aspects of war and exhibits the more 'professional' outlook that soldiering is an unpleasant job but one that has to be done. The conventional heroics are staged in the sober style associated with the director (Milestone had directed Hollywood war films such as *All Quiet on the Western Front*, 1930 and *A Walk in the Sun*, 1945) and the outcome of the mission is equivocal: Boy's own enthusiasm for blowing up German planes results in his party sustaining heavy casualties.

The 1960s saw a vogue for big-budget, all-star action adventures aimed at the international market. *The Guns of Navarone* (J. Lee Thompson, 1961) and *Operation Crossbow* (Michael Anderson, 1965) were backed by American studios (Columbia and MGM respectively) and featured top-billed American stars (Gregory Peck, George Peppard) for the world box office. They are characterised by their expansive, rambling narratives, with a degree of philosophical chat about the nature and conduct of war punctuated by elaborate action set pieces and expensive pyrotechnics. There is an identifiable trend in these films away from the conventions of psychological realism and towards a treatment that has more in common with the comic books of the 1950s and 1960s such as *Lion, Eagle, Hotspur* and *Wizard*. As Paris observes: 'The action strip offered its readers exciting visual entertainment with a minimum of explanation or character development, and rushed the reader from one action-packed image to another.'[14]

The apotheosis of the comic-strip war adventure is *Where Eagles Dare* (Brian G. Hutton, 1968), in which cardboard characterisation and preposterous plotting combine to make one of the most absurdly enjoyable action movies of all time. *Where Eagles Dare* is the cinematic equivalent of war comics such as *Victor, Warlord* and *Battle Picture Weekly*: a long but fast-moving adventure narrative in which climax piles upon climax and where the heroes never run out of ammunition or explosives. Richard Burton and Clint Eastwood (who had become a major film star through a trilogy of similarly gun-obsessed spaghetti Westerns) are sent on a mission to penetrate the *Schloss Adler* in the Bavarian

Clint Eastwood in *Where Eagles Dare* (Brian G. Hutton, 1969)

Alps. The excessively convoluted plot (ostensibly a rescue mission for a top-brass American general, but actually a triple-bluff to expose German agents in MI6) might be seen as a parody of the conventions of the adventure thriller. The last vestiges of psychological realism have disappeared from the narrative; instead the film foregrounds visual spectacle and positively wallows in the gratuitous destruction of property, vehicles and bodies, especially in the last third, which becomes one extended chase sequence in the style of the James Bond films. *Where Eagles Dare* was written by Alistair MacLean, whose books were much in demand by film-makers in the 1960s and 1970s and who spans different lineages of adventure fiction including war (*The Guns of Navarone, Force Ten from Navarone*) and the spy thriller (*Puppet on a Chain, When Eight Bells Toll*).

The Sensational Spy Thriller

The spy story became popular in Britain around the turn of the century, with stories of intrigue and con-spiracy in the courts of Europe from the pens of William Le Queux and E. Phillips Oppenheim. The spy thriller relocated the threat to the British Empire to a European context: plots to undermine British society and foiled invasions were prominent in popular fiction in the first decade of the 20th century as increased geopolitical tension between the Great Powers made the prospect of war more likely. The genre became especially prominent during and after World War I, with the novels of John Buchan and 'Sapper' (the pen-name of ex-army officer H. C. McNeile).

Michael Denning identifies two lineages within the literary spy thriller. On the one hand there are 'magical thrillers where there is a clear contest between Good and Evil with a virtuous hero defeating an alien and evil villain', exemplified by the sensational thrillers of Buchan, Sapper and Ian Fleming with their narratives of action, movement and pursuit. On the other hand there are 'existential thrillers which play on a dialectic of good and evil overdetermined by moral dilemmas', exemplified by the morally ambiguous spy stories of Graham Greene, Eric Ambler and John Le Carré.[15] The spy film has also tended to follow these two lineages, and while the latter falls outside the ambit of this essay, revolving around 'mole-hunt' narratives and stories of treachery and betrayal, the sensational spy thriller shares the ideologies of patriotism and duty that characterise other variants of the adventure film.

The spy thriller was prominent in British cinema during the mid- and late 1930s when there were adap-

tations of Buchan (*The 39 Steps*), Sapper (*The Return of Bulldog Drummond, Bulldog Drummond at Bay*), W. Somerset Maugham (*Secret Agent*) and Edgar Wallace (*The Four Just Men*).[16] As the threat posed by the newly resurgent Nazi Germany became apparent in the late 1930s, the spy thriller became a vehicle for urging military preparedness and criticising the foreign policy of appeasement. Two films especially represent the narrative ideologies of the eve-of-war spy thriller. *The Four Just Men* (Walter Forde, 1939) completely realigns the 1905 Edgar Wallace novel on which it was based, turning the Just Men from European vigilantes committed to help-ing foreign nationals seek refuge in Britain into an Anglicised society seeking to protect Britain from for-eign dictators. The villain of the novel, a British Foreign Secretary introducing an 'Aliens Political Offences Bill', becomes in the film a foreign-born MP who is feeding military secrets to an unnamed foreign power (implicitly Germany). *Q Planes* (Tim Whelan, 1939), an original screen story, concerns the attempts of an unnamed for-eign power (again clearly meant to be Germany) to hijack a new British fighter plane. There are two pro-tagonists in *Q Planes*, representing the convergence of the 'amateur' and 'professional' archetypes of the English gentleman hero: test pilot Tony McVane (Laurence Olivier) is the amateur, displaying courage and ingenu-ity in an unfamiliar situation, while Major Hammond (Ralph Richardson) is the professional secret agent who combines dedication to duty with the eccentricity that personifies English individualism. Landy interprets Hammond's umbrella as 'a satiric allusion to [Neville] Chamberlain' and there is a strong theme, as there is in *The Four Just Men*, that appeasement is misguided and that Britain needs to prepare vigorously for war.[17]

It was through the success of the James Bond films beginning in 1962, however, that the sensational spy thriller reached its widest audience not only in Britain but throughout the world. The Bond films are significant not only for their longevity but also for their place within the generic lineages of adventure fiction. On one level, as Raymond Durgnat observes, the films are a throwback to an earlier heritage: 'Bond J. is the last man in of the British Empire Superman's XI. Holmes, Hannay, Drummond, Conquest, Templar *et al.* have all succumbed to the demon bowlers of the twentieth century, while The Winds of Change make every ball a googlie.'[18] The first two Bond films, especially, are strongly reminiscent of pre-World War II fiction. In *Dr No* (Terence Young, 1962) Bond combats an oriental villain cast in the mould of Fu Manchu,

Casino Royale (Martin Campbell, 2006)

Casino Royale, the twenty-first 'official' James Bond film in the sequence stretching back to *Dr No*, represented a significant transitional point in the history of the series. The first vehicle for new leading man Daniel Craig (the sixth actor to assume the role), it marked something of a departure for the series in terms of style. The Bond series has always negotiated a path between 'realistic' action thrillers on the one hand (*From Russia with Love, On Her Majesty's Secret Service, For Your Eyes Only*, 1981, *Licence to Kill*, 1989) and implausible out-of-this-world fantasy adventures on the other (*You Only Live Twice*, 1967, *The Spy Who Loved Me, Moonraker, Die Another Day*). *Casino Royale* was marketed as a 'back-to-basics' Bond after the visual and technological excess of *Die Another Day* (2002), which, with its ice palace and invisible car, was felt by many critics to have overdosed on CGI special effects. In contrast *Casino Royale* is rooted in contemporary geopolitics – Bond's principal antagonist this time around is no madman bent on world domination but rather 'private banker to the world's terrorists' – and the action sequences are notable for their bruising visual and aural realism.

Blond Bond: Daniel Craig in *Casino Royale*

Casino Royale is also only the second Bond film (after *Dr No*) where the credits state 'Based on the novel by Ian Fleming'. Fleming's first novel had in fact been used twice before – first in a much underrated live American television adaptation in 1954 and then as an extravagant but only intermittently funny spoof produced by Charles K. Feldman in 1967 – and had been the only Bond title to which producers Eon did not own the screen rights. It was the acquisition of those rights in 2002 that prompted Eon to produce a 'straight' version of the novel. Structurally *Casino Royale* seems like two films in one. The middle section is a reasonably close adaptation of the original, updating the narrative from the Cold War to the post-9/11 'War on Terror' but maintaining crucial Fleming incidents such as the pivotal card game (Bond has to beat his opponent at the gaming table) and the gruesome torture sequence (in which villain Le Chiffre makes both a figurative and literal assault on Bond's manhood). This middle section of the film is book-ended, however, by three elaborately staged action set pieces that have become *de rigeur* for the series since the opening sequence of *The Spy Who Loved Me*. This results, like other Bonds, in a tension between narrative and spectacle in which attempts at psychologically plausible characterisation (there is much talk of Bond's ego) are overwhelmed, like the audience's senses, by the explosive pyrotechnics.

Casino Royale is a revisionist Bond narrative in so far as it is set in a fictional world in which the events of previous films have not taken place: it dramatises Bond's first mission upon achieving his 'licence to kill'. The pre-title sequence, documenting his first two 'kills', is shot in grainy low-contrast monochrome, though thereafter the cinematography of Phil Méheux (returning to the series, with director Martin Campbell, for the first time since 1995's *GoldenEye*) adheres to the glossy high-contrast style established in the 1960s by Ted Moore. Craig's Bond is not yet the fully formed article: the film charts the process whereby a 'blunt instrument' acquires Bond's familiar accoutrements such as his Aston Martin and trademark vodka martini 'shaken not stirred'. Craig's performance, aided by some well-written 'character' dialogue by script doctor Paul Haggis, suggests a greater depth to Bond than previous actors, while his buffed-up physique, revealed in several entirely gratuitous swimming-trunk shots, makes Bond rather than his women the object of the spectator's gaze. Perhaps the most interesting facet of the film, however, is its reversal of the traditional gender politics of the series, to the extent that Craig's Bond is beleaguered by women in positions of authority, including Eva Green's curiously accented Treasury agent Vesper Lynd (she holds the purse strings in his big game against Le Chiffre) and Judi Dench's acerbic M, the only link back to the preceding films. It is M who symbolically endows Bond with his phallic authority when he takes possession of an automatic pistol with an implausibly large silencer.

The commercial and critical success of *Casino Royale* – it grossed over $450 million worldwide (a new record for the series) and received the best reviews for a Bond movie since *The Living Daylights* (1987) – confirmed that the longest-running franchise in cinema history has been successfully reinvigorated for the 21st century. Even more significantly, however, its nomination for 'Outstanding British Film of the Year' for the British Film and Television Academy Awards (it lost to *The Queen*) and its selection for the prestigious Royal Film Performance (only the second Bond to be chosen, after *Die Another Day*, though others had royal premières) suggests that the Bond series has finally been accepted by a British film industry that had for so long looked down upon it as being everything that British cinema is not supposed to be: big, brash, loud, extravagant, spectacular and highly commercial.

FURTHER READING

James Chapman, *Licence to Thrill: A Cultural History of the James Bond Films*, 2nd edn (London: I. B. Tauris, 2007).

Jonathan Romney, 'The Man with the Golden Grunt', *Independent on Sunday*, 19 November 2006.

while in *From Russia with Love* (Terence Young, 1963) he travels on that symbol of pre-war luxury, the Orient Express. It was the third film, *Goldfinger* (Guy Hamilton, 1964), that established the blend of technological modernity and parodic humour that was to become the hallmark of the Bond series. The combination of sex, violence and spectacle (most apparent in the lavish set designs of Ken Adam) in the Bond films set the style for other action-adventure movies in the 1960s and beyond.

The Bond films successfully recast the clubland hero of Ian Fleming's novels as a modern, classless hero whose attitudes towards sex and consumerism were more in tune with the 'cultural revolution' of the 1960s. While the Bond films have continued to express the themes of patriotism and duty – most explicitly in the much underrated *On Her Majesty's Secret Service* (Peter Hunt, 1969) – they have also transformed Bond from a specifically British hero into a sort of International Mr Fix-It who is frequently employed to save western civilisation from the diabolical designs of terrorist syndicates and avaricious capitalists. The relatively taut thriller narratives of the early 1960s films quickly gave way to the massive visual spectacle and elaborate pyrotechnics that reached their fullest expression in *The Spy Who Loved Me* (Lewis Gilbert, 1977) and *Moonraker* (Lewis Gilbert, 1979). Having saved the entire world from destruction at the hands of deranged megalomaniacs in those films, Bond came back down to earth – and back into identifiable geopolitical tensions – in the films of the 1980s and 1990s.

The Decline of the British Adventure Film

The action-adventure film continued into the 1970s, though it was undergoing a significant ideological change. The patriotic hero serving king and country was still in evidence, but he was now confined to films set in the past such as World War I adventure *Zeppelin* (Étienne Périer, 1971) and two handsomely mounted adaptations of early spy classics, *The Riddle of the Sands* (Tony Maylam, 1979) and *The Thirty-Nine Steps* (Don Sharp, 1978). The contemporary adventure hero was now more likely to be a mercenary whose motivation was pecuniary rather than patriotic. There was also a general increase in the level of violence and brutality, exemplified by films such as *Shout at the Devil* (Peter Hunt, 1976), in which two soldiers of fortune (Lee Marvin and Roger Moore) wage a private war against the German army in Africa during World War I, and *The Wild Geese* (Andrew V. McLaglen, 1978), in which a motley band of mercenaries (Richard Burton, Roger Moore, Richard Harris, Hardy Kruger) are hired to rescue an imprisoned political leader in a central African state.

Like all artefacts of popular culture, films are tracts for their times. The last flowering of the British action-adventure film can be seen as an early response to the political tone of Thatcherism. Unlike the socially critical cinema of the 1980s, however, the action film is explicitly right-wing in its narrative ideologies. *North Sea Hijack* (Andrew V. McLaglen, 1979) concerns a terrorist threat to the North Sea oil fields – an energy source vital to 'the economic life of Great Britain'. Rufus Excalibur Ffolkes (Roger Moore), a misogynistic, cat-loving eccentric who leads his own special unit of underwater commandos, reinforces to the Prime Minister (Faith Brook) the importance of not giving in to terrorists: 'If you do not stand firm on this issue then you will simply encourage every villain with a rowing boat to hold this country to ransom again'. The same

The Wild Geese (Andrew V. McLaglen, 1978)

The Wild Geese was the most successful of a cycle of action-adventure films produced by the British film industry in the 1970s and intended for the international market – a cycle that also includes *Puppet on a Chain* (1971), *When Eight Bells Toll* (1971), *Fear Is the Key* (1972), *Caravan to Vaccares* (1974), *Gold* (1974), *The Eagle Has Landed* (1976), *Shout at the Devil* and *The Dogs of War* (1980). These films were all adapted from best-selling novels by authors such as Alistair MacLean, Wilbur Smith, Jack Higgins and Frederick Forsyth. If, on one level, this demonstrates the prevailing economic and cultural conservatism of the British film industry during this period – the logic being that the marketing of the films would draw upon audiences' familiarity with the titles and authors – on another level it also represents the continuing presence in British cinema of a strand of adventure yarns adapted from popular literature. These authors can be seen as the heirs of nineteenth-century adventure writers such as Haggard and Henty: the difference is that the protagonists have become hired mercenaries rather than gentleman adventurers and the books, reflecting changing cultural attitudes, are more violent in content. Their cultural and racial politics, however, remain much the same as their predecessors. This is particularly evident in *The Wild Geese*, based on a novel by Daniel Carney, which sends a team of ageing mercenaries to a (fictional) African state to slaughter hundreds of black Africans in the name of 'freedom'.

The Wild Geese was a commercial success that, predictably, was derided by critics. Whether it is a good or bad film is largely irrelevant. It is certainly an ideologically confused one, but this confusion is endearing and to an extent reflects the uncertain political and economic conditions of the 1970s. The film posits an alliance between western corporate finance and African military dictatorships. Mercenary Alan Faulkner is hired by banker Sir Edward Matherson to extract an imprisoned democratic leader, Julius Limbani, from a military jail in an unnamed central African state. Faulkner assembles his team and carries out a daring rescue mission, only to find himself and his men abandoned when Matherson concludes a deal with Limbani's rival, General Undofa, who has offered concessions in the copper-mining industry in return for Limbani's death. The country itself is unnamed, though references to borders with Uganda and Burundi would suggest the Democratic Republic of Congo – as would the presence of East German 'military advisers'. The fact that actor Winston Ntshona bears a passing resemblance to the Rhodesian nationalist leader Joshua Nkomo is probably coincidental. *The Wild Geese* legitimates the idea of western military intervention in post-colonial Africa: the mission has the tacit approval of the government. This turned out to be a very plausible scenario given the revelations two decades later that British military consultancy Sandline had been involved in *coup* attempts in Sierra Leone and Liberia. Rather like Robert Aldrich's *The Dirty Dozen* (1967), *The Wild Geese* includes a sequence that seems like an endorsement of cold-blooded murder as Undofa's men, asleep in their barracks, are gassed with cyanide. At the same time, however, the film's reactionary politics are mixed with an unconvincing dose of liberalism as the racist South African Pieter Coetzee comes to admire the 'kaffir' Limbani. The film's title song, performed by Joan Armatrading, refers to the possibility of democracy for Africa and a better understanding between races. This makes it rather ironic that location-shooting for the film took place in apartheid-era South Africa.

A lame-duck sequel, *Wild Geese II*, directed by Peter Hunt, followed in 1985, in which the mission was to rescue Rudolf Hess (Laurence Olivier) from Spandau prison. It featured none of the original stars, with Edward Fox stepping in as a late replacement when Burton died and playing Faulkner's brother. The Italian-produced *Codename: Wild Geese* (1984) was entirely unrelated, a straight-to-video vehicle for Lewis Collins, from the television action series *The Professionals*, who had also starred as SAS captain Peter Skellern in *Who Dares Wins* (1982). *The Wild Geese*, for its part, remains very much a guilty pleasure: the sort of film that a film studies academic is not supposed to like but in fact rather does.

FURTHER READING

Robert Stam, 'The Wild Geese', *Cineaste*, Winter 1978/9, pp. 50–1.

Alexander Walker, *National Heroes: British Cinema in the Seventies and Eighties* (London: Harrap, 1985).

anti-terrorist message informs *Who Dares Wins* (Ian Sharp, 1982), a blatantly exploitative action movie glorifying the SAS and celebrating the clinical use of force in disposing of enemies of the state. It was made in the wake of the storming of the Iranian Embassy by the SAS, sanctioned by Mrs Thatcher; *Sight and Sound* detected 'hawkish politics poking unappealingly through a thin cloak of fiction'.[19]

In the last two decades the adventure film has all but disappeared from British cinema – only the evergreen James Bond series keeps the tradition alive. The reasons for its demise are both economic and cultural. In economic terms, the scaling-down of the British film industry and lack of investment since the 1970s makes the production of such films virtually impossible. The vast budgets and production resources required for the international market have put the adventure film beyond the scope of British producers, who have concentrated instead on more modestly budgeted heritage films, realist dramas and romantic comedies. The only exception is the Bond series, backed, as it always was, by American money (MGM/United Artists), but maintaining a British production base (Pinewood Studios) and rooted within a British generic tradition. Following a hiatus in the early 1990s, the Bond films returned to the forefront of popular cinema with *GoldenEye* (Martin Campbell, 1995), *Tomorrow Never Dies* (Roger Spottiswoode, 1997) and *The World Is Not Enough* (Michael Apted, 1999), responding to geopolitical change (the end of the Cold War, Middle Eastern terrorism) and maintaining Bond's status as a contemporary rather than a period hero.

In cultural terms, moreover, the archetypes incarnated in the adventure film no longer possess much currency with cinemagoers. The most successful archetypes in contemporary Hollywood action cinema are not the patriotic, chivalrous gentleman heroes of yesteryear, but the aggressively masculine muscle-men such as Arnold Schwarzenegger and Sylvester Stallone and the cynical, swearing, blue-collar heroes of Mel Gibson and Bruce Willis in the *Lethal Weapon* and *Die Hard* films. The nearest approximation of the old-fashioned adventure hero in recent times has been Indiana Jones, whose adventures are located in a comic-book 1930s past involving lost treasures and hissable Nazi villains, but who exhibits a cynical edge more in tune with the modern era: faced with a sword-wielding warrior, Jones's response is to shoot him. And, moreover, these are American films with an American hero. The age of the *Boy's Own* tradition in British cinema would long seem to have passed.

Notes

1. Marcia Landy, *British Genres: Cinema and Society, 1930–1960*, p. 97.
2. This is illustrated by the brevity of the following bibliography, which includes works that touch only tangentially on the adventure film in its various forms. In a *Screen* article of 1990, Steve Neale called 'for more attention to genres hitherto neglected in genre studies, such as the adventure film, the war film, and the epic' – a call that has been only partially heeded in recent work on British cinema. See Neale, 'Questions of Genre', *Screen* vol. 31 no. 1, Spring 1990, pp. 45–66.
3. I am, of course, aware that by focusing on these lineages I am excluding other types of narrative that could be placed in the adventure category, particularly costume swashbucklers. On the whole, however, and despite the national myth of Robin Hood, the swashbuckler has been less prominent in British cinema than the other lineages identified. The pioneering – and to date still the only – study of the costume swashbuckler is Jeffrey Richards's *Swordsmen of the Screen* (London: Routledge & Kegan Paul, 1977).
4. Alan Williams, 'Is a Radical Genre Criticism Possible?', *Quarterly Review of Film Studies* vol. 9 no. 2 (Spring 1984), p. 124.
5. Michael Paris, *Warrior Nation: Images of War in British Popular Culture, 1850–2000*, p. 69.
6. A partial exception is Tom Ryall, *Alfred Hitchcock and the British Cinema*, pp. 115–40. The literary sources of Hitchcock's thrillers are discussed in Charles Barr, *English Hitchcock* (Moffat, Dumfriesshire: Cameron & Hollis, 1999).
7. See James Chapman, *Licence to Thrill: A Cultural History of the James Bond Films*.
8. Jeffrey Richards, *Visions of Yesterday*, p. xvi.
9. Ibid., p. 133.
10. Karol Kulik, *Alexander Korda: The Man Who Could Work Miracles* (London: W. H. Allen, 1975), p. 214.
11. Paris, *Warrior Nation*, p. 9.
12. The story was remade as *Singlehanded* (Roy Boulting, 1953) – known as *Sailor of the King* in the USA – starring American Jeffrey Hunter and updating the narrative to World War II.
13. Quoted in Jeffrey Richards, *The Age of the Dream Palace: Cinema and Society in Britain, 1930–1939* (London: Routledge & Kegan Paul, 1984), pp. 293–4.
14. Paris, *Warrior Nation*, p. 231.
15. Michael Denning, *Cover Stories: Narrative and Ideology in the British Spy Thriller*, p. 34.
16. See James Chapman, 'Celluloid Shockers', in Jeffrey Richards (ed.), *The Unknown 1930s: An Alternative History*

of the British Cinema 1929–39 (London: I. B. Tauris, 1998), pp. 75–97.

17. Landy, *British Genres*, p. 129.

18. Raymond Durgnat, *A Mirror for England: British Movies from Austerity to Affluence*, p. 151.

19. Quoted in Paris, *Warrior Nation*, p. 251.

Bibliography

Chapman, James, *Licence to Thrill: A Cultural History of the James Bond Films*, 2nd edn (London: I. B. Tauris, 2007).

Denning, Michael, *Cover Stories: Narrative and Ideology in the British Spy Thriller* (London: Routledge & Kegan Paul, 1987).

Durgnat, Raymond, *A Mirror for England: British Movies from Austerity to Affluence* (London: Faber and Faber, 1970).

Harper, Sue, *Picturing the Past: The Rise and Fall of the British Costume Film* (London: BFI, 1994).

Lambert, Gavin, *The Dangerous Edge* (London: Barrie and Jenkins, 1975).

Landy, Marcia, *British Genres: Cinema and Society, 1930–1960* (Princeton, NJ: Princeton University Press, 1991).

Murphy, Robert, *British Cinema and the Second World War* (London: Continuum, 2000).

Paris, Michael, *Warrior Nation: Images of War in British Popular Culture, 1850–2000* (London: Reaktion Books, 2000).

Richards, Jeffrey, *Visions of Yesterday* (London: Routledge & Kegan Paul, 1973).

Richards, Jeffrey, *Films and British National Identity: From Dickens to Dad's Army* (Manchester: Manchester University Press, 1997).

Ryall, Tom, *Alfred Hitchcock and the British Cinema* (London: Croom Helm, 1986; reprinted with a new introduction by Athlone Press, 1996).

Walker, Alexander, *Hollywood, England: The British Film Industry in the Sixties* (London: Michael Joseph, 1974; reprinted by Harrap, 1986).

Walker, Alexander, *National Heroes: British Cinema in the Seventies and Eighties* (London: Harrap, 1985).

11
Traditions of the British Horror Film

IAN CONRICH

In *A Heritage of Horror* (1973), David Pirie wrote that the British horror film is 'the only staple cinematic myth which Britain can properly claim as its own'.[1] He charted an area which until then had been part of a 'lost continent' of British cinema, but while his study remains invaluable it focused mainly on Hammer films.[2] It was not until the late 1990s that a wealth of new studies on the genre began to emerge with an ever-growing understanding of the broad range of British horror film productions.

Trick Films, Transformations and True Crime

As early as 1898 elements of horror were being presented in G.A. Smith's series of trick films. These comic shorts employed double exposure, which enabled the creation of transparent images to represent spirits or ghosts. Labelled the 'spectral effect', it was demonstrated in Smith's 1898 films *The Corsican Brothers*, *Photographing a Ghost* and *Faust and Mephistopheles*.[3] More sophisticated effects enabled film-makers to present detached heads and limbs, for example in James Williamson's *The Clown Barber* (1899) in which a man who has been accidentally decapitated is seen being shaved. 'Transformation narratives' such as *The Vampire* (1913) and *Heba the Snake Woman* (1915), the latter showing, for example, women metamorphosing into snakes, while *The Fakir's Spell* (1914) had a man turning into a gorilla.

Silent film productions based on true crimes foregrounded violence and employed the 'whodunit' narratives developed in popular detective dramas. The murder of Maria Marten in 1827 was a source for three

early films (in 1908, 1913 and 1923), and *In the Grip of Iron*, based on the Paris Strangler, was filmed in 1913 and 1920.

Horror Films and Horror Film Censorship, 1930–50

Tod Slaughter is one of the key figures of British horror film before 1950. A theatre actor, he specialised in stage productions of familiar horror and crime dramas, which were known as 'Strong Meat' melodramas. Film versions, most of them directed by George King, were made of a number of his most memorable productions including: *Maria Marten, or The Murder in the Red Barn* (1935), *Sweeney Todd, the Demon Barber of Fleet Street* (1936), *The Face at the Window* (1939) and *The Curse of the Wraydons* (1946).

Slaughter's films deal with gruesome subjects. *The Crimes of Stephen Hawke* (1936), for instance, features a notorious murderer known as 'The Spine Breaker', who at the beginning of the film bends the back of an inquisitive boy over his knee and breaks his spine. One of the few Slaughter films that appears to have been censored after it was made was *The Greed of William Hart* (1948), where the grave-robbers Burke and Hare had to be fictionalised as Moore and Hart.[4] Deriving from the popular forms of Victorian theatre, the films were marked by sensationalism, a heightened theatricality, and Slaughter's larger-than-life villains. By mixing elements of sadism and Grand Guignol with pantomime, the films gave 'a none-too-subtle leering wink at the audience, letting the viewer in on the fact that no one concerned considered this anything but good fun'.[5]

The Ghoul (T. Hayes Hunter, 1933)

The Ghoul is a horror film for non-believers: its many mysteries, in the fog-free light of day, are revealed to be sleights of hand, and merely the stratagems of a reassuringly commonplace criminality. The activation and maintenance of old myths by those with a vested interest in deceiving others might be said to constitute a sceptic's strain in mysteries and thrillers but, with a startling level of sophistication, *The Ghoul's coup de théâtre* suggests even more daring lessons for the gullible. Ralph Richardson's country parson is a crook, distracting the others (and the viewers) with his singsong tones and daft otherworldliness, and the resurrection of Karloff's Professor Morlant is nothing of the sort – merely an awakening from a coma. Ancient curses and life-giving forces emanating from the other side – in other contexts, the very substance of Christianity – are a powerful opiate when utilised by those seeking to get their hands on the Egyptian loot. And the film revels in such pseudo-miracles: the body arises and bursts out its tomb in one of the most arresting sequences of any horror film of the 1930s, and the false god worshipped by the mad Morlant finally does (seemingly) come to life. Such jaw-dropping moments point to the distinguished pedigree of *The Ghoul*: US-born director T. Hayes Hunter combines Universal-style horror (Karloff as the eponymous monster makes just such an inescapable, and welcome, connection), an English eccentricity of milieu and sensibility (the setting of an old dark house on the Yorkshire moors), and European, specifically Expressionist, stylisation (cinematography and art direction were in the hands of master German émigrés Günther Krampf and Alfred Junge).

Another set of questionable beliefs – in the alluring/barbaric otherness of the uncivilised races, continually voiced by a wide-eyed and clearly aroused

The first film to receive an 'H' rating: *The Ghoul*

spinster – masks the more mundane goal of cheating gullible westerners of their cash. Such a narrative twist is much more edifying than the eroticisation/demonisation/criminalisation of the dark-skinned other intruding in polite society, apparent in films such as *The Devil Rides Out* (1968) and *The Oblong Box* (1969), where the strong implication is that Satanism arises from the colonial masters having 'gone native'.

So when the smoke and mirrors of *The Ghoul* glitter and dazzle (only now properly apparent in the recent restoration of the film), it is more than just aestheticisation. The visual quality of the film weaves the spell upon which the film's entire conceit is founded.

(Benjamin Halligan)

FURTHER READING

James Chapman, 'Celluloid Shockers', in Jeffrey Richards (ed.), *The Unknown 1930s: An Alternative History of the British Cinema 1929–39* (London: I. B Tauris, 1998).

Ian Conrich, 'Horrific Films and 1930s British Cinema', in Steve Chibnall and Julian Petley (eds), *British Horror Cinema* (London: Routledge, 2002), pp. 58–70.

The British Board of Film Censors (BBFC) was more critical of the influx of American horror films that began in 1931 with Universal's *Dracula* and *Frankenstein*. In January 1933 it added an 'H' classification to the 'U' and 'A' certificates. Purely advisory and not yet a form of certification, the 'H' stood for 'horrific', and covered non-horror films such as Abel Gance's 1938 anti-war film *J'Accuse* and the 1945 United Nations War Crimes Film as well as the American horror film.

The first British film to receive an 'H' rating was *The Ghoul* (1933), starring Boris Karloff; *The Tell-Tale Heart* (1934) and *The Man Who Changed His Mind* (1936, also starring Karloff) were similarly rated. An 'H' rating created immediate difficulties for a film: some cinemas and local councils refused to exhibit any movie with this rating. *The Ghoul's* distributors took care to reassure exhibitors about its content, declaring in the publicity booklet that, 'while perhaps, it is not exactly the type of film which a very sensitive person should see, it most decidedly is not on the horrific plane of other mystery thrillers'.

An official BBFC 'H' certificate (the first official 'adults only' film certificate) was introduced in June 1937. The 1939 film *Dark Eyes of London*, with Bela Lugosi, was the first British film to receive the certificate, but in 1940 horror films came under renewed criticism. It was argued that 'there was enough horrifying action in the world today without having to pay to see it at the cinema'.[6] The BBFC banned all 'H' films in 1942, and over the next three years twenty-three films were denied certificates. In January 1951 the 'H' certificate was subsumed into the newly created 'X'.

Even before the war, problems with censorship meant that film-makers tended to import horror into comedies and thrillers rather than attempting to make outright horror films. In comedy-horror films actors such as Will Hay, Arthur Askey, Arthur Lucan or Herbert Mundin, would find themselves at a train station, an old house, a lighthouse or an inn, which would then be revealed to be haunted by real or fake ghosts. By the film's conclusion the comedian would have solved a mystery and uncovered a group of criminals who had been using the haunting as a cover for their fiendish activities. These films – *What a Night!* (1931), *Immediate Possession* (1931), *Forging Ahead* (1933), *Ask a Policeman* (1939) and *Old Mother Riley's Ghosts* (1941) – are similar to the American films *The Cat and the Canary* (1939), *The Ghost Breakers* (1940), *Ghosts on the Loose* (1943) and *Ghost Catchers* (1944), though the American films are often recognised as horror films, while their British equivalents are regarded as comedies.

Psychopaths and murderers featured in a number of gruesome thrillers, such as *Condemned to Death* (1932), *The Frightened Lady* (1932 and 1940) and *Sabotage* (1936). The production of these films increased during and just after the war, with films such as *Gaslight* (1940), *Tower of Terror* (1941), *Wanted for Murder* (1946), *Daughter of Darkness* (1948) and *Obsession* (1949) reflecting a British fascination with morbidity at a time of social and economic instability. A possible comparison can be made between these films and the brooding films noirs that were being simultaneously produced by Hollywood. *The Night Has Eyes* (1942) is a notable example of this type of film. It featured murders on the Yorkshire moors, death by quicksand and James Mason as a reclusive composer who could be a killer. The film's British pressbook declared, 'Death strikes at full moon

as the mad killer seeks his victims in the lone house on the moors.'

Another kind of horror can be seen in films built around séances and the role of clairvoyants. The contacting of spirits was presented in a number of films, including *At the Villa Rose* (1930 and 1939), *The Barton Mystery* (1930), *The Clairvoyant* (1935) and *Latin Quarter* (1945). *Spellbound* (1941) and *Things Happen at Night* (1948) both featured evil spirits and possession. The former film was temporarily banned by the BBFC and was only passed once a foreword had been provided by the Spiritualist Church. The period between 1944 and 1946 saw the production of two of the most famous British pre-Hammer horror films *Halfway House* (1944) and, in particular, *Dead of Night* (1945). As Robert Murphy puts it, with death part of everyday life during World War II, 'it is not surprising that there should have been an upsurge of interest in spiritualism and the supernatural'.[7]

Hammer Horrors

In 1935, Enrique Carreras and Will Hinds (stage name, Will Hammer) formed the distribution company Exclusive Films. Their sons, James Carreras and Anthony Hinds, joined later and in 1947, Hammer, a small independent production company, was formed.[8] The company's identity was strengthened by the decision to buy a country house to act as its own studio. The building and its surrounding land served to provide a multitude of sets and consequently reduced production costs.

Many of the early productions were adaptations of radio plays such as *Dick Barton Special Agent* (1948), *Celia* (1949) and *Meet Simon Cherry* (1950) or genre films patterned on Hollywood successes. In 1951, Hammer moved to a large Gothic house at Bray. It was from here that their most famous horror films were produced.

The popular reaction to their science-fiction films, *The Quatermass Experiment* (1955) and *X The Unknown* (1956), led Hammer to produce the first of their horror films. *The Curse of Frankenstein* (1957) was even more profitable; made for approximately £65,000, it grossed around £300,000 in Britain, £500,000 in Japan and £1 million in America.[9] Previous British horror films had relied on shadows, mysteries, suspense, spectral figures and the viewer's imagination. Hammer's films, generally made in colour, used excess, explicitness, sensuality and violence. Derek Hill's attack on the new British horror films, in 1958, was primarily aimed

Characteristics and Tendencies of the British Horror Film

In general British horror eschews apocalypticism – a tendency mostly manifest elsewhere, in Cold War yarns and science-fiction thrillers. The supernatural assaults minds and moral fibre, not cityscapes or civil systems of law and order. The threat of the supernatural, therefore, is more theological than ideological; it is the soul, not the things under the sun, which is endangered. And even British beasts tend to ravish rather than eviscerate, preying on invisible and moral qualities (virginity, sometimes coupled with a nobility of birth – the 'chosen one' still in an innocent, even newborn, state) as much as flesh and blood. And yet the arsenals of Christian defence that come so readily to hand in the combat that ensues are rarely endowed with any particularly spiritual quality. Here, Bibles are for lobbing rather than consulting, crucifixes for wielding (even melting down into bullets and firing) rather than as the loci of meditation and prayer. The foot soldiers in the fight against evil incarnate seem to lack piety, and the films often haphazardly mix Roman Catholic and Anglican imagery and tropes. In fact, the religious props and concerns of the British horror need to be considered as little more than set dressing and narrative decoration. The films themselves help to facilitate such a reading; the hectoring lectures on the corporeality of evil in *The Devil Rides Out* are rapidly dramatised and once the devil himself materialises, in the guise of the Goat of Mendes, doctrinal matters are swiftly put to one side.

The spread of the horror itself remains confined to its immediate environs, with the unfortunate innocents drawn, mostly unwittingly, into the coven as in: *The Wicker Man* (1973), *Vampyres* (1974), *House of Whipcord* (1974), *Black Candles* (1982), *Darklands* (1997); the Satanic or deviant circle as in: *Night of the Eagle* (1962), *Scars of Dracula* (1970), *Don't Look Now* (1973), *The Last Great Wilderness* (2002); the beast's nest as in: *The Horror of Frankenstein* (1970), *Tower of Evil* (1972), *Death Line* (1972), *Alien* (1979), *Inseminoid* (1981), *The Lair of the White Worm* (1988), *The Descent* (2005); or away from the beaten track as in: *Trog* (1970), *And Soon the Darkness* (1970), *Lighthouse* (2000). There they disappear, die, are rendered insane, or are transformed into abominations. Whereas North American and Italian horror films have mounted plagues and threatened to lay waste to swathes of civilisation, the British horror prefers to imperil the individual, or assail the small group now surrounded by the unfamiliar.

The polity of the hidden cult or secret societies – conspiratorial whispers and unusual goings-on, subtexts and intimations – is effectively the terrain that stretches from the world of Miss Marple to that of Harold Pinter. In all such outwardly quiet comings and goings are the dark thoughts behind the jovial exterior, the power struggle for family wealth or sexual access, the sham respectability of the middle-class milieu, the malevolent deployment of bread knives and rat poison, and so forth. It is the pervasiveness of such everyday settings that is apparent when considering a further characteristic of British horror: with few exceptions, events impact less on exuberant teenagers, transgressing the norm for kicks, more on civil servants, scientists, politicians, policemen and fire-fighters, builders and caretakers, who have to work together to overcome the threat.

At the 'high-brow' pole of British horror – *Dead of Night* (1945), *The Innocents* (1961), *Night Must Fall* (1964), *Repulsion* (1965), *Blue Blood* (1973), *Afraid of the Dark* (1991) – it is the psychological realisation of horror that is predominant, expressing an unease that, at its most progressive, offers the potential to spread length-wise, undermining the class-derived notion of social respectability. At its least progressive, such unease can be predicated from a position of a reflex distrust of the other, engendering racist (the subgenre of murderous yokel inbreeds, and Celtic pagan-barbarism), quasi-homophobic and objectifying-misogynist (virtually institutionalised in horror film as a whole) tendencies.

'Low-brow' British horror offers a less problematic dynamic: the evil personified principally in the figures of Count Dracula, variants on Frankenstein's monster, and vampires, is awakened, invoked or loosed, and runs riot, usually in the surrounding countryside. Yet if this populist horror starts at one remove from contemporary, recognisable society (the castle in the woods, the unregulated laboratory, the distant and often 'Continental European' past), a connection with the present is soon made. Concomitant with the unleashing of evil is an unleashing of passions, and the dashing of inhibitions. The Dracula, Frankenstein and vampire cycles of British horror, from the moment of their inception in the mid-1950s, are characteristically orgasmic: the deep breathing of imperilled women, the body, often exposed, offered in the surrendering to the 'dark side', the instincts of the flesh gaining the upper hand over the council of the mind. And such *jouissance* remains, tantalisingly, in the domain of evil.

Thus horror interlocks with sex, synchronised at the moments of their climax and release; sex is not the fall, to be puritanically (and pruriently) revenged in many North American horror films, particularly of the 1970s. Rather, it is the recognisably human element in an otherwise fallen world. The films display a fascination with sex, which dovetails with a vantage point of moral (if not visual) detachment from this subject matter. Such a position on sexuality could only exist within a recreated Victorian constellation – the predominant house style of Hammer during its 1960s heyday, in which the identity of British horror was forged. But even here a hypocrite's days are inevitably numbered; the rapidly approaching permissive age would reveal the limitations of this moral code, to the extent that the horror film would not survive in the 'low-brow' form in which it had developed.

(Benjamin Halligan)

at this switch to a more visceral approach: 'instead of attempting mood, tension or shock, the new Frankenstein productions rely almost entirely on a percentage of shots of repugnant clinical detail. There is little to frighten . . . but plenty to disgust.'[10] Further attacks on the early Hammer horrors included a call for an 'SO', 'Sadists Only' certificate.[11]

In 1931, Hollywood had adapted Mary Shelley's *Frankenstein*, Bram Stoker's *Dracula* and Robert Louis Stevenson's *The Strange Case of Dr Jekyll and Mr Hyde*. But the success of *The Curse of Frankenstein* (1957) led to Hammer acquiring from Universal the rights to their Gothic horror films. According to Pirie, 'even Universal had realised by this time that England was reclaiming its own myths'.[12] *Dracula* was Hammer's second horror production, released in 1958; *The Mummy* (1959), the Jekyll and Hyde story *The Ugly Duckling* (1959) and *The Curse of the Werewolf* (1961) followed. Hammer was to produce a further six Frankenstein films, six Dracula and nine vampire films, three Mummy films and two more Dr Jekyll and Mr Hyde films.

Most of Hammer's Gothic horrors operated within strong moral frameworks depicting the struggle between the forces of good and evil, the spirit and the flesh, science and superstition and the familiar and the unknown. Carnal desire is presented as dangerous; characters, in particular women, are susceptible to its power and therefore need to be contained. It is only with the destruction of monstrous or deviant sexuality that social order and normality can be reinstated.

Hammer was also responsible for a series of psychological thrillers. These 'invisible' Hammer horrors are either ignored in the stampede to examine the monster horror films, or, as in Denis Gifford's *The British Film Catalogue*, listed as crime and not horror films. The first such film, *Taste of Fear* (1961), scripted by Jimmy Sangster, was inspired by the recently released *Psycho* (1960). Of the ten films that followed, eight – *Maniac* (1962), *Paranoiac* (1963), *Nightmare* (1963), *Hysteria* (1965), *The Nanny* (1965), *The Anniversary* (1967), *Crescendo* (1969) and *Fear in the Night* (1972) – were scripted by Sangster; *Fanatic* (1965), was scripted by Richard Matheson and *Straight on till Morning* (1972) by Michael Peacock.

In these films an individual, generally female, is trapped in a large, isolated house. Here she is tormented and scared by scheming relatives or associates, who require her to be punished, destroyed or made to appear deranged. The narrative is structured upon a systematic series of persecutions and night-time disturbances and occasionally broken by an hallucination or nightmare sequence. Plot twists, a choice of suspects and false moments of terror, are closer to the 'whodunit' narratives of the early British horror films than to the explicitness of Hammer's recognised horrors.

The Proliferation of the Horror Film

The box-office response to *The Curse of Frankenstein* inspired many other British production companies to produce horror films.[13] Amicus, managed by the Americans Milton Subotsky and Max Rosenberg, employed an omnibus format similar to that of *Dead of Night* in such films as *Torture Garden* (1967), *Dr Terror's House of Horrors* (1965), *The House That Dripped Blood* (1970), *Asylum* (1972), *Tales from the Crypt* (1972), *The Vault of Horror* (1973), *From beyond the Grave* (1974) and *The Monster Club* (1980). In these films individuals find themselves gathered together in a group (in catacombs, a railway carriage, a fairground sideshow or a basement room), where they are made to listen to or recount unusual stories. Alternatively, a character enters somewhere (a house, club or antique shop) and themselves sets off an episode. The films resemble the style of the American EC comics (from which *Tales from the Crypt* and *The Vault of Horror* took their names) and the stories frequently conclude with an ironic twist, or a deliberately gory or shocking image.

The episodic structure can also be observed in the Vincent Price 'revenge-with-a-theme' horror films of the early 70s – American International's *The Abominable Dr Phibes* (1971) and *Dr Phibes Rises Again* (1972) and Cineman's *Theatre of Blood* (1973) – establish a link with the past where Price's theatrical performances, the sardonic humour and the interest in macabre methods of death are reminiscent of the Tod Slaughter films of the 30s and 40s.

Anglo-Amalgamated is most famous for its 'Sadean' trilogy – *Horrors of the Black Museum* and *Circus of Horrors*, both produced by Herman Cohen in 1959, and Michael Powell's *Peeping Tom* (1960). Their treatment as a trilogy and the concentration on the hysterial reaction to *Peeping Tom*, however, is misleading.[14] Other Anglo-Amalgamated films such as *Cat Girl* (1957) and *Konga* (1961) and the Herman Cohen productions *Berserk!* (1967), *Trog* (1970) and *Craze* (1973) have been overlooked, as has the fact that *Circus of Horrors* was part of a larger group of British horror films that featured operations, surgery and biological experimentation. Derek Hill described the films as being part of a 'clinical cult', though the term 'surgical horrors' is preferable.[15] *Circus of Horrors* borrowed both Anton Diffring and his role as a crazed surgeon from Hammer's *The Man Who Could Cheat Death*, made the previous year. It told the story of a sadistic plastic surgeon who assembles around him in his circus disfigured and ugly women upon whom he operates. Dramatic deaths are arranged for those women who exhaust his interest. The idea of a circus psychopath and spectacular deaths as part of the performances was re-used by Herman Cohen for *Berserk!*

Another surgical horror film, *Corridors of Blood* (1958), made by Producers Associates, is even more sadistic than *Circus of Horrors*. A surgeon, played by Boris Karloff, who works quickly and without anaesthetic, only succeeds in horribly mutilating his patients. Filmed back-to-back with another Karloff film, *Grip of the Strangler*, the gory and, for some, unpalatable proceedings were an indication of the future form of exploitation. Titan's *Corruption* (1968) added elements of Jack the Ripper, with the plastic surgeon played by

Peter Cushing displaying a compulsion to mutilate and decapitate women. Its gratuitous violence, graphic surgery and nudity, made it unpalatable to most critics, yet it represents an important strand. Director Robert Hartford-Davis and screenwriters Derek and Donald Ford had acquired their experience making British sexploitation films, and the lurid mix of sex and violence was to dominate the next decade.

Flesh Films and the Dark Decades

Between 1967 and 1974, the relaxation of censorship and the import of more explicit foreign films led to an increasing reliance on nudity and graphic violence in British horror productions.[16] Individuals who had previously worked on sexploitation films – such as Pete Walker, Norman J. Warren and Antony Balch – switched to horror and brought with them a willingness to foreground sensational elements.

The film producer and distributor Tony Tenser is representative of the way elements of the British sex film permeated British horror. His first company, Compton-Cameo, was formed with Michael Klinger, who later produced the Robin Askwith *Confessions* series of sex comedies. Compton-Cameo distributed early sexploitation films and produced their own examples such as *Saturday Night Out* and *The Yellow Teddybears*, both in 1963. Their first horror film, *The Black Torment* (1964), generated a sufficient financial return for Compton to invest in Roman Polanski's *Repulsion* (1965) and *Cul-de-Sac* (1966). In 1967, Klinger and Tenser parted and Tenser formed a new company, Tigon.

Tigon's biggest critical success was *Witchfinder General* (1968), directed by the twenty-four-year-old Michael Reeves, who died of a sleeping-pill overdose soon after finishing the film. The company attempted to exploit its rustic horror theme with the more macabre and gruesome *Blood on Satan's Claw* (1970). But Tigon seemed torn between the market demand for lurid pornographic films and its desire to make costume horrors such as *The Blood Beast Terror* (1967) and *The Creeping Flesh* (1972). In 1972 Tenser sold Tigon, 'tiring of the explicit violence he was having to inject into his films'.[17]

Reeves's first film for Tigon, *The Sorcerers* (1967), had shown two old people attempting to control, manipulate and experience the vibrant sensations of youth. Similar themes are explored in Pete Walker's nihilistic horrors in which youth's hedonism is repressed. Individuals are seized, punished and destroyed by ascetic

Individuals are seized, punished and destroyed by ascetic elders: *House of Whipcord* (Pete Walker, 1974)

elders apparently jealous of the sensation-based experiences of a counter-culture. Institutions such as law and order (*House of Whipcord*), the church (*House of Mortal Sin*) and the family (*Frightmare*, 1974) are exposed as corrupt. David Sanjek points out that similar 'anti-establishment paranoid narratives' can be observed in *Scream and Scream Again* (1969) and *The Wicker Man*.[18]

Hammer itself had moved from Bray to the confines of Elstree Studios in 1966. By 1968, when the company received the Queen's Award for Industry, it had already begun to decline. Required to transgress further in order to compete, Hammer produced two lesbian-vampire films, *The Vampire Lovers* (1970), *Lust for a Vampire* (1970) and *Twins of Evil* (1971), which all presented scenes of soft-core pornography. Vampirism was combined with martial arts in *The Legend of the 7 Golden Vampires* (1973); *Captain Kronos – Vampire Hunter* (1972) mixed vampirism with elements of the adventure film; Dracula, meanwhile, was injected with new blood to increase his commercial viability. Fresh methods by which he could be destroyed were introduced, such as lightning and hawthorn bushes, and the stories were modernised – *Dracula AD 1972* (1972), originally titled *Dracula Chelsea '72*, placed him among the youth of Swinging London.

The success of the American trio of demon films, *Rosemary's Baby* (1968), *The Exorcist* (1973) and *The Omen* (1976), led to a spate of films featuring satanism, demonic children and the occult. Most British imitations, such as *I Don't Want to Be Born* (1975), *Satan's Slave* (1976) and *The Godsend* (1980), were small independent productions. Hammer's *To the Devil a Daughter* (1976) was a European co-production, employing a

large budget and American stars, but it was poorly received and Hammer, sharing in the general decline of the British film industry, gave up feature production.

The new wave of American horror films, which emerged between the late 70s and mid-80s, overshadowed British horrors. The advances made in special effects created a largely American subgenre of horror films fascinated with exploding, bleeding and mutating bodies. British attempts to imitate these films failed both commercially and critically. *Dream Demon* (1988), *Beyond Bedlam* (1994) and *Funny Man* (1994), which patterned themselves on the *Nightmare on Elm Street* series, appeared clumsy and derivative.

Americanised British horror films such as *Hellraiser* (1987) and *Hardware* (1990) foregrounded spectacle and action sequences. They reduced the narrative to a secondary role and consciously opposed the theatrical and literary tradition of British cinema, epitomised by *Dracula* (1979), *The Awakening* (1980), *The Bride* (1985), *The Monk* (1991) and *Mary Shelley's Frankenstein* (1994). Gothic literary adaptations such as *The Company of Wolves* (1984) and *Shallow Grave* (1994) were more interesting and better received. Neither film required a large budget and both drew strongly on British culture rather than imitating the style of the American horrors.

Small-budget Exploitation

British horror film production did not cease after the mid-70s, but many of these 'Lost Continent' films are submerged at a depth at which critics have assumed that nothing can exist. Andrew Higson, for instance, sees a termination of production after 1980: 'This was the end of the low-budget British genre film, one of those cinematic forms that proved to be no longer commercially viable.'[19] On the contrary, the dramatic growth in the home-video market since the early 80s has helped support the production of a number of small-budget, exploitation, British horror films. *Screamtime* (1983), *Don't Open till Christmas* (1984), *Rawhead Rex* (1986), *Bloody New Year* (1987), *Goodnight, God Bless* (1987), *Hand of Death Part 25* (1988), *I Bought a Vampire Motorcycle* (1989), *Living Doll* (1989), *Edge of Sanity* (1989), *Cold Light of Day* (1990) and *Revenge of Billy the Kid* (1991) may have experienced limited theatrical exhibition, but for such cult films, sale to a video distributor is generally its main source of income.

Most of these films are part of a counter-cinema which is actively transgressive, challenging standards of cultural acceptability and definitions of good taste, what

The Last Great Wilderness (David Mackenzie, 2002)

At first sight, *The Last Great Wilderness* incorporates elements of *The Wicker Man* into a contemporary variant of *The Old Dark House* (1932). Unlike Julian Richards's *Darklands* (1997), which transplanted *The Wicker Man*'s pagan cult to Wales and improbably linked it with Welsh nationalism, *The Last Great Wilderness* does without borrowed spectacles and set pieces. Rather, the film retains a modest originality throughout. The substance of the horror is predicated on the idea of isolation: the introspective and Armani-clad protagonist Charlie (Alastair Mackenzie), whose life has evidently fallen apart around him, is caught between the vastness of the wintry Scottish highlands and the thrown-together cranks and misfits who inhabit a remote retreat house. As in *The Wicker Man*, where Paul Giovanni integrates the music and songs of the Summerisle pagans into his score, David Mackenzie relies on Scottish C86 stalwarts the Pastels to provide the lilting pop and folktronica soundtrack, and to turn up at the retreat house to play for the final night drag party.

Charlie's unease at his inhospitable and spooky surroundings gradually defuses his flailing attempts to regain control of his life; we soon discover he is on his way to avenge the pop star who has cuckolded him. The pop star's hit song, a catalogue of seedy metaphors and euphemisms about his seduction of Charlie's wife (delivered in a lazy and satiated drawl by Jarvis Cocker) taunts Charlie, and evidences the torture that life has dished out to this otherwise amicable young professional, and the quiet bloodlust that now propels him to this remote corner of Scotland. In these respects, the horror, and torture, is more psychological than visceral; indeed, the crucifixion, castration and blinding of Charlie's accidental travelling companion at the film's close lacks the dramatic intensity deftly established elsewhere in the film.

A rich ambience and atmosphere, captured with a Dogme 95-type intimacy, is established for the Moor Lodge Wilderness Retreat setting ('Normal rules don't apply around here – especially in Winter'; the house is signposted 'Leave your troubles behind'). The film drops numerous clues as to the nature of this rundown abode: a former or still active hotel; a free-love commune; a hospice; the remnant or an outpost of a

The road of life: Alastair Mackenzie and Jonny Phillips in the *The Last Great Wilderness*

Reichian treatment centre (an Orgone Accumulator is seen at one point with anti-fascist graffiti scrawled on the side, bringing to mind the radical political agendas associated with Reich in the late 1960s); a 'Stone Tape' psychic hotspot; a clinic or observational laboratory; a cultish, neo-pagan secret society; and a mad professor–voyeur's lair, with the professor/landlord/guru (David Hayman) himself reminiscent of R. D. Laing. This accumulation of tantalising red herrings works to obscure the way in which the house is little more than the proverbial haunted house, lost deep in the forest, and the protagonist the quintessential fish out of water.

While the film is firmly grounded in the milieu of the Celtic fringe, it does not rustle up an angry mob of murderous yokels along *Wicker Man* or *Straw Dogs* lines; it is the outsiders – including Charlie – who bring murder and mayhem in their wake. Rather, all the indigenous elements (people, ghosts and places) are eminently understanding; and Charlie, after a bout of emotional love-making, and the dispatch of hitmen, does leave with his troubles now behind. Despite appearances (and genre expectations) to the contrary, this old dark house with its ragtag commune of outcasts comes to be a safer, and more welcoming, proposition than the unforgiving modern world; ghosts and the mentally unstable infinitely preferable to homophobes and hired heavies. (Benjamin Halligan)

FURTHER READING

Andy Richards, 'The Last Great Wilderness', *Sight and Sound*, June 2003, p. 49.

Jonathan Romney, 'The Last Great Wilderness', *Independent on Sunday*, 18 May 2003.

Jeffrey Sconce calls paracinema 'a most elastic textual category' which would include 'Japanese monster movies, beach-party musicals, and just about every other historical manifestation of exploitation cinema from juvenile delinquency documentaries to soft-core pornography'.[20]

The more aggressive and excessive forms of British exploitation, in particular those films that emerged in the early 70s, have been deemed lacking in value and consequently banished from the critical agenda. In comparison to the popularisation of Hammer, whose horror films have gradually been reclassified as worthy and acceptable, sensational films such as *The Beast in the Cellar* (1970), *Horror Hospital* (1973), *The Mutations* (1973), *Scream and Die* (1973), *Symptoms* (1974), *The Beast Must Die* (1974), *Exposé* (1975) and *Killer's Moon* (1978) still await serious examination.

Postscript

Since this article was written in 1996 there has been a renaissance of the British horror film, which has seen traditional generic forms enlivened by innovative interpretations, particularly in *My Little Eye* (2002), *28 Days Later* (2002), *Shaun of the Dead* (2004), *Creep* (2004) and *The Descent* (2004), films which have attracted international commercial and critical attention. *Shaun of the Dead* and *28 Days Later* form part of a post-millennial revival of zombie movies, which includes Paul Anderson's *Resident Evil* (2002) and *Resident Evil: Apocalypse* (2004), and George Romero's *Land of the Dead* (2005). The zombie film (with the notable exception of John Gilling's *The Plague of Zombies* in 1966) has been a subgenre rarely explored by British cinema. Yet these new films were able to compete in the US market by paying homage to American horror classics such as Romero's *Dawn of the Dead* (1978) while asserting a strong British identity. Both *28 Days Later* and *Shaun of the Dead* offer London-centred narratives that effectively utilise the urban and suburban spaces of the metropolis, the former capturing images of Central London in scenes of apocalyptic abandonment that more than match those of *Dawn of the Dead*'s deserted Pittsburgh. *Shaun of the Dead*, shot in and around London's Crouch End, manages to unite the ethos of Ealing comedy with the horror of Romero's *Night of the Living Dead* (1968).

The film-makers involved in this renaissance demonstrate an expert knowledge of American horror traditions, but they also excel in their deployment of British locations as a site for horror. In *Creep*, Christopher Smith makes as good use of the claustrophobic tunnels of the London underground system as had Gary Sherman in his cult classic *Death Line* (1972). In *Dog Soldiers* (2002), where British soldiers find themselves pitted against vengeful werewolves, Neil Marshall makes the open wilderness of the Scottish Highlands eerily atmospheric. *The Descent* (2005), Marshall's impressive follow-up, is ostensibly set in the American Appalachian Mountains, but that too was shot in Scotland. Like *Creep* with its intrepid heroine trapped underneath London, *The Descent* with its all-female cast, lost in an unexplored cave system, demonstrates the effectiveness of the modern slasher film in creating claustrophobia and unease when it is able to move beyond the formulaic nature of the narrative. Genres appear in cycles and with the British horror film so much a part of its national cinema it was perhaps only a matter of time before it would awaken from its slumber.

Notes

1. David Pirie, *A Heritage of Horror: The English Gothic Cinema 1946–1972*, p. 9. An updated and expanded edition, *A New Heritage of Horror: The English Gothic Cinema*, was published in 2007.
2. See Julian Petley, 'The Lost Continent', pp. 98–119.
3. Rachael Low and Roger Manvell, *The History of the British Film 1896–1906* (London: George Allen & Unwin, 1948), pp. 44–5.
4. Denis Gifford, *A Pictorial History of Horror Movies*, p. 204.
5. Ken Hanke, 'Tod Slaughter', *Films in Review* vol. 8 no. 4, April 1987, p. 207.
6. *Today's Cinema*, 29 May 1940, p. 16.
7. See Robert Murphy, *Realism and Tinsel: Cinema and Society in Britain 1939–49* (London: Routledge, 1992), pp. 168–9.
8. A film production company, Hammer Productions Ltd, had been registered in November 1934. Its chairman was Will Hinds and it produced four films, *The Public Life of Henry the Ninth* (1935), *The Mystery of the Marie Celeste* (1935), *The Song of Freedom* (1936) and *Sporting Love* (1937).
9. Robert Murphy, *Sixties British Cinema*, p. 162.
10. Derek Hill, 'The Face of Horror', *Sight and Sound*, Winter 1958–9, p. 9.
11. Pirie, *A Heritage of Horror*, p. 99.
12. Ibid., p. 43.
13. Tyburn, an important British company, produced *Persecution* (1974), *The Ghoul* (1974) and *Legend of the Werewolf* (1975); the team of Robert S. Baker and Monty Berman produced *Blood of the Vampire* (1958), *Jack the Ripper* (1958) and *The Flesh and the Fiends* (1959).

14. Derek Hill considered that 'the only really satisfactory way to dispose of *Peeping Tom* would be to shovel it up and flush it swiftly down the nearest sewer'. *Tribune*, 29 April 1960, quoted by Ian Christie, 'Criticism: The Scandal of *Peeping Tom*', in Ian Christie (ed.), *Powell, Pressburger and Others* (London: BFI, 1978), p. 54.

15. Hill, 'The Face of Horror', p. 9.

16. One useful text that has attempted an examination of this period is David Sanjek, 'Twilight of the Monsters: The English Horror Film 1968–1975', pp. 195–209.

17. Mike Wathen, 'For Adults Only! Home-Grown British Crud, 1954–1972', in Stefan Jaworzyn (ed.), *Shock Xpress 2* (London: Titan, 1994), p. 102. See also David McGillivray, *Doing Rude Things: The History of the British Sex Film 1957–1981* (London: Sun Tavern Fields, 1992), p. 130.

18. Sanjek, 'Twilight of the Monsters', p. 197. For a discussion of Pete Walker, see McGillivray, *Doing Rude Things*, pp. 58–65; and Alan Jones, 'House of the Long Shadows – The Terror Film Career of Pete Walker', *Starburst* no. 57, May 1983, pp. 16–20; and Steve Chibnall, *Making Mischief: The Cult Films of Pete Walker*.

19. Andrew Higson, 'A Diversity of Film Practices: Renewing British Cinema in the 1970s', in Bart Moore-Gilbert (ed.), *The Arts in the 1970s: Cultural Closure* (London: Routledge, 1994), p. 224.

20. Jeffrey Sconce, ' "Trashing" the Academy: Taste, Excess, and an Emerging Politics of Cinematic Style', *Screen* vol. 39 no. 4, Winter 1995, p. 372.

Bibliography

Bryce, Allan (ed.), *Amicus: The Studio That Dripped Blood* (Liskeard, Cornwall: Stray Cat Publishing, 2000).

Chibnall, Steve, *Making Mischief: The Cult Films of Pete Walker* (Guildford: FAB Press, 1998).

Chibnall, Steve and Petley, Julian (eds), *British Horror Cinema* (London: Routledge, 2001).

Conrich, Ian, 'The Contemporary British Horror Film: Observations on Marketing, Distribution and Exhibition', in Harvey Fenton (ed.), *Flesh and Blood. Book One* (Guildford: FAB Press, 1998).

Eyles, Allen, Adkinson, Robert and Fry, Nicholas (eds), *The House of Horror: The Complete Story of Hammer Films* (London: Lorrimer, 1984).

Gifford, Denis, *A Pictorial History of Horror Movies* (London: Hamlyn, 1974).

Hamilton, John, *Beasts in the Cellar: The Exploitation Career of Tony Tenser* (Guildford: FAB Press, 2005).

Hutchings, Peter, *Hammer and Beyond: The British Horror Film* (Manchester: Manchester University Press, 1993).

Larson, Randall D., *Music from the House of Hammer: Music in the Hammer Horror Films 1950–1980* (Lanham, MD: Scarecrow, 1996).

Meikle, Denis, *A History of Horrors: The Rise and Fall of the House of Hammer* (Lanham, MD: Scarecrow, 1996).

Murphy, Robert, *Sixties British Cinema* (London: BFI, 1992).

Petley, Julian, 'The Lost Continent', in Charles Barr (ed.), *All Our Yesterdays: 90 Years of British Cinema* (London: BFI, 1986).

Pirie, David, *A Heritage of Horror: The English Gothic Cinema 1946–1972* (London: Gordon Fraser, 1973).

Pirie, David, *A New Heritage of Horror: The English Gothic Cinema* (London: I. B. Tauris, 2007).

Sanjek, David, 'Twilight of the Monsters: The English Horror Film 1968–1975', in Wheeler Winston Dixon (ed.), *Re-Viewing British Cinema, 1900–1992: Essays and Interviews* (New York: State University of New York Press, 1994).

Smith, Gary Allen, *Uneasy Dreams: The Golden Age of British Horror Films, 1956–1976* (Jefferson, NC: McFarland, 1999).

12
Traditions of British Comedy

RICHARD DACRE

British cinema has a rich history of comedy which divides into two traditions: films which rely on the writer and films which rely on a star entertainer. Literary comedies prospered in the early days of sound, drawing on the thriving light comedy theatre of the day and a large pool of established theatrical and popular writers. But it was paralleled by a music-hall tradition which took its stars from the variety stage, from revue, and later from radio and television.[1] In the silent period the heritage of the British music hall had been ignored or wasted as raw material for the cinema. Film was used to record sketches, but anyone with more ambition was either frustrated in their aims or – like Charlie Chaplin and Stan Laurel – went to America. It was not until the coming of sound, coupled with the production boom resulting from the Cinematograph Films Act of 1927, that comedy began to come into its own. Both traditions benefited. Sound meant that writers were encouraged to pen pages of witty repartee as audiences were thought hungry for dialogue. Variety artists were placed under contract and expected to bring humorous characters and situations (and an audience) to their films with a minimum of investment.

From Ruritania to the Aldwych

Many of the literary comedies were indifferent adaptations of popular stage successes or novels written by people with little interest in the film medium. Their class-based plots have dated badly and rapid turnover ensured a depressing recurrence of a limited number of ideas – rich young gentleman impersonates member of the lower classes to court woman of his dreams; country mansion overrun with thieves and/or blackmailers;

the hero mistaken for a thief etc. There were also Ruritanian comedy-romances and musical comedies though these at least provided incidental pleasures of performance from such revue stalwarts as Jack Buchanan, Gene Gerrard and Stanley Lupino.

The main exception to this disappointing output were the Aldwych farces. Farce is a curious combination of the literary and the music-hall traditions. Laughs come from the multiplication of plot absurdities but the best farces utilise a vaudevillian slapstick professionalism in their performance. The series began with *Rookery Nook* (1930), scripted from his play by Ben Travers and one of the first commercially successful British sound films. Other Travers farces followed, including *Thark* (1932), *A Cuckoo in the Nest* (1933) and *Dirty Work* (1934). The Aldwych team revolved around a small number of skilled players – Tom Walls, Ralph Lynn, Mary Brough and Robertson Hare. Walls, who also directed, usually played a crusty gentleman with a roving eye and a shady past; Lynn was the classic 'silly ass', forever blundering into trouble with women. Michael Balcon, who resented the autonomy Walls and his team enjoyed at Gaumont-British, complained that Walls 'did not understand films in any technical or creative sense'.[2] But Walls understood better than Balcon that doing away with the theatricality of a farce would undermine the very nature of the form.

Triumph of the Clowns

The music-hall tradition was at its richest in the 1930s. On stage specific characters were born, with laughs springing from the physical, facial and verbal resources of the comics and even when they did not write their own sketches, they reworked them to make them their own. Cinema transferred these skills to the big screen, creating feature-length stories for both physical clowns such as George Formby and verbal comedians like Max Miller. A whole army of clowns came into films between 1929 and 1939, recruited from music hall, variety, musical comedy and the radio. The majority of those from the halls shared roots with and maintained the allegiance of their predominantly working-class following. Often their films – like Formby's *Off the Dole* (1935) – were set in working-class communities and the sense of solidarity between performer and audience enabled them to command first-feature status, on at least a regional basis, despite their low budgets.

When Gracie Fields made her first appearance on film in *Sally in Our Alley* (1931), she already possessed vast experience in music hall, concert party and revue. Her character had a volatile Lancashire directness and this, coupled with a fine singing voice and a natural exuberance, was well captured by the cinema.[3] She had been signed up by Basil Dean, the theatrical impresario who founded Ealing Studios and her immensely popular films in effect subsidised Dean's more expensive but less profitable theatrical adaptations. In 1934 he recruited George Formby and set about maximising his comic potential.[4] Formby's stage persona of the Northern simpleton with an inhibited boyish sexuality was retained but made acceptable to Southern audiences by dressing Formby smartly and placing the action outside his own stamping ground of industrial Lancashire. (The first of Formby's Ealing films, *No Limit*, 1935, had him competing in the Isle of Man TT motorcycle race). Though forever bewildered by the dizzying events into which he was pushed, Formby's screen character was a natural survivor who foiled the villains and won the girl at the end. Formby's popularity was enhanced by his songs, self-accompanied on his ukulele or banjulele, which revealed an impish, sexually active *alter ego*, and he became Britain's most popular male film performer.

The South's chief rival to the Lancashire comics was Max Miller, 'The Cheekie Chappie', but capturing his appeal on film was something of a problem. On stage he hardly ever did sketches or revues, and he was seldom to be seen in pantomime. His act was brash, rapid-fire, front-cloth patter – delivered with impeccable timing and keen awareness of his audience – which he would intersperse with a few songs and a laconic dance routine. In his best films, such as *Educating Evans* (1936) and *Hoots Mon!* (1939), he was allowed to do

what he did best – tell jokes. As he later confessed: 'I never paid much attention to the script. It was agreed that I put the speeches into the sort of words I could get across.'[5]

Though he is now virtually forgotten and most of the twenty-six films he made between 1930 and 1945 are lost, Kent-born Leslie Fuller was once popular enough to purchase his own studios at Elstree. Fuller's background was that of the seaside concert-party and with the coming of the talkies he took himself into a string of broad, homely comedies. His character, Bill, was known for his jovial ever-changing rubber face and for being plunged into plots riddled with misunderstandings in such films as *Doctor's Orders* (1934), *The Stoker* (1935) and *One Good Turn* (1936). According to one of his directors, he portrayed 'a character . . . brimful of cheerful spirits . . . loveable disposition . . . intensely human in a simple, unintelligent way . . . a "dumb-bell"'.[6] But like Formby's grinning simpleton, his character was more crafty and less gullible than he seemed.

The idea for the Crazy Gang stemmed from the appearance of three double acts on the same bill at the London Palladium. In 1933 the first of seven Crazy Shows was mounted with the classic line-up of Flanagan and Allen, Nervo and Knox, Naughton and Gold, abetted by Monsewer Eddie Gray. The double acts had different styles which made them a potent mix: Flanagan and Allen's sophisticated cross-talk and lilting songs; Nervo and Knox's knockabout physical slapstick and juggling; Naughton and Gold's juvenile buffoonery. With such films as *O-kay for Sound* (1937), *The Frozen Limits* (1939) and *Gasbags* (1940) the Gang's surreal unpredictability led to comparisons with the Marx Brothers, but cinema inhibited rather than enhanced the inventive spontaneity of their stage work.

Hay and the Hulberts

Will Hay came to the cinema in 1933 but it was only with his third starring role in *Boys Will Be Boys* (1935) that he used the schoolmaster character he had developed on the stage over many years. Though born in the North of England, he covered up his roots to portray a variety of bogus authority figures – the headmaster in *Good Morning Boys* (1937), the stationmaster in *Oh, Mr Porter!* (1937), the police sergeant in *Ask a Policeman* (1939) – who aspire to a middle-class respectability beyond their reach and are never able to shake off the remnants of a mysteriously disreputable past. Depth of characterisation, strong plots, expert supporting players and Hay's extraordinary timing have assured his films an enduring popularity.[7] Hay always saw himself as a comic character actor, and he can be seen as bridging the gap between music-hall comedies and comedies populated by character actors playing comic roles. Hay took an interest in the mechanics of the cinema, eventually co-directing his later films, but his ability to make bits of business out of mundane props and his extraordinary visual timing derived from his music-hall training.

The music-hall tradition embraced other comics of middle- and upper-class persuasion, notably Claude Dampier, a twittering 'silly ass' or occasional country bumpkin; the bald old-Etonian Ronald Frankau; and Oliver Wakefield who told stories and gave lectures, missing out the crucial words and flowing off at a tangent. The most successful of them all from this period, however, were the brothers Jack and Claude Hulbert, the only ones to have a series of films built around them. Jack Hulbert's background was one of revue and musical comedy, stemming from his university days as a member of the Cambridge Footlights, but Hulbert never eschewed slapstick. He was blessed with a suitably comic face, was capable of good comic delivery, could carry a tune and was a superb dancer. Unlike many artists whose first love was the theatre, Hulbert saw the cinema as more than just a grind for the money. He brought the same care and creative imagination to his films as he had done to his stage work, eventually taking both dialogue and director credits. His big-chinned, goofy, happy-go-lucky character breezed his way through a series of films including *Sunshine Susie* (1931), *Love on Wheels* (1932), and *Jack of All Trades* (1936). Hulbert's wife, Cicely Courtneidge, a major musical-comedy star in her own right, made a number of films with him, including *Jack's the Boy* (1932) and *Falling for You* (1933).

Claude Hulbert, also a Footlights graduate, made several appearances with the Aldwych team early in his career. He managed to extend the range of his 'silly ass' character beyond the farces and made a series of films for Warner Bros. at their small British studio at Teddington. Serious consideration of his talents is hampered by the fact that much of Warners' British output has been lost, but his bumbling, eager-to-please character enhanced many movies and he proved an ideal partner for Will Hay in *The Ghost of St Michael's* (1941) and *My Learned Friend* (1943).

Wartime Populism

The Second Cinematograph Films Act of 1938 encouraged American companies to make fewer but more expensive films which could be marketed internationally. This, coupled with a new financial crisis, helped squeeze out the independent producer and as a result film production was halved. The upper-class comedies and comedy-thrillers were among the main casualties. From 1933 to 1938 between twenty-five and sixty-one literary comedies were produced each year. Only thirteen appeared in 1939 and the number dropped to single figures between 1941 and 1947 when conditions were exacerbated by wartime economies and controls.

World War II did away with Ruritanian comedies and upper-class fripperies were reduced to the occasional adaptation of West End plays such as Esther McCracken's *Quiet Wedding* (1941) and *Quiet Weekend* (1946) and Noël Coward's *Blithe Spirit* (1945). Terence Rattigan and Anatole de Grunwald's *The Demi-Paradise* (1943) and *English without Tears* (1944) were rather more relevant to the war effort, showing the upper middle classes discarding barriers of class, nationality and ideology in the spirit of wartime populism. Established film comedians such as Will Hay and George Formby also did their bit. Formby socked Hitler on the jaw in *Let George Do It* (1940) and Hay stole the Nazis' secret weapon in *The Goose Steps Out* (1942). However, they had to face competition from comedy stars who had made their name on the wireless and from regional variety performers who proved unexpectedly popular during the war years.

By the late 30s the wireless was producing innovative shows such as *Band Waggon* (1938–9) with Arthur Askey and *ITMA* (*It's That Man Again*, 1939–49) anchored by Tommy Handley. Askey made his starring début in the film version of *Band Waggon* (1940) which successfully combined a putting-on-a-show format with a far-fetched yarn about spies and fifth columnists. *ITMA* (1943) also used a putting-on-a-show format which helped to go some way in preserving the radio series' anarchic feel engendered by its multiplicity of characters, catchphrases and topical allusions.[8] Handley, like Max Miller, was a verbal comedian and was uncomfortable with the film medium, but Askey made a run of eight films during the war and later became a popular television performer.[9] Both had a national appeal which crossed class boundaries, but the enduring vitality of working-class culture was attested by the success of two more vulgar variety performers: Arthur Lucan and Frank Randle.

Lucan from Boston, Lincolnshire, developed the character who would become Old Mother Riley while

Frank Randle waged a lifelong war against anything that reeked of respectability: *Somewhere in England* (John. E. Blakeley, 1940)

touring and brought her to the cinema in 1937. A cantankerous Irish washerwoman, she washed and cleaned in various institutions and kept a close eye on her daughter's virtue. Her sordid workplace conditions were never shunned and certainly never glamorised and she attacked them with a strident working-class rebelliousness. Another thirteen films followed – from *Old Mother Riley in Paris* (1938) to *Mother Riley Meets the Vampire* (1952) – all of which paid dividends at the box office especially in the North.[10]

That Randle, the North's most popular comedy star, is not better remembered is partly a consequence of Southern critical neglect, but it is also posthumous revenge on a man who waged a lifelong war against anything that reeked of respectability. Randle's background included a spell as a circus acrobat and clown and he perfected his command of the stage with a long apprenticeship in revue and music hall in a wonderfully crude act. He made his first film *Somewhere in England* in 1940 for the Manchester-based Mancunian Films of which he later became a director. Randle's films were not as scandalously offensive as his much-prosecuted stage manifestations but he nevertheless proved to be one of the most successful transfers of a music-hall comedian onto the screen. The method at Mancunian was to spend as little as possible, keep the camera steady and let the comic get on with it. This suited Randle, who brought to his films bits and pieces of the famous stage creations which had sustained him for most of his professional life. His act seems at least in part to be drunkenly improvised and the conversations with his stooges in broad Lancashire dialect meander all over the

place in hilarious disregard for the norms of comic development.

Ealing Comedy

About two-thirds of the comedies made during the war were from the slapstick music-hall tradition, but things altered dramatically with the coming of peace. Though they produced no comedies between Will Hay's *My Learned Friend* in 1943 and *Hue and Cry* in 1947, Ealing Studios were at the centre of this change. In 1949 they released, *Whisky Galore, Kind Hearts and Coronets, A Run for Your Money* and *Passport to Pimlico*, which was scripted by T. E. B. Clarke, the architect of Ealing's popular image of cosy whimsicality. Most of Clarke's comedies – which include *The Lavender Hill Mob* (1951) and *The Titfield Thunderbolt* (1953) – depict a Britain of shopkeepers, friendly spivs, jolly coppers, incompetent but honest bureaucrats, kind-hearted squires, contented old-age pensioners and eccentrics. If there are villains, they tend to be hard-nosed businessmen – most other sections of society are ignored or are minor irritants. The Clarke structure can be taken as a crystallisation of Ealing's values and the films of Robert Hamer – *Kind Hearts and Coronets* – and Alexander Mackendrick – *Whisky Galore!, The Man in the White Suit* (1951), *The Maggie* (1954), *The Ladykillers* (1955) – a dark commentary on those values.

Ealing comedy brought the literary comedy tradition to the fore, demanding actors with a gift for comedy who could flesh out the well-constructed scripts. The chief beneficiary was Alec Guinness; a man

Passport to Pimlico (Henry Cornelius, 1949): Ealing's world of shopkeepers, friendly spivs, jolly coppers and assorted eccentrics

one would not expect to see on a variety bill. Guinness was a master interpreter of comic scripts and could undertake a wide range of roles as proven by his finely delineated performances as a family of eight doomed aristocrats in *Kind Hearts and Coronets*. Subsequent comedies cast him as a timid bank robber (*The Lavender Hill Mob*); a naive scientist (*The Man in the White Suit*); a detective-priest (*Father Brown*, 1954); and a psychopath (*The Ladykillers*).

The classic Ealing comedies were made over a very short period of time. With the exception of the two Mackendrick films, *The Maggie* and *The Ladykillers*, the post-1951 Ealing comedies either work to a different set of commands (and are seldom revived or even remembered as Ealing comedies) or are tepid re-workings of Clarke's earlier successes.[11] But the influence of the studio on popular comedy films of the 50s is pervasive. As Ealing itself began to falter the trend was taken up by others. Indeed such films such as *Brandy for the Parson* (1952), *Fast and Loose* (1954) and *Alive and Kicking* (1958) could easily be mistaken for Ealing product.

In 1953 the Rank Organisation released *Genevieve* with Kenneth More, John Gregson, Dinah Sheridan and Kay Kendall (a project turned down by Ealing) and its huge success accentuated the move towards middle-class comedy epitomised by *Doctor in the House* (1954) and its successors.

Doctor in the House (Ralph Thomas, 1954)

Doctor in the House exemplifies the literary tradition in post-war British cinema comedy. A fine script from a popular novel interpreted by a wonderful ensemble cast now seems a winning formula, but both the subject matter (medical students gaining their first experience as doctors in an NHS hospital) and the source novel (an anecdotal and partly autobiographical account by Richard Gordon) were regarded as unsuitable for the cinema.

When producer Betty Box acquired the rights to Gordon's novel she discovered that another company had already abandoned their option after failing to come up with a satisfactory script. She called on Nicholas Phipps to solve the adaptation problems. Phipps had been writing for the cinema since the 1930s, and had his greatest success with the sophisticated London romances of Anna Neagle and Herbert Wilcox. Comedy was not his obvious forte, but Box's intuition paid off and Phipps became the mainstay of the first five films in the resulting Doctor series. He discarded the minutiae of medical life, firmed up the anecdotal nature of the novel, fleshed out the narrator (renamed Simon Sparrow), and focused on his friendship with three very different male students (played by Kenneth More, Donald Sinden and Donald Houston) as Sparrow discovers women and they all train to be doctors.

Against opposition from the head of Pinewood Studios, Earl St John, who thought him unsuited to light comedy, Box cast Dirk Bogarde as Sparrow. After Robert Morley's agent demanded too high a fee, James Robertson Justice was cast as the eccentric surgeon Lancelot Spratt (he was the only actor to play in all seven films in the series). Muriel Pavlow, Suzanne Cloutier, Joan Sims and Kay Kendall provided memorable female interest. Also glimpsed in the cast are Phipps as the magistrate and Gordon as the anaesthetist, but sadly not Tommy Cooper whose magic routine – sawing a lady in half before shouting 'Is there a doctor in the house?' – was sadly excised before release.

The finished film, efficiently directed by Ralph Thomas, exhibited an infectious *joie de vivre* which not only characterised the interaction of the cast, but also displayed a confidence in the future of the National Health Service, which had survived the re-election of a Conservative government in 1951. Few films up to then had captured the British public's appreciation of the institution and the popularity of this film would pave the way for other affectionate comic forays into hospital life, most notably those of the *Carry On* team beginning with *Carry On Nurse*, direced by Ralph Thomas's brother Gerald and produced by Box's husband Peter Rogers, in 1959.

Doctor in the House was judged top box-office money-maker of 1954 and its influence on literary comedy was matched only by Henry Cornelius's similarly exuberant *Genevieve* as others film-makers tried to duplicate its success.

FURTHER READING

Box, Betty, *Lifting the Lid* (London: The Book Guild Ltd, 2000).

Gordon, Richard, *Doctor in the House* (London: Michael Joseph, 1952).

Farceurs and Eccentrics

Another popular series emerged from the writer/producer/director team, Frank Launder and Sidney Gilliat who had contributed to Gainsborough's stream of comedies in the late 30s before their directorial debut, *Millions Like Us* (1943). *The Happiest Days of Your Life* (1950), based on John Dighton's farce about a girls' school being accidentally billeted with a boys' school, starred two great eccentrics of British cinema, Margaret Rutherford and Alastair Sim and was a huge success. The *St Trinian's* films followed, based on the cartoons of Ronald Searle, which worked to a similar pattern. In *The Belles of St Trinian's* (1954) Alastair Sim appropriated Rutherford's role as the headmistress and a wonderful cast of supporting players led by Joyce Grenfell, George Cole, Richard Wattis, Eric Barker and Terry-Thomas was built up to enhance two further films, *Blue Murder at St Trinian's* (1957) and *The Pure Hell of St Trinian's* (1960).[12] Though these films were developed directly for the cinema they are an extension of the farce tradition skilfully utilising strong comic plots while showcasing the comic adroitness of the performers.

Similarly, a group of films made by John and Roy Boulting utilised a sparkling ensemble of actors led by Ian Carmichael, Peter Sellers, Richard Attenborough and Terry-Thomas. The scripts generally involved the contribution of one of the brothers in collaboration with Frank Harvey or Jeffrey Dell. The best were broadly played satires: *Private's Progress* (1956) dealt with skiving and graft in the army; *Lucky Jim* (1957), snobbery in universities; *I'm All Right, Jack* (1959), bloody-mindedness in industry; *Carlton-Browne of the F.O.* (1959), ineptitude in the diplomatic service and *Heavens Above!* (1963), hypocrisy in the Church. Ironically, this cycle petered out just as the satire boom heralded by television's *That Was the Week That Was* (1962–3) took off.

The great discovery of the Boultings was Ian Carmichael, whose characterisation as the well-meaning blunderer is best seen in *I'm All Right, Jack*. Though more restricted in his range of characterisations than Alec Guinness, given the chance, as in the Boulting films and Robert Hamer's *School for Scoundrels* (1960), he could be equally impressive. Another of the mainstays, Peter Sellers, played a far wider range of characters. His films with the Boultings marked a stage in his quest for world stardom. His background was stage and radio variety, and fine performances in *The Smallest Show on Earth* (1957) as a drunken projectionist and in *The Naked Truth* (1957) as a murderous family entertainer confirmed his promise in the cinema. Sellers combined skilful interpretation with a clown's ability to work in pieces of business. Where Guinness was a straight actor taking on comic roles, Sellers was an insecure clown voluntarily submitting himself to the confines of a script. In 1963, when cast as the bumbling French detective Inspector Clouseau in *The Pink Panther*, he discovered a comic persona – one wholly within the music-hall tradition – strong enough to maintain a series.

Windmill Survivors and Radio Stars

The end of the war had marked a major change in the fortunes of the established stars of the music-hall tradition. Will Hay made his last film in 1943, George Formby bowed out with *George in Civvy Street* in 1946 and the Crazy Gang came together only for a nostalgic reunion, *Life Is a Circus*, in 1958. Arthur Lucan, Arthur Askey and Frank Randle struggled on into the 50s but the coming of peace had seen an influx of new talent hoping to make their names as comedians. People whose careers had been interrupted by the war rubbed shoulders with those who had gained a taste for entertaining in army concert parties, with ENSA or with the Gang Shows. They were lucky in having the remnants of a variety circuit in which to work, since perfecting routines through practical experience was and is indispensable for developing knockabout slapstick comedy, timing and audience control.

The most celebrated of the theatres giving a chance to up-and-coming comedians was the Windmill, where they had the thankless task of filling in between the nudes. The roll call of those who trod its boards is a 'Who's Who' of post-war comedy. Some failed the audition like Norman Wisdom, Benny Hill and Charlie Drake, many were sacked, most famously Morecambe and Wise, but some survived for a run like Tommy Cooper, Richard Murdoch, Arthur English, Tony Hancock, Peter Sellers and Jimmy Edwards. To perform at the Windmill was a tremendous training opportunity. Jimmy Edwards recalled:

> I certainly learned a lot . . . the frequency with which
> I had to do my act turned out to be a good thing, for
> it meant that I could modify my lines and my 'business' from hour to hour, retaining the successful bits
> and throwing out the failures . . . as the show was
> continuous, from 12.15am to 10.35pm.[13]

Radio provided another training ground. The rise to fame could be accelerated by appearances on such programmes as *Henry Hall's Guest Night*, *Workers'*

Playtime and *Variety Bandbox*. The oddest was Peter Brough's *Educating Archie* (1950–60), centred as it was on a ventriloquist's dummy, a curious concept for the radio. Of all the series popular on radio at the time it was the most important in launching or establishing names: Hattie Jacques, Max Bygraves, Tony Hancock, Harry Secombe, Benny Hill, Ronald Shiner, Bruce Forsyth, Sid James, Alfred Marks, Beryl Reid, Dick Emery, Jerry Desmonde, Warren Mitchell, Bernard Bresslaw and Marty Feldman all played a part in giving the dummy an education.

Most of the early comedy shows on television were in the variety format, generally one-off specials, though series such as *Val Parnell's Sunday Night at the London Palladium* (1955–67) later emerged. Veteran Arthur Askey was joined by newcomers Norman Wisdom, Arthur Haynes, Tommy Cooper, Benny Hill, Frankie Howerd, Ken Dodd, Charlie Drake, Jimmy Edwards and Morecambe and Wise, many of whom were given their own series in the 50s and early 60s.

These newcomers had surprisingly little effect on the cinema. Ken Dodd made no films before his brief appearance in Kenneth Branagh's *Hamlet* (1996), Arthur Haynes played only cameos and Tommy Cooper was confined to supporting roles except in Eric Sykes's semi-silent *The Plank* (1967). Jimmy Edwards showed cinematic potential in *Treasure Hunt* (1952) as did Frankie Howerd in *Jumping for Joy* (1956) but their subsequent films were disappointing. Charlie Drake's cocky self-confident character was well served in his first three films, *Sands of the Desert* (1960), *Petticoat Pirates* (1961) and *The Cracksman* (1963), which allowed him plenty of space to display his witty and inventive slapstick, but he was never able to match his small-screen success. Benny Hill made no real effort in the cinema after appearing in *Who Done It?* (1956) and *Light up the Sky!* (1960). His cheery unsentimental characterisation could have had a huge impact, but he preferred to work in television. Eric Morecambe and Ernie Wise remained a front-cloth, cross-talk act in the old tradition even on television. A film series was envisaged starting with *The Intelligence Men* (1965), but they were over-constrained by the plots and only two more were completed: *That Riviera Touch* (1966) and *The Magnificent Two* (1967). Similarly, a later television feature, *Night Train to Murder* (1984), failed to build on their strengths and proved only fitfully amusing.

Wisdom and Hancock

The one exception to this cinematic misuse of talent was Norman Wisdom, who went on to become the

most successful of all the post-war screen clowns. Wisdom entered the business after the war, working his way through an apprenticeship in variety and pantomime. He was on television by 1947 and he rapidly became the small screen's top comedian. Film soon beckoned and *Trouble in Store* (1953) made him a major cinema star and led to a string of successors such as *Up in the World* (1956), *There Was a Crooked Man* (1960) and *A Stitch in Time* (1963). Wisdom's key success was in incorporating acrobatic physical comedy within a logical narrative framework. His character, known as 'the Gump', was remarkably consistent over the years – a little man who wants to fit in but whose childlike trust in people, coupled with his need for love and acceptance, make him easy prey for the less than honest, the unkind, or the unthinking. Like Formby, Wisdom achieved worldwide popularity but little critical acknowledgment in Britain.[14]

By the mid-1950s television series with some sort of narrative framework began to emerge and, as with their radio predecessors, some like Denis Norden and Frank Muir's *Whack-O!* (1956–60) and Sid Colin's *The Army Game* (1957–61) led to feature films.[15] Television also provided opportunities to comedians outside the variety format: most notably for Tony Hancock. Ray Galton and Alan Simpson created *Hancock's Half Hour* for the radio in 1954 and the series was transferred to television in 1956 with Hancock visually perfect for his comic persona as a pretentious middle-class remnant amid the new affluence. Galton and Simpson also scripted *The Rebel* (1961) which extended the familiar Hancock format into a feature-length film by casting him as an amateur painter who assumes the mantle of a genius. It is a fine film, with the script giving Hancock ample space to display his comic abilities within a coherent narrative. By the time he made *The Punch and Judy Man* (1963), Hancock had lost writers Galton and Simpson and was losing his battle with alcohol. The film still works well, with Hancock superb as the downtrodden seaside entertainer, but an aura of melancholia finally overwhelms it.

With the radio and the television *Hancocks*, Galton and Simpson had paid little attention to continuity of plotlines or logic from episode to episode. Instead they had concentrated on the basic consistency of the Hancock character, allowing him to react to a wide range of situations to get the laughs. Freed of the constraints of writing for a comic, Galton and Simpson developed *Steptoe and Son*, where the humour emerged from character interaction – the love–hate relationship between father and son – played by straight actors (Harry H. Corbett and Wilfrid Brambell) rather than comedians. The creative tension between the comic and the literary that had been evident in *Hancock's Half Hour* gave way to the literary in *Steptoe and Son*, setting the pattern for future television sitcoms and mirroring what had happened in film the previous decade.[16]

Carry On

Sidney James, memorable as Hancock's crooked sidekick in *Hancock's Half Hour* on radio and television, found even greater popularity as part of the *Carry On* team which he joined for their fourth film, *Carry On Constable* (1960). Kenneth Williams, Charles Hawtrey and Kenneth Connor had been there from the beginning, in *Carry On Sergeant* (1958); Joan Sims was recruited for *Carry On Nurse* (1959) and the final key member, Barbara Windsor, for *Carry On Spying* (1964). The early films, written by Norman Hudis, work to a basic formula in which a group of incompetents are let loose in an instantly recognisable institution – an army camp, a hospital, a school – and then succeed in muddling though to some level of sanity with a subsidiary romance woven in to give the film a happy ending.

Once Hudis left, the scripting was taken over by Talbot Rothwell, and it is from his films that most people take their image of the series. Hudis's scripts had become increasingly ribald, but Rothwell eschewed all subtlety, broadening the basic concept and delighting in a peculiarly British bawdiness and use of *double entendre*. Running out of institutions to mock he generally resorted to pastiche and parody, *Carry On Spying*, *Carry On Cleo* (1964) and *Carry On . . . Don't Lose Your Head* (1967) being the best examples. After *Carry On Up the Khyber* (1968) the *Carry Ons* allowed themselves more leeway in explicit nudity while maintaining a basic innocence. Rothwell maintained Hudis's exploitation of expert ensemble slapstick while emphasising the individual development of the performers into a set of distinct comic personae. This, coupled with strong dialogue but loose plotting (which separates the *Carry Ons* from the farces), marked a further straddling of the music-hall and literary traditions.

The loss of Talbot Rothwell in 1974 was a blow from which the *Carry On* films were never to recover, and Britain's most successful and long-lived series spluttered to an ignominious close. It is unlikely, though, that even Rothwell's skills could have sustained the series. Other companies put together more explicit sex-romp comedies, notably the *Confessions* films and the

Adventures films with which the ageing *Carry On* team could not hope to compete.[17]

By the mid-60s, British pop music and television were at their most inventive, London was in full swing and American finance encouraged British cinema to ride the surf of Britain's cultural centrality. Most British comedies were unaffected by all this, but some producers did react to what was going on around them. *Please Turn Over* (1959) was a jaunty debunking of 'Angry Young Men'; *The Pot Carriers* (1962) and *Sparrows Can't Sing* (1963) carried the new realism into comedy; and *Billy Liar* (1963), *Smashing Time* (1967), *Alfie* (1966) and the Beatles films *A Hard Day's Night* (1964) and *Help!* (1965) combined comedy with the ethos of the Swinging Sixties.

Oxbridge, Alternatives and the New Mainstream

In a decade of low production after the withdrawal of American financial support, the 1970s produced few new comedy personalities. The main comic input was from television spin-offs.[18] These died out as the 1980s progressed, with feature-length Christmas specials replacing the big-screen outings. The only other comedies fighting for screen time were the last *Carry Ons* and the *Confessions/Adventures* sex romps.[19]

Perhaps paradoxically, genuine heirs to the clown tradition hailed in greatest strength from the rarefied climes of Oxford and Cambridge Universities, with the 'Oxbridge Mafia' emerging from the Cambridge Footlights and the Oxford University Dramatic Society. The *Beyond the Fringe* team of Jonathan Miller, Alan Bennett, Peter Cook and Dudley Moore had spawned the satire boom of the 1960s and exerted an enormous influence on British comedy. The next generation of Oxbridge graduates shone initially on the radio with *I'm Sorry I'll Read That Again* (1965–73), which included among its writers/performers Tim Brooke-Taylor, John Cleese, Graeme Garden and Bill Oddie, who were explicitly inspired by the music-hall tradition and reacting against the satirical movement. The transfer of this strand of humour to television yielded *At Last the 1948 Show* (1967), which featured Brooke-Taylor, Cleese, and another Oxbridge man, Graham Chapman among its cast; and *Do Not Adjust Your Set* (1968–9), which included Oxbridgers Eric Idle, Terry Jones and Michael Palin. The casts of these shows recombined to create *Monty Python's Flying Circus* (1969–74) and *The Goodies* (1970–8). *Python,* with its cast of Chapman,

Cleese, Idle, Jones and Palin, plus animated interludes from the American Terry Gilliam (who had worked occasionally on *Do Not Adjust Your Set*), broke through to the cinema, and after the rehash of old television material in *And Now for Something Completely Different* (Ian MacNaughton, 1971) provided the richest comic contributions of the decade: *Monty Python and the Holy Grail* (Terry Gilliam/Terry Jones, 1975) and *Monty Python's Life of Brian* (Terry Jones, 1979). All the members of the Python team would have significant film careers – in particular John Cleese with his masterly *A Fish Called Wanda* (Charles Crichton, 1988) and its underrated follow-up *Fierce Creatures* (Robert Young/Fred Schepisi, 1997), and Michael Palin, with a string of successes including the Alan Bennett-scripted *A Private Function* (Malcolm Mowbray, 1984) and *The Missionary* (Richard Loncraine, 1982), which he wrote himself.

Another Oxford University graduate was Rowan Atkinson, who developed his inventive live act on stage before moving to television in *Not the Nine O'Clock News* (1979–82) alongside Pamela Stephenson, Griff Rhys-Jones and Mel Smith.[20] Atkinson's comic persona Mr Bean, written with fellow Oxford graduate Richard Curtis, was honed through a number of television specials (with input from writer Ben Elton) before hitting the big screen in *Bean* directed by Mel Smith in 1997.[21] As a performer Smith continued to work extensively with Rhys-Jones and together they made *Wilt* (Michael Tuchner, 1989) and *Morons from Outer Space* (Mike Hodges, 1985).

The alternative cabaret club circuit pioneered by London's Comedy Store and Comic Strip provided another platform for new comedians. The privileged and much-criticised route to television from Oxbridge was now complicated by the success of these clubs and the exposure of acts at the Edinburgh Fringe Festival, where sketch shows and reviews faded out to be taken over by stand-ups as the 1980s progressed. But the route, for those who attempted it, from stand-up to situation comedy to feature-length cinema was as hazardous as ever. The most successful in making the passage were a loose ensemble of players (including Rik Mayall, Adrian Edmondson, Robbie Coltrane, Nigel Planer, Alexei Sayle, Dawn French and Jennifer Saunders), under the leadership of Peter Richardson, labelled the Comic Strip. After a series of successful television comedies they progressed to the cinema with *The Supergrass* (1985), *Eat the Rich* (1987) and *The Pope Must Die* (1991), all directed by Richardson and scripted by Pete Richens.

Lee Evans, a prodigiously talented physical comic of the old school also developed his act through the live circuit. While he has yet to regain the heights of his masterly début *Funny Bones* (Peter Chelsom, 1995), such films as *Mousehunt* (Gore Verbrinski, 1997) and *The Martins* (Tony Grounds, 2001) confirm he has the makings of a great screen comedian.

The next generation, which specialised in satirising the styles and formats of radio and television, produced Steve Coogan, a talented character comedian rather than a physical clown whose own personality became difficult to disentangle from his most famous creation, the incompetent chat-show host Alan Partridge. In an effort to get away from the awful Partridge, Coogan accepted an eclectic range of film roles ranging from Mole in *The Wind in the Willows* (Terry Jones, 1996) to Phileas Fogg in *Around the World in 80 Days* (Frank Coraci, 2004). But his most resonant and satisfying comic performances – in Jim Jarmusch's *Coffee and Cigarettes* (2003) and Michael Winterbottom's *A Cock and Bull Story* (2005) – effectively deploy Partridge-like pomposity, egocentricity and tactlessness.

Sacha Baron Cohen was much faster in exposing his *alter ego* Ali G to cinema audiences. *Ali G Indahouse* (Mark Mylod, 2002) proved embarrassingly juvenile, with little of the outrageous wit shown in the television shows, where he interacted with real people to humorous and sometimes revelatory effect. Cohen did much better with *Borat: Cultural Learnings of America for Make Benefit Glorious Nation of Kazakhstan* (Larry Charles, 2006), a mock documentary featuring his benignly sexist, anti-Semitic Kazakhstan journalist Borat. Crudity failed to blunt its outrageous humour and it proved an international success. The other major television-generated success was the spoof horror *Shaun of the Dead* (2004), which came from two of the creative team behind the offbeat situation comedy *Spaced* – writer-director Edgar Wright and writer-performer Simon Pegg.[22]

To the wider world, it is the literary tradition of British comedy that has fared best. It recurred fitfully through the 80s particularly in the films of Bill Forsyth: *That Sinking Feeling* (1980), *Gregory's Girl* (1980), *Local Hero* (1983) and *Comfort and Joy* (1984). In the late 1990s *The Full Monty* (Peter Cattaneo, 1997), scripted by Simon Beaufoy, proved a huge international success. But attempts to recreate the film's combination of realism, pathos and tragicomedy failed to yield much box-office allure. Beaufoy's *Among Giants* (Sam Miller, 1998) was too earnest and his *Blow Dry* (Paddy

Funny Bones (Peter Chelsom, 1995)

Funny Bones is an inspired ragbag of ideas about comedy which both makes us laugh and analyses the meaning of comedy. The film is exclusively about the clown tradition with, at its heart, the idea that although some people are innately funny and others have to learn how to be funny, both are dependent on a rich cultural heritage for their inspiration.

The film pits two half-brothers against one another. One, Tommy (Oliver Platt), the rich offspring of a famous American comic, travels to Blackpool, the old stomping ground of his father George (Jerry Lewis), to buy routines in order to follow in his father's footsteps. The other, Jack (Lee Evans), Blackpool-based and unaware of his progeny but with a natural ability to create laughter, is manic, naive and depressed. Tommy views possible turns to purchase – the attempted privatisation of comic tradition – only to recognise the very routines that launched his father's immensely successful career. By appropriating these routines his father not only destroyed careers but thwarted the rich organic traditions which created the comedy in the first place. The one act that Tommy craves is performed by Jack – but he understands that even if he was capable of doing it, he would be re-enacting the crime of his father.

Director Peter Chelsom and scriptwriter Peter Flannery's stylish thesis-film required an embodiment of 'funny bones' at its centre; this was provided by Lee Evans in his film début. Evans, a slapstick comic with physical skills honed on the live circuit, more than holds his own in genuine funny bones company including that of Freddie 'Parrot Face' Davies, a graduate of the Northern clubs, and the astounding septuagenarian American clown George Carl, former resident of the Crazy Horse Saloon in Paris, also making his feature début.

Along the way, the film touches on many aspects of comedy, but the most challenging in its execution is

A heritage of comedy: George Carl, Freddie Davies and Lee Evans in *Funny Bones*

also the most familiar, the relationship between the comic and the tragic, both in terms of the things that make us laugh and its exposure of the toll exacted on the funny bones comedian. The film starts with a man chopped to death by a boat's propeller and finishes with Jack performing a death-defying, potentially self-destructive routine. In between we witness the event that stymied Jack's career: his killing of a fellow performer in the circus ring when fake violence becomes real violence (discernible only in its outcome, not in its execution – the crowd laughs on). Lee Evans inextricably links Jack's frail mental condition, and his unpredictable propensity for violence to his comic ability. In an equally knowing performance, Jerry Lewis implies that George gave up the physical visual comedy for the verbal precisely because he preferred to keep his sanity.

FURTHER READING

Andy Medhurst, 'Unhinged Invention', *Sight and Sound*, October 1995, pp. 6–10.

Breathnach, 2001) too silly; Peter Cattaneo's *Lucky Break* (2001) proved inconsequential, and producer Uberto Pasolini's *The Closer You Get* (Aileen Ritchie, 2000) incompetent. Better were two films by Mark Herman, *Brassed Off* (1996) and *Purely Belter* (2000), though humour here was subsidiary to social concern and the promise of a new type of social comedy

remains largely unfulfilled. It has been broader, simpler comedies – notably Kirk Jones's *Waking Ned* (1998) and *Nanny McPhee* (2005), and Nigel Cole's *Saving Grace* (2000) and *Calendar Girls* (2003) – which have enjoyed popular success.

Similarly the quirky originality of Richard Curtis's *Four Weddings and a Funeral* (Mike Newell, 1994), and

Notting Hill (Roger Michell, 1999) was followed by the dismayingly simple-minded Bridget Jones films – *Bridget Jones's Diary* (Sharon Maguire, 2001) and *Bridget Jones: The Edge of Reason* (Beeban Kidron, 2004), and the syrupy sentimentality of *Love Actually* (Richard Curtis, 2003). Thus British comedy remains vibrant but its successes continue to be elusive and unpredictable.

Notes

1. A non-scientific rule of thumb to distinguish between the comic actor and the clown is whether or not the performer is likely to be able to do a comic turn on stage.

2. Michael Balcon, *Michael Balcon Presents . . . A Lifetime of Films* (London: Hutchinson, 1969), p. 92. Theatrical farce depends on sharp timing and the effect of this is difficult to recreate in a 'non-live' situation. Note, for example, the failure of the film versions of Ray Cooney's *Not Now Darling* (1973) and Michael Pertwee's *Don't Just Lie There, Say Something* (1974).

3. Fields's honest brassy character was seen to transcend her background and 'make good', a characteristic that brought her to the attention of Hollywood. She signed to 20th Century-Fox but insisted on shooting the films in Britain.

4. Formby was provided with his own production unit under Anthony Kimmins.

5. Quoted in John M. East, *The Cheeky Chappie* p. 134.

6. Norman Lee, *Money for Film Stories*, p. 53.

7. Hay's sidekicks in the 30s films were Moore Marriott and Graham Moffatt who went on to support Arthur Askey, Ben Lyon and Bebe Daniels and Tommy Handley in the 40s.

8. The putting-on-a-show format is a convenient way to incorporate short sketches into a film without rupturing the narrative. Askey's *I Thank You* (1941) used this formula as did another wartime radio transfer *Happidrome* (1943) starring its writer Harry Korris.

9. Tommy Handley only completed one more feature before his death in 1949. This was a mildly amusing time-travel spoof, *Time Flies* (1944).

10. Old Mother Riley's daughter was played by Lucan's wife, Kitty McShane. The couple had to wait until 1949, with *Old Mother Riley's New Venture*, for a West End film opening.

11. The former include *Meet Mr Lucifer* (1953), *The Love Lottery* (1954), *Touch and Go* (1955) and *Who Done It?* (ironically scripted by Clarke); the latter include *The Titfield Thunderbolt* and *Barnacle Bill* (1957).

12. The final two films – *The Great St Trinian's Train Robbery* (1966) and *The Wildcats of St Trinian's* (1980) – lacked most of the regulars, and were dismal affairs.

13. Jimmy Edwards, *Take It from Me*, p. 149.

14. Richard Dacre, *Trouble in Store*, is the only book-length study of Wisdom's films. Wisdom triumphed on Broadway with his Tony-nominated performance in *Walking Happy* (1967), which led to an American feature *The Night They Raided Minsky's* (1968), but his British films failed to appeal to American audiences. He was knighted in 2000.

15. *Bottoms Up!* (1960) and *I Only Arsked!* (1958) respectively.

16. The historic importance of Galton and Simpson is unquestionable. However the generally accepted relationship between their split with Hancock and the comic's subsequent decline is far more problematic. By the time they left, Hancock's well-documented insecurity was already exacerbated by chronic alcoholism which would lead to his suicide. Moreover, Galton and Simpson never cracked writing for the cinema and their television work outside of the *Hancocks* and the *Steptoes* is unmemorable.

17. *Carry On Columbus* (1992), made by the regular director/producer team of Gerald Thomas and Peter Rogers, tried to cash in on a renewed interest in the series, but without any of the central acting team it was a critical and commercial flop.

18. The best of these are *Dad's Army* (Norman Cohen, 1971), *Steptoe and Son* (Cliff Owen, 1972), *The Likely Lads* (Michael Tuchner, 1976), *Porridge* (Dick Clement, 1979) and *Rising Damp* (Joseph McGrath, 1980).

19. The *Confessions* films were based on the books by Timothy Lea (Christopher Wood), starred Robin Askwith and began with *Confessions of a Window Cleaner* (Val Guest, 1974). The *Adventures* series were the brainchild of director/producer Stanley Long and débuted with his *Adventures of a Taxi Driver* (1976).

20. Chris Langham was in the original line-up but was quickly replaced by Rhys-Jones.

21. A further adventure emerged in 2007: *Mr Bean's Holiday* (Steve Bendelack).

22. The third key person behind *Spaced*, co-writer and co-star Jessica Stevenson, appeared briefly in *Shaun of the Dead*, but is otherwise best known for her regular appearances in Caroline Aherne and Craig Cash's ground-breaking TV sitcom *The Royle Family* (1998–2006). Her impressive film credits include *Harry Potter and the Order of the Phoenix* (David Yates, 2007). The *Spaced* team's next film *Hot Fuzz* (2007), proved even more popular than *Shaun of the Dead*. Christopher Smith's sharply witty *Severance* (2006) is also a horror spoof but unlike *Shaun of the Dead*, it is better classed as horror than comedy.

Bibliography

Brown, Geoff, *Launder and Gilliat* (London: BFI, 1977).
Busby, Roy, *British Music Hall* (London: Paul Elek, 1976).

Carpenter, Humphrey, *O.U.D.S.: A Centenary History of the Oxford University Dramatic Society* (Oxford: Oxford University Press, 1985).

Clarke, T. E. B., *This Is Where I Came In* (London: Michael Joseph, 1974).

Connor, John, *Comics: A Decade of Comedy at the Assembly Rooms* (London: Macmillan Papermac, 1990).

Cook, William, *The Comedy Store* (London: Little, Brown and Company, 2001).

Dacre, Richard, *Trouble in Store* (Dundee: T. C. Farries, 1991).

Dean, Basil, *Mind's Eye* (London: Hutchinson, 1973).

East, John, *The Cheeky Chappie* (London, W. H. Allen, 1977).

Edwards, Jimmy, *Take It from Me* (London: Werner Laurie, 1953).

Fisher, John, *Funny Way to Be a Hero* (London: Frederick Muller, 1973).

Foster, Andy and Furst, Steve, *Radio Comedy 1938–1968* (London: Virgin, 1996).

Hewison, Robert, *Footlights! A Hundred Years of Cambridge Comedy* (London: Methuen, 1983).

Hulbert, Jack, *The Little Woman's Always Right* (London: W. H. Allen, 1975).

Kavanagh, Ted, *Tommy Handley* (London: Hodder & Stoughton, 1949).

Kendall, Henry, *I Remember Romano's* (London: Macdonald, 1960).

Lee, Norman, *Money for Film Stories* (London: Pitman, 1937).

Lewisohn, Mark, *Radio Times Guide to TV Comedy* (London: BBC Worldwide, 1998).

Montgomery, John, *Comedy Films* (London: George Allen & Unwin, 1954).

Moules, Joan, *Our Gracie* (London: Robert Hale, 1983).

Nathan, David, *The Laughtermakers* (London: Peter Owen, 1971).

Nobbs, George, *The Wireless Stars* (Norwich: Wensum, 1972).

Quinlan, David, *Illustrated Directory of Film Comedy Stars* (London: Batsford, 1992).

Rix, Brian, *My Farce from My Elbow* (London: Secker and Warburg, 1975).

Seaton, Roy and Martin, Roy, *Good Morning, Boys* (London: Barrie and Jenkins, 1978).

Smith, Leslie, *Modern British Farce* (London: Macmillan, 1989).

Travers, Ben, *Vale of Laughter* (London: Geoffrey Bles, 1957).

Walker, Alexander, *The Mask behind the Mask* (London: Weidenfeld and Nicolson, 1981).

Williams, Philip Martin and Williams, David L., *Wired to the Moon: Frank Randle – A Life* (Ashton-under-Lyne: History on Your Doorstep, 2006).

Wilmut, Roger, *Tony Hancock 'Artiste'* (London: Eyre Methuen, 1978).

Wilmut, Roger and Rosengard, Peter, *Didn't You Kill My Mother-in-Law?* (London: Methuen, 1989).

13
British Cinema and Black Representation

Jim Pines

The objective of colonial discourse is to construe the colonised as a population of degenerate types on the basis of racial origin, in order to justify conquest and to establish systems of administration and instruction.[1]

Black representation in British cinema is inextricably bound up in colonial and race-relations discourses. Typically, narrative stress tends to be on ideological constructions of 'blacks' as either exotic or threatening 'Other'. This Eurocentric motif, moreover, is usually articulated with equally divisive constructions of 'whiteness' or 'Britishness' (the two identities are conflated in this context), in which Empire looms large as a kind of Manichean framing device.[2] The articulation of racial difference in terms of sharply differentiated and easily recognisable character (or racial) types and dramatic situations thus plays a crucial role in structuring colonial and race-relations narratives. The racially motivated oppositions in colonial/race-relations stories tend not to be satisfactorily resolved, however, either at the fundamental human level or in terms of social idealism.

The history of black representation in British cinema is marked by discontinuities, along with intermittent moments during which particular racial and/or colonial motifs might feature prominently. The first of these moments was the cycle of popular colonial adventure films made in the 1930s, which included *Sanders of the River* (1935), *King Solomon's Mines* (1937), *The Drum* (1938) and *The Four Feathers* (1939), and culminated in the propaganda classic *Men of Two Worlds* (Thorold Dickinson, 1946). However, the core themes and images that define the genre are already evident in the silent film *If Youth But Knew* (1926), which centres

on an English doctor who goes to work as a regional medical officer in colonial Africa (Nigeria). The twin themes of personal sacrifice and character-building are much in evidence in this drama – as, for instance, in the doctor's decision to leave his fiancée behind with the promise that he will save enough money for them to marry and buy a house when he returns to England. An inter-title – 'The Dawn of the New Century – After four years' hard work in the land of the white man's grave!' – reminds the audience that this is not a cosy romantic adventure. The personal danger which the English colonialist doctor faces and overcomes is central to the story, although this epitaph can also be read as an oblique pathologisation of the African setting. 'Empire . . . provided one of the conditions under which men and women could be expected to use their mental and physical resources to the full.'[3] The notion that the Empire also provided a setting for certain classes of Europeans to 'find themselves' not only defines the film's colonialist doctor 'hero', but also drives the narrative. Typical scenes show the doctor caring for the sick (during what appears to be an epidemic of some kind), and longing for his fiancée and England. But his personal sacrifice is underpinned by a clearly articulated sense of his moral superiority and political domination over the natives.

While the first half of *If Youth But Knew* centres round paternalistic colonialism, epitomised by the English doctor, the second half focuses on white colonial domination and the representation of natives as 'degenerate types'. This shift in narrative focus is signalled by the arrival (eighteen years later) of big-game hunters, which is quickly followed by a series of provocative vignettes involving witchcraft, native rebellion and the exercise of white authority. *If Youth But Knew* begins to take on a rather nasty tone at this point, reminiscent in some respects of Griffith's *The Birth of a Nation* (1915): we see the natives using American plantation idioms, such as referring to the white male authority figure as 'massa', being whipped, and so on.

Curiously, there is even a hint of miscegenation in the film – between an Englishman and an African woman (played by a white actress in blackface, of course) – but this subplot is largely framed in terms of the European's sense of Christian missionary duty. Despite her expressed devotion to 'massa', the 'African' woman is still denied the possibility of their relationship being consummated. Needless to say, the colonialist doctor hero emerges from all these experiences a new man, returning to England to resolve the failures of past relationships with all the stoicism and chivalry that befits the classic colonial hero.

One of the features of cinematic colonial narratives is that they are located in 'other' places, and invariably centre on white characters' predicaments. *If Youth But Knew* is a little unusual in this respect, in that England itself features as an important location, to which the doctor hero eventually returns. Otherwise, the film conforms to the generic conventions. The colonial setting provides the backdrop against which European adventures and melodramas can be played out. Questions of racial or cultural equality, or of the integration of the European into the social and political sphere of the 'Others', or vice versa, are not propositions that the genre ever seriously entertains.

The Europeanised African: Robert Adams (with topee) in *Men of Two Worlds* (Thorold Dickinson, 1946)

British colonial film policy was concerned with promoting an acceptable image of Empire, largely through the Colonial Film Unit, set up by the Ministry of Information in 1939 'to make and distribute propaganda films designed to encourage the colonial war effort, chiefly in Africa'.[4] This strand of colonial representation existed alongside more popular – or more commercial – orientations, but it was different in two important respects. First, it was highly institutionalised within the official discourses of government colonial policy; second, it had strong undertones of paternalism with regard to images of the colonial subject. *Men of Two Worlds*, for example, was originally commissioned by the Colonial Office, and was intended not only to boost domestic morale, but also to represent colonial development as a humane policy.[5]

The film's story centres on an African concert pianist living in Britain who returns to his village on a humanitarian mission to assist colonial administrators in a mass resettlement operation, following an outbreak of sleeping sickness. He is immediately thrown into conflict with the local 'witch-doctor', who is leading local resistance. The battle of wills that ensues between these two Africans is mediated, or, more accurately, stage-managed by the British District Commissioner, a paternalist figure who is represented as working for the welfare of the villagers as a whole. The film's view of colonial power relations and authority turns on the relationship between these archetypal figures – the Europeanised African, the local 'witch-doctor', the colonial District Commissioner – but, more significantly, it is delineated in terms of colonial notions of cultural identity. The Europeanised African's cultural identity and allegiance are constantly called into question by the witch-doctor figure, who regards him as a European with black skin and therefore as an instrument of colonial rule. The dramatic tension between the two Africans serves to heighten the Europeanised African's cultural angst, his sense of dislocation. Colonial mediation enters into the equation in the form of the District Commissioner, who promotes the idea of the 'New Africa' in terms of a synthesis of 'the best of Africa' (its spirituality) and 'the best of Europe' (its rationalism).

This imposed definition of Africa is only partly personified by the film's Europeanised African 'hero'; but in any case the mediation is fundamentally Eurocentric, designed to work primarily in the interest of the European colonial power. Significantly, the District

Commissioner figure never directly confronts the local power of the witch-doctor; instead, he is able to defeat this source of opposition through the control he exercises over his Europeanised African protégé. Colonial authority is thus maintained through a form of indirect rule.

Men of Two Worlds is an excellent example of the way in which a colonial narrative attempts to rework and 'liberalise' ideological constructions of the colonial 'Other', in order to reposition itself in relation to the new political (neo-colonial) circumstances that were beginning to emerge by the end of World War II. But like the earlier films in the genre, *Men of Two Worlds* does not question the basic premise of Empire, nor is it suggesting the possibility of (say) the cultural assimilation of colonised subjects. The film reaffirms notions of 'cultural difference', but in terms of its reconfiguration of the interests of neo-colonialism. Despite its liberalism, the film is unable to articulate an alternative vision of the 'New Africa'.

The demise of Empire more or less coincided with the first major influx of immigrants from the Caribbean and the Indian subcontinent, with all the social and political implications that were to follow. Although many of the old colonial constructions persisted intact, small shifts had already started to appear in relation to cinematic black representation. *Pool of London* (1951), one of the earliest post-war British films to focus on the theme of racial intolerance in Britain, signalled this shift within the context of an otherwise non-racial storyline. It wasn't until the Notting Hill 'race riots' of 1958, however, that issues concerning race relations became central themes. The two landmark films from this period, *Sapphire* (Basil Dearden, 1959) and *Flame in the Streets* (Roy Baker, 1961), belong to the cycle of British 'social-problem films' made between the late 1950s and the early 1960s.[6]

These two films are especially interesting for the way in which they dramatise early anxieties about the 'black presence' in post-war Britain; that is, before immigration became the dominant theme in race-relations discourses. This is thematised partly in terms of white racial prejudice and partly in terms of blacks being represented either as 'victims' (*Flame in the Streets*) or as 'social problem' (*Sapphire*). Neither film is particularly concerned with notions of social justice, integration or assimilation, although both can be read as liberal humanist pleas for racial tolerance. The thematic focus of the films centres on how the white characters are affected by, and come to terms with, the

presence of 'race' in their lives. Black characters in the films tend to function primarily as catalysts for the expression of white characters' anxieties. These anxieties are not rooted in race or racial prejudice as such, but they are activated as a direct result of encounters with blacks.

Two aspects of this representation of British race relations should be noted here. First, the representation of blacks as 'victims' or 'social problem' limits the possibility of developing black characterisation beyond the narrow parameters of this dual stereotype; it also reinforces the broader notion of 'black communities' representing marginal, alien and potentially threatening positions on the fringe of civil society. This is a quite explicit undercurrent in both *Flame in the Streets* and *Sapphire*. Second, the theme of racial prejudice is constructed mainly in terms of individual psychopathology, the white working-class domestic setting becoming the primary site of racist angst and tension. The wider social context of racial interaction is suggested, but functions primarily as a backdrop against which the domestic melodramas unfold.

Both films end on a similar note: the traumatised white family facing the reality of 'race' in their lives. And, interestingly, both films identify a female member of the family as the primary source of familial and racial angst. The men at the centre of the drama are seen to possess the capacity for 'rationality' – i.e. they are able to reason their way out of difficult situations and overcome their prejudices. The 'irrationality' of prejudice is explicitly located in the realm of women's anxieties, triggered by the threat of direct interracial contact. In both films this threat appears in the form of an interracial sexual relationship between a member of the white family (not the traumatised woman) and a black person.

This imaginary threat to the stability of the family unit, which the interracial encounter triggers, provokes the films' troubled women characters to play out a series of familial and racial set pieces with a neurotic intensity. But their racism is more than just a fear of blacks as such; it is rooted in a deeper sense of insecurity that these characters articulate within and about their family. It turns on their sense of unfulfilment both as mothers and as wives, which the racial element dramatically activates.

One of the effects of this representation of race relations is that it clearly emphasises the marginality, and the powerlessness, of the black subjects who get drawn into the drama. The notion of blacks as the 'Other', the personification of an alien and disruptive presence, goes unchallenged in both films, it is merely exploited for dramatic purposes. While it could be argued that black representation in *Flame in the Streets* and *Sapphire* is more sophisticated than hitherto in British cinema, it is still not developed to the extent where black characters themselves assume a more proactive role. Black characters are marginalised within the narrative, which is shaped by its focus on white characters' anxieties about their encounter with 'race'.

These examples of racial representation from the late 1950s and early 60s illustrate the post-World War II shift from colonial motifs situated in 'other' places to 'race-relations' narratives located in Britain itself. However, there was little subsequent development in the next two decades. The proliferation of films and, especially, television documentaries dealing with race-relations topics during the 1970s may suggest another major shift in racial representation in British media, but this was not the case. Like the colonised subjects in earlier colonial narratives, the metropolitan black subjects in contemporary British race-relations drama remained fixed within the narrow parameters of the 'social-problem' paradigm, with only rare instances of alternative approaches in either narrative fiction or documentary.[7]

By the 1970s television had become the dominant medium for representing British race relations, generally in the form of sociological documentaries examining various aspects of so-called immigrant life. These television programmes tended to pathologise black experiences, rather than offering new perspectives on the subject. During this period multiculturalism reached its height of influence, but although the representation of a multicultural Britain signalled a relatively progressive step forward, in the political sense, culturally it did not seriously challenge the traditional ethnocentricity of colonial and race-relations discourses. Black representation, in other words, continued to be framed in terms of its relevance to the wider white public. The threat of the 'Other' might have been less accentuated than in the past, but it remained a force in the public imagination.

One of the characteristics of colonial and mainstream race-relations discourses is the absence of the colonised subject as an active voice; that is to say, the colonised subject does not have access to the means of self-representation. This changed with the arrival of black film and cultural practitioners. Commenting on the uneasy relationship between black literature and critical practice, Henry Louis Gates, Jr writes:

> For all sorts of complex historical reasons, the very act of writing has been a 'political' act for the black author . . . And because our life in the West has been one political struggle after another, our literature has been defined from without, and rather often from within, as primarily just one more polemic in those struggles.[8]

The same observation can be made regarding black independent film-making in Britain and elsewhere, which faces a similar dilemma because it is perceived largely in terms of race relations and protest-oriented representation. Indeed, what Gates calls the received critical fallacies which frame standard readings of black literary texts also applies to problems which underlie the critical and institutional recognition of black film and cultural practices. This is evidenced partly in public perceptions of what a 'black' film is, and partly in an institutional funding policy that tends to be uncertain about the social and polemical scope of black cinematic practice. Consequently, films which attempt to break the sociological race-relations mould, or which try to explore the issue of black representation through the deployment of alternative (non-realist) narrative strategies, tend to be less easily accommodated within conventional race-relations paradigms.

In that respect, *Pressure* (1975), the first British feature film made by a black director (Horace Ové), can be read as a landmark transitional film. While it draws heavily on a number of familiar race-relations motifs, it reworks them into the film's documentary-like fictional narrative with effects quite different from mainstream black representations. More importantly, the film sets out to 'depathologise' black British experience by

The first British feature film made by a black director: *Pressure* (Horace Ové, 1975)

examining the notion of 'Black Britishness' itself. It can thus be read as a critique of British multiculturalism and institutionalised race relations. The closing image of black political protest – an image which effectively reinstates an active black voice in black representation – is nonetheless deliberately pessimistic in tone, accurately reflecting the general sense of despair over the 'failure' of race-relations politics that was felt within black communities by the mid-1970s.

Burning an Illusion (1981), the second British feature film made by a black director (Menelik Shabazz), marked another important shift in the representation of 'race'. As in *Pressure*, narrative stress is placed on the idea of black politicisation, but here there is little interest in commenting on the failure of multiculturalism, or exploring problems concerning black–white relations in the wider social context. *Burning an Illusion* focuses instead on relationships within black communities, especially those between men and women. Thus the notion of black identity is defined from within the context of a black community rather than being mediated by dominant race-relations discourses, and the question of 'Britishness' has no special significance in terms of the film's representation of black experience. This can be seen in the film's portrayal of racial victimisation, for example. Despite the deployment of this archetypal motif (blacks as victims) during key moments in the plot, it plays a relatively minor part in the main thrust of the narrative, functioning instead as a plot device that helps to move the story on. By placing narrative stress on such intra-ethnic or intra-black community concerns, *Burning an Illusion* introduced a more culturally militant tone to black representation within British narrative fiction.[9]

In the 1980s, with the emergence of a new generation of black British independent film-makers, another shift occurred, one that was part of a broader crisis in representation. Two important things had happened. First, essentialist notions of cultural identity began to be challenged, resulting in a radical reconceptualisation of cinematic black representation. Second, black independent film-makers in Britain institutionalised themselves, in response to the growing institutionalisation of film cultural policy and funding. These developments could only have happened in the context of post-multicultural Britain in the 1980s, when black film-makers abandoned traditional race-relations discourses and gained access to the means of self-representation. This resulted in a series of major cultural shifts during the decade, not only in the area of black film imagery

and representation, but also in the relationship between black film and cultural practitioners on the one hand, and dominant cultural institutions on the other.

This remapping of the black British film cultural terrain effectively helped to shift the cultural terms of reference away from the narrow scope of traditional race relations and multiculturalism and towards new ways of conceptualising the role and status of black representation. The notion of the black diaspora, for example, was mobilised in such a way as to reconfigure the geographical boundaries of 'black' film-making, giving it an entirely different political inflection. In addition, there was a tendency towards evolving a cinematic black historiography which would 'excavate' black people's own histories and re-present them through new forms of audiovisual practice.[10] Empire itself became the object of interrogation.

Three films in particular herald the arrival of this critical moment in black representation: *Territories* (Isaac Julien, 1984); *The Passion of Remembrance* (Maureen Blackwood and Isaac Julien, 1986); and *Handsworth Songs* (John Akomfrah, 1986). These films effectively changed the cultural agenda, by demonstrating that it was possible to engage in formal experimentation and to take cultural media intervention beyond the narrow bounds of race-relations iconography. Initial reaction to the films centred on their alleged elitism, a response which derived from popular assumptions about what a 'black' film ought to be *vis-à-vis* notions of realism and accessibility. But as Kobena Mercer observed, the critical debates which the films provoked – the first public debates of their kind in Britain – highlighted

> the way image-making has become an important
> arena of cultural contestation – contestation over
> what it means to be British today; contestation
> over what Britishness itself means as a national or
> cultural identity; and contestation over the values that
> underpin the Britishness of British cinema as a
> national film culture.[11]

The critical challenge to essentialist notions of 'blackness' provided the means by which black representation itself could be recast in new terms. This signalled a major shift, enabling black film and cultural practitioners to extricate themselves from traditional race-relations paradigms. As Stuart Hall states:

> What is at issue here is the recognition of the
> extraordinary diversity of subjective positions, social

experiences and cultural identities which compose the category 'black'; that is, the recognition that 'black' is essentially a politically and culturally constructed category, which cannot be grounded in a set of fixed trans-cultural or transcendental racial categories and which therefore has no guarantee in Nature. What this brings into play is the recognition of the immense diversity and differentiation of the historical and cultural experience of black subjects.[12]

The notion that cultural identities are based on a less fixed sense of 'race', and that they necessarily incorporate other identities such as class, gender and sexuality, became a primary motif in certain strands of black representation. *My Beautiful Laundrette* (Stephen Frears, 1985) and Isaac Julien's *Young Soul Rebels* (1991) both explore hitherto unspoken areas of black (gay) sexuality as one of the means of breaking the mould of social-problem representation.

There is nevertheless a general sense in which the destabilising effect of what Hall calls 'the end of the innocent notion of the essential black' has resulted in a kind of cultural eclecticism which denies the black subject any coherent sense of (ethnic) identity – that is, an identity which, in the last instance, I would suggest, is centred on the 'fact of blackness'.[13] This is not intended to reduce the totality of black experience to 'race', or to celebrate some untenable concept of 'blackness' as such, but rather to give ethnicity far more significance than is allowed for in some contemporary radical cultural theory. Indeed, the sense of ethnicity as an underlying principle, a means by which people bring structure to their lives, is implicit in both *My Beautiful Laundrette* and *Young Soul Rebels*.

It has been suggested that the emergence of new, multifarious black identities since the 1970s is bound up in the historical process of fragmentation which currently afflicts the post-modern western world. This conceptualisation has to be contested. Post-modern angst and fragmentation may well be part of the psychic experience of sections of the (black and white) creative intelligentsia, but there is little evidence to suggest that it is a common experience, or a prevalent attitude in everyday black life, or in (self-)representation, for that matter. One is therefore inclined to resist calls for assimilation through fragmentation.

This conclusion could be accused of cultural nationalism, and of aestheticising 'blackness' – a practice which results in unacceptably simplistic representation. Nothing substantive can be gained from conjuring up

images of 'pre-colonial innocence and authenticity', to use Paul Willemen's words, or promulgating essentialised symbols of a cultural identity which simply mirror dominant practices.[14] On the other hand, the 1990s have seen the emergence of a completely new cultural and political agenda in Britain, which has temporarily halted any radically new interventions in the area of black representation. This does not bode well for the immediate future.

Notes

1. Homi K. Bhabha, 'The Other Question – the Stereotype and Colonial Discourse'.
2. Abdul R. JanMohamed, 'The Economy of Manichean Allegory: The Function of Racial Difference in Colonialist Literature', pp. 78–106.
3. David Trotter, 'Colonial Subjects', pp. 3–20.
4. Rosaleen Smyth, 'Movies and Mandarins: The Official Film and British Colonial Africa', p. 132. See also Jeffrey Richards, '"Patriotism with Profit": British Imperial Cinema in the 1930s'.
5. Smyth, 'Movies and Mandarins', p. 135.
6. For an excellent study of this genre, see John Hill, *Sex, Class and Realism: British Cinema 1956–1963*.
7. The best examples are *Blacks Britannica* (David Koff, 1978), an independent production made for WGBH-Boston, which critically examined Britain's colonial legacy; and Colin Prescod's series of documentary films, *Struggles for the Black Community*, produced by the Institute of Race Relations in 1983.
8. Henry Louis Gates, Jr, 'Criticism in the Jungle', p. 5.
9. See Jim Pines, 'The Cultural Context of Black British Cinema', pp. 183–93.
10. For the role of critical theory in black film practice, see Robert Crusz, 'Black Cinemas, Film Theory and Dependent Knowledge' and Kobena Mercer, 'Diaspora Culture and the Dialogic Imagination: The Aesthetics of Black Independent Film in Britain', which carries the intentionally ironic title, 'The Last "Special Issue" on Race?'; and Reece Auguiste and Black Audio Film Collective, 'Black Independents and Third Cinema: The British Context'.
11. Kobena Mercer, 'Recoding Narratives of Race and Nation', p. 5.
12. Stuart Hall, 'New Ethnicities'.
13. Ibid., p. 28. For an interesting development of this critical reformulation, see Stuart Hall, 'Cultural Identity and Cinematic Representation'.
14. Paul Willemen, 'The Third Cinema Question: Notes and Reflections'.

Bibliography

Auguiste, Reece and Black Audio Film Collective, 'Black Independents and Third Cinema: The British Context', in Jim Pines and Paul Willemen (eds), *Questions of Third Cinema* (London: BFI, 1989).

Bhabha, Homi K., 'The Other Question – the Stereotype and Colonial Discourse', *Screen* vol. 24 no. 6, Winter 1983.

Crusz, Robert, 'Black Cinemas, Film Theory and Dependent Knowledge', *Screen* vol. 26 nos 3–4, Spring–Summer 1985. Reprinted in Houston A. Baker, Jr *et al.* (eds), *Black British Cultural Studies – A Reader* (Chicago, IL: University of Chicago Press, 1996).

Dyer, Richard, 'White', *Screen* vol. 29 no. 4, Autumn 1988.

Gates, Jr, Henry Louis, 'Criticism in the Jungle', in Henry Louis Gates, Jr (ed.), *Black Literature and Literary Theory* (New York and London: Methuen, 1984).

Hall, Stuart, 'New Ethnicities', in Kobena Mercer (ed.), *Black Film, British Cinema* (London: Institute of Contemporary Arts Document 7/BFI Production Special, 1988). Reprinted in Houston A. Baker, Jr *et al.* (eds), *Black British Cultural Studies – A Reader* (Chicago, IL: University of Chicago Press, 1996).

Hall, Stuart, 'Cultural Identity and Cinematic Representation', *Framework* no. 36, 1989. Reprinted in Houston A. Baker, Jr *et al.* (eds), *Black British Cultural Studies – A Reader* (Chicago, IL: University of Chicago Press, 1996).

Hill, John, *Sex, Class and Realism: British Cinema 1956–1963* (London: BFI, 1986).

JanMohamed, Abdul R., 'The Economy of Manichean Allegory: The Function of Racial Difference in Colonialist Literature', in Henry Louis Gates, Jr (ed.), *'Race,' Writing and Difference* (Chicago, IL: University of Chicago Press, 1986).

Mercer, Kobena, 'Diaspora Culture and the Dialogic Imagination: The Aesthetics of Black Independent Film in Britain', in Mbye B. Cham and Claire Andrade-Watkins (eds), *BlackFrames: Critical Perspectives on Black Independent Cinema* (Cambridge, MA: Celebration of Black Cinema, Inc. and MIT Press, 1988), pp. 50–61. Reprinted in Kobena Mercer, *Welcome to the Jungle* (London: Routledge, 1994).

Mercer, Kobena, 'Recoding Narratives of Race and Nation', in Kobena Mercer (ed.), *Black Film, British Cinema* (London: Institute of Contemporary Arts Document 7/BFI Production Special, 1988). Reprinted in Kobena Mercer, *Welcome to the Jungle* (London: Routledge, 1994).

Parry, Benita, 'Problems in Current Theories of Colonial Discourse', *The Oxford Literary Review* vol. 9 nos 1–2, 1987.

Pines, Jim, 'The Cultural Context of Black British Cinema', in Mbye B. Cham and Claire Andrade-Watkins (eds), *BlackFrames: Critical Perspectives on Black Independent Cinema* (Cambridge, MA: Celebration of Black Cinema, Inc. and MIT Press, 1988). Reprinted in Houston A. Baker, Jr *et al.* (eds), *Black British Cultural Studies – A Reader* (Chicago, IL: University of Chicago Press, 1996).

Richards, Jeffrey, ' "Patriotism with Profit": British Imperial Cinema in the 1930s', in James Curran and Vincent Porter (eds), *British Cinema History* (London: Weidenfeld and Nicolson, 1983).

Ross, Karen, *Black and White Media: Black Images in Popular Film and Television* (Cambridge: Polity Press, 1996).

Shohat, Ella and Stam, Robert, *Unthinking Eurocentrism: Multiculturalism and the Media* (London: Routledge, 1994).

Smyth, Rosaleen, 'Movies and Mandarins: The Official Film and British Colonial Africa', in James Curran and Vincent Porter (eds), *British Cinema History* (London: Weidenfeld and Nicolson, 1983).

Trotter, David, 'Colonial Subjects', *Critical Quarterly* vol. 32 no. 3, Autumn 1990.

Willemen, Paul, 'The Third Cinema Question: Notes and Reflections', in Jim Pines and Paul Willemen (eds), *Questions of Third Cinema* (London: BFI, 1989).

Young, Lola, *Fear of the Dark: 'Race', Gender and Sexuality in the Cinema* (London: Routledge, 1996).

14
Exiles and British Cinema

KEVIN GOUGH-YATES

European exiles dominated British film production in the 1930s. In his now notorious review of a Max Schach production, Graham Greene, then film critic of the *Spectator,* wrote in 1936 of 'the dark alien executive tipping his cigar ash behind the glass in Wardour Street, the Hungarian producer [Alexander Korda] adapting Mr Wells's ideas tactfully at Denham, the German director [Karl Grune] letting himself down in his canvas chair at Elstree', and asked whether *The Marriage of Corbal* (1936) could be considered an English film at all, directed as it was by 'Karl Grune and F. Brunn, photographed by Otto Kanturek, and edited by E. Stokvis [sic], with a cast which includes Nils Asther, Ernst Deutsch and the American, Noah Beery'.[1] Greene, grossly misrepresenting the Cinematographic Act of 1927, writes that the

> Quota Act has played into foreign hands . . . there is nothing to prevent an English film unit being completely staffed by technicians of foreign blood. We have saved the English film industry from American competition only to surrender it to a far more alien control . . . it is not English money that calls the tune, and it is only natural that compatriots should find jobs for each other.[2]

Greene argues that there are perfectly good 'English technicians capable of producing films of a high enough standard to take their place in the international markets', technicians who had made *Song of Ceylon* (1934), *BBC – The Voice of Britain* (1935), *The Turn of the Tide* (1935), *Night Mail* (1936) and *Midshipman Easy* (1935).

The sometimes acrimonious debate about aliens in the British film industry was not only about employ-

ment, it was concerned with the concept of national identity as expressed through the cinema. Documentary film-makers, perhaps self-servingly, have wanted to see Britain's national cinema as having its roots within films such as *Song of Ceylon* and *Night Mail*, made at the Empire Marketing Board and the GPO Film Unit in the 1930s. Basil Wright, for example, writes of how 'the great period of the British feature film, which was during and immediately after the Second World War, owes a tremendous amount to the influence and example of the documentary film'.[3]

This chapter questions whether a national cinema can be constructed by following so narrow a trajectory. What is generally forgotten in writings about the development of British cinema, particularly those which focus on the documentary film movement as providing the inspiration for its 'classic period', is that for the ten years before World War II the production context outside of the documentary film movement was fashioned by non-British film-makers – producers, writers, cinematographers, directors and designers – most of whom had been driven out of Nazi Germany. Not only were they engaged in all capacities in the production of British films, they trained the future generation of native-born film technicians; they were, for the most part, not economic migrants seeking employment, but experienced film-makers who helped develop a nascent industry.

Producers: Korda and Schach

Alexander Korda made films in his native Hungary and in Austria, Germany, Hollywood and France before settling in England in 1931 and establishing himself as

Britain's foremost independent producer. Although his career to this point was relatively undistinguished, with fifty films behind him his understanding of the international market was unique in Britain. He created London Film Productions and scrambled together the money to make *The Private Life of Henry VIII* (1933), which became a great success, the first British film to make a breakthrough into the American market. His achievement encouraged major financial investment in the industry and he was able to build Denham Studios with the financial backing of the Prudential Assurance Company.

Korda was a visionary with regard to British cinema, and set about correcting its fundamental weaknesses: underinvestment in equipment, studios and manpower, and inadequate distribution. He built Denham Studios along Hollywood lines and brought in leading technicians from abroad to work on such films as *Sanders of the River* (1935), *The Ghost Goes West* (1935), *Things to Come* (1936), *The Scarlet Pimpernel* (1934), *The Man Who Could Work Miracles* (1936), *Farewell Again* (1937) and *Knight Without Armour* (1937). Not only did he successfully negotiate a distribution arrangement with United Artists, he continuously sought an innovatory marketing edge, entering into an early contractual agreement with Technicolor, for example, and using the process to maximum effect in *The Four Feathers* (1939). For the first time numerous fledgeling British technicians and directors were able to receive training from major cinematographers, editors and designers. Several of Korda's leading actors and actresses became stars: Laurence Olivier, Ralph Richardson, Vivien Leigh, Sabu, Merle Oberon, Robert Donat, Flora Robson and Charles Laughton all established their film-acting careers at London Films.

On the back of Korda's success in America, 'hot' money, much of it from banks, was recklessly invested in the film business. Among the many beneficiaries was the producer Max Schach, who had been forced out of Emelka Studios, Munich, in December 1931 because of his lack of financial control. He came to Britain as a refugee in 1934 and soon established a string of film-production companies, the Capitol Group, which included Trafalgar, Buckingham, and Cecil Films. According to the journalist Hans Feld, who as film editor of *Film Kurier* in Germany knew Schach, reputable figures such as the producer Erich Pommer steered well clear of him.[4] Rachael Low considers Schach's companies 'tramp' operations, travelling from studio to studio without homes of their

Austrian sophistication, Austrian extravagance: Karl Grune's *The Marriage of Corbal* (1936)

own, but it should be emphasised that Denham was designed to be available to such tenant companies, and the money that the banks were only too ready to lend was not intended for studio infrastructure; it was speculative money riding on individual films. Korda's prosperity depended on a thriving non-studio-owning industry which hired space from him at Denham. Schach's and Korda's fortunes were, therefore, intertwined in a complex speculation in which the banks as much pursued film-production companies as were sought out.

Where Korda was said to favour Hungarians, Schach's associates were generally Austrian: the singer Richard Tauber, the actor Fritz Kortner, the actress Elisabeth Bergner, the writer Rudolf Bernauer, the cinematographer Otto Kanturek, the designer Oscar Werndorff, and the director Karl Grune. His films, which include *Abdul the Damned* (1935), *Land without Music*, *The Marriage of Corbal* and *Pagliacci* (all 1936), were failures, because Schach, duplicating his Emelka experience, was cavalier with budgets and failed to secure satisfactory distribution. Korda's films invariably exceeded their projected costs; *Things to Come*, for example, finally cost £258,000, two-and-a-half times as much as Schach's *Pagliacci*, but Schach's film lost all its money, while Korda's took £350,000 at the box office.[5]

Korda and Schach both possessed a major talent for charming money out of people. Monja Danischewsky, who was employed by Schach in the publicity department of Capitol, describes him as a man with 'immense charm and an irrepressible sense of humour'.[6] Tales abound of Korda's ability to calm the most irate of bankers and the most fragile of star temperaments. Rachael Low makes an unfavourable comparison between Schach and Korda. Schach, she feels, contributed nothing to the industry. Money went directly into people's pockets. Korda created stars, built Denham Studios, provided opportunities for writers and directors, and encouraged the industry to find a significant place for itself in world markets.[7] But Schach, though less deliberately and thoroughly than Korda, also helped forge a national industry out of a combination of experienced mid-Europeans and eager but inexperienced British actors, directors and technicians.

When Twickenham, a company that produced little of lasting interest, went under in 1937, there was a rash of bankruptcies. Schach's companies collapsed and Korda lost control of Denham to the Prudential and, ultimately, to Rank. Korda was blamed by City financiers for the failure of their own reckless speculation. The journalist Robert Bruce Lockhart, whose anti-Semitic views were well known, wrote in his diary:

> Last night Bayliss-Smith, who is a leading chartered accountant and represents the creditors in some of the biggest cinema financial messes in this country, says the cinema industry here has cost the banks and insurance companies about £4,000,000. Most of this is lost by Jews – like Korda and Max Schacht [sic]. Latter already lost a packet for the German Government before Hitler. He has now done the same here. In Bayliss-Smith's opinion, and he would not say so lightly, Korda is a much worse man than Schacht. Schacht is just a slick Jew who sees financial moves ahead of the other fellow. Korda is a crook and, according to Bayliss-Smith, an evil man.[8]

Cinematographers and Art Directors

The major writers, photographers, producers and even directors of feature films in Britain throughout most of the 1930s were not British, or at least were not British-born.[9] A glance at the 'Technical Section' of *Spotlight* for Winter 1935 reveals that no major British production company failed to have at least one European cinematographer under contract. Gaumont-British sported Mutz Greenbaum, London Films listed Georges Périnal and Hans Schneeberger. The small, under-financed company Criterion Film Productions, which had been created by Douglas Fairbanks, Jr with the Romanian producer Marcel Hellman, listed Günther Krampf.

Even Basil Dean's Associated Talking Pictures, at its very English Ealing Studios, listed Jan Stallich as its studio photographer. The only significant company not to list a European cinematographer was Herbert Wilcox's British and Dominion.

Of the British-born cinematographers listed in this edition of *Spotlight* only three had notable careers: Freddie Young, Ronald Neame and Desmond Dickinson. Desmond Dickinson 'was so good', wrote Adrian Brunel, the director and writer, that 'it seemed incredible that he should have been relegated to shooting cheap films only, while foreign cameramen, infinitely less talented, were freely admitted into the country to shoot in our studios'.[10] Another British cinematographer, Erwin Hillier, was in fact born and educated in Berlin, and began a long film career in 1931, as assistant to Fritz Arno Wagner on Fritz Lang's *M*.

Most of the art directors who made creative interventions in the British film industry were Europeans. Léon Barsacq, in *Caligari's Cabinet and Other Grand Illusions*, his book on film design, writes of 'the apathy and ignorance pervading British film studios' and of the encouragement Vincent Korda, a key figure at his brother's London Films, offered a generation of young, aspiring art directors.[11] The Hollywood art director Holmes Paul identified the transformation that was taking place in British studios when, in 1932, he wrote:

> A valuable advance in realism has been attained through the closer co-operation of the director and cameraman with the art director. This essential co-operation has been lacking in this country. . . . German producers, ever in the forefront where scenery is concerned, have always insisted on the closest attention to the building of sets which are intended to help the camera to secure the utmost realism. . . . The German studios have always realised that large sums of money and a great deal of time can be saved if the director, camera staff, and art director work in the closest harmony.[12]

As with photographers, each of the European art directors had an individual style, which was incorporated into a broad knowledge of film-making. Michael Powell observed that Alfred Junge, whom he had first encountered at the Gaumont-British Studios, was a good organiser, a tremendous disciplinarian, and a very good trainer of young people . . . besides being a very great designer himself'.[13] This view of Junge is confirmed by the cinematographer Christopher Challis:

Alfred was a martinet, he ran the art department like a hospital . . . it was immaculate . . . they literally wiped up your footprints as you went in . . . Alfred was brilliant with matte shots, hanging miniatures and all that sort of thing . . . He would mark on the set with a cross the position of the camera for the main shot and woe betide anyone who tried to shift it . . . . He'd designed it from that position and that was it. There was this cross and the size of the lens put on it.[14]

European Influences: The Powell–Pressburger Partnership

Europeans were less dominant in the areas of directing and editing, although here too they were well represented. Paul Stein, Friedrich Feher, Hans Schwartz, Karl Grune, Ludwig Berger, Berthold Viertel and the brothers Alexander and Zoltan Korda are among those with major directorial credits. Feher's *The Robber Symphony* (1936), for example, which was designed by Ernö Metzner, is described by Elliot Stein as 'one of the great and delightful eccentricities of European cinema in the thirties'.[15] It was said to be the first 'composed' film, the first film shot to a pre-recorded soundtrack. Michael Powell claims that, although he never saw the film, he was 'haunted by it and longed for a film subject where music was the master'.[16] It inspired him to create the atmospheric end sequence of *Black Narcissus* (1947), the ballet in *The Red Shoes* (1948) and the whole of *The Tales of Hoffmann* (1951).

In the spectrum of debate, Powell, who considered the collective truth of documentary no more valid or verifiable than his own personal one, was firmly at the European end. He worked as second-unit director on Korda's *The Thief of Bagdad* (1940) which, until war and Korda's financial problems forced its evacuation to Hollywood, was directed by Ludwig Berger at Denham. *Kinematograph Weekly* noted that Berger, who 'is also a great musician and has produced several operas on the Continent, has a revolutionary scheme for shooting the music first on *The Thief of Bagdad*'. It was to be 'the first time that a full musical score would be played back and the sound "mixed" on the set'.[17] 'In the end the only sequences shot to pre-composed music were those involving special effects – the gallop of the Flying Horse and the Silvermaid's Dance.'[18] But the chaos associated with the experiment excited rather than dampened Powell's aesthetic enthusiasms.

The European film-maker in Britain during the 1930s was frequently better read and better educated than his British counterpart. Powell felt that the European could converse on a wide range of subjects. He was 'cultivated': Feher was a trained composer, Vincent Korda a reputable painter, Berthold Viertel a poet and Walter Goehr, Allan Gray and Hanns Eisler students of Arnold Schoenberg. Powell was one of the few British-born film-makers who was seduced, and not shamed, by this wealth of experience and erudition. He recognised that the particular combination of imagination and technical skill which the Europeans brought to the cinema could help create a less parochial British cinema. Whenever he could, he associated with European artists. His partnership with the Hungarian-born scriptwriter Emeric Pressburger began in 1938, when Korda introduced them to each other at a script conference for *The Spy in Black* (1939). Thereafter Powell's designers were always European: Vincent Korda, Alfred Junge and Hein Heckroth; and his main cinematographers were Georges Périnal and Erwin Hillier until his collaboration with Jack Cardiff began with *A Matter of Life and Death* (1946).[19] It could be argued that during the war, with Korda in America and British cinema turning towards a form of British realism, they alone kept the Korda flag flying, using Korda stars and technicians whenever they could.

European actors and writers were also surprisingly important. Anton Walbrook, Fritz Kortner, Conrad Veidt, Oscar Homolka, Frederick Valk and others all had to battle with the English language. Dolly Haas was given parts which made her Russian or Hungarian; on one occasion her accent was supposed to be Australian. Both Valk and Walbrook appeared successfully on the London stage in 1939, the latter in Noël Coward's *Design for Living*, but accent remained a determining factor in the parts they were offered. Conrad Veidt was compelled to speak his lines phonetically in his first British film. According to the actor Robert Morley, who worked with him briefly as dialogue director on *Under the Red Robe* (1937), he 'was a master at delivering lines. . . . He always spoke them very slowly when everyone else spoke rather fast, and softly when everyone else spoke loudly.'[20] He also knew about lighting and always carried a small pocket mirror in order to see how his face was lit, so that he could make suggestions to the cinematographer.[21] But his distinctive accent, meant that Gaumont-British, to whom he was under contract, had problems finding him suitable parts and he became stereotyped as a German spy or a mysterious foreigner. Even when he moved to London Films, Korda found it difficult to find roles for him and, in the end, resorted to using him in much the same way.

In *The Spy in Black*, Emeric Pressburger created a character which enabled Veidt to be located in an English film while retaining elements from his parts in German cinema. Powell put it this way:

> I knew all the German Expressionist films he had done and . . . [Veidt] said '. . . let him wear black overalls as the motorcyclist, make him a black figure'. . . . The way he comes out is just as much the myth of Veidt as the myth of the German spy.[22]

Pressburger makes use of the possibilities arising from a situation where one person speaks faltering English and the other speaks it perfectly. Valerie Hobson is a schoolteacher and a double agent, Veidt a U-boat commander who has just been landed on the coast. When they meet, they establish their credentials by exchanging a few words in German, but she loses no time in insisting on English and in correcting Veidt's pronunciation.[23]

In *The Life and Death of Colonel Blimp* (1943), Pressburger's most personal film script, he makes manifest the anxieties of a refugee from Nazi Germany. Anton Walbrook, as Blimp's friend, Theo Kretschmar-Schuldorff, is interrogated at an aliens tribunal by A. E. Matthews. The once patriotic, exuberant army officer of World War I is now noticeably down-at-heel and depressed. In a statement transplanted from Pressburger's own experience and spoken without interruption, Theo explains why he has left Germany for Britain. He (unlike Pressburger himself) was not obliged to leave Germany, he had nothing to fear from Hitler. When Matthews observes that it took him some time to discover where he stood with regard to Hitler, Theo points out that the British, too, seem to have been in no great hurry. Matthews is taken aback and has to acknowledge the validity of Theo's remark. Pressburger's comment on this sequence in 1970 emphasises the intensity of his feelings:

> I wanted to express this feeling of mine that though my mother had died in a concentration camp and I was pre-conditioned about the whole thing, I always believed . . . that there are also good Germans . . . who didn't have to go away from Germany but chose to go away. . . . I had that kind of experience [in immigration control] obviously. England is a very, very difficult country for foreigners to come to. Of

course, when I came my intention was to stay in England but you have to lie straight away . . . to the question, 'How long do you intend to stay here?' You mustn't say, 'I intend to stay forever' . . . so you answer, 'Six months', and then you extend the six months. . . . I believe that anyone that comes to the country under the same circumstances cannot love the Immigration Officers.[24]

The difficulties of adjustment to Britain and its language were never entirely solved by Pressburger himself, and this theme reappears throughout his career. *A Canterbury Tale* (1944) and *I Know Where I'm Going!* (1945) are conventionally seen as examples of Powell's neo-Romantic sensibility, but they also disclose Pressburger's sensitivity to being a stranger, confronted by an alien language and culture. In *A Canterbury Tale*, the stranger is an American GI, Bob Johnson, played by a real one, Sgt John Sweet. Pressburger here displaces the problems of the refugee in Britain on to two characters: an English-speaking but foreign soldier and Alison (Sheila Sim), a Londoner, but now a land girl. Officially, the GI was a welcome guest in Britain, but the number of films that were made to help him adjust to its alien conventions suggests that difficulties were not easily overcome. Pressburger modulates the GI's problems with trains, telephones and tea-drinking with a more deeply rooted cultural difference embodied by two English characters – Alison, who worked in a department store before the war and Peter (Dennis Price), a cinema organist – urban aliens in a rural environment that the American, a country boy from Oregon, is more attuned to. In one of the most effective sequences in the film, Alison and Bob meet again at a wheelwright's yard. Alison is teased by the blacksmith for her ignorance of country matters, but an immediate rapport is reached between the wheelwright and the American soldier because of their shared knowledge and understanding of wood. As Bob and Alison ride off in the mended cart, Bob explains his acceptance (he has been invited to share the wheelwright's midday dinner) by telling her, 'We speak the same language.' To which she responds, 'I'm English and I don't speak their language.'

In *I Know Where I'm Going*, a prissy English girl (Wendy Hiller) travels to Scotland to marry a rich industrialist. She finds herself in a country where she is bemused by the language and bewildered by the people she meets. She is transported to Scotland in a montage

A stranger confronted by an alien language and culture:
Wendy Hiller on Mull in *I Know Where I'm Going!* (Michael
Powell and Emeric Pressburger, 1945)

sequence which suggests Powell's fascination with *The
Wizard of Oz*, but which, for Pressburger, is a further
attempt to exorcise the painful experience of his
forced flight to Britain. The film is a supreme example
of the ways in which an émigré writer and an English
director are able to harmonise their concerns and
obsessions. The brilliant, almost show-off sequence of
the journey from London to the Isle of Mull gives way
to a journey of discovery for the protagonist once she
arrives. Gaelic may substitute for English as the incom-
prehensible language of *I Know Where I'm Going*, but
there is the same sense of bewilderment and difficulty
that Pressburger's other 'alien' characters experience.
Underneath the stand-offish character played by
Wendy Hiller lies a yearning to understand and
belong.

The Enduring Contribution
of European Exiles

World War II did not kill off the 'international' film, but
a British interpretation of realism gradually asserted
itself. Basil Wright and others believed that the documentary film contributed significantly to the development and maturity of British feature films during the
war. The producer Michael Balcon thought it 'the
greatest single influence in British film production
[which] more than anything helped establish a national
style'.[25] Sir Arthur Elton, too, felt that the 'old school'
was effectively left behind: 'Korda, who was a wonderful man, didn't finally come into the battle, which was
between the old and the new. The attack was to get the

Ministry of Information to base its policies on realism
rather than 1914 romance.'[26] But matters were less
simple than this. Cavalcanti, the Brazilian who headed
the GPO Film Unit at the outbreak of the war, took a
number of figures from documentary into feature film-
making when he joined Balcon at Ealing. But Ealing
and the Crown Film Unit were responsible for only a
fraction of wartime feature films and many of the
wartime realist classics – Powell and Pressburger's *One
of Our Aircraft Is Missing* (1942), Sidney Gilliat's *Waterloo
Road* (1945) and David Lean and Noël Coward's *In
Which We Serve* (1942) – owed little to the documentary film movement.

Although there was frequently a nostalgia for
Germany, European émigrés associated themselves with
the Allied cause during the war. Their experience and
knowledge of Hitler's Germany reinforced their feelings for Britain and, despite the indignity and unfairness
of internment, many of them embraced British values
and contributed what they could to the war effort.
Some of them undertook official responsibilities:
Rudolf Bernauer, the co-writer of the screenplay for
Hatter's Castle (Lance Comfort, 1941), was involved
with 'black' propaganda broadcasts to Germany from
Woburn Abbey; the composer Mischa Spoliansky and
the actors Lucie Mannheim, Herbert Lom, Gerard
Heinz and Walter Rilla worked for the BBC on 'white'
propaganda broadcasts such as *Aus der freien Welt*. Korda,
who was in the USA during the early part of the war,
acted as a courier and gathered intelligence information
for the British government.[27]

By 1946 Korda had re-established London Films
and he gradually attracted back talented film-makers
like Powell and Pressburger, Launder and Gilliat,
Carol Reed, and David Lean, who had made films for
the Rank Organisation during the war. Reed's *The
Third Man* (1949) and Powell and Pressburger's *The
Red Shoes* and *Gone to Earth* (1950) show a flowering
of sophisticated European-influenced British cinema.
But by the end of the decade, as financial crisis stalked
the industry, horizons contracted and smaller-
budgeted, cosier, more parochial films became the
norm. If the European exile can be said to have established the British cinema in the 1930s, *The Tales of
Hoffmann*, Powell and Pressburger's homage to
Friedrich Feher's *The Robber Symphony*, might be seen
as the last gasp of that ambitious, expansive cinema
which they brought to Britain. The 1950s was the
decade of Ealing and Pinewood, whose very names
betoken little England.

Notes

1. Graham Greene, *Spectator*, 5 June 1936, reprinted in *The Pleasure Dome* (London: Secker & Warburg, 1972), pp. 78–9.

2. The facts are quite opposite. The Cinematographic Films Act of 1927 defines a British film, for the purpose of the Act, as one that has 'been made by a . . . British subject', where 'the studio scenes must have been photographed in a studio in the British Empire', where the 'author of the scenario must have been a British subject' and where not less than seventy-five per cent of the salaries, wages and payments for labour and services in the making of the film (exclusive of payments in respect of copyright and of the salary or payments to one foreign actor or actress or producer, but inclusive of the payments to the author of the scenario) has been paid to British subjects or persons domiciled in the British Empire. The review is quite clearly anti-Semitic.

3. Basil Wright, *The Long View*, p. 109.

4. Interview with author, 12 July 1986.

5. Paul Tabori, *Alexander Korda*, p. 178. The producers' revenue was, therefore, much smaller (£137,500), so the film still made a considerable loss.

6. Monja Danischewsky, *White Russian, Red Face* (London: Gollancz, 1966), p. 105.

7. Rachael Low, *Film Making in 1930s Britain* (London: George Allen & Unwin, 1985), pp. 218–29.

8. Sir Robert Bruce Lockhart, *The Diaries* (London: Macmillan, 1973), p. 105. Bayliss-Smith was on the board of some of Schach's companies. Bruce Lockhart's attitudes towards Jews did not prevent him exploring the possibilities of working with Korda after the war. He eventually decided against becoming an adviser to Korda at £12,000 a year. 'Films are unclean and having anything to do with them is moral and physical degradation,' he wrote to his son on 8 January 1948. See *The Diaries: Volume Two, 1939–65* (London: Macmillan, 1980), p. 646.

9. Korda, who arrived in Britain in 1931, became a British citizen on 28 October 1936, having been in Britain for the required minimum of five years; others, like the director Paul Czinner and the actors Elisabeth Bergner and Conrad Veidt, followed suit.

10. Adrian Brunel, *Nice Work*, p. 180. Brunel, like others, found himself with divided loyalties for, on another assignment, *The Return of the Scarlet Pimpernel* (1937), much of its effectiveness was due to Lazare Meerson, 'that genius amongst art-directors, as well as to the photography of "Mutz" Green', ibid., p. 181.

11. Léon Barsacq, *Caligari's Cabinet and Other Grand Illusions: A History of Film Design*, p. 220.

12. *Kinematograph Weekly*, 11 February 1932.

13. Michael Powell, interviews with author, 22 September 1970 and 30 August 1973, in Kevin Gough-Yates, *Michael Powell in Collaboration with Emeric Pressburger*; Kevin Gough-Yates, *Michael Powell* (Brussels: Filmmuseum/Palais des Beaux-Arts, 1973).

14. Christopher Challis, interview with Rex Stapleton, 7 January 1984, in Stapleton, *A Matter of Powell and Pressburger: Group Dynamics and Notions of Authorship* (MA thesis, Polytechnic of Central London, 1984), p. 17.

15. Ibid., p. 228.

16. Michael Powell, *A Life in Movies*, p. 582. Privately, to the author, 20 July 1987, Powell admitted to having seen it at the Palace Theatre.

17. *Kinematograph Weekly*, 8 July 1939.

18. Miklós Rózsa, *Double Life* (Tunbridge Wells: Baton Press, 1986), p. 84.

19. Hillier was actually British, as his father had become naturalised. He first worked as a camera assistant on Fritz Lang's *M* (1931).

20. Robert Morley and Sewell Stokes, *Responsible Gentleman* (London: Heinemann, 1966), pp. 89f.

21. Hillier, interview with author, 16 April 1987.

22. Powell, interview with author, in Gough-Yates, *Michael Powell in Collaboration . . . .*

23. Cf. Richard Tauber taking English lessons from Paul Graetz in *Heart's Desire* (Paul Stein, 1936), Anton Walbrook and Walter Rilla practising their English in *Victoria the Great* (Herbert Wilcox, 1937).

24. Pressburger, interview with author, in Gough-Yates, *Michael Powell in Collaboration with Emeric Pressburger*.

25. Michael Balcon, *Michael Balcon Presents . . . A Lifetime of Films* (London: Hutchinson, 1969), p. 130. Balcon adds that he turned towards the documentary school of film-makers because Ealing was 'denuded' of 'so many of our people' (through conscription or internment). Henry (Heinz) Cornelius producer of *Hue and Cry* (1947), *It Always Rains on Sunday* (1947), and director of *Passport to Pimlico* (1949) was born in Berlin, not as commonly thought, in South Africa, and studied under Max Reinhardt. He trained as an editor at Korda's London Films and his own work shows the influence of René Clair, for whom he worked on *The Ghost Goes West*. *Hue and Cry* is a British variation on the famous Erich Kästner Berlin story, *Emil und die Detektive*, and *It Always Rains on Sunday* is firmly in the Carné-Prévert tradition of the 1930s.

26. Elizabeth Sussex, *The Rise and Fall of British Documentary: The Story of the Film Movement Founded by John Grierson* (Berkeley: University of California Press, 1975), p. 120.

27. For 'black' propaganda from Woburn Abbey, see especially Denis Sefton Delmer, *Black Boomerang: An Autobiography,*

Vol. Two (London: Secker & Warburg, 1962), and
Lawrence C. Soley, *Radio Warfare, OSS and CIA Subversive
Propaganda* (New York: Praeger, 1989), pp. 123–55.

Bibliography

Barsacq, Léon, *Caligari's Cabinet and Other Grand Illusions:
A History of Film Design* (New York: Little, Brown, 1976).

Brunel, Adrian, *Nice Work* (London: Forbes Robertson, 1949).

Gough-Yates, Kevin, *Michael Powell in Collaboration with Emeric
Pressburger* (London: BFI, 1971).

Low, Rachael, *The History of British Film 1929–1939* (London:
George Allen & Unwin, 1985).

Macdonald, Kevin, *Emeric Pressburger: The Life and Death of a
Screenwriter* (London: Faber and Faber, 1994).

Powell, Michael, *A Life in Movies* (London: Heinemann, 1986).

Richards, Jeffrey (ed.), *The Unknown 1930s: An Alternative History
of the British Cinema 1929–1939* (London: I. B. Tauris, 1998).

Tabori, Paul, *Alexander Korda* (London: Oldbourne, 1959).

Wright, Basil, *The Long View* (London: Secker & Warburg,
1974).

This chapter derives from an earlier article that appeared in
Günter Berghaus (ed.), *Theatre and Film in Exile: German
Artists in Britain 1933–45* (Berg Publishers, 1989).

15

Where Are Those Buggers?
Aspects of Homosexuality in Mainstream British Cinema

Stella Bruzzi

The question in the title, for those who do not recognise it, is adapted from *My Beautiful Laundrette*, when uncle Nasser (Saeed Jaffrey) asks of his mistress Rachel (Shirley Ann Field) 'but where are those two buggers?' as he is trying to find his nephew, Omar (Gordon Warnecke), and his friend Johnny (Daniel Day Lewis) at the grand opening of their laundrette, Powders. Omar and Johnny have been having sex in the back office. Nasser comes in and finds them rushing to put their clothes on and asks, 'What the hell are you doing? Sunbathing?', to which Omar replies: 'Asleep uncle, we were shagged out'. Nasser looks confused and put out; either he does not realise what is going on or is repressing that he does. Nasser's confusion and the multiple ironies of this exchange seem symptomatic of how homosexuality often appears in mainstream cinema: it is there, but not always openly confronted. In this chapter I wanted to examine the portrayal of same-sex relations between men in mainstream British cinema and explore how individual films negotiated the narrative and representational complexities of showing non-mainstream sexualities in general audience movies. The films under discussion fall into two broad traditions: heritage (*Maurice*, *Another Country*) and realist (*Sunday Bloody Sunday*, *My Beautiful Laundrette*), traditions that have, as amply illustrated elsewhere in this volume, proved fundamental to British cinema, but also traditions that have been 'surprisingly hospitable to homosexual representation'.[1]

As I will go on to discuss in relation to *Maurice* and *Another Country*, there is a sense that the visual opulence of heritage cinema offers a natural home for homosexuality, especially the tension between the visual pleasures of heritage – its detailed and lavish representation of the past, the importance of costume and appearance and the genre's frequent focus on aesthetics, artists and aesthetes – and the often explicit homophobia of the society the films inhabit. Realist cinema has been likewise surprisingly hospitable to homosexual characters and narratives but maybe for different reasons. As illustrated by a film such as *Victim* (Basil Dearden, 1961), homosexuality became a legitimate issue for cinema to tackle, a 'social problem' alongside illegitimacy and delinquency. *Victim* is somewhat heavy-handed in its treatment of homosexuality, its telegraphed sincerity masking an underlying evasiveness. In later films, such as *Sunday Bloody Sunday* and *My Beautiful Laundrette*, homosexuality becomes almost incidental, integrated into a wider realist narrative.

The issue of the films I have chosen being mainstream is important, as mainstream culture in general has not been historically hospitable to homosexuality, lesbianism or bisexuality. Despite having been 'evasive on detail', *Victim* was a turning point here.[2] Stephen Bourne quotes Dirk Bogarde (Melville Farr in *Victim*) remarking at the time of its release: 'Better one film like *Victim* than a dozen of those negative white telephone films full of dashing chaps wearing sporting cravats and driving pretty popsies around in Bentleys.'[3] *Victim* was made after the Wolfenden Report of 1957 recommended the de-criminalisation of homosexual practices in private between consenting adult males, but before these recommendations became law ten years later. Andy Medhurst, like Bourne, views Farr's admission to his wife Laura that he 'wanted' Jack Barrett as 'a radical act'.[4] The gap between allusion and evasiveness in

Victim to the kiss ten years later in *Sunday Bloody Sunday* (1971) is, though, immense. Wolfenden's recommendations had become law; John Schlesinger, the film's gay director, had moved from the hints of sexual ambivalence around Alan Bates in *A Kind of Loving* (1962) to the openly gay but incidental character played by Roland Curram in *Darling* (1965) to a psychologically complex gay central character (Daniel Hirsch played by Peter Finch) in *Sunday Bloody Sunday*.

Before embarking on my discussion of the films, a few notes on what this chapter is not about. First, it is not about, to quote Andy Medhurst, 'looking for queers' in 'pre-gay British film', an activity that 'carries no immediate health risks, and might indeed qualify as the safest sex ever invented'.[5] Medhurst's sparkling essay can hardly be bettered in this respect, although it means that I will not be engaging in that favoured fruit fly as well as queer activity of proffering covert queer readings of mainstream films. Other critics, notably Alexander Doty in *Flaming Classics* and Bourne in *Brief Encounters*, have likewise focused on the erotic and identificatory possibilities offered by 'pre-gay' cinema. Both Doty and Bourne mount a challenge to the repressive instincts of much classical cinema – and those who have critically interpreted it; as Doty explains: 'to think that all texts produced within dominant capitalist systems are (supposed to be) straight, is pretty naive'.[6] For Doty, Bourne and others, alternative readings of mainstream films are infinitely legitimate and queering the canon a necessary critical, political and personal pursuit. As Doty points out:

> Queerness is frequently expressed in ways other than by nude bodies in contact, kissing, or direct verbal indicators; the reasons for finding different means of expression are many – psychological (fear, repression), cultural (oppression), and institutional (censorship, commerce). Even aside from the constraints imposed by these considerations, however, queerness is often (and freely) expressed in subtle ways.[7]

I would posit, however, that it is equally important to register that more explicit representations of homosexuality in mainstream cinema can also offer points of identification for non-queers, an opening up of the mainstream text that seems hugely important.

Second, this chapter is not about the arrival of queer cinema on the independent 'art cinema' scene, which has meant leaving out, among others, Derek Jarman. Although the films that comprised 'New Queer

Cinema', a term coined by B. Ruby Rich in her formative essay of 1992, were explicitly and essentially gay, lesbian and transsexual (*Paris Is Burning, Poison, My Own Private Idaho, Edward II*), 'queer' as an affirmative term of reappropriation carries with it multiple and non-essentialist connotations. Michele Aaron argues in her Introduction to the edited volume *New Queer Cinema*: 'To be queer now, then, means to be untethered from "conventional" codes of behaviour. At its most expansive and utopian, queer contests (hetero- and homo-) normality.'[8] The negotiation between 'normality' or 'conventional codes' and homosexuality underpins my discussion. I have been particularly interested in how certain mainstream British films have not necessarily entirely resisted 'heteronormative' assimilation, while at the same time proving capable of soliciting 'queer modes of interpretation'.[9] What ultimately became particularly interesting was how, within a mainstream context, the politically necessary attachment to essentialism in much early queer cinema criticism (for example Rich's argument that Jarman's *Edward II* is 'a bit complicated' for women because the 'heroes are men and the main villain is a woman', as if women would only be able to identify with the female villain) could be relaxed.[10]

Heritage: *Maurice, Another Country*

It is far from unusual for heritage films to take an overt interest in homosexuality, most obviously in films about Oscar Wilde (*Oscar Wilde*, 1960, *The Trials of Oscar Wilde*, *Wilde*), that most cherished of heritage queers, or adaptations of his works (the various versions of *An Ideal Husband* and *The Importance of Being Earnest*, for example).[11] The shift from pre- to post-gay films, to use Medhurst's term, is exemplified by the differences between *The Trials of Oscar Wilde* (Ken Hughes, 1960) and *Wilde* (Brian Gilbert, 1997). Whereas in the earlier version a rather hysterical fixation on Wilde's renowned verbal wit takes the place of explicit acknowledgment of his sexuality, the later biography is almost wearily fixated upon Wilde's relationships with men, particularly Bosey, to the virtual expense of everything else. Glyn Davis argues that, despite this, 'sweeping claims made in favour of the heritage genre and its accommodation of homosexuality need to be somewhat tempered', going on to note that, 'although heritage cinema may feature lingering images of attractive male bodies, sexual activity is extremely rare in these films: when present, it is usually depicted in a muted, "sensitive" fashion'.[12] In heritage films in which characters' homosexuality is not in any doubt, the sexual act itself is conveniently and artfully disguised, often by being very brief (*Another Country*), blurred (*Wilde*) or through being supplanted by pre- and post-coital embraces (*Maurice*). Keith Howes notes that *The Servant* (1963) is 'much queerer than *Victim*', just as it is the case that *Victim* is much queerer than *The Trials of Oscar Wilde*.[13] The conclusion to be drawn, though, is not that explicitness necessarily suppresses eroticism and queerness.

The attraction of the repressed or coded allusion to homosexuality as opposed to its physical presence is dramatised in *Maurice* (James Ivory, 1987) which concludes with a poignant juxtaposition between Maurice Hall (James Wilby) going to the boathouse at Pendersleigh for sex with Alec Scudder (Rupert Graves) in front of a raging fire and Clive Durham (Hugh Grant) perfunctorily hugging his wife Anne in their bedroom at the main house before moving away to close the window shutters. At one window Clive pauses, prompting a flashback to Maurice waving up at him during their more contented days of platonic homosexuality at Cambridge. Framed by the window, Anne comes to rest her head on Clive's shoulder (an image of steely serenity) and the film's closing image is of an unhappy husband closeted within Pendersleigh and self-imposed heterosexuality. At Cambridge Maurice had said to Clive that he would have 'gone through life half awake if you'd had the decency to leave me alone'; it is therefore ironic and poignant that it is Clive who remains only 'half awake', having bowed to conservative convention.

Maurice, as if absorbing the gay liberation movement, becomes a testament to the importance of coming out. Dyer maintains that 'homosexual heritage cinema may point to antecedents to gay liberation itself. These are most often manifested in two of the cardinal principles of the gay movement: being oneself and coming out'.[14] In *Maurice* the juxtaposition between the un-liberated Clive and the liberated Maurice is fundamental. The point at which their polarisation is complete is when Clive comes into Maurice's bedroom while he is a guest at Pendersleigh. Maurice is writing a journal detailing his sexual history which, because he hides it away as Clive enters the room, Clive takes to be a love letter to a woman. Clive is happy for Maurice and kisses his hand to demonstrate he has not 'forgotten the past'; he then retires to his bedroom. As Clive is undressing, Anne, already in bed, glances over at him, as aghast at the sight of her husband's buttocks peeking out from below his shirt, as Clive had been when

Maurice had last tried to plant a kiss on him. Anne then screws up her eyes as Clive comes to bed and kisses her. The Durhams' mutual awkwardness is then juxtaposed with Maurice's freer physicality as he thrusts his head out of his bedroom window into the rainy night air, an act witnessed by Alec, who seems to be aware from then on of Maurice's sexuality. Maurice's window comes to symbolise sexual freedom, and later can be contrasted with Clive's own entrapment behind a closed window at the end of the film. It is via his window at Pendersleigh that Alec first comes to Maurice's bedroom; it was also the means by which Maurice had entered Clive's rooms at Cambridge, to kiss Clive.

Although the sex in *Maurice* remains 'sensitive' as Davis argues, the fleeting glimpses of buttocks are important here to an interpretation of the differences between Maurice and Clive. Anne's repugnance at the sight of her husband's buttocks contrasts neatly with Maurice and Alec's nakedness in the scenes in which they make love; especially the casual way in which a naked Rupert Graves strolls in front of the camera after their afternoon together in London (James Wilby, perched stiffly on the edge of his bed, one leg conveniently up so as to shield his penis, is rather less casual). The fleeting glimpse of the bottom half of Hugh Grant's buttocks becomes suggestive of the relative poverty of the unsatisfactory heterosexual union. The heady, aching sensuality of Maurice's university encounters with Clive, in particular the mute scene in which Clive rests his head on Maurice's lap as they both run their fingers through the other's hair, finds its ultimate expression not in yet more scenes of non-consummation, but in the intense physical relationship Maurice enjoys with Alec. The earlier scenes would have remained perfect heritage – the elegant folds of natural fibres, the sheen of youthful floppy hair, only a bare wrist here or an unbuttoned shirt there to signal the lurking carnality of desire – but been far less powerful if they had not ultimately led, on Maurice's part at least, to sex.

The balance between allusion and consummation also underpins another 1980s example of queer heritage, *Another Country* (Marek Kanievska, 1984). The film opens in Moscow with an ageing Guy Bennett (Rupert Everett playing a very thinly veiled caricature of spy Guy Burgess) being interviewed by an American journalist. The role of this rather perfunctory interview is to prompt the flashback to Bennett's schooldays that comprises almost the entire film and which starts with two gay schoolboys being caught together while the

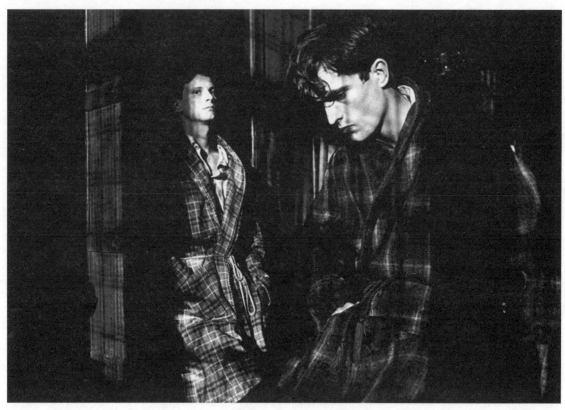

Love in the shadows: Colin Firth and Rupert Everett in *Another Country* (Marek Kanievska, 1984)

rest of the Eton-esque school has lined up in the quad to sing 'I vow to thee my country'. One of the boys, Martineau, commits suicide before he can be punished, leaving little doubt of this England's homophobia, although – and herein lies the paradox of much homosexual heritage – what is also clear in *Another Country* is that the rich, beautiful world of 1930s privilege is far more receptive towards and redolent of homosexuality than the drab, grey Moscow Bennett's politics and sexuality have condemned him to.

Throughout the flashback Bennett's flamboyance has stood in defiance to his ostensibly repressive surroundings, and by the end he offers himself up as a Communist spy on the grounds that there can be no better disguise than 'total indiscretion'. However, when the flashback comes to an end (at the nadir of the youthful Bennett's relationship with the English establishment) and the interview in Moscow resumes with him being asked what he misses of the old country, it becomes clear via Rupert Everett's wistful looks into the middle distance that he hankers after everything about it. For all the explicit homophobia, the aesthetics and beauty of England (the cobblestones and quads of

Oxford, for example) better suit homosexual sensibilities, as Bennett's final moroseness implies, than the featureless Communist interiors his politics have led him to inhabit.[15] This most significant paradox of homosexual heritage is also related specifically to Guy Burgess in John Schlesinger's television film *An Englishman Abroad*, made the year after *Another Country*, in which Alan Bates's more dishevelled, drink-sodden Burgess hankers after a new Savile Row suit.

In a notably Foucauldian manner, homosexuality in *Another Country* thrives under an excessively repressive 1930s regime, exemplified by Fowler, the proto-fascist prefect. One of Fowler's obsessions is with trying to catch Bennett in the act of getting a note passed to James Harcourt, the pupil with whom he is in love; the other is with commanding younger boys to polish things, whether the comical horn-shaped trophy or the cadets' uniforms before an inspection. In Fowler's twin obsessions lies an ironic acknowledgment of the role repression plays in the nurturing of closeted sexuality, for each act of over-zealous cleaning is invariably laid side by side with Bennett being rebellious, for instance, passing Harcourt a note or showing up for parade in a crumpled uniform. However forcefully Fowler orders the phallic trophy to be scrubbed until it shines, however ardently the boys attack the boots and uniform buttons, Bennett's colourful ostentation, like the newly be-suited Burgess's swaggering stroll through Moscow at the end of *An Englishman Abroad*, proclaims the irrepressibility of the queer forces of heritage.

Realism: *Sunday Bloody Sunday*, *My Beautiful Laundrette*

What links the heritage and realist films under discussion here is how they all, though in different ways, seek to address the traditional repression of homosexuality by normalising and de-marginalising it. Both *Sunday Bloody Sunday* and *My Beautiful Laundrette* effect the 'normalisation' of homosexuality by refusing to single it out, instead placing gay characters within narratives in which several issues and strands coexist and interrelate, thus displacing homosexuality as *the* determining feature of either story or character, which is what it is in *Victim*. *Sunday Bloody Sunday* might contain British cinema's first on-screen gay kiss, but it is the contextualisation of this otherwise extraordinary moment within the, at times documentary-like, ordinariness of its portrait of middle-class London in 1971 that characterises Schlesinger's depiction of homosexuality. *Sunday Bloody Sunday* centres on the triangular relationship between Daniel, Alex Gréville (Glenda Jackson) and Bob Elkin (Murray Head), whom the other two share. Daniel is not too dissatisfied with this arrangement, while Alex by the end has had enough of it.

The integration of this potentially heightened sexual situation into the realist narrative is exemplified from the start as *Sunday Bloody Sunday* opens with close-ups of Daniel, a doctor, examining a middle-aged male patient's stomach. After this appointment he calls the telephone messaging service to see if Bob has rung, having tried Bob's number and found it engaged. There is no message and as he tries Bob again – over a montage of shots of Bob's studio – there is no reply. The ringing starts up again, but this time it is shown to be Alex trying to get hold of Bob, then leaving a message with the same messaging service used by Daniel to tell him that she is running late. It is an incidental detail (and one of many such asides) but the class similarities between Daniel and Alex and the implied social differences with Bob are asserted here as both patronise the hapless woman who takes their messages. Both the quotidian messiness and the liberated and radical nature

of their mutual love of Bob is exemplified by the repeated close-up shots of the colourful complex of entwined telephone wires running through the vaults of the messaging centre. The radicalism of *Sunday Bloody Sunday* becomes embedded within the intricate observation of mundanity.

This continues to be the case when it comes to 'the kiss', which happens a little over twenty minutes into the film, after Bob has deserted Alex for the day, leaving her alone to look after the five children of mutual friends. Bob lets himself into Daniel's house as Daniel, despite it being Saturday, is with a patient (a tearful, depressed wife played by June Brown). The appointment comes to an end, Daniel sees Bob downstairs and they kiss: tenderly, intensely but briefly on the lips, a far less telegraphed moment than the kiss between the gay priest and Robert Carlyle in Antonia Bird and Jimmy McGovern's *Priest* (1994), with its breathless, circular camera moves.

That homosexuality in *Sunday Bloody Sunday* is not set apart, but is exemplified by the two sides of Bob's bisexuality being not so much contrasted as rendered comparable. There are two bed scenes, for instance, that illustrate this. The first comes just after the kiss. Bob and Daniel are in bed, Bob on top; Daniel's hands, fingers apart, push down into his youthful, slightly spongy back, his older fingers squashing, displacing Bob's flesh. The ostensible specialness of this moment is completely and ironically undercut only a few minutes of screen time later, after Bob has returned to the home of the five children he and Alex are babysitting for the weekend. Alex and Bob have just argued, their row having culminated in Bob saying 'OK, I know you're not getting enough of me, but you're getting all there is.' He then takes a shower (to the strains on the soundtrack of the trio from *Cosi Fan Tutte*) with Alex looking both admiringly and quizzically at the blurred curves beyond the shower curtain. She then embraces Bob, and her hands knead the flesh on his back in much the same way Daniel's had done not half a day (in narrative time) earlier.

Sunday Bloody Sunday steadfastly refuses to offer up homosexuality as a heightened state of being. The ostensible ordinariness of the triangular relationship is further exemplified by the characterisation of Bob, the object of the intersecting passions as in no way worthy of them. He is superficial, callous and self-absorbed, soaking up the love lavished on him by both Daniel and Alex, just as the flesh on his back absorbs their hands. Much more so than the mouths-only kiss between Bob and Daniel, the physicality of homosexual desire, as well as its comparability to heterosexual desire, is manifested by the brief intensity of Daniel's embrace. The vulnerability of this attachment to one so superficial and narcissistic foreshadows its demise.

That the relationship is not particularly special, at least not to Bob, is neatly demonstrated through the narrative use made of his glass tube sculptures. Filled with coloured liquid that bubbles up to each bulbous head, these are rather obviously phallic, and in their obviousness function as apt metaphors for both Bob's vacuity and for what he feels for Daniel. Just after their kiss, we see one of these sculptures in Daniel's garden. Bob admires his own sculpture and declares 'I think it's the best thing I've done', before thinking it is too small and that he should make a bigger one. He then goes to tend it, topping up its blue liquid as Daniel (comparably to Alex at similar moments, for instance while Bob is taking a shower) gazes on longingly. Later, we see different versions of the sculpture: in Habitat's window as Daniel is driving to the all-night chemist with the seedy acquaintance played by Jon Finch, and later in Bob's studio as Daniel is nursing Bob's fever, caused by his smallpox vaccination. The version of the tube sculpture in Daniel's garden is the smallest and least important of the three. That this also represents how Bob feels about Daniel is confirmed when the final, larger version of the sculpture in Bob's studio is revealed, just at the moment Daniel finally realises that Bob is going to New York to further his career rather than staying in London with him (and Alex).

We are made to mind more than Daniel that Bob finds it so easy to leave. *Sunday Bloody Sunday* concludes with Daniel delivering a soliloquy in which he discusses the nature of his relationship with Bob. In it Daniel turns to camera and remarks that, although friends tell him 'what's half a loaf, you're well shot of him', he misses Bob, because despite not being the 'someone courageous and resourceful' he had searched for all his life, together they 'were something'. Daniel then remonstrates with his friends and no doubt with the audience too that 'You've no right to call me to account.'

Sunday Bloody Sunday is compassionate and affectionate about society's – even liberal society's – fraught and too often tentative inclusion of homosexuality. What marks *Sunday Bloody Sunday* out from some other films in terms of tone is its casual confidence in its handling of the triangular relationship. Homosexuality and bisexuality thus become integrated

Peter Finch hosts a party in *Sunday Bloody Sunday* (John Schlesinger, 1971)

into the broader portrait of London society in the early 1970s. Schlesinger's nuanced sensitivity towards class sensibilities, his fluid merging of the extraordinary and the mundane, and his attention to detail form the backdrop to *Sunday Bloody Sunday*'s portrayal of Daniel's homosexuality. When compared to the melodramatic, tortured Mel Farr in *Victim*, Daniel seems warmly unexceptional; the film itself though is exceptional for the easy manner in which he is integrated – his and Bob's kiss sitting alongside Alex's grimace as she swigs down a cup of instant coffee mixed hastily with water from the hot tap.

In *My Beautiful Laundrette* (Stephen Frears, 1985) homosexuality is just one of a series of issues and problems the film encompasses. As John Hill observes, in both *My Beautiful Laundrette* and *Sammy and Rosie Get Laid* (Stephen Frears, 1987), Stephen Frears and Hanif Kureishi give preference to a 'loosely structured and episodic' narrative, so the central stories in the narratives (such as the relationship between Johnny and Omar) are 'interwoven with a series of other characters and stories to convey a network of social relations and diverse social identities'.[16] This narrative fragmentation also impinges on *My Beautiful Laundrette*'s creation of complex and decentralised identities. Kenneth MacKinnon argues that the film's handling of homosexuality is 'highly unusual' because it refuses 'to foreground the categories of homo/hetero any more than those of Pakistani and white-British "identities"'.[17] But it is limiting to assume that a film can only be 'about' sexual or racial identity if these identities are specifically foregrounded so they become a narrative's all-defining feature. Just as *Sunday Bloody Sunday* is not 'about' homosexuality or bisexuality, but about how such sexual identities collide and contribute to a particular strata of white middle-class London society in the late 1960s/early 1970s, *My Beautiful Laundrette* raises a number of issues around and about Johnny's relationship with Omar, through which their homosexuality is contextualised and comprehended.

The most important of these is the background of Thatcherite Britain and the racial tension that arose as a more or less direct result of the Conservative election victory of 1979. Johnny has been a National Front supporter, and on the day Powders opens, Omar recalls being with his father and seeing Johnny on an NF march through Lewisham, a recollection that, in turn, becomes the catalyst to their lovemaking, as a penitent Johnny slides his hand into Omar's partially unbuttoned shirt, telling Omar that while he cannot make it up to him, 'I am with you'. In part, therefore, the central relationship in *Laundrette* becomes an act of racial reconciliation, pointedly contrasted with the film's other clandestine relationship between Nasser and Rachel. That these two relationships are intended to reflect on each other is made clear at the laundrette's opening, as the kisses of both couples – Omar and Johnny lying naked on a table one side of the office's glass screen with Nasser and Rachel clearly visible on the other – are synchronised. While the heterosexual couple, however, are waltzing under the bright lights and gaudy décor of the refurbished laundrette very much in the open, Johnny and Omar (in public) are prudent.

Gritty in its treatment of racism and the corrupting effect – on Nasser and Salim in particular – of 1980s capitalism, *My Beautiful Laundrette* becomes potentially soppy in its idealisation of Omar's relationship with Johnny. Although Omar too is driven to make a success of Powders by the thought of making money, his love of Johnny has led Johnny away from his white supremacist friends and coincided with him wanting to forget his past. One night, before the renovations and grand opening, Omar and Johnny are kissing in a shady back alley, interrupted by the sound of Johnny's former friends about to trash their laundrette. They remonstrate with Johnny that it is demeaning to be 'grovelling to Pakis' and plead with him not to cut himself off from his 'own people' because 'everyone has to belong'. But Johnny now 'belongs' to a different group, through his friendship with Omar, though this switch in his affiliations and the suggestion that he has found himself is questioned towards the end of the film when he (and Omar) have moments of both affirming their sexuality and fighting it.

The final scene exemplifies this fraught ambivalence. Earlier, Johnny had offered a defiant affirmation of his sexual identity when Tania, who has arrived at Powders suitcase in hand, asks him to go with her. Johnny replies: 'I couldn't leave him, not now. Have you ever touched him?' Tania, who along with Salim has been one of the characters to realise what has been going on between Johnny and Omar, walks off alone. A fight then ensues outside Powders between Johnny's erstwhile white friends and Salim, who is in danger of being killed until Johnny – despite hating him – intervenes on his behalf. Salim crawls away and Johnny is left badly beaten up, this concluding fight being intercut with Nasser finally going to visit his brother, Omar's 'Papa', who concludes lugubriously that 'this damn country has done us in'. After the fight, Omar tends to Johnny's wounds. The fight has made Johnny ambivalent about his relationship, when earlier he had seemed so sure; he threatens to walk out of Omar's life as he has done before and brushes aside Omar's tending of him as he says: 'I'm serious. Don't keep touching me.'

My Beautiful Laundrette is persistently preoccupied with notions of belonging or not belonging, with group affiliation and identity. As Kureishi's comment about his own intentions with the script suggest, however, such identities are far from fixed. Papa had come to England looking for 'another country' that would be receptive to his socialist intellectualism and would give Omar an education, but that country has moulded and been far more welcoming towards his capitalist brother; likewise the 'other' country of homosexuality is where Johnny and Omar 'belong', but they both fight against it. Christine Geraghty opens her analysis of *My Beautiful Laundrette* by categorising it as 'a cross-over film'; one that 'literally takes crossing over and hybridity as its subject matter'.[18] As Geraghty goes on to discuss, many of the personal problems explored in the film stem from changes in identity and shifts in group affiliations, to the extent that social and cultural certainty is missing. These uncertainties are expressed throughout via both narrative and *mise en scène*. The concluding scene is fraught with masochism and uneasy contradiction. Omar's optimism about his and Johnny's future as he tends Johnny's wounds, for example contrasts sharply with Johnny's rejection of him, just as this rejection appears to ignore the fact that Johnny at this moment is being nursed for having come to the defence of that 'scum' Salim against his 'own people'. This exchange complements an earlier scene (the night of the grand opening) when Omar finds Johnny in his room, having left Powders after hearing a drunk Omar propose to Tania. The ostentatiously chiaroscuro lighting, deriving here from the contrast between Johnny's angle-poise lamp and his otherwise dark room, is used to eroticise and emphasise the contours of Daniel Day Lewis's torso, just as the similarly dim lighting earlier in the day had silhouetted both their torsos against the window onto the brightly lit laundrette. At the end of the film Johnny and Omar again occupy a darkened space, and again Johnny's chest is pointedly and erotically on show. *My Beautiful Laundrette* ends positively with Omar and Johnny reconciled and playfully splashing each other with water, but this is only the film's microcosm; the larger social concerns remain as unresolved as the equivocal *mise en scène*.

The representation of homosexuality in mainstream British cinema is, in certain respects, bound to be a compromise; James Wilby shields his penis in *Maurice* just as moody lighting shades Daniel Day Lewis. Still, the step from mere insinuation and actual representation of same-sex intimacy is a significant and interesting one. Does the emergence, however, of the 'sensitive' moments of homosexuality Glyn Davis criticises simply mean that homosexuality has been subsumed into the dominant heterosexual culture? Although I have focused on films that adopt a broadly liberal aesthetic, the alliance between homosexuality and liberation and liberalism is clear and fundamental. What all these heritage and realist films achieve is both the inclusion of and the de-marginalisation of 'deviant' forms of sexual identity; this is not quite synonymous with homosexuality being subsumed by a dominant heterosexual culture. The films' shared plural patterns of identification, their focus at both a narrative and an aesthetic level upon the difficulties of 'coming out' or self-identifying as homosexual and their refusal to only see homosexuality as a social 'problem' or 'issue' mark the films out as not merely 'sensitive' but receptive to homosexuality. In *Sunday Bloody Sunday* Daniel is called away from his nephew's bar mitzvah in order to visit a patient in hospital. He assures her worried relatives that 'People can manage on very little'. This indirect comment on Daniel's contentment with Bob, also says something about homosexuality in mainstream cinema: that not much is made to go quite a long way, that the films selected here, with their de-radicalisation of homosexuality, say more than they – being 'mainstream' – could show.

Notes

1. Richard Dyer, *The Culture of Queers*, p. 204.
2. As John Hill observes, *Sex, Class and Realism: British Cinema 1956–1963*, p. 91.
3. Andy Medhurst, 'Homosexuality and British Cinema: Representations and Readings (MA Film Studies at University of East Anglia, 1982)', quoted by Stephen Bourne, *Brief Encounters: Lesbians and Gays in British Cinema, 1930–1971*, p. 155.
4. Quoted in Bourne, *Brief Encounters*, p. 161.
5. Andy Medhurst, 'In Search of Nebulous Nancies: Looking for Queers in Pre-gay British Cinema', p. 21.
6. Alexander Doty, *Flaming Classics: Queering the Canon*, p. 5.
7. Ibid.
8. Michele Aaron, *New Queer Cinema: A Critical Reader*, p. 5.
9. Robin Griffiths, *British Queer Cinema*, p. 3.
10. B. Ruby Rich, 'New Queer Cinema', p. 32.
11. For an excellent recent précis of what constitutes 'heritage films' see Dyer, *The Culture of Queers*, p. 205.
12. Glyn Davis, 'Taming Oscar Wilde: Queerness, Heritage and Stardom', p. 198.
13. Keith Howes, 'Are There Stars Out Tonight?', p. 64.
14. Dyer, *The Culture of Queers*, p. 207.
15. Cf. John Hill, *British Cinema in the 1980s*, p. 87, for another discussion of this contrast between Burgess's Moscow apartment and the 'seductive allure' of the flashback.
16. Ibid., p. 207.
17. Kenneth MacKinnon, 'Intermingling under Controlled Conditions: The Queerness of *Prick up Your Ears*', p. 122.
18. Geraghty, *My Beautiful Laundrette*, p. 5

Bibliography

Aaron, Michele (ed.), *New Queer Cinema: A Critical Reader* (Edinburgh: Edinburgh University Press, 2004).

Bourne, Stephen, *Brief Encounters: Lesbians and Gays in British Cinema, 1930–1971* (London: Cassell, 1996).

Davis, Glyn, 'Taming Oscar Wilde: Queerness, Heritage and Stardom', in Robin Griffiths (ed.), *British Queer Cinema*.

Doty, Alexander, *Flaming Classics: Queering the Canon* (London and New York: Routledge, 2000).

Dyer, Richard, *The Culture of Queers* (Routledge: London and New York, 2001).

Geraghty, Christine, *My Beautiful Laundrette* (London: I. B. Tauris).

Griffiths, Robin (ed.), *British Queer Cinema* (London and New York: Routledge, 2006).

Hill, John, *Sex, Class and Realism: British Cinema 1956–63* (London: BFI, 1986).

Hill, John, *British Cinema in the 1980s* (Oxford: Clarendon Press, 1999).

Howes, Keith, 'Are There Stars Out Tonight?', in Robin Griffiths (ed.), *British Queer Cinema*.

MacKinnon, Kenneth, 'Intermingling under Controlled Conditions: The Queerness of *Prick up Your Ears*', in Robin Griffiths (ed.), *British Queer Cinema*.

Medhurst, Andy, 'In Search of Nebulous Nancies: Looking for Queers in Pre-gay British Cinema', in Robin Griffiths (ed.), *British Queer Cinema*.

Rich, B. Ruby, 'New Queer Cinema', *Sight and Sound*, September 1992, reprinted in Michele Aaron (ed.), *New Queer Cinema*.

PART THREE

British Cinema 1895–1939

16

Before *Blackmail*: Silent British Cinema

CHARLES BARR

To most people other than specialist academics and historians, British silent cinema is an unknown country. No British feature films from the silent era belong to an internationally known repertoire, or to a national tradition that is absorbed by, or at least known to, later generations of film-makers and cinephiles. Our film culture has no roots in, and no memory of, the formative silent period. For a country which was to become a major producer in the sound period, this is extraordinary.

It is now common to divide pre-1930 film history into three main stages:

1. Early or primitive cinema, from 1895 to around 1907.
2. A period of rapid transition, at the level both of film form and of production methods.
3. A more settled period, starting around 1916, by which time certain standardised patterns of production and marketing were in place.

During the transitional second stage, or early in the third, all the obvious rival countries to Britain managed to produce at least one set or strain of films whose national character was distinctive and attractive enough to make a strong, lasting impact, abroad as well as at home. When America came to dominate the world market, it continued to import films from Europe and to learn lessons from European countries, and often to sign up their directors, like Lubitsch and Murnau from Germany and Sjöström from Sweden. No British film of this time made any significant impact, nor was any British film-maker head-hunted by Hollywood. If Britons worked and prospered there – Chaplin for

instance – it was not because of any experience in their native film industry.

The balance of power was different in the early years of cinema. The medium was a novelty. Films were cheap, short, and varied in form. If they told a story it was only a rudimentary one: they might just as well present a view, or a joke, or a brief record (or restaging) of a public event. Production was a small-scale local enterprise. Films were shown by the men who made them, or else copies were sold outright to showmen. They were shown not in special buildings but in fairgrounds or shops or lecture halls, or as part of music-hall programmes.

There was no such thing yet as a 'national cinema', because nothing was organised or standardised or marketed on a national scale. But we can claim that the new medium was explored as energetically and imaginatively in Britain as anywhere in the world.

Already, by the time of the first Lumière show in London in February 1896, a range of English experimenters were active. There are even British candidates for the title of 'inventor' of the moving picture: Augustin Le Prince, who disappeared mysteriously in 1890 soon after making some successful experiments in Leeds, and William Friese-Greene.[1] Two London-based collaborators, Birt Acres (still photographer) and R. W. Paul (scientific instrument maker), seem to have worked more or less in parallel with the Lumières, constructing their own equipment and shooting actuality material; they could immediately exploit the interest aroused by the Lumière show, by programming their own films in the West End. A variety of photographers, lantern-slide men and other showmen now diversified into moving pictures, seizing the moment energetically.

Discovering Early Cinema

There seem to have been three main centres for sustained production in these early years: London and its suburbs; Brighton, or more accurately its affluent neighbour, Hove; and Yorkshire.

A lot of films from this period survive. Since prints were then sold outright, not rented, many copies of popular films were disseminated; and when the British Film Institute was founded in 1933 and launched a National Film Library, it was able to get hold of plenty of early material. These early film-makers, notably the Brighton School, were given the status of important pioneers. British cinema might, for much of its history, be a subject of embarrassment, but we could take pride in the period (albeit before cinema took on a 'national' dimension) when our men led the world.

Standard histories of the medium went on dutifully acknowledging these pioneer British films, without showing or inspiring any great interest in them. For a long time, the early years of cinema constituted a minority antiquarian concern. Film scholarship and film education, as they developed in the 1960s and 70s, preferred to deal with the medium in its more accessible maturity. Silent films were not easy to see or to contextualise. When they were shown, they were generally in poor condition and lacked any sound accompaniment.

In the late 1970s this changed rapidly. The reasons are complex, but the key factor is a convergence of interests on the part of three separate groups: film archivists, academics and popular historians like Kevin Brownlow.[2] While Brownlow and his collaborators began to create a new market, in cinema and on television, for the experience of mature silent film, archivists and scholars put equal energy into exploring the medium's pre-history and early years. The landmark event was the 1978 conference mounted in Brighton by FIAF (the International Federation of Film Archives), which showed all the material it could find in the world's archives from the period before 1906. For the first time, historians looked systematically, analytically, comparatively, at early material from all over the world. The event itself generated a flood of scholarly publications and has led to additional conferences and research projects.[3]

One might expect the British film pioneers to have been put in a humbler place by this sort of event, this new scholarly assessment – decentred and even debunked. And yet they were not. Scholars as diverse in their methods and ideologies as Barry Salt, Noël Burch and the American team of David Bordwell and Kristin Thompson continue to give the early British film-makers a privileged place. Like other exponents of the 'new film history', they make abundant use of the British pioneers in tracing the early material development of the medium.

These early films express a native eagerness to embrace and explore the new medium, and a craftsmanship in handling it, that flourish briefly and then are blocked off, before surfacing again in different forms, a long way in the future, in British film and television.

All the new histories refer to *The Big Swallow*, made in around 1900 by the Hove chemist/photographer James Williamson. A man is out walking, catches sight of the camera (i.e. the camera that is shooting the film), and advances menacingly towards it, then opens his mouth to swallow it. We see a camera, a tripod and an operator fall into a black hole; the man moves away, munching in triumph. This can be read as a visionary playing out of the aggression inherent in the camera–subject relation; at the same time (and the two things are not mutually exclusive) it's a brilliant little joke in the manner of a Monty Python TV sketch of around 1970, designed for inclusion within a similar programme of short, distinct items, each constituting an independent 'attraction'. The Monty Python slogan, 'And Now for Something Completely Different', echoes the way in which the short early films seem habitually to have been yoked together.

Cecil Hepworth made a comparable *tour de force* of aggression in *How It Feels to Be Run Over* (1900). A car advances along a road from extreme long shot to, indeed, run us over; almost subliminally, the words 'Oh Mother Will Be Pleased' flash on the screen. There is a great abundance of early one-joke films, generally done in a single shot (like the many one-view films in the actuality mode). It might be inferred that film-makers in Britain exploited the medium effectively at the level of isolated effects or attractions but were left behind when representations became less bitty and the medium started to acquire a 'grammar' – to move towards the 'classical narrative' model that America was destined to impose and dominate. But this is not so at all. The early British film-makers are pioneers at this level too. Those early years are an island not just of Monty Python inventiveness but of an editing ingenuity that looks ahead, in its way, to the craftsmanship of a David Lean.

A consummation of all this early ingenuity, and possibly the high point historically for cinema in Britain relative to the rest of the world, is marked by a short narrative made by the Cecil Hepworth company in 1905.

Rescued by Rover

The baby of a well-off couple is looked after by a nanny. Out in the park, she flirts with a soldier, and the baby is stolen from its pram by a gypsy woman. While she is explaining this to the mother, the family dog, Rover, senses what has happened, speeds through the town, and locates gypsy and baby in an attic room. Rover then returns home and persuades the baby's father to come back with him. Father retrieves the baby, leaving the gypsy to swig from her gin bottle. The family is happily united, Rover included.

What is remarkable about the film is its systematic organisation. The camera scarcely moves, and there are no inter-titles: a story of some seven minutes is told through a lucid succession of visual images.

There are four basic locations: the opulent family home, the park, the tenement block where the gypsy lives, and the route from the family home to the tenements. Setting the narrative out in tabular form enables the structure to be clearly read. There are eleven separate camera set-ups, here designated by the letters A to K (in the horizontal plane); and twenty-one shots, designated by successive numbers (in the vertical plane). The 'Time' column gives the approximate length of each shot, in seconds.

In more detail, the camera set-ups are as follows:

Park:	A and B: adjacent angles	
Family home:	C: close shot, living room.	D: wider shot, living room
	E: father's study	F: exterior, window
Route:	G: street, long shot	H: street corner
	I: river (with boat)	
Gypsy home:	J: exterior, street door	K: attic interior, with bed

PARK		FAMILY HOME				ROUTE			GYPSY HOME		Time	
A	B	C	D	E	F	G	H	I	J	K		
		1									8	Rover and baby
2											16	nanny with pram: spurns gypsy
	3										42	– flirts: gypsy steals baby
			4								25	nanny tells mother: exit Rover [R]
					5						4	R out of window
						6					8	R runs towards/past camera
							7				4	R likewise
								8			20	R swims river, passes camera
									9		12	R pushes open street door: in
										10	63	gypsy/baby: R in, sees, exits
									11		5	R exits by street door
								12			15	R away from camera, swims river
						13					5	R away from camera
					14						4	R in through window
				15							22	father depressed, R in: exeunt
						16					11	father led by R . . .
								17			30	. . . across river (in boat)
									18		13	. . . to the right door: in
										19	22	father takes baby, gypsy drinks
		20									20	bereft mother joined by all three
21											10	happy family group

The analysis lays bare a pattern of repetition and symmetry which is pleasurable in itself, in the way that metre and rhyme can be in a poem. The action moves in a linear way from house to attic across a series of locations (shots 4 to 10), then back to the house (11 to 15), and thence back again to the attic (16 to 19). Repetition and variation – the variation comes from what is shown (dog coming, dog going, then dog and man coming) and from the unobtrusive shortening of the sequence: the street-corner shot (7) is missed out of the second journey, and the window shot (5/14) is missed out of the third. A fourth journey would be one too many, and is elided.

Form and content are beautifully matched. The confidence of the shot-by-shot construction is an ideal vehicle for the confidence of the narrative, as it moves in the classic manner from equilibrium to disruption to restoration of equilibrium in the happy ending; and, in turn, for the ideological confidence it expresses. Man is the hunter, women are transgressive or subservient; gypsies are menacingly other. Middle-class family values rule.

It's easy to see why this film became so celebrated and so widely imitated. So many copies were made for sale at home and abroad that the negative twice wore out, necessitating shot-by-shot remakes. I have neither seen nor read about any other film from this period that is constructed with this machine-like efficiency. It's a clear precursor of the short films made by D. W. Griffith for the Biograph Company in America between 1908 and 1913, based on the same structural principle of repetition and variation, of permutations worked upon a limited number of camera set-ups. Griffith is likely to have seen *Rescued by Rover*, and it may be no coincidence that his own first film, *The Adventures of Dollie*, tells of the loss and rescue of a small child.

What Griffith would soon make into his trademark was parallel editing, a dimension that *Rescued by Rover* lacks. Looking at the narrative chart, we can see that the movement is purely linear, following a single path. The Griffith of 1909 would assuredly have kept cutting back and forth between two and probably three centres of interest: Rover's journey, the helpless baby, the anxious mother.

It's not surprising Hepworth didn't go this far in 1905: *Rescued by Rover*, for its time, is extraordinary enough. Among other things it is a visionary model of economy in film-making. A complex narrative can be constructed on the basis of a limited number of fixed camera set-ups. The system lends itself to advance

scripting and to unproblematically delegated editing. In theme, tone and organisation, *Rescued by Rover* seems the very model of the way mainstream popular cinema was destined to develop.

The Long Decline

The question that does arise, though, is what happened to Hepworth and to the pioneer spirit in British filmmaking, after 1905. Why was it Griffith and not Hepworth himself who developed the system further, using it for films of greater range and depth? Why was it America and not Britain that built a production system on this model of structural economy? Hepworth continued as a director and producer for some twenty years; to judge from the films I have seen, he effectively turned his back on the line of development represented by *Rescued by Rover*. It's as if he and Smith and Williamson and the others ran the first lap, passed on the baton to the Americans, and then stopped exhausted.

Rescued by Rover may point the way to the future but it also belongs firmly to the primitive years. First, it was a cheaply shot family affair. The family are the Hepworths, and Rover is their dog, even though the other parts are played by actors hired for the day. Second, copies were still sold outright. Third, for all the claims one may make for it, it does undeniably have the childish quality that its title implies.

Momentous changes were taking place in cinema, with more organised patterns of production, renting of films and exhibition – and an increase in production values. This is the point at which the British input falters: the stage when cinema begins to acquire genuinely national dimensions.

The next two decades were depressing ones. British production ceased to have much of an export market, except to some extent in the countries of the Empire; even in the home market, it supplied only a minor – and decreasing – proportion of the films shown. By the start of World War I, the figure was around 15 per cent; by 1926, it was down to 5 per cent. The reputation of British films among audiences and critics had sunk to a low level, and remained there in spite of intermittent efforts by the film trade to promote them and to mount special events and campaigns.

The 'cottage industry' which produced *Rescued by Rover* could not survive the new developments in the international film market. The American industry organised itself in 1908 to form the powerful oligopoly of the MPPC (Motion Picture Patents Company),

Square-on, tableau-like shooting: Cecil Hepworth's *Comin' thro' the Rye* (1924)

laying down a system that would enable it to service its own very large home market and to set strict controls on foreign imports. Williamson and Hepworth were among the film-makers who had relied on selling a lot of prints in America. Hepworth did manage to survive, and stayed active until the mid-1920s. Other pioneers, Williamson included, soon abandoned production and went back to their day jobs. But in other countries likewise, most of the early innovators had dropped out around this time, and dynamic new people took over, to work within the new structures. There seems no obvious reason why British production could not have organised itself in such a way as to serve its home market more effectively, and to do better in countries other than America. But it failed either to match the dynamism of American production, or to find an effective alternative style that could give it a distinctive niche in the world market. Not for the last time, British cinema was caught awkwardly between American and European modes of operation.

Tantalising as it is to see D. W. Griffith taking over the baton from Hepworth, and extrapolating ruthlessly and prolifically from the *Rescued by Rover* model of construction, it is pointless to regret that Hepworth himself did not go on in that way, or that no other British film-maker emerged to do so. Griffith's success resulted not just from his own talent but from a framework unavailable in

Britain: a combination of the size of the American market, the security of the investment behind him, and other things about the history, landscape and culture of the nation. The 400-plus films that Griffith made for the Biograph Company between 1908 and 1913 are not much longer than *Rescued by Rover* and its British successors, but they have a stunning dynamism, maturity and range (from Westerns to domestic dramas). They are the dramatic equivalent of the comic energy and fertility of early American comedy. The most sensational of the comedians, Charlie Chaplin, was of course British, and moreover had learned his comic craft in the British music hall – as had Stan Laurel. Britain could supply not only 'talent' like these two, but the popular forms that fostered them. What it evidently could not do was to provide an appropriate cinematic framework for them, either institutionally or formally.

But if Britain could not compete with America, it might have operated in the manner of, say, Sweden. As Thompson and Bordwell remind us in their global survey of *Film History*:

> The Swedish cinema initially had little impact abroad, and so its film-makers were working without the larger budgets made possible by export. Sweden was among the first countries to create a major cinema by drawing deliberately upon the particular traits of its national culture. Swedish films were characterised by their dependence on northern landscapes and by their use of local literature, costumes, customs, and the like.[4]

There were indeed many attempts in Britain to capitalise on the indigenous landscape, literature and general 'heritage'. But to compare the silent British versions of Shakespeare, Dickens, etc., with the Swedish adaptations from stage and literature, notably the novels of Selma Lagerlöf, is to understand why they had such different status and staying power. According to a Swedish film historian, these Lagerlöf films

> became national events and drew the public to the cinema on a scale previously undreamed of. Victor Sjöström's film version of *Ingmarssönerna* (*The Sons of Ingmar*) was seen by 196,000 in Stockholm, a city which at that time had only 400,000 inhabitants. The picture ran for twenty years in the capital and surpassed both Douglas Fairbanks and Charles Chaplin in popularity.[5]

The Hepworth company's one-hour film version of *Hamlet* in 1913, in contrast, had some warm patriotic reviews but limited box-office appeal. Like many early British adaptations, it presents 'scenes from' the original, trading on the prestige appeal of the text and the performers, rather than, like the films of Sjöström and his colleagues, reworking the play in film terms. And the landscapes are a backdrop rather than an organic part of the work. The Swedes had carefully acquainted themselves with international developments in film style, absorbing what was appropriate rather than imitating. The equivalent British efforts are insular in comparison.

What, in more precise terms, was wrong with British films in these two decades, what made them so consistently unsuccessful? Commentators have identified a variety of reasons. James Park puts most emphasis on the script:

> Writing, it's true, isn't thought of as one of the problems of British cinema. It's the one thing the nation that produced Shakespeare thinks it can do rather well. But writing screenplays is something the British do very badly indeed.[6]

For Park, this failing goes right back to the years before World War I. Rachael Low puts particular emphasis on the crudity, for most of the silent period, of the British approach to film editing and to film acting. Editing was all too often seen as a purely technical process of joining scenes together, while the dominance of stage work in the lives of most film actors meant that 'there was neither motive nor opportunity for actors to adapt themselves to the silent screen and discover a suitable style'.[7] Alfred Hitchcock, discussing with François Truffaut the low opinion he formed of British films as a consumer in the 1910s, singled out the unvaryingly flat quality of British lighting and photography.[8] Finally, Iris Barry, looking back in 1926, was exasperated by a regular directorial failing:

> the one, common in England, of using the screen as though it were a stage with exits left and right, the actors free to move only across a circumscribed oblong area, with a low skyline and the movements all parallel to the plane of the screen, not, as they should be, for the sake of depth-illusion, at angles to it.[9]

Writing, editing, acting, lighting, directing – that covers just about everything. The complaints fit together to create a sense of a total filmic system that is ponderous and literal-minded. The common criticism is of a failure to rethink material in film terms, or to consider what 'film terms' amount to. Material is mechanically transcribed or condensed from a stage or literary original: the actors act it, the camera shoots the scene, the editor joins the scenes together, and you have a film. And the audience endures it, perhaps thinking of it as a patriotic duty. Or it stays away.

New Shoots

By 1926, the year of Iris Barry's book, things were starting to change on several fronts:

1. A new and more businesslike body of film-makers was emerging. It's as if enterprise and innovation had skipped a generation, but now returned. These are some of the people who came on the scene after 1920: Michael Balcon, Victor Saville, Herbert Wilcox, Graham Cutts, Anthony Asquith, Alfred Hitchcock, Ivor Montagu, Adrian Brunel. All of them combined ambition, and generally a degree of idealism, with a realistic knowledge of the film world, and an awareness that that world stretches beyond Britain. Balcon and Saville started as film distributors in the Midlands, Montagu and Brunel made their name as editors. Apart from Balcon, all of them were – or would at some point become – directors. Though many of them initially met obstacles from producers and exhibitors, they persevered.

2. The Film Society was founded in London in 1925, to show important new films from abroad as well as significant revivals, and to act as a forum for discussion. Again it met some opposition, from the established film trade, but it too persevered. Many of the new generation of film-makers belonged to it. Alongside this, belatedly, the medium started to get more sustained and informed critical attention in print – in Iris Barry's book, in the specialist magazine *Close Up* (from 1927), and in a few newspapers and magazines.

3. There was growing awareness of the existence of a branch of film-making which Britain might be in a position to lay a special claim to. Barry referred to 'documentary films' as 'a department of cinematography in which England is still unbeaten'.[10] Throughout the barren years from 1908 Percy Smith had been turning out, for a succession of companies, his studies of plant life, using close-up and slow-motion. Entitled *Secrets of Life* or *Secrets of*

Nature, these films appealed both to popular and to high-brow audiences; and there had been much more in the broad documentary mode. This work did not, yet, have a very high profile, but a young Scot named John Grierson was spending 1926 in America, studying the role of the mass media in influencing public opinion. Soon he would return to extend the role of documentary film considerably, and to attract a lot of publicity both to it and to himself.[11]

4. The British government was at last sufficiently disturbed by the hegemony of American films on British screens to prepare some protective legislation: the first Cinematograph Films Act was passed in 1927.

These four factors between them set an agenda for the 1930s, and indeed beyond. Committed film-makers, looking to make an effective career in an unstable industry. A strong critical and intellectual discourse about cinema. A concern for documentary and the realist film. And an involvement, however uncertain, on the part of the government.

One of the recurring debates around British cinema is between the concepts of the national and the international. British producers had already begun to toy with the strategy of aiming directly at the international market by bringing over American stars. Balcon did so for his first British feature, *Woman to Woman*, in 1922; the strategy was successful, but didn't work so well when repeated. After burning his fingers a few times like this, Balcon was to argue that 'we shall become international by being national'.[12] But it seems more plausible to rework the terms of this opposition: the lesson of the silent period is that we became national by being international. It was only when Britain became intelligently open to international influences that it began to be able to find a strong, meaningful, national identity for its own production.

Grierson needed to go to North America in order to formulate his ideas about the role documentary film could play in British society and British cinema. Michael Balcon made some of his early productions in German studios. Anthony Asquith spent six months on a study trip in Hollywood, before returning to make the sharp and precocious *Shooting Stars* for British International Pictures in 1927; set partly in a film studio, it's one of the few British silent films that would stand up to revival with full orchestral honours. Ivor Montagu travelled in Europe and in the young Soviet

Union, and brought Eisenstein and Pudovkin, both in person and through their films, to the Film Society in London. The Society itself was a major medium for the dissemination of ideas from abroad.

This international dimension is crystallised in the person, and the work, of two young directors of the time. One is Michael Powell, who served an intensive European/American apprenticeship in the Victorine Studios in Nice, working mainly with two directors from Hollywood, Rex Ingram and Harry Lachman, and then came back to England, initially working as stills photographer on the Alfred Hitchcock film *Champagne* (1928). The other is Hitchcock himself.

Hitchcock

No one could be more obviously, tenaciously English than Hitchcock. At the same time, no one could be more international. He had gone to work, as a teenager, not for a British company (having a low opinion of British standards), but for the London office of an American firm. The films he remembered being impressed by were mainly American and German. When his first employers pulled out of London, he moved to a British company (Balcon's Gainsborough), worked on their German-based productions, and watched Murnau shooting *The Last Laugh* (1924) at the UFA Studios in Berlin. The first two films he directed were again shot in a German studio, as well as on Italian, French and Austrian locations. One of his main early colleagues was Ivor Montagu, the friend of the Soviet directors, and Hitchcock encountered them and their work at the Film Society. And his films are, unmistakably, the meeting place of stylistic influences from America, Germany and the Soviets. Hitchcock made no secret of this. He would always refer, in articles and interviews, to the impact made on him by Soviet montage editing and to the satisfaction he took in using devices drawn from Pudovkin and Kuleshov. For the magazine *Close Up*, reviewing *Blackmail*, he was already notorious for his use of 'the almighty German technique', at the level of image composition.[13] And early in his career he wrote an article in the *Evening News* expressing a shrewd sense of his own relation to the dominant American cinema.

> The American directors under their commercially
> minded employers have learned a good deal about
> studio lighting, action photographs, and telling a story
> plainly and simply in moving pictures. They have

learnt, as it were, to put the nouns, verbs and adjectives of the film language together. . . . It is obvious that what we must strive for at once is the way to use these nouns and verbs as cunningly as do the great novelists and great dramatists, to achieve certain moods and effects in an audience.[14]

Nouns, verbs and adjectives. I think one can interpret the linguistic analogy at three levels.

1. The basic grammar of cinema: the way shots are composed and combined.
2. The grammar of narrative: economical and coherent storytelling, moving purposefully from beginning to middle to end, with no loose ends.
3. What one might call the grammar of story psychology: motivation, relationships, particularly between couples, and between parents and children, worked out across the narrative.

Between them, these constitute the grammar of what historians now describe as the 'classical Hollywood system': a highly purposeful and consistent model of film-making, seen as the basis of Hollywood's success in, at one end of the process, organising its production methods efficiently, and, at the other, appealing to wide audiences.

Long before the concept of classical Hollywood was named and analysed, Hitchcock had formed his own understanding of how it operated; and the film he was making at the time is a fine example of the judicious application of its principles to British material. *The Farmer's Wife* (1928) might sound unpromising: a film of the long-running West End comedy by Eden Phillpotts, much of it shot on rustic locations. It could easily, in other hands, have been stagey in all the wrong ways, with the occasional insertion of picturesque bits of local scenery. Hitchcock is not disrespectful of the original, but reworks it deftly in terms of the 'nouns, verbs and adjectives' of popular cinema.

The grammar of narrative: subplots and diversions are cleared away, along with most of the dialogue, to give a lucid central storyline – the quest by the newly widowed farmer Samuel Sweetland to find a second wife. Story psychology: a quite new emphasis is put on Sweetland's relationship with his only daughter (there are two daughters in the play). The death of the wife is quickly (in film time) followed by the daughter's marriage. Lonely after hosting the wedding feast and seeing her depart for her new home, he at once starts

A stage play reset with the nouns, verbs, adjectives of popular cinema: Hitchcock's *The Farmer's Wife* (1928)

the search for a new wife. The ultimate choice will be his housekeeper, who is aligned both with the first wife (through her job) and with the daughter (through her youth – she is much younger than any of the other women whom Sweetland considers). The drama is thus given a clear though delicate Oedipal dimension, of a kind that was already thoroughly familiar in Hollywood narrative. Finally, the grammar of film language. The intensity of feeling between father and daughter is conveyed not in inter-titles but by visual means: point of view, and the shot/reverse shot construction. They exchange looks across the crowded scene of the wedding feast: shots of him are intercut with shots from his viewpoint of daughter and son-in-law, at the other end of the table. The pattern is repeated when the couple depart from the house (and thus from the film).

These linked devices – point of view, shot/reverse shot and matching of eyelines – have been convincingly identified by historians as the cornerstone of 'classical' Hollywood's spatial system. It is a radical break from the mode of direction criticised by Iris Barry as typical of retrograde British films (square-on, tableau-like shooting). It doesn't simply 'open up' the play technically, make it more cinematic: it affords a new level of intimacy between audience and characters. Interestingly, it is a strategy against which Cecil Hepworth explicitly held out, to the end of his life. See the notorious passage in his memoirs of 1951:

Smoothness in a film is important and should be preserved, except when for some special effect a 'snap' is preferred. The 'unities' and the 'verities' should always be observed, to which I should add the 'orienties'. Only the direst need will form an excuse for lifting an audience up by the scruff of the neck and carrying it round to the other side, just because you suddenly want to photograph something from the south when the previous scene has been taken from the north.[15]

It may seem ironic that this is the same Hepworth who in 1905, in *Rescued by Rover*, had offered such a precocious model of a cinematic system. In 1924 his most ambitious film, *Comin' thro' the Rye*, helped to bankrupt his company. Although revisionist claims have been made on behalf of this film, it signally failed to make an impact with critics and audiences, or to carve out any sort of niche for its version of a national cinema. On his way out in the mid-1920s Hepworth passes Hitchcock coming in.

Postscript 2007

Ten years after it was first published, this confident account of British silent cinema – a narrative of rapid rise, catastrophic decline and tentative recovery – seems altogether too slick and schematic. As soon as I began, shortly afterwards, to research the early career of Alfred Hitchcock in detail, it became clear that his predecessors and earlier collaborators could not be so easily written off, and that he owed much more to them, and in particular to his early screenwriter Eliot Stannard, than Hitchcock himself, or his auteurist critics, ever admitted. I have redressed the balance somewhat in the early part of *English Hitchcock*, and in an essay, 'Writing Screen Plays: Hitchcock and Stannard', for Andrew Higson's collection *Young and Innocent*; meanwhile, the British Silent Cinema Festival, held annually at the Broadway cinema in Nottingham, has provided the focus for a much wider work of rediscovery and reassessment.[16] Some of the results are already evident in this new edition of *The British Cinema Book*. Above all, Christine Gledhill's *Reframing British Cinema*, thoroughly researched and convincingly argued, has made the old critical orthodoxy look altogether untenable. The value of letting this chapter stand, rather than radically rewriting it, is that it does express, with unusual conciseness, a view of this period of British film history that was dominant, and scarcely challenged, for many decades; as such, I believe it has a historical interest.

Notes

1. For Augustin Le Prince, see Christopher Rawlence, *The Missing Reel* (London: Collins, 1990); also his film of the same title broadcast on Channel 4. For Friese-Greene, see especially Michael Chanan, *The Dream That Kicks*, 2nd edn (London: Routledge, 1995).

2. Brownlow has had a remarkable influence at three levels:
   a) as author of books on the silent period, starting with *The Parade's Gone By* (London: Secker & Warburg, 1968);
   b) as co-director, with David Gill, of many TV series about silent cinema, starting with the thirteen-part *Hollywood: The Pioneers* (for Thames Television, 1979);
   c) as (again with Gill) restorer and exhibitor of silent film prints, with orchestral accompaniment, in cinemas and then on television.

   It's ironic, and symptomatic, that while these activities are based in Britain they have virtually ignored the British cinema of the silent period, although their series *Cinema Europe: The Other Hollywood* (Channel 4, 1995) does devote one programme to it. None of their choices for orchestral presentation has been a British film.

3. Details of the conference are given in *Cinema 1900–1906* (edited by Roger Holman, Brussels: FIAF, 1982). Some of the scholarly work directly and indirectly inspired by it is collected in Thomas Elsaesser and Adam Barker (eds), *Early Cinema: Space, Frame, Narrative*.

4. Kristin Thompson and David Bordwell, *Film History: An Introduction* (New York and London: McGraw-Hill, 1994), p. 65.

5. Bengt Idestam-Almquist, *Nar Filmen Kom Till Sverige* (Stockholm: P. A. Norstedt, 1959; Swedish text, with summary in English), p. 608.

6. James Park, *British Cinema: The Lights That Failed* (London: Batsford, 1990), p. 14.

7. Rachael Low, *The History of the British Film 1918–1929*, p. 301. On editing, see pp. 267ff.

8. François Truffaut, *Hitchcock* (1st English edn, London: Secker & Warburg, 1968), p. 27.

9. Iris Barry, *Let's Go to the Movies*, p. 233.

10. Ibid., p. 220.

11. See Forsyth Hardy (ed.), *Grierson on Documentary* (London: Collins, 1946, and subsequent editions). Other important books written from within the documentary movement, by early collaborators of Grierson, include Paul Rotha, *Documentary Diary* (London: Secker & Warburg, 1973) and Basil Wright, *The Long View* (London: Secker & Warburg, 1974).

12. Michael Balcon, *Michael Balcon Presents . . . A Lifetime of Films*, p. 61.

13. Review of *Blackmail*, *Close Up* vol. 5 no. 2, August 1929, p. 134.

14. London *Evening News*, 16 November 1929, cited in Donald Spoto, *The Life of Alfred Hitchcock: The Dark Side of Genius* (London: Collins, 1983), p. 102.

15. Cecil Hepworth, *Came the Dawn*, p. 139.

16. Charles Barr, *English Hitchcock* (Moffat: Cameron & Hollis, 1999).

Bibliography

Balcon, Michael, *Michael Balcon Presents . . . A Lifetime of Films* (London: Hutchinson, 1969).

Barry, Iris, *Let's Go to the Movies* (New York: Arno Press, 1972, first published in 1926).

Burch, Noël, *Life to Those Shadows* (London: BFI, 1990).

Chanan, Michael, *The Dream That Kicks* (London: Routledge, 1995).

Elsaesser, Thomas and Barker, Adam (eds), *Early Cinema: Space, Frame, Narrative* (London: BFI, 1990).

Gledhill, Christine, *Reframing British Cinema, 1918–1928: Between Restraint and Passion* (London: BFI, 2003).

Hepworth, Cecil, *Came the Dawn* (London: Phoenix House, 1951).

Higson, Andrew, *Waving the Flag: Constructing a National Cinema in Britain* (Oxford: Clarendon Press, 1995).

Higson, Andrew, *Young and Innocent? The Cinema in Britain 1896–1930* (Exeter: Exeter University Press, 2002).

Low, Rachael and Manvell, Roger, *The History of the British Film 1896–1906* (London: George Allen & Unwin, 1948).

Low, Rachael, *The History of the British Film 1906–1914* (London: George Allen & Unwin, 1949).

Low, Rachael, *The History of the British Film 1914–1918* (London: George Allen & Unwin, 1950).

Low, Rachael, *The History of the British Film 1918–1929* (London: George Allen & Unwin, 1971).

Salt, Barry, *Film Style and Technology: History and Analysis* (London: Starword, 1992).

17
Big Studio Production in the Pre-quota Years

Jon Burrows

A *Kinematograph Weekly* cartoon showing Sir Oswald Stoll about to rescue the British film industry from an American stranglehold

Charles Barr points out in 'Before *Blackmail* ' that in the latter half of the 1920s a 'new and more businesslike body of film-makers', including Herbert Wilcox, Michael Balcon and John Maxwell, came to the fore.[1] Most of them had entered the industry early in the decade, but they were given new opportunities to expand on the back of a wave of unprecedented City confidence in the industry, inspired by the protective legislation contained in the 1927 Films Act. In spite of numerous subsequent travails, revivified companies like Gaumont and newer ventures like British International Pictures nurtured personnel, studio buildings, distribution facilities and exhibition circuits which would persist for several decades.

The transition between the pre- and post-quota eras has been typically characterised as a drastic return to

year zero in the history of silent British cinema. Rachael Low presents it as a Darwinian pruning exercise during which, between 1924 and 1927, 'the old guard of producers were weeded out and the ground was cleared for more highly capitalized companies with modern business methods and a modern style of production'.[2] The virile and strong naturally succeeded the weak and infirm. But who exactly were the 'old guard'? Low refers to production concerns like the Hepworth Manufacturing Company and the British and Colonial Kinematograph Company (B & C), both of which had been operating long before the feature-film era began in the early 1910s, and both of which went bust in the early 20s. Most American companies of a similar vintage had been wound up by the end of the preceding decade and, without wishing to dismiss the interest or merit of their output, the inadequate levels of capitalisation and antiquated production facilities of companies like Hepworth's and B & C lent an air of inevitability to their demise.

Stoll's Challenge
However, not all British production companies which failed to see the new quota dawn can be so easily lumped into the category of the ancient and old-fashioned. This chapter will investigate the history of the dominant British production concern in the nine years or so before the introduction of the Films Act – the Stoll Film Company. Stoll comfortably qualifies as the biggest and most ambitious British studio between the end of the 1910s and the middle of the 20s and the ultimate demise of the company's film-making arm, right on the cusp of the quota era, was the result of more

complex and contingent factors than those usually adduced. An analysis of Stoll's rise and fall sheds light on key events such as the Goldwyn dispute, and the 'British Film Slump' and suggests that previous characterisations of British film production in the early 1920s have been too crudely reductive.

Stoll's bore the name of its chairman, the music-hall impresario Sir Oswald Stoll, who was a founding partner of Britain's biggest music-hall chain, Moss Empires, and the independent power behind London's biggest variety theatre, the Coliseum. He branched out to launch the Stoll Film Company in April 1918 as a semi-vertically integrated production-and-distribution concern.[3] The market this venture was launched upon was one in which American films hogged something like an 85 per cent share of British screens.[4] Rather than seeking to challenge this dominance, Stoll adopted a strategy which took account of the structural weaknesses of the British film industry. The intention was to profit from the distribution of American movies while producing a limited number of its own 'niche' brand of British pictures. By the end of 1919 Stoll had completed seven films, a number of which were clearly designed as 'event' productions, boasting a unique selling point in their strong affiliation with the legitimate theatre; several of them featured stage performers, such as Lily Elsie and Matheson Lang, who had appeared at the Coliseum. But from the outset, the prestige British titles were outnumbered by a large volume of American films which Stoll had negotiated the rights to, including all of Samuel Goldwyn's 'Star' pictures.

This may well have made for an effective business model within the inequitable conditions faced by the native production industry, and it followed a pattern already practised successfully for the duration of World War I by the Ideal Film Renting Co.[5] Hollywood's post-war export plans suddenly caught up with Stoll, however. American firms had become increasingly keen to take complete responsibility for the overseas distribution of their films. Cutting out local middlemen enabled them to block-book large numbers of films directly to British exhibitors, many of whom proved willing to commit themselves to show titles not yet produced in order to ensure a continuity of supply and access to dependable star vehicles. With their distribution agreement due to end in August 1919, the Goldwyn Corporation stunned its British agent, and provoked the first major transatlantic film-industry squabble, by exploiting a loophole in their contract and withholding the last six pictures it was due to deliver.

There would seem to have been various motives behind this move. Stoll itself – stung with a blow to its commercial credibility and reputed losses of £25,000 in cancelled bookings for the six defaulted films – claimed that Goldwyn subsequently demanded vastly increased and punitive fees to ship the remaining films over. This demonstrated that 'the attitude adopted by the Goldwyn Corporation [was] an attempt to force the British exhibitor to pay higher prices for his films at the muzzle of a pistol'.[6] It is worth noting, though, that by April 1920 Goldwyn had followed the example of its peers by establishing its own British distribution office. Seen in this light, its previous actions smack of an impatience to reap the commercial benefits that Universal, Fox and Famous Players-Lasky were already enjoying by directly distributing their own films in Britain.

At any rate, this unanticipated turn of events demanded a complete overhaul of Stoll's film-making policy. It had previously shown no inclination to challenge American dominance of the British market as long as some of the profits came its way, and a space remained for its own 'speciality' product. But in one fell swoop a renting operation built with the expectation of handling twenty-five or more films a year had lost its main supplier. Faced with this blockage of its pipelines, Stoll's response was swift and dramatic. 'The action of the Goldwyn Corporation is a challenge', an editorial in the company's own trade paper *Stoll's Editorial News* declared:

> a challenge to the whole trade. It is a challenge which
> the Stoll Film Co. accepts. We are going to produce
> upon a large scale. We are going to prove to the
> British exhibitor that he can procure at home the
> films his patrons will flock to see. British films by
> British producers, breathing the British spirit are what
> the public really want.[7]

Stoll now set its sights on making significant inroads into the American stranglehold, and keeping its own exchanges and its regular customers in business with a supply mostly made up of home-grown films.

Eminent British Authors

Its strategy for achieving this aim was both ambitious and highly distinctive. The Stoll Film Company possessed one of the youngest and most energetic managing directors in the British film industry at this time in Jeffrey Bernerd (aged only twenty-six when he took up the position), and he quickly set about floating a new separate production division, Stoll Picture Productions Ltd. It was capitalised with £400,000-worth of new shares, which made it the country's biggest production outfit by a considerable margin. The initial plan was to expand Stoll's small existing mansion studio in Surbiton, with a £200,000 development of its seventeen-acre grounds to provide enough studio space for six production teams to work simultaneously. But when the Ministry of Health and Housing Committees refused to grant planning permission, it was forced to quickly look elsewhere and bought an enormous former aeroplane factory at Cricklewood. Once the extensive refit was completed in February 1921, Stoll possessed a facility with 27,993 feet of floor space, which was heralded as 'the largest and best equipped in Europe'.[8]

Maurice Elvey, Stoll's first contract director, was now joined by a team comprising British industry veterans (F. Martin Thornton, A. E. Coleby, Harold Shaw) and younger staff with experience in both Europe and America (Sinclair Hill, René Plaisetty, George Ridgewell). As 'auteurs', however, they were largely overshadowed by the most striking element of Stoll's scheme. The company embarked upon a sustained purchasing spree to secure the film rights to a huge library of contemporary British novels. Works by A. E. W. Mason, Edgar Wallace, E. Phillips Oppenheim, Jeffery Farnol, Rafael Sabatini, 'Rita', Marie Corelli, H. G. Wells, Sax Rohmer and Ethel M. Dell, among many others, were acquired in bulk to provide the scenarios for films that would be marketed under the banner of Stoll's 'Eminent British Authors' Series'. The practice of literary adaptation, of course, was nothing new, but the scale of this enterprise was unprecedented. Out of 128 feature films or film serials that Stoll was directly responsible for producing between 1919 and 1928, 118 were adaptations of modern works of English literature. In regular public affirmations of the firm's direct links with its distinguished writers, authors like Wells, Wallace and Mason appeared together at Stoll dinner functions, and occasionally went on location with the relevant film crews to 'supervise' productions.

Stoll's literary ties were foregrounded to the detriment of any attempt to foster a star system. Although a number of authentic British film stars, like Ivy Close and Stewart Rome, did occasionally feature in Stoll productions, the company never sought to keep them under contract. Maurice Elvey confidently delineated their corporate belief that stars were simply not needed

and would actively compromise the aims behind the whole 'Eminent British Authors' concept:

> The stellar system depends for its success upon what is known as the 'original scenario'; but the trouble about the original scenario is that there is nothing original about it. It is, practically speaking, a machine-made duplicate of all the other 'original' scenarios which have been constructed round the star for whom it is intended. . . . We have gone in for the filming of famous novels, which, as I maintain, is wisdom, because there is infinite variety in novels, and a big story is immeasurably better than a big star. Now, when you film a novel, you have to suit your cast to the characters in that novel, and this, surely, is a far better thing than to order scenarios that shall contain characters to suit your cast.[9]

But could such a tactic pay off? There is evidence to suggest that, initially at least, it did. Some exhibitors openly applauded the commercial logic of making films 'based on novels written by authors who are popular with the crowd – authors who are commanding very big prices with the editors of popular magazines, for the very excellent reason that their names . . . ensure a big circulation'.[10] In its share prospectus, Stoll's production division had predicted gross profits of £80,000 a year from a slate of twenty-four films.[11] After the first 'Eminent British Authors' Series' had done the rounds, the Stoll Film Company proudly revealed it had more or less met its targets with gross profits of over £75,000, allowing a net return of £55,669.[12]

Literary Cinema

The kinds of Stoll films which produced such positive results have been subsequently dismissed by Rachael Low as 'unsuitable stories mechanically adapted'.[13] Kenton Bamford argues that Stoll's 'interpretation of eminence' amounted to the perpetuation of a 'wearisome litany of middle-class prejudices' way out of step with the tastes of a mass audience.[14] A viewing of some surviving prints does not confirm such assumptions, however. The films frequently display careful and imaginative attempts to find visual equivalents for the literary qualities of the source texts. Maurice Elvey's adaptation of A. E. W. Mason's *At The Villa Rose* (1920), for example, was extensively (and attractively) shot on location in Monte Carlo. It also preserves the original novel's unusual method of unravelling the machinations of a murder after the case has actually been solved

'A thoughtful literary adaptation': Manora Thew in *At the Villa Rose* (Maurice Elvey, 1920)

midway through, but substantially reshapes its narrative structure to append a fittingly suspenseful climax. What is more, the detective Hannaud's verbal asides, which offer clues to the puzzle in the novel, are cleverly adapted to a mute medium by the inclusion of disconcerting 'bridging' shots. We are given, for example, an apparently narratively redundant glimpse of the (as yet unsuspected) murderer waving to the two detectives on their way to interview a female witness – but when later revisited in flashback, this shot turns out to be the prelude to her death. In several of the surviving Stoll films, a striking number of images are framed with vignettes, as if to signpost the presence of an omniscient narratorial voice, conspicuously showing its hand in the overt framing. One scene towards the end of the NFTVA's half-length print of *The Prodigal Son* (1923) begins with a medium two-shot of a sick mother who has been neglected by her husband and is being comforted by a devoted admirer. A circular mask is imposed on the image, which emphasises her reaction to the news he brings, while obscuring and marginalising the speaker at the edge of the frame. This is not simply a lazy equivalent for a cut to a closer view, because, when a subsequent shot does provide a medium close-up of

the woman, she is framed by another circular vignette. The effect is to self-consciously underline the selective acts of a cinematic narrator fully admitting responsibility for motivating the shifts in viewpoint.

This attempt to stylistically simulate a literary mode of narration in the films does not mean that the adaptation process slavishly respected all original authorial intentions. Bamford's inference that Stoll pandered to 'middle-class antecedents' and made 'no attempt to bridge the divide which was based specifically on class division, class-specific forms and tastes in entertainment' might be challenged with reference to its adaptation of Ethel M. Dell's short story *The Tidal Wave* (1920).[15] The source text presents a narrative in which a young woman leaves the care of her schoolmistress aunt in a Kent village to move to the coast, where her heart and life are nearly lost in the attempt of an ambitious artist to paint her in the midst of a crashing wave. The film rewrites this story to fashion a more starkly melodramatic conflict. In Stoll's version the heroine is a working-class girl from the slums of Birmingham (images of which haunt her in flashback), transplanted to a wild Cornish fishing village. Here she is almost ensnared by the seductive wiles of a more distinctly aristocratic artist/dandy, who mounts trophies of former sexual conquests alongside a talismanic skull in his rooms. A new class dynamic has been specifically inserted to replicate exactly the kind of dramatic sympathies and extreme polarities that Bamford bemoans the absence of.

It is worth noting that among all Stoll's affiliated authors, Ethel M. Dell's works were by far the most regularly adapted. Dell was the pre-eminent British romance writer of the day, and her readership was overwhelmingly female. Despite Maurice Elvey's defiant speeches in the name of literary originality and variety, another Stoll publicist made no bones about the fact that Dell and her ilk were attractive story sources precisely because they recycled

> the same old familiar and agreeable ingredients every
> time, reduced to their elements . . . . The sort of story
> 'that appeals to women and girls by the thousand'
> cannot be a bad story . . . . And to come down to
> brass tacks and business, it suits the exhibitor and the
> bookseller to perfection (no matter how imperfect
> you may deem it) because – it pays![16]

It suited Stoll to distinguish its films from American competition by advertising a product that appeared to be directly bottled from some of the more rarefied well-springs of British cultural life. But while the firm undoubtedly placed great store by the idea of cultivating a hitherto reluctant middle-class following, the 'national card' was played in such a way that it regularly deferred to a determinedly popular local heritage as well.

Distribution Strategies

Stoll still faced considerable obstacles, however, in trying to make significant inroads into Hollywood's dominant share of British screen time. Its all-British line-up of twenty-five or more films per year required a more demonstratively patriotic exhibition sector than had hitherto been evident. The notable success of Stoll's first 'Eminent British Authors' Series' can be partly attributed to one of its more ambitious gambits. Trading on the steady popularity of its early films, Stoll took the extraordinary step for a British supplier of making cinema managers take a complete package of 'Eminent British Author' films sight unseen. In other words, it block-booked its films just like American distributors. A related, but slightly less aggressive, strategy was demonstrated in Stoll's commitment to serial film production. Beginning with its 1921 *Adventures of Sherlock Holmes* series of fifteen two-reel episodes, Stoll was responsible for launching a total of nine different serials in just over three years. As with its feature films, all were adapted from modern literary sources which included Sax Rohmer's *Fu Manchu* stories and a series of *Thrilling Stories from the Strand Magazine*. The aim was transparently to get exhibitors hooked on a successful instalment pattern that they would tie themselves to for several months. This may seem a backward step in the light of the increasing critical stigmatisation and commercial downgrading of serials and series film production in America from the late 1910s onwards.[17] But, as Richard Abel has shown, the serial format retained a pronounced strategic value for beleaguered European producers; the French had their own direct equivalent of Stoll's serialised literary adaptations in the output of *cinéromans*, which 'shored up the French film industry' in the early 1920s.[18]

Serials represented a relatively benign form of block-booking in that exhibitors could always accurately anticipate the kind of formula-driven episodes they would be receiving each week. Straight block-booking of feature films was a more contentious policy, and one that was always likely to be aggravated by the fact that Stoll's films generally cost more than their American rivals' (which were effectively subsidised by profits already reaped in the vast US market). In 1924 a Brixton cinema manager complained that although Stoll's first slate of films contained a number of quality money-makers, it also delivered rather too many that constituted 'a very poor article, and this applies to their releases from January 3rd to September 19th 1921, and was a blot on the British film industry'.[19] Perhaps not surprisingly, Stoll had struggled to spread its resources effectively and consistently over the entirety of what was, for a British firm, an unprecedentedly large slate of feature films. The resentment of exhibitors who had lost money on some of these films was exacerbated by the fact that Stoll took advantage of the profits earned by its first 'Eminent British Authors' to pay out the notably large dividend of 15 per cent to its shareholders. This was deemed necessary to maintain and encourage the interest of City investors whose confidence in the film industry had always been shaky. Even so, the move provoked raised eyebrows among trade commentators, who complained that the profits should have been reinvested into production.[20] The bad feeling was reflected in a lower net profit of £42,144 garnered from Stoll's 1922 programme of films – though this didn't stop the company awarding another 15-per-cent dividend.

The protest message had patently been absorbed, however, because Stoll announced a substantially different kind of programme and general policy for 1923. All block-booking practices were dropped. And although two new serials went into production, the 1923 season of 'Eminent British Authors' feature films was otherwise half the size of previous years, with only twelve new titles. Several of these films were promoted as 'super-productions', having had significantly more time, money and effort lavished upon them than more recent Stoll efforts. They were to be hired out territory-by-territory to an agent with exclusive exploitation rights. Jeffrey Bernerd declared that 'the so-called "programme" picture has had its day and ceased to attract'.[21]

The change in direction was undoubtedly directly influenced by Stoll's success the previous year in handling British distribution of the French film *L'Atlantide* (1921). Based on a best-selling contemporary French novel, shot in the vast expanses of the Sahara desert at a cost of nearly 2 million francs, and with a running time of over three hours, Jacques Feyder's mammoth production had helped to revive an ailing French industry by providing it with its first post-war international hit. Stoll attempted to emulate its bold ambition with the centre-piece of its 1923 programme, a four-hour adaptation of Sir Hall Caine's epic novel of the shifting fortunes of two Icelandic brothers, *The Prodigal Son*, directed by A. E. Coleby. At a cost of well over £30,000 it was, at the time, the most expensive British production ever mounted, and featured extensive location shooting in Iceland, Paris, Nice and northern Italy.

Rachael Low's barbed comment that *The Prodigal Son* 'must have seemed tiring even to people used to Stoll films' stems from a misapprehension that the film was intended to be screened in one sitting.[22] It was actually released as two films, *The Prodigal Son* and *The Return of the Prodigal*, which were to follow each other at participating cinemas in successive weeks. Coleby confidently predicted that such an exploitation plan would soon become the norm, with 'big themes to be treated in a big way and, if necessary, to be put out in two – or even in three – pictures'.[23] Obviously this was not an accurate vision of the future, but it was not the isolated folly it might now seem either. The French had also been simultaneously experimenting with super-productions intended to be screened in more than one weekly instalment. Such a policy acknowledged the impossibility of matching the volume and overall quality of American imports by concentrating resources in a select number of monumental productions. The risk that this entailed was softened, however, by retaining some of the security of the old serial format: exhibitors who took one instalment of an epic would have little choice but to hire subsequent 'chapters' to complete the viewing experience.

Individual cinema managers who booked *The Prodigal Son* testified to its pulling power.[24] But the heavy investment in a smaller number of films to be exploited in staggered release patterns meant that it would take longer for returns to trickle in. Partly as a consequence of this, profits for the year 1923 were substantially down, with a final figure of £11,496. Even in these circumstances, appeasing shareholders remained a central priority and a reduced but still respectable dividend of 10 per cent was paid out. Their anxieties also seem to have panicked Stoll into prematurely abandoning its super-film strategy, and in 1924 the company tried to step up output levels once again and produced sixteen feature films and four serials. An exasperated Jeffrey Bernerd quit the company and his disagreement with his Boards on matters of policy were widely reported by the trade press.[25] This internal fighting and equivocation about its future direction signalled the

beginning of the end of Stoll's term of office as industry trailblazer.

The British Film Slump

Since 1924 was Stoll's most traumatic season to date, it is interesting to map its tribulations against one of the most notorious and apparently catastrophic events in the British film industry of the 1920s, the so-called British Film Slump of the same year. Sir Oswald Stoll was certainly directly involved in the crisis talks that suddenly engulfed the British film industry in November of 1924. The British Film Slump reported in the press at this time has come to be seen as a defining moment in the history of silent British cinema. Kenton Bamford, for example, has described it as the inevitable consequence of (what he sees as) the industry's abject failure to accommodate the tastes of its core working-class consumer base. Its manifold failings now saw it limp to the brink of complete obsolescence.[26] Given the status of this event in historical accounts of British cinema in the 20s, it is surprising how sketchily it has been investigated. The supposed crisis began with a report carried in *Kinematograph Weekly*, in the middle of November, which pointed out in alarmist rhetoric that every British studio had ground to a complete halt, and 'not a camera, so far as we can ascertain, is being turned; a state of things unprecedented in the whole quarter of a century's existence of film-making in this country'.[27] Broadsheet newspapers like the *Daily Mail* quickly leapt on the bandwagon and ran doom-laden updates on the situation for a whole week. The most significant admission of disaster was deemed to come in an interview Oswald Stoll himself gave in the *Daily Mail*, in which he openly assented to the claims 'that British films are in a quite desperate way'.[28]

These disclosures were, however, greeted with considerable scepticism from knowledgeable contemporaries. The *Bioscope* flatly denied that any such emergency existed:

> no firm with any commercial sense would attempt to produce films in this country during the months of November, December, January and February . . . . [O]nly Sir Oswald Stoll's own studios . . . are closed at the present moment, and for no other reason. For the same reason, other British firms are at present producing British pictures on the Continent.[29]

The *Westminster Gazette* similarly observed that seasonal London fogs traditionally halted British film production in November.[30] A number of commentators detected no small amount of coincidence in the timing of this 'crisis', coming as it did straight after the October inauguration of Stanley Baldwin's new Conservative government. Certainly, Stoll himself was not shy about taking advantage of this opportunity to direct the new administration's attention to his proposed scheme for imposing heavier import duties on American films.[31] Overall, there is little evidence of any shutdown reflected in Stoll's production totals: significantly more titles were released in 1924 than in 1923, and this increased output was matched in 1925. It might, therefore, be more appropriate to view the supposed great 'British Film Slump' less as the industry's self-inflicted death knell than as its own (surreptitious) self-help campaign.

When the 1927 Films Act was finally introduced, however, it was perceived to be too little too late for Stoll's investors, and the firm withdrew somewhat bruised and battered from British film-making almost directly afterwards. A severely curtailed production programme had been followed in 1926 and 1927, and the increasing disgruntlement of shareholders made for some notoriously stormy annual general meetings.[32] Stoll himself maintained in August 1927 that the company still 'had plenty of funds' to continue making films.[33] But he only advocated such a plan to his backers on the strength of an anticipated clause in the Films Act imposing a per-reel tax on the exhibition of foreign films.[34] Without this direct incentive for booking native product (which never materialised) the company was not prepared to gamble on a return to higher output levels. In 1928 it acted in a dramatic fashion to wipe out its debit balance and mollify its investors by transferring all their shares into a new holding company, the Stoll Theatres Corporation, which would henceforth concentrate solely on the management of its property assets. These now included the established theatres and music halls previously owned by other parts of the Stoll empire.[35] In the same year, Stoll's last major feature film limped out on release.[36]

It is fair to say that Stoll's fate exemplifies the stuttering, congenital weaknesses of British film-making prior to the introduction of the 1927 Films Act: but its cessation of production should not lead one to conclude that it displayed an inadequate understanding of its audience or merely fashioned incompetent responses to severe pre-existent handicaps. Stoll had been prematurely provoked into launching a bid to overturn the long-established market leaders without adequate resources or preparation. The company made too many sudden policy shifts and was unable to sustain its initial phase of measured growth. Above all, it was handicapped by the need to appease and encourage investors who, before the 1927 Films Act (and even after it became law), were impatient and inconstant in their commitment to British film production. As a final coda, though, it is worth noting the way in which British International Pictures (BIP) – the biggest and most aggressive of the new companies that were partly capitalised on the strength of the new quota legislation – selected and promoted its first slate of films. Displaying the portraits of thirteen distinguished British authors who had been either adapted or directly employed by BIP, the firm announced a programme of 'Best Sellers'.[37] Clearly, the 'Eminent British Authors' concept had not outlived its usefulness. As these kinds of issues and facts are exposed, it becomes possible to identify important continuities between production before and after the Films Act and to disperse the cloud of shame and disappointment which has gathered around British silent cinema of the post-pioneer and pre-quota years.

Notes

1. 'Before *Blackmail*: Silent British Cinema', Chapter 16 in this volume, p. 150.
2. Rachael Low, *The History of the British Film, 1918–1929*, p. 156.
3. In *Distorted Images: British National Identity and Film in the 1920s*, Kenton Bamford implies that Stoll also owned its own chain of cinemas, but the Stoll 'circuit' only consisted of five affiliated theatres, and thus was not a major consideration in its film-making policy decisions.
4. See the *Moving Picture World*, 2 June 1917, p. 1427, for an analysis of the British market.
5. For a detailed discussion of Ideal's success in the 1910s see Jon Burrows, *Legitimate Cinema*, pp. 180–224.
6. *Stoll's Editorial News*, 27 November 1919, p. 1.
7. Ibid.
8. See *Stoll's Editorial News*, 14 July 1921, pp. 3–5.
9. Ibid., 5 August 1920, p. 7.
10. A quotation from the *Rochester Journal* – reprinted in *Stoll's Editorial News*, 22 September 1921, p. 12.
11. See *Stoll's Editorial News*, 13 May 1920, p. ii.
12. Ibid., 12 January 1922, pp. 15–16
13. Low, *The History of the British Film, 1918–1929*, p. 125.
14. Bamford, *Distorted Images*, p. 74.
15. Ibid., p. 89.
16. *Stoll's Editorial News*, 16 September 1920.
17. See, for example, Ben Singer, 'Serial Melodrama and Narrative *Gesellschaft*'.

18. Richard Abel, *French Cinema: The First Wave, 1915–1929*, p. 44.
19. *Bioscope*, 10 January 1924, p. 27.
20. Ibid., 11 December 1924, p. 32.
21. *Stoll's Editorial News*, 28 December 1922, p. 7.
22. Low, *The History of the British Film, 1918–1929*, p. 127.
23. *Stoll's Editorial News*, 1 February 1923, p. 3.
24. See the correspondence reprinted in *Stoll's Editorial News*, 26 April 1923, p. 23; 10 May 1923, p. 22.
25. *Bioscope*, 11 December 1924, p. 45.
26. Bamford, *Distorted Images*, p. 88.
27. *Kinematograph Weekly*, 13 November 1924, p. 66.
28. *Daily Mail*, 19 November 1924, p. 7.
29. *Bioscope*, 27 November 1924, p. 3.
30. *Westminster Gazette*, 19 November 1924, p. 6.
31. *Daily Mail*, 19 November 1924, p. 7. Interestingly, two weeks after it broke the news of the British Film Slump, *Kinematograph Weekly* ran an article which disputed the factual basis of the original story, while pointing out the benefits to be gained from such scaremongering by drawing national press attention to the problems faced by the industry. See P. L. Mannock, 'Slump or No Slump?', *Kinematograph Weekly*, 27 November 1924, p. 6.
32. At the company's infamous seventh AGM its executive managers were unceremoniously sacked – see *Kinematograph Weekly*, 4 August 1927, pp. 25–6.
33. Ibid.
34. Ibid., 6 January 1927, p. 69.
35. Ibid., 26 July 1928, p. 36.
36. This was not officially the end of Stoll's role in British film production. Its Cricklewood studio was eventually converted for sound and remained in use until 1937. Stoll itself occasionally made the odd regulation picture in the 1930s to keep its sound stages fully active, but it remained resolutely on the fringes of mainstream production.
37. *Kinematograph Weekly*, 26 January 1928.

Bibliography

Abel, Richard, *French Cinema: The First Wave, 1915–1929* (Princeton, NJ: Princeton University Press, 1984).

Bamford, Kenton, *Distorted Images: British National Identity and Film in the 1920s* (London: I. B. Tauris, 1999).

Barker, Felix, *The House That Stoll Built: The Story of the Coliseum* (London: Frederick Muller, 1957).

Burrows, Jon, *Legitimate Cinema: Theatre Stars in Silent British Films, 1908–1918* (Exeter: University of Exeter Press, 2003).

Crowhurst, Andrew, 'Oswald Stoll: A Music Hall Pioneer', *Theatre Notebook* vol. 49 no. 1, 1995.

Gledhill, Christine, *Reframing British Cinema, 1918–1928: Between Restraint and Passion* (London: BFI, 2003).

Higson, Andrew, *Young and Innocent? The Cinema in Britain 1896–1930* (Exeter: Exeter University Press, 2002).

Low, Rachael, *The History of the British Film, 1918–1929* (London: George Allen & Unwin, 1971).

Singer, Ben, 'Serial Melodrama and Narrative *Gesellschaft*', *The Velvet Light Trap* no. 37, Spring 1996.

Thompson, Kristin, *Exporting Entertainment: America in the World Film Market 1907–34* (London: BFI, 1985).

18
Late Silent Britain

CHRISTINE GLEDHILL

By the second half of the 1920s many commentators on cinema believed that a new art form – the silent moving picture – had come to maturity. In Britain such convictions were supported by the emergence of a lively critical culture, with film critics employed by many newspapers. In 1925 the Film Society was established, introducing a rich variety of foreign films to London. Two years later *Close Up*, the first English-language journal devoted to cinema, was launched along with an experimental production wing, POOL films. However, British films figured little in discussions of a film art largely associated with European cinemas, while Hollywood dominated the mainstream. This chapter explores in what way the development of British film-making represented a 'maturing' of practices derived from a British cultural context largely disregarded in subsequent film histories.

This is not to propose a homogenous national identity or cinematic style. While demands for a national cinema were made, these emerged from specific contexts, representing different interests. As James Donald argues, culture produces the national, not the other way round.[1] Moreover local cultures are never hermetically self-contained but draw in ideas and practices from elsewhere. Equally, the shift between 'primitive' and 'mature' rarely constitutes a definitive break. In this volume, Jon Burrows questions the use of the so-called studio shut-down of Black November 1924 as an economic caesura which knocked out the old-fashioned and allowed the modern to appear. If the late 1920s marks a consolidation on both economic and cinematic fronts, its achievements can only be fully explored by recognising continuities as well as change. The maturing of late

1920s film-making derives not only from greater economic confidence leading up to and following the 1927 Films Act, but from reinvention, within the stabilising practices of a new international medium, of inherited pictorial, theatrical and storytelling traditions. To take account, then, of the cultural-aesthetic horizons of British film-makers raises the question not only of what 'British' means when prefacing cinema, but what 'cinema' means when British is attached to it.

Fantasy and Document

Contrary to the notion of a collapsing film industry, 1926 saw a remarkable crop of films made by already established film-makers – Maurice Elvey, Graham Cutts, Herbert Wilcox, Walter Summers, Sinclair Hill, George Cooper, George Pearson – as well as Hitchcock's first three films as solo director. This output included romantic melodrama, naval romance, zany comedy, crime melodrama, historical romance, marital problem melodrama, wartime romance and battle-field documentary reconstructions. Against the predominance of fantasy in Romantic or melodramatic vein, Michael Balcon remarked ruefully of the interwar years that hardly a film 'reflects the agony of those times'.[2] Thus the films of the 1920s have been castigated for evading the social changes that were accelerated by the Great War and climaxed in the class struggles of the General Strike. Found equally lacking is any substantial engagement with the modernist practices explored by the European avant-garde. Rather these films adopt a whimsicality or feyness of tone, espousing romanticist escape into costume and disguise, using late Victorian and Edwardian popular, middle-brow sources and aesthetic predilections. As 'signs of the times', then, these films reveal their engagement in indirect, implicit ways.

In *Reframing British Cinema*, I looked for the aesthetic and imaginary frameworks or mental-emotional horizons within which such engagements might be made. If early 20s films made heavy use of the iris, masks and internal framing (curtains, doorways, arches), treating shots as pictures; if sets constructed spaces as social stages for public acts, favouring tableaux effects and frontal shooting; if acting demanded either the 'restraint-and-passion' mode, splitting public from private, self from role or, in the interests of extending representation, the caricature of social typing and character acting; and if characterisation and plots were elaborated through cultural references, quotation, parody, such practices shared an investment in the defining power of frame, boundary and document. An emphasis on articulation and demarcation suggests the primacy of a geographic over a biographic aesthetic. Unlike the American imaginary, emerging from the egalitarian ideals of revolution and valorising the heroic trajectory of the individual overcoming both natural and social obstacles, British cultural production, embedded in a long history of social division but undergoing democratisation, invests in mapping and demarcating protagonists defined by social difference. This practice responds to the pressure, both political and commercial, to extend representation, recognising while managing social difference: the aesthetic pay-off lies in the dynamic of the boundary and in the reflexivity of the articulated image. For the boundary not only defines and separates, but initiates contact with consequent frissons of danger and transgressive desire, while the process of definition foregrounds markers of class, gender, race and region (home, workplace, dress, leisure pursuits, artefacts) as cultural documents and reference points. Thus documenting and fictional practices form a mutually reflexive continuum: pictures, stories and entertainment practices become themselves cultural references within film fictions, instituting a process of cultural recycling and circulation between differently constituted audiences. Arguably, this endemic re-use of past materials and practices enabled the cinema of the 1920s to engage with the trauma of the Great War and the class and gender changes it accelerated in indirect, sometimes heavily symbolic and sometimes whimsically playful ways, a contention explored in the analysis of films and film-makers below.

Theatricality and *The Rat* (1925)

The most celebrated film of 1925 was *The Rat*, based on a stage play written (with Constance Collier) by Ivor Novello. Michael Balcon, head of Gainsborough studios, gave the project to his commercially successful but temperamentally erratic director Graham Cutts as a means of separating him from his pushy young assistant Alfred Hitchcock. Cutts had proved his pictorial skills in *The Wonderful Story* (1921), where the predicament of a man paralysed on the eve of his wedding, watching from his bed the courtship of his erstwhile fiancée by his brother, taught Cutts the power of the camera to project jealous desire interlaced with sadistic voyeurism. In *The Rat*, he exploits this power in sinuous tracking shots and cross-cut looks between playing areas of the multi-level White Coffin, the Rat's underworld haunt, instigating movements of transgressive desire. Early in the story we find Zelie (Isabel Jeans), a high-class courtesan bored by the legitimate theatre's variety shows, looking for new sensations at the proletarian White Coffin. Seated on the mezzanine, Zelie's fashionable crowd look through coffin-like openings down onto the bar area below, where the Rat (Novello) is soon provoked into a knife-fight. Thus a working-class ritual becomes an enactment for the upper-class viewers, framed in reverse shot in the arches above, leaning excitedly forward to watch. However, the 'performance' refuses to stay within the bounds of its own stage. The two combatants, followed by their supporters, push up the steps onto the floor above, galvanising Cutts's mobile camera and bringing a nonchalant Rat under Zelie's desiring gaze. Retreating to the lower floor, he responds by dancing a violent tango with one of his admirers. Zelie sends him a tip. He replies by using it to light his cigarette. Thus the tension between the containment of pictorial framing and movement in theatricalised space provokes cross-class eroticism.

Ivor Novello, Stardom and British Film Acting

As a boundary figure the Parisian Apache was much in vogue in the 1920s. But the popularity of *The Rat* and its two sequels was equally vested in the screen presence of its star, Ivor Novello.[3] As one of the few British film actors to attain cinematic stardom, Novello's charisma rested in a specific performance style which, concealing a gay identity that could not be publicly expressed, dramatised the tensions of British film acting. For if stardom depends on the 'illusion of the first time' whereby the performer appears not to be acting but revealing the self, both the underplaying of the 'restraint-and-passion' mode and the foregrounded skills of character acting depend on the visibility of performance – the first in order to separate public from an implied but hidden inner life and the second to produce delight in recognition of character construction. If Novello offered body and persona to the camera, inviting uncharacteristically intimate and sexualised writing by critics, he nevertheless aspired to the Romantic stage of melodramatic expression and rhetorical flourishes.[4] These contrary tendencies were held together by his making a performance out of *not performing*: by tossing off in camp manner the flamboyant gestures of the Romantic stage or retreating into the passivity of self-display enabled by cinematic devices – framing, close-up and lighting – which served to present the star performer as himself a projection, exemplified in his celebrated profile. Hitchcock's *Downhill* (1927), plays neatly on the ambiguity of such projection and the tension between theatre and cinema, visible and star acting. We watch Novello as Roddy Berwick, disgraced public-school boy driven from the family home, apparently stealing a cigarette lighter from a café table, only to see him line up with a number of other waiters in a jigging dance routine as the camera pulls back to reveal him playing in the chorus of a theatrical musical.

Remembering the War

In *The Rat*'s paradoxically named sequel, *The Triumph of the Rat* (1926), the combination of Novello's penchant for suffering roles and Cutts's voyeuristic camera produces a sadistic edge as the Rat, subject to an underworld frame-up instigated by the jealous Zelie, is accused of treachery by his erstwhile White Coffin compatriots and driven into destitution under their hostile gaze. If such scenarios of sado-masochistic suffering suggested an androgynous and ambivalent sexuality, they could also, Michael Williams argues, focus traumatic memories of the War. Taking a lead from the *Picture Show*'s Edith Nepean, Williams reads Novello's image in terms of the 'war touch' she discerned in the 'horror-haunted' figure found in *The Rat* and its two sequels, also exploited by Hitchcock in *The Lodger* (1927) and *Downhill*.[5] Novello's associations with the War – he composed 'Keep the Home Fires Burning,' while his youthful Grecian profile recalled the dead poet Rupert Brooke – and his scenarios of self-destruction spoke in different ways to the images, losses and nightmares of the War. But the 'war-touch' ran like

a nerve-twanging seam through many of the films of the 1920s.

Producer Bruce Woolfe's reconstructions of key battles constituted explicit acts of remembrance that increasingly mixed war footage with re-enactment and fictionalised episodes as a dignifying frame within which to revisit the War while recognising its solemn pathos. *Mons* (Walter Summers, 1926) played at the Pavilion, Marble Arch for many weeks to record audiences, familiarising new generations with the pain undergone by their fathers on the front and suggesting an anti-war message.[6] Scenarios that highlighted the novelty of social reversals and relationships resulting from the rise of former servants through the ranks and from defiant daughters emancipated into war work – for example Maurice Elvey's *Comradeship* (1919), Thomas Bentley's *General Post* (1920), and Adrian Brunel's *Blighty* (1927) – were paralleled by stories focused explicitly or by implication on wounded, psychologically maimed or neurasthenic men, beginning with the crippled hero of *The Wonderful Story*, continued in Cutts's *The Passionate Adventure* (1924) and Novello's 'war-touched' protagonists, and on to Sinclair Hill's wartime melodrama *Guns of Loos* (1928), Miles Mander's stylish marital melodrama *The First-Born* (1928) and Victor Saville's *Kitty* (1929) at the end of the decade.

Guns of Loos combined warfront reconstruction – realised through the pyrotechnic effects of Hill's inventive cameramen – with melodramatic conflict between competing heroes for the homebound heroine. At the beginning of the film, John Grimlaw (played by Henry Victor, master of upright restraint) has turned from 'Ironmaster' to 'Slave Driver' under pressure from the ministry to produce more shells. However, he is confronted not only by a striking workforce but by disapproval of his ruthless tactics from Diana Cheswick (Madeleine Carroll), daughter of the local aristocracy. She is courted by both John and her more socially adept adopted brother, Clive, but withholds her answer while they go to the front as officers, along with servants from the Cheswick mansion as 'Other Ranks'. This mix of document and melodrama registered social change through the clash of class-based social forms and performance practices. The night of departure contrasts the high-toned farewells and repressed longings of the Cheswick gathering; below stairs a raucous party acknowledges, while attempting to blot out, the realities of the battlefront.

In one of the few private moments in the film, Grimlaw, till now characterised by the restraint that belies inner passion, retreats into a dugout in a state of 'funk', his breakdown expressed in a montage of dissolves between the factory, battlefront and Diana. He is then found and challenged by Clive, who persists in high-flown heroic rhetoric. Responding to Clive's goading, Grimlaw returns to service. Now he physically collaborates with the Cheswick staff, his shoulders spread, crucifix-like, under the yoke of the field gun they struggle to move. Such Christian references, part both of the mythology and artistic response to the war, thread through these films, hovering also around the war-touched sufferings of Novello in *The Lodger* and the Rat films. Grimlaw's recovery, registered in his volunteering to replace the dead Forward Observation Officer, is played by Henry Victor with the restraint associated with upper- and officer-class characters. In marked contrast the camp show performed on a makeshift stage by 'Other Ranks' draws on music-hall traditions of parody, burlesque and drag, and ends with communal singing of 'Keep the Home Fires Burning' in which, no doubt, the audience would have joined. While this hilarity is underway we see through the back of the shed soldiers preparing for the 'real' theatre of war. Through this combination of theatrical performance and documentary, social observation and symbolism, *Boy's Own* heroics confronts war as industrialised destruction, raising questions about class, masculinity, capitalism and war, while making the competition between John and Clive for Diana a struggle for England's future.

Maurice Elvey and the Picture Story

Besides documentary reconstructions and obliquely 'war-touched' films, 1926 saw a return to more overtly heroic war stories, including earlier forms of swashbuckling romantic naval melodramas with Maurice Elvey's *The Flag Lieutenant* and Dinah Shurey's *Second to None* (which raised some eyebrows at Britain's then only woman director's apparent endorsement of military heroics).[7] As an industry veteran with an early background in romantic and experimental theatre, Elvey drew from a range of cultural and aesthetic influences to make a remarkable series of films in the late 1920s. Following a disastrous spell with Fox in America, his fortunes revived in 1926 with *The Flag Lieutenant*, which starred the infectiously debonair Henry Edwards as the playful, but stiff-upper-lipped lieutenant who nobly shoulders a charge of cowardice – thereby threatening to lose the respect of the admiral's daughter whom he is

courting – in order to protect the honour of his closest but less charismatic and competent friend.

Mademoiselle from Armentieres (1926) – an equally unlikely story of love and misrecognition in the trenches – depends on Elvey's development of editing techniques capable of integrating pictorial shots and cultural vignettes into a narrative progression. Through a form of flicker-book montage, he alternates sets of repeated carefully composed shots in progressively changing series, intensifying the pace of shot change as dramatic and emotional tensions rise. Two effective instances include Mademoiselle's scanning and then running alongside the troops setting off for the front, desperate to dispel her soldier lover's mistaken perception that she has betrayed him, and the later build-up in the trenches to the moment of attack. But equally important to the film's wholehearted reception was its incorporation of the myths, songs and stories of trench warfare – including Mademoiselle herself (Estelle Brody) as a combination of estaminet barmaid and Angel of Mons – as documents of the experience of the war.[8] A moment particularly resonant for critics and filmgoers shows a Bruce Fairbairns-like older soldier (Humberston Wright) phlegmatically cleaning his fingernails with his bayonet as he waits for the signal to go over the top, and then, noticing the trepidation of his juvenile companion, encouraging him to join in singing 'Old Soldiers Never Die'.

Elvey's command of British cinema's heterogeneous practices, whereby images, stories, performance modes, social documents and character types function as cultural reference points, underpinned two of his best films. *Hindle Wakes* (1927) opens with a montage between a knocker-up waking factory workers in Cotton Street, and the cosseted awakenings of the mill-owner's son in Midas Street. The tale of cross-class philandering is integrated into extended location sequences shot in Blackpool's funfairs and ballrooms as setting for Stanley Houghton's social drama, which concludes with the assertion of independence by mill-girl Fanny (Estelle Brody) refusing respectability by marriage into the mill-owner's family. *Palais de Danse* (1928), scripted by Jean Jay, utilises the new phenomenon of the commercial dance hall for a replay of the Cinderella story, in which the aristocratic King family, let down by the celebrity actress supposedly taking the role of Cinders in their charity tableau, purloin the daughter (Mabel Poulton) of a war-crippled night watchman from across the street, and so set in motion a re-enactment of the class antagonisms of the fairytale in the sleazy context of the thinly disguised call-girl industry then emerging in the dance halls. The film offers a near-perfect balance between pictorial image and story, cultural document and fairytale, visible acting and Poulton's starry luminescence. This enables it to render sympathetically the fantasies, dreams and down-to-earth expectations of the working-class denizens of the dance hall – particularly as performed by a sceptical, gum-chewing Chili Bouchier – while casting a cold eye on the commercialisation of sex and status in the figure of the duplicitous No 1 played by John Longden, controlling with lizard-like insidiousness his teams of male and female 'partners' to be purchased for a shilling, while masquerading as Count Alban in order to seduce Lady King.

Fantasy and Child's play

Palais de Danse reveals just how serious the fairytale and the associated child's play of play-acting, dressing-up, disguise and role-reversal could be in the 20s. The image of Lady King and her daughters hacking into the war veteran's daughter's frock with their flashing scissors to make her more Cinders-like speaks potently of the overweening class presumptions that divided British society. Child's play runs alongside the 'war touch' as its sometimes rhubarbative, sometimes healing counter-side, with a concomitant role for the 'child' in many of the decade's film stories. Significantly the 1920s saw the publication of A. A. Milne's *Winnie the Pooh* and his theatrical adaptation, *Toad of Toad Hall*. While Milne was desperate to be recognised as a serious dramatist, his neighbours ran Pooh Parties to which Christopher Robin was sent along to play himself. Many of the decade's film-makers had seen war service and none were untouched by the devastating losses of the war. In such a context, the child became a key figure through whom the dysfunction of parents and their recovery could be expressed, from George Pearson's *Nothing Else Matters* (1921), which introduced Betty Balfour as the scatty, romance-reading babysitter who allows the toddler of warring parents to get lost, to the neurasthenic widower in Hepworth's *Pipes of Pan* (1923), whose return to normal life is effected through Alma Taylor's Polly, found helping his little son summon up fairies in the woods. By the end of the decade the theme darkens in the distorted maternity of upper-class Mrs St George, who in Victor Saville's *Kitty* seeks to confine her crippled air-pilot son to his bed and so to her side away from the shopkeeping, pragmatically

cheerful Kitty (Estelle Brody again) and in Miles Mander's performance of malignant masculinity as the estranged husband looking for an heir in *The First Born*.

Against the fantasies woven around these boy children, Walter West's social drama of 1925, *A Daughter of Love*, is rare in its concern with broken promises that leave its Irish heroine (Violet Hopson) pregnant as her doctor lover pursues social advancement, and in imagining the cross-class solidarity of women, uniting to promote the well-being of the daughter. *Kitty*, on the other hand, uses the trauma of the war-wounded to dramatise social change in a conflict between women opposed through a set-construction that makes Mrs St George's country seat somewhat improbably abut the lower-middle-class street where Kitty and her mother run a tobacconist's shop. In a face-to-face confrontation with Mrs St George, Kitty's mother (Marie Ault) stoutly asserts that her daughter can respectably earn her own as well as her war-crippled husband's living. The film resolves its country seat/urban back street opposition by annexing the values of country life to the broken-down Thames-side cottage which Kitty turns not only into a successful tourist venue as a riverside café but a home for the war-damaged Alex where he learns to walk again. Like the rose-entwined cottage which bookends *Mademoiselle from Armentieres*, or the fairy-filled woods where reconciliation takes place in *Nothing Else Matters* and *Pipes of Pan*, such images of suburban pastoralism speak of escape into the magical places of childhood imagination as a necessary retreat to origins in order to return, recuperated, to the modern world.

The First-Born, however, finds no such comfort in a story disliked by the trade press for its sordid and degraded central character – a lecher and would-be MP. However, Miles Mander clearly had much invested in the project – not only did he undertake direction for the first time and co-produce with Michael Balcon, but he worked with Alma Reville and Ian Dalrymple on adapting the script from his stage play, *Those Common People*, and undertook the leading role. Drawing on his reputation for characterising upper-class libertines, Mander, as Sir Hugo Boycott, twists and turns his wiry body in a palpable embodiment of class-bound masculine dysfunction. The cause of his torture is his desire for a child and his doubt about the paternity of his first son. That both his tortured masculinity and its cause implicitly reference war-touched themes is suggested when, following news of his fatal accident as the election results make him an MP, his portrait in officer's uniform falls from the wall. That this seamy melodrama – like *Palais de Danse* and *Kitty* – offers an unflattering portrait of a society stymied by distorted class and gender relationships is suggested not only by trade-press reactions, but by Mander's declared conversion to Fabianism through his wartime 'contact with real people'.[9] The Expressionist camerawork and deft editing of seduction across overladen upper-class dinner tables, Boycott's desertion of his wife for colonial decadence, his wife's secret adoption of her hairdresser's illegitimate baby in order to lure him home with an heir (as it turns out genuinely his), and his cynical perpetuation of nineteenth-century electioneering rhetoric combine to offer a bitter portrait of the social hierarchy which oversaw the Great War and hung onto its position through the 20s.

Girls at Play: Britain's Queen of Happiness and the Constant Nymph

At its most light-hearted child's play generated a kind of infectious rejuvenation – exemplified in Betty Balfour's rise to stardom as 'Britain's Queen of Happiness' on the back of Squibs, the rumbustious Cockney flower seller, supporting a reprobate drinking-and-betting father while courting her stolid policeman boyfriend to the disapproval of his snobbish lower-middle-class parents. Created by George Pearson and Eliot Stannard out of a tragicomic rollercoaster of music-hall turns and vignettes of working-class life, Squibs generated four films in the early 20s, but proved difficult for Balfour to escape.[10] New outlets for her good-humoured scattiness included Cutts's adaptation *The Sea Urchin* (1926), where she was matched by an equally scapegrace aeronautical rescuer (George Hackathorne). Hitchcock's *Champagne* (1928) played Balfour against type as a spoilt little rich girl, while Geza von Bolvary's *The Vagabond Queen* (1929) combined Balfour's boarding-house skivvy with her comical impersonation as coronation stand-in for a Ruritanian queen abducted by political enemies. Betty Balfour continued, alongside Ivor Novello, to dominate the British star polls at the end of the 1920s.[11] But she remained identified with Squibs who, like Novello perhaps, represented too whimsical an image of delayed adolescence for a culture that by the 1930s had adopted synchronised sound and established new registers of class and gender realism.

The only performer of the decade who came near the transparency of stardom was Mabel Poulton, whose defining role was the pubescent Tessa in Adrian Brunel and Basil Dean's film adaptation of Margaret Kennedy's widely popular, *The Constant Nymph* (1928). Here Poulton played opposite Novello as the irresponsibly playful composer-musician, Lewis Dodd, who grows up only in recognising, at the moment of Tessa's death, the quality of her child-woman's devotion to him. The film, emerging from fraught production circumstances dominated by disagreements between theatrical producer and film director, was declared a triumph for Brunel and its two main stars, and voted the best British film of 1929 by *Film Weekly*'s readers.[12] Paradoxically it is the film in which Novello, donning owl-like reading glasses and confronting the problems of a too-hasty marriage, tempers his non-performing performance with a degree of character acting. Equally Brunel finds a balance between well-composed cinematography, comic vignettes and story development that combines his sense of the absurd – here caught in the quirky performance gestures and facial tics of supporting characters – with genuine pathos and yearning evoked in the ineffable desire that runs between child and composer. This is vested in particular in Poulton's projection of child-wise transcendence. In a scenario focused on the attempt by Lewis Dodd/Novello's ambitious wife to turn his creative talent to social account by making him 'grow up', this is perhaps the last time that a 1920s child-redeemer is able to perform – in this case *her* – magic, making a fittingly nostalgic farewell to what George Pearson in reminiscence would call the 'twilight twenties.'[13]

Play and Modernity

Though the lack of a modernist avant-garde among British film-makers has been pondered, this prevailing attitude of 'play' fostered a spirit of experimental 'trial-and-error' by small post-war companies formed around actors, writers and would-be film-makers who saw in cinema new opportunities for play-acting and story-telling. Acting as role-playing, pictures as cultural documents, and stories as make-believe, coupled with protagonists who either could not or would not grow up, resulted in pastiche and parody with a silly-ass satirical edge. Adrian Brunel made a series of burlesques for Gainsborough in the mid-1920s while he waited for feature-length assignments, in which he also performed in various guises. Made on a shoestring budget, using his own back garden as setting and found footage as linkage, his parodies were spun out of verbal-visual punning and chop-logic juxtapositions playing on the absurdities to be drawn out of a range of popular cultural forms and practices: the travel film in *Crossing the Great Sagrada* (1924); film newsreels in *The Pathetic Gazette* (1924) and *The Typical Budget* (1925); the boxing film and tourism in *Battling Bruisers* (1925); censorship in *Cut It Out: A Day in the Life of a Censor* (1925), and so on.

In *Crossing the Great Sagrada*, Brunel poses alternately as Sweet the intrepid film director, 'specially supervising, carefully watching and partially controlling' the production, and as the twins, Holmes and Holmes – one of them 'of Scottish origin' – who together with Sweet set out on the expedition. The by-now familiar documentary inter-titles, explanatory diagrams and maps are juxtaposed illogically with reality shots of local London life and/or exotic or outlandish foreign customs; inter-titles are underscored by parodic signatures making punning jokes at the expense of the British film industry: 'An artless production', 'A Pathetic film' and so on. *Battling Bruisers* exploits the satiric value of pursuing an idea from one national arena to another, with Brunel appearing both as announcer and various dignitaries at boxing matches played out in different national guises. In Spain the 'Tantalising Toreador of Toledo' confronts a pantomime horse, while the journey to Soviet Russia to attend 'The Smighti Fightski' is filmed in a pastiche of montage, including diagonally dissolved, criss-crossing railway lines, and at one point Lenin, leaning across the screen, making speeches in Hyde Park.

In these parodies, acerbically inclined child's play brings down the adult world of respectable authority figures and cultural forms, whether representing governments, nations or film industries. Later in the decade, Brunel's protégé and soon partner in his film editing company, Ivor Montagu (founder of the Film Society, campaigning film critic and combatant against censorship), together with H. G. Wells's son Frank, produced two short parodies: *Blue Bottles* (1928) and *Daydreams* (1928). These films similarly used pantomime sets, knock-about antics of the music-hall skit, and Elsa Lanchester's spiky performance of dotty femininity to cut down to size the authority of respectively the police force and the society gossip magazine. Like *Battling Bruisers*, *Daydreams* exploits the comic potential of the national in the adventures of his celebrity honeymooners, which involve them in fash-ionable holiday resorts of different European and North African countries. The verbal-visual game-playing and illogical silliness of Brunel and Montagu's films, sliding cheerfully between parody and pastiche, bring culturally grounded stereotypes and attitudes into public visibility.

Piccadilly and Film Europe

Growing up for the British film industry meant not only modernising themes but accommodating to the production values and narrational techniques established by Hollywood and engaging with the expressive potential of the European art film. Consequently the second half of the 1920s saw British studios increasingly employing American and European talent and entering international co-production and distribution deals, in particular with Germany under the aegis of the 'Film Europe' movement which sought to encourage collaborative resistance to domination by Hollywood.[14] Most notable among European signings was the arrival in December 1926 of the German director, E. A. Dupont as a key player in British International Pictures' bid for the international market. After working with Herbert Wilcox on *Madame Pompadour* (1927) – a spirited costume picture romanticising French royal history, starring Dorothy Gish – and directing the distinctly Expressionist *Moulin Rouge* (1928), Dupont worked on a more hybrid collaboration, *Piccadilly* (1929). Its German production team, which besides Dupont included cameraman Werner Brandes and art director Alfred Junge, was noted for an integrated use of mobile camera and set design focusing on spectacle and psychological extremity in the Expressionist manner. Flamboyant visual style encountered BIP's home-grown literary *coup*: a first-time scenario and dialogue titles from Arnold Bennett, a British novelist with an eye for social nuances of place and type and for the telling power of detail. Thus 'Piccadilly' references both a fashionable if risqué club and its location, Piccadilly Circus, centre of London nightlife – both conceived as sites of social, racial and sexual cross-boundary encounters.

Such encounters are literally and figuratively carried in the different embodiments and performance styles of the actors, brought into juxtaposition in the nightclub sequence that generates the film's plot. British actor Jameson Thomas, playing Valentine Wilmot, owner of the club, excels in what the *Bioscope* praised as 'power and restraint'.[15] American-Polish Gilda Gray, playing his mistress Mabel, the club's female dancing attraction, offered what critics and fans found lacking in the English film actress: 'pep', 'vim' and 'sex appeal', realised in Gray's performance of the 'shimmy'. Her about-to-become rival, Chinese scullery-hand, Shosho – denizen of Limehouse, signifying an East End underclass and immigrant community – is played by American-Chinese Anna May Wong. A source of considerable fan-magazine fascination, Wong is discussed as a 'hybrid persona' who combined American flapper with Eastern enigma.[16] Graham Hodges suggests that Wong's dance, developed from lessons in Chinese acting traditions, created an androgynous performance by combining gestures of both genders.[17] As narrative link between these protagonists, Charles Laughton, in his first feature-film appearance, offers a grotesque caricature of a diner disgruntled by a dirty plate.

This mix of performance and filmic styles suggests the productivity of interactions between different national practices. Approaching the taboo racial boundary, *Piccadilly* turns on the tension between desire and danger in the encounter with otherness. Thus Bennett's scenario, enlivened by pointed dialogue titles, juxtaposes socially demarcated spaces and the protagonists who inhabit them. However, the mobile fluidity of Werner Brandes's camera works against such 'geographic' demarcations. So the ironic peeling back of social-class distinctions in Wilmot's progress from dance-floor to kitchen to scullery (in search of the perpetrator of the dirty plate) is halted by the tunnel-like perspective through which his glance is diverted to his first vision of Shosho, perched on a table, entertaining the kitchen hands with oriental gyrations. This momentarily destabilises the 'power-in-restraint' of Jameson Thomas's gaze, till now delivered in a pattern of cut-in quizzical looks through which his authority has been established over staff, including Mabel on the dance-floor. Elsewhere Dupont's use of the close shot unsettles the professional polish of the American dancer – documenting the shaking of arm flesh and her almost galumphing body – to expose the effort involved in giving a 'star' performance, and thereby undermining the unity of actor and role on which stardom depends.

A further clash of performance signs occurs in the filming of Shosho's table-top dance, where a standard western camera movement, travelling up Anna May Wong's body to sexualise eastern allure is blocked by the illegibility of her Chinese mime and her inward mocking gaze. Such illegibility may underscore trade- press complaints about British story values being over-whelmed by Continental technique.[18] However, the film's success with audiences suggests that in the trans-national encounter between the German team's practice of integrated mobile camera and set design and a British scenario invested in socially demarcated protagonists, another story, not explicitly told, begins to emerge: about western fascination with a cross-racial kiss, scripted by Bennett and lost to censorship.[19] However, if such a sexually charged encounter was ideologically taboo, approaching the boundary ensures the power of its possibility, resonating in the tension between camera-work and script and between acculturated performance styles which animates the pull of alterity on which identity depends.

George Pearson and the Art of Cinema

George Pearson, the advocate of film art most respected among film industry members, was thirty-five before he abandoned his respected position as headmaster to enter the risky world of film scripting and directing in the early 1910s. He approached cinema with a sensibility steeped in the imagery and practices of popular Victorian and Edwardian culture. But at the same time he grasped film-making as a new expressive freedom, writing presciently in the *Bioscope*: 'I tell you this Cinema is going to fight Old Time and knock him out. There won't be any Past . . . it will all be Present . . . The thing the cinema can do no one has dropped on yet.'[20] Pearson's sense of the break, however, was not that of the modernist avant-garde. Rather, he was an idealist populist, who saw in film the possibility of an aesthetic and emotional enrichment for popular audiences not available through a rigid school-board curriculum and sanctioned forms of culture. In a series of polemical lectures and writings he argued for a cinema that would free itself from the constraints of stage and literary sources, prepared 'directly for the . . . screen, told not merely *on* it but *by* it'.[21] Endlessly inventive within the straightened means of the post-war film companies with whom he worked, it was in the now lost *Reveille* (1924) and the mutilated but still powerful *The Little People* (1926) that Pearson was able to put into practice his belief that 'Cinema, if true to itself, should be a lawless medium, as free as the vision of the human eye . . . as free as a bird in flight.'[22] Focusing his camera on human face and gesture, inter-cut with symbolically resonating images, Pearson aimed to build films 'emotion by emotion' rather than conforming to the sequential logic of continuity, 'that shibboleth from America'.[23]

The Little People details the encounter of two English tourists with a traditional puppet troupe in southern Italy. Into his creative team Pearson drew the young Thorold Dickinson as his assistant, charged with keeping a modern eye on script development, Alberto Cavalcanti as his set designer, and expert puppet-maker Henri Gad. Shot in France and Italy by Percy Strong, the world of make-believe spun by the puppets is lovingly evoked in a montage that cuts between the puppet stage and close-ups of children's faces, absorbed in wonderment. But while the puppet show means different things to each of the Englishmen – Walery is a writer looking for inspiration, Lyn a showman looking for a commercial proposition – the troupe itself is fraught with generational strife as its leading stars Gian and Lucia pull in different ways towards the modern world. To this the puppets contribute also by returning adults to childhood, while making ironic comment on grown-up activity and forewarning of impending problems. Crucially, the puppets represent both the attraction and threat of the past and tradition. For Lucia, puppeteering spells overwhelming oppression, conveyed in ever-intensifying rhythmic cutting between close-ups of the drum calling up an audience and her agonised face, hands clasped to her ears. To Gian's discontent she declares: 'That's just it – you're a man: but I want to do big things too.'

Lucia is enticed to London by prospects of stardom. But her Mayfair début is a disaster and she is abandoned by Lyn. Refusing protection from Walery, Lucia contemplates her mirror, and a visionary epiphany leads her back to the puppet-show. Similarly when Lucia displaces Gian at his drawing board, Pearson refuses the reverse shot that would explain her modernising vision. As in *Reveille*'s two-minute silence (reinforced by stopping the cinema orchestra), which reunites the bereaved with the returning dead, Pearson's cinema reaches for the ineffable, unsayable.

The Maturity of Late Silent British Cinema

By the end of the decade it was clear that Britain could boast two remarkable film-makers, Alfred Hitchcock and Anthony Asquith. Their subsequent fates – Hitchcock moving to America and becoming absorbed into film history as a Hollywood auteur, and Asquith remaining behind to become aligned with the ups and downs of a febrile British film industry – have obscured the degree to which their late silent films found in British cinema's pictorial, theatrical and storytelling practices a culturally sympathetic and flexible source of expression from which to construct powerful bodies of work.

While Hitchcock's *The Lodger* established the generic vein he is most associated with, the thriller, a range of silent films either based on stage plays or novels – *Downhill, Easy Virtue* (1928), *The Farmer's Wife* (1928), *The Manxman* (1929) – or generated from scenarios co-written with Eliot Stannard – *The Ring* (1927), *Champagne* – saw Hitchcock honing out of the materials and practices of British cinema's heterogeneous sources the means to achieve emotional effects and perceptions that only cinema could achieve. The separation of private and public performance, by which outward restraint is subjected to the probing of the moving camera, provided means to break through the codes and constraints of public discourse – often represented in the semi-caricatured social role-playing of supporting character actors – to bring undercurrents of unnameable desire, fascination, dread into play. Through such means Hitchcock developed the pictorial montage that he termed 'pure cinema'. In his scenarios of crime or marital dramas of highly charged emotions, Hitchcock's combination of pictorialised shot and moving camera opened up in cinema the seam of perverse sexual curiosity and sadistic voyeurism that David Pirie and Alan Lovell among others have identified running through English culture from the 18th century onwards.[24]

Much has been made of Hitchcock's lower-middle-class background and his theatrical, artistic and cinematic self-education as reinforcing the obsessions of an outsider, both penetrating and excluded from English social protocols. Anthony Asquith – privileged son of a British prime minister, Oxford-educated and treated to trips to German and American studios – approached film-making from opposite circumstances. If Hitchcock used cinema to penetrate the surfaces of British life with an acerbic perception generated from the outside, Asquith looked from the inside outward to the relief offered by a populist medium into which he could escape. In his three major silent films, *Shooting Stars* (1928), *Underground* (1928) and *A Cottage on Dartmoor* (1929), popular cultural forms offered vehicles for primary emotional conflicts: marital, sexual and criminal. Equally he used the forms of popular culture as a means

The Manxman (Alfred Hitchcock, 1929)

The Manxman explores the dynamic of the image as focus of desires drawn across socially divided spaces but at the same time subjected to public codes of legibility and misreading, involving both protagonists and audience in the perils of spectatorship. Eliot Stannard's script from Hall Caine's popular novel provides a storyline, familiar in the 1920s, of rivalry between boyhood friends – Pete Quilliam, the fisherman (Carl Brisson), and Philip Christian (Malcolm Keen), the rising lawyer – for the love of the same woman, Kate Cregeen (Anny Ondra), barmaid in her father Caesar's pub. Her father's rejection of Pete causes the latter's disappearance to seek his fortune, while Philip becomes entangled with Kate. False news of Pete's drowning and his unexpected return generates emotionally piquant situations between the trio.

In The Manx Fairy, Pete and Philip have gathered with the local fishermen to sign a petition against encroaching steam trawlers. Two playing areas are set up opposite each other: Pete at the bar in flirtatious chat with Kate, and Philip at the other end of the room, progressing the petition. Flicker-book editing between frontal close-ups of Philip, increasingly aware of Pete's closeness to Kate in the brightly lit bar area, trying to attract his attention, and Pete, absorbed in his easy intimacy with Kate, light-heartedly waving away Phil's call, set in motion an intensifying interaction between pictures. This not only utilises the space that separates them as a dramatic dynamic, but also uses audience position, sandwiched between frontal shots, as a relay in the exchange. The increasing urgency of this flick between pictures eventually triggers a reconfiguration, as the fishermen, following Philip's gaze, part to allow Philip to join them.

The news of Pete's death takes this entrapment of the spectator in emotional cross-currents a stage further. From Philip's perspective we see Kate framed

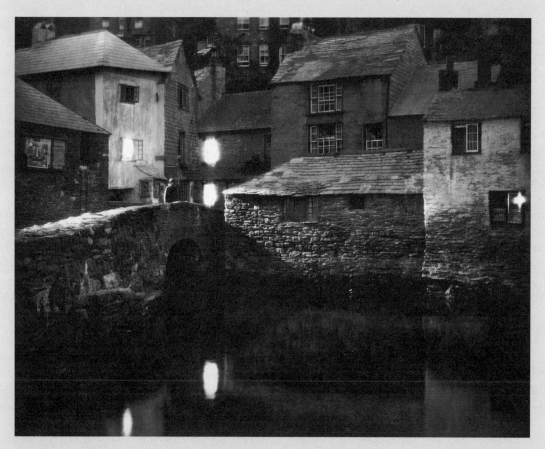

Illusory tranquillity: Anny Ondra prepares to break her love triangle in *The Manxman*

through a doorway in a room beyond, stock still, her back to us, a tableau of frozen emotion. Cuts between Philip's cautious approach and her frontal close-ups, lips pursed, looking into the camera, breathing heavily, catch the viewer in an astonishing reconfiguration – 'Philip we're free!' Not only does this demand that Philip and we re-read the previous scene of tragic loss, it abruptly throws emotional and moral expectations into confusion.

Kate's later suicide attempt following her flight from marriage to Pete, brings her to court on the day of Philip's inauguration as Deemster. The courtroom provides the tightly regulated public place where intimate truths become official statements. The key to the trapped momentum locked in the protagonists' inner desires is turned by Kate's declaration, 'I am not going back,' leading to Caesar's climactic revelation of Philip's guilt. As in a kaleidoscope the solution to the whirling pictures of shock and astonishment that follow is the retrospective re-configuration and re-reading of what has gone before. Pete turns to the camera, eyes unfocused, to be met by Caesar's cry: 'Can't you see Pete? Can't you see?' Finally Philip makes a public confession, resigns his position as Deemster and sets out to make amends to Kate.

FURTHER READING

Charles Barr, *English Hitchcock* (Moffat, Dumfries & Galloway: Cameron and Hollis, 1999).

Tom Ryall, *Alfred Hitchcock and the British Cinema* (London: Croom Helm, 1986).

of sympathetic access to his very ordinary characters' lives and modes of expression: going to the cinema in *Shooting Stars* and *A Cottage on Dartmoor*, underground travel, department-store shopping, Saturday afternoon bus excursions to the park in *Underground*. But if their cultural and entertainment practices define the horizons of his characters' lives, the reproduction of these practices as dramatic signifiers introduces a reflexive dimension through which Asquith developed an increasingly inward rendering of the conditions and processes of cultural imagination.

Thus *Shooting Stars*, woven out of the materials and practices of a popular culture in which Hollywood played such a significant role, dramatises both the conditions of British cinema and the emotional horizons it sets for those who inhabit it whether as producers or consumers. Set in a multiple stage film studio, with a Western in progress alongside a music-hall farce, its husband-and-wife star team are caught up in a melodrama that turns illicit romance into tragedy. Mae Feather (Annette Benson) – a would-be British star with her eyes set on going to Hollywood along with her lover, Andy Wilkes (Donald Calthrop), star of music-hall routines – substitutes a real bullet in the stage gun to be fired at her husband, Julian Gordon (Brian Aherne). The guns get swapped between sets, and in a moment of high farce, Andy Wilkes is shot dead while swinging from a chandelier. Through its intersection of Hollywood and British genres and performance styles with Expressionist lighting, symbolic compositions and satirical word-image juxtapositions, the film poses questions about British cinema's past and its future. Mae, forgotten by her audience, returns years later as an extra, unnoticed by Julian, now installed in the chair of the male 'auteur' in a studio transformed by a cathedral set. However, Julian's fixed inward gaze suggests the loss associated with obsessive desire, which Asquith would dramatise in *Underground* and *A Cottage on Dartmoor*.

Exploring the achievements of late silent British film-making underlines the heterogeneity of cinema – a medium that, ingesting all others, can show how cultural practices themselves contribute to making our realities. In British cinematic practice, the boundary and the cultural document become cornerstones of an aesthetic, drawing on picture-making, play-acting and storytelling. In the process the intermingling of fantasy and document draw from the cultural materials of our lives the emotional charges and ineffable insights invested in them. In late silent Britain such insights turn on war-touched dramas of wounded masculinity, the return to a world of play for make-believe or the challenge of chop-logic, and an investment in the child and sprightly girlhood as sources of rejuvenation and hope. Through film-making construed in different ways as play, these different elements and practices are kept in process, held in suspension, releasing liminal signs of change in social perceptions and emotional values.

A Cottage on Dartmoor (Anthony Asquith, 1929)

A Cottage on Dartmoor was released in 1929 as a silent film and in 1930 with a part-talking soundtrack. Its simple story – a crime drama of unrequited love – is played out between three ordinary English types, a barber, Joe (Uno Henning), a manicurist, Sally (Nora Baring) for whom he has fallen, and the stolid farmer, Harry (Hans Schlettow), a customer whom she marries. Told in flashback, when Joe, having escaped from Dartmoor Prison, confronts Sally alone with her baby in her moorland home, the main action takes place in the hairdressing salon depicting Joe's nervous attempts to interest Sally by inviting her to a movie, and his increasingly destabilising jealousy as she becomes attracted to Harry. The daily life of the hairdressing salon, Sally's boarding-house, where polite songs round the piano prevent Joe from talking to her, a traumatic visit to the (talking) pictures are documented with

gently satirical humour through Asquith's acute eye for the social types and leisure practices which both express and contain lower-middle-class lives. But at the same time Asquith's sensitivity to the emotional force of moving camera, angle, lighting and techniques such as dissolves and superimpositions invests a banal story of social inadequacy, frustration, and the unimaginative indifference of others with an intensity of feeling that supersedes the personalities and actions involved.

This combination of cultural documentation and raw feeling achieves extraordinary expression in the celebrated sequence at the talkies, when, his own invitation ignored, Joe now sits behind Sally and Harry. Here not only does cinema feature reflexively as a medium through which his characters experience their lives, but Asquith dramatises his own relation to an art form which at the height of its maturity is about to be superseded by synchronised sound. Silent cinema was

Norah Baring empathises with distraught convict Uno Henning in *A Cottage on Dartmoor*

never silent, the image always accompanied by music and sometimes sound effects. And for Asquith the moving image was musical in its power to short-circuit logical motivations articulated in speech. So to have his protagonists go to a talkie in a silent movie confronted the ultimate challenge: not to eliminate sound, but to have the visual image stand in place of sound and speech. Following the silent short which plays on the screen, Asquith's farewell begins as the now redundant three-piece band packs up and its members, indifferent to the talkie, play cards. We too are denied a view of the film. But we follow the emotional drive of a romantic melodrama in which murder threatens in the play of reactions across the audience's faces. At the same time a second movie unfolds, distilling the quintessence of silent movie art that reaches for movements of feeling beyond speech, as Joe, watching Harry press closer to Sally, projects his own drama that will ultimately destroy him.

Commenting on the film's closing, Asquith stressed the power of movement to convey an 'ecstatic feeling'. Tracking camera, inter-cut with lyrical images of breaking waves, wind-shaken cornfields and blossom against the sky carry Joe's impulse to ignore his chance of escape by running back towards the farmhouse, now surrounded by armed police. Against narrative logic, Asquith's camera releases cinema into an expression of untrammelled desire.

FURTHER READING

R. J. Minney, *Puffin Asquith* (London: Leslie Frewin), p. 58.

Murray Smith, 'Technological Determination, Aesthetic Resistance and *A Cottage on Dartmoor*. Goat-Gland Talkie or Masterpiece', *Wide Angle* vol. 12 no. 3, July 1990, pp. 80–97.

Notes

1. James Donald, 'How English Is It?', in *Sentimental Education: Schooling, Popular Culture and the Regulation of Liberty* (London: Verso, 1992), p. 50.

2. Michael Balcon, *Michael Balcon Presents . . . A Lifetime of Films* (London: Hutchinson, 1969) p. 99.

3. The film led to an epidemic of 'Rat mania' according to Michael Williams. Michael Williams, *Ivor Novello: Screen Idol*, pp. 16–17.

4. *Picture Show*'s columnist, Edith Nepean declared 'his hair is black satin, his eyes slumbering fires, his skin pale, his lips passionate': *Picture Show*, 13 November 1926, p. 13. James Agate, reviewing the stage play, *Liliom*, speaks of Novello's 'beautiful profile and baby grace . . . his body a river of grace, his thighs a cascade of loveliness', in *The Contemporary Theatre, 1926* (London: Chapman and Hall, 1927), pp. 84–5.

5. Michael Williams, 'War-torn Dionysus: The Silent Passion of Ivor Novello', in Andrew Higson (ed.), *Young and Innocent? The Cinema in Britain 1896–1960* (Exeter: University of Exeter Press), pp. 256–70, and *Ivor Novello*, Chapter 2.

6. See: *Daily Telegraph*, 19 October 1926: '*Mons* has been seen by 120,000 during its first four weeks' and *Daily Express*, 12 November 1926: '*Mons* . . . estimated to have brought nearly 2 million new "recruits" to the cinema, continues its wonderful career', among numerous press clippings on war documentaries in Sidney Carroll's Scrapbook, BFI Special Collections. See also *Yorkshire Observer*, 30 July 1926; Edward Wood, 'Love and War', *Picture Show*, 13 November 1926, p. 15; James Agate, *The Contemporary Theatre, 1926*, p. 350.

7. See *Yorkshire Post*, 30 November 1926 in Sidney Carroll's Scrapbook, BFI Special Collections.

8. The mix of document, fiction and myth is registered in press reviews. See *Evening News*, 26 July 1926: 'As famous and mythical in the war as "the Angel of Mons", *Mademoiselle from Armentieres* comes to life in a new British film . . . and is proving to be a very charming person as played by Estelle Brody'. *Yorkshire Observer*, 30 July 1926, notes: 'Now *Mademoiselle from Armentieres* is in preparation . . . to introduce that gracious lady whose memory has been perpetuated in song (if somewhat doggerel)'.

9. See *Kinematograph Weekly*, 13 December 1928, p. 70 and *Film Weekly*, 5 April 1930, p. 12.

10. *Squibs* (1921); *Squibs Wins the Calcutta Sweep* (1922); *Squibs M.P.* (1923); *Squibs' Honeymoon* (1923).

11. *Film Weekly*, 14 January 1929, p. 5.

12. *Film Weekly*, 22 April 1929, p. 5.

13. George Pearson, 'Memories – Into The Twilight Twenties, and What Then?', *Royal Academy Bulletin* no. 13, 1951.

14. See Andrew Higson and Richard Maltby (eds), '*Film Europe' and 'Film America': Cinema, Commerce and Cultural Exchange 1920–1939*.

15. *Bioscope*, 6 February 1929, p. 37.

16. *Picturegoer*, May 1930, pp. 26–7.

17. Graham Hodges, *Anna May Wong: From Laundryman's Daughter to Hollywood Legend*, pp. 93–4. For Wong's dancing lessons, see also *Picturegoer*, September 1928, p. 25.

18. *Kinematograph Weekly*, 7 February 1929, p. 55 and pp. 56–7.

19. Hodges, *Anna May Wong*, p. 95.

20. *Bioscope*, 27 November 1912, Item 12 in George Pearson: BFI Special Collections, also quoted in Pearson, *Flashback*, p. 24.

21. Ibid., p. 140.

22. Ibid.

23. Pearson, *Flashback*, p. 185; Address to the Faculty of Arts, 14 October 1923 – typescript in George Pearson: BFI Special Collections.

24. David Pirie, *A Heritage of Horror: The English Gothic Cinema 1946–1972* (London and Bedford: Gordon Fraser, 1973); Alan Lovell, quoted in Tom Ryall, *Alfred Hitchcock and the British Cinema* (London: Croom Helm, 1986), pp. 179 and 181–2.

Bibliography

Carroll, Sidney, Scrapbooks for 1926–7, BFI Special Collections.

Gledhill, Christine, *Reframing British Cinema, 1918–1928: Between Restraint and Passion* (London: BFI, 2003).

Gledhill, Christine, 'Remembering the War in 1920s British Cinema', in Mike Hammond and Michael Williams (eds), *Goodbye to All That: The Great War and Early British Cinema* (Exeter: University of Exeter Press, forthcoming).

Higson, Andrew and Maltby, Richard (eds), *'Film Europe' and 'Film America': Cinema, Commerce and Cultural Exchange 1920–1939* (Exeter: University of Exeter Press, 1999).

Hodges, Graham Russell Gao, *Anna May Wong: From Laundryman's Daughter to Hollywood Legend* (Basingstoke: Palgrave Macmillan, 2004).

Low, Rachael, *The History of the British Film 1918–1929* (London: George Allen & Unwin, 1971).

Pearson, George, *Flashback* (London: George Allen & Unwin, 1957).

Ryall, Tom, *Anthony Asquith* (Manchester: Manchester University Press, 2005).

Williams, Michael, *Ivor Novello: Screen Idol* (London: BFI, 2003).

19

The British Documentary Film Movement

Ian Aitken

In many respects the British documentary film movement can be considered a touchstone for debates on the nature and achievement of British cinema. If, as many have argued, one of the central paradigms of British national film culture is realism, then the documentary film movement is one of the principal sources of that tradition. However, despite this apparent record of achievement the movement has often been the subject of criticism, even condemnation, both for the role which it is perceived to have played in the 1930s, and for the influence which it is perceived to have had on contemporary film and broadcasting practices. This chapter will attempt to address these criticisms and also try to assess the value of the documentary movement's achievements.

The founder of the documentary movement, John Grierson (1898–1972), believed that film, and documentary film in particular, could play a crucial role within society by providing an effective medium of communication between the state and the public. Grierson's views on the cinema were formed against the background of the economic slump and the slow build-up to war in the 1930s. In this context of mounting national and international instability he felt it was vital for relatively new mass communications media such as film and radio to play a role in helping to stabilise society. He was, therefore, concerned to a considerable extent with questions of the civic and social purposiveness of film. However, this did not mean that he ignored questions relating to the aesthetic qualities of film. On the contrary, part of Grierson's importance for film theory lies in the fact that his ideas on documentary can be traced back to a complex set of systematic aesthetic theories.

In 1927 Grierson joined the Empire Marketing Board (EMB), a government organisation whose brief was to publicise trade links between Britain and the countries of the Empire. Grierson's job involved the development of a programme of publicity films for the Board, but his first film, *Drifters* (1929), became a far more ambitious project than the Board had originally envisaged. The film quickly became a critical success, and its combination of naturalistic images and formative editing has influenced traditions of documentary film-making in Britain ever since. *Drifters* also illustrates what was to become the central strategy of the documentary movement during the 1930s: to seek sponsorship from government bodies with limited remits, and then, whenever possible, to make films which went far beyond those remits.

Following the success of *Drifters*, Grierson founded the documentary film movement as such, by establishing the EMB Film Unit and by recruiting young directors such as Basil Wright, Arthur Elton, Edgar Anstey, Harry Watt and Paul Rotha. Grierson and the Unit remained at the EMB until it was abolished by Act of Parliament in 1933. After this the Film Unit moved to the Post Office, where they were re-established as the GPO Film Unit. New film-makers were also appointed, the most prominent of whom were Humphrey Jennings and Alberto Cavalcanti.

In 1936, frustrated by the restrictions increasingly imposed on the Film Unit by the GPO, Grierson left in order to establish other documentary film units and a co-ordinating body called Film Centre. In 1938 he left Britain to become first Film Officer of the National Film Board of Canada. In the meantime, following the

A film of considerable aesthetic interest: John Grierson's
Drifters (1929)

outbreak of war, the GPO Film Unit was transferred to
the Ministry of Information, and was renamed the
Crown Film Unit. After the war the movement's
importance diminished, and its personnel and ideas
were dispersed into mainstream cinema, and into the
burgeoning industries of public relations and television.

In order to fully understand the documentary film
movement it is essential to view it within its historical
context: that of Britain in the 1930s. The period has frequently been characterised as one in which radical politics were widespread, and several histories have painted a
picture of the 'red decade'. However, this is misleading.
Although radical political movements and organisations
certainly existed in Britain during the 1920s and 30s (and
one of them – the 'Red Clydeside' movement – had a
direct influence on Grierson) none of them developed
into a genuine mass movement. In fact, throughout the
decade conservative ideas dominated social and political
discourse, and Conservative-dominated national governments continued to be elected. Had war not intervened
in 1939, the Conservatives would have been re-elected in
the coming election.

This conservative hegemony was not absolute, however, and from 1931 to 1939 various strands of opinion
gradually converged to form a social democratic consensus which eventually achieved political ascendancy
in 1945. It is this strand of political and cultural discourse, described by one of its Conservative proponents, Harold Macmillan, as 'the middle way' between
unfettered capitalism and a nationalising socialism, with
which the documentary film movement, and Grierson
in particular, must be associated.[1] Although radical and
Communist figures such as Paul Rotha, Ralph Bond

and Ivor Montagu were associated with the movement,
its overall political profile was in fact similar to that of
other pressure groups of the period, such as the Next
Five Years Group and Political and Economic Planning,
who were concerned to build up support for a new
social democratic corporatist consensus. The documentary movement is best understood, then, as social democratic and reformist in relation to the dominant
conservatism of the interwar period, but not as occupy-
ing any explicitly socialist position.

Grierson

John Grierson was concerned with the potential which
documentary film had as a medium for communicating
social information, but he was also interested in exploring the aesthetic qualities of the medium.[2] The first formulation of his theory of documentary film, in an
official memorandum written for the EMB in 1927,
argued for the creation of a new genre: films of thirty to
forty minutes which through creative editing of actuality footage would enable stories to be 'orchestrated into
cinematic sequences of enormous vitality'.[3] This first
definition of the 'Griersonian documentary' contained
both formalist and naturalist elements, but it is the
former which have the ascendancy. Grierson believed
that these films, the first of which would be *Drifters*,
would 'mark a new phase in cinema production'.[4]

The documentary movement is sometimes accused
of being too close to the establishment. Grierson was
strongly influenced by forms of neo-Hegelian philosophy which placed considerable importance on the value
of the state and corporate institutions. He believed that
the institutions of state possessed intrinsic merit because
they were the culmination of long-drawn-out historical attempts to achieve social integration and harmony.
This led him to the view that the proper function of
documentary film was to promote an understanding of
social and cultural interconnection within the nation.[5]

These views led Grierson to place great emphasis on
notions of duty and service, and to argue that documentary film-makers should not merely follow their
own individual predispositions and inclinations, but
should also devote themselves to the social duty of
revealing and describing social interconnection. He also
argued that ideologies which promoted social integration were 'good propaganda', while ideologies which
promoted social division were 'propaganda of the
devil'.[6] Consequently, he believed that documentary
film-makers must discipline themselves to work within
what he called 'the degree of general sanction': the

sphere of consensual discourse generally circulating within society. This 'discipline' of consensual practice inevitably worked against the development of a radical, critical documentary film culture.

Grierson's beliefs about cinema and society can be described as corporatist and consensual, and the theory of documentary film within which they are contained can be characterised in the same terms. However, this is not the whole story. Grierson made a fundamental distinction between what he called the 'institutions of state' and the 'agents of state'. While the institutions of state possessed intrinsic historical value, he believed that circumstances could exist in which the agents of state could subvert those institutions for sectional, class purposes.[7] In these circumstances it was permissible for documentary film-makers to oppose the state, and to make radical, critical films. Grierson believed that, in the 1930s, rather than working for the benefit of the nation as a whole, the establishment was encouraging processes of unregulated capitalist development which reproduced its own interests and threatened social stability. Consequently, he argued, documentary film had to play a role in promoting social reform and, above all, in providing positive images and stories of working-class individuals and communities: in Grierson's own phrase, the documentary film must 'put the working man on the screen'.[8] In relation to the historical context of the inter-war period, then, Grierson's ideas on social change and documentary film can be characterised as reformist and progressive.

The Films and Film-makers

The films made by the documentary movement from 1929 to 1939 fall into a number of categories. On the one hand there were routine films commissioned in order to publicise government services – films such as *Cable Ship* (1933), which dealt with the laying of submarine telephone cables. On the other hand there were more ambitious projects, such as *Night Mail* (1936), which attempted to realise Grierson's objectives for the documentary film more fully. During the EMB period of 1930–4 the most important films made were Grierson's *Drifters*, and *Industrial Britain* (1931), a film shot and partly edited by Robert Flaherty, the Canadian film-maker who had made *Nanook of the North* (1922). When the documentary movement moved to the GPO in 1934 two other major projects begun at the EMB – Arthur Elton's *BBC The Voice of Britain* (1934) and Basil Wright's *Song of Ceylon* (1934) – were continued and completed. The latter film, which won first prize at the

1935 Brussels Film Festival, remains one of the most technically and aesthetically accomplished films made by the documentary movement.

Paul Rotha was one of the most important of the young film-makers employed by Grierson. Rotha was rather semi-detached from the movement, coming and going over the period and occasionally at odds with Grierson. In general, Rotha can be characterised as politically to the left of Grierson, and as an individualist who experienced difficulties in working under Grierson's omnipresent tutelage. He was opposed, in particular, to Grierson's encouragement of 'group' film-making, a practice first employed during the editing of *Industrial Britain*. In addition to his work with Grierson, Rotha also made a number of films with the commercial documentary film company British Instructional Films and its successor Gaumont British Instructional, including *The Face of Britain* (1934), inspired by a reading of J. B. Priestley's *English Journey* (1933). His most important film for the documentary movement was *Today We Live* (1937), about the social hardship caused by unemployment in a Welsh mining community. He was also the author of one of the first major English-language books on cinema history, *The Film till Now* (1930).

One of the aims of the documentary film movement was to influence the production of socially purposive and aesthetically innovative art across a range of artistic fields. To this end relationships were established with many individuals and organisations during the period, and several artists and film-makers, later to become prominent in their own right, worked on films made by the documentary movement. These included the poet, W. H. Auden, the composer Benjamin Britten, the painter William Coldstream, the writer J. B. Priestley, and film-makers such as Robert Flaherty, Carl Dreyer and Ernst Meyer. Others associated with the movement during the period included H. G. Wells, Julian Huxley, Graham Greene and the painter/designer László Moholy-Nagy. This attempt to connect with other cultural movements of the period was also fostered by the house journals of the documentary movement: *Cinema Quarterly* (1932–6), *World Film News* (1936–8) and *Documentary Newsletter* (1940–7), all of which regularly featured articles written by those mentioned above.[9]

A number of the movement's best-known films emerged from this context of association with artists and intellectuals of the period. *Coal Face* (1935), with music composed by Britten, employs modernist techniques such as non-synchronous sound and montage editing, in conjunction with a critical commentary on

Modernist techniques in conjunction with a critical commentary on the harsh working conditions in the mines: Cavalcanti's *Coal Face* (1935)

the harsh working conditions in the mines. *Night Mail*, although conventional in terms of its overall narrative structure, contains the well-known sequence in which the poetry of Auden and the music of Britten accompany close-up montage images of racing train wheels, as the postal express journeys to Edinburgh.

Most of the films made by the documentary movement were collaborative projects, sometimes involving as many as six people, each engaged in several activities. This was a practice strongly encouraged by Grierson because it helped to foster and disseminate production skills. Grierson also placed less importance on the emergence of individual 'auteurs' from the ranks of his film-makers than he did on using them to promote the ideals and aspirations of the movement as a whole.

Perhaps because of this, few important film-makers emerged from within the documentary movement, and few managed to sustain a high level of achievement throughout their careers. Grierson himself directed only one film, *Drifters*, after which he became a producer. Paul Rotha's best work was carried out in the 1930s and 40s, with *Shipyard* (1935), *The Face of Britain*, *Today We Live*, and *World of Plenty* (1943), but he did not produce or direct any important films after the war. Basil Wright's career followed a similar trajectory. His best film is *Song of Ceylon* and he also made a contribution to *Night Mail*. *The Country Comes to Town* (1931) and *The Face of Scotland* (1938) are also interesting, but like Rotha, Wright neither produced nor directed anything of significance after 1946.

Younger film-makers like Philip Leacock, Jack Lee and Pat Jackson made intelligent, modestly budgeted

films in the 50s, and Watt enjoyed considerable commercial success with films set in Australia and Africa such as *The Overlanders* (1946) and *Where No Vultures Fly* (1951). But the two major film-makers who emerged from the documentary movement were Alberto Cavalcanti and Humphrey Jennings. Cavalcanti, who was Brazilian, had worked with the French avant-garde of the 1920s, alongside directors such as René Clair and Jean Renoir. He brought much- needed technical and aesthetic expertise to the movement, as well as a knowledge of recent developments in the pictorial arts. He was appointed head of the GPO Film Unit in 1936, when Grierson left to form Film Centre, and during the war joined Ealing Studios, where he directed *Went the Day Well?* (1942), *Champagne Charlie* (1944), *Dead of Night* (1945) and *Nicholas Nickleby* (1947). Along with Harry Watt, Cavalcanti can also be credited with helping to develop the documentary-drama form which had such an influence on the British cinema of World War II, and which first appeared in Watt's *The Saving of Bill Blewitt* (1937), *North Sea* (1938) and *Target for Tonight* (1941).

Humphrey Jennings began work with the GPO Film Unit in 1934. During the late 30s he became involved with Mass-Observation, and brought the study of popular culture associated with that organisation to bear on his film-making activities. His *Spare Time* (1939) and *Listen to Britain* (1941) remain impressive, marked by a lyrical humanism and a sensitivity to the ordinary which stands out from the often stereotyped representations of working-class people found in some of the films made by the documentary movement. Indeed, Jennings's ability to portray the working class literally and authentically often put him at odds with Grierson, who preferred more idealistic images of working-class people.[10] Jennings went on to make a number of important films in the 1940s, including '*Fires Were Started —*' (1943) and *A Diary for Timothy* (1945). His career was cut short by a fatal accident in 1950.

The Critical Reputation of the Documentary Film Movement

Over the decades the reputation of the British documentary film movement has fluctuated considerably in debates on its role in and influence on British cinema and society. Initially, the movement was promoted as a heroic struggle by gifted and principled film-makers against both the banality of the commercial industry and the interference of corporate bureaucrats. The early literature on the movement reflects this position, particularly Paul Rotha's *The Film till Now* and *Documentary Diary* (1973). Other works in this tradition include Elizabeth Sussex's *The Rise and Fall of the British Documentary Movement* (1975), James Beveridge's *John Grierson: Film Master* (1986), Harry Watt's *Don't Look at the Camera* (1975) and Forsyth Hardy's *John Grierson: A Documentary Biography* (1979). In two edited collections of essays by Grierson, *Grierson on Documentary* (1946) and *Grierson on the Movies* (1981), Grierson's official biographer, Forsyth Hardy, has also attempted to promote a conception of the movement as principled, socially purposive and successful.

By the 1970s new traditions of film theory were emerging in Britain, influenced by work in the fields of semiotics and structuralism, and by translations of early Russian and German writings on film – writings which advocated an anti-realist and formalist aesthetic. The new film theory was often critical of Grierson's ideas on documentary naturalism and the need to work within 'the system'. Writing in 1983, Alan Lovell argued that the 'basic thing was to break open the prison of Griersonism', and in 1980, Paul Willemen summed up the prevailing attitude:

> Official film culture has enshrined the documentary film movement as the high point of the British cinema.... Consequently, criticism of the documentary movement and of the Griersonian ideology runs the risk of being regarded, not only as heresy, but as an attack on great artists and film-makers.[11]

The criticisms levelled at the documentary movement during the 1970s and early 1980s can be divided into three main categories. The first consists of opinions to the effect that the movement's reputation has obscured the achievements of more progressive film-making traditions in the 1930s. Critics holding these opinions gradually turned their attention away from the documentary movement in an attempt to recover these lost traditions. In *Traditions of Independence*, published in 1980, an attempt was made to reassess the work of radical organisations such as the Workers Film and Photo League, Kino, the Progressive Film Institute and the Workers Film Association; and to consider the achievements of radical film-makers such as Ivor Montagu, Norman McLaren and Ralph Bond.[12]

However, this view that the documentary movement was of less consequence than other, supposedly more valuable documentary traditions in the 1930s is problematic. The films made by the organisations and film-makers mentioned above were seen by far smaller audiences than the films made by the documentary movement. The evidence which we have suggests that they were largely consumed by minority audiences already committed to the political views which the films expressed. The documentary movement's films, on the other hand, were seen by a much more extensive and varied audience, and therefore had the potential to alter opinion across a far greater spectrum.[13] Distinctions made by critics such as Claire Johnstone and Paul Willemen between the documentary movement and leftist documentary organisations during the 1930s are overstated. In fact, there was a great deal of interaction at the time between the movement and leftist film-makers such as Ivor Montagu, Norman McLaren, Ralph Bond and Sidney Cole. These film-makers did not see the documentary movement as the enemy, but on the contrary as an ally, and as a progressive oppositional film practice.[14]

A second major criticism of the documentary movement to emerge during this period was that the reputation and ideology of the movement had been used by a conservative media establishment to reinforce consensualist ideas. Stuart Hood, for example, has argued that Grierson's belief in working within the general sanction helped to institutionalise doctrines of 'balance' and 'due impartiality' in British television, and led to the establishment of a politically toothless current affairs media, unable to carry out critical, investigative work.[15] While there is some justification in this criticism, it also needs to be set against an understanding of the historical context from which the documentary film movement emerged. It is necessary to understand the politics of the movement in relation to the 1930s, rather than to judge those politics from the standpoint of political problems and criteria in the late 1970s and early 1980s.

The third major criticism of the documentary movement to emerge during the 1970s and early 1980s revolved around questions of aesthetics. In 1976, writing in *Screen*, Bill Nichols associated Grierson's ideas with various forms of naturalistic cinéma-vérité filmmaking.[16] Two years earlier, Andrew Tudor had argued that Grierson's theories were based on an ideology of social persuasion, and had no implications for an aesthetic of film.[17] In a similar vein, Alan Lovell, writing in 1983, argued that Grierson had subordinated aesthetics to social persuasion.[18]

These criticisms are largely unfounded. A close study of Grierson's writings reveals that his theory of documentary film did not imply the subordination of aesthetics to social and political instrumentality. Grierson himself makes the point well: 'Most people . . . when they think of documentary films think of public reports and social problems. . . . For me it is something more magical. It is a visual art.'[19]

The documentary movement's reputation suffered further damage in a body of work which emerged from the history and communication departments of some British universities during the late 1970s and early 80s. This work was primarily (though not exclusively) concerned with the exploration of film as a form of historical record rather than as an aesthetic object. Within this tradition the work carried out on the documentary movement was based on the empirical analysis of archival records held at the Public Records Office and elsewhere, rather than on the application of critical theory to the movement. These archival documents, generally written by middle-ranking civil servants and political figures during the 1930s, furnished an account of the movement as a group of well-meaning but politically naive individuals who frequently frustrated the attempts made by enlightened civil servants to create a permanent state film unit. Historians writing in the 1980s, who accepted this version of events because it was inscribed within archival sources of evidence – conventionally regarded as the most 'objective' form of evidence – then began to rewrite the history of the documentary movement, placing lesser emphasis on the achievements of the film-makers and greater emphasis on the role of largely forgotten government officials.[20]

There is some truth in this account of the documentary movement. Grierson, for example, was an extremely dogmatic and obsessive individual who often generated friction with the officials for whom he was supposed to be working. Similarly, the film-makers around Grierson had little experience of how to work within bureaucratic government organisations like the EMB and the GPO, and often incurred official displeasure through their naivety. Nevertheless, there is no real evidence to suggest that, even had Grierson and the film-makers been paragons of civil-service propriety, a permanent and influential state documentary film unit would have been established in the 1930s. The historical context remained that of an establishment which was hostile to any substantial amount of reform-oriented film-making taking place within government

organisations. Given this overriding context, Grierson's tactics at the time seem justified, and the view that he should have let the civil servants just get on with it seems faintly absurd.

More recent reconstructions of the documentary movement's reputation have taken a number of different directions. In *Film and Reform* (1990), I have argued that it is of primary importance to understand Grierson's ideology, and to relate the documentary movement to the context of Britain in the interwar period. I have viewed the movement as progressive in relation to the dominant conservatism of the period, and I have argued that Grierson's ideology was related to a sophisticated and liberal branch of Continental idealist philosophy. I have also argued that this relationship to a philosophical tradition of real substance distinguishes Grierson – in a positive sense – from any other figure within British film culture.[21] Other commentators, mainly in Canada, have attempted to argue that there was a relationship between Grierson's ideas and various totalitarian philosophies prevalent in Europe during the interwar period.[22] This is a misconception. Grierson was neither a fascist nor any other sort of totalitarian: he was a democratic corporatist, whose ideas can be related to other corporate, centre-progressive political ideologies of the period.

Finally, what is the legacy of the British documentary movement today? The movement is no longer a focus of debate in the way that it was between 1975 and 1990. Few new publications on the movement have appeared since 1990.[23] With many of the film-makers themselves now dead, the sources of biographical information have been significantly reduced.[24]

Nevertheless, one can still trace the influence of the movement on contemporary film culture in a number of ways. One result of the work done on Grierson and the movement in the late 1980s has been to emphasise the modernist nature of both Grierson's ideas and the films produced within the movement. Grierson's theory of documentary film is now of more interest to film-makers and film theorists. It is a complex theory, informed by several strands of early modernism, as well as by various philosophical positions. With this in mind, the films themselves can be looked at anew. What emerges from such a reappraisal is a realisation that, despite the difficulties which the movement experienced, the films are of considerable aesthetic interest and quality. *Drifters*, *Song of Ceylon* and *Listen to Britain*, in particular, stand as major achievements of British cinema.

Notes

1. Paul Addison, *The Road to 1945* (London: Quartet, 1977), p. 29.

2. John Grierson, 'I Derive My Authority from Moses', (Grierson Archive papers, University of Stirling, 1957–72) G7A.9.1, p. 3. Cited in Ian Aitken, *Film and Reform: John Grierson and the Documentary Film Movement*, p. 7.

3. John Grierson, 'Notes for English Producers', Memorandum to the EMB Film Committee (April 1927), PRO BT 64/86 6880, p. 2. Cited in Aitken, *Film and Reform*, pp. 97–9.

4. Ibid., p. 22. Cited in Aitken, *Film and Reform*, p. 98.

5. John Grierson, 'The Challenge of Peace', in H. Forsyth Hardy (ed.), *Grierson on Documentary*, p. 174.

6. John Grierson, 'Preface', in Paul Rotha, Richard Griffith and Sinclair Road, *Documentary Film* (London: Faber and Faber, 1952), p. 2.

7. John Grierson, 'Byron and His Age' (Grierson Archive papers 1898–1927) G1.2.10, p. 9. Cited in Aitken, *Film and Reform*, p. 190.

8. John Grierson, 'The Course of Realism', in Hardy, *Grierson on Documentary*, p. 77.

9. H. Forsyth Hardy, *John Grierson: A Documentary Biography*, p. 84.

10. Aitken, *Film and Reform*, p. 147.

11. Paul Willemen, 'Presentation', in Don Macpherson (ed.), *Traditions of Independence*.

12. Macpherson, *Traditions of Independence*.

13. Precise information on the audiences for the documentary films is unobtainable. An EMB Film Committee memorandum of 19 March 1932 suggests an audience of 1.5 million by that date at the Imperial Institute Cinema alone. By October 1932 bookings had been received across the country for 4,380 film screenings. A fairly conservative estimate, based on these figures, would suggest a possible audience of between 10 and 15 million by 1939, although the actual figure could well be higher.

14. Ivor Montagu, *Film World* (Harmondsworth: Penguin, 1964), p. 281.

15. Stuart Hood, 'A Cool Look at the Legend', in Eva Orbanz (ed.), *Journey to a Legend and Back: The British Realistic Film*, p. 150.

16. Bill Nichols, 'Documentary Theory and Practice', *Screen* vol. 17 no. 4, Winter 1976–7, p. 35.

17. Andrew Tudor, *Theories of Film* (London: Secker & Warburg/BFI, 1974), p. 75.

18. Alan Lovell, 'The Grierson Influence', *Undercut* no. 9, Summer 1983, p. 17.

19. John Grierson, 'I Remember, I Remember' (Grierson Archive papers 1957–72), G7.17.2, pp. 10–11. Cited in Aitken, *Film and Reform*, p. 11.

20. See, for example, the work of Paul Swann, including his *The British Documentary Film Movement 1926–1946*.

21. See Ian Aitken, 'Grierson, Idealism and the Inter-War Period', *Historical Journal of Film, Radio and Television* vol. 9 no. 3, 1989; and Aitken, *Film and Reform*.

22. See, for example, Peter Morris, 'Re-thinking Grierson: The Ideology of John Grierson', in Pierre Verronneau, Michael Dorland and Seth Feldman (eds), *Dialogue Canadian and Quebec Cinema* (Montreal: Mediatexte, 1987), pp. 25–56.

23. A collection of writings by members of the documentary movement can be found in Ian Aitken, *The Documentary Film Movement: An Anthology*.

24. Brian Winston's *Claiming the Real: The Griersonian Documentary and Its Legitimations* (London: BFI, 1995) makes the point – repeatedly – that the documentary movement was not radical enough. It seems odd that this argument should still be thought tenable, following the detailed historical work on the movement carried out in the 1980s. Winston also makes a connection between Grierson's ideas and nineteenth-century French realism, without offering any convincing grounds for such a connection. Grierson was influenced by ideas emanating from the German, not the French, intellectual tradition and made no reference to French nineteenth-century realism in any of his writings or reported conversations.

Bibliography

Aitken, Ian, *Film and Reform: John Grierson and the Documentary Film Movement* (London: Routledge, 1990).

Aitken, Ian, *The Documentary Film Movement: An Anthology* (Edinburgh: Edinburgh University Press, 1998).

Aitken, Ian, *Alberto Cavalcanti: Realism, Surrealism and National Cinemas* (Trowbridge: Flicks Books, 2001).

Aitken, Ian, *European Film Theory and Cinema* (Edinburgh: Edinburgh University Press, 2001).

Beveridge, James, *John Grierson: Film Master* (London: Macmillan, 1979).

Ellis, Jack C., *John Grierson: Life, Contributions, Influence* (Illinois: Southern Illinois University Press, 2000).

Hardy, H. Forsyth (ed.), *Grierson on Documentary* (London: Collins, 1946).

Hardy, H. Forsyth (ed.), *John Grierson: A Documentary Biography* (London: Faber and Faber, 1979).

Hardy, H. Forsyth (ed.), *Grierson on the Movies* (London: Faber and Faber, 1981).

Hillier, Jim and Lovell, Alan, *Studies in Documentary* (London: Secker & Warburg/BFI, 1972).

Jarvie, Ian and Pronay, Nicholas, 'John Grierson: A Critical Perspective', *Historical Journal of Film, Radio and Television* vol. 3 no. 3, 1989.

Macpherson, Don (ed.), *Traditions of Independence* (London: BFI, 1980).

Orbanz, Eva (ed.), *Journey to a Legend and Back: The British Realistic Film* (Berlin: Edition Volker Spiess, 1977).

Rotha, Paul, *The Film till Now: A Survey of World Cinema* (London: Cape, 1930).

Rotha, Paul, *Documentary Diary: An Informal History of the British Documentary Film, 1928–1939* (London: Secker & Warburg, 1973).

Sussex, Elizabeth, *The Rise and Fall of the British Documentary Movement* (Berkeley, Los Angeles, London: University of California Press, 1975).

Swann, Paul, *The British Documentary Film Movement 1926–1946* (Cambridge: Cambridge University Press, 1989).

Watt, Harry, *Don't Look at the Camera* (London: Elek Books, 1974).

Wright, Basil, *The Long View* (London: Secker & Warburg, 1974).

20
British Film and the National Interest, 1927–39

Sarah Street

Only by creating a centre, a home for the industrial art of the cinema, will it be possible by study and experiment to try out the economic, aesthetic and technical issues and the social, political and moral values implicit in them. . . . To place the industry on a footing of equality with its foreign competitors we must contribute something of our own. . . . There can be no national tradition of the film until there is an ideological nucleus.[1]

During the 1920s the financial health of the British film industry was examined by official and quasi-official groups who reached a consensus that a film industry was such an important component of national culture that the government must protect it. There was considerable debate as to how this protection and concern could best be achieved, but there was agreement on the need to reduce Hollywood's domination of Britain's cinema screens. These debates on the protection of the British film industry raised, but did not always answer, fundamental questions about the role of film as an expression of national identity.

The Cinematograph Films Act (1927)

The Cinematograph Films Act (1927) was the first case of the government intervening to protect the commercial film industry. Its intention was to foster production so that a larger percentage of screen time would be devoted to the exhibition of British films. It did not do this by providing a subsidy for producers, or by ensuring that they received a larger share of box-office receipts, but instead imposed a statutory obligation on renters and exhibitors to acquire and show a minimum 'quota' of British films out of the total number they handled, British and foreign. Up to 1927 the majority of films exhibited in Britain had been American. In 1914, 25 per cent of the films shown were British, but by 1923 this had dropped to 10 per cent and by 1925 it was only 5 per cent. In 1924 the total number of British films 'trade shown' (films shown to exhibitors before hiring) was fifty-six. In 1925 only forty-five were shown, and in 1926 the figure had slumped to thirty-seven.[2] It was this state of affairs that the first Films Act aimed to rectify.

The Act provided that in the first year the renters' quota should be 7.5 per cent, and the exhibitors' 5 per cent. The renters' quota was higher because exhibitors wanted to be offered an adequate selection of films. Both quotas were to increase by stages to 20 per cent in 1936, and remain at that level until 1938 when the Act expired. A British film was defined as one made by a British subject or company. The definition did not specify that control had to be in British hands, but only that the company had to be constituted in the British Empire and that the majority of the company directors should be British. All studio scenes had to be shot in the Empire, and not less than 75 per cent of the labour costs incurred in a film production, including payments for copyright and to one foreign actor, actress or producer, had to be paid to British subjects, or to persons domiciled in the Empire. The 'scenario' – a term never clearly defined, so that the provision became a dead letter – had to be written by a British subject. The Act also regulated booking practices in an attempt to open up more of the home market to British films. The Board of Trade, whose Industries and Manufactures Department was responsible for the film industry, was to register the films, and to consult with an Advisory Committee consisting of trade and independent members.

The Films Act was passed before Britain adopted a major programme of general protective industrial tariffs in 1931. In the late 19th and early 20th centuries a policy of free trade had been pursued, even though Britain's share of the world export trade in manufactured goods fell from 35.8 per cent in 1890 to 28.4 per cent by 1900, and in 1921–5 was only 23.8 per cent.[3] The rise of competing industrial economies meant that Britain gradually lost its traditional role as the 'workshop of the world' to Germany and the United States, who protected their newly developed industries and began to supply markets previously dominated by British goods. Britain's trade deficit widened and by 1929 the leading export trades were suffering high levels of unemployment. It is in this context of gradual but limited pressures for protection that the Films Act should be seen.

Competition from Hollywood was overwhelming, and consolidated by booking practices which favoured the distribution and exhibition of American films in Britain. With British production at a low ebb in the mid-1920s, exhibitors were forced to rely on a plentiful supply of cheap and popular Hollywood films: as British production declined, exhibition boomed. In the 1920s the outstanding development in the structure of the film industry was the growth of the circuits. Whereas in 1917 there were ninety circuits (429 cinemas), by 1926 there were 139 (856 cinemas).[4] The optimism created by the prospect of quota legislation accelerated the trend towards vertical integration – the grouping of small companies into a combine which amalgamated the three main sectors of the film business: production, distribution and exhibition. By 1933 two combines dominated the British scene: the Gaumont-British Picture Corporation (GBPC) controlled 287 cinemas, and the Associated British Picture Corporation (ABPC) had 147 cinemas.[5] Financed by Maurice and Isidore Ostrer, GBPC was registered as a public company in 1927. It was an amalgamation of several important concerns: Gaumont, Ideal Films, the W & F Film Service, the Biocolor circuit, Denman Picture Houses and the General Theatre Corporation; in addition, the large Provincial Cinematograph Theatres (PCT) circuit was purchased in December 1928. ABPC was formed by John Maxwell in 1928

and consisted of his production company, British International Pictures, Wardour Films, First-National Pathé and the Scottish Cinema and Variety Theatres. The major advantage enjoyed by vertically integrated companies was that their studios were able to launch more ambitious production programmes, secure in the knowledge that the films would be shown in their cinemas and that box-office profits would finance subsequent productions. State protection was therefore responsible for a fundamental change in the structure of the industry and a revival in production.

Despite complaints that the Films Act encouraged 'quota quickies' (cheap British films financed by American renters to satisfy quota regulations while not affecting the number of American films they handled), British films increased their share of the market from 4.4 per cent in 1927 to 24 per cent by 1932.[6] British exhibitors consistently exceeded their quota requirements well into the 1930s, which would appear to contradict the view expressed by many at the time and subsequently by critics and film historians that British films were universally unpopular. Undoubtedly many poor-quality films were produced in the post-quota boom and in the awkward period of adjustment to sound, but 'good' British pictures, usually produced by highly capitalised companies like GBPC or ABPC, were welcomed by exhibitors, and many directors, technicians and actors gained valuable experience by working on British films, cheap or expensive. As John Sedgwick's statistical work has shown, by 1934 the industry was doing well, with British producers achieving 'comparable performance results per film product as their more renowned Hollywood counterparts', which supported the case that Britain could create a 'viable national cinema'.[7]

The 'Talkies'

The rush to exploit the novelty of the 'talkies' encouraged many companies to extend themselves beyond their means. While the arrival of sound attracted capital to the industry and hastened the trend towards vertical integration, it also caused confusion and panic. It is clear that some of the companies which had been formed in the immediate post-quota boom went under because of the coming of sound. Costs escalated – the average cost of a silent film production was £5–12,000, whereas a 'talkie' cost £12–20,000. Many of the new companies did not have the capital to produce on that scale and sound-recording equipment was expensive. The quota helped the larger companies adjust to sound, but could not save the smaller, more precarious companies which had been set up between 1927 and 1930. Despite the expense of equipping cinemas for sound, exhibitors fared better. Britain was the first European country to convert its cinemas: 22 per cent of UK cinemas were wired by 1929, and by 1930 the figure had risen to 63 per cent; that is, 980 cinemas by 1929, but as many as 3,151 by the end of the following year.[8]

The Americans thought it was the coming of sound, more than the quota, that rescued the British film industry. They thought particular types of film were more suited to British audiences, especially comedy-farces. One study in 1931 revealed that a higher proportion of farces and murder mysteries made by British companies were shown in Britain than similar American films. The report went on to say: 'The farces were among the most successful of British pictures, while most of the American were relatively unsuccess-ful . . . Farce is a form of humor more appreciated on its native heath than elsewhere.'[9] American Westerns and dramas were still very popular, but clearly sound gave British producers the opportunity to develop cer-tain types of film that audiences found more acceptable than has been supposed.[10] The quota helped in the process of adjustment to sound because the influx of capital which it encouraged enabled the larger compa-nies to equip their cinemas and studios for sound. This required a considerable capital outlay, and it is doubtful whether the industry, in its moribund state before the quota, could have attracted the finance necessary for the changeover.

Korda and Film Finance

The revival of the British film industry in the early 1930s enabled Alexander Korda to develop one of the most important British film companies, London Film Productions. Korda was an experienced Hungarian film-maker who came to England in 1931 after work-ing in Vienna, Berlin and Hollywood. In 1933 he made *The Private Life of Henry VIII*, an irreverent his-torical comedy starring Charles Laughton, which raised the question of whether the goal of encourag-ing indigenous 'British' film styles and themes was compatible with achieving box-office success at an international level. *Henry VIII* certainly scored as far as the latter was concerned: it broke box-office records in America, taking over £7,000 in its first week at the Radio City Music Hall in New York and over £500,000 on its first world run, and was praised for showing the world that Britain could produce inter-

Alexander Korda's *The Private Life of Henry VIII* (1933): showing the world that Britain could produce internationally successful films on British subjects

nationally successful films on British subjects.[11] But it was also accused of dictating an expensive style (it cost £93,710) and giving other producers and their finan-ciers false optimism about the type of films which made money and the accessibility of the lucrative American market.

In the wake of *Henry VIII*'s success, production boomed and Korda was able to build lavish studios at Denham. Between 1935 and 1937 new studios mush-roomed. In 1928 there were nineteen stages in British studios with a total area of 105,650 square feet; by 1938 there were seventy with 777,650 square feet.[12] Korda's success inspired others to make films for the American market. This was a dangerous policy, because if a film failed to recoup its production costs, losses could be cat-astrophic, especially if the picture was a lavish venture intended to appeal to British and American audiences. *World Film News* anticipated problems in July 1936 when it commented: 'It is generally admitted in the film trade that a collapse is imminent and that it may come any time within the next six months.' By January 1937 there were signs that the bubble would burst. Julius Hagen's Twickenham group of companies went bank-rupt after an attempt to make pictures for world release. Hagen claimed that he had been promised £40,000 for the American sales of *Scrooge* (1935), but had received only £1,200.[13] In March 1937 Gainsborough published a loss of £98,000 for 1936, and it was announced that the Gaumont studios at Shepherd's Bush would close. In the summer of 1936 Gaumont-British had an over-draft with the National Provincial Bank of £1,149,785, of which £247,904 was in respect of film production.

Hagen claimed that he had been promised £40,000 for the American sales of *Scrooge* (Henry Edwards, 1935) but had received only £1,200

By May 1936 Korda's London Films showed a loss of over £330,000.

It was clear that in a space of months the industry had passed from boom to bust.[14] In July 1937 the *Financial Times* declared that production losses were likely to be over £1 million and that financial support would be withdrawn from film production.[15] Since film production was a speculative venture, especially in Britain where the producer received by far the smallest share of box-office receipts, ordinary channels of finance were wary of investing money. Although costs had risen and producers had lost money when their films failed in America, the root of the problem in 1937 was the unstable method of film finance that had developed in the boom period. In the first six months of 1937 over £4 million was borrowed by production companies, mainly by short-term financing. *Money behind the Screen*, an exposé written by documentary film-maker Stuart Legg and Marxist art historian F. D. Klingender, concluded that:

> One of the most striking features of this expansion
> from a financial point of view is the fact that on the
> production side it is based almost entirely on expecta-
> tion without any concrete results to justify that opti-
> mism . . . the expansion has with few outstanding
> exceptions been financed not by increases in the
> companies' own working capital, but by a spectacular
> increase in loans.[16]

The financial crash of 1937 exposed the industry's weak foundations and company after company went

into liquidation. Between 1925 and 1936, 640 production companies had been registered: by 1937 only twenty were still operating.[17]

The Cinematograph Films Act (1938)

In 1936, with only two years to go before the 1927 Films Act expired, amid widespread criticism of quota quickies and discussion of Korda's international strategy, an official committee chaired by Lord Moyne reported on the film industry's affairs. In 1932 Britain had abandoned Free Trade for a system of Protection and Imperial Preference. Henceforth politicians, businessmen and civil servants began to show more enthusiasm for state intervention in industry, and many hoped that this mood would be reflected in the new Films Act. The Moyne Committee's report highlighted the strengths and weaknesses of the 1927 Act and made some key recommendations, some of which reached the statute book in 1938.[18] The ones that did not are extremely interesting and pinpoint some of the industry's fundamental problems in the 1930s. One recommendation was that the government should encourage the formation of a Films Bank to bring order to the chaotic world of film finance, and that it should keep a close watch on transfers of interests in British film companies 'to prevent control passing abroad'.[19] However, the published minutes of evidence to the Moyne Committee did not indicate that American companies had substantial interests in the British film industry, except in the renting sphere. R. D. Fennelly, who gave evidence for the Board of Trade, said that apart from 20th Century-Fox's holding in Gaumont-British there was little foreign capital invested in British production.[20] Warners and Fox had studios at Teddington and Wembley, but the only recent financial deal between a British and an American company mentioned was Universal's decision to distribute its films in Britain through General Film Distributors (GFD). GFD was controlled by the General Cinema Finance Corporation (GCFC), which had been established in March 1936 by J. Arthur Rank. As a result of the deal, which gave GCFC a 25 per cent interest in Universal, GFD was the main distributor of Universal's films in Britain, and the growing Rank group hoped the link would facilitate better exploitation of British films in America.

The 1938 Films Act was surprisingly modest. Quotas were set for another ten years and short films were protected as well as features, but despite support from the press a 'quality test' to ensure a certain standard of British film was rejected. Instead the 1938 Films Act tried to resolve the 'quickie' problem by insisting that quota films cost a certain minimum sum. The most curious aspect of the Act, however, was that it eased rather than increased quota burdens for American renters. Special 'multiple quota' concessions were available to those who wanted to make fewer, but more expensive, quota films which, it was hoped, would be distributed abroad. To register for renters' quota a film had to have cost a minimum of £1 per foot in labour costs, with a minimum total of £7,500 per film. If a film cost three times the minimum – at least £3 per foot with a total of not less than £22,500 in labour costs – it could count twice its length for renters' quota. A film of over £37,500 or £5 per foot in labour costs could count three times. Why was the Board of Trade prepared to do this when there had been so much agitation for tougher legislation, criticism of lavish, Kordaesque productions aimed at foreign markets, and anxiety about the dangers of a further wave of Hollywood domination?

Since the government was unprepared to commit itself to a policy of state subsidy for film production, finance had to be found elsewhere. Still recoiling from the shock of the 1937 crash, the City was unprepared to burn its fingers again. At the same time American companies were showing an interest in establishing production units in Britain. MGM was making bold plans for its new unit headed by Michael Balcon, and Warner Bros.–First-National continued to produce at Teddington. Paramount announced plans for a series of films for the world market.

In February 1938 the Foreign Office sent a telegram to the British ambassador in Washington, Sir Ronald Lindsay, disclosing that 'certain amendments' (triple quotas and reciprocity) would be introduced when the Films Bill was in Parliament to meet some of the American demands. This was designed to appease the Americans, and the telegram stressed the importance of secrecy:

It would be extremely embarrassing if news of these proposals reached either the industry here or the press before the President of the Board of Trade has had an opportunity to mention them. . . . Any suggestions here that HMG were in receipt of formal representations from the US Government on the subject of the Bill while it was still under consideration by

Parliament might well destroy any sympathy in Parliament for the proposals.[21]

The pro-American clauses were designed to lure more American dollars to Britain as a means of injecting capital into the ailing industry. It was hoped that American production in Britain would provide employment for British technicians and encourage production standards which would appeal to international audiences. Links with American companies also promised favourable distribution contracts in the USA. At the risk of threatening the British film industry's independence in financial and, possibly, aesthetic terms, the Board of Trade therefore welcomed American finance as a tempting solution to its chronic financial problems.

Apart from the financial argument, the international situation and British anxiety about Germany and Japan would not allow the British to be too hard on Hollywood. As the 1927 Films Act had played a major role in the Free Trade versus Protection controversy, the 1938 Act was in the forefront of discussions about Anglo-American economic and political relations. The debates on the new Bill coincided with negotiations for an Anglo-American Trade Agreement, and both sides were anxious not to allow a dispute over film to prejudice more important issues. The US Secretary of State, Cordell Hull, launched a trade agreements programme as part of his campaign to reduce international tension via 'economic appeasement' and an agreement with Britain was considered to be a cornerstone of this policy. On the British side, the situation was delicate because politicians, particularly Foreign Secretary Anthony Eden, were keen to court American support against fascism.

Britain was Hollywood's most lucrative overseas market, especially since the coming of sound and the virtual exclusion of American films from Soviet Russia, Germany and Italy. American producers culled as much as 30 per cent of their income from Britain and Will Hays, representing Hollywood's major producers, encouraged Cordell Hull to use the film dispute as a lever in the wranglings over trade. The State Department backed Hollywood's bid to make the 1938 Films Act as innocuous as possible. Hays even threatened the State Department with an anti-British press-and-newsreel campaign based on the injustices of the film quota, to be conducted by the major film companies. Hull was receptive to such tactics because his trade agreements programme was already being severely criticised in Congress: the last thing he wanted was for

Hollywood's plight to provide his opponents with ammunition against greater Anglo-American co-operation. In March 1938, while the Films Bill was being debated in the House of Lords, Oliver Stanley, the President of the Board of Trade, had a crucial meeting with Joseph P. Kennedy, the new American ambassador. Stanley promised to secure the pro-American amendments to the Bill, an astonishing move, especially since he had just made a speech in the Commons professing: 'I do not want our defences to be made in Hollywood. I want the world to be able to see British films true to British life, accepting British standards and spreading British ideas.'[22] Even so, Hollywood did not have things entirely its own way. Hull wanted film quotas to be discussed in the trade negotiations, but this time the Board of Trade dug in its heels and insisted that the topic should be excluded because film was an internal cultural responsibility rather than an ordinary industrial commodity. The Board of Trade argued that Britain did not intend to discriminate against American films, but wanted

> only to ensure a certain percentage of English films being shown for cultural reasons. The American film industry expects to have things too much its own way. Unfortunately . . . the US Government continues to look on films as a purely commercial item in the trade negotiations . . . while we regard them partly at least as a cultural responsibility.[23]

Using this argument the British succeeded in keeping film out of the discussions on trade, though the Americans tried to introduce it on several occasions. From the way the Board of Trade legislated for the film industry it is hard to imagine that it took cultural arguments seriously; but in the negotiations it was found expedient to present a cultural face.

The new Films Act became law in March 1938. The quotas for long films were to be 15 per cent for renters and 12.5 per cent for exhibitors. In the Lords they had been raised by Lord Moyne to 20 per cent and 15 per cent, but Stanley made sure, after considerable pressure from both the Americans and the exhibitors, that they were brought down again in the Commons. The quota for 'shorts' was 15 per cent for renters and 12.5 per cent for exhibitors. Studio wages and labour conditions were safeguarded in the Act, and other provisions included the multiple quotas; the reciprocity clause; the inauguration of the Cinematograph Films Council to 'keep under review the progress of the British film industry

and report to the Board of Trade'; and a stipulation that the Board could vary, within limits, the quota percentages and the cost test. The new Films Act followed the lines of the 1927 Act, but revealed the government's willingness to rely on American finance rather than try to reorganise the industry. The Association of Cinematograph Technicians' (ACT) Annual Report commented that the new legislation was 'fundamentally unsound in that the basis of the Act is not primarily concerned with the development of a flourishing British film industry independent of foreign control'.[24]

The industry's crucial infrastructure had been established and it is inconceivable that the film industry would have made such strides in the 1940s if its basic foundations had not been laid in the 1930s. As far as the government was concerned, it is remarkable that despite the orthodoxy of Free Trade there had been a response to the 'Hollywood invasion' that involved a degree of protection for the British film industry, albeit limited. British cinemas still needed Hollywood's movies and the US majors had the support of the State Department in their quest to 'Americanise the world'. In the late 1930s, with the shadow of war just around the corner, Britain was not in a position to be Hollywood's reluctant and ungrateful customer. By 1939, therefore, the ideal of a strong British film industry had been compromised by complex economic and political realities, realities which did not go away but remained firmly on the agenda of subsequent debates about the protection of the film industry.

Notes

1. *The Times*, 25 February 1926.

2. *Parliamentary Debates* (Lords), vol. 69 (1927), col. 272, and Rachael Low, *The History of the British Film, 1918–1929*, p. 156.

3. W. A. Lewis, 'International Competition in Manufactures', *American Economic Review*, Papers and Proceedings, XLVII (1957), p. 579, and S. Pollard, *The Development of the British Economy, 1914–80*, 3rd edn (London: Arnold, 1983), p. 116.

4. Low, *The History of the British Film, 1918–29*, pp. 40–1.

5. Political and Economic Planning, *The British Film Industry*, 1952, p. 56.

6. US Department of Commerce reports, 1927–32.

7. John Sedgwick, 'The Market for Feature Films in Britain, 1934: A Viable National Cinema', pp. 28–9.

8. Douglas Gomery, 'Economic Struggle and Hollywood Imperialism: Europe Converts to Sound', *Yale French Studies* no. 60, 1980, p. 92; US Department of Commerce reports, 1929–31.

9. US Department of Commerce report, 1931, p. 8.

10. See Tony Aldgate, 'Comedy, Class and Containment: The British Domestic Cinema of the 1930s', in James Curran and Vincent Porter (eds), *British Cinema History* (London: Weidenfeld and Nicolson, 1983).

11. For a study of the enthusiastic American reception of the film see Sarah Street, 'Stepping Westward: The Distribution of British Feature Films in America, and the Case of *The Private Life of Henry VIII*', in Justine Ashby and Andrew Higson (eds), *British Cinema, Past and Present* (London: Routledge, 2000).

12. Political and Economic Planning, *The British Film Industry*, p. 67.

13. *Morning Post*, 15 January 1937.

14. Karol Kulik, *Alexander Korda: The Man Who Could Work Miracles*, p. 170.

15. *Financial Times*, 13 July 1937.

16. F. D. Klingender and S. Legg, *Money behind the Screen*, p. 54.

17. *Kinematograph Weekly*, 13 January 1938, p. 139.

18. Report of the Committee on Cinematograph Films (1936), Cmd. 5320.

19. This recommendation was rejected largely because an inquiry into the film industry's affairs conducted by the Bank of England in 1937 warned the government against subsidising producers. See Margaret Dickinson and Sarah Street, *Cinema and State: The Film Industry and the British Government, 1927–84*, pp. 81–8.

20. Minutes of Evidence to the Committee on Cinematograph Films (HMSO, 1936), 5 May 1936, p. 5, para. 39.

21. Public Record Office: Foreign Office records, FO 371 21530/A 791.

22. *Parliamentary Debates* (Commons), 4 November 1937, vol. 328, col. 1173. For a full account of the interaction between American diplomacy and the Films Bill, see Sarah Street, 'The Hays Office and the Defence of the British Market in the 1930s'.

23. Public Record Office, Foreign Office records, FO 371 21530/A175, minute by Beith, 10 January 1938.

24. *Kinematograph Weekly*, 5 May 1938, p. 29.

Bibliography

Dickinson, Margaret and Street, Sarah, *Cinema and State: The Film Industry and the British Government, 1927–84* (London: BFI, 1985).

Hartog, Simon, 'State Protection of a Beleaguered Industry', in James Curran and Vincent Porter (eds), *British Cinema History* (London: Weidenfeld and Nicolson, 1983).

Klingender, F. D. and Legg, S., *Money behind the Screen* (London: Lawrence & Wishart, 1937).

Kulik, Karol, *Alexander Korda: The Man Who Could Work Miracles* (London: W. H. Allen, 1975).

Low, Rachael, *The History of the British Film, 1918–1929* (London: George Allen & Unwin, 1971).

Low, Rachael, *The History of the British Film, 1929–1939* (London: George Allen & Unwin, 1985).

Murphy, Robert, 'The Coming of Sound to the Cinema in Britain', *Historical Journal of Film, Radio and Television* vol. 4 no. 2, 1984.

Murphy, Robert, 'A Rival to Hollywood? The British Film Industry in the Thirties', *Screen* vol. 24 nos 4–5, July–October 1983.

Political and Economic Planning, *The British Film Industry* (London: PEP, 1952).

Sedgwick, John, 'The Market for Feature Films in Britain, 1934: A Viable National Cinema', *Historical Journal of Film, Radio and Television* vol. 14 no. 1, 1994.

Street, Sarah, 'The Hays Office and the Defence of the British Market in the 1930s', *Historical Journal of Film, Radio and Television* vol. 5 no. 1, 1985.

Street, Sarah, 'Alexander Korda, Prudential Assurance and British Film Finance in the 1930s', *Historical Journal of Film, Radio and Television* vol. 6, no. 2, 1986.

Street, Sarah, Transatlantic Crossings: British Feature Films in the USA (London: Continuum, 2002).

Wood, Linda (ed.), *British Films, 1927–1939* (London: British Film Institute Library Services, 1986).

This chapter reworks material that first appeared in Sarah Street and Margaret Dickinson's *Cinema and State*, BFI, 1985.

21

A Despicable Tradition? Quota Quickies in the 1930s

LAWRENCE NAPPER

The most curious result of the quota war has been the new orientation in British film values. Before it, our eyes were focused on Denham and the 'bigs'. Today the big pictures, like the dinosaurs, appear to be too big to be economic and are heading for extinction. We are all interested now in what can be done with fifty thousand pounds . . . we are even interested in what can be done with twelve thousand pounds. The record of these cheaper pictures is a lot better than the more pretentious ones. I do not mean better in production values, I mean better in essence . . . without any pretensions to those values, some of the cheaper pictures have a vitality which the luxury ones lack. My theory is that this vitality comes almost invariably from the English music hall, and this is true British cinema's only contact with reality.

John Grierson, *World Film News*, 1937

Film criticism has viewed quota quickies as an anomaly in British film history, their existence only worth recognising in the context of the industry's relationship to the state or as the 'primitive' forerunners of the mature British cinema of the war years. My own interest in the quota quickies is not that they were sometimes made by directors who later went on to make more 'interesting' films, but rather that they represent almost half of the British film output of their period. Their fate at the hands of critics is indicative of a more general problem that has pervaded thinking and writing about British films since the 1920s, and I would argue that it is these traditions of thought, unable to accommodate specifically British films in a meaningful way, which are responsible for the poor reputation of the British cinema. Before undertaking a reassessment of quota production, it is perhaps necessary to lay these critical ghosts to rest.

Films and National Identity

Since its inception with *Close Up* in 1927, serious film criticism in Britain has displayed an almost unseemly passion for denigrating the British film. This tradition can be seen as the result of various concerns operating on the critical community itself, rather than a reflection on the films that they saw. From the 1920s to the 1970s the paramount tendency was to judge British films not in terms of British culture, but in the light of international movements stemming from Europe and America. Internationalism on the part of critics led them to bemoan British cinema partly because it was so very British, retaining the popular culture of Britain as its inspiration rather than aspiring to the cinematic culture of Russia, Germany or America. A consensus emerged that an expression of the British national identity must necessarily make for bad cinema.[1]

In this chapter I wish to take a different tack, looking at British films not in terms of their poverty in relation to British film criticism, but rather in terms of their richness as a reflection of the society and culture that produced them. This approach appears to be particularly suitable with regard to the quota quickies produced as a result of the 1927 Films Act.

The Films Act hoped to provide a space in the distribution monopoly of the American majors for a genuinely national cinema to emerge – one which dealt with British issues and retained or created a sense of national identity in opposition to what was seen as a cultural onslaught from America. The domination of this space by low-budget British films funded by American distributors led to claims of a deliberate attempt by the Americans to sabotage the British industry. However, despite the financial interest of the American majors, their influence on the content of the quota quickies was minimal, and it is possible to argue that these films did present a British national identity which was appreciated by certain sections of the audience. While figures such as Balcon and Korda strove to produce a British cinema that was international in outlook and appeal, the quota-quickie producers were content to make small-scale productions with limited and purely national appeal.

Given the significance of the cinema as a site of mass consumption in Britain during the interwar period, it is worth considering what kinds of consumer attitudes American films (which still constituted 80 per cent of all films shown) themselves contained. The startling glamour and wealth visible in American films is often accounted for by critics and historians simply as a function of their 'escapism'. However, I would argue that the differences run deeper than this. The American films, not only in their more fantastic mutations, but also at their most realist, presented a kind of consumer society that British audiences could barely even dream about. Sue Bowden has shown that by 1939 in the United States 60 per cent of households owned a washing machine, whereas in Britain the figure was a paltry 3.5 per cent, which even by 1958 had not risen above 25 per cent. In the same year, 56 per cent of American households owned a refrigerator; the figure in Britain was 2.4 per cent and did not rise to 25 per cent until 1960. Most significantly, in 1939 70 per cent of American households owned a car, whereas even by 1956 the figure was only 25 per cent in Britain.[2] Given the starkness of these contrasts, it is hardly surprising that British commentators were concerned about the messages audiences might receive from American films.

The connection between American films and mass consumption was seen as an alarming phenomenon. As V. F. Perkins states:

> For some British commentators, the image of the popular audience as threateningly other was matched by the foreignness of popular films, overwhelmingly American. If the clients were an undiscriminating class, their supply came from a whole society which was held to lack class and culture.[3]

As English as tripe and onions: George Carney and imprinted soubrettes in John Baxter's *Music Hall* (1934)

The specific threat was that the Americans might import this classlessness, with its corrupting influences, into British society. Advertisers were quick to realise the potential of linking their products to the popularity of American – and even British – stars. Advertisements in magazines such as *Picturegoer, Film Weekly* and *Women's Film Fair*, claimed, for example, that 'beautiful Binnie Barnes, now playing Catherine Howard in the film *The Private Life of Henry VIII*, finds "Sphere Oval-octo" suspenders "thoroughly reliable"'; or that 'Jessie Matthews says her love for OVALTINE is EVERGREEN'.[4] The most galling thing for many commentators was the spectacle of the wage-earning classes wearing the styles, buying the goods and adopting the mannerisms associated with American movie stars. This presented a threat not only to the British way of life but, as a result of the introduction of sound, to that most sacred of cows, the English language. Jeffrey Richards, writing about a campaign to regulate cinemagoing in Birmingham in the early 1930s, quotes G. A. Bryson, the deputy chairman of Birmingham Justices: 'We don't want our children to go about saying "Oh yeah" and "OK kid" and there is no doubt a tendency to Americanise the English language throughout the film that is, I think, deplorable.'[5]

Such attitudes reflected important concerns among that section of the cinema audience who had an interest in maintaining the nuances of class in British society. For other sections of the audience, however, the American cinema, and the cheap clothing and cosmetics that went with it, represented a welcome relief from the constant process of demarcation and judgment which the British class system entailed. As Jerry White suggests: 'This borrowed "style" was a self-conscious identification with a more democratic discourse than anything British society (including the Labour movement) had to offer them.'[6] Unfortunately for these filmgoers, their very attempt to escape meant they were marked out as contemptible in certain eyes. In 1933, a journalist from the *Islington and Holloway Press* visited 'Islington's most notorious café' and reported that: 'Nearly every girl there was acting a "hard-boiled Kate" role. Nearly every youth with a very long overcoat and a round black hat on the rear of his head, was to himself a "Chicago nut".'[7] Cinema became the symbolic focus, both economically and culturally, of fears of the American threat to Britain's national life and her international status. On the one hand, the British film was expected to represent an indigenous and unchanging version of British national identity, specifically distinct from the alternative presented by Hollywood. On the other it was to export this message, gaining a place for itself in the competitive domestic and international markets by becoming more efficient and versatile, but without compromising its essentially British nature by taking on the characteristics of its foreign competitor.

Throughout the early 1930s, the British cinema was the subject of competing discourses in the trade papers and among popular critics. It was criticised for being too parochial and too internationalist; for its primitive style and its 'slavish imitation' of Hollywood; for being too reliant on stage and literary adaptations, and for its inability to draw on the richness of British literature and history; for being too slow and picturesque, and for failing to use the settings provided by the British landscape; for being too reliant on foreign stars and technicians, and for the poverty of its native talent.

The 1927 Act was certainly successful in giving the British production industry the boost it so badly needed. Only thirty-four films were made in 1926, but in 1928 production leapt to 131 films. After the difficulties of converting to sound had been overcome, production rose again, with a boom in film-making around 1934–5 which reached a peak in 1937 with 228 films.[8] The industry of this period is often portrayed as consisting of two irrevocably separate halves: on the one hand, quality producers such as Balcon, Herbert Wilcox and Korda making ambitious films for international markets, and on the other the notorious quota-quickie companies which came into being as a result of the

sudden demand among the big American majors for British films to fulfil their quota obligations.

Quota Quickies?

The legend of quota quickies is that they were so much dud footage, unwatched and unwatchable. Margaret Dickinson and Sarah Street consider that the films are 'best forgotten', and Michael Balcon claimed that they were shown early in the morning when only the cleaners were in the cinemas.[9] In the mid-1930s the quota quickie seemed to represent an even greater threat to British national pride than Hollywood, since while Balcon and co. were struggling to provide a bona fide quality British cinema, the quota producers were operating to 'bring the name of British films into disrepute' through their production of cheap, unambitious films.[10]

The success of Korda's *The Private Life of Henry VIII* in late 1933, and the resultant release of a large amount of finance capital, enabled producers such as Balcon, Korda and Wilcox to aim at a wider international market, and in the years that followed they strenuously sought to distance themselves from the quota section of the industry. However, before 1934 the situation was less well defined. During the early 1930s many companies operated a dual policy – Wilcox's British and Dominions attempted to make quality pictures, but also ran a quota department under Richard Norton, producing twelve 'quickies' a year for Paramount.[11] Other companies which have since been identified as quickie producers also made more ambitious films intended for an export market. Julius Hagen ran such a policy at Twickenham, operating under two different brand names: Real Art for his quickies (sold to Radio and Fox), and Twickenham Film Productions for more ambitious 'supers', distributed variously by United Artists, Gaumont and Wardour.

The annual round-ups in January editions of *Kinematograph Weekly* for the early years of the decade are remarkably free of negative references to the 'Quota' Act. The main concerns of the exhibitors were not to do with the unpopularity of the British film, but rather with the question of Sunday opening and the Entertainments Tax. In discussions of British production by producers and critics, no distinction is made between quota and quality producers, although concern is expressed over the quality of the British product as a whole and its perceived inability either to portray national life effectively or to appeal to the majority of filmgoers over and above the product of Hollywood. By the summer of 1934, however, controversy over

The Ghost Camera (Bernard Vorhaus, 1933)

"This is absurd!", declares the hero of *The Ghost Camera* early in the film, "We're beginning to talk like characters in a mystery melodrama . . .". He is excitedly developing the photographs in a camera he has found, one of which he is convinced is a record of a murder. As the image of a woman emerges he speculates that she will have 'golden hair and large lustrous eyes . . . . The heroine of a mystery drama is always a ravishing creature.' The photograph in the tray resolves itself into an image of the heroine, played by Ida Lupino, looking exactly as he has described, and motivating him to search for her so that together they might solve the mystery which has resulted in her brother's wrongful arrest for murder.

This self-conscious acknowledgment of the excessively generic nature of the pleasures offered by *The Ghost Camera* is typical of the middle-class mystery dramas produced by Julius Hagen's Twickenham Studios. The film is rightly celebrated for the way in which its director, Bernard Vorhaus, and its editor (a young David Lean), managed to overcome the economic and practical restrictions of 'quickie' production to create a film that breaks away from the 'filmed dialogue' style of less-ambitious quota directors. A number of scenes are shot in real locations, and some striking sequences of fast, imaginative editing clearly indicate an interest in the potential of cinema as a unique visual language. The deft sequence in which the word 'Murder' is spelt out across the wireless and telegraph to a representative range of different audiences, for example, bears comparison with the more famous (but no more economic) sequence in Hitchcock's *The Lodger* (1932) which is surely its inspiration. Geoff Brown has also noted the crisp use of close-ups and imaginative point-of-view shots in the trial sequence.

Nevertheless these innovations are only one aspect of the film. They are balanced by equally important elements that demonstrate its continuing allegiance to older theatrical and literary traditions. Indeed, as the scene quoted above demonstrates, these elements are offered to the audience in all their hoary unoriginality as something to recognise and take pleasure in. 'Stock' characters such as Henry Kendall's silly-ass detective and Davina Craig's idiotic maid are repeated across a range of Twickenham's films – performances which are offered as 'star' turns.

Jefferson Farjeon's story provides a thriller structure with an intriguing lineage. He had been responsible for the 1920s stage play *Number 17*, the second cinematic adaptation of which was directed by Alfred Hitchcock in 1932, and is nominated by Charles Barr as a turning point in Hitchcock's career – the point at which all the most distinctive elements of his romantic-thriller cycle come together for the first time. This is not to suggest that *The Ghost Camera* is on the level of Hitchcock's best work, but it certainly has its roots in similar dramatic traditions. A comparison with Hitchcock's later British films is instructive, for instance in the handling of the opening sequence establishing the mystery (*Young and Innocent*, 1937), or in the development of the relationship between the male and female leads (*The 39 Steps*, 1935).

When we first meet him, the hero of *The Ghost Camera* complains about how mundane his holidays have been, 'just the usual sort of people and happenings – unexciting like myself'. Before long he is retracing his steps, armed with a pretty girl and a murder to solve. In style as well as narrative, it is this combination of the mundane and the unexpected which marks out the best of the quota quickies.

FURTHER READING

Charles Barr, *English Hitchcock* (Moffat: Cameron and Hollis, 1999).

Geoff Brown, 'Money for Speed: The British Films of Bernard Vorhaus', in Jeffrey Richards (ed.), *The Unknown 1930s* (London: I. B. Tauris, 2000).

Dramatic scenes and the chance of becoming a Hollywood star: Ida Lupino in *The Ghost Camera*

quota quickies filled the pages of the trade papers and the fan magazines. A leading article in *Film Weekly* complained that:

> For over six years the British film industry has borne the brunt of these pictures with great fortitude, regarding them as necessary evils. But at last the time has come for plain speaking . . . as long as the present quota regulations remain in force [the British film-goer] is in danger of having his time wasted and his patience exhausted by inferior British pictures which have been produced, not to stand on their own merits as entertainment, but to enable some American film company to fulfil its legal obligations. In his own interests the filmgoer should learn to recognise such pictures – to know them for what they are – and to voice his disapproval of them so forcefully that the authorities who framed the obsolete quota law will be compelled to make sweeping reforms.[12]

What is interesting about this article is that it creates the quota quickie in the mind of the filmgoer. It calls for filmgoers to 'learn to recognise' such films, connecting them explicitly to the American distributors. Only a month before it denounced the quota quickie, *Film Weekly* had carried stories in its 'In British Studios' column – with no sense of outrage – about productions at Twickenham being filmed through the night for American distributors.[13] And in *Picturegoer*, E. G. Cousins had written an approving column entitled 'Putting England on the Screen' which praised (albeit faintly) the efforts of John Baxter and Bernard Vorhaus. Cousins argued that low production values enabled the British producer to 'turn aside for a moment from his proper employment of slavishly imitating Hollywood, and to put on British screens British themes in British scenes'. And he went on to argue that Baxter's *Say It with Flowers* (1934) was as English as 'tripe and onions'.[14] What he appears to be suggesting is that the much-despised quota section of the industry held the key to the problem of 'putting England on the screen'.

The Q-Q Audience

I would argue that as a direct result of their stringent finances and the limited release patterns open to them, the quota producers sought to portray England for two specific markets: the lower middle class and the older generations of the working class. Both were defined by their reluctance to partake in the optimistic visions of a consumerist society embodied in Hollywood and

'quality' British films. The lower middle classes were ambivalent about consumption, as they were about the cinema. The 'cloth-cap' working class looked back nostalgically to music hall. As a result of their portrayal of sections of British society which identified themselves not through processes of consumption but through British notions of class and community, the quota quickies produced for these markets responded exactly to the intentions of those who had created the Films Act of 1927.

The specific audiences for quota quickies are often difficult to identify because surveys of cinemagoing during the period are usually skewed towards the more numerous young working-class film fans in the bigger cities. However, close attention to their likely release patterns suggests that an audience for these smaller British films was there. In 1937 a report in *World Film News* about a symposium on box-office appeal suggested that audiences generally appreciated films 'dealing with people like themselves whose lives they can understand and whose reactions they can appreciate'.[15] While among younger working-class film fans Hollywood remained king, Richard Carr noted of the East End of London that 'middle-aged and elderly men continue to find their main relaxation in pigeon clubs, in darts, and in their working men's clubs'.[16]

Here, Carr said, 'music halls have vanished', but this was not so in the North. Leslie Halliwell recalled that in Bolton in the 1930s the Grand Theatre was still operating successfully as a music-hall venue, attracting crowds with great names such as 'George Robey, Frank Randle, Gillie Potter, Old Mother Riley . . . and Florrie Forde'. While the young Halliwell and his mother were devoted cinemagoers, his father preferred to patronise this music hall, and when he did go to the pictures it was significantly 'to see one of the broader Comics'.[17] The *Bolton Standard* of 1934 reveals that the Grand booked George Formby (then virtually unknown outside Lancashire) as a top biller twice during the year, and Florrie Forde appeared at the top of the bill during the summer. When these stars appeared in their respective quota quickies (*Boots! Boots!*, 1934 and *Say It with Flowers*), the cinema advertisements and local reviews made the most of their music-hall connections. While it is true that in predominantly working-class areas such as Bolton, which boasted no less than forty-seven cinemas, the more middle-class quota quickies were often used as programme supports to American films, this was not always the case. In September 1933 the Queen's Cinema in Bolton showed *The Shadow*, with Henry

Kendall, as its main feature, and in June 1934 *The Ghost Camera*, also with Kendall, was the main feature at the Rialto, unashamedly publicised as a British film with 'English scenes and English humour'.[18] In other areas the middle-class quota quickies fared even better, for outside the big cities, in places where there were fewer cinemas, the culture of the young film fan was not as dominant.

Between them the three largest cinema circuits in Britain – Odeon, ABPC and Gaumont-British – accounted for the exhibition of the four more celebrated producers of 'quality' British films.[19] Their cinemas were the sites we usually associate with filmgoing in 1930s Britain – the opulent picture palaces with 2,000 or more seats situated in and around large cities. Because of their status and their situation in populous areas, the large cinemas were able to get big features quickly after their release and run them in popular 'double-feature' programmes, often pairing British and American films. However, despite their high visibility, these cinemas were in fact in a minority, as Simon Rowson points out:

> The general view of the cinema has been formed and is maintained by the large, brightly coloured, brilliantly illuminated picture palaces, built and building, which are the constant experience of those who live in London and the large provincial towns. To all, the surprise must be profound when asked to credit the information that more than one half of the seating accommodation in the cinemas throughout the country will be found in houses containing less than 100 seats, and that the number of these houses is more than 70% of the total.[20]

For these smaller independent cinemas the situation was very different. Unable to get the 'quality' British films from British distributors, either because they could not afford them or because they were in competition with a large picture palace, the independent exhibitors were reliant on the American renters for their British quota. Furthermore, Rowson's figures on opening hours seem to suggest that while a double feature was the norm in the large houses, which opened at midday and ran a three-hour programme three times, the smaller house could only afford to open at about 6 p.m., running its programme twice with a length averaging two and a quarter hours. Despite the fact that feature films were shorter in the 1930s, it seems unlikely that a full programme lasting only two and a quarter

hours could accommodate two features (even if one was only a sixty-minute 'quickie').

This evidence suggests that, although *Kinematograph Weekly* regularly recommended British quota productions as fillers 'suitable for programme material in large popular houses', many exhibitors would be showing them as their main feature. This is confirmed by research into cinemagoing in the rural areas and coastal towns of Norfolk in the 1930s, where the *Norfolk Gazette* advertisements for programmes at cinemas in Sheringham, Holt and Cromer show a pattern of single-feature programmes changing twice a week and frequently centring on British films made by quota producers. If Balcon's claim that the British cinema was a cinema of 'disrepute' among picturegoers is correct, one would have expected these cinemas to play down the British aspect of what was on offer. Instead the opposite is the case – 'British to the backbone', says the Regent Hall cinema in Sheringham of *East Lynne on the Western Front* (1931), while of Julius Hagen's *The Crooked Lady* (1932), the Central Cinema in Cromer says, 'Thrilling, romantic, dramatic, and humorous by turns, it boasts one of the greatest casts of British stage and screen personalities ever seen.'[21]

Discovering a small independent cinema in Tooting in 1937, Richard Carr could hardly conceal his incredulity at what appeal it might offer:

> A small and rather depressed audience visits this cinema. One fancies them lost, hovering helplessly between the cinemas they knew in the ill-lit novelty days, and the new 'supers'. These are neither the simple, easily satisfied audiences of the pre-war days, nor the sophisticated movie fans of today. Perhaps too old or tired to go further than just round the corner to the pictures, or too conservative to accept change, or too dazed and bewildered by the luxury of the 'super' and the speed and complexities of the modern film. Some are people from small provincial towns and villages who find the less luxurious cinema more like home.[22]

Despite Carr's disparaging image, it is important not to underestimate the intelligence or the values of the audiences of such houses. Carr's experience was repeated at Lyme Regis. It appears that in spite of the dominance of the young film fan, the quota quickies did find an audience, not necessarily as sad as Carr imagines, who may have constituted that section of the public, whom Simon Rowson thought 'there must be in considerable numbers', who visited the cinema 'once every fortnight or even less frequently'.[23]

While the fever for exporting British film lasted, the quota quickies were seen as irretrievably contemptible. It was not until 1937, when Gaumont-British, sustaining a loss of £97,000 for the previous year, finally accepted the failure of their international policies, that cheap, indigenous culture once more became acceptable.[24]

Whodunits

Formally, quota quickies are defined by their lack of high production values – sophisticated editing, emphasis on action, economic storytelling. Instead they use slow narratives told through dialogue rather than editing, and styles of acting and presentation taken from the theatre and the music hall. These characteristics enabled quota quickies to appeal to that section of the British audience that felt ill at ease with American films. In their thematic concerns quota quickies dramatise the fears of a threat to indigenous British cultural values. This 'threat' is characterised as being to do with the modernity, classlessness and instability implied by the impetus towards social mobility that was an increasingly visible aspect of Britain in the 1930s.

The two most significant genres of quota production (indeed of British production generally) during this period were the comedy and the crime picture, comprising 38 per cent and 26 per cent of total output respectively.[25] In the hands of British quota producers these developed into genres which were distinctively different from their Hollywood counterparts. In contrast to the Hollywood gangster film, British crime pictures tended towards sedate English-country-house detective stories. British comedy films drew substantially on the music-hall tradition.

Of the fifty-six films made at Twickenham between 1932 and 1934, half are 'crime dramas' such as *The Shadow* (George Cooper, 1933), *Shot in the Dark* (George Pearson, 1933) and *Tangled Evidence* (George Cooper, 1934). They portray upper-class families, homes and manners, and structure themselves around the creation and resolution of a threat to that class. Their likely audience was the lower-middle or salaried class who, having made the leap of social mobility, had a vested interest in cementing their new status, which they expressed through a fetishisation of the unchanging class order embodied in Stanley Baldwin's rural idyll. It is within this idyll that the whodunit films are

Another threat to the class structure averted: *Tangled Evidence* (George Cooper, 1934)

situated, providing a spectacle of traditional upper-class wealth and manners, and narrating the threatened destruction, but final reaffirmation, of that world through the story of a murder.

All these films portray a wealthy family; however, in contrast to the wealth and cosmopolitanism defined by consumption portrayed in, for example, Jessie Matthews musicals, this is a wealth which is directly in opposition to modernity. The money is old money, and wealth is portrayed not through the spectacle of consumption but rather through that of tradition, specifically signified not by fashionable clothes or expensive goods but in James Carter's sets (described by Baynham Honri as 'miracles of plasterwork') denoting the English country house. These films open on a moment of crisis over inheritance, precipitated by the murder (or in the case of *The Shadow*, the threatened murder) of the family patriarch. The various family members gather to resolve this crisis, both literally through an inquest and the reading of a will, and symbolically by defining who are legitimate carriers (and inheritors) of class status and who is the impostor – the murderer who precipitated the crisis. The murderer is characterised quite literally as a threat to the class structure, though since all the members of the cast are suspects they are all connected in different ways with that threat. Working-class barbarity and female sexuality unsettle the established order, but the most serious threat stems from modernity, urbanity and consumption.

In all three films the villain is represented as an interloper. While he is part of the family, his influences are not those of the tradition, stability and insularity valued in the rural idyll, but rather those of fluidity, sophistication, cosmopolitanism and consumption represented by the urban scene which he occupies. Significantly, in both *The Shadow* and *Shot in the Dark* (and to a lesser extent in *Tangled Evidence*), he is represented by the fey young man, conspicuously well-dressed and 'debonair'. This figure is defined by his acts of impersonation, most importantly by his construction of himself as 'a very modern young man', who in a phrase used by Beverley Nichols (constructing himself in the same vein) has 'seen through things'.[26] It is this modernity and cynicism with regard to the old class structure that mark him out as such a potential threat. Both *Tangled Evidence* and *The Shadow* contain strong blackmail plotlines, in which the villain turns conservative respectability (which he himself flaunts) to his own profit. In *Tangled Evidence* the villain steals the manuscript of a novel written by his victim, which he then proceeds to pass off as his own with great success and profit. Significantly, the title of the novel is *Tradition*.

Thus the whodunits reveal the urban consumer society as the most potential threat to the British class system, even as they recontain it by the final exposure and capture of the killer. Perhaps the most important characteristic of the threat represented by this figure is the fact that he is disguised as a member of the family and economically as a member of the right class, for he is certainly rich. The minor threats which have been assigned to other suspects, particularly those to do with the working-class characters (for instance the chauffeur in *Tangled Evidence* and the criminal son of the butler in *The Shadow*), are easily containable because they are clearly visible. It is the interloping consumer who must be most vigorously resisted. His capture enables the resolution of the crisis of inheritance and the reinvestment of tradition and stability with the value that they hold as the most privileged indices in the construction of middle-class identity.

Vestiges of the Music Hall

The semantic struggle over 'value' is also a characteristic of the films dealing with music-hall performances. Music-hall artists and acts formed the main attraction in many quota quickies of the period, as is shown by the numerous shorts made by Widgey Newman, the Max Miller films made at Teddington, the films made by Stanley Lupino, Lupino Lane, Flanagan and Allen, Sandy Powell and Arthur Lucan. They operate in roughly similar ways in their negotiation of the thematic issues of consumption, in that they organise

themselves around themes of work and leisure, consistently privileging production over consumption in both areas.

This is most explicitly stated in *Music Hall* (John Baxter, 1934), which tells the story of a music hall which has fallen on hard times as a result of the competition of other, newer, more commercialised entertainments – cinemas and dance halls. The backstage staff decide that it is up to them to save their jobs by revitalising the hall, making it popular once more. They identify the recent failure of the hall with a new manager who has been attempting to run it on more commercial lines by turning it into a business. Stage staff turn instead to the previous manager, now an old man, whose attitude to entertainment is far more emotive: 'I've put a lot into that place,' he says, 'and I've drawn something more than money out of it.'

Throughout *Music Hall* and *Say It with Flowers* the music-hall tradition is privileged precisely because its relationship with its audience is emotional rather than commercial. It is a crucial signifier of class identity, which is inward-looking rather than outward-looking. Whereas Hollywood films represent a culture of aspiration, music hall, it is implied, represents a culture of affirmation. Its performers are of the same class as the audience, and the whole activity is one of production. This is represented by the community singing which forms the highlight of several of the films, and also by the fact that music-hall gags are told 'spontaneously' throughout the film and constructed as being part of the conversation patterns of their 'real' characters. This connection is portrayed as aggressively indigenous, arising from the difficulties of living a life defined by the inability to consume because of poverty. The problems implied by poverty are solved through the productive activity of the music hall. Thus the plot of *Say It with Flowers* revolves around the flower seller Kate, whose illness can only be cured by a holiday at the seaside. She is too poor to be able to afford that luxury and so her friends at the market and in the halls conspire to put on a benefit concert to raise the money to enable her to go. This is only possible because the music-hall performers are 'our own people'. As one of the characters observes, 'They have always looked after our class.'

It might be argued that the 'crime' whodunits and the music-hall 'comedies' constitute, in both their formal and thematic concerns, narratives of resistance to American values of mass consumption in exactly the ways intended by the 1927 Films Act. They addressed their audiences with an intimacy and intensity unavailable to American films. Unable, because of their minuscule budgets, to construct worlds of glamorous fantasy or protagonists defined by conspicuous consumption, they relied on portraying the spartan worlds of the British defined by class.

Quota quickies, contrary to their traditional reputation, represent a corpus of British films which are constantly surprising in their ability to entertain, intrigue, engage and fascinate any historian with a little imagination and a passion for the popular culture of the 1930s.

Notes

1. Charles Barr, 'Amnesia and Schizophrenia', in Charles Barr (ed.), *All Our Yesterdays*, pp. 1–29.
2. Sue Bowden, 'The New Consumerism', in Paul Johnson (ed.), *Twentieth-Century Britain: Economic, Social and Cultural Change* (London: Longman, 1994), p. 247.
3. V. F. Perkins, 'The Atlantic Divide', in Richard Dyer and Ginette Vincendeau (eds), *Popular European Cinema* (London: Routledge, 1992), p. 197.
4. *Film Weekly*, 4 May 1934, and *Woman's Filmfair*, July 1934.
5. Jeffrey Richards, 'The Cinema and Cinema-going in Birmingham in the 1930s', in James Walton and John K. Walvin (eds), *Leisure in Britain 1780–1939*, p. 46.
6. Jerry White, *The Worst Street in North London*, p. 166.
7. Quoted in ibid., p. 166.
8. Tom Ryall, *Hitchcock and the British Cinema* (London: Croom Helm, 1986), p. 48.
9. Margaret Dickinson and Sarah Street, *Cinema and State: The Film Industry and the British Government, 1927–84*, p. 42, and Michael Balcon, *Michael Balcon Presents . . . A Lifetime of Films* (London: Hutchinson, 1969), p. 16.
10. Balcon, *A Lifetime of Films*, p. 16.
11. Rachael Low, *The History of the British Film, 1929–1939*, p. 188.
12. 'Plain Speaking about Quota Pictures', *Film Weekly*, 29 June 1934, p. 3.
13. Stephen Watts, 'In British Studios', *Film Weekly*, 11 May 1934, p. 18.
14. E. G. Cousins, 'Putting England on the Screen', *Picturegoer*, 23 June 1934, p. 28.
15. 'Conflicting Tastes of British Filmgoers', *World Film News*, February 1937.
16. Richard Carr, 'People's Pictures and People's Palaces', *World Film News*, January 1937.
17. Leslie Halliwell, *Seats in All Parts*, p. 31.

18. This material is taken from issues of the *Bolton Standard* (a local evening newspaper) for 1934, held in the British Newspaper Library at Colindale.
19. Namely Gaumont-British, ABPC, British and Dominions, and London Films.
20. Simon Rowson, 'A Statistical Survey of the Cinema Industry in Britain in 1934', *Journal of the Royal Statistical Society* vol. 99, 1936.
21. This material is taken from various local papers held in the Norwich Central Library.
22. Richard Carr, 'Cinemas and Cemeteries', *World Film News*, May 1937, p. 18.
23. Rowson, 'A Statistical Survey'.
24. Low, *The History of the British Film, 1929–1939*, p. 143.
25. Denis Gifford, *The British Film Catalogue 1895–1985*.
26. See Beverley Nichols, *Are They the Same at Home?* (London: Jonathan Cape, 1927), p. 191. Nichols is defending himself against an attack on the 'modern young man' by the Baroness Clifton in the *Daily Express*.

Bibliography

Barr, Charles (ed.), *All Our Yesterdays: 90 Years of British Cinema* (London: BFI, 1986).
Branson, Noreen and Heinemann, Margot, *Britain in the 1930s* (London: Weidenfeld & Nicolson, 1971).
Brunel, Adrian, *Nice Work: The Story of Thirty Years in British Film Production* (London: Forbes Robertson, 1949).
Chibnall, Steve, *Quota Quickies: The Birth of the British 'B' Film* (London: BFI, 2007).
Dickinson, Margaret and Street, Sarah, *Cinema and State: The Film Industry and the British Government, 1927–84* (London: BFI, 1985).
Gifford, Denis, *The British Film Catalogue 1895–1985* (Newton Abbot: David & Charles, 1973).
Halliwell, Leslie, *Seats in All Parts* (London: Granada, 1985).
Higson, Andrew, *Waving the Flag: Constructing a National Cinema in Britain* (Oxford: Clarendon Press, 1995).
Johnson, Paul (ed.), *Twentieth-Century Britain: Economic, Social and Cultural Change* (London: Longman, 1994).
Jones, Steven, *Workers at Play* (London: Routledge & Kegan Paul, 1986).
Low, Rachael, *The History of the British Film, 1929–1939* (London: George Allen & Unwin, 1985).
Nichols, Beverley, *Are They the Same at Home?* (London: Jonathan Cape, 1927).
Pearson, George, *Flashback* (London: George Allen & Unwin, 1957).
Powell, Michael, *A Life in Movies* (London: Heinemann, 1986).
Richards, Jeffrey and Sheridan, Dorothy, *Mass-Observation at the Movies* (London: Routledge & Kegan Paul, 1987).

Richards, Jeffrey, *The Age of the Dream Palace: Cinema and Society in Britain 1930–39* (London: Routledge, 1984).

Walton, James and Walvin, John K. (eds), *Leisure in Britain 1780–1939* (Manchester: Manchester University Press, 1983).

White, Jerry, *The Worst Street in North London* (London: Routledge & Kegan Paul, 1986).

Wood, Linda, *The Commercial Imperative in the British Industry; Maurice Elvey, A Case Study* (London: BFI, 1987).

Wood, Linda, *Low-Budget Film-Making in 1930s Britain* (M.Phil. thesis, Polytechnic of Central London, 1989).

22

A British Studio System:
The Associated British Picture Corporation and
the Gaumont-British Picture Corporation in the 1930s

Tom Ryall

The 1940s are conventionally regarded as the 'golden age' of British film whereas the interwar years have been more a matter of cultural embarrassment. Despite the fact that the British film industry was effectively constructed in the 1930s out of the ruins of the 1920s, the cinema of these years was harshly judged by contemporary commentators, as it has been subsequently by film historians. It has been dismissed as trivial and escapist, unduly dependent on the West End theatre for its sources, inattentive to social realities, dominated by cheaply made pictures and, at best, a pale copy of Hollywood. Above all, despite modern purpose-built studios, generous production funding and guaranteed exhibition outlets unavailable to earlier British filmmakers, a distinctive national cinema did not emerge. Sometimes this failure was explained in xenophobic terms and laid at the door of the numerous foreigners – Hungarians, Germans, Americans and others – who came to England during the period and exerted a considerable influence on the course of British cinema. Sometimes it was attributed to the shortage of entrepreneurial and creative skills necessary to the business of creating art in the cinema and possessed in abundance by the Hollywood production bosses. 'Unless we find our Schulbergs and Thalbergs it is no use having our millions,' wrote one commentator as production funds – 'our millions' – began to flow into the industry following the passage of the Cinematograph Films Act of 1927.[1]

The Act, designed to stimulate an ailing production industry, included a requirement for exhibitors to screen a quota of British-originated films, beginning at 5 per cent but rising to 20 per cent by 1937 and offering protection to a production industry almost extinguished by American competition. Production firms mushroomed in the wake of the act, and although many of these were short-lived, two large production bases were established by the Gaumont-British Picture Corporation and the Associated British Picture Corporation (British International Pictures, BIP, until 1933), along with smaller though significant companies such as London Films, British and Dominions and Associated Talking Pictures. New studios were built at Ealing, Shepperton, Pinewood and Denham, while the Elstree complex was expanded and the Shepherd's Bush studio rebuilt.[2] The main British renter firms merged into two large distribution networks, and a third important firm – General Film Distributors – was set up in 1936.[3] The number of cinemas increased from just under 4,000 in the mid-1920s to just under 4,500 in the mid-1930s, with many of these organised into circuits; and the period also saw the emergence of a new influential force in exhibition – Oscar Deutsch's Odeon chain.[4] A modern film industry had emerged with two large vertically integrated 'majors' with interests in production, distribution and exhibition, a string of medium-sized production companies, and a number of small firms specialising in low-budget films designed to meet the quota requirements of the powerful American distributors. The 1927 Act was responsible for the emergence of a 'studio system' not dissimilar to that of Hollywood with its interrelated cluster of major, minor and 'B' picture companies.

During the years following the 1927 Act the industry moved from a total of 34 British-produced films in 1926 to over 200 a year by 1936 – equivalent to about

40 per cent of the American industry's output.[5] In addition, a British film – *The Private Life of Henry VIII* (1933) – was a box-office success in the USA, and its star, Charles Laughton, won the Oscar for the best actor of 1933. The ten-year life of the Act saw a dramatic increase in the number of British films, with some 1,600 films produced and Britain becoming the most substantial source of production in Europe.[6] Critical judgment of the British entertainment cinema of the 1930s, however, has been severe. Although production expanded dramatically during the period, it has been estimated that 'approximately half the enormous number of films turned out by British studios up to 1937 were produced at minimum cost simply to exploit the protected market or, at worst, to comply with the law'.[7] These cheaply made films were sometimes made outside Britain – in Australia, Canada and India for example – and they were often designed simply to fulfil the distribution and exhibition quotas as they increased during the decade. Quota quickies – as such films were called – sometimes remained unscreened, and in general these low-budget pictures gave the British cinema a poor reputation with both critics and the cinema-going public.[8]

When it came to the character and quality of the films actually produced it was argued that too many films – whatever their budget – were based upon middle-class, middle-brow stage plays and failed to reflect social reality. According to many it was a trivial, escapist cinema in a volatile social and political period; Michael Balcon, who had presided over the Gaumont-British output, reflected in his autobiography that hardly 'a single film of the period reflects the agony of those times'.[9] The strict codes of the British Board of Film Censors effectively inhibited social and political comment in the entertainment film, and consequently the British cinema failed to 'bring to the screen something of the life, tradition and culture of Britain and its Empire' which many considered a vital objective of the quota legislation.[10]

Studio Formation

The two film combines set up in the late 1920s consolidated operations in the different branches of the industry into unified enterprises, a process the Hollywood film industry had undergone some years earlier. British International Pictures (Associated British Picture Corporation) and the Gaumont-British Picture Corporation grouped together specialist firms from all branches of the industry into companies that were to produce just over 20 per cent of the feature films made between 1928 and 1937, establishing distinctive and contrasting profiles both as powerful forces in the indigenous industry and as international film companies.[11]

British International Pictures (BIP) amalgamated John Maxwell's Wardour Films (distribution), British International Pictures (production) and subsequently Associated British Cinemas (exhibition), and in 1933 the group set up a new concern – the Associated British Picture Corporation – as a holding company for the group's various interests. Despite the subsequent image of the company as a medium- or low-budget producing concern, when first established, BIP had the ambition to match its size.[12] The company employed some of the most important British directors – Alfred Hitchcock, Victor Saville and Thomas Bentley – but true to its international aspirations, also recruited directors from overseas, including the Americans Harry Lachman and Tim Whelan, the Germans E. A. Dupont and Arthur Robison, and an Italian who had acted in Hollywood and was to become a prolific director in the British cinema of the 1930s, Monty Banks. The company signed up major British stars such as Betty Balfour, but more important were the foreign stars – Maria Corda, Syd Chaplin, Tallulah Bankhead, Lionel Barrymore and Anna May Wong from Hollywood, Carl Brisson, Anny Ondra, Olga Tschechova from continental Europe – who seemed to guarantee access to the international market. The company's international aspirations were also reflected in the setting-up of an American distribution base – World Wide Pictures – together with companies in Germany and Austria for both production and distribution purposes. In addition, BIP pioneered the 'multiple-language version' production technique in which different language versions of a picture were shot, usually simultaneously with a change of director and/or actors as appropriate.[13] The head of production at BIP was Walter Mycroft, former film critic for the *Evening Standard* and a member of the Film Society Council.

The Gaumont-British Picture Corporation was formed in 1927 from the Gaumont Company – originally an agency for the famous French firm but since 1922 a British-owned production/distribution concern – and two of the leading British distribution firms, Ideal and W & F Film Services. Subsequently the company acquired exhibition interests, and its underwriting of the public flotation of Michael Balcon's Gainsborough Pictures brought in additional production facilities. The

enterprise was financed by the Ostrer Brothers merchant bank, which had organised the British buy-out
of the original Gaumont Company from its French
parent. Gaumont-British had a production pre-history
at both Gainsborough and the Gaumont Company, but
the decision in 1929 to rebuild the Shepherd's Bush
studios meant that output from the newly formed combine was small and it was not until the opening of the
new studio in 1932 that the corporation was able to
mount its ambitious export-oriented programme of
around twenty films a year.

The Arrival of Sound

In October 1927, the release of *The Jazz Singer* in
America ushered in a period of profound change in
the global film industry. In Britain, production
expanded dramatically to meet the demands of the
'quota' Act, but by early 1929 it became clear that there
had to be a shift to expensive sound production as
well.[14] Many in the industry were cautious, judging
sound pictures to be passing fashions. John Maxwell,
chairman of BIP, predicted their co-existence with
silent films, suggesting that 'there will arise the general
principle of showing one sound picture and one silent
picture wherever there is a two-picture programme'.[15]
Despite Maxwell's caution, the BIP company report
for 1928–9 announced that plans for the installation of
'sound-proof studios for the production of talking pictures' had been agreed during 1928.[16] The critical and
commercial success of BIP's first 'talkie', Hitchcock's
Blackmail, released in June 1929, confirmed that the
future lay in sound pictures – although the film was
also made in a silent version for cinemas not yet
equipped for sound.[17]

The Gaumont-British combine was not as quick off
the mark, although Gainsborough, its associate production company, began adding sound to silent films and
preparing part-talking pictures towards the end of
1929. Its first two full-talking pictures – *Woman to
Woman* (1929) and *Journey's End* (1930) – were made in
America in conjunction with the small Tiffany-Stahl
studio. Neither of the corporation's studios was suitable
for the production of sound films. Gainsborough's
Islington studio was a converted power station;
Gaumont's Shepherd's Bush studio dated from 1915
and, since it was surrounded by housing, the only way
of expanding it was to build upwards.[18] A further complicating factor was the combine's ownership of a
sound-equipment company, British Acoustic, which
meant pressure to equip from within despite the

superior technology available from the American companies. Balcon resisted this, with the result that the
Islington studio, which handled the combine's production while Shepherd's Bush was out of action, was not
ready for sound production until late in 1929 when
American RCA equipment was installed. A studio fire
at Islington early in 1930 brought further problems and
production was shifted on a temporary basis to Elstree.

The commercial and critical success of *Blackmail*
appeared to give BIP the edge over its rival and in
this transitional period 1928–31 BIP released more
than twice as many features as Gaumont-British/
Gainsborough.

Divergent Paths in the 1930s

In 1931 BIP presented itself in the trade press as 'the
first company to establish a film-producing organisation
capable of becoming an international force in the film
business and worthy in scope and dignity to rank with
the great concerns in other industries and in other
countries'.[19] In its formative years, the company had
recruited an impressive roster of experienced creative
and technical staff. They included directors such as
Dupont, Robison and Hitchcock, the art director Alfred
Junge, who had worked on some twenty films in
Germany, and the cinematographer Charles Rosher,
who had shot Murnau's *Sunrise* (1927). The studio's
artistic ambition was demonstrated by the European
sophistication of Dupont's *Moulin Rouge* (1928) and
Piccadilly (1929) and Hitchcock's boldly experimental
Blackmail. According to Rachael Low, the studio 'spent
money in something like the Hollywood manner', allo-
cating £150,000 to six productions in 1927–8, including Hitchcock's *The Ring*, Dupont's *Moulin Rouge* and
the Betty Balfour vehicle *A Little Bit of Fluff*.[20] Prestige
production continued into the early 1930s with adaptations of stage plays by Shaw (*Arms and the Man*, 1932),
Galsworthy (*The Skin Game*, 1931) and O'Casey (*Juno
and the Paycock*, 1930), together with ambitious pictures
such as *The Informer* (1929, directed by Arthur
Robison), the espionage tale *The W Plan* (1930), and the
historical drama *Dreyfus* (1931).[21] However, these films
represented the tail-end of BIP's production strategy of
balancing 'prestige and profit', and as early as the middle
of 1929 the trade press was carrying news of impending staff cuts at the studio and suggestions of retrenchment.[22] The investment in sound production had been
considerable and the company needed a 'pause in production while economies were made to recoup the
expense of converting to sound'.[23]

Piccadilly (E. A. Dupont, 1929)

Piccadilly, a melodrama of intrigue and jealousy set in London's sophisticated café society and in its Chinese immigrant quarter, mixes sex, class, race, and violence in an early attempt by British International Pictures to produce an 'international' film. The film is a key example of the 'Film Europe' trend of the 1920s, which sought through collaborative production to establish a pan-European cinema that could compete with Hollywood. *Piccadilly* was written by English novelist Arnold Bennett but the other major creative and technical roles were taken by Germans. It was directed by E. A. Dupont, one of Germany's top film-makers. Dupont had gained international fame with *Varieté* (1925) and had already completed another international title for BIP, *Moulin Rouge* (1928). The cinematographer, Werner Brandes, and the art director, Alfred Junge, were also German with extensive experience, and had worked with Dupont on *Moulin Rouge*. The film featured the British star Jameson Thomas, the Australian-born musical-comedy star, Cyril Ritchard, and a cameo by Charles Laughton. However, its main selling ploy was two Hollywood stars, Gilda Gray and Anna May Wong. Gray, a Ziegfeld Follies dancer in her early career, was credited with developing the body-shaking 'shimmy' dance movement, and has top-billing on the film; Anna May Wong was a rarity, a Chinese-American star.

Despite her lower billing, Anna May Wong's performance dominates. She plays Shosho, a dishwasher who rises to stardom as a dancer in the Piccadilly nightclub ousting the current star performer, Mabel (Gray), from the position. She also begins a romance with the Piccadilly's owner and Mabel's lover, Valentine (Jameson Thomas), who falls for her after seeing her impromptu tabletop dance in the nightclub scullery. Shosho, a mixture of femme fatale and ingénue, meets a tragic ending in which she is killed by her jealous Chinese boyfriend. The heady amalgam of race, class and sex, represented by Shosho's character provides the film's distinctive centre (*Piccadilly* could be classed as an early film noir); and her usurping of Gilda Gray's Mabel is confirmed in their contrasting dance sequences. Despite her brief 'shimmy', Gray's energetic though cumbersome floor-show duet with Cyril Ritchard is far less evocative than Anna May Wong's sensuous dancing whether in her work clothes in the dingy surroundings of the scullery or in her scanty oriental costume in the nightclub.

The film also contrasts Valentine's world of the sophisticated nightclub with Shosho's own 'Piccadilly', a public house in the exotic, racially mixed Limehouse area of the East End where Orientals and others mingle inharmoniously with roughhouse English types. Critical opinion at the time the film was released – at the end of the silent period, when sound films were already beginning to emerge – was mixed. Paul Rotha thought it, 'the best film of its type to be made in this country' and the American National Board of Review called it, 'the first serious contender of our American product to reach these shores from English studios'; *Close Up*, with its customary contempt for the British film, dismissed *Piccadilly* as 'one of the world's worst'. When a restored version of the film was made available in 2003, the crassness of such a verdict on this slow, sensual, fascinating film became apparent.

FURTHER READING

Andrew Higson and Richard Maltby (eds), *'Film Europe' and 'Film America': Cinema, Commerce and Cultural Exchange 1920–1939* (Exeter: University of Exeter Press, 1999), Chapters 12 & 13.

Anna May Wong in *Piccadilly*, guaranteeing access to the international market

It was a pause that led to a significant reorientation of the studio's production strategy and thereafter, despite its name, the company concentrated upon the domestic market, operating 'a policy of cut-price window dressing, trying to make cheap films which looked like expensive ones'.[24] From around 1932, the studio's production schedules were dominated by comedies, musicals and crime films. BIP drew extensively on the established popular formats of variety theatre and musical comedy, and much of its output featured comedians and musical performers such as Leslie Fuller, Ernie Lotinga, Stanley Lupino and Lupino Lane. But their films never achieved the critical or commercial success of the comparable offerings of Gracie Fields, George Formby, Jessie Matthews, Jack Hulbert, Jack Buchanan and Tom Walls. The company also developed a thriller/horror strand of low-budget film-making, utilising its second-string studio at Welwyn, but it no longer had a Hitchcock to bring these to the attention of the critical establishment. There was a foray into big-budget production in the middle of the decade with a small number of musical and historical costume pictures: *Blossom Time* (1934), starring the Austrian tenor Richard Tauber; *Mimi*, a version of Puccini's La Bohème; *Drake of England*, *Royal Cavalcade* and *Abdul the Damned* (all 1935).[25] But such ventures were uncharacteristic and the predominant strategy was to make modestly budgeted productions, to supply the needs of the company's growing cinema circuit. BIP's sustained though variable profitability during the 1930s was based mainly upon the earnings of its cinemas, and the shift in emphasis from production to exhibition was marked in 1933 when the company was reorganised as the Associated British Picture Corporation, the new name highlighting the ABC cinema chain rather than the BIP production arm.

In contrast to BIP, Gaumont-British, with Balcon established as 'general manager of film production', moved in the opposite direction, pursuing an explicitly internationalist policy during the period 1932–6 while its chief rival was in the process of retrenching.[26] With studio facilities rebuilt at Shepherd's Bush, and Gainsborough fully integrated into the combine, the studio recruited extensively within Britain and from continental Europe and Hollywood. Indeed, a description of Gaumont-British in this period sounds a little like that of BIP in the late 1920s. It can be argued that one of the key differences was that, in Michael Balcon, Gaumont-British had a very skilled and experienced producer at the helm. By contrast, Maxwell had

entrusted supervision of production to Walter Mycroft, who proved uninspiring despite his intellectual credentials. From the start of his career Balcon had been an internationally oriented film-maker, targeting films at America and organising European co-productions. During the 1920s he had established a team of colleagues which included Hitchcock, Victor Saville, Ivor Montagu and the scriptwriter Angus Macphail, and many of these joined Gaumont-British in the 1930s, together with a number of figures previously at BIP.[27] Hitchcock rejoined Balcon in 1934 to make his best-known British films – *The Man Who Knew Too Much* (1934), *The 39 Steps* (1935), *Secret Agent* (1936), *Sabotage* (1936), *Young and Innocent* (1937) and *The Lady Vanishes* (1938); Jessie Matthews, whose first starring role had been in *Out of the Blue*, made at Elstree in 1931, moved to Shepherd's Bush and became one of the most popular British stars of the time; and Alfred Junge brought a Germanic sensibility to the design of many of the best-known Gaumont-British pictures of the period.

In his autobiography, Balcon divides Gaumont-British output into vehicles for its most popular stars – Jack Hulbert, Jessie Matthews and George Arliss – Hitchcock's thriller sextet, Anglo-German films, and epics 'made with an eye on the American market'.[28] The Gaumont-British comedies and musicals, like their BIP counterparts, drew upon theatrical traditions and turned stage performers like Jack Hulbert and Cicely Courtneidge into film stars. Jessie Matthews came from the world of the West End musical revue and, after appearing in dramas such as *The Good Companions* (1933) and *Friday the Thirteenth* (1933), established herself with the stylish musical *Evergreen*, which combined elements of Edwardian music hall, with the Warner Bros. backstage musical and the art deco *mise en scène* of the Fred Astaire/Ginger Rogers films.[29]

Anglo-German co-production began in 1932, as part of an international co-production strategy that included English-language versions of successful films from France (*The Battle*, 1934) and Italy (*The Divine Spark*, 1935). Anglo-German pictures like *Happy Ever After* (1932) and *FP 1* (1933) were filmed abroad (though with largely British casts), but they were not a success and Balcon preferred to remake German films such as *Sunshine Susie* (1931) and *Marry Me* (1932) in England.[30]

Hitchcock's thrillers – now the studio's best-remembered contribution to British cinema – were part of a vigorous tradition which included Walter Forde's *Rome Express* (1932), the first thriller to use an

Evergreen (Victor Saville, 1934)

In the 1930s, Gaumont-British pursued a policy of making films designed to attract American audiences and established a distribution office in New York to sell its films in the US market. *Evergreen* reflects the studio's international ambitions by drawing upon contemporary American entertainment trends such as the Broadway musical revue and the Hollywood backstage musical. The film was based on *Ever Green*, a Rodgers and Hart stage musical written by British dramatist/screenwriter Benn Levy, and presented on the London stage in 1930 with Jessie Matthews, by then a well-established star of West End musical revue, in the leading role.

The film, directed by Victor Saville, was clearly calculated to showcase Matthews's talents, while at the same time providing the kind of entertainment that would appeal to the American public. Fred Astaire was approached to partner Matthews, though in the end she had to make do with the less agile Sonny Hale. Levy's original dramatic material was adapted for the screen by actor/writer Emlyn Williams, new production numbers were devised, and the original musical material was augmented with a couple of songs written by Harry M. Woods, one of which, 'Over My Shoulder', became Matthews's signature song and provided the title for her autobiography. *Evergreen* opened in Britain late in 1934 and in New York early in 1935 at the Radio City Music Hall where it became the first British film to play in America's largest cinema.

Evergreen begins in an Edwardian music hall where Harriet Green (Matthews) is giving her last performance before her marriage to an English nobleman. However, her plans are thwarted by her previous lover's blackmail threats and she emigrates leaving her illegitimate daughter in the care of her dresser. The narrative moves on to the present and into the world of the backstage musical with the daughter, also played by Matthews, a struggling chorus girl looking for work.

Her resemblance to her mother prompts a publicity stunt in which she is presented to the public as the Edwardian Harriet Green making a comeback in perfect youthful physical condition despite her age. The deception is eventually exposed but by that time 'Harriet junior' has established herself as a star. Both sections of the film exploit Matthews's versatility as a singer and dancer, ranging from the large-scale spectacle of the 'Springtime in Your Heart' sequence, to the intimate solo performance in the 'Dancing on the Ceiling' number. The *mise en scène* presents her in a variety of ways – elaborate Edwardian dresses, diaphanous nightgowns – and the dramatic exposure of the deceit is achieved through an energetic tapdance-cum-striptease during which she sheds her Edwardian dress to reveal her young woman's body. The film's elaborate finale with its tiers of chorines and its reprise of the film's principal songs, is reminiscent of a Busby Berkeley routine though without the bravura camera angles.[1] British audiences attuned to Hollywood spectacle were happy to accept this slightly more dowdy domestic variety and several more Matthews musicals followed in *Evergreen*'s wake. American audiences were slower to respond, though industry professionals were impressed by Matthews's talent and Saville's proficiency.

NOTE

1. The choreographer was the black American dancer Buddy Bradley, who had worked with Berkeley but found his opportunities restricted by colour prejudice.

FURTHER READING

Andrew Higson, *Waving the Flag: Constructing a National Cinema in Britain* (Oxford: Clarendon Press, 1996), Chapter 4.

Roy Moseley, *Evergreen. Victor Saville in His Own Words* (Carbondale, IL: Southern Illinois University Press, 2000), Chapter 5.

Jeffrey Richards, *The Age of the Dream Palace: Cinema and Society in Britain 1930–39* (London: Routledge, 1984), Chapter 12.

---

international train journey as its setting; early horror films such as *The Ghoul* (1933) and *The Man Who Changed His Mind* (1936), both starring Boris Karloff; and Berthold Viertel's *The Passing of the Third Floor Back*, which in its combination of mid-European sophistication and English realism prefigured the collaborations of Michael Powell and Emeric Pressburger.[31]

Gaumont-British made a much more determined attempt on the international market than BIP, and films like *Jew Süss* (1934), *The Iron Duke* (1935), *Rhodes of Africa* (1936), *King Solomon's Mines* (1937) and *The Tunnel* (1935) had budgets of £100,000 or more. In the tightly controlled American market these films fared badly, but they should not necessarily be dismissed as

Gaumont-British goes international: Leslie Banks and
Richard Dix prepare to cross the Atlantic in *The Tunnel*
(Maurice Elvey, 1935)

extravagant follies. A large-budget British film like *Jew
Süss*, costed at £125,000, was not much more expensive than the routine standard-budgeted 'A' features of
the big American studios, and much cheaper than the
top-budget ($1 million and more) American films.[32]
American producers, of course, with an internal market
several times larger than the British market, could afford
to spend a great deal more on production.

Michael Balcon, along with Alexander Korda, was
probably the nearest British equivalent to the prominent
Hollywood production chiefs such as Schulberg and
Thalberg, but despite its relatively successful production
policies, Gaumont-British, along with Korda's London
Films and others, had to curtail production and close
down studios in 1937. However, production did continue at Gainsborough, and whereas BIP's Elstree studio
was requisitioned during the war, Gainsborough – relocated at Shepherd's Bush – developed a strong studio
identity and enjoyed considerable commercial success.[33]

British Films of the 1930s:
Appeal, Popularity
and Critical Success

The view that the films of the 1930s failed to win favour
with the ordinary cinemagoing public or to construct a
distinctively British cinema has come under scrutiny
recently in two different ways. First, statistical information
from the period has been used to argue that quality
British films – those made for reasons other than simply
quota requirement – were in fact popular with audiences.[34] British audiences may have preferred American
films but this did not preclude approval of British films.[35]

The exhibitors' quota in the years 1932–6 was exceeded,
indicating that 'the cinemas were showing of their own
volition a good deal more British films than the 1927 Act
required of them'.[36] Second, film historians have argued
that national cinematic specificity can be located in the
less respectable areas of British cinema, in non-realist
genres such as horror, comedy and melodrama, in an
introspective self-reflexive cinema of fantasy rather than a
realist cinema of observation. This reorientation, although
based largely on the 1940s and after, on Gainsborough
melodrama and Hammer horror, invites a critical recon-
sideration of the British cinema of the 1930s. It can be
argued that the vigorous strands of popular culture evident in the music-hall-based comedies of Gracie Fields,
George Formby and Will Hay, in Hitchcock's thrillers, in
the Jessie Matthews musicals and in horror/fantasy films
such as *The Ghoul* (1933), *The Ghost Goes West* (1935) and
The Clairvoyant (1935) do constitute a distinctive cinema
of national identity. It would not have been one to find
favour with intellectual and socially committed critics
who searched in vain for the direct reflection of social
realities more common in the documentary films of the
time, but it might be equally valid.

The Legacy of the 1930s

Despite the financial crises and the poor reputation that
the industry acquired from quota production, the foundations for the subsequent 'golden age' of British
cinema in the 1940s had been laid. As Linda Wood has
observed:

> By 1939 Britain possessed the necessary facilities and
> personnel with the relevant expertise to produce the
> kind of quality films which could not have been
> made in this country ten years previously and on a
> sustained basis. For many film-makers, the Thirties
> provided the apprenticeship which made possible the
> flowering of British production in the Forties.[37]

The large combines provided a substantial infrastructure
for the industry and the Gaumont-British empire with
its studios and cinemas became the core of the Rank
Organisation in the early 1940s. Numerous film-makers
– Anthony Asquith, Michael Powell, David Lean, Frank
Launder, Sidney Gilliat, Ronald Neame, Charles Frend,
Arthur Crabtree and Leslie Arliss – emerged from
Elstree and Shepherd's Bush, from Islington and
Welwyn. By 1939 the ground had been prepared for 'the
appearance of a British cinema that was original and free
from influences from Hollywood'.[38] The historical

costume pictures, the popular musicals and comedies, the 'quickie' productions that drew their material from the indigenous popular culture focused on crime, fantasy and horror, together constitute a rich cluster of traditions in which a number of the key film-makers of the 1940s were nurtured and out of which the post-war British cinema emerged.

Notes

1. *Kinematograph Weekly*, 6 January 1927, p. 99.
2. See Patricia Warren, *British Film Studios*.
3. General Film Distributors was the foundation of the Rank Organisation, which was to dominate the British cinema in the post-World War II period.
4. Statistics on the number of cinemas are drawn from James Curran and Vincent Porter (eds), *British Cinema History*, p. 375. It is worth noting that the figure for the 1930s probably represents a significant increase in seating capacity as the small 'penny gaffs' were replaced by 'picture palaces'.
5. Political and Economic Planning, *The British Film Industry*, p. 41.
6. Film statistics are approximate and derived from Denis Gifford, *The British Film Catalogue 1895–1985*, and an unpublished digest of British film statistics by Simon Davies. See also Simon Hartog, 'State Protection of a Beleaguered Industry', in Curran and Porter (eds), *British Cinema History*, p. 65.
7. Rachael Low, *The History of the British Film, 1929–1939*, p. 115.
8. Films made in countries under British Imperial rule were regarded as 'British' for the purposes of the quota.
9. Michael Balcon, *Michael Balcon Presents . . . A Lifetime of Films*, p. 99.
10. See Jeffrey Richards, 'Controlling the Screen: The British Cinema in the 1930s', *History Today*, March 1983, p. 12.
11. Only one other company – British and Dominions – approached the level of production of the two large combines, but it operated solely as a production concern.
12. The name itself with the word 'international' implies this, as did the company trademark displayed at the beginning of a BIP film – Britannia seated in front of a revolving globe.
13. See Ginette Vincendeau, 'Hollywood Babel', *Screen* vol. 29 no. 2, Spring 1988, for a discussion of this phenomenon in Hollywood and Europe.
14. For a detailed analysis of the way in which sound was introduced in Britain see Robert Murphy, 'Coming of Sound to the Cinema in Britain', *Historical Journal of Film, Radio and Television* vol. 4 no. 2, 1984, pp. 143–60. See also Tom Ryall, *Blackmail* (London: BFI, 1993).

15. See John Maxwell's comments in *Kinematograph Weekly*, 25 April 1929, p. 21.
16. Ibid., 27 June 1929, p. 30.
17. See Charles Barr, '*Blackmail*: Silent and Sound', *Sight and Sound*, Spring 1983, for a comparison of the sound and silent versions.
18. Warren, *British Film Studios*, pp. 138–9.
19. Advertisement in *The Kinematograph Year Book 1931*, quoted in Political and Economic Planning, *The British Film Industry*, p. 68.
20. Rachael Low, *The History of the British Film, 1918–1929*, p. 278.
21. Around half the films made at the studio between 1928 and 1937 were based on theatrical sources and even a 'cinematic' director like Hitchcock based six of his ten features for the company on plays.
22. For example, *Kinematograph Weekly*, 29 August 1929, p. 18.
23. Low, *The History of the British Film, 1929–1939*, p. 117.
24. Ibid., pp. 116–17. *Abdul the Damned*, in particular, seems to be a departure from BIP's cost-conscious budgeting policy, but it was a co-production and the then large budget of £500,000 was partly met by co-producer Max Schach.
25. See ibid., p. 142.
26. *Kinematograph Weekly*, 19 May 1932, p. 19.
27. See Geoff Brown, 'A Knight and His Castle', in Jane Fluegel (ed.), *Michael Balcon: The Pursuit of British Cinema*, p. 17.
28. Balcon, *A Lifetime of Films*, pp. 62–3. As at BIP, a high proportion of Gaumont-British films came from the three most popular genres: comedies, *c.* 31 per cent; musicals, *c.* 16 per cent; crime, *c.* 15 per cent.
29. See Andrew Higson, *Waving the Flag: Constructing a National Cinema in Britain*, Chapter 4, for an extended analysis of *Evergreen* in the context of British production strategies of the 1930s.
30. See Low, *The History of the British Film, 1929–1939*, p. 133.
31. Powell made a number of films at Gaumont-British, including *The Fire Raisers* (1933), *The Night of the Party* (1934) and *The Phantom Light* (1935).
32. The budget figure for *Jew Süss* is taken from Sue Harper, *Picturing the Past: The Rise and Fall of the British Costume Film*, p. 31, although both Balcon and Low suggest a lower figure of £100,000.
33. As indicated by his subsequent appointment to head the new MGM-British set up in 1936. However, a number of the key studio decisions, including the internationalist policy and the acquisition of performers and stars such as George Arliss, were taken at board level by the Ostrers and C. M. Woolf rather than by Balcon

himself. See Geoff Brown, 'A Knight and His Castle',
pp. 19–22.

34. See John Sedgwick, 'The Market for Feature Films in
Britain, 1934: A Viable National Cinema'. Sedgwick's
paper is based partly on Simon Rowson's 1936 paper
'A Statistical Survey of the Cinema Industry in Great
Britain in 1934'.

35. See Jeffrey Richards and Dorothy Sheridan, *Mass-
Observation at the Movies*, pp. 33–4, for survey material on
audience preferences during the period.

36. Tony Aldgate, 'British Domestic Cinema of the 1930s', in
Curran and Porter (eds), *British Cinema History*, p. 262.

37. Linda Wood, *British Films 1927–1939*, p. 6.

38. André Bazin, 'The Evolution of Film Language', in Peter
Graham (ed.), *The New Wave*, p. 33.

Bibliography

Balcon, Michael, *Michael Balcon Presents . . . A Lifetime of Films*
(London: Hutchinson, 1969).

Curran, James and Porter, Vincent (eds), *British Cinema History*
(London: Weidenfeld and Nicolson, 1983).

Durgnat, Raymond, *A Mirror for England* (London: Faber and
Faber, 1970).

Fluegel, Jane (ed.), *Michael Balcon: The Pursuit of British Cinema*
(New York: Museum of Modern Art, 1984).

Gifford, Denis, *The British Film Catalogue 1895–1985*
(Newton Abbot and London: David & Charles, 1986).

Grierson, John, 'The Fate of British Films', *The Fortnightly*, July
1937, p. 5.

Harper, Sue, *Picturing the Past: The Rise and Fall of the British
Costume Film* (London: BFI, 1994).

Higson, Andrew, *Waving the Flag: Constructing a National
Cinema in Britain* (Oxford: Clarendon Press, 1995).

Landy, Marcia, *British Genres: Cinema and Society, 1930–1960*
(Princeton, NJ: Princeton University Press, 1991).

Low, Rachael, *The History of the British Film, 1918–1929*
(London: George Allen & Unwin, 1971).

Low, Rachael, *The History of the British Film, 1929–1939*
(London: George Allen & Unwin, 1985).

Political and Economic Planning, *The British Film Industry*
(London: PEP, 1952).

Richards, Jeffrey, *The Age of the Dream Palace: Cinema and
Society in Britain, 1930–39* (London: Routledge, 1984).

Richards, Jeffrey and Sheridan, Dorothy, *Mass-Observation at
the Movies* (London: Routledge & Kegan Paul, 1987).

Rowson, Simon, 'A Statistical Survey of the Cinema Industry
in Great Britain in 1934', *Journal of the Royal Statistical
Society* vol. 99, 1936.

Sedgwick, John, 'The Market for Feature Films in Britain,
1934: A Viable National Cinema', *Historical Journal of Film,
Radio and Television* vol. 14, no. 1, 1994.

Warren, Patricia, *British Film Studios* (London: Batsford, 1995).

Wood, Linda (ed.), *British Films 1927–1939* (London: British
Film Institute Library Services, 1986).

23

Low-budget British Films in the 1930s

LINDA WOOD

The Cinematograph Films Act (1927), which came into effect on 1 January 1928 was interpreted as a *de facto* acknowledgment by the government of the importance to the national interest of an indigenous film-production industry.

However, the film production sector itself lacked the necessary economic clout to strongarm the government into action, and it is unlikely that anything would have happened had not producers successfully wooed the Imperialist/nationalist lobby into their corner. This lobby had powerful friends both within the government and among Conservative backbench MPs. That trade followed film was an article of faith reinforced by US success in both. Business leaders were convinced that if they could show off British wares in British films this would go a long way to fight off US competition. But for the Imperialist lobby it was not simply a matter of trade; the need to promote British cultural values was considered of equal importance.[1]

The Quality Issue

This background is important when looking at the reaction to the films produced in the 1930s. If British films were to fulfil the roles used as the justification for legislation, there would appear to be an implicit commitment to the production of quality films. Poor films would fail to attract audiences overseas, and the association of 'British' with inferior products would not help in the promotion of the nation. Yet the Cinematograph Films Act did not incorporate a quality threshold, despite repeated calls for the inclusion of such a measure. While the Imperial/trade lobby exerted immense influence, a number of counter-pressures were operat-

ing on the government. There was the opposition of the film trade: both the exhibition and the distribution sectors did very nicely out of American films, which had long since proved more popular with audiences than British films. The American film companies had hinted that they were ready to boycott Britain if the burden placed on them was too onerous.

The prevalent political ethos made the Board of Trade keen to avoid any measures that might require a day-to-day involvement in the film industry. Accustomed to dealing with easily quantifiable matters such as weights and measures, it was wary of setting 'quality' guidelines and making value judgments. Since very large sums of money would be needed to build up the film industry and any provision of government finance was rejected from the outset, the Act deliberately excluded anything which might discourage private investment.

However, the government's bland assurances that it was fully behind the efforts to establish a British film industry, and the rhetoric of the production lobby, fostered the illusion that legislation would instantly result in the creation of a British Hollywood. When this didn't happen, blame was laid at the door of the Films Act. In the years that followed it was derided for giving rise to the heinous practice of the quota quickie while failing to help 'legitimate' producers such as Alexander Korda and Michael Balcon who were trying to produce the sort of film envisaged by the Act's promoters.

Quickies were films made at minimal cost – generally £1 per foot – which enabled distributors to comply with the letter of the Films Act while flouting its spirit. The cost of a sixty-minute film (with 35mm film running at ninety feet a minute) would be about £5,400, many times less than that of even a modest British feature production. Criticism of the American companies – widely perceived as being responsible for these films – might not have been so virulent had it not been for the large discrepancy in cost between their British and their Hollywood films. According to Howard T. Lewis, around this time the US companies were spending between $170,000 and $250,000 (£40,000–£65,000 at the then exchange rate) on their Hollywood films.

Because of the distributors' quota – set 2.5 per cent higher than that for exhibitors – an American company like MGM with a slate of forty or fifty of its own films on its books would also have to offer exhibitors four or five British films when the quota was 10 per cent, and eight or ten by the time it was 20 per cent. In order to fulfil these quota requirements the American renters quickly and unanimously adopted the strategy of producing low-cost films of the second-feature class. As early as June 1928, within months of the Act coming into force, the trade press was commenting on the poor-quality films being acquired by the American renters. *Kine Weekly* observed: 'American distributing houses are making arrangements to make British pictures at a low cost incompatible with good quality. These films are doomed to be "duds" before they start.'[2]

Looking at the production schedules for the years that followed, it is possible to pinpoint a handful of films which fall outside the low-cost category: in 1933, for example, Gloria Swanson came to Ealing Studios to make *Perfect Understanding*, whose £70,000 budget exceeded the combined cost of all the other films made at the studio that year. But these were the exceptions that proved the rule, one-offs that never formed part of any coherent policy to produce quality production.

What is less clear, however, is to what extent these cheaply produced films were booked to cinemas. While initially some American distributors seemed prepared to shelve the worst examples and write off their cost as a straight loss, it would appear that others were including them in packages of films being block-booked to cinemas. And as the percentage of British films required to be screened increased with each year, the more these films were shown. In 1932, Seton Margrave, who regularly argued the need for 'quality' British films to save the Empire from disintegrating, pointed out in an article severely criticising American distributors for acquir-

ing sub-standard films that 'now with the quota at 15 per cent this buying-registering-shelving dodge has become too expensive'.[3]

Because the US distributors had become the only significant source of finance for the independent producer the policies they followed acquired a crucial importance. In 1933, for instance, they were responsible for 53 per cent of British films. This key role was not one which they had sought, or welcomed.

The attitude of the American distributors to the Films Act was understandable: they were commercial organisations who owed no loyalty to the British film industry. From their standpoint, they were being forced to use their resources to help foster a rival to their home industry. Moreover, Britain was just one of many markets in which the US majors came under attack for undermining the local industry; and they were very aware that concessions made in one territory were liable to be demanded in others.

In the post-legislation euphoria a large number of film-production companies were floated on the stock exchange. Of these, only two had any real success, Gaumont-British and British International Pictures. They were larger than other British companies, and with their own cinema chains they could guarantee that their productions reached an audience. The remaining companies soon found themselves facing severe financial problems, and bankruptcy became commonplace: it had been drastically underestimated just how much reviving a dormant industry would cost. In the wake of large losses on investments in film, funds from City institutions dried up.

Better British Films

In 1933 the Board of Trade, faced by a well-organised and unrelenting campaign attacking the quality of British films produced under the Films Act, set up an internal inquiry. Its findings, based on British films produced in 1932, provide firm evidence that the vast majority of low-cost films could be laid at the door of the American distributors: sixty out of eighty-three American-sponsored films, compared with fifteen out of seventy-three British films, cost less than £75 per 100 ft (and only eight out of eighty-three American-sponsored films cost over £125 per 100 ft). But the inquiry was not just concerned with cost; it also attempted to assess the entertainment value of films, adopting the points system used by the Cinema Exhibitors Association (CEA), the trade organisation representing exhibitors (every film trade-shown was marked on a scale from one to ten: the 'better' the film, the higher the mark). Surprisingly it found that as many as 45 per cent of the pictures handled by US distributors were 'good programme pictures'.

When looking at the performance of individual companies operating specifically within the low-budget context, the committee discovered considerable variation. United Artists and Paramount had on the whole 'acquired better pictures than most US renters . . . . Although their expenditure has been by no means lavish, they can certainly be regarded as doing their share'. Fox, Radio and Warners had 'a definite policy of producing second features of about 4,000 ft which vary in quality but some of them are acceptable second features for the ordinary cinemas'. Warner Bros.–First National and Fox had both recently set up their own production units with mixed results. MGM was taken to task: 'They have acquired at times good pictures and at others sheer rubbish.' Given that only two out of nine of their films were marked by the CEA at eight points and above, the rubbish appeared to predominate. Universal was castigated as a black spot. 'So far as films made in this country are concerned, they only acquire rubbish.'[4]

Although with the proper resources it is easier to turn out a watchable film, money in itself does not guarantee a 'good' film, nor a low budget automatically result in a 'poor' one. For instance, the MGM film which obtained the company's highest CEA marking was made by Sound City for only £1,100. The CEA points system also reveals that the entertainment value of certain companies' films was far higher than would be expected, given the level of expenditure: at Radio, seven out of ten films were marked eight points or over; at Paramount, all films were seven or over; at Fox, seven out of eleven films received eight or over. Interestingly only three films out of twenty made by Warners were marked at eight points and over, and 'although their films cost more money than Fox's, they are not nearly so good'.

Though warning of the need for continuing vigilance, overall the committee found the progress made by the British film industry to be satisfactory and that the quality of British films was improving. In fact, remarkable progress had been made in the previous five years. Despite the unwillingness of the City to make funds available for film production and despite the unenthusiastic response of the US distributors to their quota obligations, production was expanding rapidly. In the year ending September 1932, while the quota requirement was only 15 per cent, 25 per cent of the films registered were British. A revitalised production sector exuded confidence and was eager to take on new challenges.

The year 1933 marked a turning point in many ways for the British film industry. Certainly from that year on it became possible to detect a greater effort being put into their quota production by the US companies. Whereas in the early years films had been contracted out to a wide range of independent producers, from this point the American companies either set up in-house production operations or became closely tied to one producing outfit. 20th Century-Fox made major improvements to its recently acquired Wembley Studios and instituted a training programme. Warner Bros.–First National upgraded its Teddington Studios and brought over the energetic young producer Irving Asher to run the operation. In October 1935, the trade press carried the story that Universal was to have its own studios at Sound City (Shepperton). In November 1935, Sam Eckman, head of MGM (UK), announced that MGM was to produce 'quality' films in Britain. As adept businessmen, the company chiefs recognised that the time had come to adopt a new strategy.

The situation they faced had drastically altered. The City was once more making finance available to independent British producers. British technicians had learnt their trade and were being supplemented by top European film-makers fleeing the Nazi threat. As the general quality of British films improved, the US distributors could no longer blame any shortfalls in the standard of their quota films on the incompetence of British film-makers. Moreover, the period had witnessed the growth of strong British circuits which were less willing to take the poorer type of quota films. Also, as the quota requirement increased, it made little commercial sense to spend money unproductively and there was an incentive to put the films to better use. A final factor associated with the new vigour displayed by the US companies towards their quota obligation was the imminent expiry of the 1927 Films Act. With good cause to fear what might replace it, the American companies made a belated effort to convince the Board of Trade that they were committed to making good British films.

Low-budget Production

Up to the mid-1930s, if the independent producer was to survive he had little alternative than to take on the making of quota films for the American distributors. Anthony Havelock-Allan, who produced Paramount's quota films at British and Dominions, recalled that its films were usually made for a flat fee:

> The profit to the maker was whether we could supply them to Paramount at a price that enabled us to make a profit. Sometimes if something was especially good we would try and bargain for a little more money than the £6,500. But in the main what we were doing was making them for about £5,000, £5,500. Somehow we managed to make an average of £625 or £500.[5]

The flat-rate system of payment seemed to remove any incentive to make better films – there was no reward for effort or penalty for the lack of it. As Norman Loudon, who ran Shepperton Studios, pointed out: 'The producer hands over the picture to the American distributor with no thought of making additional money and that is what makes a quickie.'[6] Though the system actively encouraged producers out for a quick profit there were few instances of this occurring. Most producers took the only work they could get, the production of low-cost films, and used this as a means of building up their operation, with the long-term objective of moving on to something better.

While the producer would often have liked to make more money available for his productions – after all, it was his name that went on the credits and his reputation which suffered if a film was sub-standard – he faced the problem of convincing a sceptical and unsympathetic American distributor that spending a little more to produce a better film might boost its box-office takings.

Richard Norton typifies the enthusiasm of quota producers at this time, and his experience at United Artists demonstrates the generally negative response to anyone pursuing their duties over-zealously: he was called in to see his boss, Murray Silverstone, who suggested he might be happier with another company. In his autobiography Norton recalled:

> I knew, of course, that Murray wanted to get rid of me. I had got obsessed with the idea of doing something for British films: and of course to Murray, a middle man entirely interested in distribution, and unwillingly saddled with a Quota Act, I was simply a continual nuisance. Every time he looked round, there I was making another picture.[7]

George Pearson, one of Britain's foremost silent directors who during the 30s directed many quota films, observed:

> To make a talking film with £6,000 only to meet the cost of studio space, subject, script, director, technicians, film stock, lights, artistes, overheads, and end up with a profit needed a spartan economy and a slave-driving effort. All vaunting ideas of film as an art had to be abandoned; only as a capable and speedy craftsman could one survive in that feverish and restless environment.[8]

The need for economic stringencies had a range of practical implications for film-makers. Only stories which could be made cheaply were used. The most popular types were comedies, crime/detective stories and domestic melodramas, which required few sets, small casts and no elaborate costumes. There was also a tendency to be conservative in the choice of subject matter as producers wanted to avoid having their films rejected by the American distributors, or a censor quick to ban anything vaguely straying in the direction of sex, violence or politics.

Films were often adaptations of novels or plays which could be quickly converted into film scripts. Terence Rattigan, for instance, wrote a screenplay for Paramount British. But according to Norman Lee, quota quickies proper made wide use of original scripts since these could be bought from unknown writers more cheaply – purportedly for as little as £25 – than the rights of a West End play.[9]

The need to cut financial corners frequently resulted in inadequate preparation time being allowed. John Paddy Carstairs, later a director but at that time a scriptwriter, recalled working on a Columbia picture called *Boomerang* (1934):

> They were in a frightful hurry and simply had to have a complete shooting script; that is the whole picture cut up into screen terms and dialogued all within a week as they had booked studio space. I agreed to take on the job provided I was given every kind of clerical assistance – a relay of girls for dictation and typists available at all hours of the day and night to bat out the stuff. The picture was no world beater, but the reviews were favourable and I had the satisfaction of doing the whole job within three days.[10]

There are innumerable references in accounts of film-making during this period to writers sitting in a corner and changing the script as filming proceeded. While the situation was not an ideal one, there comes across a sense of pride in the ability to do a good job of work under difficult circumstances.

Career Opportunities

Although economic expediency meant that directors rarely had the opportunity to rehearse their casts properly, good performances could markedly reduce the damage arising from other deficiencies. Consequently, producers were usually prepared to be a little more generous in their budgeting for casts than for other areas. Bernard Vorhaus, who directed a couple of quota quickies at Twickenham, recalled that studio boss Julius Hagen

> left me completely free to choose who I wanted so long as it wasn't wildly expensive. One thing they were quite ready to pay money for was to engage good actors. You had to shoot with them damn fast. He didn't mind them getting a lot of money a day as long as there were only a few days involved.[11]

Indeed producers were fortunate in that they could turn to the rich array of talent provided by the theatre, and stage actors were relatively cheap to hire. Jack Hawkins recalled the time he was working on the remake of *The Lodger* in 1932:

> When I was drawing my £8 a day during the month I was filming, I little thought that in future years I would be earning £100,000 a year. After all, at a time

A rich array of theatrical talent: A. W. Baskcomb and Barbara Everest in Maurice Elvey's *The Lodger* (1932)

when the average wage in Britain was £2.10s, £8 a day was a princely sum indeed.[12]

Because of the high stakes at play when it came to big-budget film-making, producers would generally try to reduce their risk by using established stars, and it was exceptional for an unknown to be given a lead role. Producers of low-cost films were prepared to be a little more experimental – apart from anything else they could not afford the salaries commanded by the top players. Consequently many British actors and actresses – for example Jack Hawkins, Jessica Tandy, Merle Oberon, Geraldine Fitzgerald, John Mills, James Mason and Margaret Rutherford – gained valuable experience and exposure early in their careers by appearing in low-budget films. Ida Lupino from Twickenham Studios, Richard Greene and Roddy McDowall from Wembley and Errol Flynn from Teddington were given Hollywood contracts on the strength of their performances in low-budget British films. There were many more. Editor Peter Tanner recounts that while he was at Wembley the studio was always experimenting with young actors, and all the pictures went to Fox in America. Low-budget production played the vitally important role of allowing the industry to find out whether particular actors photographed well or came across sympathetically. The players themselves were very much aware of the possibility of being asked to appear in 'quality' films if they were seen by the right person. John Mills recalls of his part in *The Ghost Camera* (1933):

> I liked the script and I thought my part was outstanding – dramatic scenes, accused of murder, wrongly of course – and felt I had a chance of really making a mark. By this time I was fascinated by the new medium and decided that, as I'd turned down the chance of becoming a Hollywood film star, nothing was going to stop me from becoming an English one.[13]

The introduction of a quota requirement had resulted in a substantially increased demand for film personnel, both on and off screen. When it came to finding their actors, producers could call on theatre, music hall and radio. While they still needed to learn how to adjust to working for the camera, these actors were relatively skilled before they passed through the studio gate. However, there was no equivalent pool of trained and experienced technicians in Britain. The shortfall had to be met through the import of personnel, initially from Hollywood, subsequently in the shape of émigrés from Hitler's Germany and elsewhere in Europe.

The Love Test (Michael Powell, 1935)

Michael Powell made over twenty low-budget films in the 1930s, twelve of which survive. They are remarkably various, ranging from Agatha Christie-like whodunit *The Night of the Party* (1934) and Bertie Wooster-like comedy *Lazybones* (1935), to lurid criminal dramas *Rynox* (1931) and *The Fire Raisers* (1933), to neat comedy thriller *The Phantom Light* (1935) and serious shipyard drama *Red Ensign* (1934). The two most interesting are *Something Always Happens* (1934), an enjoyably optimistic tale about a penniless adventurer (played by Ian Hunter, a Powell stalwart whose cheery masculinity is similar to that of Roger Livesey in later Powell and Pressburger films) who comes up with the idea of developing a network of user-friendly petrol stations; and *The Love Test*, where jealous men plot to sabotage the career of a hard-working young female chemist who is promoted over their heads.

Both films benefit from the efficient production regimes instituted by the American companies – *Something Always Happens* for Warner Bros. at Teddington, *The Love Test* at the Fox-British studio in Wembley. *The Love Test*'s story is thinner and the half-dozen sets allowed the film would hardly seem to encourage visual pyrotechnics, but Powell is flexible enough to turn things to his advantage. He boosts his supporting cast with bright beginners Bernard Miles and Googie Withers (who reappear in more significant roles in *One of Our Aircraft Is Missing*, 1942); he encourages his talented cameraman Arthur Crabtree to track around the chemistry laboratory, displaying the paraphernalia of this modern, white-coated side of British industry; and he visualises the problem the chemists have to solve – finding a way of fire-proofing celluloid (as well as indicating their sadistic attitude to women) – by making the test samples cute but alarmingly combustible dollies.

The leading man John Gregg is sulky, virginal and vulnerable, qualities rarely seen in Powell's men; but as played by Louis Hayward (who went on to play

Can men be trusted?: Judy Gunn ponders the possibility that there might be more to life than chemistry in *The Love Test*

'The Saint' in Hollywood) he is convincing and like-able. Heroine Mary Lee (Judy Gunn) is a very crude precursor of the strong women of later Powell and Pressburger films (she tells the hapless Gregg that she'd like the world to be run like a beehive, with useless males stung to death) and she proves to be remarkably gullible. But her naivety is well matched to that of Gregg – who despite his admiration for her allows himself to be drawn into a plot to seduce Mary from her single-minded dedication to work. While he is taught to kiss (by Googie Withers's irre-pressibly sensual Minnie), she allows herself to be made up by her glamorous neighbour, her face framed in languorous close-up in a sequence that prefigures the transformation of Sister Ruth in *Black Narcissus* (1947).

Mary's access to her femininity proves beneficent: from being 'a serious-minded little frump' 'with all the appeal of a Bunsen burner' she becomes a swish beauty without any surrender of her independence; Gregg's defiance of his male colleagues has more painful con-sequences. They use his part in the plot to blacken his name with Mary, who angrily rejects him; he is sacked when his equipment is tampered with and causes an explosion; and he is locked in the boiler room as a bur-glar when he breaks back into the lab to perfect the fire-proofing formula which will save Mary's job. But as in many subsequent Powell films, this odd but like-able couple are allowed to overcome the obstacles keeping them apart. Profundity might be too much to expect from a 'quota quickie', but Powell imbues this simple story with enough resonance, visual flair, and sly humour to make *The Love Test* a very satisfying little film.

FURTHER READING

Steve Chibnall, *Quota Quickies: The Birth of the British 'B' Film* (London: BFI, 2007).

Michael Powell, *A Life in Movies* (London: Heinemann, 1986).

Most British technicians accepted that they would have to go through a training period, and the expan-sion in production brought about by the 1927 Films Act provided them with the opportunity to be trained by film-makers of international standing. When making the transition to editor, cameraman, etc., they would hone their skills on low-budget productions. Oscar-winning cinematographer Oswald Morris recalled of Wembley:

> During those two or three years at Fox I was pro-moted from assistant to operating. But what we did was that we alternated. On one picture I was allowed to operate and the assistant, he'd assist, and on the next picture he would operate and I would assist. They insisted we did this but it was quite good training.[14]

Among the directors who got their initial directing experience through working on films commissioned for quota purposes were Michael Powell and Walter Forde. Other directors who first learnt about film-making from working as technicians on low-budget productions included Michael Relph, Thorold Dickinson, Guy Green, David MacDonald, Ronald Neame and Leslie Norman. Frank Launder worked on BIP's low-budget Josser films and was briefly in charge

of the script department at Shepperton. Adrian Brunel concluded:

> For most British film-makers, it was this or nothing . . . many technicians and artists got continuity of employment for the first time and became expert performers in their various fields, a number of them graduating to big production . . . quickies became a training ground for film-makers.[15]

Although British films of this period were widely dis-paraged, many people – from glamour seekers to intel-lectuals – were attracted to the idea of working in film-making. A few dilettantes found their way in, but the work was demanding and only the tough and the dedicated were able to stay the course. Working condi-tions were unpleasant. Studios were icy cold in winter and unbearably hot in summer. The producers' need to maximise studio resources resulted in very tight shoot-ing schedules which often involved working into the early hours of the morning. Indeed, many of the studios on the outskirts of London had sleeping facilities for those who were required to work after public transport had closed down. Yet despite strenuous working condi-tions, all the evidence indicates that those working in films were capable, committed and even enthusiastic. Director Bernard Vorhaus recalled:

At Twickenham it was extraordinary that the crews
had considerable enthusiasm. I say that because they
were so overworked. The films were knocked out in a
ridiculously short time. When a director finished one
of these films, certainly terribly exhausted, he could
have a rest; next morning the crew were immediately
on to another. It was extraordinary they made the
effort they did. If they saw a director was trying to
make something good and not just churn out footage
they responded marvellously.[16]

Although there were grumbles, mainly about the
absence of overtime payment, most film workers
knew that, while the producers made a better living,
they were on the whole unable to make better
resources available because they could not afford to,
not because they were milking the system. Many who
worked in films at the time have stories of the ingenious ways they got round problems created by
working with very basic equipment: home-made
attachments to cameras, makeshift fog machines, dub-
bing from gramophones, wall sections which could
be slotted together and rearranged to create whatever
set effect was required. Low-budget films benefited
enormously from the dedication of the people working on them.

Quota Quickies?

At times it seems that all British films made in the 30s
that fall outside a handful of prestigious titles get
lumped together under the designation quota quickie.
And were it not for the pejorative undertones of cheap
and nasty, it would be a very useful banner to cover
what turns out to be a wide and complex continuum
within the low-cost spectrum. Early quota films suffered from the fact that they had been made by
fledgeling film-makers in inadequately equipped studios who were trying to come to terms with the new
medium of sound, but the later ones were far more
technically assured. Throughout the 30s some dreadful
films continued to be made: renters discovered a
sudden shortfall and deliberately went out to buy
something as cheaply as possible; producers with commissions for six films found that by the time they
reached the sixth most of their fees had gone, so they
knocked out the last film with minimal resources.
Some of these films got shelved, to the relief of all concerned; others deserved to be shelved but were
screened, to the detriment of the reputation of British
films. But this was a minority; more typical were the

solidly made second features, and judged as such they
were of a reasonable standard. In the era before television when there was little by way of home entertainment, the supporting feature was a welcome addition
to the programme. And it often incorporated distinctively British elements, such as popular music-hall and
radio performers.

While the American companies deliberately pursued a policy of producing low-cost films which offered
no competition to their own first feature, they did not
maliciously cut costs to the core. Certainly they paid
their staff better than the British majors: Oswald Morris
recalled that when he left BIP for Wembley his salary as
a camera assistant doubled. Similarly Ronald Neame
remembered that when he moved to Wembley 'they
offered me the fantastic salary of £25 a week'.[17] Once
they set up their own in-house production operation,
the American outfits set about making their quota films
with the same professionalism that they applied to their
Hollywood films.

The quota quickie officially came to an end with
the passing of the Cinematograph Films Act (1938),
which introduced a minimum cost requirement. The
government, guided by interest groups primarily interested in promoting the production of 'quality' films,
omitted to include measures necessary to safeguard the
'bread-and-butter' end of the film-production industry
and production slumped.

Although the Cinematograph Films Act of 1927 had
failed to incorporate the full scope of measures envisaged by its supporters, it had provided a major stimulus
to British film production. In 1927 only twenty-seven
films were made in Britain; by 1936 there were over
200. In 1928, the average cost of films produced in
Britain was £5,374; by 1932, it was £9,250; and in
1936 it was £18,000. Average figures disguise the wide
variation in costs between films but do give an indication of the steady increase in the general quality of
British films during these years. While giving birth to
the quota quickie, the Films Act was also responsible for
building up the kind of infrastructure required to support first-feature production on a regular rather than an
ad hoc basis.

It had been unrealistic to expect the outcome of
political intervention to be the transformation of the
British film industry from being one of the most backward in Europe into becoming one which could
instantaneously rival Hollywood. But as Anthony
Havelock-Allan has pointed out, 'On the basis of these
small pictures, a sort of industry grew up.'[18]

Notes

1. Fifteen years later the ideological importance of film was still being put forward as a reason for government involvement: 'A film production industry is essential to this country both in peace and war for purposes of direct and indirect propaganda, commercial advertising and prestige.' Public Records Office, BT64/61/17793/1941.
2. *Kine Weekly*, 21 June 1928, p. 83.
3. *Daily Mail*, 1 April 1932.
4. Public Records Office, BT64/97.
5. Anthony Havelock-Allan, BECTU History Project.
6. Evidence to the Moyne Committee, 12 May 1936.
7. Richard Norton, *Silver Spoon* (London, Hutchinson, 1954), p. 184.
8. George Pearson, *Flashback*, p. 193.
9. Norman Lee, *Money for Film Stories* (London: Pitman, 1937), pp. 71, 75.
10. John Paddy Carstairs, *Honest Injun*, p. 85.
11. Interview with author, 23 October 1986.
12. Jack Hawkins, *Anything for a Quiet Life* (London: Elm Tree Books, 1973), p. 49.
13. John Mills, *Up in the Clouds – Gentlemen Please* (London: Weidenfeld and Nicolson, 1980), p. 117.
14. Oswald Morris, BECTU History Project.
15. Adrian Brunel, *Nice Work: The Story of Thirty Years in British Film Production*, p.166.
16. Interviewed, 23 October 1986.
17. Ronald Neame, BECTU History Project.
18. Anthony Havelock-Allan, BECTU History Project.

Bibliography

Ackland, Rodney and Grant, Elspeth, *The Celluloid Mistress* (London: Allan Wingate, 1954).

Brunel, Adrian, *Nice Work: The Story of Thirty Years in British Film Production* (London: Forbes Robertson, 1949).

Carstairs, John Paddy, *Honest Injun* (London: Hurst and Blackett, 1942).

Chibnall, Steve, *Quota Quickies: The Birth of the British 'B' Film* (London: BFI, 2007).

Dean, Basil, *Mind's Eye* (London: Hutchinson, 1973).

Klingender, F. D. and Legg, Stuart, *Money behind the Screen* (London: Lawrence & Wishart, 1937).

Kulik, Karol, *Alexander Korda: The Man Who Could Work Miracles* (London: W. H. Allen, 1975).

Lee, Norman, *Log of a Film Director* (London: Quality Press, 1949).

Low, Rachael, *The History of British Film 1929–1939* (London: George Allen & Unwin, 1985).

Moyne Committee, The, Cinematograph Films Act 1927: Report of a Committee Appointed by the Board of Trade (London: HMSO, 1937).

Pearson, George, *Flashback* (London: George Allen & Unwin, 1957).

Powell, Michael, *A Life in Movies* (London: Heinemann, 1986).

Richards, Jeffrey, *The Age of the Dream Palace: Cinema and Society in Britain 1930–39* (London: Routledge & Kegan Paul, 1984).

Richards, Jeffrey (ed.), *The Unknown 1930s: An Alternative History of British Cinema 1929–1939* (London: I. B. Tauris, 1998).

Robinson, Martha, *Continuity Girl* (London: Robert Hale, 1937).

Shafter, Stephen Craig, *Enter the Dream House: The British Film Industry and the Working Classes in Depression England 1929–39* (University of Illinois at Urbana-Champaign, 1982).

Wilcox, Herbert, *25,000 Sunsets* (London: Bodley Head, 1967).

Wood, Alan, *Mr Rank* (London: Hodder & Stoughton, 1952).

PART FOUR

British Cinema from World War II to the 70s

24

The Heart of Britain: British Cinema at War

ROBERT MURPHY

Patriotism and the Brains Trust, fighting the Nazis and lunchtime concerts were different expressions of the brief period when the English people felt that they were a truly democratic community.[1]

The Legacy of the War

It is easy to look back on World War II with a rosy glow of nostalgia, particularly while watching films such as *The Way Ahead*, *In Which We Serve* and *Millions Like Us* which seem to capture that ethos of people pulling together, sacrificing class boundaries in the common effort to defeat the enemy. The good-heartedness and optimism, the striving towards a better society, make it all seem so admirable that it is easy to forget the boredom, the queues, the shortages, the general inconvenience of life under the blackout and the Blitz. Some 35,000 members of the merchant navy, 60,000 civilians and 300,000 servicemen and women lost their lives in the war and if these numbers look small compared to the millions of Russians killed or the millions of Jews massacred in concentration camps, they are still huge enough to leave a deep scar. Most people lost neighbours, friends, family, and bombing brought the war home to everybody except the few who escaped to quiet little hotels in Cornwall and the Lake District. Yet for many people the war was a high point of intensity and excitement when things seemed possible which wouldn't normally be possible. And these wartime films are something more than empty propaganda: the characters wrestle with difficult moral and physical problems, and when they win through it is at some cost.

Several of the films deal with the transforming effect of the war, turning timid, ineffectual civilians into warriors and war workers, as if the war were a blessing which enabled people to realise their potential. The protagonists of *Millions Like Us*, *Perfect Strangers*, *The Gentle Sex*, *The Way Ahead*, *The Bells Go Down*, *The Lamp Still Burns*, *English without Tears* become more confident and capable, more mature and fulfilled, even when they have to endure tragedy and loss. Films like *Ships with Wings*, *We Dive at Dawn* and *The Rake's Progress* have characters who redeem themselves through heroic self-sacrifice. But more typical of the later war films is the stoical, unmelodramatic death of Jacko the newsagent in '*Fires Were Started –*' (1943), holding the ladder steady so that his injured colleague can be saved, or of Tommy in *The Bells Go Down*, sharing a fag with the fire chief who reprimanded him for smoking on the job, before they both plunge to a fiery death.

The war opened up a range of experiences – travel, the use of complex machinery, meetings with people from different regions and backgrounds – which would not have been open to most people in peacetime. The normal patterns of family life were disrupted, but the war made possible a greater range and availability of sexual liaisons. The separation from regular partners, the removal of the restraining influence of parents and neighbours, the opportunities for chance meetings at dances and improvised get-togethers, the cover of the blackout, the feeling of 'live now, for tomorrow we die', worked a profound change in sexual mores.[2]

War and Romance

British wartime films reflect these changes, though, in chaste and diluted forms. Chance meetings in *Piccadilly*

Incident (during an air raid), *In Which We Serve* (on a crowded train), *Millions Like Us* (at a dance organised for the factory women and the men from the nearby RAF base) lead to romance. But caring, committed relationships, not brief sexual flings, grow out of these meetings. The war effort tends to nudge romance out of its central position in the narrative, and wartime films either under-romanticise their lovers, making them ordinary, decent and not very glamorous, or mark their relationship as passionate but impossible, using the war as a device to hurl them away from one another.

In several films, harmonious, friendly relationships between men and women are stressed. Maggie (Rosamund John) and her exhausted colleagues in *The Gentle Sex* find their already crowded railway carriage invaded by noisy, inquisitive soldiers, but she quickly makes friends with them and berates the sourpuss who complains that they are loud and disruptive. Alison (Sheila Sim), threatened by the 'glueman' in *A Canterbury Tale* (1944), forges solid, non-sexual friendships with her fellow 'pilgrims' Bob and Peter. When romantic relationships do develop they are easily confused with friendship. In *Perfect Strangers*, Robert (Robert Donat) and Cathy (Deborah Kerr), separated by the war and transformed into dynamic, successful people, both think they have found someone more suitable to their new selves. But when they finally meet again and realise that they have both grown and changed, their marriage is redeemed and their new romances downgraded into friendship. In *Waterloo Road*, Tilly (Joy Shelton) is vulnerable to seduction precisely because she thinks smooth-talking Ted Purvis (Stewart Granger) is a sympathetic friend whom she can trust and confide in.

Though the war brings lovers together in films, it also endangers their happiness: the ever-present threat of death, the separation that leads to misunderstandings and new temptations, the injuries (Gordon Jackson's blindness in *The Captive Heart*, for example) that cast doubt on the viability of a relationship. Here ordinariness is no guarantee against tragedy, as Celia (Patricia Roc) in *Millions Like Us* and Walter Hardy (Bernard Miles) in *In Which We Serve* discover. The possibility of relationships between working-class men and upper-middle-class women is explored in *Millions Like Us*, where the antagonism between languid, lazy Jennifer (Anne Crawford) and her dour, pipe-smoking foreman (Eric Portman) flowers into something akin to love; and in *English Without Tears*, where posh Joan Heseltine (Penelope Dudley Ward) is

united with her ex-butler (Michael Wilding), whom the war has transformed into an officer and a gentleman.[3] GIs are also shown as acceptable partners for respectable English women in *I Live in Grosvenor Square* and *The Way to the Stars*, but in both cases they are fliers whose planes are shot down, enabling them to die heroic deaths before any cross-cultural complications set in.

Representing Britain
British wartime cinema is characterised by realism, but as Sidney Bernstein points out:

> Story films . . . are bound to concentrate for their subjects to a large extent on violence and passion, because such is the raw material of drama. Except for isolated attempts to break the rule, as with *Millions Like Us*, films deal with the exceptional in life rather than the usual. It is the unusual which exercises a strong appeal to the sense of curiosity which is innate in us.[4]

During the war even the most mundane people could find themselves involved in life-endangering adventures, and the exceptional was the usual. Films that dealt with such wartime adventures had to pay attention to detail if they were not to offend the credulity of a knowledgeable audience. Realism was an appropriate method for telling the story of the war – though the popularity of films like *Dangerous Moonlight* and *Mrs Miniver*, which present a blatantly romanticised view of the war, showed that audiences were not averse to a degree of glamorisation.

Gainsborough's popular melodramas, with the exception of *Love Story* and the framing story of *The Man in Grey*, ignored the war and were critically disparaged for their escapism. But their star-crossed lovers torn apart by conflicting demands are subject to the same burdens of sacrifice and loss as the protagonists of war films. William Whitebait, film critic of the *New Statesman*, wrote warmly about *Western Approaches*, a flagship of the new documentary realist cinema, before turning to *Madonna of the Seven Moons*, one of Gainsborough's most improbable melodramas, starring Phyllis Calvert as the wife of an Italian banker who periodically changes identity and becomes the gypsy mistress of a Florentine bandit. He complains that 'we slip back almost as far as it is possible to slip. It is notably bad. . . . Everything in *Madonna of the Seven Moons* is treacly: characters, dialogue, situation.'[5]

Madonna certainly has none of the virtues of *Western Approaches* (meticulous attention to detail, a believable set of characters, an exciting but authentic-seeming story), but despite being a farrago of impossible events it deals with deep and disturbing issues of sexual identity and the expression of seemingly inexpressible desires.

Andrew Higson argues that 'Under the unique circumstances of World War II, the documentary idea came to inform both much commercial film-making practice and the dominant discourses of film criticism.'[6] But this is more true of film criticism than of commercial films: what was 'realist' was assumed mistakenly to be 'documentary'. Realism was not simply transfused from the documentary movement to the commercial industry; it was something that came from greater involvement with the real world by film-makers from both sectors. Humphrey Jennings, writing to his wife from Wales where he was making *The Silent Village* (1943), told her:

> I really never thought to live to see the honest Christian and Communist principles daily acted on as a matter of course by a large number of British – I won't say English – people living together. Not merely honesty, culture, manners, practical socialism, but real life: with passion and tenderness and comradeship and heartiness all combined. . . . On this I feel at least that we have really begun to get close to the men – not just as individuals – but also as a class – with an understanding between us: so they don't feel we are just photographing them as curios or wild animals or 'just for propaganda'.[7]

The movement towards realism was part of a more general feeling that it was right and necessary for the cinema to show people from all walks of life pulling together for the common good. This ethos penetrates such disparate films as *The Bells Go Down* and '*Fires Were Started –*', *Millions Like Us* and *In Which We Serve*. People felt this way – that differences and difficulties could be overcome – at least some of the time during World War II. Undoubtedly there was betrayal, injustice, abuse and exploitation, but people were fighting a cruel and oppressive enemy and they gained knowledge and self-respect in that struggle. If this was truly a 'people's war', then films can be seen to reflect, as much as they helped to create, the mood of populist pulling together.

With the survival of Britain at stake, it became possible to ask fundamental questions. In his BBC

The England of unemployment, misery, deprivation and squalor: John Baxter's *Love on the Dole* (1941)

'Postscript' broadcast on 21 July 1940, J. B. Priestley invited his audience to consider whether the concept of private property wasn't now outdated; and George Orwell was convinced that 'We cannot win the war without introducing Socialism, nor establish Socialism without winning the war.'[8] In 1941 Orwell saw this as a winnable struggle: 'Everywhere in England you can see a ding-dong battle ranging to and fro – in Parliament and in the Government, in the factories and the armed forces, in the pubs and the air-raid shelters, in the newspapers and on the radio.'[9] In December 1942 the government published the Beveridge Report, which outlined plans for a comprehensive welfare scheme: children would be financially supported by means of a family allowance; a national health service would be provided; and the unemployed would be eligible for benefits until they could return to work. The report sold 635,000 copies, and a Gallup poll two weeks after its publication reported that nine out of ten people thought its proposals should be carried out. The most popular policy of a new political party, Common Wealth, launched in July 1942, was full and immediate implementation of Beveridge's proposals. Priestley, who had helped to create the party, resigned in the autumn, but Common Wealth won its first by-election victory in April 1943 and continued to harry and embarrass the government until it was swamped by the Labour landslide in July 1945.

Anthony Howard, writing in 1963, thought that:

> 1945 was not merely a political watershed: it had at least the potentiality for being a social one too. The war had not only buried the dinner jacket – it had

reduced famous public schools to pale, evacuated shadows, it had destroyed the caste system in the Civil Service, it had eroded practically every traditional social barrier in Britain.[10]

But the new Labour government was saddled with a grossly distorted economy, a huge American debt, and an Empire it could no longer afford to police, and social change proved more difficult to sustain than had been hoped. Howard concludes that 'Far from introducing a "social revolution" the overwhelming Labour victory of 1945 brought about the greatest restoration of traditional social values since 1660.'[11] Howard's judgment is coloured by the impatient desire for political and social change prevalent in the early 1960s, after more than a decade of Conservative government. Fifty years on from the end of the war, the post-war Labour government can be seen to have worked a massive transformation of British society. The post-war desire for tranquillity and affluence may have slowed things down, but there was no return to the rigidly class-divided society of the 30s.

English Journeys

The struggle between traditionalism and radicalism – often ending up as an odd mixture of both – can be seen in the ways in which film-makers attempted to represent Britain on the screen. As Antonia Lant explains, the way in which British society, character and culture should be portrayed was not something that could be easily agreed upon:

> War produced the need for images of national iden-
> tity, both on the screen and in the audience's mind,
> but British national identity was not simply on tap,
> waiting to be imaged, somehow rooted in British
> geology. 'National characteristics' could not simply be
> 'infused into a national cinema', however much later
> writers wished that version of the story to be true.
> Instead, the stuff of national identity had to be win-
> nowed and forged from traditional aesthetic and nar-
> rative forms, borrowed from the diverse conventions
> of melodrama, realism, and fantasy, and transplanted
> from literature, painting, and history, into the
> cinema.[12]

Film-makers were very aware of these problems. Ian Dalrymple, the producer of *The Lion Has Wings* (1939), a propaganda film rushed out by Alexander Korda in the early months of the war, tried to give some durability to

the film by concentrating on abstract virtues: 'I opened our film with the suggestion that there was a British ideology arising from our national character; that it was valuable to the world; and that it should not be lost.'[13] Merle Oberon's final speech – 'We must keep our land, darling. We must keep our freedom. We must fight for what we believe in: truth and beauty and fair play and kindness' – which she declaims to her snoozing husband under an oak tree, now seems risible. But the picture of Britain conjured up by the film's documentary footage is more persuasive.

The new flats, happy people, swimming pools and health centres seen in *The Lion Has Wings* belie our view of the 30s as a depressed and demoralised decade. The evils of unemployment, the Jarrow March, the Means Test, were an important part of the 1930s, but so too were economic growth and rising living standards for those in employment. J. B. Priestley, in his 1933 *English Journey*, discovered three Englands, one of which was something like that depicted in *The Lion Has Wings*:

> This is the England of arterial and by-pass roads, of
> filling stations and factories that look like exhibition
> buildings, of giant cinemas and dance halls and cafés,
> bungalows with tiny garages, cocktail bars,
> Woolworths, motor coaches, wireless, hiking, factory
> girls looking like actresses, greyhound racing and dirt
> tracks, swimming pools and everything given away for
> cigarette coupons.[14]

This England was confined to prosperous pockets of the country, however, and could not properly represent the nation. A national identity which attempted to build upon it would contradict the reality of most people's lives in England, not to mention the rest of the United Kingdom. Priestley's second England was

> nineteenth-century England, the industrial England
> of coal, iron, steel, cotton, wool, railways; of thousands
> of rows of little houses all alike, sham Gothic
> churches, square-faced chapels, Town Halls,
> Mechanics' Institutes, mills, foundries, warehouses,
> refined watering-places, Pier Pavilions, Family and
> Commercial Hotels, Literary and Philosophical
> Societies, back-to-back houses, detached villas with
> monkey trees, Grill Rooms, railway stations, slag-
> heaps and 'tips', dock roads, Refreshment Rooms,
> doss-houses, Unionist or Liberal Clubs, cindery waste
> ground, mill chimneys, slums, fried-fish shops, public
> houses with red blinds, bethels in corrugated iron,

good-class draper's and confectioners' shops, a cynically devastated countryside, sooty dismal little towns, and still sootier grim fortress-like cities.[15]

This is the England of unemployment, misery, deprivation and squalor, the England depicted in John Baxter's adaptation of *Love on the Dole* (1941) and Norman Walker's *Hard Steel* (1942), but in precious few other British films. During the war full employment, high wages, factories working to full capacity brought it back to life. But it still seemed grim, the 'dark satanic mills' of Blake's 'Jerusalem', not something to celebrate. Humphrey Jennings's *The Heart of Britain* (1941), which in contrast to most wartime documentaries is set in the industrial Midlands and North, concludes with a warning: 'Out of the valleys of power and the rivers of industry will come the answer to the German challenge, and the Nazis will learn once and for all that no one with impunity troubles the heart of Britain.' But the film's fiery furnaces and smoking factory chimneys are outweighed by images of concert halls and cathedrals.

The Heart of Britain?

If there was an England worth fighting for, it seemed more likely to lie in the countryside – in what was left of England's green and pleasant land. Priestley had seen rural England in 1933, and had not been impressed:

Old England, the country of the cathedrals and minsters, and manor houses and inns, of Parson and Squire; guide-book and quaint highways and byways England . . . we all know this England, which at its best cannot be improved upon in this world. That is as a country to lounge about in; for a tourist who can afford to pay a fairly stiff price for a poorish dinner, an inconvenient bedroom and lukewarm water in a small brass jug.[16]

He concludes that 'It has long since ceased to earn its living.' But the myth of an idyllic rural England was important to both right- and left-wing ideologies. Conservative nostalgia for a stable, hierarchical society where everyone knew their place ('the poor man with his yard of ale, the rich man in his castle', as Tommy Trinder mockingly sings in the 1944 Ealing film *Champagne Charlie*) had to be set against an equally powerful left-wing yearning for a time when every man had his acre of land and his pig. William Morris and the Arts and Crafts movement, Robert Blatchford's *Merrie England* (1894) – described by G. D. H. Cole as 'the most

effective piece of popular socialist propaganda ever written' – led directly to the Clarion Clubs, the mass trespasses on the moors and mountains of the Peak District, and the innumerable working-class hiking and cycling clubs. One can glimpse this working-class enthusiasm for the countryside in *Love on the Dole*, when Larry asks Sally to come out with him on a Sunday ramble with the Labour Club. Relaxing on a hillside, she is overwhelmed by the beauty of the countryside, declaring, 'Oh, I never knew anywhere could be so lovely. It doesn't seem that this and Hankey Park can be same world.'

There was something for everyone in the countryside. Right- and left-wing versions of the myth were by no means mutually exclusive. Angus Calder draws a composite picture:

The ideal village – it may be in Sussex or in the Cotswolds, or in Jane Austen's Hampshire – contains a pleasant Anglican vicar, an affable squire, assorted professionals, tradesmen and craftsmen, many of whom will be 'characters', plus a complement of sturdy yeomen and agricultural workers learned in old country lore. It has a green, on which the village team plays cricket, with the squire or his son as captain.[17]

The reality of country life between the wars was very different. The import of grain from North and South America meant that small-scale British farms could only compete in the most fertile areas. Some switched to livestock farming, but not enough to prevent a general agricultural depression between the wars. Farm labourers suffered unemployment just as urban workers did. When they were working, wages were low and picturesque thatched cottages concealed primitive and squalid living conditions. There was very little mechanisation of farming and many rural areas were still without gas and electricity in 1939. Drains, ditches and fences were neglected, water meadows fell into disrepair and disuse, and: 'In almost every part of Britain, there were large tracts of total dereliction, where bracken, gorse and briars had encroached on good grassland, or where fertile soil had been abandoned because it paid no one to cultivate it.'[18]

War transformed the countryside. The dangers to shipping and the need to preserve foreign exchange made it imperative that Britain grow its own food rather than import it. Farmers were encouraged (by a subsidy of £2 per acre) to plough up grassland. War Agricultural Committees ensured that derelict farms were brought back into production, forests were cleared, fenland drained. In 1939 there were 12 million acres of arable land; by 1944 this had increased to 18 million acres. Agricultural workers who were called up were more than replaced by the 80,000-strong Women's Land Army and the 40,000 Italian prisoners-of-war who were set to work on the land. Mechanisation helped too. The number of tractors increased from 56,000 in 1939 to 253,000 by January 1946. According to Angus Calder, 'A degree of modernisation had occurred in six years of war which might have taken decades in peacetime.'[19]

During the war the countryside became less remote, the divide between town and country less sharp. Army camps and RAF bases rapidly spread over what might once have been isolated rural areas. If most soldiers and airmen confined themselves to the local pubs, land girls and evacuees permeated the marrow of rural existence, and no film set in the countryside seems complete without them. In the towns, the blackout reclaimed the night, parks and waste ground were utilised for allotments, vegetables replaced flowers in gardens and pigs and chickens proliferated.

This Pleasant Isle

Calder's caustic judgment that 'the more picturesque parts of Britain were inhabited by increasingly demoralised and often remarkably incestuous communities' was unlikely to have been true of many parts of the country in the latter days of the war.[20] But it does strike a chord with David MacDonald's *This England*, released in March 1941. In the present-day village where the film begins, the villagers seem servilely deferential to their squire, and flashbacks to key points in history – 1086, 1588, 1804 and 1918 – are unexpectedly gloomy. In the first episode the villagers murder the Norman lord, in the second a shipwrecked gypsy is hounded to her death, in the third the lord of the manor complains about 'this sticky, clinging, damnable creeper of an English past', and in the fourth the three central characters are too disillusioned to join in the jingoistic celebrations at the end of World War I. Perhaps, with the threat of invasion imminent, it was impossible in *This England* to articulate a satisfying and convincing rural myth. A group of films made between 1942 and 1944 were much more successful.

In *Went the Day Well?* (1942), directed by the documentary film-maker Alberto Cavalcanti for Ealing Studios, a platoon of soldiers who arrive unexpectedly in a typical English village turn out to be German paratroopers in disguise. The villagers are chirpy and do not

A resolutely democratic rural community: *Tawny Pipit*
(Bernard Miles and Charles Sunders, 1944)

seem to have incestuous relations. They appear to have adapted to the war and to the modern world but they are a little too comfortable in the security of their idyllic community. The Home Guard refuses to heed the warning of the church bell which signals that Germans have landed, and are shot down as they cycle along a leafy lane. The postmistress's distress call is ignored by chattering switchboard girls in the next village and she is bayoneted before they bother to answer. Most significantly, no one can bring themselves to believe that Oliver Wilsford, the gentlemanly leader of the Home Guard, could be a traitor – except the clergyman's daughter, who finally overcomes her romantic illusions about him, faces up to the truth, and kills him.

Tawny Pipit (1943), directed by the actor Bernard Miles for Filippo del Giudice's company, Two Cities, is about a recuperating airman and his nurse who discover a couple of rare pipits and mobilise a village community against an array of threats which might prevent the birds from successfully hatching their eggs. It is the sort of film which, if made in the 50s, would have been regarded as a typical Ealing comedy. But in 1943 there is something resolutely democratic in the way the whole community – from crusty colonel to Cockney evacuees – unites to protect the birds.

Like Anthony Asquith's *The Demi-Paradise*, *Tawny Pipit* was made at the height of pro-Russian feeling, when Mrs Churchill spearheaded fund-raising schemes to aid the Russians and elaborate pageants were held in the Albert Hall to celebrate Anglo-Russian friendship. But in contrast to Asquith's film, which uses its Russian hero (Laurence Olivier) as a conduit for celebrating the endearing eccentricities of the English character, *Tawny Pipit* uses the visit of a Russian woman soldier to suggest a new and better alignment of class and sexual relationships. Here, as in *Went the Day Well?*, with its land girls who gamely turn their hand to sniping, is a countryside mobilised for war.

Even an upper-class, country-house comedy like *Don't Take It to Heart*, directed by Jeffrey Dell for Two Cities, was not immune to the new spirit. The lord of the manor happily doubles up as tour guide for visitors to his crumbling stately home, and his daughter is a socialist, determined to marry a boy from the village. In the event, the village boy prefers a parlourmaid and she is free to marry an aristocratic lawyer. But since he is a radical who drinks with the locals and champions their cause against a nouveau riche incomer, this doesn't seem like a betrayal of her principles.

Don't Take It to Heart shows little respect for the countryside either as landscape or as the repository of true values. The villagers are rough and tough enough not to be demoralised but, at least until the lawyer has reclaimed their rights, they are poor and – as they are all part of an extended family called Bucket – probably incestuous. Energy and vitality come from the radical lawyer and the city-educated lady socialist.

Powell and Pressburger's Vision

Powell and Pressburger's *A Canterbury Tale* is much more thoroughly immersed in the mythology of rural England. A land girl, a GI and an English army sergeant meet in a village ten miles from Canterbury. After the girl is attacked they team up to unmask the local magistrate Thomas Colpeper (Eric Portman) as 'the glueman', a mysterious assailant who throws glue in women's hair. Colpeper is more complex and more sympathetic than villainous Oliver Wilsford of *Went the Day Well?*. His motivation is to discourage women from going out at night with soldiers from the local army base, thus leaving them with nothing to do but come to his slide-show lectures on the English landscape and its significance for modern man. Logically weak though the plot is, there is an emotional resonance to the film which stifles rational objection. As Clive Coultass explains:

> The clue lies in an appreciation of the sense of the miraculous that attaches itself to the film. Perhaps only those who are antipathetic to British cinema can fail to recognise the ways in which Powell, in *A Canterbury Tale*, anticipates the surrealism of Italian film-makers like Fellini and Antonioni . . . . Its romantic, arguably parochial and certainly conservative,

vision of the kind of country and society the British had been fighting to preserve from fascism is allied to the disturbing eccentricity and misogyny of a man like Colpeper, defender of the faith against the uncaring materialism represented by the military he has to educate at all costs.[21]

It is Colpeper's misogyny and eccentricity which makes the film so interesting. Is this a right-wing film showing that change is bad, women are trouble and only a return to traditional values can bring happiness? Or is it a left-wing film showing traditionalists as sexually disturbed psychopaths? It certainly confused the critics. Caroline Lejeune of the *Observer* set the tone of lip-pursed disapproval which would characterise much criticism of Powell and Pressburger's films henceforth:

> *A Canterbury Tale* is about a Kentish JP who believes so deeply in the message of his native soil that he pours glue on girls' hair in the blackout lest they distract the local soldiery from his archaeological lectures. That's the theme, and to my mind, nothing will make it a pleasant one. This fellow may be a mystagogue, with the love of England in his blood, but he is also plainly a crackpot of a rather unpleasant type with bees in the bonnet and bluebottles in the belfry. Only a psychiatrist, I imagine, would be deeply interested in his behaviour.[22]

Other reviewers, such as Richard Winnington, were more sympathetic, but the film was not commercially very successful and it was drastically recut for the American market. It was not until the National Film Archive issued a restored print in 1977 that *A Canterbury Tale* began to be seen as a peculiarly powerful and resonant evocation of wartime Britain.

Coultass, contrasting the elegiac nostalgia of Asquith's last war film, *The Way to the Stars*, with *A Canterbury Tale*, comments: 'Powell and Pressburger, in *A Canterbury Tale*, at least understood the potential power of the upheaval in Britain that the war had stimulated, and they tried to absorb it into the common stream of English culture.'[23] It is possible to discern a vision of the future in *A Canterbury Tale*, though it is an unusual one. As Priestley had forecast, his third England – of arterial roads and Woolworths and factory girls looking like actresses – spread out from the prosperous Southeast, slowly absorbing the old Victorian England of grimy factories and red-brick terraced houses, which was modernised by continuing prosperity and

full employment in the post-war period. Powell and
Pressburger never had anything to say about industrial
Britain. The only film Powell made which was supposed to be set in this industrial landscape was *Red
Ensign*, one of the low-budget films he made for
Michael Balcon in the mid-30s. It stars Leslie Banks
(whose tweedy Englishness masks the German identity
of Oliver Wilsford in *Went the Day Well?*) as a progressive ship-builder who arouses the hostility of the workers by his cost-cutting methods. It is a potentially
interesting film but has none of the vitality of Powell's
other 'B' movies such as *The Love Test* and *Something
Always Happens*, which are set among entrepreneurs and
new industries, or *The Phantom Light*, which is set in an
isolated Welsh lighthouse. Powell was perfectly at home
in the urban world, and Pressburger ('I like a startling
car, a startling film, a startling woman') was equally
attached to the conveniences of modern living. Powell's
idea of country life was to get the sleeper from London
to Dumfries, spend the day visiting his mother in a
shepherd's cottage and have a brisk walk in the fresh air
before returning to the metropolis the following
night.[24]

A Canterbury Tale's view of the countryside, despite
the blacksmith and wheelwright and lyrically beautiful
landscapes, is essentially a modern one. Its fusion of
magic, mysticism and naive Freudianism (the glue-
throwing, the moths eating away the contents of
Alison's caravan) reaches beyond realism and simple
moralities. And in its ending, where the three pilgrims
finally get to Canterbury and are granted miracles
which restore them to happiness and fulfilment, it
realises that gift bestowed by the war of making the
impossible possible.

Notes

1. A. J. P. Taylor, *English History 1914–45*, p. 668.
2. See John Costello's impressively comprehensive *Love, Sex and War*.
3. As one might expect with Rattigan, things are not quite this simple. Joan is smitten with Gilbey when he is the aloof, formal butler, his transformation into just another amiable 2nd lieutenant is something of a disappointment to her and passion is only reignited when he becomes a fire-eating major and she has to work under him.
4. Sidney Bernstein, *Film and International Relations* (Workers Film Association, 1945), p. 7, quoted in Robert Murphy, *Realism and Tinsel: Cinema and Society in Britain 1939–49*, p. 96.
5. Quoted in Murphy, *Realism and Tinsel*, p. 51.
6. Andrew Higson, 'Britain's Outstanding Contribution to the Film: The Documentary Realist Tradition', in Charles Barr (ed.), *All Our Yesterdays*, p. 72.
7. Mary-Lou Jennings (ed.), *Humphrey Jennings: Film-maker, Painter, Poet*, p. 33.
8. 'Near where I live is a house with a large garden, that's not being used at all because the owner of it has gone to America. Now according to the property view, this is all right, and we, who haven't gone to America, must fight to protect this absentee owner's property. But on the com-munity view, this is all wrong. There are hundreds of working men not far from here who urgently need ground for allotments so that they can produce a bit more food. Also, we may soon need more houses for billeting. Therefore, I say, that house and garden ought to be used whether the owner, who's gone to America, likes it or not.' J. B. Priestley, BBC Radio 'Postscript', 21 July 1940. Quoted in Angus Calder, *The People's War*, p. 160.
9. George Orwell, 'The Lion and the Unicorn', *The Collected Essays, Journalism and Letters of George Orwell, Vol. 2*, p. 118.
10. Anthony Howard, 'We Are the Masters Now', in Philip French and Michael Sissons (eds), *Age of Austerity* (London: Hodder & Stoughton, 1963, reprinted Oxford: Oxford University Press, 1986), p. 18.
11. Ibid., p. 19.
12. Antonia Lant, *Blackout: Reinventing Women for Wartime British Cinema*, p. 31. Her reference is to Dilys Powell, *Films Since 1939*, p. 8.
13. Ian Dalrymple, *Cine Technician*, February–March 1940, p. 10.
14. J. B. Priestley, *English Journey* (Harmondsworth: Penguin, 1979), p. 375.
15. Ibid., p. 373.
16. Ibid., p. 372.
17. Angus Calder, *The Myth of the Blitz*, p. 188.
18. Calder, *The People's War*, p. 485.
19. Ibid., p. 488.
20. Ibid., p. 484.
21. Clive Coultass, *Images for Battle: British Film and the Second World War*.
22. *Observer*, 14 May 1944.
23. Coultass, *Images for Battle*, p. 182.
24. Michael Powell, *A Life in Movies* (London: Heinemann, 1986), p. 445.

Bibliography

Aldgate, Anthony and Jeffrey Richards, *Britain Can Take It: British Cinema in the Second World War* (Edinburgh: Edinburgh University Press, 1994).

Badder, David, 'Powell and Pressburger: The War Years', *Sight and Sound*, Winter 1978.

Calder, Angus, *The People's War* (London: Granada, 1971).

Calder, Angus, *The Myth of the Blitz* (London: Jonathan Cape, 1991).

Chapman, James, *The British at War: Cinema, State and Propaganda 1939–1945* (London: I. B. Tauris, 1998).

Christie, Ian, *Arrows of Desire* (London: Faber and Faber, 1994).

Costello, John, *Love, Sex and War* (London: Pan 1985).

Coultass, Clive, *Images for Battle: British Film and the Second World War* ((London: Associated University Presses, 1989).

Higson, Andrew, 'Britain's Outstanding Contribution to the Film: The Documentary Realist Tradition', in Charles Barr (ed.), *All Our Yesterdays* (London: BFI, 1986).

Higson, Andrew, *Waving the Flag: Constructing a National Cinema in Britain* (Oxford: Clarendon Press, 1995).

Houston, Penelope, *Went the Day Well?* (London: BFI, 1992).

Hurd, Geoff (ed.), *National Fictions: World War II in British Films and Television* (London: BFI, 1984).

Jennings, Mary Lou (ed.), *Humphrey Jennings: Film-maker, Painter, Poet* (London: BFI, 1982).

Landy, Marcia, *British Genres: Cinema and Society, 1930–1960* (Princeton, NJ: Princeton University Press, 1991).

Lant, Antonia, *Blackout: Reinventing Women for Wartime British Cinema* (Princeton, NJ: Princeton University Press, 1991).

Murphy, Robert, *Realism and Tinsel: Cinema and Society in Britain 1939–49* (London: Routledge, 1992).

Murphy, Robert, *British Cinema and the Second World War* (London: Continuum, 2000).

Orwell, George, 'The English People' in Vol. 2 and 'The Lion and the Unicorn' in Vol. 3 of *The Collected Essays, Journalism and Letters of George Orwell* (Harmondsworth: Penguin, 1970).

Ponting, Clive, *1940 – Myth and Reality* (London: Sphere, 1990).

Powell, Dilys, *Films Since 1939* (London: Longmans Green, 1947).

Richards, Jeffrey, 'Why We Fight: *A Canterbury Tale*', in Anthony Aldgate and Jeffrey Richards (eds), *Best of British: Cinema and Society 1930–1970* (Oxford: Basil Blackwell, 1983).

Taylor, A. J. P., *English History 1914–45* (Harmondsworth: Penguin, 1970).

Taylor, Philip, (ed.), *Britain and the Cinema in the Second World War* (London: Macmillan, 1988).

25
Melodrama and Femininity in World War II British Cinema

Marcia Landy

> Let's give in at least and admit we really are proud of you, you strange, wonderful, incalculable creatures. The world we shape is going to be a better world because you are helping to shape it. Silence, gentlemen, I give you a toast. The gentle sex.
>
> Leslie Howard, voice-over in *The Gentle Sex* (1943)

The Consoling Pleasure of Fantasy

David Lean's *Brief Encounter* (1945), one of the best-remembered British films of the 1940s, is set in everyday surroundings, and the focal point of the film is the disjunction between the protagonist's inner fantasy world and the world of domestic duties. Laura Jesson (Celia Johnson), a respectably married woman with two children, gets a piece of grit in her eye while waiting for a train after her weekly shopping trip to town. Alec Harvey (Trevor Howard), who removes the grit, is a doctor. They meet illicitly until she realises that she has neglected her familial responsibilities. Narrated in flashback by Laura, the film does not hinge on whether the relationship she is describing has ever actually happened. What matters is that life exists apart from her family. The implication is that women cherish a private fantasy life; that their lives are split between the romantic and the banal.

The repetition of Rachmaninov's second piano concerto reinforces Laura's fantasies, accompanying her narration and prodding her memories. It is the music that arouses her – music accompanies her narration, evokes her memories – but the most disturbing sound in the film is the sound of laughter. Laura and Alec's relationship is linked to their common bond of laughter at a woman who plays the cello in the background

while the couple lunch together. And when Laura talks to her husband, she laughs as she seeks to allay her feelings of guilt. Increasingly her laughter begins to border on tears and hysteria as she narrates her story, and it appears that laughter is the tell-tale sign of her inability to bring together her inner and her outer existence. Constrained by her marital and maternal responsibilities, she is forced to live in her mind and to talk to herself.

The film reproduces the plight of the feminine figure seeking a voice, while at the same time silencing her as the text constructs a world of conventional morality in which feminine desire is inhibited. In its use of memory and recollection, the film suggests that the telling is all: the enactment of the fantasy is superior to its fulfilment. Romance is engendered by deprivation. There is no question that the film portrays the feminine domain as stultifying, if not hostile, but in the final analysis the narration aestheticises the pain, making that pain the basis of pleasure – the pleasure of telling a story that would not be half as engaging if it had a 'happy ending'.

In its indirect allusions to the war, its yoking of realism and fantasy to its feminine protagonist, *Brief Encounter* is symptomatic of how the wartime cinema did not create new concepts of femininity; it enabled old ones to circulate. Melodrama is the medium through which these concepts travel, fused with and animating discourses of familialism, community and nation. However, melodrama is also a medium that exposes the problematic and tenuous nature of social constructions of femininity, and it is through their melodramatic style and forms of narration that the films shed light on conceptions of femininity circulating in the 1940s. This chapter examines the value of the uses of various forms of melodrama as the unstable circuit through which social and political codes centring on representations of femininity erupted in World War II.

Mobile Women?

Sue Aspinall writes that 'the realist films of the early 1940s were trying to provide a more faithful reflection of common experiences than British fictional films had hitherto attempted'.[1] What the narratives promulgated and sought to valorise was fidelity to the common cause. Films such as *Millions Like Us* (1943), *The Gentle Sex* (1943) and *2000 Women* (1944) are part of a concerted effort to portray the contributions of women to the war effort, providing images of women's competence often in situations that parallel men's. While certain subjects still continued to be censored in accordance with pre-war guidelines, there was relaxation in some areas, particularly concerning the portrayal of workers and of women. An examination of the narrative strategies of these films reveals how the texts cannot contain a cohesive affirmative stance apropos of woman. The metaphor of mobility, often invoked as a means for describing the conscription of women and their assumption of new activities outside the home, exceeds its pragmatic uses, signalling conflicting responses to present exigencies.[2]

In speaking of *Millions Like Us*, Frank Launder and Sidney Gilliat said, 'We were very impressed with the fate – if you like to call it that – of the conscripted woman, the mobile woman'.[3] A mixture of documentary footage and fictional narration, the film sets up a series of contrasts between home and work, abundance and scarcity, familial unity and separation, pre-war forms of leisure and relationships and changing wartime patterns of social life. The altering face of British society is conveyed through images of mobility, in the conscription of the women, the scenes of their training as they learn to do work that was formerly the province of men, and the portrayal of growing solidarity among women of different classes and backgrounds.

Millions Like Us alternates between scenes of work and scenes of leisure. The dances, the concerts, the pub scenes, and Fred and Celia's honeymoon trip to Eastgate dramatise accommodation to change within wartime constraints. The unstable parameters of the 'mobile woman' are measured by melodramatic affect, specifically by the incommensurability between desire and gratification. The film portrays romantic entanglements but the relationships serve to underscore the problem of balancing continuity and change. In one relationship, the man dies; in the other, he refuses to commit himself until he knows whether the changes wrought in class relationships by the war are permanent. The question of continuity or change extends to the patterns of women's lives. Is the war merely a temporary disruption, or will wartime experience have an impact on their lives – in the breaking of familial ties, moving out of the home, living collectively with others, and working at non-domestic labour?

Female Solidarity

The Gentle Sex (Leslie Howard/Maurice Elvey) also focuses on the conscription, training and acclimatisation of women to a new and demanding way of life. The women form relations with other women and perform vital activities under stress in an efficient manner, though the film cannot resist including romantic entanglements with men. The women's separation from civilian life is handled through scenes of individual partings at the train station filtered through the commentary of Leslie Howard. In its focus on different women, the film breaks down the exclusive preoccupation with one dominant character so typical of pre-war films.

The women are representative of different classes in the same way that the male war films seek to provide a picture of co-operation across class lines. By introducing an older woman who was active during World War I, the film indicates the historical antecedents of women's involvement in war as well as the sense that this involvement arises under exceptional circumstances. The question raised by this film, as articulated by several of the characters, and in ways similar to *Millions Like Us*, concerns change – whether the world after the war will return to its former patterns or whether society will alter its direction, specifically in relation to feminine sexuality and woman's position. While the nature of the desired changes remains ambiguous, there is the implication that the war's promotion of greater equality in sexual and class relationships is of primary concern. This anxious question is one that will appear in many films of the period, though not always as explicitly as in this film and in *Millions Like Us*.

The film, *Two Thousand Women*, directed by Frank Launder for Gainsborough, explores personal relations among women and is set in an internment camp in France. Its female characters are of different ages and occupations – from nuns to nurses to striptease artistes – and are portrayed in less stereotypical terms than usual.

The women stand up to the enemy, outwit their jailers, and help two British fliers to escape, with a minimum of tears and hysteria. They organise entertainment, too: in a reversal of the usual female impersonation acts of the conventional prison-camp drama, the women do male impersonations. They are also mutually supportive in the face of the privations of the internment camp. In the scene in which the arriving women are brought to their rooms and baths are prepared, the film avoids the temptations of voyeurism. The female body is not fetishised. In place of the conventional portrait of a masculine fascination with the vision of the feminine body, the women are seen through each other's eyes. Women's mobilisation is presented as an outgrowth of mutual assistance rather than an externally enforced service. The grapevine, usually presented as evidence of woman's garrulousness, is here presented as a survival strategy, as when the women warn each other of the spy in their midst. The text unsettles any unified sense of woman and by extension any coherent sense of national unity in relation to the role of femininity. The cross-dressing, the mimicry of male prison-camp dramas, the suggestion of lesbian relations, all are tell-tale signs of excess that undermine realism's strategies of containment, revealing that in its reliance on the necessity of incorporating woman into the national scenario the film has inevitably introduced spectres of irreconcilable differences in gendered and sexual representation.

In Times of Old, When Women Were Bold . . .

The highly stylised, anti-realist melodramas produced during the war by Gainsborough provide a complementary, not antithetical, perspective on woman in the 'realist' melodramas. The success of *The Man in Grey* (Leslie Arliss, 1943) was dependent on the creation of a definitive visual style, developed by the art department of Gainsborough, which 'viewed history as a source of sensual pleasures, as the original novels had done'.[4] The sets and the costumes were not produced with an eye to authenticity. As Sue Harper suggests, 'The affective, spectacular aspects of mise en scène are foregrounded, to produce a vision of "history" as a country where only feelings reside, not socio-political conflicts.'[5] Similarly, the costuming, make-up and coiffures of the characters were orchestrated, to enhance the affective elements.

The stars who appeared in these films were equally responsible for the films' popularity. Margaret Lockwood projected an

image of a woman who was not part of the upper-class establishment. Although she was by no means working class, she did not possess the kind of poise that comes from knowing one's place in the world and from expecting respect. There was an edge of bravado and insecurity in her personality as she appeared on film.[6]

Not only are women at the centre of these films, but the point of view appears more explicitly feminine. While the resolutions often appear to recuperate female domesticity, disciplining the women who violate social mores, the films are daring in their willingness to explore constraints on women. Unlike the historical films, which claim to re-enact the lives and actions of prominent individuals, the costume dramas are fictional and play loosely with historical contexts, transposing history into romance. The films' remote historical settings allow for greater latitude in dramatising departures from portraits of conventional femininity, portraying conflicts surrounding choice of partners, marriage, motherhood and female companionship. Like the realist dramas, the narratives depend on the existence of a dual discourse that sought to dramatise the social changes affecting women while maintaining a continuity with traditional values.

The Man in Grey, the first of the Gainsborough melodramas, featured such Gothic elements as the old manor house with its brooding and cruel lord, the imprisonment of a high-born woman in this forbidding world, hints of the supernatural in the form of a fortune-telling gypsy, and the animistic uses of nature. The film functions by means of polarisation and splitting. There are two female protagonists: Clarissa (Phyllis Calvert), who is high-born and privileged, and Hesther (Margaret Lockwood), who is poor but ambitious and worldly. Two types of masculinity are also represented: the unscrupulous Lord Rohan (James Mason) and the socially ambiguous but romantic Rokeby (Stewart Granger). Clarissa's world is a feminine world of acceptance and trust, whereas Hesther's world is a phallic one of seduction, aggression.[7] Clarissa is associated with social legitimacy, with marital and familial responsibility. Hesther is an adventuress. Bereft of social status, she attempts to usurp Clarissa's position. The upper-class Rohan prefers lower-class women. He marries Clarissa because he must have an heir, and sees Hesther complementing his own aristocratic rejection of middle-class morality and sentiment. Their contacts are characterised by passion and physical aggression, leading finally to his beating her to death when he learns she has caused Clarissa's death. The film is unrelenting in its portrayal of the component of cruelty inherent in masculine and feminine relationships. A big commercial success, *The Man in Grey* led to a cycle of films with similar ingredients.

Gainsborough's 1944 costume melodrama *Fanny by Gaslight*, directed by Anthony Asquith, is a female initiation drama. Fanny (Phyllis Calvert) is called upon to confront one obstacle after another in her path to self-discovery. As a child she discovers a brothel in the basement of her home, and is dispatched to boarding school. On her return as a young woman she sees the man she looks on as her father trampled to death by Lord Manderstoke's horse. Her mother's death follows, and Fanny becomes the archetypal orphan of melodrama until she meets her real father, Clive Seymour (Stuart Lindsell), an MP and cabinet minister. Seymour's wife, Alicia (Margaretta Scott), unaware of Fanny's identity, takes her as a lady's maid and Fanny is initiated into Alicia's world of intrigue. Here Fanny again encounters Lord Manderstoke (James Mason), with whom Alicia is having an affair. When Alicia asks Seymour for a divorce so that she can marry Manderstoke, he refuses. Seymour commits suicide, and again Fanny loses a father. Fanny thereupon falls in love with her father's solicitor, Harry Somerford (Stewart Granger). His mother and sister (he, too, is fatherless) are adamantly opposed to the marriage, warning him that it will ruin his career. For the sake of his future, Fanny disappears. Harry finds her and takes her to Paris, where they accidentally encounter Manderstoke. Harry is provoked to a duel in which he kills Manderstoke and is himself seriously wounded. His sister arrives to tend Harry, forbidding Fanny to see him, but Fanny triumphs and, with the doctor's urging, dedicates herself to restoring Harry's health.

This film can be read as a straightforward legitimation of middle-class morality and the idealisation of the female as the stabiliser of familial values. The narrative presents female 'promiscuity' as a threat to the family. Fanny is the offspring of her mother's earlier sexual impropriety. The Hopwoods' comfortable Victorian house sits atop a brothel, suggesting the dangerous proximity of promiscuity to middle-class family life. The Seymour family is similarly destroyed by the wife's extramarital affairs. Fanny's cousin (played by the voluptuous Jean Kent), unlike virtuous Fanny, tries to use her sexual charms to gain material advantage. The film is not, however, as strait-laced as these examples of straying female virtue might suggest. Female suffering is

traced not to the women's actions but to Manderstoke, the aristocrat. His sensuality, cruelty and indifference to social decorum are a source of fascination for the women he seduces, who are rendered helpless by his charms. He offers a striking contrast to the other masculine figures in the film, who are portrayed as vulnerable, if not ineffectual. While he represents the arrogant, lawless and sadistic side of masculine power, he is also attractive, and the women who associate with him are free from conventional constraints. Fanny resists him, partly because her docility requires a more romantic, pliable and chivalrous lover like Harry, but also because she hates him as the killer of her two father figures. Nonetheless, this film, like *The Man in Grey*, invests sexuality with power and, rather than marginalising it totally, allows it to be seen in attractive as well as destructive terms.

The Housewife's Dilemma

Madonna of the Seven Moons (1944), another Gainsborough melodrama directed by Arthur Crabtree, is a maternal drama, focusing on mother-and-daughter relations, not on marriage. The film is structured around oppositions between past and present, traditional and modern attitudes towards sexuality, action and paralysis, respectability and nonconformity, and repression and sexuality. Competing conceptions of femininity are highlighted through the convention of split identity. In one identity, Phyllis Calvert's Maddalena is the wife of a respectable Italian banker; in her other identity she is Rosanna, the passionate lover of a gypsy thief, Nino (Stewart Granger). The protagonist's self-division is traced to her upbringing in a convent, where she was raped by a peasant. She remains there until marriageable age, and the film picks up her story many years later when her daughter, Angela, is an adult. A contrast is set between the constrictions of the mother's life and the daughter's freer attitudes. The mother is excessively religious, her nun-like clothing indicative of her sexual restraint and repression. Angela tries to bring her mother into her (modern) world, counselling her on clothing, make-up and jewellery. Maddalena suffers a breakdown, faints, and when she awakens assumes the identity of Rosanna. Dressed as a gypsy with peasant blouse and skirt, bracelets and long, dangling earrings, like a seductive Carmen, Rosanna re-enacts an earlier disappearance and returns to her lover, Nino.

The daughter assumes an active role in the second part of the film, piecing together clues about her mother's disappearance and putting herself in danger in

Phyllis Calvert, changed from dutiful wife to passionate lover of gypsy thief Stewart Granger in *Madonna of the Seven Moons* (Arthur Crabtree, 1944)

order to find her. In the vein of maternal melodrama, the mother sacrifices herself for her daughter. The conflict between desire and repression is represented by the final image of Maddalena-Rosanna's corpse with both the cross and the rose resting on her breast. The daughter, who has been closer to the father, is now free to pursue her life untroubled by the question of her mother's identity. It has been argued that Angela is representative of a more progressive lifestyle for women than her mother, but Sue Aspinall finds that the film's 'proposal of a modern "enlightened" sexuality as the solution to the dilemma of the virgin/whore/mother/mistress dichotomy fails to satisfactorily resolve the contradiction. This new sexuality is still romantic marriage, dressed in modern, less class-bound clothes.'[8] Where the film more cogently captures the sense of feminine subjection is in its portrayal of Rosanna's hysterical symptoms. As in many of the woman's films, illness becomes the strategy for expressing antagonism towards or resistance to the physical, psychic and moral constraints on women's lives. In the case of Maddalena, her illness represents one way in which her body manages to elude the control of her husband and family doctor by becoming a text that can be read for its symptoms rather than as an object of erotic contemplation. The male protagonist's inability or unwillingness to interpret, explain or 'cure' these symptoms indicates the limits of control by social institutions of the feminine body.[9]

Defining Femininity

The transgressive and unstable nature of femininity is central to *The Wicked Lady* (Leslie Arliss, 1945).

Margaret Lockwood's Barbara violates all the conventional expectations of women. She plays an adventuress who steals her best friend's fiancé, marries him, tires of him, seeks adventure disguised as a highwayman, has an affair with Jerry Jackson (James Mason), a notorious highwayman, poisons and kills a moralistic servant who has learned her secret, falls in love with another man, Kit (Michael Rennie), and dies at his hands after killing Jackson. Her 'wickedness' consists in her hedonism, her contempt for the law and others' private property, her lack of sentiment, and her flouting of prescribed notions of femininity.

The film is built on the classic melodramatic chain of unfulfilled desire. Caroline (Patricia Roc) loves Sir Ralph (Griffith Jones), who loves Barbara, who loves Kit. The familiar Gainsborough strategy of polarising and splitting is evident in this film. The narrative makes clear-cut oppositions between Barbara and Caroline, between chaste and passionate femininity. Differences between the women are signalled by their wardrobes and hairdos. For Sue Harper, 'the film signals two sorts of female sexuality by carefully differentiating between the two wedding veils. Roc's has cuddlesome, kittenish "ears", whereas Lockwood's is a mantilla, redolent of passion.'[10] The film also contrasts the men. Ralph is assigned to the category of ineffectual, if not masochistic, masculinity; Jerry Jackson to the category of passionate, witty and unsentimental masculinity; Kit, like Rokeby in *The Man in Grey*, is the feminised masculine fantasy figure of romances, the tender rescuer.

While Barbara is also aligned with masculinity in her apparent lack of sentimentality and conventional notions of loyalty, she maintains an attachment to her dead mother. At first, she recklessly gambles away a brooch that had been her mother's, but then the brooch becomes the pretext for her to take to the highway and reclaim it during a raid. Sue Harper suggests that Barbara is 'identified with the mother – rather than the father – principle'.[11] Her identification with the 'mother principle' expresses itself in her protean behaviour, her disregard for rules, conventions and boundaries as opposed to the maternal virtues of service, sacrifice and commitment to home and family associated with Caroline. Having only the subversive dimensions of the mother principle, Barbara is eliminated from the narrative, rejected by all as the subverter of social stability, upper-class cohesiveness and domestic rectitude.

Competing definitions of femininity are central to *They Were Sisters* (1945), a Gainsborough melodrama in contemporary garb, directed by Arthur Crabtree. This film dramatises the impossible position in which women are placed by the conflict between their own desires and the expectations of others. The narrative apportions facets of femininity among three sisters, two of whom represent extremes while the third is a mediating figure. Charlotte (Dulcie Gray) portrays one face of woman: suggestibility, masochism, the absence of a strong ego: the Victorian middle-class woman who tries to be an angel in the house but becomes the madwoman in the attic. She allows herself to be bullied, abused, humiliated and silenced by Geoffrey (James Mason), her husband, and when she seeks to escape, he cajoles her to remain only to repeat his cruelty. By contrast, Vera (Anne Crawford) is a modern independent woman who scorns conventional relationships. Brian (Barrie Livesey), the man Vera marries, is Geoffrey's opposite, earning her contempt for his pliability and permissiveness. If Charlotte overvalues marriage and overestimates her dependency on family, Vera undervalues and underestimates its importance. She is disciplined to proper familial attitudes through the temporary loss of her lover and her daughter. When she meets a man who is dominating, she settles down to domesticity.

The images of the two women unable to conform to the demands of family life sit uncomfortably with the film's formulaic solutions. But the film does dramatise, especially through Charlotte's situation, the impossible burdens placed on women in family life. The alternatives that the film has to offer – self-discipline, familial responsibility and maternal sacrifice – are in Charlotte's case clearly unworkable. Her husband's humiliation of her before the children, his toying with her sanity, his mockery of her behaviour, his refusal to relinquish her, her alcoholism, and her retreat into herself, all unbalance the tripartite structure of the film and call into question the third sister Lucy's role as successful intermediary between extremes of femininity.

The film's discourse seems to argue for a more enlightened attitude towards marriage. The alternative to the asymmetrical relations of both Charlotte's and Vera's marriages is presented through Lucy (Phyllis Calvert) and her husband William (Peter Murray Hill), but their desexualised relationship, signified by their lack of progeny, does not address the disrupting nature of unfulfilled feminine desire. Lucy's role in particular is illuminating for the ways in which she seeks to ameliorate Charlotte's dilemma, indicative of contemporary 'solutions' to feminine discontents. She enlists the aid of

a psychoanalyst to protect Charlotte from Geoffrey; she also fights Geoffrey in court and publicly exposes his cruelty – thus breaking his hold over his eldest daughter, who now recognises his maltreatment of her mother – and she creates a conventional familial environment for the children of her sisters. Thus she enlists the major institutional forces in society to ensure the stability of the family. With the sisters eliminated, one dead and one banished to South Africa, the narrative abandons the schema of tripling and moves into the 'ordinary' world, leaving the one family – Lucy, William and the children.

The doctor is a pivotal figure in melodrama, serving to identify and cure the physical and psychic maladies of femininity. In *Madonna of the Seven Moons* and *They Were Sisters,* his role is understated. In *The Seventh Veil* (1945), he becomes central. Directed by Compton Bennett, the film copied Gainsborough's flamboyant style with an emphasis on extraordinariness, hysteria and exaggeration. Francesca (Ann Todd) is another of melodrama's orphan figures. Adopted by her uncle Nicholas (James Mason), this unwanted female child is reared to become a great artist, like Nicholas's mother. Nicholas, resentful of his mother's rejection, her running off with a lover rather than facing the responsibilities of marital life, displaces his rage onto his niece. In the name of art and excellence, he subjects her to his discipline until she is able to become a successful concert pianist. As in a fairytale, an ugly duckling turns into a swan, wins acclaim, and chooses her Prince Charming among three suitors. Her attempted drowning becomes the means to her rebirth, for with the help of the magical figure of the psychoanalyst she is brought to a new definition of herself and of Nicholas. The film is replete with father figures – Nicholas, Francesca's suitors, and the psychoanalyst, all competing for Francesca. Maternal figures are absent except as they appear as surrogate figures in Francesca's childhood in the guise of her disciplinary schoolmistress and in allusions to Nicholas's mother.

The film problematises the relationship of femininity to language. Nicholas gives Francesca speech and direction, assumes her voice, and even harnesses her musical expression. Her refusal to speak and play after her accident and her separation from Nicholas portray her as bereft of both verbal and non-verbal language in the absence of the masculine figure. When she seeks to express herself, she can only speak through the symptoms of her illness. Francesca is presented as the object of male doctors' scrutiny, exposed as helpless before their inquisition, but the doctors' omnipotent position is disrupted by her gaze at them, undermining the naturalness of her subordinate position. As intermediary, the psychoanalyst provides her with language and hence is instrumental in restoring her to Nicholas. Her choice of Nicholas does not, however, constitute a 'happy ending'. Rather it underscores the impossibility of other alternatives, since they would position her outside language and hence outside society.

Femmes Fatales?

The genre of the 'woman's film' features rebellious representations of femininity, foregrounding women who do not conform to models of supportive maternal or conjugal behaviour. They are at war with men and with domesticity, guilty of harbouring secret desires and of seeking to gratify their longings. While marriage and family life may be presented in *They Were Sisters* as woman's domain and as the guarantor of tradition and stability, many of the films, especially those produced in the post-war period, also reveal the constraints of domesticity. The home is a prison which headstrong women seek to subvert or escape. The popularity of domestic melodrama during this period is not surprising, given the emphasis on the privatisation of family life which came with rising incomes, changes in housing conditions, and increasing social mobility. According to John Stevenson, 'these tendencies reinforced ideals of domesticity and private life which, ultimately, frustrated the fuller emancipation of women'.[12] The melodramas portray the greater drive towards reinforcing personal relations within the family, but they also dramatise social forces that undermine the realisation of these ideals.

The mid- and late 1940s provide striking instances of the transformation of the woman's film into film noir. *Bedelia* (1946), written by Vera Caspary, who also wrote the novel *Laura*, and directed by Lance Comfort, is a portrait of the femme fatale, the fascinating and dangerous disrupter of domestic harmony. *Bedelia* opens with a familiar film noir strategy: the image of a painting of a woman and a man's voice describing Bedelia as the film moves into a flashback. The voice says: 'This was Bedelia, beautiful and scheming. She radiated a curious innocence, eager to fascinate those she attracted like a poisonous flower.' The speaker is a detective intent on discovering Bedelia's whereabouts and her identity, and bringing her to justice.

The narrative portrays Bedelia (Margaret Lockwood) as rising in the world by marrying men, poisoning them, and getting their insurance money. As she

Margaret Lockwood as a fascinating and dangerous disrupter of domestic harmony: *Bedelia* (Lance Comfort, 1946)

puts poison in the men's food, she uses the traditional woman's vehicle of nurture to wreak her revenge on men. The film begins in France in an urban setting, but ends in an English village where Bedelia comes to live with her latest husband, Charley (Ian Hunter). Transplanted to the English pastoral environment, she is represented as the proverbial snake in the paradisiacal garden. She resents her husband's association with Ellen (Anne Crawford), a professional woman, but masquerades as the perfect wife – a good cook, gracious at parties, eager to help her husband – and provides no clue to her malevolent intentions. Pursued by the detective, posing as a painter, she is thwarted in her scheme to poison Charley; instead Charley forces her to take the poison intended for him.

On the one hand, the film can be read as a parable of housewifery run amuck. On the other, it can be read as an inevitable outgrowth of feminine resistance to domestication. In many ways, Bedelia's character seems to represent a reaction to conventional portraits of cultural expectations of femininity. For example, she resents being photographed and painted, which on the level of the narrative indicates her attempts to escape detection, but on a more culturally profound level signifies woman's resistance to being scrutinised and exposed. She admonishes Charley, 'Haven't you something better? You have me.' If Bedelia is 'a love story gone bad', it dramatises the 'impossible position of women in relation to desire in a patriarchal society'.[13] Reviewers objected to Lockwood's portrayal of the femme fatale, lamenting her lack of extreme villainy.[14] But Bedelia's ordinariness makes her 'sordid' domestic schemes typical rather than exceptional.

The 1940s preoccupation with the 'gentle sex' reveals a fusion of femininity with the national interest. In their narratives and styles, the films make visible the constructed nature of femininity, exposing it as multivalent, always circulating but subject to variation and permutation. Femininity as a fabrication of mobility – rather than the idealised 'mobile woman' of wartime rhetoric – can be seen through the melodramas in the partial and contradictory subject positions the films assign to woman. Whether the films utilise realist or escapist scenarios, adopt accommodating or disciplinary strategies, the excess generated by the various figurations of woman reveals a continuing crisis – not a rupture – in representations of femininity.

Notes

1. Sue Aspinall, 'Women, Realism and Reality', p. 280.
2. See Dana Polan, *Power and Paranoia: History, Narrative and the American Cinema, 1940–1950* (New York: Columbia University Press, 1986), p. 9.
3. Geoff Brown, *Launder and Gilliat* (London: BFI, 1977), p. 108.
4. Sue Harper, 'Historical Pleasures: Gainsborough Melodrama', in Christine Gledhill (ed.), *Home Is Where the Heart Is: Studies in Melodrama and the Woman's Film* (London: BFI, 1987), p. 178.
5. Ibid., p. 179.
6. Aspinall, 'Women, Realism, and Reality', p. 276.
7. Sue Aspinall, 'Sexuality in Costume Melodrama', in Sue Aspinall and Robert Murphy, *Gainsborough Melodrama*, p. 33.
8. Ibid., p. 36.
9. Mary Ann Doane, *The Desire to Desire: The Woman's Film of the 1940s* (London: Macmillan, 1987), pp. 62–4.
10. Harper, 'Historical Pleasures', p. 184.
11. Ibid.
12. John Stevenson, *British Society, 1914–1945* (Harmondsworth: Penguin, 1984), p. 467.
13. Doane, *The Desire to Desire*, p. 122.
14. See *Time and Tide* review reprinted in Aspinall and Murphy, *Gainsborough Melodrama*, p. 77.

Bibliography

Aldgate, Anthony and Richards, Jeffrey, *Britain Can Take It: British Cinema in the Second World War* (Edinburgh: Edinburgh University Press, 1994).

Aspinall, Sue, 'Women, Realism and Reality', in James Curran and Vincent Porter (eds), *British Cinema History* (London: Weidenfeld and Nicolson, 1983).

Aspinall, Sue and Murphy, Robert (eds), *Gainsborough Melodrama* (London: BFI, 1983).

Cook, Pam (ed.), *Gainsborough Pictures* (London and Washington, DC: Cassell, 1997).

Harper, Sue, *Picturing the Past: The Rise and Fall of the British Costume Film* (London: BFI, 1994).

Harper, Sue, *Women in British Cinema: Mad, Bad and Dangerous to Know* (London and New York: Continuum, 2000).

Higson, Andrew, *Waving the Flag: Constructing a National Cinema in Britain* (Oxford: Clarendon Press, 1995).

Hurd, Geoff, *National Fictions: World War II in British Films and Television* (London: BFI, 1984).

Landy, Marcia, *British Genres: Cinema and Society, 1930–1960* (Princeton, NJ: Princeton University Press, 1991).

Lant, Antonia, *Blackout: Reinventing Women for British Wartime Cinema* (Princeton, NJ: Princeton University Press, 1991).

Murphy, Robert, *Realism and Tinsel: Cinema and Society in Britain 1939–49* (London: Routledge, 1992).

This chapter reworks material that first appeared in Marcia Landy's *British Genres*, Princeton University Press, 1991.

26

No Place Like Home: Powell, Pressburger Utopia

Andrew Moor

At the end of Michael Powell and Emeric Pressburger's 1951 fantasy, *The Tales of Hoffmann*, Sir Thomas Beecham closes Offenbach's score for the opera and the words 'Made in England' are rubber-stamped onto its cover. This may be ironic, but it is still a gesture of the directors' pride that so international a venture, and so extravagant a visual spectacle, could be claimed for England. Offenbach was French; Hoffmann, German. Few of the film's leading players are English (even Moira Shearer is Scottish). Among the technical crew, Hein Heckroth, whose contribution as designer was crucial to the film, was German too. Yet the force with which a signifier of Englishness is grafted onto the work pinpoints a problem in defining national culture, and hints at a wider concern about the nation's sense of identity.

Powell and Pressburger have been seen as rogue outsiders because of the fantasy elements in their work and the European profile of their collaborative team. They do not fit into the understated 'quality realist' cinema which has been taken to represent our authentic national cinematic style. The industry they had entered as young men was one where international factors continually interacted with the national. Through into the 1930s, for example, the European cinema industry was notable for its multilingual co-productions and remakes of foreign successes; and its workforce was highly mobile, with key personnel shifting or being displaced from one country to another for professional, economic or political reasons. This is the culture to which Powell and Pressburger belong and it is not surprising that they interrogate nationhood rather than simplistically celebrate it.

Their canon of work is impressive and inventive by any standards. *The Life and Death of Colonel Blimp* (1943), *A Matter of Life and Death* (1946), *Black Narcissus* (1947) and *The Red Shoes* (1948) would stand out as important moments in any cinema history, and to paraphrase Boris Lermontov in *The Red Shoes*, most of their other films contain things of which no one need be ashamed. They made sixteen feature films together between 1939 and 1957, another two late collaborations in 1966 and 1972, and their production company, The Archers, was responsible for two other films in the mid-40s which were directed by others. Though they often shared the credits as writers, producers and directors, the billing is a rhetorical gesture, expressing confidence in the collaborative process. Storylines and dialogue were certainly developed through discussion, but Pressburger was the screenwriter, while Powell took responsibility for directing.[1]

Powell's film career began in the South of France. After a comfortable childhood in Kent, he took himself to Cap Ferat where his father ran a hotel. He was introduced to the Americanised Dubliner Rex Ingram, who was making films for MGM at the Victorine studios in Nice. After a spell with Ingram, Powell returned to London and underwent a rapid apprenticeship making quota quickies, emerging as a mature director with *The Edge of the World* (1937), a saga inspired by the evacuation of St Kilda and ambitiously filmed in the Shetlands. There is a cosmopolitanism to Powell, and a European sensibility which is the confident product of his class position. He is a cultural tourist, a tweed-clad Englishman with an avaricious interest in the foreign and an inventive appreciation of cinema's creative potential. His imagination embarks centrifugally from England, and he develops a baroque, inventive and exotic visual style.

Emeric Pressburger's trajectory is very different. Born in Hungary, he studied in Prague and Stuttgart and in 1930 began writing screenplays for the UFA conglomerate in Berlin, where he worked with, among others, Robert Siodmak, Max Ophuls and Reinhold Schünzel. He escaped to Paris when working conditions at UFA became less congenial, and then found refuge in Britain in 1935.[2] Pressburger scored his first British success writing the screenplay for *The Challenge* (1938), a curious Anglo-German amalgam about the English climber Edward Whymper's ascent of the Matterhorn in 1864. *The Challenge* was produced by Günther Stapenhorst (Pressburger's friend and colleague from his UFA days), and its executive producer was another Hungarian, Alexander Korda, into whose fold Pressburger had gravitated on his arrival in London. The film is the product of a Continental industry, but the fact that it was distributed by United Artists is a reminder that transatlantic factors always impacted upon European cinema. Made in both English and German, it was co-directed by Milton Rosmer – an English actor-director who appeared in Powell's *The Phantom Light* (1935) and the Powell–Pressburger collaboration *The Small Back Room* (1949), and by Luis Trenker – a German actor-director who specialised in mountaineering films and who stars in the film as the Italian mountain guide Carrel. *The Challenge* splices together Rosmer's often staid, English-language footage, much of it shot at Korda's Denham Studios, with location material from the Matterhorn itself, directed primarily by Trenker.

The unlikely combination of English staginess and Trenker's impressively spectacular location work makes *The Challenge* a curiosity, but it is chiefly interesting as an early indication of what would make Pressburger so distinctive a writer when he came to collaborate with Powell. He reworks narratives of frontiers, inscribing his own geographical and cultural displacement – from Hungary, from Germany, from France. The Matterhorn stands on the Swiss-Italian border and, as told in the film, the race to its summit in the 1860s is nationalistically driven. Rivalry builds up between Whymper's ascent from Zermatt in Switzerland, and the Italian Alpine Club's attempt from Breuil on their side of the border; much is made of how a nationalistic contest (over potential tourist income) threatens to destroy the mutual respect which

Ascending the Matterhorn: *The Challenge* (Milton Rosmer, 1938)

has been established between Whymper and Carrel. Their friendship is a neat prolepsis of the Anglo-Prussian bond which forms the basis of Pressburger's satirical wartime epic *The Life and Death of Colonel Blimp*. It is not, however, just the image of the Whymper–Carrel friendship which the author carries forward and develops. The symbolic function of the Matterhorn itself clues us to another of Pressburger's traits – his tendency to romanticise, to idealise, to envisage the utopian through landscape. Towering over the squabbling nationalist dialogue at lower altitudes, the peak is figured as something beyond the merely cultural-material-historical.

Pressburger thus turns topography into something dramatically meaningful, the snow-covered natural landscape mocking the notion of territorial borders. His vision is comparable with that of Jean Renoir in *La Grande Illusion* (1937), a film which examined conflicts between friendship and national loyalty during World War I. In the closing sequence, a pair of escaped French POWs approaches a border made invisible by a blanket of snow. 'Are you sure that's Switzerland – it looks just the same,' says one. 'Frontiers are made by men; nature doesn't give a damn,' the other replies. A German soldier fixes the POWs in the sights of his rifle, but so efficiently has he internalised the national boundaries that he is stopped from shooting them by the realisation that they have indeed crossed the border.

A glance at Pressburger's 1961 novel *Killing a Mouse on Sunday* reveals that the fascination with liminal territory stayed with him. In the aftermath of the Spanish Civil War, Pablo, the child-narrator of part of the tale, is taken to the border country by his uncle Luis to find safe shelter with Spanish refugees living in France. He recounts his disappointment:

> I have always thought that the frontier ran on the highest ridge of the mountain, but Uncle Luis said it was stupid. The border between countries depended solely on the fancy of capitalists . . . . [T]hey carved up the place, not giving a hoot what the poor people of the district suffered, splitting families, leaving a village without pasturage, houses without a road, men and beasts without water . . . . From below came the purr of a brook . . . . 'It's called the Verderiz,' Uncle Luis whispered. 'The other side is France.'
>
> What a terrible let down it was! There were the same trees, the same grass, the same sky. The wind played the same tune among the leaves high up in the foliage. I thought, it should be a French tune which I couldn't understand, something I had never heard before.[3]

The key themes here – the journey, the trauma of enforced displacement, the encounter with alien territory, the curious way in which the existence of borders is admitted yet disavowed – predominate in many of the films which Pressburger wrote with Michael Powell in the 1939–57 period.

Questions of Geography: The Exile's Tale

As Charles Barr has pointed out, 'the dominant structural element in the Powell–Pressburger films is the entry of a leading character into a strange land'.[4] Barr tidily catalogues the recurrence of this motif, and he is right to note its consistency. He thinks through this cross-border theme in terms of the author-directors' biographical experience of travel and relocation, the importance of territory and vigilance during the war years, the tension between the national and the international in debates about national cinema, and in terms of narratives which either construct a touristic gaze at the landscape or which cross a boundary into a protagonist's private subjective space. Powell and Pressburger began working together in 1939 and their first films

address the immediacies of the war years, but the discourse of exile which can be found running through Pressburger's work parallels and intermingles with the rhetoric of the 'people's war'.

Exile is a lonely and traumatic banishment from a native land. The wandering exile is positioned in relation to a stable centre from which he or she is singularly expatriated. Because of this, the exile's experience brings a sense of alienation, and this feeling of loss triggers compensatory desires for home and for a homeland, where roots can be put down and where a stable sense of identity can be re-established. This desire is nostalgic (nostalgia literally means homesickness) and it is often utopian, because the imagined home is so often idealised. Like exile, nationhood can be conceived of in terms of an 'imagined community'.[5] Home, homeland, community, utopia: these key terms for the exile are also ideologically charged symbols within wartime Britain, and are part of the way in which the nation represented its struggle to its people.

Pressburger's concerns take him close to this national 'grand narrative' but as an exile he inflects his wartime storylines with a strange, alien twist. His early protagonists cross boundaries at their peril, often because it brings them face to face with their enemies. Powell and Pressburger's first shared project, *The Spy in Black* (1939), is a Hitchcockian spy story in which the anti-Nazi German actor, Conrad Veidt, plays a German officer ordered out of his naval uniform and made to venture behind enemy lines to the Orkneys during World War I. He is uncomfortable in his disguise, and is disoriented by subterfuge and counter-espionage. With its atmosphere of Gothic unease, the film dramatises the anxieties of displacement; simple national loyalties are confused for the audience by identification with the charismatic German anti-hero. In *Contraband* (1940), Veidt returns to alien turf, this time as a Danish skipper chasing German spies in blacked-out London during World War II. It is a journey into a noir-ish cityscape, but light relief is found in a Danish enclave, the Three Vikings restaurant, whose immigrant inhabitants retain an exaggerated sense of Danishness. Ambiguously, they have settled in London, but have not assimilated. Instead they have found security by artificially creating a microcosm of their Danish homeland as a sign of their allegiance to it. At the same time they support the British cause by helping Veidt defeat the Nazi infiltrators.

This theme is explored further in *49th Parallel* (1941), where communities which have made homes in Canada find their peace and freedom disrupted by a marauding U-boat crew struggling to get back to Hitler's Germany. This scenario is inverted in *One of Our Aircraft Is Missing* (1942) where a British bomber crew crashes in a Holland made strange by German occupation. The airmen are helped back home by the spirited effort of the Dutch underground movement. As these four films rework ideas of exile and migration, an idealised sense of home becomes increasingly central to them. Through the performances of Eric Portman (as the leader of the Nazis) and Anton Walbrook (as the head of a community of German pacifists), *49th Parallel* pits the visionary zeal of its Nazi protagonist against a clearly articulated love of peaceful democracy. *One of Our Aircraft Is Missing* records a spirit of resistance through Jo de Vries (Googie Withers) who helps the British crew and who fights to rid her Dutch homeland of its alien occupiers.

As Kevin Gough-Yates has observed, Pressburger explicitly writes his autobiography of displacement into *The Life and Death of Colonel Blimp*, where Anton Walbrook's role as the Prussian Theo Kretschmar-Schuldorff is clearly informed by Pressburger's own experience as a refugee in wartime Britain.[6] At his tribunal pleading his case to stay in Britain, the widower Theo crystallises the exile's paradoxical sense of nostalgia by stating that he is 'homesick' for England. Although this has never been his home, its pastoral scenery reminds him of his English wife, Edith (Deborah Kerr), and of his oldest friend, Clive Wynne-Candy (Roger Livesey). The film is not, then, restricted to a literal evocation of geographical exile. It also considers the theme metaphorically. The English protagonist, Clive (the Colonel Blimp of the title), is banished from his imagined and complete sense of self. In an extended Edwardian sequence, he recognises too late that he has failed to win the love of his 'ideal', Edith, the young English governess he met in Berlin, who has now married his friend Theo. Clive half perceives the magnitude of his loss when he attends a stage production of *Ulysses*. One of Western culture's more notable exiles, Ulysses is declared on stage to be 'the most unhappy of mankind . . . [longing to] view the smoke of his own fire curling blue . . . [and] touch at last his native shore'.[7] Without Edith as a wife, Clive, like Ulysses, has neither home nor hearth, and he spends the rest of his life seeking compensatory fulfilment, either in masculine pursuits such as hunting and soldiering, or by finding physical substitutes for his lost love in surrogates for Edith (all of them played by Deborah Kerr). By the closing shot of the film, the aged Clive has also

lost his literal home during the Blitz. He stands in the street where his house once was, and turns at last to salute the British army marching by off screen. This street scene is a spatial expression of the importance of the public over the private during the war, and Clive's invigorated salute, with a military march tune accompaniment, expresses a faith in communal, shared endeavour which is clearly utopian.

Although *Blimp* attracted Winston Churchill's opprobrium, it marks Powell and Pressburger's commitment to the hegemonic ideals of wartime British cinema, characterised as it was by elements of propaganda and often by a mode of direct address used to foster recognition or to educate the population. When Clive faces the camera and salutes, it is an intimate yet public gesture of respect to the soldiers passing by within the narrative, but more significantly his look crosses the boundary of a 'fourth wall' and directly acknowledges a dispersed mass cinema audience. It admits an impossible sense of community with them, and is the final act of incorporation in a film which has striven to unite all ages, all classes, both genders and even a 'good German' in an allied hostility to Nazism.

Their next feature film, *A Canterbury Tale* (1944), is set in Powell's home county of Kent, but it is viewed through Pressburger's exile's sensibility. The film is a fond, if quizzical, portrait of half-timbered village Englishness made dark and strange because of the warped misogyny of its protagonist Thomas Colpeper (Eric Portman). The name of the village in the film captures the ambiguity: Chillingbourne, a cold domain, where a series of nocturnal attacks have taken place on girls stationed nearby. Much of the film was shot (by Erwin Hillier) on location in the idyllic countryside where Powell spent his childhood. In part it is his nostalgic paean; in part he now shares his collaborator's fascination with a landscape where he no longer feels at home. The film's neo-Romantic aesthetic argues that the disruptive frenzy of urban modernity needs the curative properties of the English landscape to regain a true sense of perspective. A trio of young protagonists – a Land Army girl, a British soldier and a GI – are exiled from their loved ones, their homes or from their youthful hopes. They have failed to fulfil their ambitions and now conscription has uprooted them. Delayed in Chillingbourne by their wish to investigate the attacks on the girls, they acclimatise to rural England and gain a sense of its history.

As with *49th Parallel*, there is a conflict between staying and going, between stasis and mobility. The

Chaucerian trajectory of the protagonists towards Canterbury invests the journey motif with the spiritual weight of pilgrimage and urges them forward, while their enjoyment of the visual spectacle of the Kent countryside arrests their journey. Complicating this dialogue between the picaresque and the picturesque is their involvement in the plot to prove that the mystery attacker is Colpeper. The film's tensions allegorise the condition of the exiled. The stress on images of domesticity and permanence throughout the film implies a need to belong; but the irrational motivation of the 'glueman' is suggestive of an hysterical fear of assimilation, and asserts a case for remaining outside this otherworld. Finally, the utopianism to be found in Canterbury Cathedral sublimates those anxieties and fixates them onto an ideal future.

At the end of the film, when the trio at last reach Canterbury, miracles seem to occur. The Land Army girl learns that her fiancé, feared dead, is alive; the GI receives letters from the girlfriend he thought had forgotten him; and the British soldier realises a long-abandoned ambition to play the Cathedral organ before he and his battalion are shipped into battle. The image of Canterbury Cathedral becomes a symbol of spiritual blessing. It also stands for tradition and permanence, stoicism and defiance: actuality footage (reminiscent of Humphrey Jennings's images of St Paul's in the Blitz) documents the Cathedral standing proud above the bombed streets of Canterbury. Pilgrimage thus becomes a metaphor for the common purpose of the war effort. There is a temporal ambiguity in the last images of the film. The Cathedral stands for the past; like the Matterhorn, its longevity is a cause of wonderment and it silently passes judgment on modern ephemera and transitoriness. But, like the 'Boots the Chemists' shop sign in the narrow street through which the soldiers march, the Cathedral looks the same in 2001 as it does in these 1944 images and the footage of Canterbury seems strangely contemporary.[8] This is appropriate, for the Cathedral also stands for the future: the ringing Cathedral bells chime for an anticipated victory and peace, for the new Jerusalem of the welfare state, and for utopia.

Questions of Fantasy: The Artist's Tale

The transcendental tendency evident in *A Canterbury Tale* and its successor, *I Know Where I'm Going* (1945), is re-channelled in Powell and Pressburger's post-war work. In the trio of women-centred melodramas they make after the war, *Black Narcissus*, *The Red Shoes* and *Gone to Earth* (1950), we find desire thwarted, neuroticised and Gothicised: narratives of aspiration are distorted, to become narratives of blockage. *A Matter of Life and Death* is a transitional film. Released after the war, it mixes an idealised and happily resolved wartime romance with spectacular shifts between Heaven and Earth, parading fantasy elements rich in visual inventiveness.[9] This film ushers in a new phase in their career: as Powell writes in his garrulous autobiography, 'Now the war was over, *The Red Shoes* told us to go out and die for art.'[10] The idealism of the war story continues, but the structure is reworked and often reality is abandoned in favour of a regime constructed around fantasy or 'Art'.

Raymond Williams has argued that because Romantic art purports to transcend the material economic base, and sets itself up as a marvellous, sequestered thing, it is constructed as a 'magic' space, resisting through its appeals to culture. It is specialised, abstracted from the quotidian. Along with this comes the notion of Art as a 'superior reality'.[11] This is the position to which Powell subscribes. With a gift for self-mythologisation, he appointed himself as 'a high priest of the mysteries' and declared that for him 'the end was art, the end was to tell a story; the end was to go out into the real world and turn it into a romantic fantasy world where anything could happen'.[12] Pressburger's first draft screenplay for *The Red Shoes*, written in the 1930s for Korda, realistically narrated the tale of aspiring dancers and revolved around a love triangle between the heroine Vicky, the composer Julian and the impresario Lermontov. When the project was revived after the war, Powell encouraged him to write it up as a metaphysical meditation on the conflict between Art and Life, and Lermontov was imbued with seemingly magical powers.[13]

Lermontov's ballet troupe is a creative team, and it expresses the same collaborative ethos of Powell–Pressburger's own company, The Archers. *The Red Shoes* is less a film about ballet than about Art in general, and the transformative power of cinema in particular. The kernel of the original 1930s screenplay survives as a backstage drama portraying the hard work behind a theatrical production. At one point, Lermontov is called a magician for achieving a great success with his protégée Vicky, but he is quick to point out that a magician can only pull a rabbit out of a hat if the creature is already in there to begin with. Although what he voices here suggests a very materialist approach to Art, he embodies a far more mystical view of its power. This reflects the supernatural theme in the Hans Christian Andersen tale of a girl whose red shoes force her to continue dancing. The style and the narrative of the film are broadly realistic until a central sequence in which Vicky dances in the première of 'The Red Shoes' ballet. Once she is in the red shoes the real theatre-space is left behind and we enter a surreal fantasy. Jack Cardiff's camerawork, and Hein Heckroth's imaginative designs create special effects which combine with music and dance to create pure cinematic spectacle. *The Red Shoes* is Powell–Pressburger's first art–film, and it demonstrates that the utopian possibilities which were rendered topographically in the war films are now to be sought in Art, and in imaginative cinematic illusions.

As an artistic ideal Powell was pursuing the 'composed film' which would form an 'organic whole', a synthesis of music, dialogue, sound effects and images.[14] Prior to *The Red Shoes*, The Archers' chief designer had been Alfred Junge, whose work is exemplified in the architecture of the studio set for *Black Narcissus* and the Bathers' Pool in *Colonel Blimp*. Junge trained in Germany, worked at the State Opera and Theatre and at the UFA Studios on films such as Paul Leni's *Waxworks* (1924). Most of his work, however, is conventional and solid. Hein Heckroth, who replaced him as The Archers' production designer on *The Red Shoes* and its successors, boasted more modernist credentials. He worked with the avant-garde Kurt Joos ballet company, which was exiled from Europe to Dartington in Devon during the war, and carried the flag for anti-realism in the theatre. Heckroth helped Powell realise his ambition for the composed film, where design, blocking, shots

'A romantic fantasy world where anything could happen': *The Red Shoes* (Michael Powell/Emeric Pressburger, 1948)

and editing all synchronised to match a pre-recorded musical score. In the pastel shades, the ephemeral gauzes and the gossamer airiness of his designs in the ballet sequence of *The Red Shoes* – and in *The Tales of Hoffmann*, an entirely fantastical film from which reality is banished – we see the influence on him of Adolphe Appia, the French-Swiss writer whose chief artistic interest had been with staging and capturing the musical fluidity of Wagner's operas. Heckroth creates a similarly fluid cinematic space in *The Red Shoes*, in which, as Lermontov insists to Vicky, 'nothing matters but the music'.

In the context of the late 40s, the fantasy elements of the Powell–Pressburger aesthetic are a rejection of the austerity of the time. Britain's status on the world stage was shrinking, and the paucity of the national coffers meant that despite the welfare state, times were hard. The arrival of the Labour government was less of a revolution than it seemed. Many of its senior figures perpetuated a staunchly patrician set of values not too distant from those of Old Toryism, and its appeals to 'the people' reinvented wartime 'One Nation' politics within the context of welfare capitalism. The state's attitude towards the nation's culture can be seen in the direction taken by the newly established Arts Council, which, like the BBC's 'Third Programme', clung to ideas of 'high art' but fostered the notion that it could be trickled down to be enjoyed and appreciated by all the people.

Although Powell and Pressburger's art-films exist within the commercial film sector, they are part of that cultural mission. Their incorporation of elite art forms into a popular medium chimed with the state's wish to popularise high culture for the masses. But the film industry received only minimal support from the state and was governed by the market. The Archers' often-voiced wish for creative freedom from their financial backers marks a desire to be shielded from this truth, and is part of a bourgeois tradition which can seem both self-indulgent and commercially untenable. It can also seem brave, cosmopolitan and international because it allows for an allegiance with art movements which are no respecters of commercial markets or national frontiers.

Cinema can be both national and international. When its images and narratives direct themselves to a national community which can use and understand them – such as Powell and Pressburger's treatment of the British army, Canterbury Cathedral, Sadler's Wells, the English and Scottish countryside – and when it suggests that one can simultaneously belong to a nation and respect the best of foreign culture, as in *The Red Shoes* and *The Tales of Hoffmann*, then the cinema's link to the nation is secure. However, the boundaries of cinema cultures rarely coincide with those of the nation-state. They may more comfortably follow regional demarcations; they may address subcultures for which a sense of nation is not the most salient point of identification; or they may overspill the containing strategies of national culture and situate themselves, as Powell and Pressburger do, within an international framework. None of the above are mutually exclusive. This is why we need to use the 'national cinema' paradigm guardedly, and be alert to its problematical nature.[15]

Notes

1. Powell's work outside his partnership with Pressburger includes impressive films such as *The Edge of the World* (1937), the Spanish/British production *Honeymoon* (1959), the Gothic *Peeping Tom* (1960), and his little-seen West German production of Bartók's opera *Bluebeard's Castle* (1964).

2. See Kevin Macdonald, *Emeric Pressburger: The Life and Death of a Screenwriter*; Pressburger's mother perished at Auschwitz.

3. Emeric Pressburger, *Killing a Mouse on Sunday* (London: Collins, 1961), pp. 9–10. Pressburger's novel was later filmed as *Behold a Pale Horse* (Fred Zinnemann, 1964).

4. Charles Barr, 'In a Strange Land: The Collaboration of Michael Powell and Emeric Pressburger', *La Lettre de la Maison Française*, p. 95.

5. See Benedict Anderson, *Imagined Communities: Reflections on the Origin and Spread of Nationalism* (London: Verso, 1983).

6. Kevin Gough-Yates, 'Exiles and British Cinema', in the present volume, p. 129.

7. Michael Powell and Emeric Pressburger, *The Life and Death of Colonel Blimp*, pp. 173–4.

8. Regrettably, Boots and its sign moved from Mercery Lane around 2005.

9. See Ian Christie, *A Matter of Life and Death*.

10. Michael Powell, *A Life in Movies*, p. 653.

11. Raymond Williams, *Culture and Society 1780–1950* (Harmondsworth: Penguin, 1961), p. 50.

12. Michael Powell, *Million Dollar Movie*, p. 16; Powell, *A Life in Movies*, p. 93.

13. In a similar fashion, Rumer Godden's naturalistic *Bildungsroman Black Narcissus* is transformed in the film version into a high-Gothic clash between Spirit and Flesh.

14. Powell, *A Life in Movies*, p. 581.

15. For the debate over national identity in British cinema see: Andrew Higson, 'The Instability of the National', in Justine Ashby and Andrew Higson (eds), *British Cinema: Past and Present* (London: Routledge, 2000) and John Hill, 'The Issue of National Cinema and British Film Production', in Duncan Petrie (ed.), *New Questions in British Cinema* (London: BFI, 1992).

Bibliography

Barr, Charles, 'In a Strange Land: The Collaboration of Michael Powell and Emeric Pressburger', *La Lettre de la Maison Française*, no. 11, Trinity-Michaelmas 1999.

Christie, Ian (ed.), *Powell, Pressburger and Others* (London: BFI, 1978).

Christie, Ian, *Arrows of Desire* (London: Faber and Faber, 1994).

Christie, Ian, *A Matter of Life and Death* (London: BFI, 2000).

Christie, Ian and Moor, Andrew (eds), *Michael Powell: International Perspectives on an English Film-maker* (London: BFI, 2005).

Connelly, Mark, *The Red Shoes* (London: I. B. Tauris, 2005).

Gough-Yates, Kevin (ed.), *Michael Powell in Collaboration with Emeric Pressburger* (London: BFI, 1970).

Macdonald, Kevin, *Emeric Pressburger: The Life and Death of a Screenwriter* (London: Faber and Faber, 1994).

Moor, Andrew, *Powell and Pressburger: A Cinema of Magic Spaces* (London: I. B. Tauris, 2005)

Peters, John Durham, 'Exile, Nomadism and Diaspora: The Stakes of Mobility in the Western Canon', in Hamid Naficy (ed.), *Home, Exile, Homeland: Film, Media and Politics of Place* (London: Routledge, 1999).

Powell, Michael, *A Life in Movies* (London: Mandarin, 1992).

Powell, Michael, *Million Dollar Movie* (London: Mandarin, 1992).

Powell, Michael and Pressburger, Emeric, *The Life and Death of Colonel Blimp*, edited and with an introduction by Ian Christie (London: Faber and Faber, 1994).

Screen special issue devoted to Powell – *Screen* vol. 46 no. 1, Spring 2005.

Street, Sarah, *Black Narcissus* (London: I. B. Tauris, 2005).

27

Some Lines of Inquiry into Post-war British Crimes

RAYMOND DURGNAT

This survey of British crime films from 1945 to 1949 derives from a work in progress on British cinema in the Age of Austerity. The subheadings indicate, not *pigeonholes*, inside which the films mentioned would belong, but *ad hoc* groupings around selected themes. No genre *requires* or *imposes* stereotypes. No genre has unique themes, attitudes, moods, styles or narrative structures, most of which are shared by *many* genres. Genres freely crossbreed, and generate hybrids and unclassifiables as easily as 'pedigree' specimens. To catalogue *every* appearance of *every* theme would require a very long book, but this selection may help spread attention from the usual films (critical classics, cult favourites . . .) to a wider spread of suspects.

1. The Crime Genre(s) – and Crimes in other Genres

If the crime film is a genre it's difficult to define, for crimes abound in films of all genres. The crime genres range from gangster and noir (separate, but easily overlapping) to Agatha Christie's middle-class whodunits. However, a courtroom discussion of criminal libel wouldn't qualify, unless it also involves harder, tougher action. Crime genres normally require some actual or incipient brutal or socially transgressive act, and a reaction from the machinery of law enforcement, be it official (the police), or unofficial (a private eye) or communal (a posse). The antagonism between 'crime as bad' versus 'law as good' is routinely counterpointed, complicated or reversed (by decent criminals, crooked cops, etc.) Six borderline cases may be usefully noted. *Waterloo Road* (Sidney Gilliat, 1945) is

properly classified as an 'ordinary people drama' (though this genre has no widely accepted name). Yet its decent family man, John Mills, is a serious criminal twice over, as a two-time deserter from the British army. Is this the most *insubordinate* movie from *any* of the combatant nations? *The Wicked Lady* (Leslie Arliss, 1945) would qualify as a crime story, insofar as James Mason and Margaret Lockwood are highwaypersons, yet it's usually grouped with costume melodramas. *Carnival* (Stanley Haynes, 1946) climaxes with a *crime passionel*, as Bible-black farmer Bernard Miles shoots his wife, music-hall ballerina Sally Gray, for loving aristocratic sculptor Michael Wilding, but the film's major interests make it mainly a romantic melodrama. In *Kind Hearts and Coronets* (Robert Hamer, 1949), Dennis Price kills a whole family tree of Alec Guinnesses, but the film is conventionally thought of as an Ealing comedy. In *The Winslow Boy* (Anthony Asquith, 1948), a very young naval cadet's alleged theft of a five-shilling postal order precipitates an elaborate courtroom struggle. It certainly revolves around the minutiae of a crime (which wasn't), but its main theme is not 'crime' but 'the law', and conflicts between 'Establishment' and 'private' attitudes. Rather less tangential is *For Them That Trespass* (Alberto Cavalcanti, 1949). Middle-class writer Stephen Murray is fascinated by a low-class girl, but finds her murdered, and to preserve his own respectability withholds vital evidence, thus sending lower-class Richard Todd to jail for fifteen years. Todd breaks out, hears Murray's 'fictional' radio play, recognises the case, and comes after him, to get the wrong righted. This is, I think, a crime film – even though crime does not subordinate its other interests, notably class injustice. As often, in films of our period, the upper classes wrong the lower (though the detail and reasons are beyond our scope here).

2. Criminals, Lumpen, Ordinary People, Populism

There's a large grey area, or rather overlap, between the crime film and the 'ordinary people' genre. The idea that films about ordinary, unglamorous, people (the lower-middle classes down) living everyday lives, constitute a genre, prevailed from the mid-20s on through our period, for reasons connected with leftish interests in social realism, and ranges from French Poetic Realism (like *Hotel du Nord*, 1938) to Hollywood films like *Street Scene* (1931) and *Dead End* (1937). But as the last pair of titles remind us, ordinary people, delinquents and criminals meet, mingle and interact, just as the social classes involved dovetail, overlap and shade gradually into one another. Down the *Waterloo Road*, John Mills, respectable lower class, finds himself in a sort of 'deserters' network', and as he squares up to spiv Stewart Granger, Alastair Sim, the local GP (i.e. middle-middle class), looks on, keenly and benignly. *It Always Rains on Sunday* (Robert Hamer, 1947) strikes some critics as an 'ordinary people' film, a sort of East End cross-section. Others see it rather as a 'low-life' film, and indeed most of its characters are criminals, or accomplices, or policemen. On the 'ordinary people' side, its love story can evoke *Brief Encounter* (1945), for sharing the everyday anguish of an ordinary middle-aged housewife, while trains shriek by. On the other hand, John McCallum is a violent convict, on the run, and Googie Withers, by helping him, becomes a criminal too (though we don't think of her as such).

London Belongs to Me (Sidney Gilliat, 1948) is another genre 'amphibian'. It's a tale of the shabby pseudo-genteel (a very low middle class), in a drab boarding house, who falteringly and loosely get together to protest on behalf of a mucky-handed mechanic (Richard Attenborough), who has turned luckless spiv and bungled himself into a death sentence. Their demo is 'too little and too late', the sentence having been commuted anyway, but in the process barriers between the stiffly respectable, the common and the criminal classes crumble.

3. Noir, Austerity, Traditional British Miserabilism and Other Feel-bad Factors

The heavy weight, in post-war British movies, of guilt and gloom, and broodings about crime, is very surprising for a victorious nation busily constructing a kindly welfare state. I'd diagnose not one reason, but a 'pluri-causal convergence' of factors, some long-term (like puritan pessimism and sobriety), some short-term (like war-weariness, widespread bereavement and middle-class fears of Labourist egalitarianism). Whereas Hollywood noir between 1945 and 1949 is driven by an optimism/cynicism split, the British mood owes more to a more gradual, uneasy shift of the balance between older, more traditional suspicions about human nature and more modern, lenient attitudes, spreading fastest among the middle classes, some of whom regarded Victorian harshness as a main cause of evil.

Hollywood noir must negotiate much stronger pressures to a general optimism, partly from audiences themselves, partly from censorship. So, it usually limits its noir to the underworld and its penumbra, and uses a cocktail of chiaroscuro lighting, brisk, brute violence, and temptingly evil femmes fatales to attract a wider audience than that usually reached by films imbued with moral pessimism. In myriad ways, evil is segregated from ordinary people. But in British films good and evil are more intimately connected.

4. Middle-class Noir: I: Incomes and Inheritances

Since 1914, the upper middle classes have experienced, or feared, a certain decline and fall. The Great War escalated their taxes. Slump and depression decimated their dividends. World War II saw Britain bankrupt by 1941 (though US aid averted disaster). Now Austerity and Labourism threaten to finish them off. Death duties, which ravage inheritances, crucial to many middle-class people (especially women), are a very sore point. Two films ingeniously combine 'inheritance' themes with 'social rise' themes, thus appealing to spectators in both the threatened upper and the rising lower classes. In *Jassy* (Bernard Knowles, 1947) and *Blanche Fury* (Marc Allégret, 1948), Jassy (Margaret Lockwood) and Blanche (Valerie Hobson) are female servants, with whose social ambitions we can sympathise and whose hardness of heart we can understand. Both marry into the gentry (brutal Basil Sydney, vulnerable Michael Gough) for security, wealth and property, but love another. Both, after being involved in one or two murders, convey this 'patrimony' to a more 'democratic' character (Jassy to tenant farmer Dermot Walsh; Blanche to her son by co-employee Stewart Granger). Both films feature those property-less nomads, gypsies.

Whereas gypsy Jassy is 'rising lumpen', Blanche seems 'sunken middle class' even, a 'decayed gentlewoman'. Thorn (Granger), is both a 'have' and a 'have not'. (1) As manager of this property, evicting gypsy lumpen, he's a 'have'. But (2) as merely its manager, whose duties often evoke manual labour, he's a 'have not'. He evicts the gypsies, not through 'middle-class' loyalty to its legal owners, the Fury family, but because he schemes to get hold of it. So he's (3a) *seemingly* servile middle class, but actually (3b) graspingly ambitious middle class. But he's also (4) a bastardised relative of its owners, i.e. 'sunken upper class'. Whence his obsessive, bitter fury (!) at what he considers his expropriation into servility. So he can stand as metaphor for (5) a proletarian resentment. He's an omnibus, or portmanteau, of class furies, in all directions, and can attract diverse identifications from diverse spectators. Probably the principal tension is his 'have not' animus against the property-owners. It drives him to murder Blanche's husband, and father-in-law, and he'd kill the last heir, the little girl to whom Blanche was governess. After he's hanged, she dies giving birth to their child, who will inherit the stately home. All this evokes, in personal drama, some bitterness and sufferings in British social history – the passing of power to lower-class democracy. It's a positive end, though hardly a happy one, with the hero/villain hanged and the heroine dead! Blanche's death in childbirth is not, I think, a woman being 'punished' for daring to be sexual, or be independent, or acquire property and power. Blanche's sins – adultery, a hardness of materialism, near-connivance in two murders out of three – are the understandable, maybe unavoidable, response of her mettle to the inequalities of her day and age. Most 1940s spectators well understand that movies are not moral instruction manuals to prove that sins are punished, that unhappy ends don't flow from sins whose avoidance would have brought a happy end, and that unhappiness can hit us as arbitrarily as a German bomb, or illness or fatal complications in childbirth.

5. Middle-class Noir: II: The Portman Murders

Up to 1945, Eric Portman played a nice diversity of roles. In *Millions Like Us* (Frank Launder, Sidney Gilliat,

1943) he's a factory foreman, and his intellectual forehead, hooded eyes – now cloudy, now gleaming – and tight yet sensual mouth suggest 'ordinary people' thoughtfulness, J. B. Priestley-style. In *Great Day* (Lance Comfort, 1945) he's a demoralised country gentleman, whose moment of shame is stealing, while drunk, a ten-shilling note from a working-class woman (Kathleen Harrison). (Here's another upper-class 'trespass' against the lower . . . .) From then on he's a one-man crime wave. In *Wanted for Murder* (Lawrence Huntington, 1946) he's the Hyde Park strangler, and attributes his murderous drives to his hangman forefather (hereditary tendencies? or morbid imagination? or both?). In *Daybreak* (Compton Bennett, 1946) Portman is the public hangman, and ingeniously frames, for his own murder, the bargee (Maxwell Reed) who seduces his wife (Ann Todd). But face to face in the condemned cell he can't hang him, and confesses (reprieved by censor?). In *Dear Murderer* (Arthur Crabtree, 1947) Portman kills Maxwell Reed again, for loving his wife again, though this time she's Greta Gynt.

These murders evoke *crimes passionnels*, in involving sexual jealousy, but they smack even more strongly of offended vanity (egomania), or cold pathology, which are hardly 'passionate', in the usual sense of loving attachment to an individual. The films play on such confusions. Moreover, the Portman–Reed 'duos' foreground class tensions. Portman is middle class: suave, supercilious, secretive, rational, deadly jealous. Reed is a hunk-cum-barrow-boy, virile, shifty, physically aggressive. *The Mark of Cain* (Brian Desmond Hurst, 1948) is different again. Portman's stifled, homicidal hatreds are 'all in the (northern factory-owning) family'. To win Sally Gray, he poisons his blustering brother (Guy Rolfe), but accidentally frames her and gets sussed out by another virile admirer (Dermot Walsh). In *Corridor of Mirrors* (Terence Young, 1948) he's a rich mystical aesthete who thinks he murdered Welsh beauty Edana Romney in their previous incarnations. In effect, he frames, and then hangs, himself. But he's also goaded by his possessive housekeeper (and malignant mother-figure?) Barbara Mullen.

6. Middle-class Noir: III: The Gentle Sex

Most ladies who murder prefer to quietly poison. In *Pink String and Sealing Wax* (Robert Hamer, 1945) Googie Withers is a battle-axe barmaid resolved to eliminate her husband. She coaxes poisons from a shy and innocent pharmacist's assistant (Gordon Jackson), whose religious fanatic father (Mervyn Johns) rules him with a rod of iron. In *Madeleine* (David Lean, 1950) Ann Todd is a Scottish banker's daughter resolved to preserve her respectability by poisoning her penniless French seducer when he threatens scandal. In *So Evil, My Love* (Lewis Allen, 1948) Ann Todd (again) is a missionary's widow who is seduced by immoral artist Ray Milland, with whom she schemes a convoluted path through old friendships, blackmailings and poisonings. Here, not just sexual love but all social relations, and religion, and art, become hypocritical, insidious, abusable. In *Bedelia* (Lance Comfort, 1946) Margaret Lockwood is a Riviera socialite who poisons her three husbands. In *The Wicked Lady*, as a Cavalier socialite, she poisons an oppressively puritanical old servant (Felix Aylmer) who cramps her hedonistic style. Her 'trespass' against a faithful retainer is repaid to another Margaret Lockwood in *Jassy*, where her devoted mute maidservant (Esma Cannon), thinking to help her mistress, poisons brutal Basil Sydney, inadvertently framing her. In *This Was a Woman* (Tim Whelan, 1948) Sonia Dresdel humiliates and then poisons her husband, in order to get a richer one, and ravages her daughter's life, until her son the brain surgeon, whom she idolises, turns against her. If Dresdel is a bourgeois matriarch, Siobhan McKenna in *Daughter of Darkness* (Lance Comfort, 1948) is an outcast. A nymphomaniac Irish girl witch-hunted by the village wives, she's inclined to despatch her lovers during, or just after, her sexual excitations.

Where Portman seems coldly rational but seethes with mad emotion, these lady poisoners are more socio-materialistic, and in that sense rational-realistic. Money, or respectability, looms quite large in their motivations. Lockwood as the wicked lady wants to eat her cake and have it (by enjoying social status and untrammelled independence and her bit of rough). But not all the women are calculating. Esma Cannon's motive is platonic gratitude to her kindly mistress, and Sonia Dresdel is vulnerable through her successful son (though perhaps that's more 'Oedipal' than platonic). The missionary's widow's suicide in *So Evil, My Love* suggests that her poisonings were for love of the artist, but then again, perhaps they're a case of *folie à deux*.

In these films woman's sexuality isn't often the problem and where it is, in *Daughter of Darkness*, it is a twisted sexuality as distinct from normal and generally accepted female desire. The woman here is a switch on the (normally male) sex-murderers who proliferate in plays and films in our period: Portman repeatedly, and

two charming lady-killers – Richard Greene in *Now Barabbas Was a Robber* (Gordon Parry, 1949) and Dennis Price in *Holiday Camp* (Ken Annakin, 1947), both possibly inspired by the Neville Heath case of 1946.

7. Close Pent-up Guilts

On screen at least, the respectable middle classes commit more than their fair share of murders. In *Mr. Perrin & Mr. Traill* (Lawrence Huntington, 1948), boarding-school teacher Marius Goring is blimpish, pedantic, snobbish, and so goaded by jealousy of a younger, livelier, science teacher (David Farrar) that for a few mad moments he wants to, not 'murder' him exactly, but kill him by what the French call 'non-assistance to a person in danger'. His humiliation and remorse are observed critically and compassionately. In *The October Man* (Roy Baker, 1947) chemical engineer John Mills, to clear himself of a murder charge, must overcome his shyness, self-doubt, self-restraint, and low assertiveness – conventionally, middle-class traits. The film attributes much of this 'characterology' to a work accident and brain injury inducing amnesia, but the man's style and symptoms evoke the meekly worried, middle-class character type. A similar weakness of spirit infects the protagonists of three other films. In *Take My Life* (Ronald Neame, 1947) another murder suspect (Hugh Williams) panics and runs for it, but is saved by the spunky detective work of his clever diva wife (Greta Gynt). In *The Small Voice* (Fergus McDonell, 1948) Valerie Hobson tartly criticises the self-indulgent depression of her writer husband James Donald, and braces him to outwit (with her help) the escaped convicts who hold them hostage. Richard Todd in *Interrupted Journey* (Daniel Birt, 1949) is unfaithful to his wife (Valerie Hobson), thus getting drawn into a vortex of crime; it's only a dream, but the 'nightmare' is still in his soul. These inadequate protagonists anticipate a kind of 'anti-hero', or V.O.P. (Very Ordinary Person), much rarer in Hollywood. Maybe traditional English modesty and pessimism help audiences in Britain understand, and identify with, guilty weakness and failures rather better than American audiences do.

In *The Upturned Glass* (Lawrence Huntington, 1947), bitchy gossip Pamela Kellino causes the death of brain surgeon James Mason's future bride. He plans to kill her and, backing away from him, she dies accidentally. Then he finds himself having to jeopardise his alibi to save an injured boy.[1] In *Obsession* (Edward Dmytryk, 1949) smooth Harley Street doctor Robert Newton outdoes Eric Portman in cool nasty crime. Each day he brings a hot-water bottle filled with acid into a blitzed house and pours it into an old bath beside which he has chained his wife's lover. Although it's a *crime passionel* he's so cruel, cold and gloating that, far from getting any sympathy from us, he's a powerful argument for capital punishment. On the other hand, hospital nurse Megs Jenkins in *Green for Danger* (Sidney Gilliat, 1946), accused of murdering several patients and staff by switching operating-theatre gases has a deplorably trivial motive: to conceal from nasty neighbours that her twin sister broadcasts for the Germans. But she is so poignant, with her plump motherly figure, high-pitched voice and generally distressed frailty, that we can't but sympathise with her fearful conformity, and the clinging to respectability that links her with Ann Todd in *Madeleine* and *So Evil, My Love*, and Dennis Price in *Kind Hearts and Coronets*. On a lower level of the medical classes, fairground quack Douglass Montgomery in *Forbidden* (George King, 1948) starts slow-poisoning his wife (Patricia Burke), and, just as he remorsefully desists, a chapter of accidents incriminates him.

Martha Wolfenstein and Nathan Leites point out that most Hollywood murders involve quick, brutal, impersonal methods, whereas British murderers have subtler ways of making you croak, like anaesthetic or gas-fire poisoning, and a pseudo-reasonable approach.[2] Most such films involve us so closely with their murderers as to induce an involuntary identification with them, often coupled with a certain sympathy for their motives and an antipathy towards their victims. These stories acknowledge the hostilities pervading ordinary relations, and remind us how easily civilised and coldly barbaric attitudes may intertwine. They're more pessimistic (but also more sensitive) than Hollywood noir, with its relatively simple, sharp good/bad distinctions. In *The Shop at Sly Corner* (George King, 1946), Kenneth Griffith as a sneaky and spiteful shop assistant threatens to blackmail his boss, Oscar Homolka, a foreign antiques dealer (and fence) unless he is given the hand of his musician daughter (Muriel Pavlow). Whereupon Homolka murders him – and so would I.

From one angle, this ready intimacy with criminals may de-demonise the criminal, apprise the 'honest' spectator of his own guilts, and even plead against capital punishment. But back in 1945 many spectators would react more traditionally, on lines like this: 'The more "naturally human" the act of murder is, the more strongly society must assert its disapproval and impose

awesome deterrents, even if the dividing lines get tragically arbitrary.' Such crime films accommodate audience ambivalence about the slowly tilting balance, from Victorian severities to modern leniencies.

8. Whodunits

Whodunits are relatively rare among 'A' features, but among cheaper films they abound. Three star lady detectives. In *Penny and the Pownall Case* (Slim Hand, 1948), Peggy Evans is a model-cum-amateur sleuth who exposes her boss Christopher Lee as complicit with fascists. In *Celia* (Francis Searle, 1949), Hy Hazell is a 'resting' actress who turns 'tec, 'plays' charwoman, and saves a wife from a homicidal husband. *My Sister and I* (Harold Huth, 1948) rather fumbles an intriguing idea. Set-designer Sally Ann Howes finds herself uncovering a murderer, and a very closely pent-up guilt – incest – in the family of a patron of the arts (Martita Hunt).

The liveliest 'tec 'B' films, unlike films noirs, prefer brightly normal settings. There's a fashion salon in *Death in High Heels* (Lionel Tomlinson, 1947), the one London nude show sanctioned as respectable in *Murder at the Windmill* (Val Guest, 1949), and a BBC radio quiz in *The Twenty Questions Murder Mystery* (Paul Stein, 1950).[3]

9. Ladies in Distress

Uncle Silas (Charles Frank, 1947) is a floridly Gothic piece, with rather beautiful (and expensive) décor. But, alas, its drama is limited to switches between sweetness and threats from the Victorian heroine's guardians (Derrick de Marney, Katina Paxinou), so it's a box-office flop. *Madness of the Heart* (Charles Bennett, 1949) bombs for the opposite reason: melodramatic overload. Margaret Lockwood hesitates between the convent life and marriage to a rich Frenchman, shrinks from his viciously snooty family, loses but then regains her sight, then feigns blindness to entrap her murderous rival (Kathleen Byron of *Black Narcissus*, on the rampage again). Between these two extremes, *A Man about the House* (Leslie Arliss, 1947) gets the mixture right (between domestic drama/suspense, melo/pathos). Spinsters Dulcie Gray and Margaret Johnston move into their Italian dream villa but slowly wonder if they're not at risk from their very obliging, very handsome major-domo (Kieron Moore). It's another master/servant plot, like *Jassy* and *Blanche Fury*, but with gender reversals and a softer touch.[4]

10. Thrillers: Two-fisted/Thick-ear/ Hard-boiled/Tough/Noir

By 1945 two-fisted English gentlemen like Bulldog Drummond seem a touch passé. This may be less to do with Britain's shaken self-image – appeasement having associated the toff class with weakness – and the English gentleman's socio-economic decline and fall, than with Yank private eyes having muscled in on the 'private justice' racket.

Nonetheless, the thrillers which most widely popularise American noir in France come from two British authors, specialists in faking pseudo-Yank tough thrillers. Peter Cheyney and James Hadley Chase start to churn them out in 1936. In 1948 two hit the screen with a faint plop. In *Uneasy Terms* (Vernon Sewell, 1948) gumshoe Slim Callaghan (Michael Rennie) recces the murky intrigues of a colonel's stepfamily (a soupçon of *The Big Sleep?*). In *No Orchids for Miss Blandish*, American gangsters kidnap an heiress, dope her and rape her. But in the film (St John L. Clowes, 1948) she's saved from such a fate by romantically respectful gangster Jack La Rue, a good-bad guy (made even more sympathetic by a domineering mother). As the police burst in to rescue her, she realises they've killed him and joins him in death. Miss Blandish's rejection of rich respectable boredom for the sex-and-violence life means she's a soul-sister of two Gainsborough girls: Phyllis Calvert as schizo-mum in *Madonna of the Seven Moons* (Arthur Crabtree, 1944), and Lockwood's Wicked Lady. The Gainsborough films infuse their murky and morbid intimations with a robust energy, and balance them with healthy and heartily sensitive characters whose lively sexual promise goes with normal pleasures like horse-riding and grand balls. In contrast, *Miss Blandish*, with its sleazy, sensual faces and nasty air, paraphrases the novel's porno-philosophical sadism, via visuals as bad as its prose.

11. Two Gentleman Criminals

As the Bulldog Drummond-type toff is in eclipse, so is the gentleman crook. By 1945 the confident individuality of Raffles and Blackshirt has gone the way of their classmate Blimp's chivalry. Still, two films hark back. *The Spider and the Fly* (Robert Hamer, 1949) observes, wistfully but finally with saddened cynicism, a moral duel between a gentleman crook (Guy Rolfe) and a 'civilised' policeman (Eric Portman). They're both French, which enables Hamer to combine his Francophile leanings and his moral wryness/melancholy. In *Escape* (Joseph L. Mankiewicz, 1948), officer-class Rex Harrison, chatting

to a 'Mayfair darling', accidentally kills an obnoxious bobby, gets sent to Dartmoor, breaks out, is helped by Peggy Cummins, but finally gives himself up, largely to protect a parson who has helped him.[5] It's a strange blend of Galsworthy's moral scrupulousness and Warners' man-on-the-run melo and hard to say whether the fugitive's moral punctiliousness is meant to be specific to gentlemen as a social class and how far it's a shining example of 'decency' generally.

12. Lyceum Melodrama Modernised

The Curse of the Wraydons (Victor M. Gover, 1946) and *The Greed of William Hart* (Oswald Mitchell, 1948) end a long line of George King 'B' films smacking of Victorian 'blood and thunder' melodrama. Both star Tod Slaughter (aptly named), a fine old trouper of live theatre and better, I'd say, on stage than in these films.[6] On screen, the lord of this genre is Derrick de Marney. He's juicily friendly-sinister in *Uncle Silas*; in *Latin Quarter* (Vernon Sewell, 1945), he's a mad sculptor whose work of art entombs his wife's body.

Some stories retain faintly Gothic overtones by using Bohemian milieux, like a fairground or circus. In *Dual Alibi* (Alfred Travers, 1947) Terence de Marney

Trapezist twins, Herbert Lom x 2 in *Dual Alibi* (Alfred Travers, 1947)

(brother of Derrick) cheats trapezist twins (Herbert Lom x 2) of their lottery win. He's murdered, but which Lom dunnit? Witnesses, and justice, are baffled. Lom's smooth glowerings reconcile melo and deadpan. In *The Trojan Brothers* (Maclean Rogers, 1946), David Farrar is the front half of a pantomime horse, and enjoys an affair with society beauty Patricia Burke until she dumps him, whereupon he strangles her. It's a lively comedy-of-manners, what with insults hurled across the footlights, and backchat between the horse's mouth and its other end (Bobby Howes), set in the Bohemian world of the music hall. Interestingly, too, it enlivens a traditional ambivalence about class barriers. For the one end's aspiration and rage contrasts with the other end's weary marriage to Barbara Mullen. They're like the 'heads' and 'tails' of a lower middle class: upward mobility/acceptance. *The Shop at Sly Corner*, a 'shopkeeper's tragedy', gives its contemporary settings Gothic inflec-

tions: exotically overripe acting (Oscar Homolka vs Kenneth Griffith), eerie antiques (an oriental idol and an Eastern poison unknown to science). It's 'plain-clothes' Gothickry, well adapted to what many think an old-fangled, doomed genre.

It shares pride of place with two British National movies of 1948, both co-scripted by Dylan Thomas. *The Three Weird Sisters* (Dan Birt, 1948) rejoices in highly Gothic performances by Nancy Price, Mary Clare and Mary Merrall, a trio of bitter crones out to kill their half-brother Raymond Lovell, and his pretty secretary Nova Pilbeam. Though Gothic, in a sense, it really derives from genres (or traditions) about rural evil. *No Room at the Inn* (Dan Birt, 1948) brings the idiom virtually up to date. Slatternly alcoholic Freda Jackson starves and brutalises wartime evacuees, and squanders the benefit money doled out by negligent social workers (*plus ça change . . .*).

Backchat between the horse's mouth and its other end: *The Trojan Brothers* (Maclean Rogers, 1946)

13. BBC Thick-ear Pulp

Surprisingly, the principal supplier of pulp tosh for British 'B's, 'C's and 'D's is the supposedly high-minded BBC, whose radio thriller serials are low-brow, boyish and smashingly popular. Its heroes: Dick Barton – Special Agent (Drummond's 'scrapper' successor), Paul Temple and his faithful wife Steve, The Man in Black, and Dr Morelle, star in cheapissimo 'B's, mostly from Butcher's and Exclusive. Both noir man and mournful doctor are played by Valentine Dyall, whose dark, mean voice well expresses (like, later, Edgar Lustgarten's) the mixture of libidinal fascination and moralistic gloating conspicuous in popular attitudes to crime and punishment. It's not usually just morbid, and even where it is, it's an authentic pessimism, with a philosophical pedigree going back to the atheist Hobbes and the harsh puritan Calvin. For both of them, Man, like Nature, is nasty, brutish and morally stunted.

14. Tales of the Criminous

This pessimism/severity imbues a very old, very morbid, pre-Victorian genre, the Criminal Chronicle. Here, a vicious criminal's career is retold, with no real 'interpretation' and with no real sympathy for anybody much: just archetypal, gut-instinct horror and punitiveness. It may seem Victorian but it goes much further back. It's there in the 'hanging' broadsheets, then in the *Newgate Calendar*, then in *Reynolds News*, which in Victorian times combined popular radicalism with sensationalism, then in the *News of the World*, and it gets into some early films, like *The Life of Charles Peace* (1905). It's soon pressure-grouped out of movies, and only fully resurfaces in *The Case of Charles Peace* (Norman Lee, 1949). But its spirit seeps into a whole range of films: *The Wicked Lady*, *Good-time Girl* (1948) (though overall it's too soft-heartedly reformist), *Night and the City* (1950) (though it's more drama than chronicle); and *Brighton Rock* (1947), set among the razor-slashing racetrack gangs of the 1930s.

15. Return to Civvy Street

More topical problems included demobbed servicemen finding post-war readjustment very difficult. It inspires many films in many genres, though only crime films concern us here. Most demob yarns concern the black-marketeers and spivs so useful to honest citizens throughout Austerity. In *Nightbeat* (Harold Huth, 1948) ex-commando pals sign on as bobbies: one stays straight, one goes crook. It's scripted by two ex-wartime 'Specials', Guy Morgan and Tommy Morrison, and they

tackle that rare theme, the badly bent bobby. In *They Made Me a Fugitive* (Cavalcanti, 1947) ex-officer Trevor Howard joins a gang of black-marketeers; when they're revealed as dope-peddling torturers, he wants out, which they won't allow. In *Dancing with Crime* (John Paddy Carstairs, 1947) taxi-driver Richard Attenborough sets out to avenge army pal Bill Owen and summons a horde of brother cabbies to help round up dance-hall racketeers. In *Hue and Cry* (Charles Crichton, 1947), warehouse lad Harry Fowler sets out to help save a comic from crooks, and summons a horde of kids and chums to help round up dockland racketeers. In *Noose* (Edmond T. Gréville, 1948) ex-commando Derek Farr sets out to help crusading reporter Carole Landis and summons a horde of pugilistic pals to help round up nightclub racketeers.[7] All hopefully populist, like *Man on the Run* (Lawrence Huntington, 1949), where decent deserter Derek Farr must live outside the law unless the government decrees an amnesty, but strait-laced Joan Hopkins likes his manly decency and rather than turning him in risks her reputation to help him.

16. Rackets and Gangs

On racetracks and in gambling clubs (the latter illegal until the 1960s), champagne-swish society and organised crookery can meet and mingle. *The Calendar* (Arthur Crabtree, 1948) has a sneaking sympathy for racehorse owner John McCallum's briefly shaky morality. Clever Greta Gynt helps get him off the hook. In the racing world, the underworld is the racecourse razor-slasher gang in *Brighton Rock*. Casino gambling is not underworld exactly, but 'demi-monde' – deluxe, though furtive meets in private flats, where feckless nobs, rich Mayfairites, bookies, harmless and otherwise respectable fun-lovers, and consenting victims can rub elbows with criminals, some honest, some bent, some vicious as they come. The politer, pleasanter, side, of all this, inspires *Adam and Evelyne* (1949), where orphan Jean Simmons charms professional gambler Stewart Granger, her father-figure-turned-lover, into going straight. It's much less a crime film than a café-society romance (with charmingly Oedipal overtones). The uglier, nastier, side inspires *Third Time Lucky* (Gordon Parry, 1949). Here Charles Goldner as an outraged gangster stalks Dermot Walsh as a professional gambler, and Glynis Johns his mascot (just maybe *verb sap* for 'mistress'?). Alas, violence substitutes for the subtler disillusionments implied by the title of Gerald Butler's source novel, *They Cracked Her Glass Slipper*.

British screens swarm with spivs and black-marketeers.[8] In *Dancing with Crime*, they infest the Palais de Danse, that beacon of pleasure shining over mean streets. In *Noose* they run a Soho nightclub. The tougher screen gangs tend to mix Cockney with Mediterranean ethnic types (Italian, Sicilian, Maltese, Greek), represented by George Coulouris and Charles Goldner. This is probably not xenophobia, more 'popular sociology'. For a few, very conspicuous, immigrants, from these relatively violent cultures did lead a widespread escalation from smuggling nylons to smuggling dope, from bouncing to poncing, and from fist and cosh to knife and shooter. Still, vile Brits dominate *Brighton Rock* (where Attenborough is sixteen-year-old razor-boy Pinkie), *They Made Me a Fugitive* (where gentle Griffith Jones becomes psychotically vain gang boss Narcy), and *The Blue Lamp* (Basil Dearden, 1950) where young hysteric Dirk Bogarde shoots tough but kindly PC Dixon.

British films are more interested in the failures than the successes of underworld attempts at self-regulation. Even when well intentioned, they're pitiably unstable, while treacheries, transgressions and even righteous feuds and vengeances make their Code of Honour much fiercer than the Law.[9] Tough-as-nails William Hartnell is a small-time gangster wreaking harsh vengeance for betrayal in both *Murder in Reverse* (Montgomery Tully, 1945) and *Appointment with Crime* (John Harlow, 1946), and a fat lot of good it does him. *Good-time Girl* (David MacDonald) traces, with too-distant compassion, a slum kid's sleazy rise and wretched fall. Jean Kent herself is as sharp as La Bern's writing, itself sharper than in *It Always Rains*. But alas! Censorship, formulary dialogue, and moody but somehow depersonalising visuals, blur most of it into a glum moral tale.

In *Brighton Rock* the bare rooms, smelling of bugs and damp, stand as metaphor for empty, festering minds. Graham Greene, as a pessimist Catholic, can recognise evil – slate-eyed, unreformable, inexplicable – when he sees it. A different atmosphere imbues *Night and the City* (Jules Dassin), a *ne plus* ultra of noir visual style, with every frame a painting, every character a deep-sea monster, gritty or flabby, like noir Fellini. Dassin's London makes Chandler's L.A. look like Surbiton. And yet this 'absolute' style somehow 'blacks out' the vulnerability of Gerald Kersh's characters. The story's *moves* are there (like underworld king Herbert Lom's fine concern for his father, an old-time all-in wrestler), but not the emotionality. Googie Withers strikes some regally malevo-lent poses, but you can't feel her longings, such as hit you with oven heat in *It Always Rains*. Widmark's is the only 'rounded' role, and he's ruinously miscast, always the clever wheeler-dealer, never the cunning little git, quite out of his class, of Kersh's novel.[10] So though Dassin (and photographer Max Greene) fully deserve the Gold-Plated Cosh Award, for the Harshest Atmosphere in Any Film Noir Ever; the Solid Gold Razor must go to a smaller, rougher, more uneven, film, *They Made Me a Fugitive*. Cavalcanti comes to noir from early French Poetic Realism, a tradition more sensitively melancholy than American 'deadpan Expressionism' (admirable as that is). Faces and voices are limned with a disabused sensuality (Sally Gray's sulky lips, hurt angry eyes and husky voice) or disgust (Griffith Jones's cruel, witty, irrational malice). Trevor Howard, as a cynic fallen among racketeers, is caustic, explosive, reflexive as Bogart. This sleazy brew of meanness and sadism is Cavalcanti's most poetic, gloomy mood piece since his avant-garde years. Even the advertising copy revs up into blank verse: 'Mayfair darling must have nylons, Park Lane lovely must smell sweet, But what price glamour when the guns go off. And that red smear ain't rouge!'[11]

17. Juvenile Delinquency

Post-war moralists emphasise wartime's glorifications of violence, its family dislocations, notably the wartime absence of strong fathers, and the lure of black-market profits. *Good-time Girl* adds sexual harassment (by Jean Kent's pawnbroker employer), overuse of Dad's belt, and approved schools as the most intense criminal environment of all. This brave criticism of social work has the censors very nervous, and they insist that the producers add a sermon from a kind but stern magistrate. So Flora Robson tells Jean Kent's sad story, in flashbacks, to young Diana Dors, who, deeply impressed, resolves to step off the primrose path to the condemned cell.[12] But the moralistic miserabilism of plot and style had already crushed the life out of the film (and crudified the novel's human thrust).

A similar mix of tentative criticism and respect pervades *Boys in Brown* (Montgomery Tully, 1949). This motley bunch of Borstal boys aren't all bad lots, many of them more sinned against than sinning, but one must be tough on crime, especially the rotten apples who corrupt the merely weak, and it takes all Guvnor Jack Warner's fatherly sagacity to save Attenborough, R., from the sneaky influence of Bogarde, D. This paternalist Borstal for boys is paralleled by a matriarchal remand home for girls in *The White Unicorn* (Bernard Knowles, 1947). Here Matron Margaret Lockwood encourages young mum Joan Greenwood, who has attempted infanticide and suicide, by confiding her own sad story about irresponsible men.

Even if (and it's a big 'even if'), Attenborough in *Brighton Rock* is just a poor victim of his environment, his cold loathing of one and all suggests a damned soul. It's as if the Boultings agree with Greene, against optimistic humanists, that pure evil springs eternal in the human heart.[13] Until this film, the Boultings, reputedly liberal-left zealots, made earnest, idealistic, even, perhaps, puritanical, films. But here, the only real force for good is blowsy Hermione Baddeley. Later their comedies will signal their switch to hilarious (hysterical) despair about British social morality in general.

18. Wickedness vs Moral Weakness

In *My Brother's Keeper* (Alfred Roome, Roy Rich, 1948) two convicts escape, handcuffed together: Jack Warner, cast against type, is the hardened criminal; George Cole is the innocent (simple-minded?) youth. Now wouldn't you expect some positive relation, with mutual hatred perhaps and as many complications as the scriptwriters can think of, to grow between them? But *The Defiant Ones* (1958) this is not. The old lag cuts free of his 'useless' companion, killing a farmer in the process. The horrified lad surrenders to the police, who promptly charge him with the crime. The loner keeps going and, when cornered, takes his chance in an uncleared minefield. He ends as a pillar of smoke in long-shot.[14]

This strange film is dissatisfying, yet disconcerting. Here are the two poles of criminality: one is the decent, but *weakly foolish* victim of whatever circumstance he finds himself in; the other is the *cold hard case,* whom *nothing* can influence – neither his loyal wife (Beatrice Varley), nor his attractive mistress (Jane Hylton); he calmly reduces them to his (technically criminal) accomplices. The police go aggressively wrong, and the newspaper reporter on the case is David Tomlinson, bumbling fusspot of umpteen comedies. The biblical title suggests another angle, perhaps related to Rank's earlier tries at moral-religious messages, though this film puts it in noir negative: 'All you weak lads in the audience, *don't* trust your big brother criminal mates.' The film allows a little pathos but otherwise moves in a mysterious, cold, non-identifying way – alienation by emptiness of explanation – though this could be quite inadvertent, in a 'dollar-crisis quickie' rushed into production from an underdeveloped script.

Now Barabbas Was a Robber sympathises, in various ways and degrees, with crooks of most classes (a bank cashier, an IRA man, a Cockney ticket-forger, a Negro matelot caught smuggling, a bigamist – but not the charming killer).[15] Far from rigidly distinguishing heroes from villains, or good girls from bad, British films routinely compare and contrast the wicked with the weak. In *Temptation Harbour* (Lance Comfort, 1947), railway signalman Robert Newton turns out to be a middle-way tangle of moral weakness and animal-natural ability to kill. For most of his life a considerate family man, he remains so even as temptation (weakness of will? strength of desire?) leads him ever more deeply into crime. In bare narrative synopsis, his 'sinner's progress' may sound as moral as *Good-time Girl*, but his is no social-worker sermon, but the common ground between Simenon's non-idealistic human sympathies, tabloid awareness of dirty linen in every closet, Newton's strange persona (rolling eyes and viper mouth) and Simone Simon's cat-like look, and a certain poetic realism. It might almost be a French film remade, though it's not, and it complements *It Always Rains* (by Hamer, another melancholy Francophile). Ealing shows us the 'community panorama', Simenon the intimate drama.

19. Cops and Robbers and the Moral Order

In *Brighton Rock,* Pinkie's nemesis is Ida Arnold (Hermione Baddeley), an easy-pick-up woman, who's 'no better than she ought to be' (to revive an, interesting, Victorian phrase). Her relation to upright 'law-and-order' figures, like Jack Warner, is not, I think, 'opposition', but 'complementarity'. One might postulate a certain populism, in the sense of an anarcho communitarian hope that social authority comes naturally, organically, out of everyday social interaction, free from ruling class and other outside forces. Some such longing for 'popular moral authority' can help explain the genesis and meaning of that classic homage to law and order, *The Blue Lamp*. It's produced by Balcon (a Labour voter in 1945), who buys the first script from Gainsborough, whose boss, Sydney Box, is another Labour supporter). Its major writers are Ted Willis (an authentically working-class ex-Comrade, from the left-militant Unity Theatre) and T. E. B. Clarke (an ex-policeman, whose other voices are distinctly mischievous about the boys in blue).

Jack Warner's PC Dixon emblemises – what? 'Labour's People now-in-authority'? Conformism? Working-class embourgeoisement? Petit-bourgeois authoritarianism? Working class as New Pillar of Society? The decent common man endowed with responsible authority? Whichever, as 'Dixon of Dock Green' he'll become a figurehead of the 1950s, as spreading affluence reconciles ever wider sections of the lower middle and the working classes.

The Blue Lamp may seem stodgily conformist and petit-bourgeois (there are worse things, dare one say); *Hue and Cry* may seem delightfully anarchic. But they're opposite poles of the same spirit. The very phrase 'hue and cry' suggests a sort of populist citizenship, a 'have-a-go' spirit, a 'citizen's arrest'. In *The Blue Lamp*, even crooks help hunt down the cop-killer: partly for selfish reasons (of course), but partly from an indignant, almost principled respect for some law and order. It's not so much Ealing being soft on crime, as part of Ealing's faith in 'the benevolent community'.[16] Here's a typically Ealing (and British) contradiction – not foregrounded, but palpable in tone and atmosphere.

20. Philosophical Thrillers

The criminal world, with its solitudes, distrusts, guilts, despairs, its self-appointed tasks and projects, its *ad hoc* loyalties, and its emotive, precarious subculture, of 'honour among thieves', lends itself to a certain existentialism. Though movies of this period can't yet pursue deep thoughts through labyrinthine finesses, which need philosophical writers, they can flesh out some basic propositions in movie atmospherics like the near-Expressionist idioms of two Carol Reed films, *Odd Man Out* (1947) and *The Third Man* (1949).

They're two of four crime films that offer, not 'statements', but 'meditations', agnostic and agonised, on basic, existential-religious, questions, which comfortable humanisms might answer too affirmatively. The Odd Man Out is James Mason, a patriotic terrorist, stripped, as he wanders, dying, through Belfast, of his 'terrorist' identity, but meeting precious little kindness, from a cross-section of 'ordinary people'. This pessimistic populism extends as far as visionary artist Robert Newton, who props the dying man on a model's throne to 'paint his soul' at the moment of death. Finally his girlfriend (Kathleen Ryan) pretends they're escaping together, so that he can die happy, but her loving kindness entails another betrayal. It's as if the human condition must always confuse terrorism/idealism, love/treachery.[17]

Another 'man-on-the-run' film, *Escape*, might almost be a retort to Reed's pessimism. The kindness of strangers, to its hounded hero, helps him overcome bitterness and reciprocate with self-sacrifice. The Boultings' *Brighton Rock*, like *Odd Man Out*, ends in ironic deception. Greene ends with the sad waitress (Carol Marsh) eager to play the recording, on which she will hear her dead lover saying he loathes her. In the film, the record is chipped, and the needle will always stop short of the truth. Is this a kinder, but subtler, pessimism?

The Third Man (scripted by Graham Greene) is a relatively simple narrative. What gives its simplicity popular classic status is its atmosphere: a chemistry of 'British Expressionist' visuals (realistic locations + slanting shadow-throws + deeply diagonal night-streets + Dutch tilts), strong, insolent, secretive faces, charged acting, and zithery-slithery vibrations tangling and unwinding our nerves, teasing and haunting us like a ghostly hurdy-gurdy in the key of Kurt Weill. It's another meditation on the iron law of betrayal. Orson Welles is the charming, but morally ugly, American – a racketeer, now bootlegging, not hooch, but penicillin, in cold, hungry, post-war Europe. Joseph Cotten as the innocent American, becomes culpably innocent, in refusing to betray his old friend, and when he does his moral duty, he's punished by Valli's silent rejection. If loyalty matches legality she's entirely right. Yet, as a racketeer's mistress, her moral authority is not exactly awesome. It's Trevor Howard, as a British army officer, who provides the necessarily harsh moral realism, to hold back the forces of chaos and black night. Greene and Reed share one inspiring obsession: treachery – malevolent, or righteous, or inadvertent – is the human condition. And isn't treachery (to neighbours, to society . . .) what crime is all about?

Notes

1. As a rejection of intellectual elitism, *The Upturned Glass* matches *Rope* (1948). Hitchcock's Hollywood film has strong British connections. He co-produced it with Sidney Bernstein of Granada, and it's based on a British play (Patrick Hamilton, 1929). *The Upturned Glass* is sterner, in the sense that Mason's brain-surgeon skills are socially and spiritually valuable, whereas the two young aesthetes' *fin-de-siècle*-cum-Nietzschean ideas are vain waffle and the action they inspire, mad and vile.

2. Martha Wolfenstein and Nathan Leites, *Movies: A Psychological Study*.

3. The Windmill Theatre (whose nudes never moved) had already inspired *Tonight and Every Night* (Hollywood, 1945).

4. From another angle it foreshadows *The Servant* (Joseph Losey, 1963).

5. *Escape* was first filmed in 1930, with Gerald du Maurier (father of Daphne), the West End theatre's specialist *suprême* in suavely casual, understated gentlemen. He'd created Raffles on stage, and his gentlemen ranged from the casually sensitive to raffish nobs and rascally toffs.

6. For an attempt to evoke Slaughter's great stage role, Sweeney Todd, as it will evolve by the mid-50s, cf. Raymond Durgnat, 'A Salute to Slaughter', in *Ark* (Journal of the Royal College of Art) no. 30, 1961–2.

7. *Noose*, being thick-ear comic noir, comes as a surprise after the same author Richard Llewellyn's soulful Welsh novel, *How Green Was My Valley*, filmed by John Ford in 1941. The missing link may be *None But the Lonely Heart*, about a populist-class drifter, played by Cary Grant in the 1944 film.

8. Cf. the chapter on 'The Spiv Cycle', in Robert Murphy, *Realism and Tinsel: Cinema and Society in Britain 1939–49*.

9. Some underground types might prefer a good kicking, to a year in gaol. This is more or less the attitude of Shortie Matthews in James Curtis's novel *They Drive by Night*, though it doesn't make it into the film version (Arthur Woods, 1939).

10. Kersh's 'anti-hero' defies perfect casting, but umpteen British actors would have been more suitable, in one way or another: Attenborough (in his early, spiritually stunted period), Maxwell Reed (jumped-up barrow-boy/spiv, with a swagger, a punch and low cunning), George Cole (no, don't laugh; cf. *My Brother's Keeper*), Laurence Harvey?

11. These stresses and alliterations smack of Anglo-Saxon (Old English) patterns. Eerie atavism? Doggerel drumroll-and-rap?

12. Where, maybe, Eric Portman awaits, as in *Daybreak*. Come to think of it, his wife in that film (Ann Todd) has been a bit of a good-time girl in her delicate, mournful way, though she's relieved when he makes an honest woman of her.

13. Greene's position as a left-wing, pessimistic Catholic is quite a tease. Does he credit some plain-clothes Devil, or Original Sin, or is Human Nature vile in itself (being instinctively, or inalienably, selfish or malign), or is it so easily 'confused' (aka 'twisted'), that, 'in the childhood of Judas, Jesus was betrayed'? Or is humanity so easily corruptible, by subtle, complex, tricky, trivial, intimate, concatenations of circumstance, that good without evil is as improbable as light without shadow?

14. This distant understatement is a British way to go – especially compared with James Cagney, in *White Heat*, a year later.

15. Its writer, William Douglas Home, aristocratic brother of a future Conservative prime minister, had been a wartime army officer, and had gone to prison for disobeying an order which he considered pointlessly inhumane. (Is this a crime story? Don't we admire the 'sin' he's punished for?)

16. Cf. Charles Barr, *Ealing Studios* (London: Cameron and Tayleur/Newton Abbot: David & Charles, 1977).

17. See also F. L. Green's 1939 novel, *On the Night of the Fire*, a 'backstreet' crime story, with a lowly, luckless, backstreet barber (Ralph Richardson in the 1939 film).

Bibliography

Chibnall, Steve and Robert Murphy, *British Crime Cinema* (London and New York: Routledge, 1999).

Durgnat, Raymond, *A Mirror for England: British Cinema from Austerity to Affluence* (London: Faber and Faber, 1970).

Durgnat, Raymond, 'Genre: Populism and Social Realism', *Film Comment* vol. 11 no. 4, July–August 1975

Durgnat, Raymond, 'Gainsborough: "The Times of Its Time"', *Monthly Film Bulletin*, August 1985.

Durgnat, Raymond, 'La Gainsborough e i suoi Cugini', in Emanuela Martini (ed.), *A Gainsborough Picture* (Bergamo Film Meeting, Italy, 1994).

McFarlane, Brian, *Sixty Voices: Celebrities Recall the Golden Age of British Cinema* (London: BFI, 1992).

Murphy, Robert, *Realism and Tinsel: Cinema and Society in Britain 1939–49* (London: Routledge, 1992).

Oakley, Charles, *Where We Came In* (London: George Allen & Unwin, 1964).

Wolfenstein, Martha and Leites, Nathan, *Movies: A Psychological Study* (Glencoe, IL: Free Press, 1950).

28

A Song and Dance at the Local: Thoughts on Ealing

Tim Pulleine

The production history of Ealing Studios under Michael Balcon spanned two decades, from 1938 to 1959. Yet four decades after the company's shutdown Ealing remains, with the possible exception of Rank, the likeliest response in any word-association game to the phrase 'British cinema'. Or more precisely, the response might be Ealing comedy; and while of the nearly 100 films made by Ealing, fewer than thirty are comedies, the fact is, that in the handful of 'essential' Ealing movies, comedies figure strongly.

In British film production itself, the Ealing legacy is frequently foregrounded. Among high-profile British pictures of the recent past, *A Fish Called Wanda* (1988) is the work of an ex-Ealing director, Charles Crichton, and reworks elements of its Ealing comedy predecessors, adding in the sex and violence which they excluded. *Chariots of Fire* (1981), which dramatises a true story of moral endeavour very much in an Ealing mould, bears a dedication to the memory of Sir Michael Balcon.

When Balcon took up the post of head of production at Ealing in 1938, he was already an established presence in British cinema, having filled the same position at both Gainsborough and Gaumont-British.[1] In the interim, he had briefly and unhappily been involved in inaugurating the British production arm of Metro-Goldwyn-Mayer, with *A Yank at Oxford* (1938). Balcon's personal dissatisfaction with this phase of his career assumed a wider symptomatic value with his tenure at Ealing. A continuing refrain in British film history has been the question of whether to seek to challenge Hollywood on its own ground, or to play the 'national' card by embodying qualities of 'Britishness'. Balcon was in no doubt about endorsing the latter course, although his method of doing so – creating a team of personnel and concentrating on self-sufficiency and a policy of in-house promotion – was one which echoed the tactics of Hollywood companies such as MGM.

Early Years

The first film of the new Ealing era, *The Gaunt Stranger* (Walter Forde, 1938), was a version of Edgar Wallace's previously filmed novel and play *The Ringer*, a conventional comedy-thriller of the sort that might have been made at any other British studio. Pen Tennyson's *There Ain't No Justice* (1939), about the trials and tribulations of a small-time boxer, was more significant. Though recognisably made in the studio, the film depicts its Cockney working-class community with detailed affection, and the story ends with the protagonist turning his back on the fight game in favour of an 'ordinary' life. The moral scheme (community life good/commercial machinations bad) may presage Ealing films to come, but a clearer indicator of Ealing's future is to be found in Walter Forde's *Cheer Boys Cheer* (1939), a comedy in which the family brewing firm of Greenleaf becomes a takeover target for the heavyweight Ironside company. It is with the foiling of this scheme that the plot is concerned. Greenleaf's product is advertised as 'the beer of Old England'; the Ironside owner is glimpsed reading *Mein Kampf*; given that the film appeared only weeks before the outbreak of war, the wider implications are inescapable. Charles Barr points up the correspondence between Greenleaf and Ealing itself: deliberately small, characterised by a family atmosphere and a 'benevolent paternalism'.[2]

Small cosy clans: Walter Forde's *Cheer Boys Cheer* (1939)

Forde also made *Saloon Bar* (1940), set in the precincts of a pub in a working-class area of London. A formula picture with an artificial comedy-thriller plot about clearing an innocent man's name, *Saloon Bar* has considerable incidental vitality. In particular, it draws an unpatronising picture of the *ad hoc* community of regulars, who rally round in a good cause, complete with running jokes and bits of character business. Short shrift is given to a group of rather unlikely toffs, who become the target of caustic mockery as soon as they have departed. And the coda is significant: the local bobby turns up to point out it is after closing time, only to discover that the landlord has become a father again and to be invited in for celebratory drinks. The policeman's response is a cheerful assent, and as the door closes on him the end-title appears: we are left with the sense of a small, cosy clan that may know

Bar-room regulars rally round in Walter Forde's *Saloon Bar* (1940)

its place but is not going to stand for being messed about.

Ealing at War

Most of Ealing's thirty or so wartime films are concerned with the war itself, though several are vehicles for such performers as George Formby and Will Hay as they take on spies, saboteurs and fifth columnists. In the sphere of war films proper, Ealing got off to an unsatisfactory start. Tennyson's *Convoy* (1940) made use of material shot in the North Sea, but married it uneasily to a romantic-triangle plot amid the officer class, which the casting of Clive Brook and John Clements only renders more theatrical. Much worse, though, is *Ships with Wings* (Sergei Nolbandov, 1941), a purported account of the Fleet Air Arm in peace and war which paints it as the sole preserve of what a later generation would term upper-class twits.

Balcon's recruitment of talented documentary film-makers like Alberto Cavalcanti and Harry Watt brought an influx of realism into Ealing's wartime films, and it is startling to compare *Convoy* and *Ships with Wings* with *Nine Men* (1943), the first fictional work to be directed by Watt. A film which deserves a wider reputation, it has been described by Laurence Kardish as 'the leanest, simplest and most paradigmatic of Ealing's wartime narratives'.[3] Running only sixty-eight minutes, *Nine Men* constitutes a flashback, narrated by a veteran sergeant (Jack Lambert) to men in training, describing the survival of a small patrol cut off in the Libyan desert. This is conspicuously an other ranks' war (the sole officer dies early on), with a spread of authentic-sounding regional accents, and while the language is necessarily expurgated, it achieves a vernacular, sometimes surprisingly near-the-knuckle, pastiche of soldiers' talk. The functional style mirrors the lack of rhetoric in the script; war is presented as a grimly unromantic job of work.

Coming between *Ships with Wings* and *Nine Men*, however, are a group of films released in 1942 – *The Foreman Went to France* (Charles Frend), *The Next of Kin* (Thorold Dickinson) and *Went the Day Well?* (Cavalcanti) – which negotiate a transition in attitudes. The concept which in different ways they promote is that of a people's war, of democracy in action in its own defence. In *The Foreman Went to France*, a Welsh engineer crosses the Channel at the time of the fall of France in a bid to retrieve machinery his firm has installed and keep it out of German hands. This is by its nature an amateur initiative, but that very fact is used to stress the need for a

The Cruel Sea (Charles Frend, 1953)

World War II played a key part in establishing Ealing's identity, but the post-war period brought changing concerns. After *Against the Wind* (Charles Crichton, 1948), a surprisingly authentic film about special operations agents resisting the Nazis in Belgium that failed to find an audience, no Ealing film until *The Cruel Sea*, released early in 1953, directly treated the prosecution of the war. This situation mirrored a wider one in British film: it was not until 1950, with the release of *They Were Not Divided* (Terence Young, 1950), that the retrospective World War II genre was properly inaugurated. One could argue that this awakening was provoked by response to the Cold War and to hostilities in Korea, though a more broadly plausible explanation might be that of a need to look back at what had been a seismic upheaval for Britain (and the world).

The tone of underplayed heroism for post-war films dealing with the war at sea was set by Compton Bennett's *Gift Horse* (1952), which climaxes in Trevor Howard's hard-bitten captain ramming his explosive-laden destroyer into the dock gates of the German U-boat base at St Nazaire. Nothing as dramatic occurs in *The Cruel Sea*, which was adapted by Eric Ambler from a best-selling novel by Nicholas Monsarrat, published in 1951. Monsarrat had risen from being a junior officer in the RNVR to commanding both a corvette and a frigate and knew at first hand the privations of the North Atlantic convoys, which provide a key strand in the narrative. He can thus be seen as a surrogate not only for Lieutenant Lockhart (Donald Sinden in what he considered the best role of his career) but also for his commanding officer Ericson (Jack Hawkins).

If any work came to be popularly regarded as 'the great British war novel' it was most likely Monsarrat's. Publishers Cassell subsequently issued an expurgated 'cadet edition' vouchsafing younger readers substantial doses of heroism but filtering out much of the grim realism that director Charles Frend played on in the film. The best example is the episode in which Ericson orders the depth-charging of a suspected U-boat at the expense of Allied sailors struggling in the water. Helped by Hawkins's iconic performance as a stoic, humane man faced with an impossible choice between his duty to kill the enemy and his instinct to save his fellow seamen, this sequence still rings resonantly true as an illustration of the unheroic destructiveness of war.

The episodic structure of the book, expertly conveyed in Ambler's screenplay, which incorporates subplots about the experiences of Lockhart's brother officers and subordinates, is consonant with both an epic view of historical events and with the recurring Ealing tradition of portmanteau storytelling.[1] The concluding sequence, in which Lockhart and Ericson recall lost comrades, strikes an elegiac note comparable with that of the endings of several other prominent British war movies (notably *The Dam Busters*, Michael Anderson, 1955) in a way that serves to contradict the 'gung ho' popular notion of the genre.

Two historical footnotes. By the time of filming, all the Royal Navy's corvettes had been scrapped or sold but one which had been loaned to the Greek navy was acquired by Ealing in the nick of time from Malta, where it had been sent to be broken up. With a 126-minute running time, the film was Ealing's longest production to that date; among its successors, only one was longer, the 135-minute *Dunkirk* (Leslie Norman, 1958), which was also the studio's only subsequent war subject.

NOTE

1. Ealing's portmanteau films include the classic horror film *Dead of Night* (Alberto Cavalcanti/Charles Crichton/Basil Dearden/Robert Hamer, 1945), *Train of Events* (Sidney Cole/Charles Crichton/Basil Dearden, 1949) and *Pool of London* (Basil Dearden, 1951).

FURTHER READING

Charles Barr, *Ealing Studios* (London: Cameron & Tayleur/David & Charles, 1977).

Jack Hawkins, *Anything for a Quiet Life* (London: Elm Tree Books/Hamish Hamilton, 1973).

hard-headed, professional approach. The protagonist is aided by an American woman and by two British soldiers, a Cockney and a Scot, but when a British officer appears he is revealed to be a German spy. Unfortunately the film suffers from a not-very-French atmosphere, and the conclusion, in which the democratic theme is illustrated by a vote-taking among passengers on an escape vessel over whether to sacrifice their belongings in order to accommodate the machinery, seems hollow and schematic.

The Next of Kin was initially commissioned by the War Office as a training film, and then expanded into a commercial feature. The narrative, showing how a German spy ring contrives to obtain details of a 'secret'

British raid on the French coast, is tense and convincing in itself, but also acts as a critique of the easy-going British amateur spirit: at the final fade-out, the unapprehended chief spy is still at large and going about his business. *Went the Day Well?* is equally grim. It is set in a 'typically English' Home Counties, where it transpires that the squire (played by four-square Leslie Banks) is a Nazi plant, waiting to do his bit for the Fatherland, when an invasion force of German commandos infiltrates the community in the guise of British soldiers on an exercise. Understated realism of behaviour and surroundings give the film the conviction which *The Foreman Went to France* ultimately lacks, and underscores its endorsement of the need to meet ruthlessness with ruthlessness. Fittingly, it is an old poacher (Edward Rigby), rather than any of the upper-class figures, who is most responsible for thwarting the German plan.

When Ealing returned to the war at sea with *San Demetrio London* (Charles Frend, 1943), the democratic impulse is evident. The *San Demetrio* is a merchant ship, bringing oil from the US in 1940, abandoned after being holed in a German attack. Subsequently, survivors among the crew rediscover the ship still afloat, board her and contrive to sail her home. The men function as a unified team, with decisions taken by vote, and any division between officers and the rest becomes one of function. The effort and sacrifice involved are rendered the more affecting for the ostensible matter-of-factness of the narrative.

Ealing's wartime oeuvre, seen as a whole, cannot be described as documentary in the formal sense of utilising actual locales and non-professional actors. What it does evince, though, is a distinctive form of realism, a capacity for projecting a view of British character in convincingly direct terms.

Post-war Comedy and Drama

How could this impetus be harnessed to the post-war situation? Balcon himself seemed uncertain: 'Because we felt we were at the beginning of a new era . . . we were inclined to try out our talents on different sorts of films.'[4] The British cinema in the period immediately after the war was possessed of a spirit of confidence, evidenced in particular by the work of David Lean, Carol Reed, and Michael Powell and Emeric Pressburger. To a degree, Ealing sought to follow the path of prestige, via such films as *Scott of the Antarctic* (Charles Frend, 1948) and *Saraband for Dead Lovers* (Basil Dearden, 1948). *Scott of the Antarctic*, a popular success at the time, is in its latter stages impressively

mounted, with locations in Norway, as a reconstruction of the ill-fated expedition to the South Pole, but it remains dramatically inert. *Saraband for Dead Lovers*, which was a commercial failure, is revealing in a complementary way. Again an elaborately mounted colour production, the film is a costume melodrama, recreating a doomed romance against the background of the eighteenth-century Hanoverian court. The self-consciously academic style stands in opposition to that of the Gainsborough pictures, and to the supposed vulgarity of Hollywood costume epics; the very title has an anti-popular ring to it; and the film itself unfortunately jettisons not only melodrama but drama itself. Both these films convey a striving for 'respectable' status, and a concomitant sense of inhibition.

The film from Ealing's early post-war period that with hindsight becomes most indicative is a modest comedy, *Hue and Cry* (Charles Crichton, 1947). The representative image of the film is its climax, a free-for-all amid the London bomb sites in which numerous boys, devotees of a blood-and-thunder weekly magazine, get the better of a gang of crooks who have been using a serial in its pages to disseminate information among themselves. The extensive use of locations, for all that they remain subordinate to a studio-based style, communicates a topicality patently not to be found in prestige literary pictures. *Hue and Cry* is, though, an exercise in fantasy, something which the down-to-earth surroundings serve to throw into relief; in fact, one of the most engaging sequences, in which two of the boys gain an audience with the eccentric author (Alastair Sim) of the serial in question, makes its effect through exaggeratedly mock-sinister lighting and composition. But the fantasy acts for the characters – and arguably for the audience as well – as a safety valve; at the end, they return to the quotidian round of school and work in the fantasy-free zone of austerity Britain.

Here is the genesis of Ealing comedy. Balcon commented in his autobiography: 'The bloodless revolution of 1945 had taken place, but I think our first desire was to get rid of as many wartime restrictions as possible and get going . . . there was a mild anarchy in the air.'[5] The success of *Hue and Cry* led to *Passport to Pimlico* (Henry Cornelius, 1949) and *Whisky Galore!* (Alexander Mackendrick, 1949), films whose stock in trade is mild anarchy.

Passport to Pimlico turns on the comic conceit of an ancient document which reveals that the London borough of the title belongs to the kingdom of Burgundy and is thus independent of British rule.

The film's construction is artful, with a rapid exposition and a compression in the subsequent action which gives the impression of a hectic series of events being contained within a few days, when in mundane reality they would drag on for months. Early on, the idealistic shopkeeper (Stanley Holloway), who wants to set up a children's playground, is told at a council meeting, 'This borough is in no position to finance daydreams'; but the ensuing discovery of the Burgundian treasure trove permits exactly this. The trouble is that the daydream is rapidly undercut by external events: the pubs stay open all day, but an army of spivs moves into the locality. The film turns, in a fashion that its surface speed serves partly to obscure, on a kind of double bluff: a supposed celebration of the jettisoning of wartime restrictions becomes a nostalgic evocation of the wartime spirit of solidarity. The rituals of evacuation and bundles for Britain are run through in a spirit of play. Finally, Pimlico returns to Britain, as the heatwave gives way to a downpour, a declension of mood which seems to presage a sense of relief. A contemporary comment by Richard Winnington is to the point: 'The apex of Burgundian emancipation is a song and dance in the local after hours.'[6] It is an allusion that reflects not only back to the jocular ending of *Saloon Bar* but also forward to the very last Ealing comedy, *Barnacle Bill* (Charles Frend, 1957), which concludes with a party of revellers being precipitately ejected from a drinking session under the eye of a policeman.

Drink is central also to *Whisky Galore!*. 'It's a well-known medical fact that some men are born two drinks under par,' says the doctor (James Robertson Justice) who is 'fuelling' the repressed teacher (Gordon Jackson) for a confrontation with his domineering mother. Whisky, in this story of a Hebridean island community whose stock of it has run out until a ship carrying the stuff is wrecked offshore, is seen as a liberating force. The start of the film, once past a whimsical passage of mock-documentary narration, is dark and fog-bound, and it is only the unscheduled arrival of the cargo of spirits which brings music and an acceleration of tempo. The film, deriving via Compton Mackenzie's novel from an actual incident, is set in 1943, and can be seen as 'exploiting the dramatic conventions of a war film – or to be exact, a resistance movie'.[7] The resistance is, though, against the authorities on the British mainland (the posse of revenue men in black mackintoshes imports overtones of the Gestapo), and specifically against the English commanding officer of the local Home Guard detachment,

Captain Waggett (Basil Radford), who views the plunder as contraband. Through an understated, almost elliptical style, the film illustrates the series of ruthless stratagems by which the islanders undercut Waggett's position until he is finally rejected even by his wife and is condemned in the eyes of his superiors. The misanthropy of this, allied to the fact that the island community is not cosily united (the publican, put at a pecuniary disadvantage, informs on the conspirators), contrives to give the movie a genuine, albeit mild, edge of anarchy.

The third Ealing comedy of 1949, *Kind Hearts and Coronets* (Robert Hamer), is a very different matter. This is black comedy in an Edwardian period setting, the tale of an aristocrat in reduced circumstances who murders his way through the relatives standing between him and a dukedom (with Alec Guinness playing all the victims). Literary in tone, it is a work of structural intricacy, including at one stage a flashback within a flashback. The extensive use for ironic effect of a first-person narration, together with the periodic use of Mozart on the soundtrack, make it seem like a stylistic precursor of the French New Wave. Crucially, however, this is a film that centres on that most English, but generally un-Ealing, preoccupation of class distinction (the French release title was *Noblesse oblige*), and although the plot is motivated by revenge for class-based snobbery, the impulse that sustains it is far from a democratic one. Moreover, it is defiantly amoral: despite the sop to censorship of a trick ending which suggests that the murderer may have delivered himself to subsequent justice, the tenor of the conclusion is that the claimant to the coronet has won the day.

The two melodramas which Hamer previously directed for Ealing – *Pink String and Sealing Wax* (1945), which shares the Edwardian setting of *Kind Hearts*, and *It Always Rains on Sunday* (1947), set in the contemporary East End – have in common with their successor a strongly marked formal configuration and a thematic concern with the clash between natural instinct and institutional restraint. In some respects Hamer's work invokes correspondences with that of Fritz Lang, and there is a specific association of Langian fatalism in the shot in *It Always Rains on Sunday* of the slowly spinning wheel of the bicycle discarded by the fleeing jailbreaker. Hamer refracts the studio's themes of community and togetherness through the prism of a socially agnostic sensibility, achieving a creative tension rare in British cinema. His distance from the Ealing ethos becomes apparent if one compares *It Always Rains on*

Sunday with *The Blue Lamp* (Basil Dearden, 1950), which embodies with particular directness an ideal set of Ealing values: a good-humoured, stratified community in action in the defence both of itself and of wider society.

Ealing in the 50s

What becomes apparent in the concluding decade of Ealing production is not so much the absence of auteurist projects like Hamer's, an absence characteristic of British cinema in the wider scheme, but rather the manner in which the changing circumstances of British life – the social diversification and rising consumer affluence in the 'new Elizabethan' age – were increasingly at variance with the Ealing ethos.

In the comedy sphere, *The Lavender Hill Mob* (Charles Crichton, 1951) is indicative of an encroaching parochialism. By fitting paradox, the framing sequences take place in Latin America, where millionaire-in-exile Alec Guinness is recounting the saga behind his ill-gotten fortune. But the closing scene reveals that his confidant is a Scotland Yard man, to whom he is handcuffed in readiness for the journey home to retribution. This undercuts the screenplay's contention that 'the saddest words in the world are "it might have been"', reducing the action to a game in which the powers-that-be have an inbuilt right to win.

A divorcement from reality is heightened in *The Titfield Thunderbolt* (Charles Crichton, 1953), where the very fantasticality of the stratagems involved in saving 'the oldest branch railway in the world' tends to throw into relief the odd precepts on which the story rests. In what a contemporary reviewer called a 'Toytown village' it seems to be perpetual summer, where all and sundry appear to have limitless time and energy to devote to what is in effect a philanthropic enterprise, and where a trade union official's intervention is laughed off as a truculent irrelevance.[8]

The capital and labour issue is touched on to more pointed effect in two comedies by Mackendrick, *The Man in the White Suit* (1951) and *The Maggie* (1954). But while the first film may look in its early stages as if it will anticipate the 'white heat of technology' theme which the following decade's Labour administration would seek to promote, the story ends in whimsical retreat, and the light in which both sides of industry are depicted is sour enough to make some of the humorous business of chases and explosions assume an imposed air. *The Maggie* has something of

the ruthlessness of *Whisky Galore!* in the humbling of its American tycoon protagonist, but the literally backwater nature of the setting conspires to lend this film, too, a feeling of whimsicality. However, in Mackendrick's last Ealing comedy, *The Ladykillers* (1955), one does sense a critical engagement with the project's potential for whimsy.

When it comes to dramatic subjects, 50s Ealing tends to be typified by half-hearted stage adaptations such as Dearden's *The Gentle Gunman* (1952) and *The Square Ring* (1953), or, more worthily but not much more rewardingly, by Crichton's *The Divided Heart* (1954), a tug-of-love story set in post-war Germany which uneasily straddles emotional melodrama and documentary. A counter-example, however, is *The Ship That Died of Shame* (Basil Dearden, 1955), in which three friends reunite some years after their wartime naval service, using their old motor gunboat for black-market smuggling. The loss of a wartime sense of purpose and the rise of a 'get-rich-quick' ethos (brilliantly embodied in Richard Attenborough's playing of a superior spiv) are pointedly dramatised. The semi-supernatural ending, with the vessel apparently wrecking itself, bespeaks the film-makers' lack of any sense of a positive way ahead.

The police-procedural thriller *The Long Arm* (Charles Frend, 1956) climaxes in the thwarting of a scheme to rob the Royal Festival Hall, emblem of the 1951 Festival of Britain that had once symbolised post-war optimism. Five years on, such idealism had been displaced, and *The Long Arm*, whose storyline visits various parts of the country almost as if to offer a cross-section of British life, is low key and ironic in tone. The film is efficiently mounted, but there is something dogged about its professionalism, perhaps symptomatic of Ealing's own position.

It is interesting to contrast *The Long Arm* with one of the last Ealing movies, *Nowhere to Go* (1958), the directorial début of Seth Holt, who had for many years been an Ealing editor. Here again is a fragmented society, but in this case it is an underworld with little time for the tenet of 'honour among thieves', and the central figure is not a policeman but a plausible Canadian conman (George Nader), a loner anti-hero who represents a denial of any team spirit. While the film is in its latter stages over-reliant on a quota-quickie plot, its stylistic accoutrements – jazz score, luminous camerawork – link it with the French New Wave films and another kind of cinema altogether. The disparity heightens the feeling that, over and above the economic practicalities,

The Ladykillers (Alexander Mackendrick, 1955)

It began, suitably enough for a story set in a small urban community and for a studio which cultivated the team spirit, in a pub – the Red Lion on Ealing Green, where director Alexander Mackendrick heard screenwriter William Rose recount how he had 'dreamed a film' involving five criminals in a house with a little old lady and how their decision to murder her led to their own demise. Rose, who had scripted *Genevieve* (Henry Cornelius, 1953) as well as Mackendrick's *The Maggie* was prevailed upon to develop the idea. Studio chief Michael Balcon gave the project the green light after vanquishing misgivings about a 'comedy' in which five of the six principal characters end up dead – he had presumably overlooked the acclaimed precedent of *Kind Hearts and Coronets*.

It was Balcon who pushed for the casting of Alec Guinness as the criminal 'mastermind' Professor Marcus, in preference to Mackendrick's more predictable suggestion of Alastair Sim. However, Mackendrick's instinct over the casting of seventy-seven-year-old Katie Johnson as the fragile but indomitable Mrs Wilberforce – opposed by both Balcon and producer Seth Holt (who was convinced that the rigours of Mackendrick's direction would kill her) – was vindicated by a very assured performance. Despite formidable competition from Guinness and a strong supporting cast – including Peter Sellers, Frankie Howerd, Jack Warner, Cecil Parker, Herbert Lom and Danny Green – Johnson's Mrs Wilberforce dominates the film.[1]

The film proffers a caricatural cross-section of Britain both 'old' (the camel-coated bogus major, played by Parker) and 'new' (Teddy-Boy-garbed Sellers), while design and colour styling contrive to combine the higgledy-piggledy Toytown aspects of the milieu with intimations of the Gothic world of the Hammer horror movies which would shortly make their entrance into British cinema. *The Ladykillers*, with its *reductio ad absurdum* narrative, functions as, in the older sense of the word, a cartoon; and with hindsight its implicit irony is redoubled by the knowledge that the then cosy King's Cross vicinity of London, where the story takes place, would subsequently become notorious as a red-light district.

Mackendrick's films are often marked by generic mixing. In *The Ladykillers* this manifests itself not only in a humorous slant on the heist movies prevalent in the 1950s, but in homage to the German Expressionist films he had admired as a boy. The effect is most evident in the introductory shots of Professor Marcus as a distorted warning shadow. Efforts to make Mrs Wilberforce's house Expressionistically slanted were less successful. But the stylised backcloth of the King's Cross/St Pancras railway yards made for an appropriately nightmarish setting for the sequence where the gang members – none of whom can bring themselves to murder Mrs Wilberforce – eliminate each other.

By the time the film was released in December 1955, Ealing Studios had been sold to the BBC. Ealing as a name lingered on for another two years, but *The Ladykillers* was the last Ealing film to sustain a lasting reputation.

NOTE

1. Irma P. Hall gives an accomplished performance in the Joel and Ethan Coen remake of *The Ladykillers* (2004). But as a sharp, sensible, self-confident woman under seventy she is unable to recreate the twittering absurdity that Johnson brings to 'Mrs Lop-sided'. Hall's Marva Munson is a good, simple woman; Johnson's Mrs Wilberforce conceals a propensity to create chaos wherever she goes beneath her neat exterior.

FURTHER READING

Charles Barr, '"Projecting Britain and the British Character": Ealing Studios, Part II', *Screen* vol. 15 no. 2, 1974, pp. 126–63.

Philip Kemp, *Lethal Innocence: The Cinema of Alexander Mackendrick* (London: Methuen, 1991).

Ealing itself had been left with nowhere very much to go.

It would be possible to see in Nader's lonely death an analogy with the fate of the fugitive in *It Always Rains on Sunday* a decade earlier; the crucial difference is that in the later film there is no alternative community to which the other characters, and the audience's allegiance, can be returned, and no further prospect of a song and dance at the local, after hours or not. And yet, down all the intervening years, the melody of such vanished celluloid get-togethers has proved obstinately inclined to linger on.

Notes

1. Sound film production at Ealing had begun in 1931, when the studio became the base of ATP, the company headed by Basil Dean. Dean left in 1938, and after Balcon's arrival the company's name was changed to Ealing.
2. Charles Barr, *Ealing Studios*, pp. 5, 6.
3. Laurence Kardish, 'Michael Balcon and the Idea of a National Cinema', in *Michael Balcon: The Pursuit of British Cinema*, p. 57.
4. Michael Balcon, *Michael Balcon Presents . . . A Lifetime of Films*, p. 157.
5. Ibid., p. 159.
6. *News Chronicle*, 30 April 1949.
7. Philip Kemp, *Lethal Innocence – The Cinema of Alexander Mackendrick*, p. 32.
8. Penelope Houston, *Sight and Sound*, April–June 1953.

Bibliography

Balcon, Michael, *Michael Balcon Presents . . . A Lifetime of Films* (London: Hutchinson, 1969).

Barr, Charles, *Ealing Studios* (London: Cameron and Tayleur/David & Charles, 1977, rev. edn, 1993).

Cook, Jim, 'The Ship That Died of Shame', in Charles Barr (ed.), *All Our Yesterdays* (London: BFI, 1986).

Danischewsky, Monja (ed.), *Michael Balcon's 25 Years in Films* (London: World Film Publications, 1947).

Houston, Penelope, *Went the Day Well?* (London: BFI, 1992).

Kardish, Laurence (ed.), *Michael Balcon: The Pursuit of British Cinema* (New York: Museum of Modern Art, 1984).

Kemp, Philip, *Lethal Innocence – The Cinema of Alexander Mackendrick* (London: Methuen, 1991).

Perry, George, *Forever Ealing* (London: Pavilion/Michael Joseph, 1981).

29

Methodism versus the Marketplace:
The Rank Organisation and British Cinema

Vincent Porter

The activities of J. Arthur Rank during the 1940s and 50s lie at the very heart of British cinema history, for during that period he was both Britain's chief cinema owner and its principal film producer. He had to resolve the tensions between cinema exhibition and film production; and between domestic and international distribution. But Rank was also a devout Methodist. He felt his films should promote family values at home and the British way of life overseas.

Building an Empire

Rank first became involved with the film industry in 1934 when he set up British National. The company's first film, *Turn of the Tide* (Norman Walker, 1935), was a melodrama about Yorkshire fishing folk with a moral message. Although it won third prize at the Venice Film Festival, it was denied a proper release and Rank decided to use some of his financial muscle to improve matters. In partnership with Sheffield builder Henry Boot, he built Pinewood Studios and backed C. M. Woolf, the leading film distributor, to develop his own company, General Film Distributors. But it was not until the end of 1941 that Rank emerged into the limelight. In October he bought the Gaumont-British Picture Corporation with its chain of cinemas and the Gainsborough production unit at Shepherd's Bush studios. In December, Oscar Deutsch, chairman of Odeon Cinema Holdings, which Rank already half-owned, died suddenly, and Rank became chairman. He was now the most powerful figure in the British film industry.

Rank had acted on his religious principles when he set up GHW Productions in 1937. Run by the editor of the *Methodist Times*, the Reverend Benjamin Gregory, and Norman Walker, the director of *Turn of the Tide*, GHW Productions made several feature films with a religious message, all directed by Walker. They included *The Man at the Gate* (1941), *Hard Steel* (1942), *The Great Mr Handel* (1942), a Technicolor production in which the composer is restored to royal favour after writing 'The Messiah', and *They Knew Mr Knight* (1945). Fascinating though they now seem, none of these films was successful at the box office and Rank's commercial instincts were better served by Independent Producers, which he established in 1942 to provide production finance and management facilities to a number of independent production companies. The principal beneficiaries were The Archers (Michael Powell and Emeric Pressburger), Cineguild (David Lean, Anthony Havelock-Allan and Ronald Neame), Individual Pictures (Frank Launder and Sidney Gilliat) and Wessex Productions (Ian Dalrymple). Two years later Rank acquired Two Cities Films, headed by the Italian producer Filippo Del Giudice, who was producing his films at Denham Studios, and signed a co-financing and distribution contract with Michael Balcon's Ealing Studios. Initially, Rank gave his producers a free hand, but when profits failed to materialise changes were made. At Two Cities, Del Giudice was replaced by Josef Somlo and Earl St John; and at Gainsborough, Maurice Ostrer had to make way for Sydney Box.

In 1947, the government's attempt to tax imported films led to a boycott by Hollywood and thus a shortage of films. Rank increased production, but to do so he had to restructure his empire. He used his control of

Odeon Theatres to buy the issued share capital of his production and distribution vehicle, the General Cinema Finance Corporation, which in turn owned Gainsborough, Two Cities and Independent Producers. His minority shareholders, notably the United Artists Corporation, were aghast. Suddenly their investments in the comparatively safe trade of cinema exhibition were being switched into the far more risky business of film production and distribution. By the time Rank's films were ready for release, the American boycott had ended and he had to compete with the best that Hollywood could offer. In October 1948, Odeon Theatres had a £13.6 million overdraft; the following year it rose to £16.3 million.

Rank's financial restructuring also affected his production policy. In order to increase his film output but to keep costs down, he tried to introduce new rules about budgets and the submission of scripts, progressively alienating the prestigious producer/director teams which worked under the Independent Producers' umbrella. Powell and Pressburger followed Carol Reed to British Lion, after disputes with Rank and his company secretary John Davis over the budget and the distribution plans for The Red Shoes (1948).[1] Launder and Gilliat soon followed, because of Rank's inflexibility over the distribution arrangements for The Blue Lagoon (1948).[2] Cineguild split up, as first Anthony Havelock-Allan and then David Lean moved from Pinewood to Shepperton. So did the Wessex team (Ian Dalrymple and Jack Lee), who went on to make their most successful film, The Wooden Horse (1950), for British Lion.

The differences between Rank and his most successful film-makers lay in the tension between quality and quantity. Rank and Davis wanted a steady supply of British films to fill the screens of their Odeon and Gaumont cinemas. When the financial crisis came, they were in a dilemma. What type of production should they cut back? To businessmen like Rank and Davis, the choices were contradictory. The most profitable, and most prestigious, films were those which did only moderately well at home but could be immensely profitable abroad.

The films released by Rank between January 1947 and June 1949 cost between £113,600 (My Brother's Keeper, 1948) and £572,500 (Hamlet, 1948), but the two most expensive, Hamlet and The Red Shoes, made the most profit – about £780,000 each.[3] Both did extremely well overseas, especially in the US, and the company estimated that their foreign earnings would ultimately exceed £1 million each. But only eight of thirty cheaper films, which Rank and Davis considered more typical, were expected to make a profit. Worse, three of these films, Great Expectations, Oliver Twist and The Blue Lagoon, all made through Independent Producers, cost more than £300,000 each and none of them covered their costs in the UK. Only two (Portrait from Life and Easy Money) cost less than £150,000.

Rank and Davis had to choose between a few high-budget, high-risk and potentially highly profitable pictures and a greater number of lower-budget pictures. But they also had to supply Rank cinemas with British films. To meet their quota requirements, the Gaumont and the Odeon circuits each had to show sixteen

Rank Group trading results 1950–60

Year	1950	1951	1952	1953	1954	1955	1956	1957	1958	1959	1960
					[£ Millions]						
UK Exhibition	2.8	3.5	3.3	2.9	3.3	3.6	2.7	2.7	2.2	2.4	2.2
Overseas Exhibition	0.3	0.3	0.6	0.6	0.6	0.3	0.2	0.4	0.3	0.4	0.5
Production and Distribution	−2.1	−1.3	−0.1	+0.3	+0.8	+0.7	+0.9	+0.7	−1.3	−0.9	+0.2
Manufacturing	0.3	0.8	1.1	1.3	1.3	2.2	2.0	1.5	1.1	1.4	1.5
Studio/Labs	0.3	0.2	0.2	0.2	0.2	0.3	0.4	0.3	0.4	0.4	0.4
Miscellaneous Activities	0.2	0.2	0.3	0.3	0.2	0.3	0.1	0.1	0.1	0.2	0.3
Total*	1.8	3.7	5.4	5.7	6.3	7.4	6.4	5.8	3.0	4.0	5.1

Source: Annual Reports and Accounts

*There are minor discrepancies in the totals because individual figures have been rounded up or down to the nearest £100,000. After 1952, dividends received on trade investments have been apportioned over the various activities of the group. Tax figures, and dividends payable to shareholders, have been omitted.

British films a year. Rank also needed to keep his two film studios at Pinewood and Denham turning over. His business empire was like an overloaded bicycle: if it slowed down, it would fall to the ground. A quick glance at the group's financial results during the 1950s makes the company's structural problem clear (see Table). Its main income was from domestic exhibition, which produced approximately £3 million a year. Film production and distribution could as easily make a loss as a profit. As Rank told his shareholders in 1952,

> Each film produced is in effect a new enterprise and a prototype and although much care is taken before production starts, it is impossible to know whether a successful film will be made until the film is available for showing.[4]

The first task for Rank and Davis was to secure their principal revenue base – film exhibition. They had to opt for quantity. They therefore imposed an upper limit of £150,000 on each production. Even this figure was on the high side, for only four of their recent films had recouped this sum from their UK release, although each had cost far more to produce.[5]

Restructuring Cinema Exhibition

One way in which Rank and Davis sought to improve their revenue was to increase receipts from overseas exhibition. By 1956, in addition to his UK cinemas, Rank owned cinemas in Canada, the Republic of Ireland, Jamaica and Portugal; he also had partnership arrangements with cinemas in Australia, South Africa, New Zealand, Malaya, Ceylon and the Netherlands.[6] Overseas receipts doubled in five years, but cinema exhibition was not a cash cow which could be milked at will. The habit audience, on which the lazy exhibitor had come to rely, was already starting to stay at home; and as the decade progressed the struggle to maintain revenues became ever more difficult.

For Rank, a strict Methodist, his cinemas were not merely a source of profit. They also had a social role to fulfil. He told his shareholders:

> The motion picture theatre is in many ways a local and communal institution and its success is dependent on the standing of its Manager and his staff in the local community. Our personnel are loyal, keen and enthusiastic men, who have taken a leading part in the social and economic problems of the communities in which they operate.[7]

His philosophy was to 'offer through the medium of cinema theatres, healthy entertainment under ideal conditions for all members of the family'.[8] He also promoted healthy entertainment for children with his Saturday-morning film programmes. On Good Friday 1953, he even offered the Campaign for Methodist Advance the facilities for five-minute religious talks in more than 400 of his cinemas, while in a further twenty-four cinemas, they were given permission to hold a full-scale service including a showing of the film *Which Will Ye Have?*. But altruism was also the handmaiden of commerce. *Which Will Ye Have?*, a thirty-six-minute film about the arrest and release of Barabbas the robber, had been produced in 1949 by one of Rank's own subsidiaries, GB Instructional.[9]

Rank's cinemas had access to the most popular American films through his ties with Columbia, Disney, 20th Century-Fox, United Artists and Universal. Indeed, during the 1950s American films regularly accounted for 70 per cent of Rank's circuit releases. The one significant constraint was the government's requirement for a 30 per cent quota of British films, which Rank sought to fulfil as scrupulously as possible. The only quota year in which he seriously defaulted was 1949–50, when his bookers rejected eleven films they considered so poor that they could not be played as first features without incurring additional losses.[10] Rank's only subsequent quota failures, after the national shortage of British feature films in 1950–1, were with the 25 per cent quota for the supporting programme, but the Board of Trade did not consider this worth pursuing.[11]

With the decline in cinema audiences in the 1950s, Rank began to exploit its dominant position in order to increase its share of the market. In 1952, it owned 12 per cent of UK screens, but by 1965, although it only had 330 cinemas, they accounted for 16 per cent of screens.[12] Disgruntled independent cinema owners claimed that Rank was acting uncompetitively by preventing them from obtaining access to the best films until they had been fully exploited in its own theatres. Rank cinemas often included barring clauses in the licensing agreement signed with a film's distributor, which ensured that no other cinema within a fifteen-mile radius could simultaneously show the film, thus eliminating all local competition. For 70mm films that were given longer runs in selected cinemas, the radius was often increased to twenty-five miles. In addition to distance bars, there were also time bars – seven days for most films and fourteen days for 70mm films.[13] The distributors were usually happy to comply with these restrictions because they reduced the number of prints for which they had to pay.

Even so, Rank had to close many cinemas. Between 1954 and 1963 the corporation disposed of 189 cinemas because they were making a loss, and a further twenty-five because of programming difficulties. In 1958, John Davis decided to merge the Odeon and Gaumont circuits into a single circuit. He also tried to establish a third circuit from some of his less successful cinemas and the remaining independents; but the other exhibitors declined to co-operate.[14] By 1960 there were only two cinema circuits in the UK: Odeon and ABC.

Production in the 1950s

The National Film Finance Corporation (NFFC) was established in 1949 to provide finance for independent film production, but it immediately had to loan £3 million of its funds to bail out British Lion. In order to provide continuity of production for the rest of the industry, the NFFC set up three new consortia. The Rank/NFFC consortium, British Film Makers (BFM), consisted of a group of producers who would theoretically retain their creative independence but who would also work together to ensure a properly planned and continuous production programme. The producer-director teams were advanced money to prepare a script and a budget. Rank and the NFFC then financed the films, and any profits went into a pool. BFM films received 70 per cent of their production finance from the National Provincial Bank against Rank's distribution guarantees. The remaining 30 per cent, £707,000 in all, came from the NFFC. Completion guarantees were jointly provided by the NFFC and General Film Distributors, Rank's distribution company.[15] Rank had to guarantee the distribution of BFM's films, but the only capital he had at risk was that shared with the NFFC for completion guarantees. In return, BFM provided Rank with a supply of British films for his cinemas at comparatively little cost.

Unfortunately, this semi-co-operative arrangement was torn by internal dissent. After eighteen months it had financed fourteen films – six produced by BFM alone, the other eight were co-productions with independent producers. None of the BFM films was listed as a box-office winner, although *Appointment with Venus* (Ralph Thomas) was a 'notable attraction' in 1951; and *The Card* (Ronald Neame), *Hunted* (Charles Crichton) and *The Importance of Being Earnest* (Anthony Asquith) were all 'notable attractions' in 1952. Rank's biggest

Bringing in the name of the Good Lord: Philip Leacock's *The Kidnappers* (1953)

box-office successes were two Ealing films, *Where No Vultures Fly* (Harry Watt, 1951) and *Mandy* (Alexander Mackendrick, 1952), and *The Planter's Wife* (Ken Annakin, 1952).[16]

Rank decided to establish a new production order by which he could maintain control over the subject of each film, and in late 1952 he ended his agreement with the NFFC and wound up BFM.

This was a critical period for Rank, for when his elder brother James died he also had to run the family flour business. He became less involved in the day-to-day problems of his film business, but tried to retain control over the films the company made by 'buying the brains that do know about films'.[17] He chose John Davis and Earl St John, the head of production at Pinewood, for the task. From then on they effectively managed Rank's film business. The only subsequent occasion on which Rank rejected their advice was when he allowed Philip Leacock to make *The Kidnappers* (1953), on condition that he would bring in 'the name of the Good Lord'.[18] Rank wanted films which would be representative of Great Britain and assist in upholding its prestige abroad. But they were also to have high entertainment value acceptable to world audiences. John Davis dutifully echoed his master's vision. 'The aim is to make films of high entertainment value, of good technical standards, in good taste, and with sound moral standards.'[19]

Not surprisingly, the Rank films produced during this period all reinforced family values in one way or another. Most of them were contemporary comedies, adventure pictures or dramas. In Rank crime pictures the dramatic focus of the film was often not the crime itself but the morals and motives of those who were caught up in solving it.[20] 'Adult' subjects, like John Osborne's play *Look Back in Anger* or Alan Sillitoe's novel *Saturday Night and Sunday Morning*, were rejected. There were no science-fiction films and virtually no musicals. Historical subjects, if treated at all, were normally about British heroism or adventures in World War II, and those that were set in an earlier period, such as *A Tale of Two Cities* (Ralph Thomas, 1958) or *North West Frontier* (J. Lee Thompson, 1959), often had a central hero who unquestioningly fought off the enemy in order to defend British values or British interests.

Rank's principal production organisation, Group Film Producers, was based at Pinewood. The aim was to maintain a production programme of some fifteen films a year and to co-finance around six films from Ealing. After 1955, Rank ceased to support Ealing and production at Pinewood was increased to twenty films a year. In John Davis's view there were extremely few 'independent producers', as they did not either provide their own production finance or accept the financial risks involved. He therefore established an elaborate system of financial and organisational controls that shaped and limited the production of all Rank films. In return for their production finance, all producers who worked for Rank had to accept curbs on their creative freedom. Each project had to be approved by the board in two stages. Before it would finance pre-production development, the board had to approve the general treatment of a particular subject, such as a novel or a play. At the second stage, the board had to approve a detailed package consisting of the final script, the principal players, the director, the production schedule and budget. For most films, it could take almost a year to develop an idea or a story into a fully planned production.[21] Sometimes a film project, such as *Lawrence of Arabia*, which was to have been produced by Anatole de Grunwald and directed by Anthony Asquith, would fall at the second hurdle.[22] A Rank producer was also expected to use some of the stages at Pinewood, even though most film-makers preferred to shoot on location. In addition, a producer often had to cast some of Rank's contract artists.

During the 1950s the company maintained about forty contract artists, some of whom, such as Diana Dors, Jill Ireland and Anthony Steel, had been through the Rank Charm School. They were employed on long-term contracts, usually for seven years, although Rank retained the freedom to terminate the contract if the artist's behaviour was unsatisfactory. When the artist

worked outside Rank, the contract was automatically extended to make up for any leave of absence. If a contract artist was assigned to a Rank film, the production company had to pay half the artist's annual salary. Thus assignment to two films would cover an artist's annual salary; any more, and a profit was made.[23] John Davis would frequently require a production to use Rank contract artists before he would give it the financial go-ahead. He forced Anthony Asquith to cast Dirk Bogarde, Jean Kent and Susan Shaw in *The Woman in Question* (1950), and he insisted that Powell and Pressburger use Dirk Bogarde in *Ill Met by Moonlight* (1957). Davis also insisted that contract artists be used for the leads in *Robbery under Arms* (Jack Lee, 1957), and that Virginia McKenna star in *Carve Her Name with Pride* (Lewis Gilbert, 1958).[24] Theoretically, each contract artist was entitled to accept or reject any scripts offered by the Contract Artists Department, but if the artist rejected more than two scripts, there was trouble. Even Kay Kendall, one of Rank's biggest stars, was suspended after she had turned down scripts that she and her agent felt were unsuitable for her.[25]

John Davis and Earl St John were unimaginative and conservative in their attitude to films and they appear to have had little feel for public taste. Davis was an accountant who often sought to exert control by fear; Earl St John was an old-fashioned exhibitor who drank too much. Neither understood the changes in public taste that were taking place during the 1950s.[26] They often seemed intent in imposing their conservative views upon the public, although they could also perform a rapid volte-face in order to repeat unexpected commercial successes.

Earl St John was only persuaded to support *Genevieve* (Henry Cornelius, 1953), one of Rank's most popular films, because the NFFC had agreed to participate.[27] He and Davis were extremely chary about financing both *Doctor in the House* (Ralph Thomas, 1954) and Norman Wisdom's first film, *Trouble in Store* (John Paddy Carstairs, 1953). At the preview of *Trouble in Store* at the Odeon, Camden Town, Davis and St John gave Wisdom the brush-off, but once they saw how funny the audience found the film they changed their tune.[28]

Similarly, on the first day of shooting on *Doctor in the House*, Earl St John told producer Betty Box that the Rank board did not like hospital films, or films with the word 'Doctor' in the title. They wanted the title changed and the budget reduced.[29] Even when the film was completed, they insisted that all the stars should wear sports jackets, not white coats, in the publicity photographs.

If a film was successful, Davis insisted that the formula should be repeated. But many film-makers felt trapped by the limitations imposed on their creativity. Ted Willis found Pinewood creatively suffocating because it had him firmly tagged as a gag man.[30] Norman Wisdom was condemned always to play 'the Gump' and denied his wish to play Hamlet or the Hunchback of Notre Dame.[31] Betty Box and Ralph Thomas were more astute, using their success with the *Doctor* films to their own advantage: they only agreed to make other *Doctor* films if they could be interspersed with films of their own choosing.[32]

During the mid-1950s Davis's managerial methods paid dividends, unpopular though they were with film-makers and contract artists. Between 1953 and 1957 the organisation's production and distribution activities made a small, if unspectacular, profit. In 1955, *Doctor at Sea, One Good Turn, Man of the Moment* and *Above Us the Waves* all did well at the box office.[33] The following year, the top box-office attraction was *Reach for the Sky* (Lewis Gilbert), starring Kenneth More as Douglas Bader. Two more Rank films about World War II also did well: *A Town Like Alice* (Jack Lee, 1956) and *The Battle of the River Plate* (1956), written, produced and directed by Michael Powell and Emeric Pressburger after seven years away from Rank.[34]

Rank and the International Market

Only the most popular low-budget Rank films could recover their production costs in the UK. The differences between profit and loss depended on overseas revenues. The largest overseas market was the US, but Rank's attempts at US distribution in the late 1940s had been a failure.[35] Outside the US, however, results were much better. In 1953, when production and distribution activities made a £353,000 profit, half the company's film revenues came from overseas. Demand for British films had increased and Rank's colour film of the Coronation, *A Queen Is Crowned*, was successful everywhere except in the US.[36] The following year, profits rose to £837,000. Remittances from Canada were the largest ever and demand in the Eastern hemisphere remained high.[37] In 1955 profits fell, but the following year, boosted by the sale of some older films to US television, profits from production and distribution rose to an all-time high of £925,000.[38]

In 1956, Rank announced a policy of only producing films 'which had international entertainment appeal'

and which would be 'vigorously sold in foreign markets'.[39] The following year he and Davis established Rank Film Distributors of America (RFDA) to penetrate the US market and bypass the major American distributors. By March it had set up ten offices and leased cinemas in key cities to play Rank films. By mid-1958, RFDA had more than a dozen offices in the US, but industry rumours insisted that it was absorbing great losses. In March 1959, eighteen months after it had opened for business, RFDA was closed down. At the Rank AGM in September, Davis told the shareholders:

> Our attempts to open up this market for British films through our own distribution organisation have thus failed, but I feel that at the time we commenced the venture we were justified in our efforts.
> Unfortunately, the trend of the industry has been against us.[40]

Davis seemed not to have learnt the lesson from the US successes of *Hamlet, The Red Shoes* and several Ealing films – that it was indigenous British subjects which were most successful in US markets. International subjects like *Manuela* (Guy Hamilton, 1957), *Campbell's Kingdom* (Ralph Thomas, 1957) and *Ferry to Hong Kong* (Lewis Gilbert, 1959) had little box-office appeal to either British or American audiences.

The Decline of the Rank Empire

Davis, like Rank, saw films as moral tracts and refused to show any 'X'-certificate films in Rank cinemas. He set his face against any portrayal of extramarital sex, despite his own colourful private life.[41] Even so, intellectual guerrillas like Henry Cornelius and Jill Craigie managed to smuggle subversive behaviour into the films on which they worked. Cornelius cheerfully implied extramarital sex in *Genevieve*, and Jill Craigie sneaked progressive economic and political views into *The Million Pound Note* (Ronald Neame, 1954) and *Windom's Way* (Ronald Neame, 1957). It was not until 1961 that Davis recognised that times had changed and the cinema audience had more adult attitudes. *No Love for Johnnie* (Ralph Thomas, 1961) was the first Rank film to get an 'X' certificate, although Betty Box surmised that it was the left-wing politics of the film's adulterous MP which made it acceptable to Davis.[42]

The moral attitudes of British cinema audiences were changing fast. The new generation of teenagers and young single adults that dominated the cinema audiences of the late 1950s was ready to challenge the

Sexual and political intrigue in a Rank 'X' film: *No Love for Johnnie* (Ralph Thomas, 1961)

moral values and the cultural subservience of their parents. On the ABC circuit, a new and more irreverent type of comedy had already appeared. In 1958, Anglo-Amalgamated pulled off what *Kinematograph Weekly* termed 'a staggering long-shot', with *Carry On Sergeant* (Gerald Thomas); and in the following year the same team capped their success with *Carry On Nurse*, the biggest box-office attraction for 1959.[43] The new cinemagoing public was clearly ready for bawdier and more satirical films than Davis was prepared to produce.

Rank lost £1.3 million on film production and distribution in 1958 and £0.9 million in 1959, although it did make small profits between 1960 and 1962. By 1963, Davis had had enough. He regretfully concluded that 'film production in isolation is not possible'.[44] His strategy for saving the Rank Organisation was to diversify out of film. In 1956, he had signed a joint development agreement with the Halord Company in America for the non-US rights of the Xerox process. In 1963, Rank-Xerox became a subsidiary of the Rank Organisation and its profits were incorporated into the Rank accounts. In that year, the company earned more than half its profits from non-film activities.[45] Unlike film distribution and exhibition, Xerox was a system of photographic reproduction which could make money without the need to pay for the production of an expensive original copy. Rank's Methodism had lost out to the economics of the marketplace.

Notes

1. Michael Powell, *A Life in Movies*, pp. 647–62. The film went on to become an international box-office success.
2. Geoff Brown, *Launder and Gilliat*, p. 124.
3. Public Records Office: BT 64/4490. Overhead costs and earnings of British films, Schedule VI. *The Red Shoes* cost £505,600 and the producer's share of the ultimate film hire was estimated to be £1,291,300. The profit would therefore be £785,700. *Hamlet* cost £572,500 to produce and was estimated to earn the producer £1,352,200, a profit of £779,700.
4. Odeon Theatres, Annual Report to 28 June 1952, p. 5.
5. PRO: BT 64/4490, Schedule VI. The films were *Oliver Twist*, £244,500; *Great Expectations*, £222,600; *The Red Shoes*, £156,500; and *The Upturned Glass*, £156,000.
6. Odeon Theatres, Annual Report to 23 June 1956, Appendix. In 1956, Rank owned 584 cinemas in the UK, 124 in Canada, nineteen in Ireland, twelve in Jamaica and one in Portugal. He had access to 135 cinemas in Australia, 123 in South Africa, 117 in New Zealand, forty in Malaya, twenty-two in Ceylon and eighteen in the Netherlands.
7. Odeon Theatres, Annual Report to 23 June 1951, p. 6.
8. Ibid. (the emphases are mine).
9. *The Times*, 27 March 1953.
10. PRO: BT 64/4483: R. H. Dewes (Licensing and Personnel Controller, Circuits Management Association) to R. G. Somervell (Films Branch, Board of Trade), 15 December 1950. The rejected films were *Torment*, *Bless 'em All*, *What a Carry On*, *School for Randle*, *Up for the Cup*, *Gorbals Story*, *High Jinks in Society*, *Skimpy in the Navy*, *Over the Garden Wall*, *Shadow of the Past* and *Dark Secret*.
11. Ibid. Circuits Management Association to Board of Trade, 3 November 1952; and exchange of memoranda between SS and the President, 4 and 8 December 1952. In the quota year 1951–2, only four Rank cinemas failed to meet their supporting quota. These were the Empire, Darlington and the Odeons at Bloxwich, Dunstall and Spalding, which were all small theatres in intensely competitive situations.
12. Great Britain: Monopolies Commission, *A Report on the Supply of Films for Exhibition in Cinemas* (206) (HMSO, 1966), para. 93.
13. Ibid., para. 58.
14. John Davis, 'Re-organisation of Booking Methods of Odeon and Gaumont Circuits', *CEA Newsletter* no. 15 (Cinematograph Exhibitors Association, 17 October 1958), pp. 1–11.
15. Odeon Theatres, Annual Report to 23 June 1951, p. 5.
16. *Kinematograph Weekly*, 20 December 1951, p. 9; and 18 December 1952, p. 10. The failure of some of those films that were made in 1952 resulted in a considerable loss for the NFFC. As late as 31 March 1956, it had still not recouped £181,000, over a quarter of its original investment, although the National Provincial Bank, which put up

the front money on each film, almost certainly made a profit on its loans.

17. Donald Sinden, *A Touch of the Memoirs*, p. 190.

18. Brian McFarlane, *Sixty Voices: Celebrities Recall the Golden Age of British Cinema*, p. 156.

19. John Davis, 'Intermission – the British Film Industry', *National Provincial Bank Review*, August 1958, pp. 1–12, at p. 5. He gave a similar – but different – paper to the annual conference of the Chartered Institute of Secretaries, in Llandudno in May the same year.

20. For instance, although *The Spanish Gardener* (1956) is nominally a crime film, the real centre of the film is the struggle of a stern British consul (Michael Hordern) to retain his only son's affection and to prevent him coming under the influence of his charming Spanish gardener (Dirk Bogarde), whom he distrusts.

21. John Davis, 'The British Film Industry', Chartered Institute of Secretaries, Annual Conference, May 1958, p. 3.

22. The reasons are unclear, but it was probably because the budget was about £700,000: Dirk Bogarde, *Snakes and Ladders* (Harmondsworth: Penguin, 1979), pp. 170–2, and R. J. Minney, *Puffin Asquith* (London: Leslie Frewin, 1973), pp. 172–6.

23. Sinden, *A Touch of the Memoirs*, pp. 190–1.

24. Dirk Bogarde, in McFarlane, *Sixty Voices*, p. 26; Michael Powell, *Million Dollar Movie* (London: Heinemann, 1992), p. 360. Vincent Ball and Lewis Gilbert, in McFarlane, *Sixty Voices*, pp. 24 and 98.

25. Donald Sinden, in McFarlane, *Sixty Voices*, p. 203. Dinah Sheridan turned down roles in a 'B' feature, *Grand National Night* (Talisman, Bob McNaught, 1953) and *Street Corner* (London Independent, Muriel Box, 1953) before accepting her role in *Genevieve* (see Dinah Sheridan, in McFarlane, p. 200). Davis could also hire out a contract artist to another film company, normally for a sum equivalent to the artist's annual salary. *The Times*, 22 December 1954, for Kay Kendall.

26. See for example, Sue Harper and Vincent Porter, 'Moved to Tears: Weeping and the Cinema in Post-War Britain', *Screen* no. 2, Summer 1996, pp. 38–53.

27. Michael Balcon, *Michael Balcon Presents . . . A Lifetime of Films* (London: Hutchinson, 1969), p. 168.

28. Geoffrey Macnab, *J. Arthur Rank and the British Film Industry*, pp. 222–3.

29. Betty Box, in McFarlane, *Sixty Voices*, p. 39. See also Macnab, *J. Arthur Rank*, pp. 223–4.

30. Ted Willis, *Evening All . . . Fifty Years over a Hot Typewriter* (London: Macmillan, 1991), p. 113.

31. Hugh Stewart, cited in Macnab, *J. Arthur Rank*, p. 223.

32. Betty Box, in McFarlane, *Sixty Voices*, p. 38.

33. *Kinematograph Weekly*, 15 December 1955, p. 4.

34. *Kinematograph Weekly*, 13 December 1956, p. 6.

35. Odeon Theatres, Annual Report to 24 June 1949; see also Robert Murphy, 'Rank's Attempt on the American Market', in James Curran and Vincent Porter (eds), *British Cinema History* (London: Weidenfeld and Nicolson, 1983).

36. Odeon Theatres, Annual Report to 27 June 1953, pp. 4, 6.

37. Odeon Theatres, Annual Report to 26 June 1954, p. 7.

38. Odeon Theatres, Annual Report to 23 June 1956, p. 9.

39. Ibid., p. 73.

40. Thomas Guback, *The International Film Industry* (Bloomington: Indiana University Press, 1969), pp. 75, 76.

41. Like King Henry VIII, John Davis had six wives. He metaphorically beheaded two of them by omitting them from his entry in *Who's Who*.

42. Betty Box, in McFarlane, *Sixty Voices*, p. 39.

43. *Kinematograph Weekly*, 18 December 1958, p. 6; and 17 December 1959, p. 6.

44. Odeon Theatres, Annual Report to 19 June 1963, p. 21.

45. Ibid., p. 11.

Bibliography

Brown, Geoff (ed.), *Launder and Gilliat* (London: BFI, 1977).

Davis, John H., 'Intermission – the British Film Industry', *National Provincial Bank Review*, August 1958.

Falk, Quentin, *The Golden Gong: Fifty Years of the Rank Organisation, Its Films and Its Stars* (London: Columbus Books, 1987).

Great Britain: Monopolies Commission, *A Report on the Supply of Films for Exhibition in Cinemas* (London: HMSO, 1966).

Harper, Sue, and Porter, Vincent, *British Cinema of the 1950s: The Decline of Deference* (Oxford and New York: Oxford University Press, 2003).

Macnab, Geoffrey, *J. Arthur Rank and the British Film Industry* (London: Routledge, 1993).

MacQuitty, William, *A Life to Remember* (London: Quartet, 1991).

McFarlane, Brian, *Sixty Voices: Celebrities Recall the Golden Age of British Cinema* (London: BFI, 1992).

McFarlane, Brian, *An Autobiography of British Cinema* (London: Methuen, 1997).

Mullally, Frederic, *Films – An Alternative to Rank: An Analysis of Power and Policy in the British Film Industry* (London: Socialist Book Centre, 1946).

Murphy, Robert, 'Rank's Attempt on the American Market, 1944–49', in James Curran and Vincent Porter (eds), *British Cinema History* (London: Weidenfeld and Nicolson, 1983), pp. 164–78.

Murphy, Robert, *Realism and Tinsel: Cinema and Society in Britain 1939–49* (London: Routledge, 1989).

Perry, George, *Movies from the Mansion: A History of Pinewood Studios* (London: Elm Tree Books, 1982).

Powell, Michael, *A Life in Movies* (London: Heinemann, 1986).

Powell, Michael, *Million Dollar Movie* (London: Heinemann, 1992).

Sellar, Maurice, *et al.*, *Best of British: A Celebration of Rank Film Classics* (London: Sphere, 1987).

Sinden, Donald, *A Touch of the Memoirs* (London: Hodder & Stoughton, 1982).

Wood, Alan, *Mr. Rank: A Study of J. Arthur Rank and British Films* (London: Hodder & Stoughton, 1952).

30
Bonnie Prince Charlie Revisited: British Costume Film in the 1950s

SUE HARPER

Although they both reinforce the act of social remembering, costume dramas and historical films are different from each other. Historical films deal with real people or events: Henry VIII, the Battle of Waterloo, Lady Hamilton. Costume film uses the mythic and symbolic aspects of the past as a means of providing pleasure, rather than instruction. It is a far more flexible form than historical film, and this flexibility makes it acutely unstable. It can splinter into further subgenres, such as the imaginary biopic or the historical horror film. Moreover, it can alter radically over short periods of time, and constantly reform its definitions of national identity.

My book, *Picturing the Past: The Rise and Fall of the British Costume Film*, shows how in the 1930s and 40s history was raided for political purposes by filmmakers from the right and left of the political spectrum.[1] In the 1930s, groups such as the Historical Association and the British Film Institute struggled for control over the content and style of historical films, and they bewailed the popularity of such 'disrespectful' films as *The Private Life of Henry VIII* (1933) and *The Scarlet Pimpernel* (1934), which audiences flocked to see. During World War II, the Ministry of Information was initially enthusiastic about the usefulness of history as a propaganda tool, and it favoured films which used the past to encourage and educate the public about the nation's war aims. Later in the war, another form of historical film emerged: the costume extravaganza. In films such as *The Wicked Lady* (1945) heroines wearing sumptuous frocks committed hubris, and caused mayhem among the unsuspecting populace.

Three conclusions can be drawn about British costume film from this earlier period. First, the entertainment afforded by costume films was frequently excoriated by the critical or social establishment. Costume films had especially low status because they appealed primarily to female audiences. Second, the historical and costume films that were most successful (both artistically and financially) were those made by the larger production companies such as Gainsborough or London Films. Third, popular costume films expressed a coherent position on class, but this was always combined with a strong statement about gender stereotyping and sexual pleasure. The class which was made to work hardest in the costume texts was almost always the aristocracy, which was presented as a high point of style and confidence to which all other groups might aspire.

Changing Styles and Audiences

The costume genre altered radically during the 1950s. It was always expensive to produce, and was therefore more vulnerable to market fluctuations. Throughout the decade the British film industry was riven by economic difficulties and a decline in overall confidence. Changes in government policy and adjustments in the international film market brought problems in their wake. The relationship of British films to international audiences had always been volatile, and this was particularly so for the costume genre, predicated as it was on definitions of national identity: these were compelling enough to sell at home but prone to slippage and incoherence when exported abroad. In the intensively competitive and insecure market of the 1950s, home-grown costume films were at a considerable disadvantage.

Another important determinant on British costume films was that, in the mid-1940s, the British Film Producers' Association (BFPA) brought its policy on fiction in the public domain into line with that of the Motion Picture Association of America (MPAA). All the major Hollywood companies worked on a system of registration of those novels whose authors had been dead for more than fifty years. Once a studio had registered an interest in filming such a novel, other studios were legally bound not to compete. This had profound effects on patterns of British production. It was only with the greatest difficulty, for example, that Cineguild was able to make *Great Expectations* (1946) and *Oliver Twist* (1948) in the 1940s.[2] Conversely, George Minter of Renown was not a member of the BFPA and so, although he was free to make his Dickens films in the 1950s, he stood no chance of gaining American (or even major British) distribution.[3] And the only reason Rank could make *A Tale of Two Cities* in 1958 was that Hollywood had made a successful version in the 1930s and did not wish to repeat it so soon.[4]

After the MPAA registration system took hold, costume film-makers in Britain no longer had first call on their own classic novelists. In effect, the most 'cinematic' novels of Scott, Dickens and Robert Louis Stevenson were the property of MGM and Disney, and the British were prevented from making films of them. Hence British producers' fondness for modern novelists who wrote historical fiction. One alternative was to choose a dead writer still in copyright and then negotiate with his heirs; that was how Arnold Bennett's *The Card* came to the screen in 1952. Another alternative was to commission purpose-made scripts, which was always a more risky procedure.

Besides the marketing, legal and industrial difficulties that assailed the costume genre, there were also profound changes in audience composition. The commercial success of the 1940s costume films depended largely on the fact that more women than men went to the cinema, and the genre came to be seen as a female prerogative that offered visual pleasures when other consumer pleasures were at a premium. All this changed in the 1950s, when British cinema audiences declined catastrophically. In 1950, 30 million people went to 4,500 cinemas every week; by 1960, only 10 million people went each week to 3,000 cinemas. More importantly teenagers, particularly unmarried male teenagers, were replacing female and family viewers.[5] The baby boom, commercial television and leisure activities such as do-it-yourself meant that families

stayed at home, and it was the young people who increasingly sought leisure outside.[6] The following remarks by two middle-class women are typical:

> It's different when you're single, you've nothing else to do once you've had your supper and you're itching to go somewhere. Now with the baby I'd rather sit by the fire and listen to the wireless. You either get into the habit of going regularly, or you grow away from it as I have done. I haven't been since we had the television fixed. We just switch on the television and relax. Often there's a good play on. Besides so many of the films these days are so unsuitable for children.[7]

The tastes and desires of the audience were qualitatively different from those of the 1940s. There were more males (particularly young males) in the regular audiences, the female audience which had traditionally patronised costume films now tending to stay at home; and middle-class audiences, who had been the mainstay of the more respectable historical films, were increasingly alienated from the cinema.[8]

So the costume genre was in flux and crisis throughout the decade. The National Film Finance Corporation only supported it in an erratic and inconsistent manner.[9] However, there was a remarkable shift in critical opinion. Throughout the 1930s and 40s, costume film had attracted the wrath of critics, who felt that its sensationalism impugned the historical heritage. But in the 1950s history in film was rehabilitated by journalists in the quality press. *The Times* film correspondent defended American representations of Helen of Troy, Diane de Poitiers and Catherine de Medici thus:

> The look of her dark little head set imperiously on a long slender neck will, for those that saw them, always accompany the thought of Catherine in the mind, and the possession of so bright an image is surely an enticement rather than a snare and a delusion . . . it must give people who normally never think about the past at all the conviction that at least it once existed.[10]

And Peter John Dyer produced a taxonomy of the genre in *Films and Filming* in an attempt to improve its status.[11]

What kind of costume films were produced in Britain in the 1950s? The decade opened with Gainsborough's last costume film, *So Long at the Fair* (1950). This was a far cry from the studio's early bodice-rippers, which had celebrated female energy. *So Long at the Fair* was set at the turn of the century, and dealt with a heroine whose brother contracts the plague. This is concealed from her, and the film is structured around the themes of female vulnerability and social duplicity. This pattern was repeated in such films as *Madeleine* (1950) and *Svengali* (1954). Other historical films were based on well-known literary texts, such as *Scrooge* (1951), *The Pickwick Papers* (1952), *Romeo and Juliet* (1954) and *Richard III* (1955).

Some films made in the early part of the decade tried to recapture the *élan* of earlier costume extravaganzas. *The Elusive Pimpernel* (1950), Powell and Pressburger's remake of *The Scarlet Pimpernel* suffered from an incoherent narrative which betrayed the fact that its makers were 'all pulling in different directions'.[12] The aristocratic symbolism, which had been so subtly deployed in the 1930s film, was crude and inconsistent. Herbert Wilcox, too, tried to repeat the successes of his 1930s historical films with *Lilacs in the Spring* (1954), but failed dismally. Another producer, Anthony Havelock-Allan, had tried the same technique with *The Shadow of the Eagle* (1950), which borrowed themes and settings from 1930s British films such as *Catherine the Great* and *The Dictator*. However, the film's lavish décor was no substitute for good sense. Other film-makers tried to recreate and reassess key aspects of the Victorian period in a more sober way. Unfortunately *Tom Brown's Schooldays* (1951), *The Lady with the Lamp* (1951) and *The Story of Gilbert and Sullivan* (1953) were all worthy but dull.

From 1950 to 1958 British-financed historical films tended to concentrate on periods which were politically quiescent but economically turbulent; in doing so, they avoided the spectacular aspects of the past. American producers did exactly the opposite. After 1950, American film-makers took full advantage of the Eady Levy to make prestigious costume films using British actors and technicians.[13] Their films featured heroic individuals quite different from those in the home-grown costume films. The Americans preferred the medieval period and the 18th century, and they had an interest in Scottish settings. Disney made *Treasure Island* (1950), *The Story of Robin Hood and His Merrie Men* (1952), *The Sword and the Rose* (1953), *Rob Roy, the Highland Rogue* (1953) and *Kidnapped* (1960). Warners made *Captain Horatio Hornblower R.N.* (1951) and *The Master of Ballantrae* (1953). MGM made *Ivanhoe* (1952), *Beau Brummell* (1954) and *The Adventures of Quentin Durward* (1955).[14] Despite considerable commercial

success, after 1957 the Americans gradually withdrew from making historical films in Britain and shifted to contemporary settings and stories.

In general, war films and comedies tended to dominate the British box office in the 1950s, but some costume films were successful. Hammer's costume frighteners did well at the British box-office, though they did better business abroad.[15] *The Lady with the Lamp* earned an honourable mention in the *Kinematograph Weekly* listings of box-office winners, as did *The Card* (1952); *Scrooge* and *The Pickwick Papers* did fairly well, despite their distribution problems. *The Moonraker* (1958) made a reasonable showing, as did *A Tale of Two Cities* and *North West Frontier* (1959). But none of these were smash-hits; it was the American-financed historical films that made the real impact at the British box office. *Captain Horatio Hornblower R.N.* and *Ivanhoe* were major box-office hits. *The Black Rose*, *The Master of Ballantrae* and *The Crimson Pirate* made large profits as did *Knights of the Round Table*, *Rob Roy, the Highland Rogue*, *Footsteps in the Fog* and *Kidnapped*.[16]

Class and Costume

Clearly, both British and American backers recognised the need to nuance their product so as to take account

Covert homilies about entrepreneurial skills: Alec Guinness and Glynis Johns in *The Card* (Ronald Neame, 1952)

A Tale of Two Cities (Ralph Thomas, 1958)

A Tale of Two Cities was made by the Rank Organisation during the period when John Davis was running the company and promoting films for the international market. Davis gave a degree of autonomy to directors and producers who had complied with his behests and whose films succeeded at the box office. Consequently Betty Box and Ralph Thomas were allowed to make *A Tale of Two Cities* as one of an interesting group of films sandwiched between the formulaic but profitable *Doctor at Large* (1957) and *Doctor in Love* (1960). Unfortunately they made two serious errors of judgment: shooting the film on location in France, which proved expensive and uninspiring, and shooting it in black-and-white when the story's historical romanticism required colour to attract a mass audience. Bruised by their experience, Box and Thomas respectively suggested that the film be called *I Love Lucy* or *Doctor in the Bastille*.

Nonetheless, the film is a serious interpretation of the Dickens classic. It contains an outstanding performance from Dirk Bogarde (then the idol of the Odeons), who managed to augment the psychological complexity of the novel's Sidney Carton; Dorothy Tutin's Lucie might seem vapidly sweet, but this is what is required of Dickens's heroine. Among the vivid cast of character actors Athene Seyler's sympathetic Miss Pross and Rosalie Crutchley's predatory Madame Defarge stand out. Beatrice Dawson's costumes pay little attention to historical accuracy, but they evoke a mythic past of revolutionary iconoclasm and heroic individualism. Carmen Dillon's art direction tended towards realism, which might seem inappropriate for Dickens's unremittingly Gothic urban and rural landscapes; but some of Dillon's symmetrical sets – particularly the approach to the guillotine – are impressive.

The key to understanding *A Tale of Two Cities* is the script. T. E. B. Clarke had specialised in comedy and realism, which made him an unexpected choice for the adaptation. However, he had the confidence to condense the seventeen-year timespan of the novel into three, and to contrive a spoken register that was modern without being casual. Clarke's script presents the violent convulsions of the Revolution as

'It's a far, far better rest that I go to': Dirk Bogarde makes the ultimate sacrifice in *A Tale of Two Cities*

a justifiable response to intolerable repression: a liberal viewpoint reminiscent of his best-known Ealing film *Passport to Pimlico* (1949). The lower classes are fundamentally decent and open to reasonable demands. In order for them to rebel, they have to be enraged beyond reason. Hence the weight thrown onto the performance of Christopher Lee as the foul Marquis St Evremond. In Clarke and Thomas's *A Tale of Two Cities* the bad but irresistibly charismatic aristocrat, a purveyor of lip-smacking pleasure in British costume films, is transformed into something much less attractive: the sinister oppressor of innocent people.

FURTHER READING

For an account of the scripting problems on *A Tale of Two Cities*, see T. E. B. Clarke, 'Every Word in Its Place', *Films and Filming*, February 1958 and T. E. B. Clarke, *This Is Where I Came In* (London, Michael Joseph, 1974), pp.197–9.

John Coldstream, *Dirk Bogarde: The Authorised Biography* (London: Weidenfeld, 2004), pp. 230–1, 234–5.

of shifts in audience composition. Audiences were getting younger and proportionately more masculine, and the producer of costume films ignored this at his peril. But British producers failed to capitalise on the pattern of class relationships that had characterised the costume film in the 1930s and 40s. In profitable films such as *The Scarlet Pimpernel* and *The Man in Grey* (1943), the key alliances were between the aristocracy and the working class; on a symbolic level, this alliance circumvented the power of the middle class, and the aristocracy functioned as the powerful site of hidden and repressed pleasures. Aristocratic style (careless, flamboyant and inventive) was, in 1930s and 40s films, a key resource, and a disguise in which to utter insights about the nature of social and sexual power.

But in British costume films of the early 1950s, the key classes were the middle and lower middle, and British producers used the men of those classes to engage in covert homilies about entrepreneurial skills. *The Card*, for example, directed by Ronald Neame for Rank, centres on a hero (Alec Guinness) who tackles the lack of status attending small-scale investment. History was used as a lesson about the flexibility necessary to gain and maintain financial (and subsequently social) power. In a key scene, the hero profits from his investment in a small boat. The camera moves up and down, and pans across the busy lives of those working his will. An old sea-dog, bringing the latest haul to the sedentary hero, remarks that 'It's a mighty lot of money for doing nothing.' Here the camera halts on the poised face of the entrepreneur, who ripostes, 'But you see, I did do something. I thought of it.'

The Magic Box, made by the Boultings for British Lion in 1951, was part of the Festival of Britain celebrations, and was the biography of the cinematograph pioneer Friese-Greene. Duller and less popular than *The Card*, it too used the past as a lesson about the marketplace's need for grit. The lower-middle-class hero was inventive enough but fatally lacked entrepreneurial skills and energy. The Dickens adaptations in the early 1950s followed the same pattern. Renown's *Scrooge* and *The Pickwick Papers* were both skewed, in their narrative construction and style of acting, towards the middle class and its provenance. They avoid the picturesque and sensational aspects of the past that were so evident in earlier British adaptations of Dickens, such as *The Old Curiosity Shop* (1934). This was because their directors (Brian Desmond Hurst and Noel Langley, respectively) were sufficiently persuasive, com-

bative and unconventional to impose their views on producer George Minter, who had hitherto specialised in low-budget and low-status enterprises such as the 'Old Mother Riley' films.[17]

Male Adventurers

British producers used history for slightly different purposes in the later 1950s. Several films investigated male grace under pressure, and they often presented muscular strength as sufficient for any challenge. In *North West Frontier*, the hero (Kenneth More) vanquishes Indian opposition to British Imperial power by sheer derring-do; his energy obviates the need to think. In *A Tale of Two Cities*, the protagonist Dirk Bogarde has the strength of mind to sacrifice himself for love, but the film prevaricates about the resources on which he draws. It is the same with *The Moonraker*, which deals with the English Civil War. The Cavalier hero (George Baker) displays a physical vitality which is unsullied by self-awareness. Tidy horsemanship has replaced intellectual prowess. It is instructive to compare *The Moonraker* with Hammer's *The Scarlet Blade* (1963), which has a very similar plot. In the Hammer film, the Cavaliers take refuge with a band of gypsies, and the combination of these two 'forbidden' groups gives them enormous symbolic weight. *The Moonraker* is far more conservative in its use of marginal groups, and far more mainstream in its interpretation of social power and personal motivation.

The Moonraker, like many other costume films of its period, features a hero whose cultural resources are slim and unstable. Such a hero is unable to avail himself of the aristocratic manner that was so confidently deployed in previous costume films. This is acutely at issue in Rank's *The Gypsy and the Gentleman*, directed by Joseph Losey and released in 1958. It should have worked well, since it contained a number of traditional British costume themes: the wild gypsy, the imprisoned virgin, the dissolute aristocrat, the faithful black servant. But these themes were now too residual and fossilised for the cultural job in hand. *The Gypsy and the Gentleman* was a farrago which began unpromisingly with overhead shots of the hero wrestling with a greased sow. The aristocrat (Keith Michell) behaves like a petulant ejaculator praecox, and the gypsy (Melina Mercouri) elevates nostril-flaring into an art form. However, the film's artistic failure should not be laid solely at Losey's door, even though he had the temerity to claim it as realistic.[18] Rather, the cinematic times were out of joint for such an enterprise, at least for a British company.

American producers were also preoccupied by masculinity in their 1950s history films, but they tackled it differently. Many of their British costume films were set in the medieval period, where lords, vassals and thanes could not be easily translated into the ruling/working/middle-class divide. Instead, films like *Ivanhoe*, *The Knights of the Round Table* and *The Adventures of Quentin Durward* evoked a colourful world in which the heroes are limited only by fate or political intrigue. The

medieval period has habitually been used in British literary culture (by Keats, Carlyle and Morris, for example) as a symbol of courtly love and craftsmanship. It was very rarely deployed by British film producers; whereas the Americans recuperated the period as a celebration of an energetic and classless masculinity.

The American producers also used Scottish landscape and history. Walt Disney suggested that the Scottish clans ignored the class system and permitted

---

Ivanhoe (Richard Thorpe, 1952)

Ivanhoe was made by MGM at its British studios in Borehamwood. Dore Schary, the atypically liberal new head of the studio appointed MGM veteran Richard Thorpe as director, but relied on two blacklisted writers Waldo Salt and Marguerite Rogers to prepare the script. Thorpe was a product of the old studio ethic of 'shoot as written', and never contested the producer's behests. Consequently, what emerged was an expensive and popular swashbuckler (the film cost £400,000 to make and was very successful at both the British and American box office), which puts a heavy stress on the importance of liberty, equality and tolerance.

The basic plot of Sir Walter Scott's novel is retained. Sir Ivanhoe (Robert Taylor), a Saxon knight in Norman England, finds Richard the Lionheart imprisoned in Austria, and with the help of Robin Hood and the English Jewish community, ousts his evil brother Bad King John and restores Richard to the throne. Ivanhoe is betrothed to the Saxon princess Rowena (Joan Fontaine), but the Jewess Rebecca (Elizabeth Taylor) is also in love with him, and he fights a duel with King John's champion for her life. In the novel, all the narrative and moral power lies with Rowena; but in the film she is played by Joan Fontaine, past her best by this time and labouring under the weight of heavy yellow braids and a pained expression. Elizabeth Taylor, on the other hand, was at the peak of her beauty, and her tremulous flower-like qualities make her, for the audience at least, irresistible.

The script of *Ivanhoe*, written by Noel Langley (whose previous work ranged from *The Wizard of Oz*, 1939, to *They Made Me a Fugitive*, 1947, to *Scrooge*) from the treatment by Waldo Salt and Marguerite Rogers, nuances history in a radical way. In the novel, Wamba the jester makes a fleeting appearance. In the film, Wamba (Emlyn Williams) has his serf's collar

removed by Ivanhoe, who insists that all men should be free. Producer Pandro S. Berman was fascinated by the 'Jewish angle' of *Ivanhoe* and ensured that it was given more extended treatment in the film. Rebecca is accused of witchcraft in the novel, but the film inserts a nine-minute trial scene in which she defends herself and her faith, evoking HUAC and the McCarthyite witch-hunts against supposed Communists in America.

Ivanhoe interprets medieval England as a glittering pageant. The costumes by Roger Furse are particularly interesting for the peasant clothes, which in their earthy colours and rough textures evoke a rugged organic quality; and in the robes of the heroines, which in their cut and fabric present the breasts and hips as improbably pneumatic. The sets by veteran designer Alfred Junge are lush rather than obsessively accurate, and encourage Thorpe and his cinematographer Freddie Young to present the past as a series of richly textured tableaux. The set-piece sieges and battles are aided by the solidity and imaginative coherence of Junge's designs, and the film works well as enjoyable spectacle. But the script ensures that we also learn a lesson about the historical importance of tolerance and justice.

Ivanhoe was followed by two equally colourful successors – *Knights of the Round Table* and *The Adventures of Quentin Durward*, both directed by Thorpe – but these are more orthodox films with less interesting and complex subtexts.

FURTHER READING

Vincent Porter and Sue Harper, 'Throbbing Hearts and Smart Repartee: The Reception of American Films in 1950s Britain', *Media History* vol. 4 no. 2, December 1998, pp. 175–93.

Jeffrey Richards, 'The Politics of the Swashbuckler', in James Chapman, Mark Glancy and Sue Harper (eds), *The New Film History: Sources, Methods, Approaches* (Basingstoke: Palgrave Macmillan, 2007), pp. 119–36.

the expression of an aggressive male style. He asserted that in Scotland 'it took courage and a fierce love of freedom to conquer that rugged land', just like the American frontier of old: geography and history were coterminous.[19] American producers' attentions were centred on the 1745 period, with *The Master of Ballantrae, Rob Roy, the Highland Rogue* and *Kidnapped*. They used the Stuart rebellion against the Hanoverian dynasty for their own ends. The struggle had always been a tender issue in British national consciousness. British film producers had either avoided it entirely or failed dismally with it, as Korda did with *Bonnie Prince Charlie* in 1948. Korda had used the 1745 rebellion as a symbol of failure, and his misjudgment resulted in a disaster. American producers, on the other hand, used Bonnie Prince Charlie and the 'Glorious '45' for a double purpose. First, they deployed the romantic Scottish rebellion against British rationality as a sort of 'prequel' of the American War of Independence, and were thus able to incorporate the rebellion into a debate about individualism versus legitimacy. Second, the fights and kilts afforded endless opportunities for masculine display. But the red beard and muscular calves of Rob Roy (Richard Todd) were not dished up solely for the pleasure of female viewers.

The heroes are better at running up a burn than they are at making love: Glynis Johns and Richard Todd in *Rob Roy, the Highland Rogue* (Harold French, 1953)

This was a different kind of male beauty from that presented in, say, the Gainsborough bodice-rippers. There, the languid and often feminised heroes constituted a spectacle for females. In the Scottish epics, it was male energy that was celebrated. The heroes are better at running up a burn than they are at making love. These were costume films for men.

So the Scottish films are a rich concoction of political and gender issues, in which the heroes are granted mastery over women and over geographical space. The American producers also chose to revisit historical periods that had hitherto been a British speciality. The Tudor period had been represented in the first successful British costume film, Korda's *The Private Life of Henry VIII*, in which the eponymous hero displayed human frailty and the pitfalls of political power. Disney's *The Sword and the Rose* reinterpreted Henry (played by James Robertson Justice) as a loud and virile Machiavelli. The other period which had figured largely in British costume culture was that of the Regency and the Napoleonic wars. In films such as Korda's *The Scarlet Pimpernel* and Gainsborough's *The Man in Grey*, the Regency had been represented as a period in which the aristocracy displayed a marvellous adroitness in its social dealings. MGM's *Beau Brummell*, made at enormous expense at Borehamwood, and chosen as the Royal Command Performance film of 1954, nuanced its account in a different way.

Through the work of designers who had been innovatory in previous British costume or 'fantastic' films, the American producers were able to reorient former film images of the Regency. Alfred Junge, the production designer on *Beau Brummell*, had played a key role in some of Powell and Pressburger's films. Junge's sets for *Beau Brummell* contain an unparalleled range of visual textures, in which mirrored doors, drapes, columns and *objets d'art* interpret the Regency as a period of symmetry and cultural confidence. Elizabeth Haffenden, who had constructed such skilful 'costume narratives' in the Gainsborough melodramas, designed the costumes for *Beau Brummell*. The colour coding and symbolic resonance of Haffenden's costumes are a major source of visual pleasure in the film. Her varieties of white, cream, silver and grey encourage the eye to make subtle aesthetic distinctions.[20] The male was here in sole possession of stylishness and flexibility. The historical Brummell was outrageously finicky, and reputedly effeminate; but the MGM film presents him (via Stewart Granger) as a virile adventurer whose sole flaw is to put his faith in princes.

The same period was reassessed in Warners' *Captain Horatio Hornblower R.N.* Here, the hero is lonely and riven by self-doubt, and holds himself aloof from the aristocratic powers which he challenges and vanquishes. As played by Gregory Peck, Hornblower seems to have provided a powerful role model for British males in the audience, right up to the 1960s.[21]

American 'British' films, then, were qualitatively different from the home product in the way they used history. The scripts of American costume films contained much archaic language (many 'sires' and 'forsooths'), while the British films attempted an awkward modernisation in their conversational style. American-financed costume films were based on classical novels (especially those of Scott and Stevenson), whereas the British films often had to commission custom-made scripts. American costume films were edited differently, too. They were assembled and cut on the movement of the hero, thus giving an impression of vitality and readiness. The British-financed histories tended to cut on the direction of the look, which impeded the fast flow of the narrative.

Hammer's Gothic Melodramas

There was one British company which replicated the American disposition of gender elements, and considerably to its profit. Hammer Films shifted its policy from futuristic horror (*The Quatermass Experiment*, 1955) to historical horror, with the production in 1957 of *The Curse of Frankenstein*. From that time until the early 1970s, half Hammer's output had historical settings. The historical context permitted the studio to allude to hidden or forgotten elements in British popular culture; but it also opened up a space in which notions of national identity could be examined in a new way. Significantly, the critical rehabilitation of the costume genre did not extend to Hammer's films, which were frequently attacked for their supposed immorality, so much so that the studio ceased to give press showings.[22]

Hammer Films was organised in a rigorous way, and the producers ensured that the script was the dominant discourse. This tight control over the scripts profoundly affected the way in which history was deployed. The historical periods evoked by Hammer were extensive (myth, pre-history, ancient Egypt, mid- and late-nineteenth-century Europe). Absences were important too; there were no Roman films apart from the misleadingly titled *The Viking Queen* (1967), and no treatments of the rational and elegant 18th century. All

Hammer's costume films contain an arrogant upper class and a sullen, oppressed underclass. Social relations between these two groups are never presented as contradictory in a fruitful sense: Hammer histories evoke a world in which social contradictions are absent.[23] Instead, archetypal contradictions are presented, such as those between male and female, human and animal, the quick and the dead. This shift from social to archetypal contradiction was perhaps a way of displacing and defusing the anxieties the audience may have had about social class.

Sexual anxieties are similarly displaced. Hammer's costume films do not celebrate sexual desire. They display a nervous preoccupation with the body: its orifices, its blood, its organs, its unfamiliar changes, its unratified penetration. Films such as the Frankenstein and Dracula cycles interrogate such anxieties, by broaching and breaking social taboos to do with the body. These taboos are usually dealt with by a ritual, and the films teach the audience how to distinguish between a ritual that pollutes and a ritual that ensures freedom from defilement.

Hammer costume films express intense anxiety about the female body. Some costume plots (*Blood from the Mummy's Tomb*, *The Plague of the Zombies*, *Countess Dracula*) are structured around the oozings of female blood. And others deal with manifestations of the monstrous-feminine (*The Reptile*, *The Gorgon*, *Frankenstein Created Woman*, *She*), in which the transgressive heroines are rigorously returned to the patriarchal order. The intensity of regard which Hammer costume films accord to the female body as the site of unspeakable excess suggests that the films were carefully targeted at male audiences.[24]

Hammer costume films can be said to use myth and history as a means of social as well as sexual disavowal. That is to say, they shift the audience's attention away from class difference and sexual difference, and neutralise the anxieties attending them. The manner of delivery of the films is ironic. This irony resides in the scripts, which encourage the audience to repudiate the importance of what they have seen or heard. This process of disavowal converts the potential dangers of the spectacle into something safe.

Hammer revived the motifs of popular history from previous decades, but it nuanced them differently. In Gainsborough melodramas, those on the periphery of society generated energy because they were ambiguously poised between the sacred and the profane. But in Hammer historical films such groups are profoundly disruptive. Aristocrats, wicked ladies, gypsies and pirates are like loose cannon: fun to watch but dangerous for those who get in the way.

Here we can draw important similarities between Hammer's and other costume films. British film culture of the 1950s used the historical context as a disguise in which to express disquiet about social change. The increasingly meritocratic world of the 1950s, with its radically new patterns of consumption and class allegiance, met with a conservative response from the costume genre. British costume films argued that a reformed middle class (and particularly the male of the species) was perfectly competent for the social job in hand. For them, aristocratic symbolism was a source of titillation, but nothing more. American producers working in Britain had an entirely different approach. They stripped history bare of its class resonance, and made it the threnody of an unambiguous and energetic masculinity.

Notes

1. See Sue Harper, *Picturing the Past: The Rise and Fall of the British Costume Film*.

2. Ronald Neame, 'Choosing a Film Story', in F. Maurice Speed, Film Review (London: MacDonald, 1949).

3. See, for example, PRO BT 64/4521, memo from R. Somervell to S. Golt, 1 September 1956. Here Somervell describes Minter's failure to persuade John Davis that his films should be given first-feature bookings in Rank cinemas. Somervell, expressing the official Board of Trade view, suggests that Minter's films were too expensive to be second features and qualitatively too 'indifferent' to be first features.

4. For information on the way the 1952 version of *The Pickwick Papers* was used in schools, see H. Rawlinson, 'The Pickwick Papers on Film and Filmstrip', *Journal of Photography*, 16 January 1953.

5. The Hulton Readership Survey 1950–1955, *The Spending Habits of Cinemagoers* (London: Pearl and Dean, 1956), *The IPA National Readership Survey 1956–1957, and 1959–1960*, and *The Cinema Audience: A National Survey* (London: Screen Advertising Association, 1961).

6. Clancy Sigal, 'Down at the Teenage Club: Voices in the Darkness', *Observer*, 7 December 1958.

7. Mass-Observation Report, 'Why Do They Go to the Pictures?' (1950). These remarks are from women of twenty-three and thirty respectively; they are in unsorted material in Box 15. See also *Daily Film Renter*, 10 July 1950.

8. Sue Harper and Vincent Porter, 'Moved to Tears: Weeping in the Cinema in Post-war Britain', *Screen*, Summer 1996.

9. According to the Annual Reports of the National Film Finance Corporation, the proportion of costume dramas was very small and seemingly selected at random. The 1950 report indicates that the costume films supported were *Angel with the Trumpet, The Elusive Pimpernel* and *Gone to Earth*. In 1951, they were *Tom Brown's Schooldays* and *The Magic Box*; in 1952, *The Card* and *The Importance of Being Earnest*; in 1953 *Gilbert and Sullivan*; in 1954, *Hobson's Choice* and *Svengali*; in 1957, *The Curse of Frankenstein*; in 1958, *Dracula* and *The Revenge of Frankenstein*; in 1959, *The Man Who Could Cheat Death, The Hound of the Baskervilles, The Mummy* and *The Stranglers of Bombay*; in 1960, *Sword of Sherwood Forest, The Two Faces of Dr Jekyll* and *The Flesh and the Fiends*; in 1961, *The Hellfire Club*.

10. *The Times*, 21 February 1956. There are many similar pieces in *The Times* throughout the decade, not all by the same critic.

11. Peter John Dyer, 'From Boadicea to Bette Davis', *Films and Filming*, January 1959, and 'The Rebels in Jackboots', *Films and Filming*, March 1959. See also James Morgan, 'Coronatiana USA', *Sight and Sound*, July–September 1953.

12. Michael Powell, *Million Dollar Movie* (London: Heinemann, 1992), p. 26. Powell had originally wanted to make it as a musical: see Powell, *A Life in Movies* (London: Heinemann, 1986), p. 669.

13. In order to be classified as British, films had to be made by a British company (which could be set up by Americans or anyone else); 75 per cent of the labour costs (excluding one person) had to be paid to British workers, and the film had to be made in Britain or the Commonwealth. The venture was attractive to US producers because British labour costs were substantially cheaper. Costume films formed a significant proportion of American output until 1957. In 1950, 3 out of 9 American-financed quota vehicles were historical. In 1951, the figures were 3 out of 4; in 1952, 5 out of 6; in 1953, 5 out of 13; in 1954, 3 out of 6; in 1955, 2 out of 6; in 1956, 3 out of 17; in 1957, 3 out of 27; in 1958, 2 out of 26 (figures compiled from Denis Gifford, *The British Film Catalogue 1895–1985*, Newton Abbot and London: David & Charles, 1986).

14. This is by no means a complete list. For example, Columbia made *The Black Knight* in 1954 and *Footsteps in the Fog* in 1955. There was a rash of swashbuckling pirate films as well: Disney's *Treasure Island* (1950), Warner Bros.' *The Crimson Pirate* (1952), RKO's *The Sea Devils* (1953). Pirates were to American producers what gypsies had been to the British.

15. Hammer gained a third of its profits from Britain, a third from America and the rest from other overseas markets. See Sue Harper, 'The Scent of Distant Blood: Hammer Films and History', in Tony Barta (ed.), *Screening the Past: Film and the Representation of History*.

16. *Kinematograph Weekly*, 14 December 1950, 20 December 1951, 18 December 1952, 17 December 1953, 16 December 1954, 15 December 1955, 13 December 1956, 12 December 1957, 18 December 1958, 17 December 1959 and 15 December 1960. See also *Motion Picture Herald*'s and *Picturegoer*'s annual surveys throughout the decade. *Films and Filming* also produced its version of box-office trends every year from 1958.

17. Langley had written some remarkable novels and had extensive scriptwriting experience. See his interview with the *Evening Standard*, 28 February 1955, on leaving for Hollywood: 'I seemed to be assessed as an alien influence . . . and this has robbed me of my confidence.' See Hurst, 'The Lady Vanishes', *Sight and Sound*, August 1950, and his unpublished autobiography in the British Film Institute Library.

18. *Films and Filming*, January 1958.

19. Interview given by Walt Disney as a trailer for *Rob Roy, the Highland Rogue* on the Disney Home Video of the film. For Disney's views on another of his British-made films, see 'Why I Filmed *Treasure Island*', *Daily Graphic*, 20 June 1950.

20. Interestingly, it was through her work with MGM-British, and particularly with this film, that Haffenden was invited to Hollywood. There, she won an Oscar for her costume work on *Ben-Hur* (1959).

21. See Graham Dawson, 'Playing at War: An Autobiographical Approach to Boyhood Fantasy and Masculinity', *Oral History*, Spring 1990. The popularity of the film may have had something to do with the fact that the star (Gregory Peck) was then at the peak of his career. By contrast, Errol Flynn in *The Master of Ballantrae* was at the fag-end of his. He was exhausted, and it showed.

22. A typically negative review is in *Tribune*, 10 May 1957. See also Walter Lassally, 'The Cynical Audience', *Sight and Sound*, Summer 1956; Derek Hill, 'The Face of Horror', *Sight and Sound*, Winter 1958–9.

23. There is one exception, the extraordinary *The Plague of the Zombies* (1965), in which the squire has learned the arts of voodoo while abroad. He uses his powers over the undead to create a compliant workforce for his tin-mines.

24. Hammer's publicity campaigns are an index of its gender orientation. The captions for posters (in the British Film Institute Library) are significant. One urges the audience to see Dracula as 'The Terrifying Lover Who Died – Yet Lived', clearly making subliminal reference to fears of *le petit mort*. Another advertises a Dracula film with 'You Can't Keep a Good Man Down', implicitly linking Dracula's revival with his tumescence, via blood, of course.

Bibliography

Barta, Tony (ed.), *Screening the Past: Film and the Representation of History* (Westport, CT and London: Praeger, 1998).

Geraghty, Christine, *British Cinema in the Fifties: Gender, Genre and the 'New Look'* (London and New York: Routledge, 2000).

Harper, Sue, *Picturing the Past: The Rise and Fall of the British Costume Film* (London: BFI, 1994).

Harper, Sue, *Women in British Cinema: Mad, Bad and Dangerous to Know* (London and New York: Continuum, 2000).

Harper, Sue, and Porter, Vincent, *British Cinema of the 1950s: The Decline of Deference* (Oxford: Oxford University Press, 2003).

Hutchings, Peter, *Hammer and Beyond: The British Horror Film* (Manchester: Manchester University Press, 1993).

Macnab, Geoffrey, *J. Arthur Rank and the British Film Industry* (London: Routledge, 1993).

Pirie, Dave, *A Heritage of Horror: The English Gothic Cinema 1946–1972* (London: Gordon Fraser, 1978).

Spraos, John, *The Decline of the Cinema* (London: George Allen & Unwin, 1962).

31

'Twilight Women' of 1950s British Cinema

MELANIE WILLIAMS

The 1952 film *Women of Twilight* opens with an unusual credit sequence: a series of head-and-shoulder shots of women against a shadowy backdrop. Some of the women meet our gaze, while some stare straight past us; some look nervous, one laughs, one smokes a cigarette, and one chews gum; some are dressed smartly in suits, others more casually, in sweaters or blouses, although one wears a glamorous spangled evening gown, contrasting with another's threadbare dress and lank hair. These are the 'women of twilight' referred to by the film's title, the inhabitants of a run-down boarding house for unmarried mothers. They vary in age, class and attitude but have one thing in common – they are hidden away from the daylight world of respectable society. Such a diverse gallery of women acts as a sharp reminder that the enduring image of 1950s femininity in terms of marriage and stay-at-home housewifery was not the whole truth, and that its resonance in the popular imagination perhaps says more about the force with which it was promulgated in the service of consumer capitalism than it does about what women's lives were actually like at the time.

As Michael Wood has suggested, the aura of blandness symptomatic of our cultural memory of the 50s is partly a legacy of 'the time's own attempt to invent itself, a contemporary cover-up. "The fifties" is what the fifties were trying to be.'[1] Wood refers to American society but his point seems equally relevant to the position of women in the 'soap-flake Arcadia' of an increasingly affluent Britain. Despite the appearance of settled gender spheres in post-war Britain, the 'orchestration of consensus on the position of women', Elizabeth Wilson has argued, was actually 'the achievement of a deceptive

harmony out of a variety of noisy voices', among them the voices 'of women in revolt, of women despised, of women despairing', adjectives that seem to fit the faces we see in *Women of Twilight*.[2]

This credit sequence is also relatively unusual for its time in offering such a plenitude of women on screen. The 1950s marks a kind of 'twilight' for women in British films, during which the female stars who had enjoyed such prominence in the previous decade, such as Margaret Lockwood and Anna Neagle, found themselves eclipsed in popularity by male stars like Kenneth More and Dirk Bogarde. This was partly determined by the sharp decline of female cinemagoing at this time, partly because the two most popular genres of the 1950s, the war film and the comedy, had a tendency to sideline women and present them as either 'childish, silly and vindictive or valorised and saintly'.[3] There are exceptions – Virginia McKenna and Kay Kendall carved out distinctive careers through their star performances in war films and comedies respectively – but on the whole, the 'chaps' were in the ascendant in the 1950s.

Yet explorations of the hidden worlds of women were not entirely absent from the British screen. Several films directed by J. Lee Thompson during this decade offered something altogether more complex than the customary female roles of 'virtuous potential homemaker' or busty soubrette.[4] Of particular interest are his two prison dramas, *The Weak and the Wicked* (1954) and *Yield to the Night* (1956), as well as *Woman in a Dressing Gown* (1957), about a hapless housewife whose husband wants a divorce, *No Trees in the Street* (1959), a tale of 1930s slum life, and *Tiger Bay* (1959), in which Hayley Mills made her début as a gun-fixated tomboy on the run with a murderer. Even his war film *Ice Cold in Alex* (1958) was unusual in the prominent role it gave to the military nurse played by Sylvia Syms, and in *North West Frontier* (1959) Kenneth More's Imperial hero meets his match in Lauren Bacall's feminist governess.

Frequently, Thompson's films depict those women who fall short of the feminine ideals of the age – the unfit mother, the convict, the jealous murderess, the slatternly housewife, the tomboy – and present their world sympathetically from within, allowing a degree of empathy rather than opprobrium. Steve Chibnall suggests that the female perspectives adopted in Thompson's films 'provide an interesting contrast to Basil Dearden and Michael Relph's more male-oriented approach' to similar material, while Sue Harper praises them for being unusually 'radical on gender matters'.[5] Furthermore, in a time of masculine ascendancy, these films were significantly popular with audiences: *The Weak and the Wicked* and *Tiger Bay* feature in the annual list of box-office successes in the *Kinematograph Weekly* while *Woman in a Dressing Gown* not only ranks highly on this list but also comes out as joint-third most popular film of 1957 in Janet Thumin's retrospective popularity ratings.[6] *Yield to the Night* gets an honourable mention in the 1956 *Kine Weekly* ratings and might have enjoyed more commercial success had it not been for the inevitable restrictions placed on it by its 'X' certificate.[7]

It seems reasonable to attribute some of these films' gender radicalism to the influence of Thompson's collaborator and subsequent spouse Joan Henry, who wrote the original source material and co-wrote the screenplays for both *The Weak and the Wicked* (based on her own experience of serving a prison sentence) and *Yield to the Night*. She also acted in an unofficial advisory capacity on several other of Thompson's films besides the ones for which she has screen credit.[8] Her personal history gave her unique insights into the continuum between respectable women and those beyond the pale, and in the preface to her prison memoir *Who Lie in Gaol* (1952) she envisages her reader as someone 'who can watch, or read of, the man or woman convicted of any crime, from petty theft to murder, and say: "There" – but for the little kink in the brain, the tiny twist in the mind, the shuffle of circumstance – "but for the grace of God, go I."'[9]

However, the impact of these films also comes from Thompson's dynamic style of direction, praised by Raymond Durgnat for using melodrama 'not gratuitously, but in determination to ram right into the complacent spectator the full pain and terror of the emotional extremes against which moral principles must assert themselves [. . .] He deals, and validly, with massive blocks of brute emotion, rather than nuances of thought.'[10] Such a departure from the restrained emotional tenor of much British cinema of the time was remarked upon by critic Isabel Quigley, noting how Thompson's vigorous depiction of British life aroused in foreign audiences 'surprise and interest and even incredulity, so unfamiliar a picture does he present of us [. . .] for his people are passionate creatures and the physical world about them, however drab, is, to match them, passionately observed'.[11]

Thompson's female-centred films are undoubtedly moving and powerful because of the bare facts of their subject matter and their historical context and because they provide fascinating glimpses into the twilight worlds of women of the 1950s. However, they would not be able to delineate the contradictions and difficulties of female experience with such eloquence and resonance, were it not for their aesthetic inventiveness. They are significant not only because of their innovative representations of women for the time but also because they are often very good films, with even the weaker ones containing 'short, but very sharp, moments worthy of the greatest directors'.[12]

The Prison House of Home

Images of imprisoned men are inescapable in 1950s British culture particularly in view of the popularity of prisoner-of-war films such as *The Wooden Horse* (1950), *The Colditz Story* (1955) and *The Bridge on the River Kwai* (1957), adaptations of memoirs and novels that were themselves best-sellers. But several literary texts dealing with civilian life also focused on male incarceration, whether it was literal, as with the young Borstal inmates of Brendan Behan's autobiographical *Borstal Boy* (1958) and Alan Sillitoe's *The Loneliness of the Long Distance Runner* (1959), or metaphorical, as with the rebellious protagonists of John Osborne's play *Look Back in Anger* (1956) and Sillitoe's novel *Saturday Night and Sunday Morning* (1958). This trend is carried through into film according to Sue Harper, who argues that Karel Reisz's 1960 film version of *Saturday Night and Sunday Morning* deploys a *mise en scène* that 'oppresses the male characters and makes the claustrophobia impinge intensely on them [. . .] with choking close-ups of Arthur as he rebels against limitation. None of the female protagonists are shot in this way.'[13] Instead, women are generally presented as the agents of

Dance Hall (Charles Crichton, 1950)

Suggestive parallels can be drawn between the opening sequences of *Dance Hall* and *Saturday Night and Sunday Morning*: the four friends in *Dance Hall*, Georgie (Petula Clark), Carole (Diana Dors), Mary (Jane Hylton) and Eve (Natasha Parry) are introduced standing behind just the same kind of noisy screeching lathe behind which Arthur Seaton makes his defiant pre-credits speech. Separated by a decade, both films deal with the same topic; what young workers do for fun once they clock off from the factory. But there are marked differences: in place of Arthur's scathing voice-over on work and his attitude to it, all we hear of the women is their plucky sing-along with the music on the tannoy, their inner thoughts remain a mystery. And while Arthur's weekend revolves around hard drinking and womanising, *Dance Hall*'s workmates flock to the more salubrious environs of their local Palais to dance and socialise.

These venues, with their 'swirl of colour and lights and music', were central to many young people's leisure at the time and provided a welcome dose of glamour and excitement in the pinched years of post-war austerity.[1] But *Dance Hall* takes pains to present the realism behind the tinsel, making us aware of the faux intimacy of the oleaginous Palais owner, the homely background of the supposedly exotic dancers Chiquita and Juan ("OK ducks?"), and the hard work behind the presentation of a slick façade: the film's first shot features a cleaner mopping the empty dance floor, accompanied on the soundtrack by the orchestra tuning up rather than in full swing. The illusory nature of the dance hall's pleasures is underlined by the film's theme song, 'You're Only Dreaming', and in the closing scenes it becomes a nightmarish place, an Expressionistic backdrop to marital breakdown and suicidal thoughts.

The struggle for young women to reconcile desire and duty is pivotal to *Dance Hall*, represented by Eve's choice between two suitors: the seductive American lothario Alec (Bonar Colleano) and the two-left-footed boyfriend Phil (Donald Houston) whom she subsequently marries. Phil may be a more suitable choice but he is no Prince Charming, pettily shushing her in favour of the football results and thoughtlessly eating several days' worth of food in a single night.

Natasha Parry is tempted from the straight and narrow by the smooth-talking Bonar Colleano in *Dance Hall*

Unsurprisingly, Eve feels trapped at home, and longs to return to the Palais and her single life. Their marriage reaches breaking point when he suspects her of resuming her affair with Alec, and during a venomous argument, Eve accuses Phil of forcing her to stay home every night being 'bored, bored, bored'.

Although Charles Barr characterised 'poverty of desire' as the emotional keynote of Ealing, *Dance Hall*'s lead couple are surprisingly fiery – Phil smashes a pint glass on the bar in a jealous rage, while Eve throws shoes, tin cans and planks of wood in various fits of anger. Indeed, much of the film's poignancy comes from its depiction of the sacrifices inherent in domesticity; the sadness of passionate young women having to relinquish the tango for a night in with the ironing.

NOTE

1. Diana Morgan, the film's co-writer, interviewed on the Channel 4 documentary *Fifties Features* (tx 28 September 1986).

FURTHER READING

Charles Barr, *Ealing Studios* (Berkeley: University of California Press, 1998).

Melinda Mash, 'Stepping Out or Out of Step? Austerity, Affluence and Femininity in Two Post-war Films', in Christine Gledhill and Gillian Swanson (eds), *Nationalising Femininity: Culture, Sexuality and Cinema in World War Two Britain* (Manchester: Manchester University Press, 1996).

entrapment, not its victims. As Lorna Sage later reflected: 'It's galling to realise that you were a creature of mythology: girls were the enemy of promise, a trap for boys, although with hindsight you can see that the opposite was the case.'[14]

Again, the films of J. Lee Thompson offer an interesting counterbalance to this emphasis on masculine incarceration. By their very nature, the two women's prison films, *The Weak and the Wicked* and *Yield to the Night*, deal with the experience of female incarceration and use an imprisoning *mise en scène*, but crucially, so do the other films whose locales ostensibly bear no resemblance to prison at all; one thinks of the housewife of *Woman in a Dressing Gown* stuck in her cramped flat surrounded by her undone housework; and the young woman in *No Trees in the Street* trapped in the squalor of her tenement slum. Sometimes the female subject in the non-prison films is even framed behind bars: in *No Trees in the Street*, drunk on the bed and about to be seduced by the local gangster, the heroine is framed through her barred bedstead, mimicking an image used to depict the condemned woman in *Yield to the Night*; and the first shot of the girl protagonist in *Tiger Bay* shows her gazing yearningly through railings resembling prison bars. This kind of imagery of entrapment is not unique to Thompson's films. There is, for example, a striking instance of it in the prostitution drama *Passport to Shame* (1958), with a dream sequence in which the heroine finds herself trapped behind the bars of a cage. Also, Christine Geraghty notes how a sense of imprisonment is evoked in a number of post-war Ealing films – *It Always Rains on Sunday* (1947), *Cage of Gold* (1950), and *Dance Hall* (1950) – reflecting contemporary fears of women's dissatisfaction with domesticity.[15] Other 1950s films deal more directly with women's experiences of incarceration and release, such as *Turn the Key Softly* (1953), about three inmates of Holloway women's prison on their first day out after serving their sentences, and Hammer's *Women without Men* (1956), probably the only film to feature Thora Hird orchestrating a prison break-out.[16] Undeniably though, the theme is most consistently explored (and with the greatest degree of commercial success) in the mid- to late 1950s in J. Lee Thompson's films.

'I feel that it's very dramatic, to put people in confined spaces and have their characters examined', Thompson once said.[17] However, in his films about women, confinement takes on a specific meaning, corresponding with an idea that began to gain acceptance by the early 1960s: the housewife as prisoner.

'Imprisonment and escape', according to Elizabeth Wilson, became housewives' dominant metaphors to describe their situation, ranging from the middle-class women interviewed in Judith Hubback's 1957 study, *Wives Who Went to College* ('one day, when the children are bigger, I may be able to escape') to the working-class wives in Hannah Gavron's symptomatically titled book, *The Captive Wife*, who articulated similar feelings ('I'm used to an office with people coming and going, and now I don't get any company at all'; 'I feel like I'm in a cage.')[18] In so consistently invoking the experiences of women imprisoned, one might say that Thompson's films were not so much providing a fascinating entrée into an unknown world than recreating an experience that may have felt uncannily familiar to many women at the time.

Women – Barred from Men!

The biggest hit in British cinemas in 1954 was the Rank Organisation's amiable medical comedy *Doctor in the House*, with its 'air of gay, youthful, relatively modest contentment and sauciness' capturing the prevalent national mood.[19] However, another box-office success of 1954, *The Weak and the Wicked*, presented a different version of contemporary British society, although the two films share some common ground: both deal with the progress of a 'green' young protagonist through an institutional environment, learning its arcane traditions and befriending its misfit inhabitants, before eventually leaving to begin a new life. But whereas Dirk Bogarde's Simon Sparrow works his way through medical school, Jean Raymond (Glynis Johns) undergoes the rigours of a prison sentence. One might argue that both are engaged in a form of state-sponsored training, one to be a doctor and the other to be a doctor's wife. After a spell in prison, Jean recants all her earlier misgivings about marriage to her boyfriend, confessing to the prison chaplain 'to live for somebody else is the finest thing in the world . . . I want to make him a good wife'. Her change of heart is rewarded by his unexpected presence at the prison gates on the day of her release, to whisk her away and make an honest woman of her.

The insertion of a romantic subplot, absent from Joan Henry's original book, was intended to make *The Weak and the Wicked* into a commercially viable project. One reviewer felt that the 'vice, squalor, sex and life' of *Who Lie in Gaol* had been usurped by 'a pale cloying "niceness"' in its film adaptation, with Henry's sharp critique of Holloway prison (renamed Blackdown for the film) blunted in order to placate the censors.[20] However, the film still manages to make a cogent case for the innovative 'open prison' idea, focused on rehabilitation of the offender rather than retributive punishment.

Two of the film's most powerful moments address motherhood. Shortly after we learn that prisoners have to hand over their babies to the authorities at six months, usually to be given up for adoption, we are presented with the emotional reality of this. A mother and baby are framed in the doorway of her cell during their last moment together. Although the woman is reluctant to relinquish her crying, struggling child, eventually the warder persuades her, immediately taking him away. The barred gate of the cellblock slams in the shot's foreground, visually echoing the mother's irrevocable separation from her son. She hangs onto the bars, hopelessly sobbing and crying out her child's name, before finally walking back to her cell, her pitiful figure receding into the distance. Described by Michael Bracewell as a scene of 'tragedy and brutality', Thompson's emotive staging packs a punch entirely fitting for the agony of the woman's situation.[21] It is all the more powerful because we see it inflicted upon an anonymous prisoner rather than one of the film's central characters, with the mother becoming an 'Everywoman' figure, exemplifying the common experience of *all* women in prison rather than its specificity to one unlucky individual.

The difficulties of the maternal are explored further through the character of Babs (Jane Hylton). She is one of four characters among the film's female ensemble cast who enunciates a flashback detailing how she came to be in prison. Babs recalls leaving her two children home alone to go out dancing with her American boyfriend. Only intending to stay out for a few hours, but getting tipsy and throwing caution to the wind, she returns next morning to find that her baby has died during the night. On the face of it, this sounds like a harsh morality tale where a feckless woman is punished for her transgression against the sanctity of motherhood. There is a grimly punitive logic about the baby's death during the one night she is not at home, a single error of judgment having fatal consequences. Yet the situation is presented more as a terrible consequence of Babs's enforced isolation and loneliness as a single parent. Having been abandoned by her husband, she admits that she 'couldn't stand being alone night after night', and when her new boyfriend flatters her, buys her jewellery, and reminds her that 'you're only young once', she is understandably susceptible. Offered the chance to escape for one night, she mistakenly takes it.

The Weak and the Wicked presents this story of a woman who is indirectly responsible for her child's death in a sympathetic light, attempting to understand the pressures that led her to fatally neglect her baby, rather than simply condemning her. We are aligned with Jean, who reassures Babs that she's not 'dreadfully wicked' and that she should be allowed to have custody of her daughter when she's released, rather than with the angry neighbour outside Babs's flat who insists 'women like her deserve to be hanged'.

While *The Weak and the Wicked*'s poster tagline, 'Women – Barred from Men!', announces disbelief in the possibility of women's independent existence (as well as also hinting at a lesbian subtext), the film actually implies a kind of 'default sisterhood' in the all-female world of the prison, a new ability to relate to each other without the usual rivalries, as Henry suggests: 'having no background and no possessions; no men to show off to; wearing the same clothes every day . . . to each other, we were just ourselves, good, bad or indifferent'.[22] The film's key friendship is between Jean and Betty (Diana Dors), showcased when they are permitted a day out together prior to their release to help them readjust to life outside. Not much happens – they do a spot of window shopping, have lunch in a café, go to the pictures and then to the local funfair (at this point the scene takes a more dramatic turn, as Betty is tempted to run off to see her errant boyfriend back in London, but decides not to out of loyalty to Jean) – but their exchanges are permeated with a lively sense of affection, indicated by their good-humoured banter. They are conspiratorial about whipping cigarette ends from the ashtray in the cafe ('Jean, not here . . . I must say you've picked up some very nasty habits from somewhere', says Betty with an ironic raised eyebrow), adopting an arch tone and calling each other 'Miss Raymond' and 'Miss Brown'. They joke about how much to tip the waitress (an exquisitely grumpy Irene Handl) and whether they should go to the pub or not. All of this may sound rather inconsequential and banal but a scene like this, showing female friends together, is rare in British cinema of this time and merits attention.

For the Night Is Already at Hand . . .
Diana Dors is divested of all liveliness in the subsequent prison drama she made with Thompson and Henry, *Yield to the Night*, seizing the opportunity to demonstrate depths rarely required in her usual light-comedy roles and willingly undergoing a process of complete de-glamorisation to play Mary Hilton, the woman

condemned to death. While Dors got the role of a life-time, its makers got something in return: a star to entice audiences along to what might otherwise be an unappealing prospect, set for much of its running time in the grim confines of the condemned cell, and ending in an execution. Often described as a drama about Ruth Ellis, the last woman to be hanged in Britain, Joan Henry had actually written the novel on which the film was based several years before Ellis committed murder, and as Mike Nellis argues, the eerie similarities between these fictional and real-life *crimes passionnels* merely reveal Henry's 'prescient, if still inchoate understanding of the sexual and social forces that would bring an Englishwoman to the gallows in mid-century England'.[23]

The film begins by showing us the murder that in due course will be avenged by the state. It was important for the director that there is no doubt about Mary's guilt because in order to make an effective protest against the death penalty, he argued, 'you must take somebody who deserves to die, and then feel sorry for them and say this is wrong'.[24] The sequence teases us, only permitting partial images of its famous star (high heels, a gloved hand, a flash of blonde hair, her distorted reflection in a car's hubcap) deferring the revelatory close-up until she pulls out the gun to shoot the woman she believes drove her lover Jim to suicide. After Mary contemptuously tosses the spent weapon between her victim's legs in a sexually loaded action, there follows a reaction shot of a man who has witnessed the crime. Kneeling down by the victim, he looks up open-mouthed at the murderess, who makes no attempt to flee the scene of the crime.[25] Like us, he attempts to fathom her odd facial expression, which simultaneously suggests horror and triumph, but it proves impossible to read. As the camera moves closer to her face, and the timpani on the soundtrack grow louder and more insistent, the close-up finally blurs, an optical effect suggesting both the moment's emotional import – it almost looks like the view through eyes brimming with tears – and Mary's clouded mental state.

However, Mary is more than a passive object of observation in the film. Flashback sequences, inaugurated by her voice-over narration, tell the story of what led to the murder from her point of view. Yet her first voice-over words are not her own but A. E. Housman's, as she recollects lines from *A Shropshire Lad* that she first came across while thumbing through Jim's books, which now have a painful relevance: 'Since to look at things in bloom/Fifty Springs is little room./About the woodland I will go/to see the cherry hung with snow.' The poem seems deliberately to taunt her, her voice dwelling on and repeating the word 'hung', reminding her of the fate that awaits her. Mary's recitation of Housman works as an audacious appropriation of male discourse: taking his homoerotic meditations on the untimely deaths of beautiful young men and daring to apply his words to her own predicament, claiming the same tragic status for herself. Later in the film, she finds herself drawn to one particular sentence in an anthology she is given by the chaplain: 'For the night is already at hand and it is well to yield to the night.' Although never revealed in the film, the source is Book VII of *The Iliad* when warring forces agree to stop battle as night falls. They echo the prison doctor's previous exhortation for her to 'conform to the routine, however hard and futile it may seem', and come to encapsulate the advice of all those around her who urge her to reconcile herself to death, here with all the weightiness of high culture and ancient tradition adding to their authority. But finally she rejects their implied message: 'Perhaps it is well, but I can't. I want to live. I want it more than ever.'

Does Mary's crime stem as much from class envy as it does from retribution? Her job in an upmarket beauty shop promises social mobility but results in little more than dull nights out at drinking clubs and propositions from ageing roués. She can wear the same perfume as her wealthy rival but only because she can get free dabs of the expensive scent at work; she could never afford a bottle of it herself. No wonder the first thing she notices about her nemesis are her beautiful high-heeled black suede shoes, redolent of the life of ease and luxury that Mary will never enjoy, even if she worked and saved for years.[26] In the context of 1956, the high point of the 'angry young man' phenomenon, it's tempting to see her as a rare instance of an 'angry young woman' capable of sudden flashes of sullen rebellion. When a game of chess is set out by the warder who is teaching her to play, it prompts a furious outburst from Mary – 'I'm sick of everything being arranged. I don't understand this game and I never will! I don't WANT to learn!' – as she swipes the chess-pieces off the table, scattering them across the cell. The chess lessons, one of the recurrent motifs of the film along with the meticulous medical attention paid to the blister on her heel, exemplify the absurdity of Mary's situation: the irony of the state's care for the body it will soon destroy; the utter futility of learning a new skill in the shadow of the gallows.

Woman in a Dressing Gown (J. Lee Thompson, 1957) Described by Jeffrey Richards as 'a *Brief Encounter* of the council flats', *Woman in a Dressing Gown* not only takes the scenario of an extramarital relationship and relocates it to a working-class setting, it also switches the gender roles of the original: this time, it is the husband (Anthony Quayle) who is tempted to leave his wife (Yvonne Mitchell) for another woman (Sylvia Syms).

Although time and space is given over to the dilemmas faced by husband Jim and girlfriend Georgie as they struggle with their feelings for each other and their guilt about the hurt they are inflicting on others, the film's central focus is on the wife, Amy, the eponymous 'woman in a dressing gown' who is anything but the 1950s domestic goddess. She is messy, chaotic and 'all over the place', dropping sticks of firewood, leaving bits of thread on shirts, overfilling teacups, spilling beer. Even her undone housework might be seen as her

unstable excessive housewifely self spreading out and filling the cramped confines of the flat. Wherever she is, she engenders noise (the loud radio, the pub singsong) and disaster (burnt breakfasts, bad weather, ruined hair-dos, collapsing tables).

The plot synopsis in the film's publicity material encourages us to read it as a cautionary tale pitting one kind of woman against another, because, while Amy's 'slatternly ways do not make for domestic bliss', Georgie's 'calm, orderly mind and quiet beauty soothe his jarred nerves'.[1] However, the film also suggests why Amy might have become that way (grief at the death of an infant daughter, Jim's neglect) and perhaps indirectly questions some of the limitations of the housewife role to which Amy is so obviously ill suited. Although Jim returns to his wife at the end of the film, these questions hang in the air beyond their reconciliation, and just as Laura Mulvey suggests of contemporaneous American melodramas, the fascination of a

In praise of sluttishness: messy, chaotic Yvonne Mitchell in *Woman in a Dressing Gown*

film like *Woman in a Dressing Gown* lies in 'the dust the story raises along the road, a cloud of over-determined irreconcilables which put up a resistance to being neatly settled in the last five minutes'.[2]

In 1963, the same year *The Feminine Mystique* fostered feminist dissent in America by querying the housewife role, British journalist Katherine Whitehorn caused a stir by writing an article in praise of sluttishness, beginning conspiratorially with a dedication to all the women who had ever brushed their hair with a nailbrush or retrieved something from the laundry basket 'because it had become relatively the cleaner thing'.[3] Whitehorn characterised the female reaction to her 'slut' piece as one of enormous relief because previously 'any advice given to women was telling them to be perfect', whereas 'it's not like that really, let's come dirty about it'.[4] Rather than a fatal character flaw, not having the housework under control could be bran-

dished as a badge of honour (although probably only among middle-class women). In this brave new world of honest sluttery, might Amy be held up as an unwitting pioneer heroine?

NOTES

1. *Woman in a Dressing Gown* pressbook.
2. Laura Mulvey, 'Notes on Sirk and Melodrama', *Visual and Other Pleasures* (London: Macmillan, 1989), p. 40.
3. Quoted in Suzanne Lowry, *The Guilt Cage* (London: Elm Tree Books, 1980), p. 49.
4. Ibid., p. 52.

FURTHER READING

Jeffrey Richards, *Films and British National Identity* (Manchester: Manchester University Press, 1997).

Melanie Williams, 'Housewife's Choice: *Woman in a Dressing Gown*', in Ian MacKillop and Neil Sinyard (eds), *British Cinema of the Fifties: A Celebration* (Manchester: Manchester University Press, 2003).

Yield to the Night's final scenes chronicle the morning of the execution, beginning with the warders writing the final entry in the ledger – 'Prisoner slept well, no change in condition. Woke at 8 o clock.' – and the camera lingers over the bland language of official record, prompting us to consider the contrast between the basic facts and the complex emotional reality of Mary's ordeal. The entry is then blotted, emphasising the sense of finality: Mary's story is over, the record is complete and ready to be filed with the rest. The camera pans up to the light on the ceiling, symbol of Mary's torments in the cell, which is finally turned off; not out of kindness but because its job is over. True to the iconography of the condemned prisoner, one of Mary's final acts is to have a smoke, and it is the mundanity of this image of Mary sitting at the table, sipping tea and smoking, that makes it so affecting, her simple actions taking on a tragic grandeur in the face of death. The camera moves into a close-up of the texture of the skin on her throat as she swallows the tea, and her lips enclosing the cigarette. This is a body which is still (defiantly) alive and functioning and we watch it closely with a sense of awe, observing its final moments of life before the power to move and feel and smoke and drink is extinguished forever. It's a visualisation of the revelation that strikes Orwell in his essay 'A Hanging': 'This man was not dying, he was alive just as we were alive. All the organs of his body were working

– bowels digesting food, skin renewing itself, nails growing, tissues forming – all toiling away in solemn foolery.'[27]

The chaplain leads the final prayer and the film avoids any transcendental notions of Mary going onto a better place with a sickening tracking shot toward her exposed bowed neck (her hair is tied up ready for the noose) as she kneels to pray, reminding us of the horrible physical reality of the death that awaits her. As the prayers finish, we hear the off-screen sound of the door at the foot of her bed finally opening. We never see what is in that adjoining room, its horror remains a mystery, and as Mary rises and turns around, our attention is focused instead onto her face, wide-eyed and terror-stricken, as she advances towards the scaffold and towards the camera. She moves into deep shadow and finally vanishes into the place of execution, before the film cuts to her last cigarette, still smouldering in the ashtray, leaving us only with the memory of her final gaze into the abyss.

Twilight to Daylight?

In 1956, Thompson joined forces with producer Frank Godwin and writer Ted Willis to create an independent production company aiming to make films about 'ordinary working-class people'.[28] But while their first film *Woman in a Dressing Gown* was a box-office success, the follow-up, set in the East End slums of the 1930s, *No Trees in the Street* was not, despite an outstanding performance by Sylvia Syms as a girl dragged down by her degrading environment. Thompson's next significant foray into female representation came with the Rank Organisation thriller, *Tiger Bay*, which perhaps suggested the emergence of a new model of femininity.[29] While the mature woman Anya's (Yvonne Mitchell) expressions of liberated self-possession ('I'm not an animal for a little boy to keep in a cage. I'm a woman with a heart and a body that is my own to give how I like to who I like') are curtailed by her murder, the possible fate impressed upon eleven-year-old Gillie (Hayley Mills), that 'little girls dressing up as gangsters and playing with guns' end up in prison, fails to materialise. Instead *Tiger Bay* ends with its fearless young heroine still on the brink of adolescence, her destiny not yet decided, but with the sense that her womanhood might take a different path from her imprisoned predecessors in 1950s British films, not least because of larger changes in the social climate, broadening women's horizons.

Indeed, among the various representations of femininity in 1950s British cinema, it is arguably the young girls who offer the most hope; from Mandy, in the film that bears her name, stepping tentatively but courageously across the bomb site to meet her new playmates and a new future; to the terrifying carnivalesque schoolgirls of *The Belles of St Trinians* (1954) and *Blue Murder at St Trinians* (1957) flouting all sense of feminine propriety; and the tenacious young girl Lovejoy in Philip Leacock's *Innocent Sinners* (1958), who may be temporarily sent away to a children's home but still has the chutzpah to pray 'Hail Mary, Holy Mary, keep me cocky and independent.' Along with *Tiger Bay*'s Gillie, they hint at a future where twilight and night might finally yield to day.

Notes

1. Michael Wood, 'Foreword: Happy Days', in Peter Biskind, *Seeing Is Believing: Or How Hollywood Taught Us to Stop Worrying and Love the Fifties* (London: Bloomsbury, 2000), p. ix.
2. Elizabeth Wilson, *Only Halfway to Paradise*, p. 3.
3. Christine Geraghty, *British Cinema in the Fifties*, p. 159.
4. Sue Harper, *Women in British Cinema*, p. 98.
5. Steve Chibnall, *J. Lee Thompson*, p. 8; Harper, *Women in British Cinema*, p. 85.
6. See *Kinematograph Weekly* 16 December 1954, 17 December 1959, and 12 December 1957; Janet Thumin, 'The "Popular", Cash, and Culture in the Postwar British Film Industry', in Annette Kuhn and Jackie Stacey (eds) *Screen Histories: A Screen Reader* (Oxford: Clarendon, 1998), p. 43. Thumin's list makes use of additional data from *Motion Picture Herald* and *Picturegoer*.
7. *Kinematograph Weekly*, 13 December 1956.
8. Joan Henry describes rewriting scenes in *Woman in a Dressing Gown* ('I'm supposed to be rather good at dialogue and love scenes so I was always having to do these. Lee said "My God, look at what Ted Willis has written! [. . .] You'll have to change this." So I did a lot of that.') in Chibnall, *J. Lee Thompson*, p. 172.
9. Joan Henry, *Who Lie in Gaol*, p. 9.
10. Raymond Durgnat, *A Mirror for England*, pp. 243–4.
11. Isabel Quigley, 'Unfamiliar Picture', *Spectator*, 3 April 1959.
12. Raymond Durgnat, 'Cape Fear', *Films and Filming*, February 1963.
13. Harper, *Women in British Cinema*, p. 96.
14. Lorna Sage, *Bad Blood* (London: Fourth Estate, 2000), p. 234.
15. Geraghty, *British Cinema in the Fifties*, pp. 76–92.
16. Jack Lee, the director of *Turn the Key Softly*, also directed the war film *A Town Like Alice* (1956), about women taken prisoner in Malaya after the Japanese invasion. In a neat inversion of the male POW films, dealing with men trying to escape from camps, the women in this film are forced to wander the country looking for a prison camp that will let them *in*.
17. Chibnall, *J. Lee Thompson*, p. 185; the director's unrealised ambition was to set a film in a lift 'with just three people stuck in it', J. Lee Thompson, 'My Battle with the Censor', *Photoplay*, October 1962.
18. Wilson, *Only Halfway to Paradise*, p. 57; Judith Hubback, *Wives Who Went to College* (London: Heinemann, 1957), p. 75; Hannah Gavron, *The Captive Wife* (London: Routledge and Kegan Paul, 1966), pp. 118, 148. Although published in 1966, Gavron's books used interview material collected in 1961. It should be noted that recent work has queried the inevitable linkage of prison and home in feminist writing. See Lesley Johnson and Justine Lloyd, *Sentenced to Everyday Life: Feminism and the Housewife* (Oxford: Berg, 2004).
19. Durgnat, *A Mirror for England*, pp. 44–5.
20. *Sunday Chronicle*, 7 February 1954.
21. Michael Bracewell, *England Is Mine: Pop Life in Albion from Wilde to Goldie* (London: HarperCollins, 1997), p. 142.
22. Henry, *Who Lie in Gaol*, p. 78.
23. Mike Nellis, 'Remembering Joan Henry', *Prison Writing* no. 3, 1993, p. 51.
24. J. Lee Thompson, 'The Still Small Voice of Truth', *Films and Filming*, April 1963, p. 5.

25. This differs from an earlier draft of the scene where she tries to evade capture: 'As she tries to dash past the POLICEMAN grabs her. MARY fights back trying to break free . . . MARY beats against the POLICEMAN's chest with her fists.' Script of *Yield to the Night* (S1698) dated 9 August 1955, p. 114.

26. Shoe imagery is integral to *Yield to the Night*, as noted in Viv Chadder, 'The Higher Heel: Women and the Post-War British Crime Film'.

27. George Orwell, 'A Hanging', *Collected Journalism and Letters: Vol 1 (1920–1940)* (Harmondsworth: Penguin, 1970), p. 68.

28. Peter Evans, 'Three in Search of the Common Touch', *Kinematograph Weekly,* 10 April 1958.

29. See Melanie Williams, 'I'm Not a Lady!: *Tiger Bay* and Transitional Girlhood in British Cinema on the Cusp of the 1960s'.

Bibliography

Bell-Williams, Melanie, 'Shop-soiled Women: Female Sexuality and the Figure of the Prostitute in 1950s British Cinema', *Journal of British Cinema and Television* vol. 3 no. 2, 2006.

Chadder, Viv, 'The Higher Heel: Women and the Post-War British Crime Film', in Steve Chibnall and Robert Murphy (eds), *British Crime Cinema* (London: Routledge, 1999).

Chibnall, Steve, *J. Lee Thompson* (Manchester: Manchester University Press, 2000).

Cook, Pam, 'The Trouble with Sex: Diana Dors and the Blonde Bombshell Phenomenon', in Bruce Babington (ed.), *British Stars and Stardom* (Manchester: Manchester University Press, 2001).

Durgnat, Raymond, *A Mirror for England: British Movies from Austerity to Affluence* (London: Faber and Faber, 1970).

Geraghty, Christine, *British Cinema in the Fifties: Gender, Genre and the 'New Look'* (London: Routledge, 2000).

Harper, Sue, *Women in British Cinema: Mad, Bad and Dangerous to Know* (London: Continuum, 2000)

Harper, Sue and Porter, Vincent, *British Cinema of the 1950s: The Decline of Deference* (Oxford: Oxford University Press, 2003).

Henry, Joan, *Who Lie in Gaol* (London: Gollancz, 1952).

Williams, Melanie, 'I'm Not a Lady!: *Tiger Bay* and Transitional Girlhood in British Cinema on the Cusp of the 1960s', *Screen* vol. 46 no. 3, Autumn 2005.

Wilson, Elizabeth, *Only Halfway to Paradise: Women in Postwar Britain 1945–1968* (London: Tavistock, 1980).

32

Male Stars, Masculinity and British Cinema, 1945–60

Andrew Spicer

In the early post-war period a survey showed that stars were the main reason for cinemagoers' choice of film.[1] British producers and studio heads were well aware of their importance and attempted to create British stars on Hollywood lines. Both the vertically integrated combines, Rank and ABPC, kept a roster of contract players who were assigned particular roles by producers or studio executives to help create a stable image which stayed broadly the same in order to allow audience recognition. A star's image was also carefully built up and managed through active promotion, including a specific fan club for each major star, fan magazines and personal appearances at circuit cinemas in chauffeur-driven Rolls-Royces.[2] Rank trained and groomed potential stars through the 'Company of Youth' – the 'Charm School' as it was dubbed in the press.[3]

Their lack of institutional power led some stars, like Robert Donat in 1948, to renounce films and pursue careers in the theatre as actor-managers, where they had far greater artistic control; but this was exceptional. Most British actors opted for the security and wealth provided by a long-term studio contract, with occasional forays into live theatre. The most successful and clearly typecast male stars, Rex Harrison, James Mason, Stewart Granger and Michael Wilding, all left Britain to pursue careers in Hollywood, where the rewards were far greater.

Star images also circulated in widely selling journals like the fortnightly *Picture Show* and the weekly *Picturegoer*, which constructed a discourse about cinema that was largely oriented around stars. The popular press constantly commented on their lives, loves and careers, while their images also recurred in product endorsements. Though much of the attention was given to Hollywood stars, there was often a lively concern about British stars: were they getting enough promotion, recognition, the right roles?

The popularity of stars cannot be explained simply in terms of charismatic personalities or astute marketing. As Richard Dyer has argued, the most significant reason for stars' popularity is their typicality.[4] Male stars represent easily recognised types of masculinity which have been socially, culturally and historically constructed, embodying important beliefs about power, authority, nationality and class. Paradoxically, they embody the type in a way which is uniquely their own. This combination of typicality and uniqueness encourages audience identification, admiration and desire.

Because of their representativeness, images of male stars may give important clues as to the changing construction of masculinity in this period, but in a general survey I can only discuss the most popular stars. The *Motion Picture Herald* published an annual ranking of the box-office performance of the top ten British stars of either sex, based on exhibitors' returns. These returns were compiled by cinema managers who 'watch their audiences closely, studying them to see which star is making them laugh or cry. From that, they decide which of two stars in the same picture is the greater attraction.'[5] Despite this dubious basis, the *Motion Picture Herald*'s listings were highly influential, frequently quoted as authoritative evidence. *Picturegoer*'s annual 'Gold Medal' award also ranked the top ten male or female stars according to a readers' poll, but combined British and American stars. *Picturegoer*'s readers voted for a star's performance in a particular film, affording an insight into which were the key roles. There are many correlations and some interesting differences between the two lists which, taken together and supplemented where possible from *Kinematograph Weekly*'s intermittent listings (for which no criteria are given), provide a reasonable basis for discussion.[6]

Melodrama and Masculinity

The most popular male star from 1944 to 1947 was James Mason, who had a fan mail of 5,000 letters per week. Mason's popularity was based on the sex appeal generated by his performances in Gainsborough's costume dramas, which were specifically targeted at the predominantly female cinemagoing audience. As Lord Rohan in *The Man in Grey* (1943), Mason converted the traditional villain of stage melodrama – dark, menacing, deep-voiced – into a Byronic figure, often cruel and vindictive but also thrilling, fascinating and highly erotic. An article in *Picturegoer*, entitled 'Does This Man Make Villainy Too Attractive?', suggested how Mason's individuality had animated a type so decisively different from conventional male leads.

> The Marquis of Rohan could not be played by the average British screen hero. It is a part needing more strength than a typical hero's role. . . . He has the strength; and his mobile face needs no make-up to transform it from its habitual pleasing good looks to a mask of ferocity and evil which suits the part. The thick eyebrows, the curved sensuous lips and the dark, compelling eyes, the wide nostrils and patrician nose are the foundations necessary for such a part as the proud, cruel Marquis.[7]

The writer also stressed that Mason cleverly underplayed, with slow movements and *sotto voce* delivery. Mason's haunting voice was a cinematic rather than a theatrical instrument, and his performance was astutely keyed to the greater intimacy of the film medium.

Mason worked a series of variations on his Man in Grey, beginning with the sadistic Lord Manderstoke in *Fanny by Gaslight* (1944). In *The Seventh Veil*, the top-grossing film of 1945, the image was adroitly updated in a contemporary melodrama about a brooding, cruel guardian and his hapless niece. They are eventually united after he has shown signs of compassion but above all a need to be loved, which softened the image and was much more popular than his bullying husband role in *They Were Sisters*, released earlier that year. Mason was back in period costume as a romantic outlaw in *The*

Wicked Lady (1945), the highest-grossing film of 1946. The dashing highwayman Captain Jerry Jackson has some moral scruples but offers an unbridled sexuality.[8]

The use of costume melodrama allowed Gainsborough the licence to construct flamboyant, erotic male figures as objects of female desire, their costumes displaying the male form in tight trousers and unbuttoned shirts. As Mason's opposite in several of these films, Stewart Granger, the second most popular male star, was the conventional romantic hero: honourable, dashing and brave. Granger possessed the necessary physical attributes, being tall, handsome and muscular. But there was an arrogant sensuality to Granger's performance and an irony in his delivery, which lightened the tone and slightly distanced performer from role. In those films where he was the main protagonist rather than playing against Mason, Granger's roles became more openly glamorous and erotic. *Madonna of the Seven Moons* (1944), *The Magic Bow* and *Caravan* (both 1946), all use Mediterranean settings to license an exotic, transgressive masculinity. This is perhaps most apparent in *Caravan*, where Granger plays Richard Darrell whose prolonged amnesia makes him forget his love for an English lady, Oriana, and his aspirations towards gentility. He is refashioned as the dependent lover of the Granada gypsy Rosal. The poster for *Caravan* displayed the gypsified Granger with long, dark, curled hair, earrings, even lipstick, and bearing a startling likeness to Valentino, the archetype of the erotic Latin lover.[9]

The popularity of Mason and Granger seems to indicate a female desire for fantasies about handsome but dangerous men. The appeal of Michael Wilding, also immensely popular at this time, was rather more conventional. Wilding came to prominence in Herbert Wilcox's highly successful 'London' series (1945–50), built round his wife Anna Neagle. Rex Harrison starred in the first, *I Live in Grosvenor Square* (1945), but was replaced in the remaining four by Wilding, whose image was a reworking of the debonair gentleman: idealistic, gentle, soft-spoken and 'genially amateur'.[10] Wilding was admired by one critic as possessing 'the looks and bearing of Lord Mountbatten' and the 'charm of Leslie Howard', indicating that his image could be read as acceptably masculine.[11] Less raffish than Harrison and less dreamy than Howard, Wilding produced a well-bred, well-spoken charm which was not so obviously upper class, in keeping with a more egalitarian society. Wilding suffers nobly in a tragic wartime romance (*Piccadilly Incident*, 1946), and dons a series of becoming uniforms in a historical pageant (*The Courtneys of Curzon Street*, 1947), but he is at his most charming in the musical comedies *Spring in Park Lane* (1948) and *Maytime in Mayfair* (1949), where he is as elegant and urbane as Cary Grant, able to glide through the plot contrivances as effortlessly as he dances with Neagle in the set pieces.

Troubled Men

However, *Maytime in Mayfair* was significantly less successful than its predecessor, indicating that the debonair gentleman was becoming a residual type, its appeal less relevant to audience needs.[12] Wilcox declared that his renovations of *noblesse oblige* were 'happy, unclouded pictures. We do not want sadism, abnormality and psycho-analysis.'[13] What he was referring to was a loose group of psychological melodramas (usually crime thrillers) which could be classified as British film noir.[14] The central type in these films was the misfit, often a fugitive, usually innocent and falsely accused, but always tormented, desperate, unable to find a safe haven or a secure identity. In some films these protagonists begin to doubt their own sanity, and the result is breakdown or uncontrolled violence. The emergence of this type suggests a profound social dislocation and a crisis of masculine identity.

Most of the major British male stars of the 40s appeared in these films: James Mason in *Odd Man Out* (1947) and *The Upturned Glass* (1947); John Mills in *The October Man* (1947); Rex Harrison in *Escape* (1948); Richard Todd in *For Them That Trespass* (1949) and *The Interrupted Journey* (1949); Trevor Howard in *They Made Me a Fugitive* (1947); Robert Newton in *Temptation Harbour* (1947), *Obsession* (1949) and *Waterfront* (1950); and David Farrar in *Frieda* (1947), *The Small Back Room* (1948), *Cage of Gold* (1950) and *Night without Stars* (1951). But the actor who most often embodied this type was Eric Portman.

Portman, who had come to prominence through his performance as a fanatical Nazi in *49th Parallel*, the top-grossing film of 1941, starred in *Great Day* (1945), *Wanted for Murder* (1946), *Daybreak* (1946), *Dear Murderer* (1947), *The Mark of Cain* (1948), *Corridor of Mirrors* (1948) and *The Spider and the Fly* (1949). In all these films he played tormented, sexually insecure failures. *Great Day* explicitly shows this as an inability to adjust. Captain Ellis (Portman), a World War I veteran used to excitement, male comradeship and command, cannot cope with the different demands of civilian life. In the climactic scene he breaks down, admitting he

The inner bitterness in a strong man's soul: Eric Portman watches Edana Romney in *Corridor of Mirrors* (Terence Young, 1948)

was 'frightened in peace', conscious of the dependency of his wife and daughter, of his failure to live up to what he understands to be a man's role: 'He's the lover, the protector, the strong man. Or he wants to be. In my case no fresh supplies came in.'

Although the appeal of these films is essentially to male spectators who could identify with these anxieties even if they could not admit to them, Leonard Wallace noted that Portman had a large female following:

> It's the strength being harried and tested by circumstances that really gets the girls suffering for him. . . . No-one is better than Portman at expressing with a haunted, tortured expression of the eyes in a face otherwise taut and immobile, the inner bitterness in a strong man's soul.[15]

Picturegoer readers, presumably from both sexes, voted him into fourth place in the 1947 poll for his performance as the tormented serial killer in *Wanted for Murder*.

The misfit, as a failed hero, was different from the other oppositional type of the late 40s, the spiv. A product of war and post-war rationing, the spiv became, in part, a kind of anti-austerity folk hero, represented as colourfully dressed, charismatic and enterprising in affectionate caricatures by comedians, cartoonists and columnists.[16] Stewart Granger's performance as Ted Purvis in *Waterloo Road* (1945) helped fix the type, a portrait clearly based on popular stereotypes of the flashy, Americanised, work-shy, petty criminal wide-boy. Griffith Jones played a much more sinister variant in *They Made Me a Fugitive* and *Good Time Girl* (1948), indicating that the spiv's image was becoming more threatening.

It was these criminal traits which were transferred to the representation of the delinquent. Several young actors played the type, including Richard Attenborough in *Brighton Rock* (1947), but it was Dirk Bogarde's engrossing performance as Tom Riley in *The Blue Lamp*, the top-grossing film of 1950, which had the most impact. Riley is neurotic, unstable and sexually threatening, his presence explicitly linked to wartime dislocation and the break-up of the family. Bogarde, despite playing such an obviously unacceptable character, gained seventh place for his performance in the *Picturegoer* poll, suggesting that the taste for the thrilling sadist had migrated to this type.[17]

Heroes of World War II

The prominence of these oppositional types in the immediate post-war period was partly due to the difficulty British cinema experienced in producing heroic roles, a problem only resolved when war films came back into favour after 1950. But the heroes of these 50s war films were different from charismatic leaders like Laurence Olivier in *Henry V* (1944) or debonair gentlemen in uniform like Noël Coward in *In Which We Serve* (1942): they were professional officers. As Harold Perkin argues, the interventionism of the welfare state promoted the growth and status of a meritocratic professionalism which cut across traditional elites and class boundaries.[18]

The first star who embodied this emergent type was John Mills, always noted for his sincerity and believability rather than for romantic qualities. He topped the *Picturegoer* poll in 1947 for his performance as Pip, the personable Everyman of *Great Expectations*. This ordinary decency was elevated in *Scott of the Antarctic* (1948) to the status of national hero. In place of the debonair gentleman's dash and charm, Mills embodies a boyish enthusiasm which is deepened by testing into a gritty determination to continue whatever the cost. In *Scott*, it is the nobility of sacrifice for others which turns physical suffering and defeat into a spiritual triumph: a victory for the team rather than for charismatic individualism. Mills was also much admired in *Morning Departure* (1950) as a similarly inspirational leader, this time a submarine captain who has to encourage three of his crew, trapped with him in their stricken craft, to face death calmly. Despite his versatility as an actor, Mills continued to achieve his greatest success in similar roles: as Commander Fraser in *Above Us the Waves*

(1955) and as Pat Reid, the head of the escape committee, in *The Colditz Story* (1955).

A similar typecasting moulded the mid-50s career of Richard Todd, who had starred in three exuberant Disney swashbucklers made in Britain: *The Story of Robin Hood and His Merrie Men* (1952), *The Sword and the Rose* (1953) and *Rob Roy, the Highland Rogue* (1953). Despite his wholesome athleticism and brio in these films, Todd's defining role was as another national hero, Wing Commander Guy Gibson in *The Dam Busters* (1955). The essence of Todd's performance is to downplay Gibson's personal charm in favour of a professionally disciplined dedication to the task in hand. Gibson succeeds through efficient organisation and teamwork.

The most successful representative of meritocratic professionalism was Jack Hawkins, the most popular male star in 1953 and 1954. Hawkins's massive physique, coupled with the deliberate, hesitating delivery of his gravelly voice, were expressive of the immense effort that war required: an unending tight-lipped vigilance, resulting in occasional hard-won victories. Though two years younger than Mills, Hawkins lacked Mills's boyishness and was cast in roles which made him a plausible father figure to the young officers who were on their first mission – a rite of passage into full manhood – in such films as *Angels One Five* (1952), *The Cruel Sea* (1953) and *Malta Story* (1953). Denied any kind of love interest in these films, the emotionalism of the Hawkins character is channelled through male comradeship. As Commander Ericson in *The Cruel Sea*, the top-grossing film of 1953, Hawkins's scarcely mobile face sheds silent tears at the loss of the drifting British crewmen, blown up by his decision to depth-charge a suspected submarine. Shortly after, having drunk himself into insensitivity, Ericson is discovered slumped in his cabin by his 'son' Lockhart (Donald Sinden), who puts him tenderly to bed.[19] Later the two toast, with pink gins, their decision to see out the war together, a decision which Lockhart cannot explain to his girlfriend. The bonds of comradeship here, as elsewhere in the war films, offer a deeper and more sustaining relationship than that of heterosexual romance.

The appeal of war films is very much to males. By the mid-50s they outnumbered females in cinema audiences and critics were offering the qualities of these male stars for their admiration and emulation. Robert Otway celebrated Hawkins's 'rocky frame [which] has become a national institution, a kind of male Britannia', an appropriately regendered national icon.[20] Otway went on to contrast Hawkins's image with Mason's wicked gentlemen, while Jympson Harmon saw him as representing 'loyalty, courage, leadership, unselfishness, compassion and all those things that used to make this such a pleasant land to live and work in'.[21] Clearly the war heroes embodied an idealised golden age, and a patriotic noble Britishness, as well as meritocratic professionalism.

Bogarde and More

The dominance of the war films at the box office in the mid-50s was interrupted by the success of *Doctor in the House*, the highest-grossing film of 1954. Josh Billings commented that the film had 'uprooted all records at the Odeon, Leicester Square. . . . What does this fantastic success signify? I suggest that a large part of the result is due to the buoyant youthfulness of the film. Here is freshness. Here is vitality.'[22] *Doctor in the House* gently debunked the do-gooding welfare-state professional, reconstructing the rather untouchable and piously noble image of the doctor into something lovable. The professional could also be fun.

The role of Simon Sparrow allowed Dirk Bogarde to break with his earlier typecasting as a delinquent and to rework the unstable juvenile into a vulnerable and sensitive romantic lead. Although he faints in the operating theatre, hears the sea in his stethoscope and engages in a series of naively unsuccessful attempts at sexual initiation, he is also capable of delivering a baby and passing his exams. The film is another rite of passage for the young male equipping him to become a doctor and a husband, ready to take up a practice and to settle down. His wife-to-be is a sensible nurse and their relationship a representation of the post-war ideal of the companionate marriage. *Films and Filming* regretted that the 'good looks which have made out of the spiv, the deserter and the petty thug creatures of mystery and fascination' should have been neutered by the 'wide-eyed diffidence' of Bogarde's role as Simon Sparrow, confirming the trend of his films towards 'niceness'.[23] But most critics celebrated Bogarde's release from shabby mackintosh roles.

The other star of *Doctor in the House* was Kenneth More as Grimsdyke, whose upper-middle-class bohemian lifestyle is eccentric rather than rakish. Although he wears a succession of lurid waistcoats and lives on an allowance, he is reliable and caring both towards the younger males and towards his Austrian fiancée, whom he treats as an equal partner. Derek Granger congratulated More on transforming the 30s stereotype of the raffish young

man, which he had employed so effectively in *Genevieve* (1953), into a rounded and convincing characterisation.[24] This suggests that More's performance must be understood as a modernisation of the debonair gentleman, a combination of tradition and the contemporary. *Films and Filming* felt that More had 'all the virtues and none of the vices' of the upper middle class, combining eccentricity and humour with sincerity and honesty.[25] In a general comment on the film, Dilys Powell enthused about these 'well-spoken' young men after all the representations of spivs and 'young workers with regional accents'.[26]

Because of their ability to embody, in very different ways, a youthful and ostensibly classless masculinity, Bogarde and More displaced Hawkins as the most popular male star and dominated the box office until the end of the decade. Their star power was exploited by deployment in a wide range of roles in which the consistency of their image was often more important than the demands of characterisation.

Bogarde was rushed into another domestic comedy, *For Better, for Worse* (1954), and Rank made him repeat the Simon Sparrow role in *Doctor at Sea* (1955) and *Doctor at Large* (1957), which were both huge successes. He also played romantic leads in action adventure (*Campbell's Kingdom*, 1957), war romance (*The Wind Cannot Read*, 1958) and historical drama (*A Tale of Two Cities*, 1958), all of which were highly popular with *Picturegoer* readers. With the partial exception of *Campbell's Kingdom*, these films exploit Bogarde's star image of the passive and sensitive male – a soft, expressive masculinity. A reviewer of *The Wind Cannot Read* commented that Bogarde with 'spaniel pathos in the eyes . . . [was] prowling the screen demanding mother love from his millions of female fans'.[27]

More's appeal was rather different, since he was not a conventional romantic lead. In an interview he commented that his female fans were 'under fifteen and over thirty . . . the others all go for a handsome bloke like Bogarde'.[28] A letter from a female admirer, unfortunately without her age given, praised his 'mature good looks' which were enough to send 'all thoughts of . . . beautiful beefcakes out of my head'.[29] His pleasant, strong face was attractive rather than strikingly handsome, and his muscular, stocky physique not graceful or dashing but pugnacious, determined, redolent of robust good health and exuding self-confidence. The domestic comedy *Raising a Riot* (1955) characteristically shows him as the harassed officer father of three rather than as

Pugnacious, determined, redolent of robust good health and exuding self-confidence: Kenneth More as Douglas Bader in *Reach for the Sky* (Lewis Gilbert, 1956)

a newlywed. He is the attractive, often charming, mature man who captures the heart of a seventeen-year-old neighbour, but he rebuffs her with avuncular tact.

This maturity and strength meant that More was able to perform effectively as the officer professional, as well as in comedies. More's key part, like that of Mills as Scott and Todd as Gibson, was as a national hero: Douglas Bader in *Reach for the Sky* (1956). More brought to this role his image as the ebullient hearty together with the introspection of his highly successful stage and film role as the maladjusted former fighter pilot Freddie Page in *The Deep Blue Sea* (1955). His depiction of Bader, more nuanced and emotional than is usually recognised, is vital to the success of a film that shows the literal smashing of the pre-war debonair gentleman and his recreation as the robust, tenacious professional officer with an indomitable will to win. As with Scott, with whom Bader was frequently compared, this story was understood as another 'victory of the human spirit'.

By the end of 1957 Josh Billings thought that More was 'unquestionably a big draw' who could 'turn an ordinary film into a box-office success mainly on the strength of his name'.[30] This allowed him to be cast in a diverse range of films: J. M. Barrie's Edwardian castaway fantasy *The Admirable Crichton* (1957); an action drama about the sinking of the Titanic, *A Night to Remember* (1958); a John Buchan adventure, *The 39 Steps* (1959); a 1905 Imperial epic, *North West Frontier* (1959); a comedy Western, *The Sheriff of Fractured Jaw* (1958); and a late naval war epic, *Sink the Bismarck!* (1960). The consis-

tency is provided by More himself, who remains largely the same, displaying a resolute, chivalrous integrity, a 'rugged spiritual health', which is tested but never found wanting.[31]

The Rise of the Working-Class Hero: Stanley Baker

But even More's presence cannot disguise the increasingly backward-looking nature of these films, and his career faltered in the early 60s along with those of other 50s stars.[32] They were replaced by pop stars like Cliff Richard, by Christopher Lee's subversively sexual Count Dracula, and above all by working-class heroes. Working-class masculinity had been conspicuously absent from British screens in the 50s. Parts that had demanded the ordinary bloke as action man had been played by fading or second-drawer American stars such as Forrest Tucker. However, towards the end of the decade such roles were played by Stanley Baker, who overtook Bogarde in the *Motion Picture Herald* ratings in 1959.

Baker – Welsh, strongly built and with a thin mouth, prominent jaw and 'falcon eyes' – was a new male type. In the early 50s he had been typecast as the villain, including the oafish bully Bennett in *The Cruel Sea*, until association with McCarthyite exiles Cy Endfield and Joseph Losey led to a series of more interesting roles. *Films and Filming* commented that he played 'hard, tough characters neither particularly sympathetic nor particularly villainous, [which proved that] ordinary men, doing everyday jobs, can be exciting and often are'.[33] As Tom Yately in *Hell Drivers* (1957) he is a resourceful ex-convict whose time inside has made him able to survive in a harsh, brutal and exploitative world. This 'hero with a sadistic streak . . . showed an enormous increase in his fan mail from girls between the ages of 17 and 20', an indication that Baker had become identified with thrilling, sexually desirable and subversive masculinity.[34]

His policemen in *Violent Playground* (1958), *Blind Date* (1959) and *Hell Is a City* (1960), in contrast to those of Jack Hawkins in *The Long Arm* (1956) or *Gideon's Day* (1958), are confused men, strangely drawn to the criminals they hunt and with unformed or unstable family lives. As Johnny Bannion in *The Criminal* (1960), his old-fashioned individual villainy is at odds with the new world of organised crime, making him again an ambivalent figure. Baker's tough, aggressive characters, confused about their social role, lead directly to the anti-heroes of the 'New Wave' films such as Albert Finney's Arthur Seaton in *Saturday Night and Sunday Morning* (1960).[35]

Michael Roper and John Tosh argue that 'masculinity has a history . . . it is subject to change and varied in its forms'.[36] The images of the popular male stars which I have sketched, illustrate this process, exhibiting a variety which changed in relation to the complex social and historical forces that shaped the needs and desires of cinema audiences. The immediate post-war period in British cinema must be understood as a transitional phase in which subversive representations of masculinity came to prominence, before a – very male – consensus re-emerges in the 50s. This consensus was represented by a caring and heroic professionalism that passed itself off as universal, effectively marginalising alternative forms of masculinity until the end of the decade, when that social formation began to break up.

Notes

1. *Kinematograph Weekly*, 20 December 1945, p. 71.
2. Several stars have written informatively about studio promotion in their autobiographies, especially Dirk Bogarde, *Snakes and Ladders* (London: Chatto and Windus, 1978); Stewart Granger, *Sparks Fly Upward* (London: Granada, 1981); Jack Hawkins, *Anything for a Quiet Life* (London: Elm Tree Books, 1973); James Mason, *Before I Forget* (London: Hamish Hamilton, 1981); John Mills, *Up in the Clouds, Gentlemen Please* (London: Weidenfeld and Nicolson, 1980); Kenneth More, *More or Less* (London: Hodder & Stoughton, 1978); Richard Todd, *Caught in the Act* (London: Hutchinson, 1986) and *In Camera* (London: Hutchinson, 1989).
3. For 'Charm School' details see Geoffrey Macnab, *J. Arthur Rank and the British Film Industry* (London: Routledge, 1993), pp. 141–6.
4. Richard Dyer, *Stars*, pp. 53–68.
5. Peter Burnup, the *Motion Picture Herald*'s London editor, quoted in an article in the *Daily Express*, 13 December 1956.
6. I have also used the *Daily Mail*'s annual listings, again based on readers' choices, which ran from 1945–9.
7. *Picturegoer*, 4 December 1943.
8. Mason's success attracted Hollywood offers, and he left for America in 1947.
9. Granger also played romantic leads for other production companies, notably Apollodorus in *Caesar and Cleopatra* (Pascal/Rank, 1945) and Count Koenigsmark in Ealing's *Saraband for Dead Lovers* (1948). Granger left for Hollywood in 1949, occasionally appearing in British

costume films such as *Beau Brummell* (1954) or in action adventures like *Harry Black* (1958).
10. Jeffrey Richards, *The Age of the Dream Palace: Cinema and Society in Britain 1930–39* (London: Routledge, 1984), p. 167. Richards argues that the debonair gentleman was the dominant British male type of the 30s.
11. Ewart Hodgson, *Sunday Times*, 23 August 1946.
12. Wilding also pursued a career in Hollywood after 1950, rather unsuccessfully. He was less adaptable than Granger and less distinctive than Mason.
13. *Kinematograph Weekly*, 18 December 1947, p. 18.
14. Robert Murphy discusses these films in *Realism and Tinsel*, pp. 168–90.
15. *Picturegoer*, 17 December 1949, p. 8.
16. David Hughes, 'The Spivs', in Michael Sissons and Philip French (eds), *Age of Austerity, 1945–1951* (London: Hodder & Stoughton, 1963; reprinted, Oxford: Oxford University Press, 1986), pp. 71–88.
17. See Andy Medhurst, 'Dirk Bogarde', in Charles Barr (ed.), *All Our Yesterdays: 90 Years of British Cinema* (London: BFI, 1986), pp. 346–54. Medhurst rightly argues that Bogarde's performance displaces the film's nominal hero, PC Andy Mitchell (Jimmy Hanley), unbalancing the film.
18. Harold Perkin, *The Rise of Professional Society* (London: Routledge, 1989), especially pp. 355–61. See also Harry Hopkins, *The New Look* (London: Secker & Warburg, 1963), pp. 158–61.
19. Sinden is one of Raymond Durgnat's keen cadets: 'grown-up boys, trusting, vulnerable, decently worried and ready aye ready'. *A Mirror for England: British Cinema from Austerity to Affluence*, p. 142.
20. *Sunday Graphic*, 10 January 1953.
21. *Evening News*, 15 October 1953.
22. *Kinematograph Weekly*, 22 April 1954, p. 5.
23. *Films and Filming*, August 1955, p. 3.
24. *Financial Times*, 19 March 1954.
25. *Films and Filming*, April 1955, p. 3.
26. *Sunday Times*, 21 March 1954.
27. Derek Monsey, *Sunday Express*, 7 August 1958.
28. *Sunday Graphic*, 3 November 1957.
29. *Photoplay*, December 1955, p. 4.
30. *Kinematograph Weekly*, 12 December 1957.
31. Quotation from the review of *The 39 Steps*, *Observer*, 11 December 1959.
32. More, Todd and Hawkins went into character roles or television leads. Bogarde effectively redefined his 'idol of the Odeons' image by appearing in less populist films by Losey and Visconti.
33. David Conrad, 'Stanley Baker: Tough at the Top', *Films and Filming*, November 1959, p. 5.

34. Ibid.

35. For a detailed discussion see Christine Geraghty's essay, 'Albert Finney – A Working-Class Hero', in Pat Kirkham and Janet Thumim (eds), *Me Jane: Masculinity, Movies and Women* (London: Lawrence & Wishart, 1995), pp. 66–72.

36. Michael Roper and John Tosh (eds), *Manful Assertions: Masculinities in Britain Since 1800* (London: Routledge, 1991), p. 1.

Bibliography

Babington, Bruce, *British Stars and Stardom* (Manchester: Manchester University Press, 2001).

Babington, Bruce, Powrie, Phil and Davies, Ann (eds), *The Trouble with Men: Masculinities in European and Hollywood Cinema* (London: Wallflower Press, 2004).

Docherty, David, Morrison, David and Tracey, Richard, *The Last Picture Show? Britain's Changing Film Audiences* (London: BFI, 1987).

Durgnat, Raymond, *A Mirror for England: British Cinema from Austerity to Affluence* (London: Faber and Faber, 1970).

Dyer, Richard, *Stars* (London: BFI, 1979).

Geraghty, Christine, *British Cinema in the Fifties: Gender, Genre and the 'New Look'* (London/New York: Routledge, 2000).

Gledhill, Christine (ed.), *Stardom: Industry of Desire* (London: Routledge, 1991).

Hill, John, *Sex, Class and Realism: British Cinema 1956–1963* (London: BFI, 1986).

King, Barry, 'Stardom as an Occupation', in Paul Kerr (ed.), *The Hollywood Film Industry* (London: Routledge/BFI, 1986).

Lowe, Vicky, '"The Best Speaking Voices in the World": Robert Donat, Stardom and the Voice in British Cinema', *Journal of British Cinema and Television* vol. 1 no. 2, 2004.

Macnab, Geoffrey, *Searching for Stars: Stardom and Screen Acting in British Cinema* (London: Cassell, 2000).

McFarlane, Brian, *An Autobiography of British Cinema* (London: Methuen, 1997).

Morin, Edgar, *The Stars* (London: Grove Press, 1960).

Murphy, Robert, *Realism and Tinsel: Cinema and Society in Britain, 1939–49* (London: Routledge, 1989).

Plain, Gill, *John Mills and British Cinema* (Edinburgh: Edinburgh University Press, 2006).

Richards, Jeffrey, *Films and British National Identity* (Manchester: Manchester University Press, 1997).

Spicer, Andrew, *Typical Men: The Representation of Masculinity in Popular British Cinema* (London: I. B. Tauris, 2001).

Walker, Alexander, 'Random Thoughts on the Englishness (or Otherwise) of English Film Actors', in *It's Only a Movie, Ingrid* (London: Headline, 1988).

33

Beyond the New Wave:
Realism in British Cinema, 1959–63

PETER HUTCHINGS

Realism is generally acknowledged to be a vital component of British cinema. But since the development of film studies as an academic discipline in the 1970s, realism has been treated with suspicion, its claim to picture things 'the way they are' dismissed as an illusion fostered in the interests of ideology. Seen from this perspective, the predominantly urban and industrial landscapes of British film realism, and the stories of the mainly working-class characters who populate these landscapes are revealed as vehicles for the expression of middle-class and patriarchal values.

New Wave Realism

This concern to deconstruct realism and the aesthetic practices associated with it impacted especially severely on the group of British films released between 1959 and 1963 collectively known as 'the British New Wave', or, more disparagingly, as 'Kitchen Sink dramas'. For an earlier grouping of realist films – the documentaries produced by John Grierson during the 1930s – the middle-class perspective has become so obvious over the years that they have lost their power to win us over to their viewpoint and their main interest now is either historical or – in the case of the more 'poetic' or visually arresting films – aesthetic. The films of the British New Wave, by contrast, are fictions that seek, often in very seductive ways, to involve us in their narratives in a manner that still has the potential to neutralise any critical distance, in effect to make us sympathetic participants in their world. Hence the stern gaze that has sometimes been fixed on them by critics and historians concerned to resist their influence.

This chapter has two aims. The first is to reconsider the roles played by realism in British cinema in the late 1950s and early 1960s. This necessarily involves reassessing the British New Wave, but the discussion can be broadened to include films and film-makers marginalised or ignored in previous accounts of this period. The second is to contextualise some of the key readings of the British New Wave and other realist films from the 1959–63 period, particularly the work of John Hill and Andrew Higson in the 1980s.

The British New Wave is usually seen as consisting of the following films: *Room at the Top* (Jack Clayton, 1959), *Look Back in Anger* (Tony Richardson, 1959), *The Entertainer* (Tony Richardson, 1960), *Saturday Night and Sunday Morning* (Karel Reisz, 1960), *A Taste of Honey* (Tony Richardson, 1961), *A Kind of Loving* (John Schlesinger, 1962), *The Loneliness of the Long Distance Runner* (Tony Richardson, 1962) and *This Sporting Life* (Lindsay Anderson, 1963), with *Billy Liar* (John Schlesinger, 1963) and *Darling* (John Schlesinger, 1965) sometimes included for good measure. Their initial claims to realism stemmed in large part from their offering what for the time of their release was a shockingly new subject matter. The focus was on the working class, but this was not the working class as envisaged by Grierson's documentaries – noble workers, worthy cogs in the social machine. Instead the New Wave's working-class heroes were aggressively individualistic and materialistic and often anti-establishment as well, and the stress in the films tended to be on their leisure activities rather than on their work. This thematic refocusing was coupled with an increased openness on the part of the films regarding the representation of sexual behaviour and other subjects previously deemed unacceptable in the mainstream cinema. All the films featured extramarital sex, for example, alongside what were for the late 1950s and early 1960s scandalously frank discussions of abortion, miscarriage and homosexuality (although, as one might expect, from our present perspective such elements now seem scandalous only in their tameness and reticence). Often shot on location in cities in the Midlands or the North of England and featuring relatively unknown actors and relatively untried film directors, these films were generally seen by critics of the time as a step forward for British cinema, a move towards a mature, intelligent engagement with contemporary British social life and a welcome breath of fresh air after the conformist entertainment provided by studio-bound British filmmakers in the first part of the 1950s.[1]

Higson and Hill

During the 1980s, John Hill and Andrew Higson produced important accounts of the New Wave that elaborated upon the formal and thematic qualities that bound together the New Wave films as a distinctive group.[2] In particular, both Hill and Higson identify what they see as a tension apparent in these films between narration and description (in Hill's terms) or narrative and spectacle (in Higson's). They both argue that the way in which New Wave films stress the pictorial or spectacular – usually in the form of shots of the city – interrupts and destabilises the cohesiveness of the narrative. Higson identifies 'the problem of the irreconcilability between an "internal" point of view of the figure in the city . . . and the "external" point of view from outside and above the city, the look of the master-cameraman'.[3] Hill notes the New Wave's 'deployment of actions and, especially, locations which are ostensibly non-functional, which only loosely fit into the logic of narrative development'.[4] Seen in this way, the films stand apart to some extent from the commercial mainstream.

Critics writing about these films at the time of their initial release often related them to the phenomenon of the 'Angry Young Man', a term devised by the media as a shorthand for a range of new developments in theatre and literature from the mid-1950s onwards expressing social disenchantment and rebelliousness. All the New Wave films were based on novels or plays associated with the movement and the connection was further validated by the involvement of John Osborne, the writer of *Look Back in Anger*, in Woodfall, the main New Wave production company.

John Hill's 1986 account of the New Wave stresses the importance of broader social trends, notably a burgeoning consumerism and the decline in Britain's status as a world power symbolised most visibly by the Suez crisis of 1956. There is a sense in Hill's account of the films as *Zeitgeist*-like expressions of change in the social fabric, albeit male-centred and potentially misogynist expressions. In particular, social instabilities in class (and especially working-class) identity and gender identity are conveyed via New Wave narratives which often focus on an alienated working-class male attempting to find a role for himself in a turbulent, materialistic world.

New Wave Variations

Seen together, Hill's and Higson's writing about the New Wave provides a cohesive package, one which defines the New Wave aesthetically but which also places it in relation both to British culture generally and to British social history. But it has tended to overstress the cohesiveness of the New Wave films and to overlook the manifestations of realism in other areas of British cinema of the period.

The New Wave films are in certain respects quite different from each other. This is most obviously the case with the first and last films in the cycle, Jack Clayton's *Room at the Top* and Lindsay Anderson's *This Sporting Life*. Unlike other New Wave directors who came to feature-film direction from backgrounds in documentary and theatre, Clayton had been working in the mainstream film industry since the mid-1930s. *Room at the Top* is more conventionally 'well made' than later New Wave projects; and its casting is more orthodox, with established star Laurence Harvey 'doing' a regional accent (criticised at the time of the film's release for its lack of accuracy) and a glamorous French woman – Simone Signoret – in the part of the sexually experienced woman. Panoramic shots of the industrial city – noted by Higson and Hill as a distinguishing feature of the New Wave – are of little significance here, and the New Wave's concern elsewhere with the depredations of modern mass culture is entirely absent. Instead *Room at the Top* offers an old-fashioned morality story in which the desire for material possessions leads inevitably to unhappiness. The film's moralistic tenor is most obvious at its conclusion where the hero finally acquires – via marriage – the woman he wanted as a way of gaining access to wealth but only at the cost of losing forever the woman he actually loved. As if to underline his own detachment from the realist cycle inaugurated by *Room at the Top*, Jack Clayton subsequently turned down further realist projects – including *Saturday Night and Sunday Morning* and *The L-Shaped Room* (1962) – and chose instead as his next film *The Innocents* (1961), an adaptation of Henry James's ghost story *The Turn of the Screw*.[5]

This Sporting Life would appear to be a more 'authentic' product of the New Wave. Lindsay Anderson

had worked in documentary in the 1950s; been the prime mover behind the 'Free Cinema' programme of screenings at the National Film Theatre; and was associated with the Royal Court Theatre, where Tony Richardson had staged *Look Back in Anger*.[6] The film itself was produced by Karel Reisz, the director of *Saturday Night and Sunday Morning*, and its two stars – Richard Harris and Rachel Roberts – were (like Albert

This Sporting Life (Lindsay Anderson, 1963)

Like earlier British New Wave films, Lindsay Anderson's *This Sporting Life* was adapted from a novel (by David Storey) with strong Northern working-class credentials. Storey was a miner's son who, like his novel's hero, had played rugby in a Northern town. However, he was also a student at the Slade School of Fine Art, and his novel was different in tone and emphasis from other social realist novels of the period. As Anderson himself noted of Storey, 'he was not interested in surface, but in essence; not in what was representative, but in what was exceptional' (quoted in Sussex, p. 42).

This disdain for the representative and the typical also informed Anderson's film, especially in its presentation of its two principal characters, the rugby player Frank Machin (changed from the novel's Arthur, possibly to distance him from Arthur Seaton, the hero of *Saturday Night and Sunday Morning*) and his landlady and occasional lover Mrs Hammond. In each case, expository biographical details are few and far between. As played by Richard Harris, Frank resonates with unfocused aggression but no explanation is given for this, nor is he connected to a social context in the manner of other New Wave heroes. One might compare him in this respect with Arthur Seaton, whose opening manifesto-monologue positions him very precisely in relation to a historical moment of social change. Storey's original novel had contained a scene with Frank's parents that had a similar function in explaining some of the character's attitudes, but there was no such scene in the film. Instead Frank just shows up – out of the blue, as it were – at a local dance and, for no apparent reason (and, it is implied, for no reason that he himself can understand) picks a fight.

If Frank is masculine aggression personified, Mrs Hammond, as played by Rachel Roberts, represents feminine self-abnegation. The reason for her husband's suicide is never spelled out, and her devotion to his

memory, which is so extreme that it borders on the pathological, also remains something of a mystery. Roberts's earlier performance as an adulterous wife in *Saturday Night and Sunday Morning* had been a nuanced portrayal of socially situated repression, but her performance as Mrs Hammond is both more grotesque and more stylised.

Indeed, the distinctiveness of *This Sporting Life* as a whole derives mainly from the distance it puts between itself and the earlier New Wave films. While some of the New Wave approaches are superficially evident – for example, in the extensive location-shooting and in an apparent focus on working-class characters – much of the social context so important to the New Wave has been drained away and replaced by something more abstract.

This Sporting Life is certainly an uneven film, with some of the domestic scenes between Frank and Mrs Hammond having a theatrical quality that sits uneasily with the location-based material. However, the quality of the film resides, in part at least, in this awkwardness, which seems to parallel Frank's own awkwardness as he struggles with emotions that he can never understand or articulate. Similarly the fractured flashback structure reflects the tumultuous emotions which destroy Mrs Hammond and leave Frank damaged and confused. A more polished and linear treatment would have lacked the raw power of Anderson's ungainly masterpiece. In any event, *This Sporting Life* demands a kind of response different from that invoked by other British New Wave films, with its apparent reliance on realist devices something of a distraction from its concern with extreme states of being.

FURTHER READING

Erik Hedling, *Lindsay Anderson: Maverick Film-Maker* (London and Washington: Cassell, 1998).

Elizabeth Sussex, *Lindsay Anderson* (London: Studio Vista, 1969).

Finney in *Saturday Night and Sunday Morning*, Alan Bates in *A Kind of Loving* and Rita Tushingham in *A Taste of Honey*), relatively new to cinema audiences.

However, some remarks made by Anderson during the production of *This Sporting Life* suggest an approach quite distinct from that adopted in earlier New Wave films. '*Saturday Night and Sunday Morning* was a thoroughly objective film, while *This Sporting Life* is almost entirely subjective,' Anderson said, adding 'I have tried to abstract the film as much as possible so as not to over-emphasise the locations and keep attention on the situation between the characters.'[7] Anderson's words are borne out by the film itself which shows little or no interest in exploring the social dimension of its characters' lives and does not make much visually of the town in which it is set. The abstraction mentioned by Anderson is more than apparent in the film's stylised rugby sequences as well as in Rachel Roberts's disturbing death scene. In fact, *This Sporting Life* probably has as much in common, thematically and stylistically, with Martin Scorsese's *Raging Bull* (1980) – another tale of a sportsman unable to come to terms with his own inner violence – as it has with *A Kind of Loving* or *Saturday Night and Sunday Morning*. Anderson, like Clayton, chose for his second feature a project with distinct fantasy elements, *If . . . .* (1968), and his subsequent critical reputation, like Clayton's, tends to put him in the 'art-cinema' mould.[8]

Room at the Top and *This Sporting Life* might represent the most visible instances of films that do not neatly embody what has become the standard definition of a New Wave film but they are not alone in this. There are significant differences even between the films directed by Tony Richardson, the most prolific of the New Wave directors. The first two, *Look Back in Anger* and *The Entertainer*, wear their theatrical origins on their sleeves and are full of declamatory speeches and 'show-stopping' performances from, respectively, Richard Burton and Laurence Olivier. By contrast, *A Taste of Honey*, although another theatrical adaptation, seems more committed to offering a non-theatrical experience. It was the first of the films to be shot entirely on location; its principal actor is an unknown – Rita Tushingham – and its style, while still featuring some expressive moments, is comparatively self-effacing. *A Taste of Honey* also stands apart from its New Wave companions (if one excludes *Darling*) in that it is the only one of them to have a female protagonist.[9] *The Loneliness of the Long Distance Runner*, based on a short story by Alan Sillitoe, has a more obtrusive cinematic

Women in the industrial landscape: Dora Bryan and Rita Tushingham in *A Taste of Honey* (Tony Richardson, 1961)

style, borrowing from the French *nouvelle vague* its shaky camerawork, staccato editing and jump-cutting. One could assign this lack of stylistic or thematic consistency to the inadequacies of Richardson as a director. But his mercurial approach to film-making can also be seen as symptomatic of a broader heterogeneity within the British New Wave.[10]

Non-New Wave Realism

If the films included as part of the New Wave are less homogenous than was once thought, the realism they purvey was by no means their exclusive preserve. In 1960, Penelope Houston, editor of *Sight and Sound*, offered a succinct definition of the 'new British film':

> Its subject means something in contemporary terms; its working-class dialogue sounds tolerably close to the way people talk; it is not afraid, on some levels at least, to call things by their right names; and there is an air of drive and energy about it enough to recharge the flat batteries of half-a-dozen studio vehicles.[11]

The film she is discussing, however, is *The Angry Silence* (Guy Green, 1960) – a film starring Richard Attenborough as a factory worker who is sent to Coventry by his fellow workers for his refusal to come out on strike – which had no connection with the New Wave. But with its mainstream director, an already established male star and an imported foreign actress in the form of Pier Angeli, it can be seen as a clearer successor to *Room at the Top* than any of the New Wave films. The writer of *The Angry Silence*, Bryan Forbes, went on to direct *The L-Shaped Room*, which, along with Peter Glenville's *Term of Trial* (1962) was an adaptation of a social realist novel made for Romulus, the company responsible for *Room at the Top*. Contemporary reviews refer to 'the new social subtlety', 'the new "traumatic" school of independent British film-making' and 'the present "tough" school of British films' when discussing films such as these.[12] But along with John Guillermin's *Never Let Go* (1960), Sidney Gilliat's *Only Two Can Play* (1962) and J. Lee Thompson's *Yield to the Night* (1956), *Woman in a Dressing Gown* (1957) and *No Trees in the Street* (1959), their realism has come to be seen as derivative and inauthentic compared to that of the New Wave films.[13]

This new realism can also be seen in crime films, comedies, science-fiction films and musicals and it is interesting to compare how such genre films were treated by the critics and the censors.[14] The 'X' certificate had been introduced in the early 1950s as an attempt to open up a space for the exhibition of artistic films (usually European art films) for a 'cultured' audience. However, it had quickly become tarnished as a convenient label for more exploitative fare. In the late 1950s and early 1960s – precisely the time when the main British cinema circuits became more willing to show 'X' films – notions of a 'good' realism and a 'bad' realism often seem to be organised around the art/exploitation dichotomy associated with the 'X' certificate. The key element in differentiating various types of realist film is genre. Genre films are condemned for exploiting the commercial possibilities of the 'X' certificate whereas those films which do not have an obvious generic identity – the New Wave films and those social-problem films that use generic conventions merely as a framework through which to consider more 'serious' issues – are treated more indulgently. *Room at the Top*, for example, rated a *Picturegoer* 'Seal of Merit' and made the 'X' certificate look like 'a badge of honour', while John Guillermin's crime melodrama *Never Let Go* 'runs full circle through every type of violence this side of an 'X'-certificate'.[15] Within such a context, the slogan used to market *Room at the Top* – 'A savage story of lust and ambition' – becomes an embarrassment, something to be explained away as industry philistinism rather than an indicator that the market for *Room at the Top* might be similar to that for 'X'-certificated genre films.[16]

The 'broadness' of British film realism in the 1959–63 period is lost in later accounts of the New Wave. In his book *Sex, Class and Realism: British Cinema, 1956–1963*, John Hill does devote considerable space

Unpatronisingly sympathetic view of teenage culture: *Beat Girl* (Edmond T. Gréville, 1960)

not only to the New Wave but also to the social-problem film. However, the more obviously generic products are either marginalised or absent, and Hill makes implicit value judgments. For example, *Beat Girl* (Edmond T. Gréville, 1960), which is unpatronisingly sympathetic towards its teenagers, is discussed as an exploitation film about youth. Hill considers it 'a more straightforwardly "commercial" attempt to "exploit" the issues involved', but it is never entirely clear from his analysis precisely how *Beat Girl* is different from an apparently more worthy film like *Sapphire* (1959) (or the New Wave films) other than in an undefined 'seriousness' on the part of the film-makers involved in the latter.[17] A similar disdain for the commercial is apparent in Hill's comment that 'It was not long before even Rank had jumped on the social problem/realism bandwagon with productions of its own like *Flame in the Streets* (1961) and *The Wild and the Willing* (1962).'[18] Elsewhere, Hill acknowledges that all social-problem films (and presumably all New Wave films as well) are exploitative in some sense, but the implications – that films like *Saturday Night and Sunday Morning* and *A Kind of Loving* are just as much part of the commercial mainstream as *Beat Girl* and other genre products – are never worked through.

The Uses of Realism

This concern to establish the New Wave as existing at some distance from the commercial imperatives of mainstream cinema is also evident in Higson's identification of the ways in which New Wave films disturb the certainties of normative narrative structures. However, this interest in the potential for some kind of resistance to the mainstream is accompanied in both Hill and Higson by an almost palpable sense of disappointment that the films concerned do not go far enough, that ultimately they are bound to and compromised by their attachment to the commercial mainstream. This disappointment can be seen as deriving from the context within which Hill and Higson produced their accounts of the New Wave. Their work grows out of film theory developed in the 1970s, which was concerned to disassemble realism and to bring into view realist film's strategies for placing the spectator in particular positions in relation to the drama.[19] In addition, the interest apparent in both Hill and Higson in exploring cultural positions of resistance in regard to representations of class, gender and national identity aligns their work with the British independent film culture of the 1970s and 80s. Higson makes this explicit at the conclusion of his piece when he compares the New Wave unfavourably with 1980s British independent film: 'it is perhaps only in some "independent" films of the 1980s that the question has been seriously confronted of how cinema might investigate a landscape historically'.[20] The distaste for materialism and consumerism in both Higson's and Hill's work can also be seen as part of a broader left-wing reaction evident in Britain in the 1980s against the unfettered capitalism promoted by the Thatcher government. From this perspective, the British New Wave – and to a certain extent the social-problem film as well – becomes a kind of failed revolution, a moment of challenge to aesthetic, commercial and social norms which ultimately led nowhere.

This is a partial reading of the films, which fixes upon particular details while ignoring others. From another perspective, the landscape shots in which Higson and Hill invest so much might be seen as explicable within the established conventions of the establishing shot, and the case for judging these films against a radical agenda which the film-makers involved did not share becomes less tenable. The readings offered by Higson and Hill are not necessarily wrong – their work carries an explanatory force and has substantially furthered our understanding of this area of British cinema – but, like all readings, they emanate from particular positions and contexts. The films can be read from other positions – such as that offered by Terry Lovell's feminist account of *A Taste of Honey* in 'Landscapes and Stories in 1960s British Realism' – which makes sense of them in a different way.[21]

Contextualisation of interpretative activity might help to explain the disparity between early 1960s readings of the New Wave realists and the Higson/Hill readings. But for Hill there is a sense that the 'real' meaning of the films was not always perceived by critics (and presumably audiences) who thought the films were primarily about class when they were really about gender. There is a danger in this sort of criticism of installing later readings as more enlightened than those made at the time the film was first shown, whereas both are delimited by contextual factors. One needs constantly to judge whatever readings one encounters in terms of their credibility and validity, but it is important to be aware that film history does not just involve the history of film but also the history of interpretation.

This chapter has generally avoided the question of what realist films 'meant' in the 1959–63 period and has sought to open up the question of realism by considering some of the ways in which readings of realism have been constructed. In the case of Higson and Hill's approach, the contemplation of the New Wave as a distinct object has to be set against more recent work on British cinema in the 1950s and 1960s, which suggests a more complex, heterogeneous relationship between realism, the New Wave and British cinema.

Within such a context, a consideration of the relation between realism and specific film genres can enhance an understanding of realism itself in a manner that is not reliant on seeing the New Wave as either source or guarantor of 'the real'. For example, in crime films such as *Hell Is a City* (Val Guest, 1960), *The Criminal* (Joseph Losey, 1960) and *The Frightened City* (John Lemont, 1961) one finds location-shooting coupled with a relatively explicit representation of violence and sexuality which separates them from the more anodyne programme-fillers that had constituted the bulk of crime-film production throughout the 1950s. Realist elements here function primarily as generic innovations, as a means of updating and 'refreshing' crime narratives in order to make them more attractive to audiences.[22]

Much the same can be said of the turn to realism in British science-fiction cinema, although here a generic incorporation of new realist elements actually predates the New Wave films and is not itself wholly determined by cinematic factors. In the early to mid-1950s, novelist John Wyndham, in novels such as *The Day of the Triffids* and *The Midwich Cuckoos*, and television writer Nigel Kneale, with the BBC TV series *The Quatermass Experiment* and its sequels, had relocated the traditional SF invasion theme within deliberately mundane contemporary English settings, often to intensely surreal

Hell Is a City (Val Guest, 1960)

During the first half of the 1950s, the Hammer company churned out a series of low-budget crime thrillers that had little critical or commercial impact and which were generally indistinguishable from all the other rather staid crime 'B' movies being produced at the time. By contrast, *Hell Is a City*, which was Hammer's return to crime after it had become a very successful horror specialist, offered a more confident and detailed visualisation of law-breaking and its consequences, with much of its distinctive character deriving from the use of realist devices.

Hell Is a City was based on a 1954 novel by ex-policeman Maurice Proctor. The narrative – about the planning of a heist and its aftermath – was not especially original, but the film's strong sense of place and characterisation clearly separated it out from Hammer's earlier vapid work in the genre. Much of the film was shot on location in Manchester, and the drama that played out in these locations exhibited what for the time was a ground-breaking explicitness, particularly about sexual matters. An outcome of this approach were individual scenes that would not have been out of place in a British New Wave film. For example, a pitch-and-toss event on the edge of Manchester has a function within the story, but the level of detail involved in its presentation also renders it a fascinated New Wave-like inspection of a proletarian public ritual. In addition, the policeman hero (played by Stanley Baker) has a brooding and earthy intensity that connects him with similarly abrasive, no-nonsense protagonists in *Saturday Night and Sunday Morning* and *The Loneliness of the Long Distance Runner*.

However, the presence of such elements in *Hell Is a City* has a particular significance relating more to the refreshing of the thriller format through an enhanced verisimilitude than it does to any New Wave imperatives. Val Guest, the film's director, had earlier brought a brusque realism to Hammer's science-fiction/horrors *The Quatermass Experiment* and *Quatermass 2*, where localised settings and a keen sense of native social mores had firmly anchored these alien-invasion fantasies within a British context. Something comparable happens in *Hell Is a City*, where generic conventions

A landmark on the road to gritty realism: Stanley Baker in *Hell Is a City*

formerly associated more with American cinema – the graphic violence, the alienated hero, the strident jazz score – are integrated into a detailed and convincing British milieu, albeit one full of national 'types' such as the shifty landlord, the affectionate barmaid, the bookie and various low-life criminals. The film's energy might derive from its American-style fast pacing and cutting, but at the same time an observational realism helps to provide a recognisably British sense of the drama.

This bringing together of generic and realist elements is not always seamless. That the main villain might be an old school friend of the policeman hero is stretching credibility a little. But having him played by an American actor (John Crawford) who does little to disguise his non-British accent breaches verisimilitude to a distracting extent. If nothing else, the awkwardness apparent here underlines how effective the rest of the film is in deploying realist techniques as a means of introducing US conventions into British cinema.

FURTHER READING

Steve Chibnall, 'Ordinary People: "New Wave" Realism and the British Crime Film', in Steve Chibnall and Robert Murphy (eds), *British Crime Cinema* (London and New York: Routledge, 1999).

Robert Murphy, *Sixties British Cinema* (London: BFI, 1992).

effect. Film versions of *The Quatermass Experiment* (Val Guest, 1955) and *Quatermass 2* (Val Guest, 1957) had already appeared before *Room at the Top*'s release.[23] To these can be added significant films like *The Damned* (Joseph Losey, 1961), *Unearthly Stranger* (John Krish, 1963), *Village of the Damned* (Wolf Rilla, 1960), based on Wyndham's *The Midwich Cuckoos*, and *The Day the Earth Caught Fire* (Val Guest, 1961), which together constitute another vein of realism, though one with a distinctly uncanny element, running through British cinema in the 1959–63 period.[24]

It is also significant that just about every ambitious British film-maker in the 1959–63 period – Roy Ward Baker, Bryan Forbes, Guy Green, Val Guest, John Guillermin and J. Lee Thompson, for example – seized upon the possibilities offered by the new realism as an appropriate way of forwarding their own professional aspirations. In the case of the pre-1959 genre films of Baker, Guest, Guillermin and Thompson, there is an intermittent engagement with realist practices and themes, which predates and in many ways emulates the realism of the New Wave films.

It is in the nature of realism that it dates, that inevitably it gives itself up to its own deconstruction and reinterpretation. Seen in this way, realism becomes strangely elusive, difficult to grasp. This is especially the case in the 1959–63 period when notions of the real were installed in a wide range of British films in a complex, multilayered way. In the past, discussions of New Wave realism have tended to place it in a position of resistance to the commercial. What a broader view of British film production of this period reveals is that realism is both more central to the commercial cinema and more dispersed across different generic and industrial contexts. Realism might well in some instances involve a 'moral' commitment to serious social issues but in the 1959–63 period it also sold films, and sometimes – in commercially successful New Wave films such as *Saturday Night and Sunday Morning* and *A Taste of Honey* – it managed to do both at once.

Notes

1. Needless to say, some critics disputed this, notably V. F. Perkins who in the first edition of *Movie* in 1962 excoriated the New Wave along with much of the rest of British cinema. It is fair to say, however, that in the period of the New Wave itself, such critical voices tended to be in the minority. See V. F. Perkins, 'The British Cinema', *Movie* no. 1, June 1962, pp. 2–7.

2. See John Hill, *Sex, Class and Realism: British Cinema, 1956–1963*; Andrew Higson 'Space, Place, Spectacle: Landscape and Townscape in the "Kitchen Sink" Film'.

3. Higson, 'Space, Place, Spectacle', p. 150.

4. Hill, *Sex, Class and Realism*, p. 129.

5. For a detailed discussion of Clayton's career, see Neil Sinyard, *Jack Clayton*.

6. For more on Free Cinema, a series of short film programmes screened at the National Film Theatre between 1956 and 1959, see Alan Lovell and Jim Hillier, *Studies in Documentary*, pp. 133–59.

7. Quoted in Tom Milne, 'This Sporting Life', *Sight and Sound*, Summer 1962, p. 115.

8. See, for example, Erik Hedling, *Lindsay Anderson: Maverick Film-maker*.

9. For a discussion of the film in these terms, see Terry Lovell, 'Landscape and Stories in 1960s British Realism'.

10. Richardson's reputation is much less established than that of Reisz and Anderson (David Thompson dismisses him as 'a wretched film director' in *A Biographical Dictionary of Film*, London: André Deutsch, 1994, p. 632). The publication of his autobiography, *Long Distance Runner* (London: Faber and Faber, 1993) and an American collection of scholarly essays, *The Cinema of Tony Richardson: Essays and Interviews* (James M. Walsh and John C. Tibbetts, eds, New York: State University of New York Press, 1999), has done something to challenge this low assessment.

11. Penelope Houston, 'The Angry Silence', *Sight and Sound*, Spring 1960, p. 89.

12. Francis Wyndham, '*The L-Shaped Room*', *Sight and Sound*, Winter 1962–3, p. 41; review of *Never Let Go* in *Monthly Film Bulletin*, July 1960, p. 93; review of *Only Two Can Play* in *Monthly Film Bulletin*, February 1962, p. 21.

13. Hill devotes a chapter to the social-problem films of Basil Dearden and Michael Relph in *Sex, Class and Realism*; and the films of Baker, Lee Thompson, Dearden and Relph *et al.* are greeted with a degree of enthusiasm by Robert Murphy in *Sixties British Cinema* (London: BFI, 1992) and Raymond Durgnat in *A Mirror for England: British Cinema from Austerity to Affluence* (London: Faber and Faber, 1970).

14. 'The British "New Wave" rides again' commented one critic on the musical, *What a Crazy World* (1963), *Monthly Film Bulletin*, December 1963, p. 175.

15. *Picturegoer*, 24 January 1959. *Sunday Express*, 25 January 1959. *Monthly Film Bulletin*, July 1960, p. 93.

16. The Hammer horror cycle that commenced with *The Curse of Frankenstein* in 1957 and *Dracula* in 1958 also relied on a certain kind of realism and was criticised both for its graphic qualities and for its exploitative nature. However, Hammer films' period settings meant that they

tended not to be lumped in with the contemporary
'tough school' of British film-making.

17. Hill, *Sex, Class and Realism*, p. 117.

18. Ibid., p. 48.

19. In Britain this sort of film theory was particularly associated with the journal *Screen*.

20. Higson, 'Space, Place, Spectacle', p. 156. Hill does not
explicitly refer to independent film in *Sex, Class and
Realism* but he explores the subject in some detail in a
subsequent publication, *British Cinema in the 1980s*
(Oxford: Oxford University Press, 1999).

21. Terry Lovell, 'Landscapes and Stories in 1960s British
Realism'.

22. For more on this, see Steve Chibnall, 'Ordinary People:
"New Wave" Realism and the British Crime Film'.

23. Kneale confirmed his 'realist' credentials by working on
the screenplays for *Look Back in Anger* and *The Entertainer*.

24. See Peter Hutchings, '"We're the Martians Now": British
SF invasion fantasies of the 1950s and 1960s'.

Bibliography

Chibnall, Steve, 'Ordinary People: "New Wave" Realism and
the British Crime Film', in Steve Chibnall and Robert
Murphy (eds), *British Crime Cinema* (London and New
York: Routledge, 1999).

Hedling, Erik, *Lindsay Anderson: Maverick Film-maker* (London:
Cassell, 1998).

Higson, Andrew, 'Space, Place, Spectacle: Landscape and
Townscape in the "Kitchen Sink" Film', originally published in *Screen* vol. 25 nos 4–5, July–October 1984,
reprinted in Andrew Higson (ed.), *Dissolving Views: Key
Writings on British Cinema* (London: Cassell, 1996).

Hill, John, *Sex, Class and Realism: British Cinema, 1956–1963*
(London: BFI, 1986).

Hutchings, Peter, '"We're the Martians Now": British SF
Invasion Fantasies of the 1950s and 1960s', in I. Q. Hunter
(ed.), *British Science-Fiction Cinema* (London and New York:
Routledge, 1999).

Lovell, Alan and Hillier, Jim, *Studies in Documentary* (London:
Secker & Warburg, 1972).

Lovell, Terry, 'Landscapes and Stories in 1960s British
Realism', in Andrew Higson (ed.), *Dissolving Views: Key
Writings on British Cinema* (London: Cassell, 1996).

Perkins, V. F., 'The British Cinema', *Movie* no. 1, 1962.

Sinyard, Neil, *Jack Clayton* (Manchester: Manchester
University Press, 2000).

34

Women and 60s British Cinema: The Development of the 'Darling' Girl

CHRISTINE GERAGHTY

Adolescents are the litmus paper of our society.
The Albermarle Report on the Youth Service, 1960[1]

This chapter is concerned with the changing position of women in 60s British cinema and in particular focuses on three films whose heroines I take to be emblematic of the changes that I am discussing – *A Taste of Honey*, *Darling* and *Here We Go round the Mulberry Bush*. But I want to place questions of narrative and representation in these films in the specific social context of British society during this period and, in particular, to look at the way in which the discourses around the sexuality of young women which were constructed and reworked in the cinema can be placed within the context of educational and moral arguments about youth and sexual behaviour that are associated with the 60s.

Understanding Teenagers

The problems posed by youth in the post-war period can be traced in the official reports which sought to provide social and legal ways of examining what was needed and providing a remedy.[2] Those working with young people – teachers, youth workers, probation officers, social workers, psychologists, psychiatrists, magistrates – began to claim a professional expertise which placed emphasis on supporting and protecting young people in their engagement with the modern world.[3] In the literature which served these professionals and, in particular, in the paperback sociology books which were aimed at them and at the interested lay reader, we can see discourses developing in which youth could be explained and understood as a species

marked off by surveys and services as being different from the adult world. Much of this work in the 50s focused on working-class young men and what was seen as their anti-social and sometimes violent behaviour. Insofar as young women entered the picture, it was as adjuncts who attached themselves to such youths; and while there was concern about their sexuality, there was also the feeling that young women could, through their desire for home and family, be part of the process of settling their boyfriends down. In his study of delinquents, *The Insecure Offenders*, T. R. Fyvel reported that the Teddy girl retained 'the basic feminine ideal of a normal home life', and commented that 'even the wildest Teddy boy . . . arrives at the point where traditional morality reasserts itself usually at the point of a shotgun'.[4]

In the late 50s/early 60s, however, the debate shifted from delinquency to premarital sex and the figure of the young woman came into greater prominence.[5] Sociologists such as Michael Schofield began to argue for a greater sympathy for young people's position; premarital sexual activity, he suggested in his 1965 study, *The Sexual Behaviour of Young People*, was not 'a minority problem confined to a few deviates. It is an activity common enough to be seen as one manifestation of teenage conformity.'[6] Schofield found that girls were more likely to associate sex with romance and love and to accept that, given the double standards applied by the boys, they had to be more circumspect than boys. Nevertheless, the survey also suggests some rather less conventional attitudes to sexual activity among the girls. Although sexual activity had traditionally been associated with working-class deviancy, Schofield reports a higher level of sexual activity among middle-class girls who 'were prepared to allow more sexual intimacies as long as these stop short of sexual intercourse'.[7] While such findings reflect the lack of access to contraception, which Schofield also reports, they may also reveal young women taking a degree of control over sexual behaviour which chimes with Schofield's comments that sexually experienced girls were strongly associated with 'a desire for freedom and independence'.[8]

It is not surprising that debates about youth can be found in films of the period since the cinema as an industry had much at stake in youth and its pleasures. Changing leisure patterns, including the arrival of television, meant that increasingly distributors and exhibitors relied on young people for their audiences. One of the attractions of cinemagoing for young people was its connection with dating and sexual behaviour. Fyvel, accompanying Teddy boys to the pictures, commented that 'the cinema is sex-dominated, the sanctioned place to take one's girl to, with sex on the screen and a good deal of it in the auditorium too'.[9] More generally, Schofield reported that 51 per cent of his sample went to the cinema on their first date and found that the cinema provided 'one of the few semi-private places a boy and a girl can go to make love'.[10] Thus filmgoing had a particular role in young people's social lives and, while the films of the 60s shared and indeed helped to shape the concepts of youth which are characteristic of the social and political discourses of the time, cinema's specificity in relation to young people's leisure activities means that the films could take a different attitude to the youth phenomenon from that of either sociological and educational treatises or the tabloid press. In addition, cinema's role in dating and sexual activity suggests a more distracted mode of viewing than that proposed by theories of 'the gaze' which have dominated much textual analysis in film study; this interrupted, 'back-row' viewing might be expected to privilege the impact of image and star rather than the logic of narrative in creating meaning.

The three films I have chosen to discuss allow us to trace some of the shifts in the representation of women in 60s films and to see how the social and moral issues which clustered round young women were reworked in the cinema. In each case I will look at the way in which certain thematic issues – the family, sexual behaviour, generational differences – are handled and suggest that in these films narrative and image may work against each other at crucial points to provide a contradictory account in which pleasures can be found in the image which the narratives try to deny.

Rita Tushingham – New Wave Woman

A Taste of Honey (Tony Richardson, 1961) belongs to the 'New Wave' of British film-making which characteristically drew on Northern settings, working-class mores and young, aggressive heroes. Films like *Saturday Night and Sunday Morning* (Karel Reisz, 1960) and *A Kind of Loving* (John Schlesinger, 1962) seem to mark a shift in attitude to young people compared with earlier films such as *The Blue Lamp* (Basil Dearden, 1950) or *The Scamp* (Wolf Rilla, 1957). While they could be critical of their youthful protagonists, the 'New Wave' films suggested that problems with their behaviour lay with society rather than in the innate delinquency of youth or the failure of their individual families. *A Taste of Honey* differed, however, by centring its narrative on a young woman, Jo, played by Rita Tushingham, a change which skews some of the characteristic themes of the 'New Wave' – consumerism, sexual energy, generational differences – and gives them a somewhat different purchase.

The narrative of *A Taste of Honey* deals with Jo's dissatisfaction with the family life created by her mother, Helen, and her unsuccessful struggle to escape from it. From the beginning, the film emphasises her mother's inadequacies as the pair do a moonlight flit to escape unpaid rent and set up a new home in impoverished and run-down rooms. Helen's fecklessness extends to her sexual activities, and her choice of Peter as a husband – based on sexual need rather than his suitability for a paternal role within the family – is used to underline her careless attitude to Jo. Helen, as Terry Lovell has pointed out, exists 'on the margins of working-class culture and community', but her pleasure in sex is firmly linked to working-class culture and Jo is excluded from both.[11] A trip to Blackpool ends with Jo being sent home alone and Helen's vivacious excitement in the pub and the dance hall is contrasted with Jo's haunting of the wastelands and canals. The effect of this elision is to associate Jo's dissatisfaction with her family with a rejection of working-class culture and the film thus links her efforts to move out of the family with an attempt to make for herself a kind of 'youth culture' in which she can literally feel at home. *A Taste of Honey* marks an early attempt at the creation of a proto-family in which support is given, often by members of the same generation, in a less restrictive but more careful way than that given by the family. Jo meets Jeff, whose youth credentials are established by an interest in art and style, and the two set up home together. Their attempt to decorate the loft/flat which they share is markedly different from Helen's careless muddle; it indicates the way in which Jo and Jeff strive to create a space in which a different form of family can emerge, one which provides emotional support but is a move away from the messy clutter of Helen's attempts at domestic comfort.

Jo's move away from home is precipitated by her sexual encounter with the black sailor Jimmy, but this occurs after she is rejected by Helen on the Blackpool trip and returns to Manchester, lonely and angry. Thus Jo's entry into sexuality is associated not with a move into adult desires but with a childlike need for help; the association with innocence and loss is underlined by the children's songs which accompany Jo and Jimmy as they walk along together and the long leave-taking scene in which Jo watches the deserted boat depart through the empty industrial landscape of the canal. Later in the film, Jo's pregnancy and Jeff's homosexuality serve narratively to prevent Jo's sexuality from being further explored and the contrast between this chasteness and her mother's lack of sexual control is a motif throughout the film.[12]

This childlike quality is reflected in Tushingham's appearance, a marked contrast to the mature women stars of 50s films such as Diana Dors and Virginia McKenna. Tushingham's Jo is a schoolgirl at the beginning of the film and never loses her childish features – thin body, big eyes, wide cheekbones, gawky stance. Jo is presented as being unconventional and quirky; she tells the truth at awkward moments, acts on impulse and is quick to express her feelings even when this might hurt others. Thus youth is associated with a transparency of purpose, a refusal to compromise or pretend. These traits which mark Jo as a character are consonant with the image of Rita Tushingham as a new kind of female star; interviewers commented approvingly on her 'wide-eyed appeal' and the natural way in which she pulls 'the sort of apprehensive face a schoolgirl might if she were caught doing something bad'.[13]

A Taste of Honey ends with Helen reclaiming Jo, the break-up of the 'youth family' and the denial of Jo's possibilities for freedom. This punishing closure suggests that Jo has lost, is trapped in 'a resigned acknowledgment of things as they are'.[14] But to place too much emphasis on their endings is to miss what these films

offered young audiences. For while the end of *A Taste of Honey* returns Jo to the situation she has fled, the combination of character and star has suggested other routes. The 'problem' of the teenage pregnancy is dealt with by the narrative, but codes of characterisation and stardom suggest other possibilities for a young audience. The emphasis throughout the film on Jo/Tushingham's unconventionality, her truthfulness and her desire for different kinds of relationships survives the film's ending. With *A Taste of Honey*, we can begin to see the emergence of a specific discourse around young women which was highly significant for 60s British cinema.

Middle-class Girls

As debates on the sexual behaviour of young people took centre-stage in the discussion of youth, the role of young women became critical. What begins to emerge from studies such as Schofield's is the figure of the middle-class, educated teenage girl who has a measure of control over her own pleasure and behaviour. Schofield's research suggested that 'it does appear that the higher up a girl is on the social scale, the more sexual experience she is likely to have'.[15] Whether this was actually the case is less important for our purposes than the change in image. The delinquent girl who can be led astray – a common figure in 50s films such as *Cosh Boy* (Lewis Gilbert, 1953) and *I Believe in You* (Basil Dearden, 1952) – becomes in these studies someone who calculates how far she can or wants to go and is more sexually active than many of the working-class boys who had formed the vanguard of youth culture up to this point.

The early 60s thus sees the creation of a set of sociological discourses which suggest that young women might be more powerful and more confident than before. Two further factors are important. First, like the working-class youth of the 50s, the 60s girl was placed firmly within the context of consumption. She was a figure around whom the wheels of marketing were spinning and liberal commentators worried about how far a desire to conform lay behind her purchases, making her prey to the designs of big business and the media. Nevertheless, in some senses the attempts of advertising, magazines and television to appeal to the young woman reinforced the impression that she was exercising choices which she could wilfully withdraw. The second factor was the Profumo affair, which had at its heart the capacity of a young woman of dubious morals to bring down a government minister. The Denning Report of 1963, which was widely read and

publicised in the popular press, painted a picture of
Christine Keeler's *demi-monde* in which she swam naked
in the swimming pool of an aristocrat, casually picked
up a Cabinet minister and was fought over by 'coloured'
lovers. The Profumo affair associated young women
with sexual power, exemplified in the ability of a girl to
destroy a man's career and the insouciance of Mandy
Rice-Davies's casual put-down when confronted with
denial: 'Well, he would say that, wouldn't he?'

Julie Christie's *Darling*

The characterisation of the young woman in *Darling*
(John Schlesinger, 1965) takes on some of this flavour as
it pushes much further representations which *A Taste of
Honey* only suggests. In *Darling*, the shift from the
North to London, from the working class to the middle
class, means that different possibilities come into play.
The family, which had been such a key point of rebellion for the 'New Wave', hardly features for the film's
protagonist, Diana (Julie Christie); a middle-class convent childhood is sketched in, as is her relationship with
her sister, but since the film treats Diana as an enigma
her family cannot be pinned down as the source of the
problem she poses.

Sometimes it's hard to be a woman: Julie Christie in *Darling*
(John Schlesinger, 1965)

Nevertheless, Diana cannot ignore the family, and
much of the film's narrative traces her failure to establish her own family. She cannot build a successful relationship with Robert or Miles and her abortion
destroys the possibility of a 'normal' family life. Her
proto-family relationship with the gay Malcolm (like
that of Jo and Jeff in *A Taste of Honey*) has possibilities of
friendship, fun and style, free of heterosexual complications, but the fantasy of living together in Capri is
destroyed by Diana's competitiveness. The family she
adopts through her marriage to the Italian prince is
dominated by conventions and rules to which she
cannot conform. Thus a narrative pattern like that of *A
Taste of Honey* is set up in which a search for a different
form of family is an important mainspring of the plot
but one which is doomed to fail.

Darling, however, differs markedly from the earlier
film in its representation and organisation of female
sexuality. Here, sexuality is associated with power rather
than innocence and Diana is presented as using her
desirability as a means of control. The film inextricably
links female sexual desire with the desire for power and
thus makes it impossible to untangle the two, to judge,
for instance, whether Diana is pursuing her own sexual
interests when she seduces Miles or furthering her
career. There are strong links to the Profumo case in the
notion that male desire for young women is linked to
the dubious and worn-out politics of the establishment
figures whom Diana meets on her way to the top.
Diana (like Keeler) mixes in the cross-over world
between politics, business and showbiz; the orgies,
masks and sexual games which Diana is drawn into by
Miles have the seedy flavour of the 'rumours' investigated in the Denning Report.[16] Rather more pro-
saically, Diana's sexual confidence in the first part of the
film recalls Schofield's findings about middle-class girls
who were sexually experienced but who seemed to
control the stages of sexual activity which they were
prepared to participate in. Described in male terms,
Diana is both powerful and a tease, a combination
which, as both Carrie Tarr and John Hill indicate, is
punished by the ending when, rejected and abused by
Robert, Diana is dispatched back to Italy.[17] From a
female viewpoint, though, the presentation of Diana's
sexuality may suggest that pleasure on one's own terms
is imaginable if not narratively possible.

The question of where this female viewpoint might
or might not be found is central to Tarr's discussion of
the film. Certainly it is hard to find in Diana's voice-
over, which is consistently undermined by the images

and serves to present her as hypocritical and self-pitying. In addition, as Tarr indicates, the identification of Diana with the media world to which she aspires means that the film's critique of that world turns into a critique of its heroine. The critical attitude of the film to its heroine was echoed by the contemporary quality press critics, allowing little space for pleasure to be taken in the representation of the young woman. Yet the impact of Julie Christie in the role was enormous. Sarah Maitland, looking back on the 60s, speaks for many, I suspect, when she refers to Julie Christie as 'the symbol of all my yearning adolescent hopes'.[18] Christie herself, musing on the character she played, recalls that 'She was extraordinary. . . . Here was a woman who didn't want to get married, didn't want to have children like those other kitchen-sink heroines; no, Darling wanted to have everything.'[19]

As with *A Taste of Honey*, the possibilities for interpretations which work against rather than with the ending are to be found in the characterisation and star image rather than the working out of the plot. Two key factors are important here – the use of fashion and the establishment of Christie's star persona outside the film. The narrative of *Darling* makes much of Diana being trapped in the artificial world of modelling but the way in which Diana/Christie is dressed speaks of a self-confidence based on but not limited to a new approach to fashion and style. Her clothes mix the mod (tartan skirt, knee-length socks, hairbands) with the traditional (her evening dress at the charity function). Both styles are worn with an individual flourish, and the emphasis in her dress is not so much on following a 60s style but creating it, controlling fashion rather than conforming to it. This sense of creativity and control potentially has the effect of assuring young women that, while sociologists might be worried about a tendency to conformity among the young, fashion can be remade to express your own personality. Christie's clothes, while marked as those of a star, would also have been available through boutiques and dressmaking patterns to young women in the audience and the emphasis on accessories – headscarves, velvet bows, handbags – made it easy to adapt styles to the individual. This emphasis on individuality and personal freedom is reinforced by Christie's star image, which built on her appearance in *Billy Liar* (John Schlesinger, 1963) and emphasised her impulsiveness, her lack of calculation, her overwhelming desire for freedom. Like Tushingham, Christie is approachable, 'friendly but honest', and she has 'real friends' who are not in showbusiness; her middle-class origins (she was

born in India) are disguised by her then 'rather nomadic' existence – 'I just dossed down in the flats of my friends.'[20]

Some of these traits can be found in Diana – the car ride round Trafalgar Square or the impulsive trip to Fortnum's – but in the main it is precisely the clash between Christie's star image and the characterisation of Diana as manipulative and cold which is significant. Kenneth Tynan remarked that Christie was 'temperamentally miscast. . . . Her niceness is blazingly evident.'[21] In this disjunction, femininity itself becomes a performance, something which is ironically played on. While Diana's voice-over reveals her to be self-pitying and deluded and the narrative tells us that she is confused and greedy, we actually see something rather different. Take, for example, the scene in which Diana and Miles enter his empty office: the changes in the register of her voice as she teases Miles, the transformation of the board table into a catwalk, the faux-naïf admiration of the 'Glass millions' refer us to the character's ambition but the star's naturalness and integrity transform this into a display of femininity which she controls even in the seat of big business. Thus, Christie's image and performance call the narrative into question by suggesting that feminine discourses of beauty and fashion are not the property of the establishment but a way of claiming a feminine identity which can be used as a mode of self-expression, particularly around sexuality.

From Star to Simulacrum – Judy Geeson

Christie thus added sexual power and confidence to the honesty and unpredictability of Tushingham and created a figure which was to be carried through in British cinema into the late 60s. But the difficulty in maintaining the possibilities of identification for young women can be seen in the rapidity with which it turned into a stereotype of what Robert Murphy identified as the late-60s figure of 'a spontaneous, vulnerable, sexually willing young woman'.[22] When the gap between star and narrative, voice-over and image is removed, there is less space for a female viewpoint and it was difficult for this figure to avoid becoming a male fantasy of sexual availability rather than a female fantasy of control. An examination of a later film, *Here We Go round the Mulberry Bush*, may show how this happened.

Here We Go round the Mulberry Bush (Clive Donner, 1968) gives the narrative voice to a teenage boy, Jamie

(Barry Evans), whose viewpoint and voice-over underpin the film. The story is a picaresque tale of pursuit that follows Jamie's clumsy efforts to lose his virginity. Thus, unlike *A Taste of Honey* and *Darling*, the film lacks a female narrative viewpoint and the story is reminiscent of the 'New Wave' narratives of male desire, although its tone and 'new town' setting are markedly different. The tone is now humorous and the girls wield power not by their conformity to the traditionally feminine aspirations of marriage and a home, but by their control over sexual behaviour. In addition, *Here We Go round the Mulberry Bush* has none of the artistic or aesthetic aspirations which mark the other two films and instead generically attempts to combine the traditional humour of a British sex comedy with the psychedelic trendiness of a 'youth' film. Here, the youth audience is being appealed to directly without the explanatory tone for an adult audience found in the earlier films.

Mary, the key female figure in *Here We Go round the Mulberry Bush*, shares many of the qualities of Diana. Her family (whom we never see) is comfortably middle class; she lives on a better part of the estate, a Jag is casually tucked into the garage, and she is comfortable in the social world of the well-to-do at the sailing club. But her manners and behaviour are classless in that, while she mixes with the crowd, she has her own unpredictable criteria for action and openly pursues her own pleasures without thought for conventional morality. Like Diana, however, she is narratively punished by being rejected by Jamie and condemned, through failing her A-levels, not to go to university. Like Diana, also, she uses fashion and style as a means of attraction and control, and the film's lighting and close-ups emphasise the similarities between Julie Christie and Judy Geeson with their blonde tousled hair, wide cheekbones and disarming smiles. This similarity

'That's the kind of girl I'd like to marry': Barry Evans ogles Judy Geeson and Diane Keen in *Here We Go round the Mulberry Bush* (Clive Donner, 1968)

means, however, that Geeson's star image cannot be authentic; she apes Christie and by doing so calls attention to her lack of the very naturalness on which Christie's star image is based.

The central joke of *Here We Go round the Mulberry Bush* is the reversal of conventional gender expectations of earlier films, the contrast between Jamie's innocence and the sexual experience of the girls who surround him. 'What are young girls coming to these days?' he muses as Mary strips off in front of him for an impromptu swim in the lake. While Jamie is bemused, Audrey, Caroline and even the church-going Paula treat sexual activity in an entirely practical fashion, something to be seized as the opportunity presents itself but not to get worked up about. It is Jamie who learns the narrative lesson of the film, that promiscuity is 'a drag' and that marriage may have something going for it after all.

The film's attitude to sexuality is split between a matter-of-fact acceptance of teenage behaviour and the lessons to be drawn from the moral journey made by its young hero. The relentlessly male viewpoint means that, while the audience is offered a position which is, in certain respects, critical of Jamie, no access can be given to the internal life of the girls he tries to get into bed. The importance of this is seen in the treatment of Mary at the end. Geeson's lack of a star image means that she can be defined through narrative in a way that Christie could not and the ending can thus dispatch her more effectively. Jamie's problem with Mary is not so much her behaviour as her frankness, the way she speaks; she makes dates with other men in front of him and refuses to be conventionally romantic about their love-making: 'I can do what I like and you can do what you like. Remember we made a bargain. . . . You can go with someone else and I wouldn't mind.' Jamie is shocked – 'That's the worst thing I've ever heard you say' – and he finishes the relationship. This rejection of Mary's frank speech is reinforced by the images with which the film ends. Jamie watches, but does not overhear, Mary talking to her friend Claire. Claire walks away in long shot so that, with Jamie, we can assess her legs, but turns to exchange glances in a close-up of her speechless, smiling face as he ponders, 'That's the kind of girl I'd like to marry.'

Despite this ending, it was the figure of Mary – like that of Jo and Diana earlier – which dominated 60s British cinema. This representation of an unpredictable, spontaneous, emotionally honest, sexually active young woman shows how cinema worked within the broader social context in its attempt to reflect contemporary attitudes to what was seen as a 60s phenomenon. But the figure of the young woman was particularly important to British cinema in this period because it fed two specifically cinematic purposes. First, it continued the trend set by 'New Wave' films such as *Saturday Night and Sunday Morning* which established British cinema as being both contemporary and shocking; this was a cinema 'for adults' in which the sexual promise of the 'X' certificate could be justified by the social examination of the young woman as a contemporary phenomenon. Second, the figure of the young woman allowed British cinema to appeal to one of its key audiences – the youth market – by offering an entertainment which, like music and fashion, marked young people as a different species. It was common for sociologists in the late 50s and 60s to see the cinema as one of the sites where a commercial 'youth subculture' was being created which had an undue influence on teenage behaviour. But the influence was not all one-way and the discourses of female sexuality in 60s film need to be understood in the context of changing behaviour and attitudes to which British cinema, with its commercial need for young audiences, had to speak. Thus while the films' narratives, as we have seen, typically punish sexual activity, the codes of stardom developed in the 60s associated female sexuality with honesty, independence and freedom and could suggest, to young audiences at least, that young women were not 'the problem' but offered possibilities for a solution.

Notes

1. Report of the Committee on the Youth Services in England and Wales (the Albermarle report), quoted in Michael Schofield, *The Sexual Behaviour of Young People*, p. 25.

2. Examples include: in 1959, the Report on the Central Advisory Council for Education in England (the Crowther report), which looked at the educational provision (or the lack of it) for fifteen- to eighteen-year-olds; in 1960, the Report of the Committee on the Youth Services in England and Wales (the Albermarle report) and the Report of the Committee on Children and Young Persons (the Ingleby report); and in 1963, *Half Our Future* (the Newsom report), looking at the education of thirteen- to sixteen-year-olds of average or less than average ability.

3. T. R. Fyvel, for instance, called for 'educational reform . . . to keep the country's adolescents right out of the racket of the commercial youth market' (*The Insecure Offenders*, p. 318), and the National Union of Teachers saw the need

for educators to encourage young people and those involved with them 'to recognise the need for discrimination in accepting the offerings of the mass media'. Denys Thompson (ed.), *Discrimination and Popular Culture*, p. 7.

4. Fyvel, *The Insecure Offenders*, pp. 136–7.
5. Jeffrey Weeks in *Sex, Politics and Society* comments that by the end of the 50s 'pre-marital sex was the subject of anxious debate' (p. 238), and that 'sexuality of youth . . . provoked the fiercest debates in the 60s and 70s' (p. 254).
6. Schofield, *The Sexual Behaviour of Young People*, p. 224.
7. Ibid., p. 55.
8. Ibid., p. 233.
9. Fyvel, *The Insecure Offenders*, p. 107.
10. Schofield, *The Sexual Behaviour of Young People*, p. 57; p. 143.
11. Terry Lovell, 'Landscapes and Stories in 1960s British Realism', p. 374.
12. Lovell (ibid.) gives a detailed account of the film in the context of the British 'New Wave' and emphasises, in her reading, the relationship between Jo and her mother.
13. *Daily Express*, 7 September 1961; *News of the World*, 7 October 1962.
14. John Hill, *Sex, Class and Realism: British Cinema 1956–63*, p. 167.
15. Schofield, *The Sexual Behaviour of Young People*, p. 117.
16. Lord Denning's 1963 report (London: HMSO) includes a chapter on 'Rumours Arising out of the Profumo Affair' and sub-sections on 'The "Darling" Letter' and ' "The Man in the Mask" ' who was one of the attractions at 'parties in private of a perverted nature' (p. 108).
17. Carrie Tarr, 'Sapphire, Darling and the Boundaries of Permitted Pleasure'; Hill, *Sex, Class and Realism*.
18. ' "I Believe in Yesterday" – An Introduction', in Sarah Maitland, *Very Heaven: Looking Back at the 1960s*, p. 4.
19. 'Everybody's Darling: An Interview with Julie Christie', in Maitland, *Very Heaven*, p. 171.
20. *Daily Mail*, 15 September 1965; *Sunday Express*, 18 July 1965.
21. *Observer*, 19 September 1965.
22. Robert Murphy, *Sixties British Cinema*, p. 154.

Bibliography
Fyvel, T. R., *The Insecure Offenders* (London: Chatto & Windus, 1961).

HM Government, Report on the Central Advisory Council for Education in England (the Crowther report) (London: HMSO, 1959).

HM Government, Report of the Committee on Children and Young Persons (the Ingleby report) (London: HMSO, 1960).

HM Government, Report of the Committee on the Youth Services in England and Wales (the Albemarle report) (London: HMSO, 1960).

HM Government, *Half Our Future* (the Newsom report) (London: HMSO, 1963).

HM Government, *Lord Denning's Report* (London: HMSO, 1963).

Hill, John, *Sex, Class and Realism: British Cinema 1956–63* (London: BFI, 1986).

Lovell, Terry, 'Landscapes and Stories in 1960s British Realism', *Screen* vol. 31 no. 4, Winter 1990.

Maitland, Sarah, *Very Heaven: Looking Back at the 1960s* (London: Virago, 1988).

Murphy, Robert, *Sixties British Cinema* (London: BFI, 1992).

Schofield, Michael, *The Sexual Behaviour of Young People* (Harmondsworth: Penguin, 1968).

Tarr, Carrie, 'Sapphire, Darling and the Boundaries of Permitted Pleasure', *Screen* vol. 26 no. 1, 1985.

Thompson, Denys (ed.), *Discrimination and Popular Culture* (Harmondsworth: Penguin, 1964).

Weeks, Jeffrey, *Sex, Politics and Society* (London: Longman, 1989).

35
Strange Days: British Cinema in the Late 1960s

ROBERT MURPHY

'Swinging London' films, though they were popular with audiences, have had a hard time with the critics. The social revolution that occurred in the 60s still rankles with conservatives, while film critics complain of the degeneration of film style and the drift into fantasy. Penelope Houston, summing up the decade, apocalyptically pronounced that British cinema 'has suggested another jaded party, dragging exhaustedly on into the night in its bedraggled fancy dress surrounded by its odds and ends of boutique bric-a-brac, and deaf to the ambulance sirens coming louder up the street'.[1] And Jeffrey Richards sees Swinging London as an increasingly frenzied saturnalia in which:

> Sober realism and earnest social comment gave way to fantasy, extravaganza and escapism; black-and-white photography and Northern locations to colour and the lure of the metropolis; Puritanical self-discipline to hedonistic self-indulgence; plain truthful settings to flamboyant, unrealistic decorativeness. Films became locked in a heady spiral of mounting extravagance, febrile excitement and faddish innovation.[2]

But the idea that most films between 1965 and 1970 promoted a mindlessly optimistic view of the world is more of a myth than the myth the films are assumed to convey. The *Time* magazine cover story that told the world about 'Swinging London' is breathlessly silly ('. . . The guards now change at Buckingham Palace to a Lennon and McCartney tune, and Prince Charles is firmly in the long-hair set') and the reaction against the 'permissiveness' of the 60s has obstructed any fair

reassessment.[3] Yet London in the 60s was at least as much a beacon of cultural creativity as Hemingway's post-World War I Paris, Isherwood's pre-Hitler Berlin, or Revolutionary Russia before Stalin stepped in to stop the fun and games. Ironically, in view of the importance attached to the 'ideological superstructure' rather than the 'economic base' by fashionable New Marxism, these cultural achievements were to fade away like Shangri-La as the economic climate worsened. But for a time it seemed that the cultural industries thriving in 60s London – music, fashion, film – showed the way forward for Britain as it shuffled off its Empire and closed down its industrial heartlands.

Revivalist radio stations ensure that much 60s music is still in circulation and the fashion innovations of Mary Quant and Barbara Hulanicki are constantly recycled. But post-New Wave cinema is still derided and neglected, at best the subject of outrageous parody in the Austin Powers films. The last few years of black-and-white cinema, between 1964 and 1966 (by 1967 the form was to all intents and purposes dead) represented a creative flowering as important, and as underestimated as that of the last years of British silent cinema.[4] Serious examinations of the bizarrer reaches of bourgeoise life like Jack Clayton's *The Pumpkin Eater* (1964) and Joseph Losey's *The Servant* (1963) rub shoulders with the first intimations of 'Swinging London' in *The World Ten Times Over* (1963), *Darling* (1965) and *The Knack* (1965), and grim dramas like Sidney Lumet's *The Hill* (1965). When colour did become the norm, fantasies like *The Bliss of Mrs Blossom* (Joe McGrath, 1968) and *Work Is a Four Letter Word* (Peter Hall, 1968) struggled to compete with the revived realism of

Joanna (Mike Sarne, 1968)

Joanna has all the essential ingredients for a 'Swinging London' film and mixes them well. *Darling*'s Diana Scott has to go to Paris to experience true decadence and ends up marooned in an Italian palazzo. Joanna (Geneviève Waïte) has an interlude in Morocco, but she finds quite enough hedonistic thrills to keep her busy in London. The sprawling story and Geneviève Waïte's flat, little-girl voice are sometimes irritating but the film's integrity, vitality and stylishness make it one of the best films of the late 60s and the only one to capture the excitement and glamour of life in London.

Joanna might be a spoilt rich girl, but like the heroine of an eighteenth-century picaresque novel, her antics are viewed with affectionate good humour. She's warm and sexy and doesn't make a fuss; open without being naive, irresponsible but not stupid, caring but unsentimental. She's careless of the feelings of others – her long-suffering granny, her lecturers, the wives of men she sleeps with – but there's no intent to harm. Sarne obviously like her and doesn't try to patronise her or put her down. Cass (Christian Doermer) her German art-school tutor complains about her unwillingness to commit herself to anything, and Donald Sutherland's terminally ill aristocrat worries about her inability to look after herself; but she's tough enough to complete her odyssey.

Sarne, then a pop singer best known for the gimmick song 'Come Outside', doesn't have much credit in his cultural bank account, but he knows what he is doing here and offers us a view of the Swinging London scene refreshingly free from prurience. He is helped enormously by Walter Lassally's cinematography, which uses colour as creatively as he had used black-and-white in Tony Richardson's *A Taste of Honey* (1961) and *The Loneliness of the Long Distance Runner* (1962) to bring a poetic lyricism to the film.

Cass tells Joanna she'll become a worthless flibbertigibbet unless she commits herself to something or someone. The man she does commit herself to, a black nightclub owner (Calvin Lockhart), is implicated in gang warfare and sentenced to ten years for

Glenna Forster-Jones and Geneviève Waïte in *Joanna*

murder, so the film is hardly a vision of unclouded happiness, but its brightness and vitality makes it endearing. There are disconcerting shifts in style – the Morocco episode built around Sutherland's ludicrously foppish Lord Peter Sanderson; the Brechtian ending with cast and crew lining up to say goodbye to Joanna as she boards a train back to her stockbroker-belt suburban home – but to condemn 60s films for their sometimes ill-advised experimentation is to miss the point. This is not a cinema concerned with classical perfection.

NOTES

Lassally saw the film 'despite its many faults as a better mirror of the 'Swinging Sixties' than such films as *Smashing Time* (1967) or *Here We Go round the Mulberry Bush* (1968). He points out that 'Mike was closer to the core of that society than the directors of those films were, and this more than made up for his lack of directorial experience.' *Itinerant Cameraman* (London: John Murray, 1987), p. 111.

Poor Cow (Ken Loach, 1967), *The Long Day's Dying* (Peter Collinson, 1968) and *The Reckoning* (Jack Gold, 1969).

Did They Have Kitchen Sinks in Swinging London?

The problem for Jeffrey Richards is that the Swinging London films seemed to betray the promise of an artistically ambitious, socially serious cinema held out by the New Wave films of the early 1960s. Forty years on the gap seems less wide. The main body of Kitchen Sink films had concentrated on the joys and terrors of being young and adventurous and imprisoned in the lower depths of British society. Though the films can hardly be called optimistic, their talented young casts – Laurence Harvey, Albert Finney, Rita Tushingham, Rachel Roberts, Tom Courtenay, Alan Bates, June Ritchie, Julie Christie, Leslie Caron, Tom Bell, Richard Harris – bring an energy and enthusiasm which prevents them from lapsing into depressing naturalism. They are essentially – and here one can include the more gloomy *Term of Trial*, *The L-Shaped Room* and *This Sporting Life* – romantic.

There was certainly a realist input into the New British Cinema of the early 60s – the use of location shooting, of naturalistic dialogue, of unfamiliar young actors, the depiction of areas of society hardly seen before in the cinema (the working class, the Northern industrial landscape), and there is a frankness about sex hitherto unknown in British cinema. Despite the accusations of lapses into fantasy, these sorts of elements characterise many of the 'Swinging London' films too, and they can be seen as valid attempts to grasp the shifting realities of mid-60s Britain.

The first crop of what are now thought of as 'Swinging London' films – *Nothing But the Best*, *A Hard Day's Night*, *The Knack*, *Catch Us If You Can*, *Darling*, *Morgan: A Suitable Case for Treatment*, *Georgy Girl* – are surprisingly closely associated in terms of actors, directors, production companies and even their thematic concerns, with the New British Cinema of the early 60s. *Nothing But the Best* (1964), made for Anglo-Amalgamated, the company responsible for *A Kind of Loving* and *Billy Liar*, is virtually a remake of *Room at the Top*, though director Clive Donner and scriptwriter Frederic Raphael have a much more sardonic and unsentimental attitude to their hero (played by Alan Bates) in his ruthless climb to the top. *A Hard Day's Night* (Richard Lester, 1964) was scripted by the young

television dramatist Alun Owen and has a refreshing realism compared to the gushy escapism of Tommy Steele and Cliff Richard musicals. *The Knack*, directed by Richard Lester, but starring Rita Tushingham and made in black-and-white for Tony Richardson's Woodfall company, has its earthy heroine reject the smooth charms of Tolen (Ray Brooks) in favour of old-fashioned romance with a shy and spotty schoolteacher played by Michael Crawford. *Darling* is no less realistic and socially relevant than Schlesinger's earlier films for being set in middle-class London. The last two black-and-white 'Swinging London' films, Reisz's *Morgan: A Suitable Case for Treatment* (1966) and Silvio Narizzano's *Georgy Girl* (1966), both centre on characters who are conspicuously out of place in a London obsessed with glamour and affluence. David Warner's shaggy, gangling Morgan, who loses his wife to an affluent art dealer, is a harbinger of the hippy counter-culture with his enthusiasm for gorillas and Leon Trotsky. In *Georgy Girl* Charlotte Rampling's Meredith, the epitome of Swinging London chic, is condemned for her amorality and our sympathies weighted in favour of Lynn Redgrave's unfashionably hefty Georgy, a girl whose warm-hearted enthusiasm makes up for her lack of glossy sex appeal. The London she inhabits doesn't seem to be swinging much more than that of *The L-Shaped Room* (Bryan Forbes, 1962).

Admittedly these early 'Swinging London' films do have fantasy sequences and use devices like direct address to camera, but one looks in vain for that 'disregard of form and structure, the visual extravagance, the devices used like purple phrases and exclamation marks in schoolgirl prose, the tourist fantasies of a colour-supplement Britain', complained of by the *Sight and Sound* critics.[5] It would be possible to argue though, that these films have a morning-of-the-world freshness about them which had not yet degenerated into cliché, and that the real 'Swinging London' films don't emerge until after April 1966 when *Time* magazine published 'London – the Swinging City' as its cover story. Ironically then, many of the later 'Swinging London' films – *Blow-Up*, *I'll Never Forget What's 'Is Name*, *Interlude*, *Twinky*, *Sebastian*, *The Strange Affair*, *Performance* – have an angst-ridden, almost elegiac quality about them. And they are interspersed with films that explore a London which isn't swinging – Battersea in *Up the Junction* and *Poor Cow*, Notting Hill in *Leo the Last* and *Otley*, Fitzrovia in *A Touch of Love*, Bloomsbury in *Praise Marx and Pass the Ammunition*, the South London suburbs in *Our Mother's House*. By the end of the decade there is no longer much sign of 'Swinging London' except in bad genre films like *Dracula AD 1972*. Realism returned with a vengeance encompassing the handheld vérité of Peter Collinson's *The Long Day's Dying*, the cynicism of André De Toth's *Play Dirty* (1968) and films like *Kes* (Ken Loach, 1969) and *The Reckoning* (Jack Gold) made by the new generation of television trained directors were marked by a socially conscious realism, harsher and bleaker than that aspired to by the 'Kitchen Sink' directors.[6]

Escape from the Kitchen Sink

None of the New wave directors was committed to making films based on working-class novels set in the North of England. Jack Clayton, whose film of John Braine's *Room at the Top* started the ball rolling, refused to take on what he considered similar topics (*Saturday Night and Sunday Morning, The L-Shaped Room, Term of Trial*) and followed up with *The Innocents* (1961), an atmospheric rendering of Henry James's *The Turn of the Screw*, and *The Pumpkin Eater*, a slim novel by Penelope Mortimer about a woman whose life falls apart when she's prevented from adding to her brood of children, given an edgy significance in Harold Pinter's screenplay and Clayton's subtly elaborate direction. His first colour film, *Our Mother's House* resolutely turns its back on 'Swinging London', using the unfashionable suburbs of South London as the setting for its strange story about children hiding the fact of their mother's death to avoid being taken into care. Superb performances from the children are not quite matched by Dirk Bogarde, returned to no-good spivvery but a little too nondescript to match the children's sharp intensity.

Clayton's stock has risen steadily since his death in 1995, though *The Pumpkin Eater* and *Our Mother's House* are still under-appreciated.[7] Karel Reisz was always treated with more respect than the other New Wave directors, and an obituary denigrating his British films brought a furious riposte from playwright and film-maker David Hare.[8] After *Saturday Night and Sunday Morning*, and a failed bid to make a film about Ned Kelly on location in Australia with Albert Finney as the legendary bushwhacker, Reisz accepted an offer from MGM to remake the melodrama *Night Must Fall* (filmed with Robert Montgomery and Rosalind Russell in 1937). Finney (who had achieved huge popularity in Tony Richardson's *Tom Jones*) relishes the opportunity to cast off his image as a lovable rogue and play a psychopath who keeps the head of one of his victims in a hatbox, but Reisz's first brush with madness

never quite finds the right pitch. Finney's monstrous creation, sexually disturbed and unsympathetically manipulative, is fascinating but unappealing and the voice of sanity and reason, Susan Hampshire's bored rich girl, makes an insipid adversary. Similar ingredients were played out more creatively and imaginatively in *Morgan*, adapted by David Mercer from his 1962 television play about a working-class writer whose existential crisis leads to mild schizophrenia and a break-up with his upper-middle-class wife (Vanessa Redgrave). Reisz was accused of stylistic gimmickry but the film resonates with sincerity and conviction. David Warner's Morgan appears endearingly outrageous rather than mad, his empathy with gorillas and gibbons a likeable reaction to society's obsession with affluence.

Vanessa Redgrave's feckless Leonie, riding through early-morning London in an open-topped sports car in *Morgan*, her silk scarf blowing in the wind (and around the head of driver Robert Stevens), is a quintessential image of Swinging London. In *Isadora* (1968) a similar image evokes tragedy. Redgrave as the American dancer Isadora Duncan who shocked pre-World War I audiences with her daringly sensual performances, drives off in pursuit of a handsome, mysterious man who has caught her eye, but the scarf gets caught in one of the car wheels and breaks her neck. Disillusion for Reisz, never an optimistic film-maker, set in early. The three-hour version of the film failed to attract big audiences and was deemed unacceptable by the distributors; the shortened version pleased no one. One might still prefer Ken Russell's brief, sharp *Isadora Duncan, the Biggest Dancer in the World* (1966), but forty years on it is easier to extend sympathy to Vanessa Redgrave's madly idealistic romantic, by turns infuriating and achingly vulnerable. If the film as a whole is unsatisfactory, some of the sequences – Duncan's love affair with Gordon Craig (James Fox), and her excursion to Soviet Russia in 1921 – are masterly demonstrations of how to encapsulate complex events into concise episodes.

John Schlesinger was the most orthodox and the least radical of the New Wave directors, but he was also the most sure-footed. *Darling* displayed with guarded disapproval the world of 'Swinging London' before it became a cliché. Though the film explores the affluence and promiscuity of the 1960s, Schlesinger and his scriptwriter Frederic Raphael remain cautiously critical, stressing the unhappiness and emptiness of this new permissive society. *Darling*'s success enabled Schlesinger to secure financial backing from MGM for a lavish adaptation of Thomas Hardy's *Far from the Madding*

Crowd (1967). Julie Christie has a narrower range than Redgrave (who now looks to be the key actress of the 60s) and her Bathsheba Everdene is rather too close to *Darling*'s Diana Scott – restless, wilful, never truly happy with her lot. But in Thomas Hardy's earthy, bucolic world (magically brought to life by Nicolas Roeg's lush cinematography) common sense in the end prevails and she's able to find happiness with solid reliable Gabriel Oak. In the early 90s, I complained that Julie Christie, Alan Bates and Terence Stamp were so closely associated with Swinging London that it is difficult to shake off the feeling that at any moment they might discard their funny voices and fancy dress and rush off to a fashionable nightclub.[9] As time passes they seem more closely integrated into Hardy's world (along with Peter Finch who always was). Bathsheba presiding over the harvest supper; Troy letting fate help him from doing his duty by arriving at the wrong church for his marriage to Fanny; Gabriel puncturing the distended stomachs of Bathsheba's sheep and deflating them like so many woolly balloons. *Far from the Madding Crowd* failed to repeat the commercial success of *Tom Jones*, Richardson's costume frolic, its slow pace and convoluted story proved too demanding, particularly to American audiences unfamiliar with Hardy, but it has better stood the test of time.

Lindsay Anderson's two feature films would seem to exemplify the split between early and late 60s British cinema. *This Sporting Life* is the last major New Wave film, black-and-white, serious, set in the North of England and centred on working-class characters. *If . . . .* (1968), in colour (though arbitrarily lapsing into black-and-white), intertwining fantasy, wish-fulfilment and surrealism (the housemaster's wife wandering naked through the dormitory, the supposedly dead chaplain turning up alive in a drawer), and set among the privileged pupils of an English public school. But *This Sporting Life* had already stretched realism to its limits with its convoluted flashback structure and lurches towards abstraction (as in the almost hallucinatory outing to the countryside, made all the more eerie by Roberto Gerhard's music); and *If . . . .* achieves much of its impact from the keenly observed depiction of public-school rituals, and is as savage and relentless as *This Sporting Life* in its social criticism.[10]

If . . . . turned out to be the first part of a trilogy: *O Lucky Man!* following in 1973, *Britannia Hospital* in 1982, bearing out Anderson's claim that *If . . . .* was less about the English public-school system than about the state of Britain. What the public-school setting does for

If . . . . is give it a sense of structure (which proved more elusive in the two subsequent films). The ethos of *If . . . .* might be the opposite to that of earlier public-school films like *Goodbye Mr Chips* (1939), *The Guinea Pig* (1948) and *Tom Brown's Schooldays* (1951), sharing a viewpoint closer to that of Jean Vigo's anarchic *Zéro de conduite* (1933). But along with the extensive literary tradition, they provide conventions, themes and characters (the initiation of the new boy into the rituals of the school, the continual testing of authority, the rivalries, bullying and conflict between the individual and the group) that provide Anderson and his young writers David Sherwin and John Howlett with a framework.[11]

Two feature films in a decade seems a meagre output for an ambitious young film-maker, but there is little argument now that both films are of lasting significance and that Anderson, for all the disappointments of his later career, is a talented auteur.[12] Tony Richardson was much more prolific, but critical opinion is less unanimous. As Sheldon Hall puts it: 'Rarely can any director's reputation have been so much at variance between his peers – to whom Richardson was brilliant, passionate, mercurial – and his reviewers, for whom his films rarely cohered as unified wholes.'[13] His reliance on literary sources, his eclecticism, his lack of abiding thematic concerns have told against him, but several of his films now seem remarkably innovative. After his four New Wave films (and an unhappy experience in Hollywood making *Sanctuary*), Richardson turned in a radical new direction with an adaptation of Henry Fielding's sprawling eighteenth-century picaresque novel *Tom Jones*, which in style if not setting seemed to set the tone for subsequent 60s extravaganzas. It proved such a huge and unexpected success that it allowed Richardson *carte blanche* to make what he wanted for the rest of the decade. He chose boldly, if not wisely: a Hollywood updated adaptation of Evelyn Waugh's satire *The Loved One*; two exotic art films starring Jeanne Moreau, *Mademoiselle* and *The Sailor from Gibraltar*; a big-budget historical reconstruction, *The Charge of the Light Brigade* and a sparse film version of his production of *Hamlet* at the London Roundhouse; an under-appreciated adaptation of Nabokov's *Laughter in the Dark*; and the much derided *Ned Kelly*, with a miscast Mick Jagger as the legendary Australian bandit.

Richardson himself expressed dissatisfaction with *The Sailor from Gibraltar*, particularly over the performance of Ian Bannen and his own inability to rein in production problems while in the midst of a turbulent love affair with Jeanne Moreau. *Mademoiselle* (1966) had been a much happier production despite the grim subject matter, and resulted in a shockingly impressive film, though it found little favour with critics or audiences at the time. David Watkin's black-and-white Panavision cinematography is stunning. Richardson's framing sometimes seems perverse but it falls into a logical pattern, expressing the voyeuristic, fetishistic viewpoint of Moreau's Mademoiselle, a small-town schoolmistress who becomes obsessed with an Italian woodcutter only to find that several of the local women are already sampling his sexual favours.

Jean Genet, upon whose story the film was based, expressed understandable reservations about the casting of Moreau – considered one of the most beautiful women in the world in the mid-60s – as his frumpy, embittered heroine; but Moreau excels in crossing the line from beauty to ugliness, turning herself into a femme so fatale she makes other femme fatales look like wholesome milkmaids.[14] Her acts of sabotage (opening sluice gates to cause a flood, setting off fires, poisoning the water supply) are thrillingly evil; her sadistic humiliation of the woodcutter's son once she has won his affection, breathtakingly cruel.

With no musical soundtrack, no camera movement and no humour, *Mademoiselle* proved too portentous for most British film critics – then as now a cynical but often frivolous bunch when viewing films collectively. Only the unabashedly high-brow Penelope Gilliatt was prepared to take it seriously.[15] Admittedly Ettore Manni with a snake wrapped round his waist and a much less sleepy one in his trousers is more of an icon than a

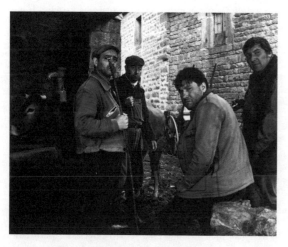

Backwoods France: vengeful farmers discuss the cause of their woes in *Mademoiselle* (Tony Richardson, 1966)

character (Brando was originally cast in the part); and the flashback Dilys Powell condemned as one of the clumsiest she had ever seen is disorienting.[16] But there is a consistency of vision here, an uncompromising intensity which takes much further the poetic realism of *A Taste of Honey* and the anarchic subversion of *The Loneliness of the Long Distance Runner*.

The Charge of the Light Brigade (1968) might be seen as a return to the big-budget mainstream – the equivalent of Schlesinger's *Far from the Madding Crowd* and Reisz's *Isadora*, though it is an edgier and more uncomfortable film than either of them. It has tended to be seen as an anti-war film, but its message is more complex. The brilliant animation sequences by Richard Williams of contemporary political cartoons revel in as much as they mock Victorian jingoism, and the film's protagonist, David Hemmings's dashing and decent Captain Nolan is intoxicated with the glories of war. Despite the senseless brutality and horrific slaughter one can see his point. Life for a light cavalry officer is colourful and thrilling. Nolan's problem is with the intolerable amateurism of a British army run by dunderheaded officers who have bought their commissions and whose only qualification is their status as wealthy gentlemen.[17] Charles Wood peppers his script with statements from the real-life Nolan's astute and sensible *Cavalry: Its History and Tactics*, first published in 1853 (such as 'horses are taught not by harshness but by gentleness'), but Richardson veers away from endorsing his reformist viewpoint.[18] The triumvirate of dozy Raglan, choleric Lucan and arrogant Cardigan would seem an easy target for our and Nolan's derision, but the performances of John Gielgud, Harry Andrews and particularly Trevor Howard dominate the film. Howard's Cardigan is no lovable eccentric: his malice towards good-hearted Sergeant-Major Corbett (Norman Rossington) when he refuses to spy on Nolan is chilling, but his absolute certainty in himself commands a sort of horrified respect rather than the contempt we might expect to feel. As the fatal battle approaches, we are gradually distanced from Nolan. His conduct in the first half of the film is unimpeachable: even his affair with his best friend's wife (Vanessa Redgrave again) appears forgivable, as in a cheeky inversion of Victorian values it is she who stifles his objections and initiates the liaison. But to avoid too close an identification with a character who would have been an exemplary officer in the modern British army, Richardson hints at imperfections. He tears up unread the letter he receives from his – now pregnant – lover and drops it into the sea when he embarks for the Crimea.[19] On an early-morning reconnoitre, he comes across a group of soldiers, including Corbett, who has been flogged and reduced to the ranks for his refusal to betray Nolan, and further alienates our sympathies by snaffling their eagerly prepared fried breakfast. Most seriously, his hastily delivered orders to Cardigan and Lucan set the Light Brigade off on their disastrously misdirected charge. Thus he is at least partly to blame, and his death 'shrieking like some tight girl' (as Cardigan indignantly puts it), as he tries to turn the charge away from the fatal valley, looks like another messy casualty of war rather than the tragic denouement an epic such as this would normally deliver. Audiences were nonplussed and box-office returns disappointing, but as with *Isadora* and *Far from the Madding Crowd*, *The Charge of the Light Brigade* can now be seen as brave and original. Richardson's fall from critical grace (he went so far as to exclude critics from previewing *The Charge of the Light Brigade*) by no means signalled a decline in his creative powers.

The Stranger's Eye

One might expect foreigners making films in London to be peculiarly susceptible to myths about 'Swinging London'. Jack Smight in *Kaleidoscope* (1966) and James Clavell in *To Sir, with Love* (1967) deploy miniskirts and red London buses to spice up their essentially old-fashioned stories, but more serious directors remained remarkably immune. If one takes three diverse but prestigious non-British views of London – Polanski's *Repulsion* (1965), Preminger's *Bunny Lake Is Missing* (1965) and Antonioni's *Blow-Up* (1966) – they are all dark and sardonic, with hardly a hint of the frivolity that supposedly characterises mid-60s British films. Admittedly it would be difficult to think of three directors less likely to be swayed by fashionable concerns. Polanski with his horrific childhood in Nazi-occupied Poland, Preminger, the Austrian Jew who survived in Hollywood by playing Nazi bullies, Antonioni the poet of Existential angst, but even so their treatment of London is surprisingly bleak.

Polanski had won international acclaim with *Knife in the Water* (1962), but his non-conformist take on Polish society upset the Communist government and after a brief period in Paris he arrived in London in 1964. Instead of persuading the Rank Organisation to let him direct an Anglo-Polish comedy or gaining backing from the BFI Experimental Film Fund to make avant-garde short films, he teamed up with Tony Tenser

and Michael Klinger, two exploitation producers who had recently had a hit with *The Yellow Teddybears* (Robert Hartford-Davis, 1963). Polanski's proposal for what would become *Cul-de-Sac* was too risky even for Klinger and Tenser (though to their credit they did finance the film). With Gérard Brach, Polanski wrote the script for a low-budget horror film about a young woman going mad when her elder sister deserts her for a fling with her married lover. The combination of Polanski's inventive direction, the adventurous cinematography of Gilbert Taylor, and the performance of Catherine Deneuve as the delicate, fearful Carole Ledoux, made for a disturbing and impressive film. Most of the memorable sequences take place in Carole's flat (one could almost say in Carole's head). But Polanski also captures a strong sense of the London setting.

Carole works in a beauty salon attempting to patch up the decaying flesh of rich old ladies. But even when she goes out into the sunny streets of South Kensington, the world seems alien and strange. At lunchtime, she has to pass an ugly, leering group of workmen. In the evening, they are gone, but their hut looms threateningly as a black hole, which Carole scurries past only to be transfixed by a large crack in the pavement. When she is eventually coaxed away by the young man who is trying (with fatal results) to woo her, a forlorn trio of buskers crosses the screen. Later they reappear beneath Carole's window. Like the boisterous nuns we hear but don't see in the convent near Carole's flat, and the inquisitive lady across the landing with her little dog, they add to the aura of disjointed reality which complements Carole's increasingly disorientated view of the world.

In 1965 Polanski was a young director, anxious to establish a career and a reputation outside Poland. Otto Preminger was at the other end of the scale, a sixty-year-old director of numerous acclaimed films (particularly the noirish *Laura*, *Fallen Angel*, *Whirlpool* and *Angel Face*), coming to the end of his career. *Bunny Lake Is Missing*, by Marryam Modell writing as Evelyn Piper and published in 1957, is a psychological thriller about a young woman, Blanche Lake, who comes to New York seeking anonymity for herself and her illegitimate daughter but finds herself in a nightmarish situation when the child disappears and nobody will believe in her existence. The resolution of the plot, which involves peripheral figures rather than the psychiatrist who falls in love with Blanche while continuing to believe her daughter is imaginary, presented insuperable script problems. Perhaps because Columbia needed projects that could be handled by their recently established London production office, the film was relocated to England, where John and Penelope Mortimer radically reworked both characters and plot.

The plausibility of the story benefits from making Miss Lake a stranger in a city where no one can verify the existence of her daughter (the relative proximity of friends and family in Rhode Island was always a problem for the novel). Blanche Lake is changed only in name (becoming Ann), with Carol Lynley bringing exactly the right combination of charismatic beauty and unhinged maternal devotion to the part, but she is given a suspiciously possessive brother (Keir Dullea), who is crucial to the plot. The Mortimers also transform the novel's peripheral characters into splendid English eccentrics. A dubious doll-maker becomes a more benevolent figure played by the ancient Finlay Currie (making his last film appearance), and Ada Ford, the scheming nursery schoolteacher, is reworked by Martita Hunt into a garrulous variation on her role as Miss Havisham in *Great Expectations* (1946). Wilson, the writer Blanche turns to for help, is transmuted into her bizarrely camp landlord played by Noël Coward, who tries to seduce her with a fertility mask, shrunken heads and a whip owned by the Marquis de Sade. Most importantly, Dennis Newhouse the psychiatrist becomes Laurence Olivier's world-weary Superintendent Newhouse, whose interest in Ann Lake is paternal rather than amorous and who proves much more astute than the love-sick doctor in disentangling reality from fantasy.

The film's locations – a big empty house and a bustling nursery in Hampstead, a flat on the fringes of Covent Garden, with a view (now blocked by the BT tower) of Trafalgar Square, the backstreets of Soho, the darkened wards and shadowy corridors of the old Charing Cross Hospital – though not particularly unusual, provide a solid and authentic setting for the film's slightly improbable action. *Bunny Lake* becomes a London story, but it is not the Swinging City celebrated by *Time* magazine. The only concession to the existence of Swinging London occurs during a sequence in a Maida Vale pub, where Newhouse takes Ann Lake to calm her down and to probe her about the missing Bunny. Their conversation, increasingly intimate as Ann talks about her illegitimate child and her jealously possessive brother, has to compete with music from the pub television set, where the then popular band the Zombies belt out their songs.

Even Newhouse might have been stumped by the plot of *Blow-Up*, though he is exactly the sort of sane

and rational witness Thomas (David Hemmings) seeks for in vain to verify the fact that he has inadvertently photographed a murder. Antonioni deliberately chose to set his film against the backcloth of Swinging London, where a new type of fashion photographer (epitomised by David Bailey) had sprung up, whose classless, rootless lifestyle fitted his story. Thomas starts the film as master of his world, discarding the tattered clothes he has disguised himself in to take secret pictures in a Salvation Army hostel and driving away in a Rolls-Royce. But his world proves to be insubstantial and unreliable. Photographing a lover's tiff in the tranquil stillness of a London park, he captures more than he bargained for. The woman, Jane (Vanessa Redgrave) chases after him, and when he refuses to give her the film, tracks him down to his studio. When he develops the film, blow-ups seem to reveal a gun poking through the bushes and a possible murder. He sees Jane in a crowd outside a shop window but when he approaches she vanishes without trace. And the body that Thomas thinks he sees in the park as dusk falls, has disappeared when he goes back in the morning.

Thomas's failure to drag his friend Ron from a drug-infused Cheyne Walk party to confirm the existence of the body is frustrating, but the bear-like Peter Bowles leading Thomas by the tie towards sex and drugs and the zombified model Verushchka (who insists that she is in Paris) wittily encapsulates the ethos of the 60s. Critics were divided at the time over whether Antonioni offered insight or had been seduced by clichés, Pauline Kael proving particularly vituperative in condemning the ageing Italian for not catching 'the humour and fervour and astonishing speed in youth's rejection of older values'.[20] But that rejection now appears petulant and ephemeral and Antonioni's vision might be afforded more respect. Elisabeth-Marie Tuson points out that: 'The settings are generally of a realistic nature, an actual London park, a street, a café and a warehouse, but the buildings are backdrops to the narrative and do not detract from the dream-like events that occur . . . .'[21] As with *Repulsion* and *Bunny Lake*, *Blow-Up* uses London locations to help create an aura – in this case of disjointed insubstantiality – to give the film a fascinating resonance.[22]

These three films contradict the idea of mid-60s films as vacuous and socially irresponsible and they can hardly be considered exceptions. *Repulsion* might be compared with Seth Holt's atmospheric *The Nanny* (1965), like *Bunny Lake* based on an Evelyn Piper novel; *Bunny Lake* is outflanked in strangeness by Jack

Deep End (Jerzy Skolimowski, 1971)

The flowering of dark, disturbing, violent British cinema reaches its apotheosis in 1971 with *A Clockwork Orange*, *The Devils* and *Straw Dogs*, and totters on with diminishing returns through the 70s. *Deep End* has macabre strands and is imbued with an aura of seedy decay – the old bathhouse in Fulham where most of the action takes place, Soho at its nadir of sleazy clubs and bars – but it is also characterised by everyday realism and surreal humour. The film was an Anglo-German co-production – half the cast are Germans, the German anarchist band Can provide part of the soundtrack (notably 'Mother Sky' over the Soho sequence), Susan's fiancé takes her to see a German sex film – and *Deep End* can be seen as a precursor to the New German Cinema of the 70s.

Mike (John Moulder-Brown) starts his first job at a swimming pool/public bathhouse and is dazzled by the sassy, bored female attendant Susan. She is played by Jane Asher, better known now for her cakes and vegetarian sausages but an actress who excels at giving poignancy and depth to seemingly unsympathetic characters (such as Charles Ryder's unwanted wife in *Brideshead Revisited*). Susan is determinedly amoral, but to Mike she is a good companion and a desirable beauty. She is older than he is and ought to be out of reach, but she is vulnerable: her pathological hostility to Mike's mother leads to a revelation that both her parents are dead, and she's associated with the cheap-looking cuddly toys that she stuffs and sews up to earn extra money. She's impulsive: slapping Mike's face when he fondles her breasts in the cinema but turning round and kissing him; meekly obeying the sports teacher with whom she's been having an affair but then berating him for ordering her about and stealing her innocence.

We gradually realise that Susan is more ordinary and less Machiavellian than Mike thinks she is. She is keenly aware that her looks and figure are marketable assets but her promiscuity is limited to the long-term affair with the schoolteacher and her relationship with her well-heeled but unappealing fiancé. Mischievously she refuses to deny that the cardboard cut-out Mike steals from outside a striptease club and which he confronts her with in a crowded tube train, is her. But if she was working as a Soho stripper she'd hardly bother with a lowly paid day job at the baths, or with earning a few shillings sewing cuddly toys.

Apart from Mike and Susan, *Deep End* is populated with mildly grotesque caricatures – the officious baths manager, the sexually predatory customer (a scarily overwhelming Diana Dors), the very polite Chinese hot-dog seller, the cheery prostitute doggedly continuing her work (at reduced rates) despite her broken leg, the alarmingly lecherous sports teacher – and Skolimowski's loose improvisational style sometimes makes one wonder where the film is going. What holds it together is Mike's obsession. It oscillates between skittish playfulness, surprising ingenuity (his plan to find Susan's diamond in the snow) and sulky resentment. But as with most obsessions it ends in tragedy.

FURTHER READING

Deep End is a good example of a film that was misunderstood and dismissed when first released but is being rediscovered by an increasing band of people linked by the internet. The (new) external reviews and most of the user comments on the IMDb are perceptive and revealing.

Clayton's *Our Mother's House*; and Peter Watkins's *Privilege* (1967) and Nic Roeg and Donald Cammell's *Performance* (1970) express an even more jaundiced view of British society than *Blowup*. It is also arguable that other visiting directors were less resistant to the Swinging London myth. Certainly not Godard in his witty, savage *Sympathy for the Devil* (1968) and *British Sounds* (1970) or Truffaut in the dystopian *Fahrenheit 451* (1966). More surprising is the view of British society presented by mainstream American directors. Apart from William Wyler's *The Collector* (1965), which seems more in tune with the England of the Moors Murderers trial than with Swinging London, it is difficult to imagine three bleaker British films from the 60s than the John Le Carré adaptations directed by Americans Martin Ritt (*The Spy Who Came in from the Cold*, 1965), Sidney Lumet (*The Deadly Affair*, 1967) and Frank Pierson (*The Looking Glass War*, 1969).

Return of the Exiles

David Greene and Eric Till both moved to Canada in the early 1950s and established their careers directing dramas for Canadian television. They both returned to England in the late 60s, Greene to make four feature films, Till two; none of them made much impact at the time though they now look idiosyncratic and original.

Greene's *The Shuttered Room* (1966) is a 'monster in the attic' thriller, but its dangers are multiplied by a gang of feral locals similar to those employed by Joseph Losey earlier in *The Damned* (1961) and Sam Peckinpah later in *Straw Dogs* (1971). The main characters, a couple played by Carol Lynley and Gig Young, are less interesting than the semi-incestuous brother and sister in *Bunny Lake*. But Greene makes his Norfolk and Kentish locations stand in convincingly for New England, and there is a pleasing symmetry in the way the threats from thuggish lotario Oliver Reed (reprising his role in *The Damned* with a bad American accent) and the screeching, shambling monster cancel each other out. Greene handles suspense well, sustaining a mood of dark foreboding, and the spectacular burning down of the mill at the end of the film works as a satisfying purging of dark secrets.[23]

Greene's other three films are less genre-bound. *Sebastian*, written by Leo Marks and co-produced by Michael Powell, has something of the morbid obsessiveness of Powell and Marks's *Peeping Tom* (1960), though Dirk Bogarde's codebreaking makes him misanthropic rather than murderous ('I'm a kind of septic tank for all the world's ugly secrets', he complains). As in *Peeping Tom*, a sensible young woman does her best to save the disturbed protagonist, though the distance between 1960 and 1968 can be measured in the staggering difference between Anna Massey's prim, modest Helen and Susannah York's Rebecca, an intelligent woman masquerading behind a display of scantily clad glamour. Bogarde is even more ill-at-ease in Swinging London than he was in *Darling* (when it was still possible to ignore it). Like Greene, his concern is not with the glittering surface but with the corruption that lies beneath.

In *Sebastian* Rebecca represents the possibility of future happiness. In *The Strange Affair*, happiness is precluded from the start, when we see PC Strange, handcuffed and dishevelled, on his journey to prison. His story, like that of Andy Mitchell in Ealing's *The Blue Lamp* (1950), is of an eager young recruit who signs up to join the Metropolitan Police. In *The Blue Lamp*, Andy suffers boredom, discomfort and occasional embarrassment before the murder of his kindly mentor George Dixon sets the film off in a new direction. His police colleagues are gruff but friendly and unimpeachably honest. Even the crooks, apart from Dirk Bogarde's teenage killer, are decent blokes who play by the rules and want no truck with murderers. Poor Peter Strange (Michael York) is pitched into a world of corruption,

madness and sadistic violence, where his superiors are the petty-minded 'chair-polisher' Superintendent Kingsley and the irredeemably corrupt Inspector Evans. Honest Sergeant Pierce (played by Jeremy Kemp, one of the original quartet of *Z Cars* policemen) looks to be a better role model, but Pierce is bitter and paranoid. If police standards have slipped, criminal behaviour has deteriorated even further. An accidental encounter with local gang boss 'Daddy' Quince and his boys leads to Strange being tortured with an electric drill. A respite of amorous pleasure in the arms of underage flower child Susan George ends up in a pornographic film made by her decadent guardians. Blackmailed into perjuring himself to further Pierce's plan to entrap the Quinces, Strange ends up the scapegoat and is packed off to prison.

Greene shoots his hellish vision of late 60s London (the first crime film to be based at the new glass and concrete Scotland Yard building) among brash new pubs, high-rise housing developments, multistorey car parks and the Battersea heliport (where the white-clad devotees of a visiting Indian guru disrupt Pierce's drug bust).[24] As with *Sebastian*, overrun by mini-skirted dolly birds and smart new technology, the brightness of the setting is contrasted with the darkness of the message.

I Start Counting (1969) is the lightest of Greene's four films, despite its story of a serial killer who targets young women. It is set in the post-war new town of Bracknell, where Sidney Lumet was to set *The Offence* (1972), a prime contender for the blackest film in British cinema. But here darkness is held back by sweet, bright-eyed Jenny Agutter, caught at her most innocent between the television and film versions of *The Railway Children*. She plays a Catholic schoolgirl passionately in love with her older foster brother (Bryan Marshall). The fact that he might be the serial killer fails to dampen her ardour. A love like hers, she rashly believes, would redeem him. Like Carol Lynley in *The Shuttered Room*, she returns continually to a ruined old house where she suffered an undefined childhood trauma. But without the distraction Lynley suffers from lascivious thugs and doting husband, she can be much more single-minded in pursuing her destiny. Her determination to uncover the truth leads her into danger but it equips her with the knowledge she will need to survive. Though her obsession with George would seem to be far more dangerous than that of Mike with Susan in *Deep End* (see case study), when it counts, she is able to distinguish between fantasy and reality. Finally confronted with psychopathic violence, she has the sense to run for her life rather than attempt redemption. As in *The Shuttered Room*, conventional elements eventually intrude, but for much of the film Greene (helped by Agutter's delicate performance) keeps them at bay by making us view the world – dangerous, exciting, full of possibilities – through the eyes of his adolescent heroine.

In *Hot Millions* (1968), Eric Till's first British film, the main creative force is Peter Ustinov, its star and co-writer. Till's influence is more apparent in *The Walking Stick* (1970), a clever melodrama based on a novel by Winston Graham with a good cast and well-chosen locations. Samantha Eggar, the most lusciously beautiful of the 60s actresses, plays a polio victim who thinks that her weak legs make her repulsive to men. She keeps herself to herself and leads a buttoned-up existence as a porcelain expert for an auction house until she's seduced by Leigh Hartley (David Hemmings), an assiduous young artist who refuses to take no for an answer. Hesitantly at first but then with increasing confidence she begins to open out and flower into an attractive and desirable woman. She moves into his warehouse flat in the then dilapidated East India Dock but she has reservations about his friends, especially jovial Ted Sandymount (Dudley Sutton) and slimy Jack Foil (Emlyn Williams). Her suspicions are confirmed when she realises that they plan to rob the auction house and want her help, but it only dawns on her gradually that the plan predates her relationship with Leigh and that his courtship of her was an elaborate ploy to trick her into co-operation.

It is a simple idea but Till brings it alive. No doubt Hitchcock, who had filmed Graham's *Marnie* (1964), would have created more suspense during the robbery and brought the characters into sharper focus. Where Till succeeds is in the complex ambiguity of the relationship between Leigh and Deborah. When she confronts him with his lies he admits all but insists that he unintentionally fell in love with her and their happy moments together are genuine. This is easy enough for the audience to believe; even when she's supposed to be a wallflower Eggar's Deborah is magnetically attractive. But should she believe him? He's tricked her and used her but he's also given her confidence, self-respect and sexual fulfilment (no one but a professional charmer could have dragged her out of her shell). With her new-found strength she shops him (and herself) to the police. It's less spite or a turn to conventional morality than an assertion of independence: a harbinger – rare enough in mainstream cinema – of the feminism that was to mushroom in the 70s.

British music and British fashion – and more briefly British films – had an international cultural impact in the 60s; but changes to society and the economy occurred more slowly and unevenly. Cinema was able to capture something of the euphoria when Britain shook off the grey legacy of World War II and become a creative, colourful, dynamic society; but when that proved to be ephemeral, British films sought out a deeper reality; it is this rather than the descent into frivolous fantasy that characterises the second half of the decade.

Notes

1. Penelope Houston, 'Seventy', *Sight and Sound*, Winter 1970, p. 4.
2. Jeffrey Richards, 'The Revolt of the Young', in Anthony Aldgate and Jeffrey Richards, *Best of British* (Oxford: Basil Blackwell, 1983), p. 159.
3. 'London – the Swinging City', Piri Halasz, *Time*, April 1966.
4. For which see Christine Gledhill, 'Late Silent Britain', Chapter 18 in this book.
5. David Robinson, 'Case Histories of the Next Renascence', *Sight and Sound*, Winter 1968–9, p. 36.
6. For more detailed treatment of the 'Swinging London' phenomenon, see Chapter 7 of my *Sixties British Cinema*.
7. See Neil Sinyard, *Jack Clayton* (Manchester: Manchester University Press, 2001).
8. Tom Milne, Obituary, *Guardian*, 28 November 2002; David Hare, letter, *Guardian* 30 November 2002.
9. Robert Murphy, *Sixties British Cinema*, p. 265.
10. Both Jeffrey Richards in 'The Revolt of the Young' and David Robinson in 'Case Histories of the Next Renascence', pp. 36–40, argue for *If . . . .* as a special case, enabling them to continue to condemn the bulk of late 60s cinema.
11. Rudyard Kipling's public-school stories – collected together as *Stalky and Co* – centre on a trio of boys who, as in *If . . . .*, don't share the hallowed values about the importance of sport, hard work and obedience to authority. The fact that two of the three look forward to army careers policing the turbulent North West Frontier of the British Empire is a less significant difference than the fact that their wily headmaster respects their rebelliousness and admires their resourcefulness.
12. For *This Sporting Life* see the case study in Chapter 33 of this book by Peter Hutchings.
13. Sheldon Hall, 'Tony Richardson', in Robert Murphy (ed.), *Directors in British and Irish Cinema* (London: BFI, 2006).

14. Terence Stamp had similarly transformed himself into the unattractive obsessive Freddie Clegg in *The Collector* (William Wyler, 1965).

15. Penelope Gilliatt, *Observer*, 15 January 1967. Between 1963 and 1968 Gilliatt was married to John Osborne, Richardson's closest collaborator until they fell out over *The Charge of the Light Brigade*. She also wrote the script for John Schlesinger's *Sunday Bloody Sunday* (1971).

16. Dilys Powell, *Sunday Times*, 15 January 1967.

17. User comments on the IMDb website for *The Charge of the Light Brigade* – as is often the case for films involving military history – are impressively erudite.

18. Wood is granted sole credit for the script, but the script by John Osborne held by the BFI Library is not structurally different from the finished film. Wood tightens up the dialogue, introduces a couple of minor characters, and makes much less obvious the borrowings from Cecil Woodham-Smith's *The Reason Why* (a brilliantly researched book first published in 1953). But the most important elements of the narrative – the (fictional) antagonism between Nolan and Cardigan, the romance between Nolan and Clarissa, the way in which the Charge is misdirected – are all there in Osborne's script.

19. Osborne's Nolan is more gallant: 'He turns it over in his hand, looks ashore, then at the letter again. With an effort, as if it were an act of self-amputation, he looks back at Morris, kisses the letter and then drops it gently, unopened into the sea.' Osborne has Nolan eating the soldiers' breakfast, but Corbett, one of Wood's creations, is not present, so the thoughtlessness seems less significant.

20. Pauline Kael's review of *Blow-Up* is reprinted in *Kiss Kiss Bang Bang* (Boston, MA: Little, Brown, 1968), pp. 31–7.

21. Elisabeth-Marie Tuson, 'Consumerism, the Swinging Sixties and Assheton Gorton', *Journal of British Cinema and Television* vol. 2 no. 1, 2005, p. 105.

22. The IMDb offers more than usual detail on the film's locations, carefully warning readers not to confuse Maryon Park, which features so evocatively in the film, with nearby Maryon Wilson Park.

23. The haunted building where the monster in the attic lurks is the Old Mill at Hardingham, Norfolk. As it had been bought by MGM, Greene was allowed to burn it down, though not without vociferous protests. He wrote to *The Times* to point out that the mill was a ramshackle ruin which nobody had considered of any architectural value and that the protestors were relying on photographs showing the picturesque but ephemeral façade created by his art director and set dressers to make it look more interesting. *The Times*, 6 June 1966. Reprinted on www.norfolkmills.co.uk/Watermills/hardingham.html. I am indebted to 'malmig' on the IMDb message board for this reference. Another contributor, 'pat-526', witnessed scenes from the film being shot near Faversham, Kent.

24. Greene's zeal for images of new London was frustrated by building delays. According to the IMDb, the exterior of the new New Scotland Yard building was incomplete when the film was shot and an empty office building in Colliers Wood was mocked up as a stand in. It fooled me.

Bibliography

Graham, Peter, *The Abortive Renaissance* (np: Axle Publications, 1963).

Hemmings, David, *Blow-Up and Other Exaggerations* (London: Robson Books, 2004).

Hewison, Robert, *Too Much: Art and Society in the Sixties 1960–1975* (London: Methuen, 1986).

Houston, Penelope, 'Keeping up with the Antonionis', *Sight and Sound*, Autumn 1964.

Lassally, Walter, *Itinerant Cameraman* (London: John Murray, 1987).

Murphy, Robert, *Sixties British Cinema* (London: BFI, 1992).

Richardson, Tony, *The Long Distance Runner* (London: Faber and Faber, 1993).

Walker, Alexander, *Hollywood England* (London: Harrap, 1986).

Welsh, James M. and Tibbetts, John C. (eds), *The Cinema of Tony Richardson: Essays and Interviews* (Albany: State University of New York Press, 1999).

36

'Tutte e Macchio!':
Excess, Masquerade and Performativity in 70s Cinema

PAMELA CHURCH GIBSON AND ANDREW HILL

The 70s, whether or not still seen as 'the decade that taste forgot', is certainly a decade that cinematic criticism has, until recently, chosen to bypass or neglect. There are general overviews of the British films of the period and a few in-depth studies of particular directors, but there seems to be an unspoken consensus that British cinema of the 70s should be bypassed or relegated to footnotes. This chapter examines a series of films that transect the decade, from *Performance* (1970) and *Get Carter* (1971), through the films of Nicolas Roeg and Ken Russell to Derek Jarman's early output. Ostensibly they are a diverse body of work, but unifying themes and stylistic qualities can be traced through their presentation of different forms of excess.

The prevalence of 'excess' suggests that these films present responses to the shared moment of their production. The 70s were a troubling time for British society – the 'three-day week', 'the winter of discontent', inflation touching 30 per cent, lengthening dole queues, the rise of the National Front, the Birmingham pub bombings, the miners' toppling of the Heath government, rampant football hooliganism – were seen as symptoms, for those on the right at least, that the nation was on the brink of a slide into chaos. It is the sense of hysteria and panic associated with the decade which fuel the excesses displayed in the films. Indeed, they could be said to present a modern version of the baroque style, echoing and updating its reflection of the febrility of seventeenth-century Europe in an expression of the disorientation and disorder that marked 70s Britain.

The grouping of these films under the rubric of 'excess' is explored here in three ways: visual extravagance, excessive forms of behaviour, and a re-staging

and reordering of traditional ideas about gender. The latter theme is the least obviously 'excessive', but the period's climate of confrontation and breakdown can be configured as undermining the certainties of traditional identities, opening up the possibilities of new forms of gendered being. The activities of both the women's movement and gay rights groups present the most direct responses to this. But it is also registered in popular music: the ephebic boys such as Bolan and Bowie with their wan faces, their dustings of glitter and long, tousled locks; the broad-shouldered but flamboyantly dressed and heavily made-up male performers of glam rock, whose appearance was redolent of the carnivalesque tradition of transvestism; and finally the confrontational androgyny of punk.

Transition

Two films stand as pivotal in understanding the transition from the 60s to the 70s: *Performance* and *Get Carter*. In *Performance*, Mick Jagger plays the former rock star Turner, who, having lost his creative energy, languishes in his Notting Hill home with his companions Pherber (Anita Pallenberg) and Lucy (Michele Breton). There they inhabit a private world dominated by the type of excesses associated with the 60s, combining sexual experimentation with a daily diet of drugs. Spliffs are smoked in the bath, magic mushrooms chopped up for supper, and heroin casually injected into a left buttock.

In the first half of the film, we see Chas (James Fox) at work for a protection racket. Having disobeyed his boss's instructions and killed his former friend Joey Maddocks (Anthony Valentine) he goes on the run and arrives at Turner's home seeking a hiding place. There he attempts to organise a ticket to New York. But his plans for escape are thwarted by the excesses of the inhabitants' lifestyle, he's unknowingly fed magic mushrooms, and then Pherber takes him to bed, to flirt and toy with him. The film ends with the 'triumph' of a different type of excess – that of violence; Chas shoots Turner through the eye, before he is delivered back into the clutches of his boss.

Across *Performance*, questions of gender and sexual identity are broached that run throughout the films surveyed here. The opening credits shows us Chas's delight in the display of his own naked body and his sexual prowess – interestingly, the mirrors are angled so that he can see his own body, rather than that of his girlfriend. He is narcissistic in his dress, and set apart in this way from the other gangsters, yet there is the suggestion that his 'masculine' excesses of behaviour, the pleasure he derives from the infliction of physical pain on his victims in his job as an enforcer, might be a way of convincing both himself and those around him of his unquestionable heterosexuality.

Certainly, Joey Maddocks and his friends know exactly how to bait Chas; they trash his pristine flat and spray 'Poof' on the walls. Their torture of him is explicitly designed to extract a confession of homosexuality – and there is some unexplained reason for Chas's anger with Maddocks, a suggestion of some shared secret. Chas represents aggressive masculinity at its most extreme – even his employers intimate that his violent tactics and tendencies make him 'an out-of-date boy'.[1] Turner, by contrast, is androgynous in appearance and demeanour, and though he feels his time is past, he points towards a different form of masculinity, that was to achieve a certain prominence in the coming decade.

Colin MacCabe proffers the notion that 'it cannot be too long before somebody recognises *Performance* as the first queer film', but he does not pursue this thought further.[2] Nor does he seem to comprehend properly the implications of 'queer' and its meaning and usage within contemporary critical theory. Moya Luckett describes the way in which Chas is dressed up by Pherber in a variety of different outfits, all chosen from Turner's extensive dressing-up box, and is finally transformed by wig and make-up.[3] But she does not indicate, as she might, that this last guise, paradoxically, has the effect of rendering Chas's appearance more conventionally masculine. In a long, frilled shirt with flowing sleeves and wearing bright red lipstick, the butch side of his persona is stressed, just as it is with later musicians from glam rock through to heavy metal.

Throughout, *Performance* displays a visual excess and stylish extravagance, mixing the conventions of *nouvelle vague* cinema and the characteristic quirks of British psychedelia, bringing the two together in an attempt to 'see' from inside Chas's head. This jettisoning of realism culminates in the final scenes from the film, where Chas is escorted out to Harry Flowers's waiting Rolls, but it is Turner who then appears in the back of the car; their identities appear to have fused.

Jack Carter (Michael Caine), the protagonist of *Get Carter*, is in a similar line of business to Chas, and he too upsets his boss by his maverick activities, but he is a much cooler and calmer figure. The film opens as he travels up to Newcastle to investigate his brother's death, and ends with his own murder at the hands of an anonymous assassin on a grey North Sea beach. The dour Newcastle setting establishes a sense of distance from Swinging London, offering instead a desolate and unsettling backdrop, from which the sense of optimism and excitement associated with the 60s have disappeared. Carter's search uncovers a pornography ring, which has ensnared his young niece, and the film confronts the concerns about the prevalence of pornography that came to mark the 70s.

The troubling portrayal of women in the film can be taken as a further comment on the anxieties of the period and its concerns about the excesses of permissive sexuality. Carter's niece is enticed by her father's girlfriend, Margaret, into appearing in the cheap porn films that the local businessman, Brumby, produces. His mistress, Glenda, despite her Ossie Clarke dresses and the chic flat in which she has been set up, is unstable and disempowered. Ironically it is while she is locked by the enraged Carter into the boot of the white sports car given her by the porn magnate, that she meets her death. Carter exploits his landlady's sexual attraction for him and puts her at risk, while Anna (Britt Ekland), Carter's mistress, has her face cut to ribbons when her liaison with Carter is revealed to her husband.

Carter uses violence with calm ruthlessness. He tips Brumby from the top of a multistorey car park, stabs Albert Swift, the luckless intermediary, once he has told his story, forces whisky down the throat of Eric Paice before battering him to death, and injects Margaret with a fatal dose of heroin. He plants her body in the grounds of his adversary's house during a party there, and makes a call to the police complaining of a drug-crazed orgy. They arrive in force, checking for evidence of drug use, separating lovers, and hauling Margaret's body from a pond. We are left with a shot of the partygoers outside the property in the dawn light: vacant, blank and still. As in *Performance* we are left with the sense that the party of the preceding decade is over and the dark excesses of the new decade have come centre stage.

Nicolas Roeg – Nothing Is What It Seems

Roeg followed *Performance* with *Walkabout* (1971) and *Don't Look Now* (1973) which, together with *Performance*, form 'a trilogy querying the whole conception of civilisation'.[4] In *Walkabout*, two children, an adolescent girl and her brother, find themselves abandoned in the Australian desert after their father's suicide. They are rescued by a young Aborigine boy, who is performing the ritual of 'walkabout' demanded by his people; he abandons this to save the lives of the two orphans of western civilization. The price he pays is that of his own life, a victim of both alien, colonising forces and his own emergent sexual feelings.

In *Don't Look Now*, John Baxter (Donald Sutherland) comes to Venice with his wife Laura (Julie Christie), some months after their daughter has drowned, and becomes involved in a series of seemingly irrational events that culminate in his bizarre and violent murder. Baxter stands as an exemplar of rational, educated western man, for whom work is inextricably intertwined with identity, and the narrative dynamics of the film work around the tension between his refusal to accept any challenge to his rationality and his wife's acceptance of a post-rational world represented by the clairvoyance of Heather (Hilary Mason), a blind medium. Rather than accepting Laura's desire to turn to the mystical and other-worldly for support in her grief over her daughter's death, he takes her to the hospital and instructs her to resume her course of tranquillisers. Ironically, though the gift of second sight is

Julie Christie and her son lead the mourners into the funeral service, which concludes *Don't Look Now* (Nicolas Roeg, 1973)

traditionally associated with the feminine, it is John rather than his wife who has the gift, enabling him to see his own funeral, just as earlier he had sensed his daughter's death at the precise moment it took place. His refusal to accept the validity of these powers, his resistance to any challenge to the rule of the Cartesian *cogito*, plays a pivotal role in bringing about his death.

Throughout the film the Baxters are portrayed as having a close marriage; but John seems powerless in the face of Laura's grief and unable to assist her in coming to terms with their daughter's death. Confined to the role of mother and helpmate, sorting out John's slides, accompanying him wherever his work takes him, she is denied the outlet of work to divert her from her sorrow. The sex sequence which is cleverly intercut with shots of the pair dressing for dinner, and smiling with post-coital contentment, serves to show them momentarily united, despite John's growing irritation with her interest in the paranormal world and her new ability to disobey him. 'Nothing is what it seems,' he tells Laura moments before their daughter's death, and this statement applies to the relationship between Heather and her sister and to the film in general. The strange shot in which the sisters appear to laugh conspiratorially in their hotel room while they wait for Laura to attend the seance she has requested, raises doubts about the genuineness of Heather's clairvoyance and intimates that Wendy (Clelia Matania), the elder sister, who is rather butch in her appearance and manner, is the dominant member of a lesbian partnership. But genuine or not, Laura's meeting with them brings her solace. There is in the film a definite sense that there is a world beyond patriarchy, which these women inhabit, and which has redemptive powers. As John tells the uncomprehending, even sinister police inspector he turns to when Laura goes missing: 'Suddenly she was herself again ... all the things I couldn't do for her, doctors couldn't do for her, these women seemed to do.' The male authority here is a senior representative of that system which fails to catch the killer and prevent John's death.

It is of course in his role as patriarch and protector that John unwittingly pursues the murderous she-dwarf into the deserted *palazzo*, locking the gates behind him to prevent their being followed. 'Don't be frightened, I can help you,' he tells her. It is because he has clung stubbornly to the masculine role he knows and understands that he dies; Laura who changes, and moves beyond her circumscribed role as wife and mother, survives.

'Tutto e macchio!' (Everything is rotten) are the first words John speaks in Venice. He is exploring the green slime and the crumbling stonework at the base of the church he has come to restore, and as he speaks these words, the camera pulls back from a close-up of the dank stonework and the dark façade of the building to show us a vista of the Venice familiar to tourists and immortalised by Canaletto – a white marble basilica is seen across the canal, saturated with light, as two gondolas pass in front of it. Roeg was, presumably, attracted to Du Maurier's short story, which forms the basis of the film, precisely because of this setting and its description of the paranormal; but he has made of it something infinitely richer, multilayered, almost overburdened with associations, like Venice itself – truly 'excessive' in every way.[5] As the film proceeds towards its relentless conclusion, the city evokes a history of literary and cultural associations; it is the embodiment of all that is sinister, corrupt and macabre, in a line that can be traced back to Elizabethan and Jacobean drama.

In Roeg's next film, *The Man Who Fell to Earth* (1976) it is the theme of alienation from place that is central. David Bowie plays Newton, an alien sent to earth to find water for his planet. Failing to find solace in a sexual relationship he turns to alcoholism. His inventive abilities are exploited for corporate gain, while his attempt to reveal his true self to his partner is met with horror and incomprehension. The casting of Bowie as Newton is again an apposite choice on Roeg's part. The theme of alienation runs through Bowie's music in this period, and is optimised both in the assumption of the alien form of Ziggy Stardust, and his deliberately *déraciné* years in West Berlin. Repeatedly, throughout his career, whatever persona he has adopted, Bowie has questioned traditional notions of masculinity. The film encountered problems with the censors because of the explicitly sexual nature of certain scenes. In its portrayal of these particular excesses, it was regarded as going too far, and showing too much.

The Man Who Fell to Earth had been shot in the United States and financed by the internationally minded British Lion. *Bad Timing* (1980) was made as part of the Rank Organisation's last significant production programme. When it emerged in the wake of films like *Wombling Free* (1977), a shocked Rank executive described it as 'a sick film made by sick people for sick audiences' and refused to allow it into Rank cinemas.[6] In fact it is the most complex of Roeg's films, both in terms of its structure and in its presentation of sexual behaviour and voyeurism. As with *Don't Look Now*, the film's setting enhances and informs everything that takes place. Much of the action takes place in Vienna, the epicentre of Europe and European culture, but a city also associated with anonymity, rootlessness and espionage.[7]

The film is organised around an intricate pattern of flashbacks depicting the progress and collapse of the affair between Alex (Art Garfunkel) and Milena (Theresa Russell), which leads to her almost successful suicide attempt, the operations which follow and Alex's interrogation by the police about what actually took place in Milena's apartment the preceding evening. At one point the police inspector Netusil (Harvey Keitel) says to Alex, 'You realise we've been talking for nearly an hour now' – and in fact the timing of Milena's admission to hospital, her operation and the police investigation lasts approximately the same length of time as the average feature film. Such is the complexity of the layering of flashbacks and the sense in which these are taken from the perspective of different characters, that we cannot at any point with certainty say what has actually taken place, or who, if anyone, is to 'blame'. If the need to impose a coherent narrative framework and to establish closure, are part of a patriarchal desire to impose authority, to order, and explain, the film breaks with these demands, just as Milena defies any attempt to restrain her behaviour.

Alex is a research psychoanalyst but he is also required to investigate Milena's past activities as part of his covert work for NATO. First he, and later Netusil, as twin representatives of the world of male authority, are confounded by the literal disorder of Milena's life. Only her much older husband, Stephan (Denholm Elliott) makes no attempt to judge or control her. Teresa de Lauretis observes that Alex and Netusil 'play by the same rules and duplicate or implicate one another as do psychoanalysis and the law, knowledge and power'. She goes on to describe Milena's refusal to be controlled or conform and to resist social demands: 'Milena's offence is against propriety, an offence not juridical but moral: her excess, the sexual, physical and domestic "disorder" that, at least in the movies, marks women who choose to be outside the family.'[8]

Alex is in Vienna, the home of psychoanalysis, to further his career, but Milena disrupts his attempts in every way. She visits him when he is working in Freud's former consulting rooms, enticing him into making love to her on the very couch where the patients of the founding father – many of them Freud's 'hysterical' women – lay to be analysed and 'understood'. She will not marry him, she will not answer his questions, she evades him so that he, the lecturer on voyeurism, is reduced to spying on her. Finally, we discover that it is only when she is in the coma induced by her overdose that he can possess her in the way he wishes. He removes his own clothes, cuts her underwear from her with the precision of a surgeon, using the tiny knife he always carries, and as she lies quiescent, near death, enters her body in an act which moves beyond the 'ravishment' of which Netusil is accusing him, to near-necrophilia. 'Milena', he pleads, 'just let it be like it was in the beginning . . .'.

Netusil, the police officer, is also reduced to the position of voyeur as he attempts to fathom the events of the last few hours. A near-sexual excitement seems to overcome him as he finds himself on the verge of forcing a confession from Alex. The orgasmic moment is interrupted as Stephan enters the room with the news that Milena will live. There is, too, one particular shot where as Netusil enters Milena's flat he seemingly glimpses the entwined naked bodies of Milena and Alex on the bed in front of him. And as he looks through her possessions, he finds some Egon Schiele postcards – in his hands, in these circumstances, they seem quasi-pornographic. The world of 'high art' is referenced right from the start: as the film begins, Alex and Milena are wandering through an exhibition of Gustav Klimt's paintings. Almost immediately, we cut violently from the gallery and the Tom Waits song on the soundtrack to the screeching of a police siren and the interior of an ambulance – chaos supersedes the world of order and the pursuit of cultural capital.

Milena also eludes attempts to interpret or control her through her chameleon-like changes of appearance, her assumptions of different hairstyles, different costumes. One moment she resembles a 50s starlet, the next she becomes Heidi; and then back to the look of Marlene Dietrich and the decadence of pre-war Berlin. This shape-shifting and penchant for constant masquerade finally spills over into her adoption of wig, and carnivalesque make-up. In this scene she has filled her flat with candles – 'Welcome to the wake Alex', she greets him sardonically. Earlier, she has presented Alex with a parodic version of the bourgeois lifestyle and compliant *Hausfrau* that she believes he secretly craves. She tidies her flat so that it is unrecognisable and resembles the meticulous, even obsessive tidiness of Alex's own apartment. She also transforms herself; wearing very little make-up, with her hair pinned neatly back, and a full-skirted orange dress, making herself look as wholesome as Doris Day. But Alex does not respond to her desire to have what she calls 'a conversation, like normal people', and he makes to leave hurriedly. Once again, as on the occasion when they very first met, she chases after him. Now, however, she goads him, lifting her skirt, shouting 'That's what you want Alex, that's all you want isn't it?', and they have swift, rough sex at the top of the stairwell.

The only man in Milena's life who accepts her volatility and does not attempt in any way to alter her behaviour is Stephan, her estranged husband, yet perversely it is his very acceptance that has driven Milena to leave him behind in Czechoslovakia and to come to Vienna in search of new experiences. When she and Alex are on holiday in Morocco and he offers her a proposal of marriage, together with a one-way ticket to New York, she asks him 'What about *now*?' She has no desire for a controlled future just as she resists all attempts to investigate her past. It is only Milena's body, which she will unguardedly offer to Alex, just as it is offered to us, the viewers, as she lies naked on the operating table. There are frequent startling cuts between the sexual activities on Milena's purple sheets and the invasive activities of the doctors as she lies unconscious on the operating table. The sounds of sexual pleasure become the choking gasps of a patient undergoing a tracheotomy; there is a cut from the sight of Alex beating her naked breasts to the doctors attacking them with paddles as she goes into cardiac arrest. We, like Alex and like Netusil have become voyeurs, we want to see more, we want to know more. At the very end of the film as Alex encounters Milena briefly in New York and is unwillingly whirled away from her in a yellow cab, we, like Alex, want explanations; but these are denied us as the closing credits roll up the screen.

Russell's Excess

Roeg's display of the body and of physical encounters was preceded by and then paralleled by the films of Ken Russell. Indeed Russell's films have become synonymous with the notion of visual excess and explicit displays of sexuality.[9] Russell's career, which began with television documentaries in the 60s, was at its most prolific in the 70s when he made no less than eleven feature-length films. His first commercially successful film, *Women in Love* (1969) is an adaptation of Lawrence's novel remarkable for its exploration of gender politics. Rupert Birkin (Alan Bates) is, of all Lawrence's characters, the one who articulates most clearly his ideas on the relations between the sexes and

on the desire for love between men to supplement that between men and women. Rupert's relationship with Ursula (Jennie Linden) is successful because she capitulates to him, sexually and in every way; she also accepts his attacks on the ugliness of modern life and the ways in which it trammels patterns of behaviour and human impulses. Gudrun (Glenda Jackson) is the antithesis of Ursula – antagonistic, capricious and destructive. Gerald Crich (Oliver Reed) is destroyed through his inability to understand or control Gudrun, and can elude her only through suicide. These excessive emotions are mirrored in Russell's cinematic presentation; the film seems to resemble a musical where the narrative is broken up by set pieces and the dialogue interrupted by 'numbers' – the lunch party, the fête, the picnic, the town square at night lit by flares, the fireside wrestling scene, and the Alpine sequences.

Russell makes several changes to the novel. In the film Gerald's mother bursts into obscene, hysterical laughter at her husband's funeral, while, to add melodrama, it is the young newly wedded couple who die together in the lake. In the novel it is a much younger sister and the local doctor who perish. Russell shows us the woman quite literally dragging the man down into the watery depths. He also inserts a scene where Gudrun and her sculptor friend act out sequences from Tchaikovsky's wedding night. In his next film, *The Music Lovers,* he would describe Tchaikovsky's life in graphic detail, and with a typical Russell touch, cast Richard Chamberlain, known internationally as the modest star of the American hospital drama series, *Doctor Kildare,* as Tchaikovsky. Throughout this decade he was to make several films based loosely on the lives of composers, provocatively casting rock singer Roger Daltrey as Liszt, and showing Cosima Wagner in fishnets and jackboots dancing on Mahler's grave. But it is for *Women in Love* and *The Devils* (1971) that Russell is best remembered and which have a lasting cinematic legacy.

If *Women in Love* is lush and pictorial, *The Devils* is theatrical and visually excessive in quite a different way. Based on John Whiting's play and Aldous Huxley's novel *The Devils of Loudun,* it describes the events that took place in the French provincial city of Loudon in 1634. The priest Father Grandier (Oliver Reed), a political liberal and sexual libertine, attempts to prevent the destruction of the city walls as demanded by Cardinal Richelieu (Christopher Logue). He believes, rightly, that persecution of the Huguenots will follow, and that the tolerant community of the city will be destroyed. As a result Grandier himself is destroyed by an alliance between aristocracy, the Church, and a convent of Ursuline nuns. Infected with sexual hysteria the nuns accuse Grandier of satanism, and the film ends with him burning at the stake.

The film is marked by every type of excessive behaviour and different forms of visual extravagance. The narrative consists of a number of extraordinary sequences where colour changes radically to suit the activities on display, from black-and-white to lurid Technicolor. The pre-credit sequence shows us a court masque that depicts the birth of Venus. Venus, who wears a cockleshell bikini, is not only a man but the king himself. Richelieu yawns as he watches the courtiers, mainly men in heavy make-up, embracing one another. In stark contrast, the first shot to follow the credits is that of the worm-filled eye-sockets of a skull; revealed as part of the skeleton of a heretic turning on a wheel. The funeral of the city governor that follows is black, white and smoke-wreathed like a Venetian carnival. We cut immediately to the fantasies of the Mother Superior as she sees Christ (Reed) walking on the water and kneels before him. As she spreads her waist-length hair across his feet, the wind blows back her robes to reveal her hunchback. Scenes of a city devastated by the plague follow: shroud-wrapped corpses are thrown into lime-pits and piled on carts while bonfires rage all around. We see two mountebanks attempting to cure a woman by applying hornets to her naked flesh; Grandier attacks them with their own medicinal crocodile. Back at court, Louis XIII has devised an elaborate game for disposing of rogue Protestants. As they pass before him in fancy dress of black feathers and yellow beak he shoots them one by one and croons to himself 'Bye-bye blackbird'. Richelieu's massive headquarters looks to be a combination of the architectural designs of Albert Speer with the buildings of the Vatican – a vast red cross is emblazoned on monumental glass doors. The last scene is the crowning set piece; Grandier climbs a hill to the stake in a deliberate parody of Christ's journey to the crucifixion. As he burns in agony a near-orgy takes place among the more affluent members of the audience. The plebeians are entertained with a theatrical reconstruction of sinners entering the Mouth of Hell.

Conclusions

The Devils ran into trouble with the censors and could not be released for over a year. In the backlash against the permissive society that accompanied the election of the Heath government in 1970, the graphic portrayal of

Nuns 'infected with sexual hysteria': Ken Russell's *The Devils* (1971)

convent orgies, and the lurid fantasy sequences, where Oliver Reed as Christ descends from the cross to couple with Vanessa Redgrave's hunchbacked Mother Superior, sending his crown of thorns flying, was deemed too excessive even for a director such as Russell.

Derek Jarman, whose set designs helped make *The Devils* so visually distinctive, made his directorial début with a similar story of pain, sensuality and religious persecution. *Sebastiane* (1976), in which the dialogue is entirely in Latin and most of the cast are naked throughout, caused precisely the scandal that Jarman desired. *Jubilee* (1978) draws upon the sense of national crisis that was to reach its apogee in the 'winter of discontent', and presents an apocalyptic vision of a London roamed by riotous punk gangs and the Albert Hall in flames. His use of Vivienne Westwood's assistant, Jordan, wearing rubber stockings and heavy eye make-up, as Britannia, the trident-wielding symbol of English nationhood, was as provocative a gesture as putting a safety-pin through the Queen's nose. The following year Margaret Thatcher was elected and Jarman turned Shakespeare's *The Tempest* into a punk carnival.

The presentation of different forms of excess evident in these films can be taken as a particular response to a society in turmoil and apparent breakdown. One might also have expected a 'realist' response to these circumstances, a continuation of that neo-realism so prevalent in the early 60s. But to find it one has to look to television drama where, because of the parlous state of the British film industry during this period, directors like Ken Loach, Mike Leigh, John Mackenzie and Stephen Frears sought a refuge. They would return in the 80s and attempt to reinstate their disparate notions of realism. Arguably, however, it is Roeg and Russell who have had the most enduring impact on young film-makers.

Notes

1. In fact his boss, Harry Flowers, has a penchant for gay soft porn, as a casual tracking shot shows us.

2. Colin McCabe, *Performance*, p. 83.

3. Moya Luckett, 'Performative Masculinities', in Pamela Church Gibson and Stella Bruzzi (eds), *Fashion Cultures* (London: Routledge, 2000).

4. Mark Sanderson, *Don't Look Now*, p. 22. Roeg's co-director, Donald Cammell, went on to Hollywood, where his own excessive lifestyle meant he was offered decreasingly few opportunities to express his undoubted talent.

5. Part of this multilayering comes from Roeg's cross-referencing to painting and music. Heather's repeated image in the mirror of the washroom of the restaurant after her first meeting with Laura seems designed to evoke the series of triptychs painted by Francis Bacon in the years preceding the film. The use of the overture to *La Traviata* when the Baxters return to their hotel room after their first encounter with the sisters, presages stoicism in the face of grief and the ultimate sundering by death of the central protagonists.

6. Alexander Walker, *National Heroes: British Cinema in the Seventies and Eighties*, p. 208.

7. In one café scene we hear music playing that is a deliberate pastiche of the Harry Lime theme from *The Third Man* (1949).

8. Teresa de Lauretis, 'Now and Nowhere: Roeg's *Bad Timing*', p. 27.

9. Barry Keith Grant, 'The Body Politics: Ken Russell in the 1980s', p. 188.

Bibliography

Butler, Judith, *Gender Trouble: Feminism and the Subversive Identity* (London: Routledge, 1991).

Butler, Judith, 'Melancholy Gender/Refused Identification', in Maurice Berger, Brian Wallis and Simon Watson (eds), *Constructing Masculinities* (London: Routledge, 1995).

de Lauretis, Teresa, 'Now and Nowhere: Roeg's *Bad Timing*', *Discourse* no. 5, 1987.

Grant, Barry Keith, 'The Body Politics: Ken Russell in the 1980s', in Lester Friedman (ed.), *Fires Were Started: British Cinema and Thatcherism* (Minneapolis: University of Minnesota Press, 1993).

Higson, Andrew, 'A Diversity of Film Practices: Renewing British Cinema in the 1970s', in Brian Moore-Gilbert (ed.), *The Arts in the 1970s: Cultural Closure?* (London: Routledge, 1994).

Hunt, Leon, *British Low Culture: From Safari Suits to Sexploitation* (London: Routledge, 1998).

MacCabe, Colin, *Performance* (London: BFI, 1998).

Petley, Julian, 'The Lost Continent', in Charles Barr (ed.), *All Our Yesterdays: 90 Years of British Cinema* (London: BFI, 1986).

Sanderson, Mark, *Don't Look Now* (London: BFI, 1996).

Walker, Alexander, *National Heroes: British Cinema in the Seventies and Eighties* (London: Harrap, 1985).

Wilson, Kristi, 'Time, Space and Vision: Nicolas Roeg's *Don't Look Now*', in *Screen* vol. 40 no. 3, 1999.

PART FIVE

Contemporary British Cinema

37

'New Romanticism' and British Avant-Garde Film in the Early 80s

MICHAEL O'PRAY

Reading the many recent studies of British cinema published in the last decade, it is remarkable how consistent they are in their discussion (where it occurs at all) of experimental film. It would seem, according to them, that the formalist/structural movement of the 1960s and 70s vanished overnight to be supplanted in the early 80s by the art cinema of Derek Jarman, Peter Greenaway and the politically concerned Black film movement.[1] In fact, avant-garde cinema remained alive and kicking throughout the 80s and especially in the years between 1979 and 1985 which saw the flourishing of the New Romantic film movement.[2] Though they had a significant impact at the time, the fact that most of their films were made on Super-8 and were never properly distributed or written about in the influential film journals meant that they failed to find their way onto film studies or art schools' curricula and have subsequently fallen into relative obscurity.

The New Romantic film-makers were active as a loose grouping for only a few years, roughly between 1981 and 1986, reaching a peak in 1983–4. The core group were Cerith Wyn Evans, John Maybury, Holly Warburton, Steve Chivers and Michael Kostiff.[3] Other film-makers and artists associated with them included Roberta Graham, Sophie Muller, Jo Comino, Cordelia Swann, Richard Heslop and Dan Landin, Jill Westwood and Derek Jarman. Wyn Evans and Maybury had held a provocative two-person film show at the ICA in 1981 titled *New Romantic Cinema or A Certain Sensibility* and their status was confirmed when both film-makers were included in the film sessions of the international New Art Show at the Tate Gallery in 1983. Between 1978 and 1986, Maybury made about twenty short films, the majority of them on Super-8, including the mesmeric *Tortures That Laugh* (1983) and *Pantomime Incubus* (1983).

New Romanticism was a cinema of what, at the time, seemed untrammelled excess: using rich colour, superimposition, continually moving camera and an elaborately theatrical *mise en scène*, which mixed high-art iconography and popular culture, and more controversially, sado-masochistic gay imagery culled from cinema, performance art, fashion and pornography. Exterior shots were abandoned in favour of controlled interiors with painted backdrops, handmade exotic costumes, Expressionist chiaroscuro lighting effects and highly orchestrated actor movements.

The New Romantics were characterised both by a particular practice of production, exhibition and distribution, and by their cultural and filmic framework. In these aspects they both shared ground with their forerunners and decidedly differed from them. Just as the 60s counter-culture gave birth to the formalist/structuralist film movement spearheaded by Malcolm Le Grice and Peter Gidal, the New Romantics were immersed in the post-punk culture of their times. They were closely associated with the energetic London club scene which developed from Steve Strange and Rusty Egan's Blitz club in Covent Garden, as well as with performance art (Leigh Bowery, Lindsay Kemp and the neo-Naturists), dance (Michael Clark who appeared in Cerith Wyn Evans's films, the Japanese Sankai Juku theatre), pop music (Throbbing Gristle and Psychic TV, the Fall, whose lead singer Mark E. Smith used Michael Clark and Cerith Wyn Evans in his play *Hey Luciano*, staged at the Riverside in 1986) and fashion.[4] It also had its fine art counterpart in the contemporary art scene, especially the work of Gilbert and George who in the late 1970s and early 80s produced a series of large-scale vividly coloured photographic collages of English subcultural life centred around images of skinheads, young male prostitutes, Union Jacks – the right-wing visual detritus of emergent fascism and early Thatcherism.[5]

The first New Romantic films were a gauntlet thrown down at the political wing of the gay movement. Social consciousness is displaced and high-art camp jostles with a swooning loss of the self. Older audiences were shocked by the sexual and cultural energy of the imagery, which seemed to express a disturbing negative passion.[6] Images of violent, provocative, lumpenproletariat youths with their Nazi tattoos were an aspect of contemporary culture the Left felt unable or unwilling to countenance except as some dark Dickensian force – the Magwitch always on the brink of the British horizon, ready to emerge from the social underworld.

Literature replaced theory as an inspiration – especially Lautréamont, Genet and Burroughs, and when theory was used (Barthes, *Pleasure of the Text*, Bataille's *Eroticism*), it was tinged with sexuality and death. Lack of a 'serious' engagement with politics and social issues led to a negative response from the older generation of gay artists and formalists who saw them as at best reactionary and at worst fascistic. However, proponents of the new Black cinema that emerged in the wake of the New Romantics were more sympathetic. As Kobena Mercer put it 'the 80s have seen a reaction against asceticism, demonstrated in the opulent excess of the "new romantics" '.[7]

While the impact of the right-wing Thatcher government is well noted in discussing films of the 80s, very little attention has been given to the explosion of 'style' culture at the time.[8] The asceticism of the 70s avant-garde was replaced by an aestheticism, which was by no means confined to film culture. In pop music and dance, commentators heralded a post-modernist outlook in which the past was pillaged by fashion, in which style, the surface of things, became paramount; in which sexuality and gender became a matter of lifestyle.

The title of 'New Romantic' had been foisted on the film-makers by curators and critics who felt, justifiably, that there was a connection between their films and the highly successful New Romantic music and fashion cult centred around pop groups such as Spandau Ballet, Depeche Mode, Duran Duran, the

Human League and Culture Club.[9] Despite Maybury and Wyn Evans's contacts with pop artists like Boy George, they had high-art aspirations which were not to be conflated with the commercial ambitions of pop music.[10] But the Blitz club culture which affected music, dance, fashion, journalism and design had introduced a visual excess which was also a characteristic of New Romantic film-making.

The New Romantics' break from an avant-garde conceptual modernism, was supported by the advocates of Scratch video, whose technological exploitation of the Sony V series and pleasurable-cum-critical plundering of mainstream cinema and broadcast television signalled a similar imagistic flow. In 1982 the video artist George Barber, its leading figure, associated the two movements in terms of their revolt against an austere modernism:

> the New Romantics explored the myriad permutations of how 'beautiful' one could make a film image – lace, snow, reflections, over- and under-exposure, wind machines, flowers etc.; while Scratch, with its customary light-fingered approach, spent more time hustling the rules of how pictures go together, searching for the aesthetic moments that have gone underrated and unappreciated when the stuff was first broadcast on TV.[11]

Barber remarks that the clubs 'helped ground an aesthetic for both the New Romantics and Scratch – one of 'visual pleasure'.[12] The clubs were also the grass-roots 'exhibition' space for both movements.

In terms of film influence and inspiration, the New Romantics were diametrically opposed to the dominant practical and theoretical model of structural/formal film-making of the mid-70s and leapfrogged back to 1950s and 60s American avant-gardists such as Maya Deren, Andy Warhol, Kenneth Anger, Jack Smith and Ron Rice. Other influences came from the poetic surrealism of Jean Cocteau's films – particularly *Le Sang d'un Poète* (1930) and *Orphée* (1950) and from the operatic extremes of New German Cinema marked by Rainer Werner Fassbinder's *The Bitter Tears of Petra von Kant* (1972) and Werner Schroeter's *The Death of Maria Malibran* (1972).

Structural film had occupied an influential position both as an art practice and in film theory. The formal film, with its emphasis on process and its call for anti-illusionism, was embraced, if at times uncomfortably, by theoretical journals such as *Screen*, where Le Grice,

Gidal and their supporters aired their views.[13] The New Romantics marked a radical break with this aesthetic and its aspirations. As John Maybury stated in the programme notes to the ICA show:

> Our criteria for visual response have been permanently altered – sophisticated advertising and slick promotional videos have picked up the line from where the surrealists and German Expressionists left it. Experimentation was side-tracked up the blind alley of structuralism which effectively murdered underground film. I see my films as an Amateur-Hour alternative to this academic death.[14]

Besides Maybury's rhetoric and his allying with 'underground film', there is a strong desire to relate film to the culture at large, to images and ideas lying outside the narrow confines of the formalist tradition. Maybury's use of the word 'amateur' indicates his alliance with the post-punk culture of self-help and anti-professionalism manifested in fanzines and the new style magazines.

It was the New Romantics, together with Jarman, who helped to give the Super-8 film gauge its strong presence in the 80s avant-garde. First marketed by Kodak in 1965 as an amateur gauge, Super-8 was cheaper than 16mm, which had been used for most avant-garde work to that date. The cameras used a 50-ft cartridge producing less than two minutes of film at normal projection speeds. The preferred camera was a Braun Nizo which had a good-quality lens and many devices for effects – fades, slow-motion, etc.[15] In the hands of visual arts-trained makers it lent the work a distinctive feel, though it was the fact that it was notoriously difficult to edit which accounts for the slowly paced block-sequences in the films. Fast montage-style editing was impractical with Super-8.[16]

The New Romantics were also very aware of the possibilities of the burgeoning video medium, especially for editing purposes and refilming. John Maybury was already working in video by 1983 with his two-hour-long *Circus Logic* and by 1984 Wyn Evans was using up-to-date video editing effects in order to manipulate the image and the colour of films such as *Epiphany*. For distribution and exhibition purposes 16mm was used, as most cinemas in the early 80s, even art-house ones, had no facilities to project either Super-8 or video. For those films not transferred to 16mm, which was most of them, distribution was virtually non-existent.[17] Transfer onto video was less often for distribution purposes than as a means of access for curators and critics. Film-makers wished to hold onto the notion of the films as transitory, personal objects, resisting the commodification that distribution demanded.

Music was hard to marry onto Super-8 prints, so music cassettes were synchronised manually to the film projections. This had the advantage of allowing different soundtracks to be used for the same film. The New Romantics sometimes used the long-established London Filmmakers' Co-op cinema and the ICA Cinematheque to show their films, but they more often relied upon non-theatrical venues – clubs, pop venues and large rooms or gallery-type spaces where multi-projection could be used to achieve improvised image-superimpositions.

In terms of style there was an engagement with artifice and images from both high art and popular culture. As with more mainstream directors like Neil Jordan and Julien Temple, there was a harking back to the Romanticism of Michael Powell and Emeric Pressburger, whose post-war extravaganzas – *A Matter of Life and Death* (1946), *Black Narcissus* (1947), *The Red Shoes* (1948) and *The Tales of Hoffman* (1951) – had a sumptuous, exotic, imagistic quality, opening on to an interior maze of performance, art and artifice.

The experience of a watershed, of a groundshift, in the early 80s was as true of art cinema as it was of the avant-garde. Peter Greenaway established himself as a recognisable European art-cinema auteur with *The Draughtsman's Contract* (1982); Sally Potter's experimental art-cinema film, *Thriller* (1979), led to her feature film début, *The Gold Diggers* (1983), although it was another ten years before *Orlando* (1992) brought her the sort of critical recognition Greenaway had enjoyed since *The Draughtsman's Contract*. Derek Jarman, who had propelled himself into art cinema in the late 70s with a trio of successful films – *Sebastiane* (1976), *Jubilee* (1978) and *The Tempest* (1979) – spent the early 80s evolving a distinctive aesthetic in a series of experimental Super-8 shorts under the influence of the New Romantics and the new video technologies – memorably *The Angelic Conversation* (1985) and *Imagining October* (1985).[18] He returned to art-cinema feature films with *Caravaggio* (1986) which he quickly followed with the more experimental *The Last of England* (1987) and three critically successful films – *Edward II* (1991), *Wittgenstein* (1993) and *Blue* (1993) – before his death in 1994.

Jarman was a key figure for the New Romantics. His Super-8 film *In the Shadow of the Sun* (made up of films spanning the 70s and completed in 1980) with its rich

'Provocative sexual imagery': Derek Jarman's *Sebastiane* (1976)

superimpositions, symbolic tableaux and sense of reverie laid some of the groundwork for the New Romantics' own imagistic aesthetics. Equally his explicitly gay erotic film *Sebastiane* opened the way for their own provocative sexual imagery. He was also invaluable for his practical and moral support especially of Maybury and Wyn Evans.

The 80s were, as Geoff Brown has remarked, a time when 'British cinema . . . was weighted towards fantasy, the surreal, and period nostalgia', with Jarman and Greenaway identified as two of the main culprits.[19] But beyond these terrible squabbling twins there was a more general embracing of a visually intense and often self-reflective film-making, found not only in the rococo excesses of the New Romantics but also in films from the black workshop movement such as Isaac Julien's *Territories* (1984) and John Akomfrah's *Handsworth Songs* (1986).[20] In a lower key and with an avoidance of excess, Patrick Keiller's short films – especially *Norwood* (1983), *The End* (1986) and *Valtos* (1987) – shared an imagistic, surrealist, albeit documentarist, approach to contemporary Britain and Europe. On the animation front, the Quay brothers

were beginning their career of baroque-excess film-making, drawing upon East European literature and film with *The Street of Crocodiles* (1986). All these film-makers appeared as an alternative to the formalist project and they all returned to the film-maker as the purveyor of meaning and beauty.

The point to be made here is that separated lineages of film within the same culture often share similar values – what differs is the attitude towards storytelling and size of budget. Though the comparison might seem unlikely, it is possible to draw parallels between pre-war British documentary films, such as John Grierson's *Drifters* (1929) and Basil Wright's *Song of Ceylon* (1934), which draw on Eisenstein's aestheticism for their overwrought Romantic images, and the New Romantics' emphasis on the body, performance and sexuality which can also be traced back to Eisenstein. In fact the shift from the materialist-realism of the Le Gricean formalists, to montage and collaging techniques in which the concatenation of images took precedence over the depiction of reality might be seen as a shift in influence from the Russian avant-garde documentary-maker, Dziga Vertov, to an aesthetic deriving from the later Eisenstein with his interest in the *Gesamtkunstwerk* and the 'synchronisation of the senses'.[21]

For the New Romantics, the notion of avant-gardism was displaced by that of an underground cinema with its implication of sexual and cultural subversion. This was a shift from a conceptual approach that addressed the essential qualities of the medium itself to one of poetics in which images were expressive artifices, though the New Romantics shared with the formalists a suspicion of narrative. The films relied more often than not on the editing together of images, depending on a poetic coherence rather than one of narrative progression (by contrast Kenneth Anger's films, cited as precursors to those of the New Romantics, always retained a narrative, often one, as in *Lucifer Rising*, deriving from mythology). If Gidal and Le Grice countenanced a Warholian stream of time, the visual flow of duration, through a primarily realist approach (long takes of interiors, people, objects and mundane events) then the New Romantics enjoyed concocting fantastic highly elaborated image streams for the camera.

If the 70s had been dominated by empty landscapes and interiors, a depopulated *mise en scène*, the screen space of the New Romantics was filled with bodies. Similarly, Greenaway's films were obsessed with the body often in a decadent form of dissolution, decay and death. *The Draughtsman's Contract* shares an interest in theatricality and the pose as a manner of critique with the New Romantics. As Greenaway admitted:

> My film is about excess: excess in the language, excess in the landscape, which is much too green – we used special green filters – there is no historical realism in the costumes, the women's hair styles are exaggerated in their height, the costumes are extreme. I wanted to make a very artificial film.[22]

The film's opening sequence with its counter-tenor soundtrack, chiaroscuro lighting and high-artifice dialogue, make-up and costume is redolent of the same mood as the New Romantic film-makers and can be contrasted with Cerith Wyn Evans's fifty-minute *Epiphany* made on video and Super-8 and then transferred to 16mm. In his treatment of sexuality in *The Draughtsman's Contract*, Greenaway is cold, cruel and distant as well as being sado-masochistic. In *Epiphany*, the emphasis is more on masquerade: the body acting out parts – performing sometimes in the regalia of the professional masochist, the skinhead, the Holy Communion girl, the masked mannequin-like gay lovers. *Epiphany* is a narcissistic tract in which figurations, actions and style set out to shock, to transgress, but in a languorous, Pateresque kind of way.

The film begins with what seems to be a young middle-class schoolboy applying stage make-up to his face before a globe of the world. The image cuts to one of an old man whose face fades in and out of a skull. The soundtrack speaks intermittently of mortality and death. In the next shot, a young man hangs naked,

'I wanted to make a very artificial film': Peter Greenaway's *The Draughtsman's Contract* (1982)

followed by slowed-down Super-8 footage of two masked young men dancing. The film has no obvious structure but is like a series of fantasies linked together through music, and works as a poetic reverie. Images drift in and out, sometimes gaining some kind of autonomy only to drift away or be obscured by other images.[23] In this way the film becomes exemplary of what Jon Savage described as the 'enclosed world' of New Romanticism in which the 'Self is now turned into an Art Object'.[24]

As with many of Jarman's and Greenaway's films, there is a painterly aspect to *Epiphany*, most apparent in its aesthetic of shallow, often confused, depth, established through swirling superimpositions. This layering of the screen plane can be contrasted with the deep-space realism of formalist/conceptual film-making in which the camera's ability to achieve the representation of 'natural' perspective is largely taken for granted. Figures 'act out' before screens on which are projected images of bodies. In one sequence, a louche young man acting as a model, and dressed in classical costume, poses in front of an El Greco painting, flirtatiously smoking a cigarette and gazing into the camera – reconstructing ironically the traditional role of the painter's model.

Like other avant-gardes, the New Romantics dispersed after the white-hot moment of hectic innovation and commitment had passed. Maybury followed a highly successful pop-video career culminating in three MTV awards for his video for Sinead O'Connor's pop hit 'Nothing Compares 2 U' (1989). At the same time he made a series of hi-tech experimental videos such as *Remembrance of Things Fast* (1993), eventually turning to art cinema with the highly acclaimed *Love Is the Devil* (1998) an exploration of the turbulent love-life of artist Francis Bacon.[25] Wyn Evans returned to sculpture in the late 80s with only odd forays into film. He re-emerged in the mid-90s as a successful conceptual artist in the Young British Art movement.[26] Steve Chivers entered the film industry as a cinematographer and Holly Warburton followed a career as a professional photographer.

In summary, the New Romantics acted as a generational response to the formalist hegemony of the 70s. They also exemplified some of the aesthetic and thematic strategies found in other strands of 80s cinema – excess and artifice, an engagement with European art cinema, irony, a fascination with the body and sexuality – which also characterises the work of Jarman, Greenaway, the Quay brothers, Isaac Julien and John Akomfrah. They also represent the last coherent grouping within the British avant-garde whose project was not only pointed towards their own futures but also engaged with a critique of the tradition as they saw it.[27]

Notes

1. See especially John Hill, *British Cinema in the 1980s*, Sarah Street, *British National Cinema* (London and New York: Routledge, 1997) and Claire Smith's 'Travelling Light: New Art Cinema in the 90s', in Robert Murphy (ed.), *British Cinema of the 90s* (London: BFI, 2000). Peter Wollen's 'The Last New Wave: Modernism in the British Films of the Thatcher Era', mentions the New Romantics in relation to Jarman.

2. Important evidence for which is the Tate Gallery show *British Film and Video 1980–85: The New Pluralism* selected by Tina Keane and myself in 1985, which was shortly followed by the Arts Council/British Council international touring show of 1987, *The Elusive Sign, British Avant-garde Film and Video 1977–1987*. See also A. L. Rees, *A History of Experimental Film and Video*, pp. 96–107. My own remarks about this period and the changes it heralded were careful not to deny the eclipse of the avant-garde but rather to suggest that there was a pluralism and hybridity of forms that emerged in the 80s.

3. Maybury had worked with Jarman on *Jubilee*.

4. See Sue Tilley, *Leigh Bowery: The Life and Time of an Icon* (London: Hodder & Stoughton, 1997), pp. 197–8.

5. See Wolf Jahn, *The Art of Gilbert and George* (London: Thames and Hudson, 1989).

6. The same sense of outrage had been expressed about Nic Roeg and Donald Cammell's *Performance* when it was first shown in 1971.

7. Kobena Mercer, 'Sexual Identities: Questions of Difference', in *Undercut* no. 17, Spring 1988, p. 19.

8. See Hill, *British Cinema in the 1980s*, especially Chapter 1.

9. On pop New Romanticism see Dave Rimmer, *Like Punk Never Happened: Culture Club and the New Pop*; Dick Hebdige, *Hiding in the Light: On Images and Things*; and Barney Hoskyns, *Glam! Bowie, Bolan and the Glitter Rock Revolution*.

10. On such contacts see Boy George, *Take It Like a Man: The Autobiography of Boy George*; and Sue Tilley, *Leigh Bowery: The Life and Time of an Icon*, op cit.

11. George Barber, 'Scratch and After – Edit-Suite Technology and the Determination of Style in Video Art', in Philip Haywood (ed.), *Culture, Technology and Creativity in the Late Twentieth Century*, p. 112.

12. Ibid., p. 114.

13. Le Grice's aesthetic is embodied in his history of formal film, *Abstract Film and Beyond* (London: Studio Vista, 1977); see also Peter Gidal, *Structural Film* (London: BFI, 1977), and essays by Deke Dusinberre, Stephen Heath, Ben Brewster, Rod Stoneman, Pam Cook, A. L. Rees and others in *Screen*.

14. ICA broadsheet for 'New Romantics: A Certain Sensibility' show, 1981.

15. Jarman used the Nizo camera as did most of the New Romantic film-makers, especially the ones who worked with the producer James Mackay.

16. On technical aspects of Super-8 in the 80s see Jo Comino's notes in *Recent British Super-8 Film* (Film and Video Umbrella broadsheet, 1985).

17. When the Film and Video Umbrella toured a three-programme Super-8 package in 1985, projectors had to be supplied to most of the regional film theatres and galleries who showed the work.

18. Jarman also made artistically interesting pop videos, particularly for the Smiths.

19. Geoff Brown, 'Paradise Found and Lost: The Course of British Realism', Chapter 4 in the present volume.

20. See Wollen, 'The Last New Wave: Modernism in the British Films of the Thatcher Era', p. 45, for Jarman's attacks on Greenaway. Stuart Hall noted that in *Handsworth Songs*, the 'documentary footage has been retimed, tinted, overprinted so as to formalise and distance it'. Stuart Hall, 'Song of Handsworth Praise', *Guardian*, 15 January 1987, reprinted in *Black Film, Black Cinema*, (ICA Documents 7, 1988), p. 17.

21. Things are never neat – Le Grice's *Berlin Horse* (1970) uses superimposition, colour, music and the collage aesthetic.

22. Peter Greenaway, 'Meurtre dans un jardin anglais', *L'avant-scène cinema* (Paris) no. 333, October 1984, translated and quoted by Peter Wollen in 'The Last New Wave: Modernism in the British Films of the Thatcher Era', p. 45.

23. In Gray Watson's notes for the New Art show he describes Wyn Evans's work as concerned with a 'phenomenology', that is to say with the desire to capture the experience of states of consciousness. *New Art: Audio Visual* (London: Tate Gallery Publications, 1983).

24. Jon Savage, *Time Travel: Pop, Media and Sexuality 1976–96*, p. 122.

25. After a long interval Maybury made an expensive, complex and ambitious American psychic thriller *The Jacket* (2005); *The Edge of Love* followed in 2008.

26. Wyn Evans was also associated (as a model) with another famous English painter, Lucien Freud.

27. This view of a 'final moment' received some support in the title of an exhibition dealing with the period and including film/video work by Jarman, Maybury, Wyn Evans and other artists alluded to in this chapter – the neo-Naturists, Michael Clark, Leigh Bowery and the Fall. See 'The Secret Public/The Last Days of the British Underground 1978–1988', ICA, London, March–May 2007.

Bibliography

Barber, George, 'Scratch and After – Edit-Suite Technology and the Determination of Style in Video Art', in Philip Haywood (ed.), *Culture, Technology and Creativity in the Late Twentieth Century* (Luton: John Libbey/Arts Council of Great Britain 1990).

Boy George (with Spencer Bright), *Take It Like a Man: The Autobiography of Boy George* (London: Sidgwick and Jackson 1995).

Bracewell, Michael, *England Is Mine: Pop Life in Albion from Wilde to Goldie* (London: Flamingo, 1998).

Hamlyn, Nicky, 'Recent English Super-8 at B2 Gallery', *Undercut* nos 10–11, Winter 1983.

Hebdige, Dick, *Hiding in the Light: On Images and Things* (London: Comedia, 1988).

Hill, John, *British Cinema in the 1980s* (Oxford: Clarendon Press, 1999).

Hollings, Ken, 'The Dead Rose: Anger and After', *Performance Magazine*, 1984.

Hoskyns, Barney, *Glam! Bowie, Bolan and the Glitter Rock Revolution* (London: Faber and Faber, 1998).

Jameson, Fredric, *Signatures of the Visible* (London and New York: Routledge, 1992).

Letcher, Piers, 'John Maybury: *Circus Logic*', *Performance Magazine*, September–October 1984.

O'Pray, Michael, *Derek Jarman: Dreams of England* (London: BFI, 1996).

O'Pray, Michael, 'The British Avant-Garde and Art Cinema from the 1970s to the 1990s', in Andrew Higson (ed.), *Dissolving Views: Key Writings on British Cinema* (London: Cassell, 1996).

Orr, John, 'The Art of National Identity: Peter Greenaway and Derek Jarman', in Justine Ashby and Andrew Higson (eds), *British Cinema: Past and Present* (London and New York: Routledge, 2000).

Rees, A. L., *A History of Experimental Film and Video* (London: BFI, 1999).

Rimmer, Dave, *Like Punk Never Happened: Culture Club and the New Pop* (London: Faber and Faber, 1985).

Savage, Jon, *Time Travel: Pop, Media and Sexuality 1976–96* (London: Chatto and Windus, 1996).

Wollen, Peter, 'The Last New Wave: Modernism in the British Films of the Thatcher Era', in Lester Friedman (ed.), *Fires Were Started: British Cinema and Thatcherism* (London: UCL Press, 1993; 2nd edn, London: Wallflower Press, 2006).

38

Internal Decolonisation?
British Cinema in the Celtic Fringe

Martin McLoone

One of British cinema's most interesting début films of recent years was Saul Metzstein's *Late Night Shopping* (2001), an understated look at contemporary urban angst and the problems of today's disaffected and disengaged twenty-somethings. The film is remarkable for the fact that it is acerbic, cynical, metaphysical and Romantic all at the same time. What is even more remarkable, however, is that this is a Scottish film that, aside from a few peripheral accents, makes little or no reference to anything that is immediately recognisable as Scotland. Despite being set in Glasgow and partly shot on location there, its stylised vision of the city is more akin to Godard's *Alphaville* (1965) and the milieu more that of dystopian alienation than anything geographically specific. The four central characters are non-specifically British and the peripheral characters a strange mixture of European, Scottish and English.

In this regard, it bears a strong resemblance to Justin Kerrigan's Welsh-set *Human Traffic* (1999), a frenetic study of a Cardiff club culture that is fuelled by drink, dope, ecstasy and dance music. Kerrigan again explores youthful alienation through a group of central characters who are similarly cast adrift in a stylised urban milieu that is more emblematic than it is real. Again, the film avoids, for the most part, any specifically Welsh references, creating characters who are Welsh by residence rather than by ethnicity and an environment that is broadly Anglo-American rather than specific to its Cardiff setting. This sense of urban placeless-ness is well illustrated in one arresting image in the film. As the central characters emerge into the pale light of dawn from their night on drugs and drink, we get a time-lapse sequence over the city, marking the slow emergence of a new day. The music on the soundtrack is a piece called 'Belfast' by English techno duo, Orbital, and its contemporary dance rhythms and spacey technological mood perfectly sum up the film's enduring atmosphere of dislocation and 'in-betweenness'.

These two films challenge traditional notions of British cinema in interesting and complex ways. Their genesis on the 'Celtic fringe' is important. In the past, British cinema represented a kind of national allegory, a homogeneous national cinema that to all intents and purposes was synonymous with 'Englishness'. This itself tended to be a very specific kind of Englishness – metropolitan, middle class and assertive – that attempted to enlist the notion of Britain behind a narrow set of political, social and ideological perspectives. In this regard, Britain's Celtic fringe (Scotland and Wales specifically but also Northern Ireland with some important qualifications) was not so much ignored as traduced into playing a peripheral and heavily circumscribed role within the larger national project. In a sense, the primitive, beautiful landscapes of Scotland, Wales and Ireland have provided a Romantic counterpoint to England's metropolitan urbanity and the Celtic peoples – those essentially irrational, but lovable rogues – have ultimately been created to reinforce the dominance of the centre and its right to rule. Many years ago, Michael Hechter described this process as a form of internal colonialism, one that depended upon a strict cultural division of labour in which England and Englishness predominated and the Celtic fringes and their primitive languages were marginal.[1]

Breaking out of British Cinema

As far as British film-making is concerned, the Celtic fringes were represented within a particular circuit of imagery and narrative that reflected this dominance. In relation to cinematic Scotland, this tradition was identified and analysed by Colin McArthur as a combination of tartanry (Romantic evocations of the Highlands) and what has been called 'kailyardism' – the representation of Scotland through village or small-town life.[2] The regressive and nostalgic nature of kailyardism is filtered through the village's wise (or naturally wily) characters whose role in life is to point out the shortcomings and worldliness of big-city life or to resist interventions from the modern world outside. In fact kailyardism has its Irish and Welsh equivalents (although less seldom associated with Northern Ireland) and one of the most successful British films of 1999 was just such a piece of Irish-set kailyardism, Kirk Jones's *Waking Ned* (in the US, *Waking Ned Devine*). In the film, the Isle of Man stood in for Ireland, but given the similarity of *Waking Ned* to such classic Scottish kailyard movies as Alexander Mackendrick's, *Whisky Galore!* (1949) and *The Maggie* (1954), it could just as easily have been Scotland.[3] The most commercially successful example of Welsh 'kailyardism' in recent years was Christopher Monger's *The Englishman Who Went up a Hill But Came down a Mountain* (1995) in which the canny natives of Wales attempt to outwit the controlling impulses of the centre represented by Hugh Grant's amiable, stammering English surveyor. A more home-grown version of Welsh small-town life was Sara Sugarman's *Very Annie Mary* (2001); but even though this approached the tradition from a decidedly non-traditional perspective, with Australian Rachel Griffiths playing the gawky Welsh heroine, many

Early-morning symmetry: Luke de Woolfson and Kate Ashfield in *Late Night Shopping* (Saul Metzstein, 2001)

of the stereotypes (of fire-and-brimstone chapel culture, for example) were invoked for the purpose.

Both *Late Night Shopping* and *Human Traffic* attempt to move beyond these dominant stereotypes and to recast the centre and the periphery differently. If one film comes across as 'anywhere-but-Scotland' and the other as 'anywhere-but-Wales' this is because they both maintain their position as 'anywhere-but-traditionally-British'. In this way, the films are best viewed as two recent examples of a now substantial body of work that represents a kind of cinematic decolonisation of Britain's Celtic fringe. A closer look at *Human Traffic* shows just how this works.

The film opens with one of the central characters, Jip (John Simm), addressing the camera directly. His talking head is framed on either side by clocks that give the time concurrently in Cardiff and in New York. (Later, we see that the clock hidden behind his head gives the time in Tokyo as well). One of the film's main themes is that Jip and his friends would rather be anywhere else than in the reality of the 'here today'. As Jip himself intimates, the weekend 'has landed', offering him and his friends a forty-eight-hour escape into the club scene with its attendant pleasures of rave music, ecstasy, dope and drink. The film, in other words, offers us a vision of Cardiff that is 'anywhere-but-Wales', a point emphasised in a scene later when Jip stops to admire a young break-dancer performing in an alleyway – in Jip's fantasy, this is Cardiff as New York. Furthermore, the main characters in the film, Jip and his druggy friends, are residents of Wales rather than Welsh by birth or ethnicity, emphasising the strange sense of dislocation or 'in-betweenness' that hangs over the whole film.

The cultural universe that these young people inhabit is, therefore, an imagined community that is Anglo American in a broad sense rather than either specifically British or Welsh. The film is peppered with many American cultural references (especially to the films *Star Wars*, 1977 and *Taxi Driver*, 1976). And yet Jip and his pals feel themselves to be on the margins, not just of society in general (as represented by their parents' generation), but also of some centre of energy and cultural activity that is located elsewhere in time and space. The drugs that fuel their weekend escape are designed to take them to this place – an ill-defined cultural universe that lies beyond the reality of their lived experience.

In one of the film's many fantasy sequences, this anxiety is articulated in a parody of the kind of British patriotism and jingoism that is characteristic of the last night of the Proms. Jip leads his friends and eventually, it would appear, the whole generation of the young in a rendition of a reconfigured national anthem ('Who Is the Queen?'). Jip's new version ('generation . . . alienation . . . virtual reality') is perhaps a little bland and obvious and it does not carry the same cultural charge as the Sex Pistols' bitterly subversive 'God Save the Queen' did back in the Silver Jubilee summer of 1977. Nonetheless, given the cultural position of Wales within the larger construct of Britain, the sentiments are full of resonance and pathos. They express an anxiety and confusion about national or cultural identity in the film that is as important to the young protagonists as questions about personal, family, generational or sexual identity.

As many critics and observers noted at the time of its release, the film that *Human Traffic* most resembles is not any of the American films it makes references to but *Trainspotting* (1996), Danny Boyle's highly successful vision of Edinburgh as 'anywhere-but-Scotland'. Indeed, while *Trainspotting* offers a particularly irreverent approach to heroin addicts and the culture of drug dependency, it locates this within a cultural milieu that is also decidedly unstable. This is an Edinburgh bereft of its normal cultural, military, political and governmental baggage and a Scotland that, as the film's main character Renton (Ewan McGregor) puts it, 'is a shite state of affairs'. Part of the film's irreverence, then, is not just its approach to the highly emotive issue of drugs but also to a set of cultural signifiers that have operated to denote 'Scotland', both the Scotland of metropolitan disdain and of Scottish nationalist rhetoric. There is in the film a (less-than-gentle) play with aspects of Scottish 'tartanry' and especially in its mild satirising of Scottish National Party supporter, Sean Connery, a critique of nationalist pretensions. In this way, the film raises a set of interesting issues around the notion of 'Britishness' and of Scotland's relationship to it, and *Human Traffic* tries to do for Cardiff and Wales what *Trainspotting* had done for Edinburgh and Scotland. What is being questioned in both films, if not rejected outright, are traditional notions of Britishness, Welshness and Scottishness and the dominant regimes of imagery that the cinema has used to represent them. If the films represent a kind of cultural decolonisation of Scotland and Wales, then the genesis of this development can be traced back to the 1980s and the long years of Margaret Thatcher's hegemony in Britain.

Thatcher's success was built on the fact that she captured the electoral support of England's Midlands and the South. She had minimal support in either Scotland or Wales, both of which endured her essentially English

nationalism with increasing irritation. Ironically, then, the Thatcherite hegemony was to resuscitate and reinvigorate Scottish and Welsh nationalism and to raise very fundamental questions about the nature of Britishness itself. As a concomitant, both countries experienced something of a cultural renaissance and more diverse and complex notions of what constituted Britishness were canvassed. In cinematic terms this resulted in an increasing devolution of metropolitan production and funding to the regions with a desire to reflect cinematically a more diverse sense of British identity. There are now substantial funding arrangements in place in Scotland, Wales and Northern Ireland, a kind of devolved film industry that has mirrored the new devolved political assemblies in Edinburgh, Cardiff and Belfast. British cinema has increasingly begun to reflect the complex identities that now exist within and between these areas and to explore especially their relationship to both Englishness and Britishness.[4]

In other words, what unites the film-making that has recently emerged from Scotland, Wales and Northern Ireland is the fact that the films have been concerned to both challenge and move beyond traditional representations of the Celtic periphery. There are, of course, subtle and profound differences in the manner in which the films attempt to do this. Nonetheless, the shared factor in the experience of all three regions is that finally, in the 1990s, sufficient funding and technical facilities were made available to sustain a concerted programme of indigenous film production.

Belfast beyond the Troubles

The case of Northern Ireland is different to that of the other regions. Although it is technically not 'British', Northern Ireland is part of the United Kingdom (of Great Britain and Northern Ireland). It is this disputed reality that has fuelled thirty years of conflict over definitions of identity (British, Irish, Unionist, Nationalist, Protestant, Catholic) in a more upfront way than in Scotland and Wales. Northern Ireland has, as a result, enjoyed a high media profile internationally as a running news story and in the 1990s the conflict featured as a narrative device for an increasing number of high-profile American and British fiction films. However, it was entirely predictable and understandable that Northern Ireland would also demand the right to produce and control its own images in both television and cinema. With the necessary infrastructure in place, a new kind of iconography has begun to emerge, one that attempts to move beyond dominant images of the Troubles (and Troubles movies).

The new cinema in Northern Ireland emerged as a cultural outflow from the protracted peace process of the 1990s rather than as a cultural response to Thatcher's Britain as was the case with Scotland and Wales. The anxieties that the new Northern Irish cinema addresses are, not surprisingly, rather less metaphysical than those of either *Late Night Shopping* or *Human Traffic*. The evidence of recent cinema would suggest that Northern Ireland is being re-imagined not as a place of angst and alienation but rather as a place of middle-class consumption – as a haven for late-night shopping which can be celebrated without guilt or fear.

The humour and irreverence for established morality that is so pronounced in *Trainspotting* and Danny Boyle's earlier Edinburgh thriller, *Shallow Grave* (1994) was deployed by David Caffrey in his black comedy of the Northern Irish Troubles *Divorcing Jack* (1998). The film is relentless in its irreverence, so that none of the institutions of the Troubles (or Troubles movies) escapes lampooning. A grubby and incompetent shoot-out involving Loyalists is accompanied by a snatch of *The Magnificent Seven*'s epic theme music; and Caffrey builds into his film a clever reference to the kind of critical challenge that irreverence and black humour pose in relation to a subject matter that is usually deemed no laughing matter. In a paramilitary drinking club, a stand-up comedian tells a joke that is decidedly uncomplimentary to the intelligence of the average terrorist. The joke is funny but there is an awkward silence while the audience gauges whether or not it is acceptable or even safe to laugh. After a few uncertain seconds, the paramilitary leader finally guffaws (now it's a double joke – such is the slowness of the paramilitary mind that it takes a minute or so for the penny to drop). The rest of the audience can now join in, relieved to have been let off the hook. Such moments of comic invention offer a devastating critique of the Romantic pretensions and macho culture of paramilitaries of all kinds.[5]

Divorcing Jack's attempt to destabilise dominant notions of Northern Ireland by approaching political instability and paramilitary violence through this characteristic 1990s trope of irreverence and black humour contrasts with more lugubrious films such as Thaddeus O'Sullivan's *Nothing Personal* (1995), Colm Villa's *Sunset Heights* (1997) or Mark Evans's *Resurrection Man* (1998). But if *Divorcing Jack* was closer in spirit to the likes of *Trainspotting* and *Human Traffic*, Northern Ireland, even in its post-Good Friday Agreement manifestation, remained a more dangerous and unpredictable setting than Scotland and Wales, and events on the ground

were liable to stifle the laughter in mid-flow. The year that *Divorcing Jack* was released was also the year that a bomb planted by dissident Republicans killed twenty-nine men, women and children as they shopped in the quiet market town of Omagh.

Michael Winterbottom's adult comedy *With or without You* (1999) and Declan Lowney's amiable romantic comedy *Wild about Harry* (2000) adopt a different strategy: both are set in a contemporary Belfast which is 'anywhere-but-Northern Ireland', at least a Northern Ireland of violence and sectarian conflict. The sectarian geography of Belfast with its dominant iconography (wall murals, slogans, Orange marching bands, and army and police Land Rovers) is here replaced with images of urban renewal and brightly lit historic buildings. The iconography of both films is that of an affluent middle class with its culture of high-spend consumerism and metropolitan aspirations. In *Wild about Harry*, Belfast is re-imagined as part of an Anglo-American media universe. Certainly there are culturally specific references and asides throughout the film; but the small provincial television station which celebrity chef Harry McKee (Brendan Gleeson) works for represents media marginality in a general rather than in a nationally or regionally specific way. In the film's climax, Harry is threatened at gunpoint on live television ensuring that his local cookery programme finally gets onto the network, eventually going international as 'breaking news'.

After a random mugging in which he is severely beaten about the head, Harry suffers from a form of amnesia that wipes out all memory of the last twenty-five years of his life. This gives him a second chance to repair his broken marriage and to find again the love and optimism of his eighteen-year-old self and around this premise, the film plays out its amusing romantic love story. In a sense, though, the film performs a similar form of amnesia about twenty-five years of political strife and violence and deliberately creates a Belfast that is both beyond and before the Troubles. Like Harry's life, it is a Belfast of reconstruction and rebuilding, an image of Northern Ireland that moves beyond dominant representations.

Winterbottom's *With or Without You* is, in many ways, the apogee of the new Northern Ireland film. One of its main locations is the Waterfront Hall in Belfast, an ultra-modern concert, conference and exhibition centre that has come to symbolise the new, aspiring and increasingly affluent Belfast of the late 1990s. The film's protagonist is Rosie Boyd (Dervla Kirwan) now thirty and desperately, though unsuccessfully, trying to start a family with her husband, Vincent (Christopher Eccleston). Rosie works as a receptionist in the Waterfront; much of the film is shot inside and outside the Hall, its art galleries and chic restaurants giving an unusually modern and cosmopolitan view of contemporary Belfast. When the French penpal of Rosie's adolescence suddenly shows up, he adds considerably to the tensions and anxieties. In one remarkable scene, shot in the roof-top restaurant of the Waterfront Hall, Rosie and the newly arrived Benoît (Yvan Attal) chat about how their lives have developed since their correspondence ended ten years earlier. As the camera pans 360 degrees around the couple we see the downtown cityscape stretched out below, and Rosie links specific landmarks to key moments in her own life. As Benoît starts to fill in some details of his life, the camera seems to assume a purpose of its own and his story is juxtaposed with a montage of shots of urban Belfast that are totally unmotivated by narrative logic. This montage seems to emphasise the ordinariness of downtown Belfast while, perversely, also underlining just how unusual this urban banality is in terms of dominant representations. The setting, iconography and themes of the film are, therefore, located in an urban milieu that is unspecifically contemporary and far removed from the representations of Northern Ireland that have dominated film and television for many years. While the film ultimately offers a conservative message about the nature of true love and the sanctity of marriage, it is hard not to read Rosie's eventual pregnancy and reconciliation with Vincent as an upbeat metaphor for the affluent, middle-class and consumerist Northern Ireland that is itself struggling to be born in the wake of the peace process.

New Wales Cinema

Like *Divorcing Jack*, Kevin Allen's Swansea-set *Twin Town* (1997) elects to tackle stereotypes and cinematic clichés directly. As its already bizarre plot rushes towards a climax of melodramatic excess and bad taste, central icons and cultural markers of Welsh identity (rugby, community and male-voice choirs) are lampooned into absurdity. *Twin Town* – anarchic, populist, youth-orientated – contrasts with a more meditatively inclined group of Welsh-language films. The best are concerned with the state of Wales and Welshness in a contemporary context: exploring the heritage of the past, the condition of the present and the prospects for the future. At the centre of the films is the place of the Welsh language itself and indeed, the most impressive aspect of the Welsh-language films in general has been the total confidence

Tudor Roberts faces a crisis of identity in Endaf Emlyn's *Un Nos Ola' Leuad/One Full Moon* (1991)

they demonstrate in the contemporary relevance of the ancient tongue.

In Endaf Emlyn's *Un Nos Ola' Leuad/One Full Moon* (1991) the relationship between the English and Welsh language is a factor in the crisis of identity that faces the film's protagonist, an unnamed boy (Tudor Roberts). In the village school, the children speak English and are encouraged to associate English with access to power and influence – the Welsh-speaking children are clearly seen as objects of exploitation and in the case of one young girl, of sexual exploitation as well. The boy is asked to read a passage of English by the schoolmaster and the local Anglican canon. He performs the task well enough in a halting, cautious manner but pronounces the word 'society' according to Welsh phonetics. This reduces his superiors to laughter. Society, the film suggests, just like community, culture and history, is recognised through the language that describes it.

It would be wrong though to see Welsh-language cinema as an unthinking nationalist response to dominant English culture or one that collapses the complexities of identity into dubious essentialist categories. *Un Nos Ola' Leuad* is as critical of the oppressive aspects of Welshness as it is of English superiority and is especially scathing about the negative impact Welsh fundamentalist religion has had on women and the young. (In this it dovetails with a tendency in recent Irish cinema which similarly attacks the abuses of religion especially as these were visited on the young and on women.) *Un Nos Ola' Leuad* is a brooding, sonorous, deeply disturbing film that reconfigures the beautiful Welsh scenery of Romantic evocation by associating it with sexual repression, murder, communal conflict and collective madness.

In his next film, *Gadael Lenin/Leaving Lenin* (1994), Emlyn considerably lightens the mood. Here, he explores contemporary Welsh identity through the device of removing his Welsh characters from Wales itself to post-Soviet Russia. A group of Welsh-speaking sixth formers go on an educational visit to St Petersburg, accompanied by their art teacher Eileen (Sharon Morgan) and her old-style Welsh Communist husband Mostyn (Wyn Bowen Harries). The deputy headmaster Mervyn (Ifan Huw Dafydd), with whom Eileen had a weekend affair once before, also travels, hoping that, as the marriage seems to be unravelling, the affair can be resuscitated. A mix-up on the train between Moscow and St Petersburg splits teachers from students and the film contrasts the two groups' adventures in parallel narratives. The dialogue is in Welsh, Russian and English and this is one aspect of the film's audacity and ambition. Here, the minority language, which has such a low profile internationally that the Academy doubted its very existence, is vying for public space with two of the great imperialist languages of the world, engaging at the same time with themes and issues of global as well as of local importance.[6]

The foreign location adds an extra dimension to the underlying theme of Welsh identity and the film explores this to great effect through the sense of loss

Exploring contemporary Welsh identity: Endaf Emlyn's *Gadael Lenin/Leaving Lenin* (1994)

and disillusionment that Mostyn feels at the collapse of the Soviet Union. His failing marriage and his failed ideals are linked (the couple had spent their honeymoon in Leningrad, as it then was, at the cusp of early 70s radicalism). The film teases out a bewildering set of contrasting debates – philosophical, aesthetic, political and personal which touch the characters with passion, humour and poignancy. Mixed up in this heady brew are issues relating to collective ideals and individualism; differing male and female agendas; the place of art and education in society; illusion, façade and reality; poverty and deprivation and sexuality and sexual preference. Perhaps the most poignant theme of all, reflecting early 1990s concerns, is the confusion and dilemmas that face today's young people, whether the youth of St Petersburg adrift in post-Soviet Russia or those struggling to adulthood in post-Thatcherite Wales. The film proposes a need for new beginnings – whether personal, political or artistic. The final irony of the film's message is that at least Mostyn in his youth had political ideals that allowed him to imagine and work towards a new beginning. This is a privilege, the film suggests, which today's young don't have and must work for. In this way, the Welsh films resemble some aspects of recent Irish cinema. As the traditional belief systems wither away: religion, patriotism, political beliefs – the loss of something to believe in, especially the loss of political hope – is particularly debilitating.

This sense of loss is evident in Paul Morrison's *Solomon and Gaenor* (1998), which returns to the pre-World War I Wales of both *Hedd Wyn* (1992) and *The Englishman Who Went up a Hill But Came down a Mountain*. This is a complex historical moment for Wales. At the beginning of the 20th century, it still carried its identity as an industrial force of nineteenth-century British expansion but was also about to assume a central role in the radical and progressive labour politics of the 20th century. Within this complex, the film plays out a Romeo-and-Juliet scenario – the Jewish Solomon hiding his identity behind an English façade to woo Gaenor from a fundamentalist Christian community. In the tragedy that unfolds the film is again scathing about the impact that fundamentalist religion has on the lives of young people in particular (in this case, both orthodox Jewish as well as Protestant Christian). But this is more than just a Welsh cry of 'a plague on both your houses'. As much as it is a commentary on one historical Welsh moment, or the exploration of long-forgotten Welsh anti-Semitism, this tragedy is also a metaphor for the failed idealism of the 20th century – call it radical,

Unorthodox Jew: Ioan Gruffudd in *Solomon and Gaenor*
(Paul Morrison, 1998)

humanitarian communalism. In this way, it links to the
failed idealism of *Gadael Lenin*'s Mostyn and, as with a
section of Irish cinema, offers a sad commentary on a
post-modern society that struggles to find a new belief
system to replace the grand narratives of yesterday.

In identifying some aspects of the cinema from the
Celtic fringes, we are identifying a cinema that has a
double focus. These films are concerned to explode
myths and move beyond the regimes of representation
that have tended to romanticise and to marginalise the
Celtic fringe. Dominant cinema portrayed the Celtic
countries as regressive and primitive and if this portrayal
was sometimes amiable and sometimes hostile, it was
always patronising. However, a second focus of this
cinema has been inwards, exploring the nationalist
responses to the representations of the centre. This has
meant that the films reflect an uncertainty, an exploration that is as conscious of internal contradiction as it
is of larger external realities. Above all, this is a cinema
that refuses to operate on the margins. These are cultures
that are no longer content to be the peripheral and
exploited partners in a strict cultural division of labour.
In fact, this new cinema has pushed peripherality into
the centre and now operates on the cutting edge of a
contemporary cultural debate about identity.

Notes

1. Michael Hechter, *Internal Colonialism: The Celtic Fringe in
    British National Development*.
2. Colin McArthur, *Scotch Reels: Scotland in Film and
    Television*.

3. For a recent discussion of these films, see Colin McArthur,
    Whisky Galore! & The Maggie (London: I. B. Tauris, 2003).
4. There are a number of recent studies of film and culture in
    the Celtic countries, proving that critical perception has
    caught up with artistic practice. For Scotland, see Colin
    McArthur, *Brigadoon, Braveheart and the Scots: Distortions of
    Scotland in Hollywood Cinema* (London: I. B. Tauris, 2003) and
    Duncan Petrie, *Contemporary Scottish Fictions* (Edinburgh:
    Edinburgh University Press, 2004); for Northern Ireland,
    John Hill, *Cinema and Northern Ireland: Film, Culture and
    Politics* (London: BFI, 2006) and for the Celtic countries in
    general, Steve Blandford, *Film, Drama and the Break-up of
    Britain* (Bristol: Intellect, 2007).
5. For a detailed analysis of *Divorcing Jack*, see John Hill's essay
    on the film in Brian McFarlane (ed.), *The Cinema of Britain
    and Ireland* (London: Wallflower Press, 2005).
6. In 1994, when Paul Turner's *Hedd Wyn* was nominated
    for an Academy Award in the foreign-language section,
    the Academy sought independent verification that the
    Welsh language did indeed constitute a bona fide 'foreign
    language'.

Bibliography

Berry, Dave, *Wales and Cinema: The First 100 Years* (Cardiff and
    London: University of Wales Press and BFI, 1995).
Berry, Dave, 'Film and Television in Wales', in John Hill and
    Martin McLoone (eds), *Big Picture, Small Screen: The
    Relations between Film and Television* (Luton: University of
    Luton/John Libbey, 1996).
Hechter, Michael, *Internal Colonialism: The Celtic Fringe in
    British National Development* (Piscataway, NJ: Transaction
    Publishers/Rutgers, 1999).
Hill, John, McLoone, Martin and Hainsworth, Paul (eds),
    Border Crossing: Film in Ireland, Britain and Europe (Belfast
    and London: Institute of Irish Studies and BFI, 1994).
McArthur, Colin, *Scotch Reels: Scotland in Film and Television*
    (London: BFI, 1982).
McLoone, Martin, *Irish Film: The Emergence of a Contemporary
    Cinema* (London: BFI, 2000).
Petrie, Duncan, *Screening Scotland* (London: BFI, 2000).
Pettitt, Lance, *Screening Ireland* (Manchester: Manchester
    University Press, 2000).
Trevor-Roper, Hugh, 'The Invention of Tradition: The
    Highland Tradition of Scotland', in Eric Hobsbawm and
    Terence Ranger (eds), *The Invention of Tradition*
    (Cambridge: Cambridge University Press, 1983).

39

Citylife: Urban Fairy-tales in Late 90s British Cinema

Each fairy tale is a magic mirror which reflects some aspects of our inner world, and of the steps required by our evolution from immaturity to maturity. For those who immerse themselves in what the fairy tale has to communicate, it becomes a deep quiet pool which at first seems to reflect only our own image, but behind it we soon discover the inner turmoils of our soul – its depth, and ways to gain peace within ourselves and with the world, which is the reward of our struggles.[1]

In the new British cinema which emerged in the late 90s, three groups of films stand out. A large number of films delved into the lives of the poor and oppressed. Young people accept drugs, crime, violence and exploitation with hedonistic stoicism in films like *Trainspotting* (Danny Boyle, 1996), *Twin Town* (Kevin Griffith, 1997), and *Human Traffic* (Justin Kerrigan, 1999). Sheffield steel workers regain self-respect through stripping in *The Full Monty* (Peter Cattaneo, 1997) and Grimethorpe miners through their brass band in *Brassed Off* (Mark Herman, 1996). Bleaker films such as Ken Loach's trilogy – *Raining Stones* (1993), *Ladybird, Ladybird* (1996) and *My Name Is Joe* (1998) – along with Gary Oldman's *Nil by Mouth* (1997) and Rob Rohrer's *Bumping the Odds* (2000), show that what the Victorians called the 'undeserving poor', lacking regular employment, tempted into criminality, plagued by loan sharks, banished to bleak, crumbling housing estates, though capable of resilience and humour, had the odds stacked against them.

'Heritage' films, were as important in the 90s as they had been in the previous decade, though the uniform tone set by Merchant Ivory was disrupted by films which delved further back in time (such as Shekhar Kapur's *Elizabeth*, 1998); presented a darker view of the past (Michael Winterbottom's *Jude*, 1996, Phil Agland's *The Woodlanders*, 1997); or introduced anachronism and humour (as in John Madden's *Shakespeare in Love*, 1998). The third group, of romantic comedies featuring youngish and generally childless people, has received less critical attention, despite the box-office success of *Four Weddings and a Funeral* (Mike Newell, 1994), *Sliding Doors* (Peter Howitt, 1998) and *Notting Hill* (Roger Michell, 1999). Along with *Jack & Sarah* (Tim Sullivan, 1995), *Martha – Meet Frank, Daniel and Laurence* (Nick Hamm, 1998), and *This Year's Love* (David Kane, 1999), they show life in Britain as exciting, glamorous and full of romantic possibilities, and are constructed like fairy-tales. It is the fairy-tale quality of these films which is most striking and which divides them from seemingly analogous films such as *Fever Pitch* (David Evans, 1996), *Maybe Baby* (Ben Elton, 2000) and *Bridget Jones's Diary* (Sharon Maguire, 2001). One of the key components of a fairy-tale is the message that:

a struggle against severe difficulties in life is unavoidable, is an intrinsic part of human existence – but that if one does not shy away, but steadfastly meets unexpected and often unjust hardships, one masters all obstacles and at the end emerges victorious.[2]

But the protagonists of *Fever Pitch*, *Maybe Baby*, and *Bridget Jones's Diary* hardly suffer at all and blunder undeservedly into happiness. Stranger films, such as *Shooting Fish* (Stefan Schwartz, 1997) and *Little Voice* (Mark Herman, 1999), qualify as fairy-tales but do not centre upon romance. Films such as Les Blair's *Bad Behaviour* (1992), Michael Winterbottom's *Wonderland* (2000) and Jamie Thraves's *The Low Down* (2001), deal with love in the city but do so in a way that eschews fantasy and wish-fulfilment and aims at authenticity in character and setting.

Fairy-tales consciously mythologise their setting and social relationships, allow coincidence and magic to determine events and structure their narratives in such a way that the protagonist of the story undergoes a series of tests or ordeals before achieving his or her goal. Traditional fairy-tales are populated by giants and dwarfs, witches and dragons and talking animals; they are set among enchanted woods and castles and allow fabulous events to occur. These modern, urban, cinematic fairy-tales are more modest and less fantastic. But in terms of their types of characters – discontented princesses, unproven heroes, put-upon Cinderellas, witches and sages, helpers and scary antagonists – as well as in their narrative structure, unreal settings and timeless ethos, these films have an affinity with fairy-tales which grim slices of life like *My Name Is Joe* or surrealistic comedy dramas like *Trainspotting* do not.[3]

The Magical Quest

Fairy-tales begin either with a lack which must be remedied (the absence of an heir, a suitable marriage partner, enough food or land or wealth); a curse which has to be removed (a spell cast by a witch, a dragon stalking the land); or a harmonious situation which is disrupted and has to be restored (death or misfortune sends a, sometimes reluctant, hero out on a quest; a father dies and his children fall out over his legacy; a family member is abducted or ensnared and has to be rescued). All of these six films fit broadly into these categories.

Jack & Sarah begins with Jack (Richard E. Grant), living a hectic but happy life as his wife prepares to give birth to a baby. The baby is born but his wife dies, and the equilibrium is destroyed. Jack sinks into drunken despair until his father, with wizardly wisdom, brings him to his senses by placing the baby on the pillow next to him as he sleeps in a drink-sodden slumber. Jack wakes in wonder at the beauty of the baby and begins to reform his life. Rejecting conventional nannies, he recruits Amy (Samantha Mathis), an American waitress, to look after the baby; and, although handicapped by his snobbery and his lingering grief over his wife's death, he falls in love with her and is finally able to reconstitute his family and regain his happiness.

In *Sliding Doors*, Helen (Gwyneth Paltrow) is sacked from her job and prepares to travel disconsolately back home on the London Underground. She arrives on the platform just as the train doors close, but then the film rewinds to show what would have happened if she had not been delayed (by a little girl blocking her path as she comes down the steps) and had caught the train. She meets James (John Hannah), a charming man who befriends her. Arriving home earlier than expected, she catches her boyfriend, Gerry (John Lynch), having sex with another woman. She leaves him; changes her appearance; successfully starts her own business; overcomes misunderstandings with James and they fall in love. But this broad and easy path ends in untimely death. In the other story, where Helen misses the train, she arrives home too late to uncover Gerry's infidelity and works in menial jobs to support him while he continues his adulterous affair. When she finally discovers what has been happening the shock leads to a miscarriage, but this narrow, winding path promises to lead, eventually, to happiness.

In *Martha*, Laurence (Joseph Fiennes) disturbs a neighbour to recount a convoluted tale of how he came to meet and fall in love with an American woman, Martha (Monica Potter), only to discover that his two best friends, Daniel and Frank, are also in love with her and expecting his help to woo her. The choice Laurence has to make between Martha and (at least one of) his friends has little dramatic weight as both Frank and Daniel are selfish and manipulative, but the real barrier to happiness and fulfilment is Laurence himself.

In *Four Weddings*, Charles (Hugh Grant) meets Carrie (Andie MacDowell), his ideal woman, at a wedding, but

The three suitors, Rufus Sewell, Joseph Fiennes and Tom Hollander in *Martha – Meet Frank, Daniel and Laurence* (Nick Hamm, 1998)

he is unable to express his true feelings and she slips away from him. When she marries someone else, Charles fails to speak out to stop her and, thinking he has lost her forever, he resigns himself to marrying a woman he doesn't love. At the wedding, his deaf and dumb brother forces him to voice his true feelings, and although the outraged bride (nicknamed 'Duckface' by Charles's friends) strikes him to the ground, he is at last able to have and hold Carrie.

In *Notting Hill*, Anna Scott (Julia Roberts), the biggest star in the world, meets William Thacker (Hugh Grant), a humble bookseller, and they fall in love. The disparity in their wealth, status and glamour, augur against the romance prospering and when William inadvertently betrays her trust she leaves him. After a period of separation, she returns and declares her love for him, but he no longer trusts her. He rejects her, but when he realises his mistake he overcomes all obstacles to confront her at a press conference and win her love.

This Year's Love tethers its fairy-tale dreams to a reality where love withers on the vine, people find it impossible to break out of destructive, repetitive patterns and neither work nor relationships provide more than fleeting satisfactions. Danny (Douglas Henshall) and Hannah (Catherine McCormack), young, attractive, trendy, seemingly ideally suited to each other, rush off to their wedding. But their marriage is blighted by a curse. A witch-like woman reveals Hannah's infidelity and the wedding feast ends in chaos, drunkenness and destruction.

Instead of working out the problems which have disrupted their happiness, Danny and Hannah go their separate ways and interact with four other characters: Marey (Kathy Burke), an insecure airport cleaner and pub-rock singer; Cameron (Dougray Scott), a compulsive womaniser; Liam (Ian Hart), a neurotic comic collector; and Sophie (Jennifer Ehle), an upper-middle-class drop-out. After three years, Danny forgives Hannah and re-declares his love. The curse on their marriage has finally been exorcised by a period of hardship and reflection and – like Charles and Carrie, Jack and Amy, Helen and James, Laurence and Martha, William and Anna – they are now prepared to embark on a new life together.

Princesses and Beggar Maids

Although these films are contemporary urban romances, a surprising number of their characters conform to fairy-tale archetypes. Male protagonists tend to be youngish, handsome and troubled by the difficulties of winning the woman they love. Female leads are either Cinderella-like waifs whose unhappy lives are complemented by the arrival of a Prince Charming (but one whose imperfections ensure that romance between them does not run smoothly). Alternatively they appear as goddesses and sprites, quixotic and elusive.

Carrie in *Four Weddings* is like a mischievous nymph, an enigmatic presence rather than a real character with thoughts and feelings of her own. She sleeps with Charles when he least expects it, disappears when he tries to get to know her, reappears when he assumes he has lost her. Though her actions – such as marrying another man – take her away from him, she never rejects him and it his inability to speak his desires which prevents him from winning her. Anna in *Notting Hill*, is a fully fledged goddess: imperious, aloof, chameleon-like in her switches of mood and appearance. Every time she appears she both looks and acts differently – coolly enigmatic on her first appearance, swishly sophisticated in her suite at the Ritz, tomboyishly playful after the dinner party, implacably furious when besieged by the press in William's flat. When she reappears unexpectedly in William's bookshop, dressed very simply, and openly declares her love, his unwillingness to accept her offer is not simply a matter of pusillanimity. She assures him that 'the fame thing isn't really real', that 'I'm just a girl, standing in front of a boy, asking him to love her'. But underlying his suspicion that she is an actress putting on a performance is the deeper fear that this powerful and dangerous woman has assumed the guise of a simple girl to ensnare him.

Amy, Martha, Helen and Hannah are all Cinderella figures. Bruno Bettelheim points out that the resonance of the Cinderella story comes not merely from its rags-to-riches transformation but from Cinderella's development through five crucial steps to self-fulfilment. She retains her basic trust (a belief in the goodness of others even when being treated unfairly); she develops autonomy (an ability to survive in difficult circumstances) and initiative (a willingness to take up challenges and opportunities); she shows herself capable of industry and she maintains her identity (her determination to be accepted on her own terms).[4]

Amy first appears as a waitress, abused by her customers and treated tyrannically by her boss whom we later discover is her boyfriend. But she refuses to submit to oppression. She storms out of her job and, when employed by Jack to look after the baby Sarah, spends his money extravagantly and resists the interference of the older characters in her responsibilities for the baby. The way she copes with unhappiness and loneliness shows that she can suffer with dignity and forbearance and is thus, despite her youth and inexperience, a suitable partner for the grieving Jack. When Jack's bigotry and snobbery cause him to treat her like a servant, she unhesitatingly walks out on him and only agrees to return when he asks her to marry him.

Martha tells Daniel she has spent her last ninety-nine dollars on a plane ticket to London in a desperate bid to escape her dead-end job in Minneapolis, and she competes with Frank to prove who has had the most awful life. But her vulnerability is combined with a shrewdness which enables her to exploit Daniel's infatuation with her to augment her financial resources and avoid being taken in by Frank's self-pitying manipulations. Her integrity and her belief in true love make it possible for her to discern the same qualities in Laurence and forgive him his sulky inarticulateness. Like Amy, she welcomes the attention of her Prince Charming, but both women act with confidence and vitality to determine their own destiny.

Amy and Martha lead a hand-to-mouth existence, but their American identity seems to work as a protective charm, shielding them from the rigours and pains their economic situation might be expected to impose on them. Cast in the role of an Englishwoman, Gwyneth Paltrow's Helen has a much harder time of it.[5] In the first version of her story she is able to build a new and better life from the ashes of the old but she is snatched away by death. In the second, she is transformed into a drudge, working as a waitress and sandwich-deliverer to support Gerry while he continues his adultery. But we know from her rejection of Gerry at the end of the 'unhappy' story that she has a proper appreciation of her worth and identity and from the 'happy' story that her bruised sense of trust will respond to James's solicitous devotion.

Hannah, who is atypically the cause of her own unhappiness through her infidelity, and is a Scot rather than an American, might be expected to suffer the most of these Cinderellas. Certainly she has the longest wait for happiness and she falls furthest in being reduced to working at a supermarket checkout and living in a squat. But she demonstrates initiative in exploring new relationships and rejects them when they seem to deny her true nature. She shows herself capable of hard work (transforming Cameron and Liam's scruffy flat) and autonomy (by living alone rather than in an unsatisfactory relationship). Like Helen, she is tarnished by disappointment, but she retains enough basic trust to be touched by Danny's declaration of love and to win a second chance of happiness.

Sleeping Princes and Frogs Waiting to Be Kissed

Although they are handsome and attractive to women, the male protagonists have none of the machismo characteristics of conventional heroes. Richard E. Grant's Jack and Douglas Henshall's Danny are the most active, but they are also the most childish. Danny throws the wedding cake at the wall when he is told of Hannah's infidelity; Jack's response to his wife's death is to smash up the furniture and become a drunk. Joseph Fiennes's Laurence and Hugh Grant's Charles and William are soft-eyed, gentle creatures, valued by the women for their endearing openness and geniality (as is John Hannah's James in *Sliding Doors*). Charles is like an unhappy prince cursed by his diffidence to lead a passionless life. He is witty and attractive and – we assume – rich, but although he is surrounded by eligible and willing women, he can find no one he wants to marry. William, though his shop specialises in travel books, is becalmed in the post-divorce doldrums and lives among old friends who compete in displaying their incompetencies. Laurence, teaching bridge to old ladies and acting like a nervous nanny to his squabbling friends, seems condemned to a sexless world until he is discovered by Martha, a woman whose vitality is such that she is capable of stirring him into action. Laurence's dilemma is about growing up and leaving his boyhood friends; Charles has to progress beyond the casual relations enjoyed by a bachelor; William has to rise to the challenge of winning the love of a dynamic and powerful woman. But different though these situations are, all three men are somnambulists drifting aimlessly through life until they are awakened by a startling woman to whom they then have to prove themselves worthy.

Wizards, Witches, Friends and Foes

Villains and adversaries are much less formidable in these films than in traditional fairy-tales. Charles's rival in love, Hamish (Corin Redgrave), is reminiscent of the sort of bully who haunted the corridors of Greyfriars in the public-school stories of Frank Richards. William has to suffer the condescension of Anna's slobbish boyfriend and confront a tableful of yuppy yobs when they make lewd comments about Anna, but he has no serious rival for her affections. Frank (Rufus Sewell) and Daniel (Tom Hollander) are so vain, egocentric and self-indulgent that they function almost as Laurence's Ugly Sisters, but they are never actively malicious towards him. Carol (Bronagh Gallagher), the woman who reveals Hannah's infidelity in *This Year's Love*, is herself betrayed and unhappy (it is her husband Hannah has slept with) and Cameron, Hannah's rebound lover, though incapable of fidelity, is discarded in turn by Hannah, Marey and Sophie.

Lydia (Jeanne Tripplehorn) in *Sliding Doors* is a more dangerous kettle of fish. As she explains to the enthralled Gerry: 'I'm, a woman. We don't say what we want. But we reserve the right to be pissed off if we don't get it. That's what makes us so fascinating. And not a little bit scary.' Helen, even before discovering she is Gerry's lover, describes her as 'Cruella de Ville's less nice sister', and she is no match for her in their two confrontations. In *Jack & Sarah*, Amy has to save Jack from the clutches of a pushy career woman with no interest in babies (Cherie Lunghi). Being young, sassy and American more than balances out her rival's wealth and sophistication. But Helen – downtrodden, English and increasingly dowdy – can't compete with the fiery, sensual and determined Lydia. Fortunately, we know from the parallel story that James is a more suitable partner for Helen and that Gerry is not a prize worth winning. Satisfaction comes not from Helen defeating Lydia – who we can assume gets what she wants – but from her irrevocable dismissal of Gerry from her life.

Helpers play vital roles in many of these films, particularly where a dozy protagonist needs pushing into action. Both Charles and William get themselves into situations where they appear to have turned their backs on their chance of happiness and a truth-telling friend (Charles's deaf and dumb brother, William's buffoonish lodger) forces them to confront their faintheartedness and reverse their wrong decisions. Jack is so obstinately wrong-headed that it takes several helpers to keep him on the right path and he needs his mother-in-law (Eileen Atkins) to free him from the guilt he feels at getting over his wife's death and reunite him with Amy. Ray Winstone's building contractor in *Martha* (whom Laurence mistakenly believes to be a psychoanalyst) refuses to make Laurence's decision for him but, by offering him a sympathetic ear and insisting that he examine his own heart, he precipitates him into pursuing Martha.

Helen and Danny don't share the diffidence of these upper-middle-class Englishmen and don't need help in making up their minds. Helen's problem is not indecisiveness but blindness and once the scales are lifted from her eyes we know from the parallel story that when she meets James at the end of the film, he is the Prince Charming who will transform her arduous existence. Danny's jealousy and unwillingness to confront his own pain is dissolved by the passage of time and we know that his fate is inextricably intertwined with Hannah's. Among the debris of the disrupted wedding feast, her friend Denise (Sophie Okenedo) tries to reassure Hannah that she will find another partner better suited to her than the explosively jealous Danny. 'It takes people seven relationships before they get it right. . . . Seven fuck-ups and then bang! You've learnt from your mistakes, and number eight – it's magic.' But Danny is Hannah's number eight and when he makes his climactic declaration of love in the supermarket Hannah accepts his forgiveness of her infidelity as a liberating exoneration.

London – City of Delights

Apart from the excursions to Somerset and Scotland in *Four Weddings*, all the action of these six films takes place in London, but the London they present is not one which found favour with critics. Whereas films like *Bad Behaviour* and *Wonderland* were praised for their fidelity to the reality of London life, *Notting Hill* was condemned for failing to show anything of the black and Portuguese communities in the area, and Peter Matthews complains about 'the impeccably bland locations, which succeed in divesting London of street life or geographically specifiable features' in *Sliding Doors*.[6] One could counter these claims by pointing out that *Sliding Doors's* locations are specific and identifiable and that *Notting Hill's* insularity reflects social reality. But such arguments miss the point: that these films deliberately recreate London as an enchanted setting where unlikely romances can blossom.[7]

This is least apparent in the pre-Cool Britannia films, *Four Weddings* and *Jack & Sarah*. Mike Newell makes interesting use of London locations such as the concrete walkways of the South Bank and the Essex borderlands, where the squat church of St Clement's, West Thurrock, provides an unexpected setting for Gareth's funeral. But it is the richly decorated interiors of the Royal Naval College at Greenwich, Luton Hoo and the Priory Church of St Bartholomew the Great, where the weddings and receptions take place, which dominate the visual world of the film.[8]

There is little sense that Charles and his set are permanent denizens of the metropolis and that their fates are determined by living in the city. *Jack & Sarah* is more obviously a London film. Jack's home (in

St James's Gardens, Holland Park) and workplace (on London Wall in the City of London) are clearly delineated and Jack balks at the idea of a weekend away thirty miles upriver to Marlow. A trip to Camden market and the sequence in the Neal's Yard café where Jack finds Amy working as a waitress, illustrate the film's awareness of London's growing trendiness, but there is no attempt to exploit or celebrate it.

By contrast, the four later films dwell upon the pleasures and excitement of living in London in ways which echo the Swinging London films of the 60s. Just as in *Catch Us If You Can* (John Boorman, 1965), the stuntman and the model share their secret delights in a rooftop swimming pool where they go snorkelling and the orange trees growing in Syon House's palatial conservatory, Martha seeks Laurence in his favourite corner of Battersea Park, where people sit and play chess in the rain; and James finds Helen on Albert Bridge, under which they exchanged their first kiss.[9] The city is represented as a cosy village community.

The re-creation of London as an enchanted village where lovers are able to find each other among the city's teeming millions and chance encounters and coincidental meetings are to be expected, is almost vindicated in *This Year's Love* by the fact that most of its action takes place in Camden Town and Chalk Farm. As Jonathan Romney explains:

> The Camden setting might seem like touristic
> opportunism. . . . But Camden Lock, for all its plastic
> counter-culture tackiness, is one of those London
> locations where people collide in a faux-carnival
> setting, so the setting is at least a plausible narrative
> excuse for getting these people together.[10]

Danny's semi-rural prefab, Sophie's houseboat, Cameron's gloomy loft flat, balance out the easily recognisable landmarks like the canal and the market to give the film a specific grounding in its locality. Though three of the main characters are Scots and a fourth Liverpudlian, they are so at home in this urban village that whenever they leave for other parts of London it seems as if they enter alien territory. Out at Heathrow, Danny, drunk and depressed, is rescued by fellow Camden-dweller Marey, who works there as a cleaner. Liam and Hannah, who have virtually ignored each other in Camden, bond instinctively when they recognise each other at a West End dating agency get-together. Sophie is happy to engage in relationships with Danny and Cameron when she is in Camden, but

once she takes them beyond its boundaries (Danny to a posh party, Cameron to meet her rich parents), their utter unsuitability as partners is exposed.

Until the 60s, fantasies of city life in British cinema, which concentrated on low life and the criminal underworld (e.g. *They Made Me a Fugitive*, 1947), high society (in Anna Neagle vehicles like *Spring in Park Lane*, 1948 and *Maytime in Mayfair*, 1949) or dramas about the lives of ordinary people (such as *Passport to Pimlico*, 1949), were largely constructed in the studios. In the 60s, as film production moved out of the studios and on to the streets, there was an exuberant discovery of London as a location. Swinging London films, from bittersweet comedies like *Georgy Girl* (Silvio Narizzano, 1966) to metaphysical investigations like *Blow-Up* (Michelangelo Antonioni, 1967), revelled in showing London as a fascinating and exciting city. The 90s films are less rhapsodic and the world they create is carefully separated off from everyday life.

Notting Hill is exceptional in having a large enough budget to build a big studio set, but it is representative in its concern to mould and control the reality it presents. One could contrast its picture of a safe and cheerful community with that of an earlier Notting Hill film, Dick Clements's *Otley* (1968), which incorporates a more raucous and haphazard reality.[11] For the title sequence, the camera meanders through the Portobello market in front of Tom Courtenay. People peer inquisitively at the camera and contact is lost occasionally as Courtenay's progress is impeded by the crowd. There is no question that this is the real Portobello Road and that the people are everyday shoppers rather than paid extras. In *Notting Hill* there is a similar tracking shot as the camera observes William walking through the studio set of the area. No one looks at the camera and as the seasons change from summer to autumn to winter to spring we see the same characters in different guises (including a pregnant woman who reappears with her baby). The purpose is not, as it is in *Otley*, to introduce us to a colourful part of London but to show time passing in William's life, cover a necessary hiatus in his relationship with Anna and facilitate the exploration of issues of fidelity and obsession, loyalty and dependence. The London background contributes to the meaning of the sequence by showing life growing and changing, but it is not a London which has an existence outside the film.

The Lessons of Love

British cinema in the 1980s and early 90s can be defined by its anti-Thatcherism. Films such as Stephen

Frears and Hanif Kureishi's *My Beautiful Laundrette* (1985) and *Sammy and Rosie Get Laid* (1987), Ken Loach's *Looks and Smiles* (1981) and *Riff-Raff* (1991), Mike Leigh's *High Hopes* (1988) and David Hare's *Paris by Night* (1988) and *Strapless* (1989) are critical of the way in which society is moving. They show life as a difficult struggle against inequality and bigotry, government as corrupt and self-serving and the rich as greedy, socially insensitive and self-satisfied. In *High Hopes*, for example, Laetitia (Lesley Manville) and Rupert (David Bamber), the upper-middle-class couple who have bought the house next door to old Mrs Bender (Edna Doré) in a gentrified street on the borders of Islington treat her with contemptuous cruelty and, unusually for characters in Leigh's world, reveal no redeeming features.

The urban fairy-tales are much less concerned with social inequality. The lovable eccentrics of *Four Weddings* might have come from the pre-war novels of P. G. Wodehouse or the plays of Noël Coward and Esther McCracken and inhabit a similarly enclosed world. Charles and his chums are funny and full of frailties. Tom (James Fleet), for example, is the seventh richest man in England and has a house with 137 rooms, but he is good-hearted, clumsy and asks little from life. Charles is rich enough not to have to work, but he and his eclectic band of friends are bound together by the fact that they are misfits and outsiders rather than by class solidarity. Tom's ineffectuality, David's deafness, Charles and Fiona's inability to fit in, make their friendship with the classless Scarlett and the flamboyant Gareth, whose surprisingly humble origins are revealed at his funeral, entirely plausible.

Four Weddings, which combines an affection for English traditions and rituals and an easy-going benevolence to its wide spectrum of characters, captures something of the ethos John Major's government aspired to as an alternative to the abrasiveness of Thatcherism. *Jack & Sarah*, made a year later, looks forward to the fashionable, media-conscious world of New Labour. Jack, a lawyer working in a glass tower in the City of London, could be a colleague of Cherie Blair's. He owns a big Georgian house in Holland Park that is far grander than that of Rupert and Laetitia in *High Hopes*, but there is no hint of anti-yuppyism here. Whereas Rupert is unkind to old ladies, Jack gets drunk with the gentleman tramp who is living in his rubble skip, and recruits him as a butler. Rupert and Laetitia go to the opera and play ridiculously childish sex games, Jack (once his drink problem has been magicked away) becomes a devoted and responsible father to his baby daughter and falls in love with the nanny.

Similar sympathetic indulgence is extended to the well-heeled characters in *Sliding Doors*, *Martha* and *Notting Hill*, though the celebration of the virtues of the rich is not unqualified. In *Martha*, Daniel, the richest of the three suitors, is also the least sympathetic. In *Notting Hill*, Bernie (Hugh Bonneville) the stockbroker and Tony (Richard McCabe) the restaurateur are both redeemed by their failure to succeed in the material world (Bernie loses his job and Tony's restaurant goes bankrupt); and William, whose bookshop attracts few book-buying customers, seems set on the same downward economic trajectory. *Sliding Doors* begins as an archetypal 'Cool Britannia' film with its trendy, prosperous, classless young people. But in the story where Helen follows the New Labour path to happiness by starting her own business she is run over by a white van – the embodiment of untamed proletarian aggression – and dies. The Helen who survives is the one who works like a dog in low-paid, menial jobs and learns the lessons of life the hard way.

Charlotte O'Sullivan, reviewing *Notting Hill* in *Sight and Sound*, contrasts it with *Four Weddings* 'where America is in thrall to cultured, wealthy Britain' and decides that in *Notting Hill* 'Britain has banana-slipped from importance to impotence'.[12] This is disingenuous. Fun though it is, *Four Weddings* panders to the myth that British society is dominated by a dottily endearing elite. *Notting Hill* is bolder. William and his friends might be interchangeable with Charles and his friends in terms of character types but they are set lower in the class hierarchy and have none of the glamour and prestige which still attaches to the English aristocracy. If *Four Weddings* is interesting for the way it shows the self-enclosed aristocratic world of the interwar years surviving, buoyant and untroubled into the 90s, *Notting Hill*, with its stress on urban life and its setting in one of London's fashionable urban villages sells a more modern image of British society. Part of William's appeal for Anna is his capacity to open up a cosier, safer, less brash and abrasive world than her own. Whereas Carrie might look forward to country life and the possibility of rubbing shoulders with royalty, Anna is lured from the vacuous superficiality of a Hollywood lifestyle by the promise of life in a city of tranquil parks (all the more tranquil for being open only to the rich), street markets she can peruse with only minimal intrusions into her privacy and friendly people who, even when in awe of her, act in a natural, unsycophantic way.

A general criticism of these films is that in their eagerness to please and entertain, they ignore the real tensions in a society where the gap between rich and poor is becoming institutionalised through high house prices and a divisive educational system. One can compare them, for example with Mike Leigh's *Naked* (1993) and Michael Winterbottom's *Wonderland*, which show a much grimmer view of the romantic possibilities London has to offer and a view of life as an angst-ridden struggle for survival. But if life in the fairy-tales is a carnival where only love really matters, within their hermetically sealed world there is still sadness, even tragedy. In *Four Weddings*, Gareth, the jolly magus figure, has a heart attack and dies, and the most memorable sequence in the film is where his lover (John Hannah) reads W. H. Auden's poem 'Stop All the Clocks' at his funeral. In *Jack & Sarah*, Jack's relationships with his baby daughter and with prospective new lovers exist in the shadow of the death of his wife. In *Sliding Doors*, the 'happy' story ends in death and in the 'unhappy' story there is a heavy stress on the pain caused by infidelity and betrayal. In *This Year's Love*, Danny, Hannah and Marey have a chance of happiness at the end of the film, but Sophie and Cameron seem doomed to an endless round of unsatisfactory relationships, and Liam has been sucked into a nightmare world where reality has slipped away and clocks go backwards. In *Martha*, there are no deaths and little hint of tragedy, but Frank and Daniel occupy opposite extremes of sulkily self-induced failure and success bought at the cost of integrity, and Laurence goes through the film in a paroxysm of anxiety. Even in *Notting Hill*, the financial failures of Bernie and Tony, and the spinal injury which confines Bella (Gina McKee) to a wheelchair and prevents her having children, reinforce the melancholy aura around William. In a gloomy set piece equivalent to the 'Stop All the Clocks' reading, William, after a dinner party where he has been introduced to an attractive and charming woman, makes a long speech about the improbability of meeting someone who feels in equal measure what one might feel for them.

If this cycle of films is remarkable for its evacuation of class conflict and its conservative representation of society, it is less a matter of sympathy switching from the poor and oppressed to the privileged and successful, than of a *rapprochement*, a papering over the rifts that had opened up between rich and poor, losers and winners in the 1980s. This is evident in *This Year's Love*, which is clearly differentiated from the other films in that five of its six main characters are working class. The exception, Jennifer Ehle's Sophie, a Roedean-educated drop-out, is manipulative, selfish and lacking

This Year's Love (David Kane, 1999): Douglas Henshall is prepared for the merry-go-round of love

in self-knowledge. But rather than being condemned and humiliated she is allowed to show an admirable forthrightness in dismissing each of her three working-class boyfriends when they prove to be boring, demanding and socially inept.

The yearning for social cohesion and harmony is also evident in the fact that all six films end with a magical resolution – Carrie casts off her husband and Charles is saved from marrying Duckface; Amy hasn't really married her ex-boyfriend and is ready to accept the offers of chastened and loving Jack; Helen has lost her job, her boyfriend and her baby, but when she meets James coming out of the hospital, we are reassured that all will be well; Laurence heads off for the Arctic winter in Reykjavik, but Martha is there waiting to surprise him on the plane; Danny forgives Hannah her infidelity and they can at last begin their honeymoon; and William realises in the nick of time that Anna is sincere and steadfast in her emotions and publicly declares his love for her.

In a society where happiness and prosperity is a realistic possibility for the majority of the population but where unemployment, sickness or bad luck consign a substantial minority to a life of poverty, and asylum-seeking immigrants act as a reminder of a much harsher world beyond, there is an inevitable anxiety about the right to happiness. In the cocooned world of perfect love visited by these fairy-tale films, uncertainty, hardship, suffering and loss can be confronted, defied and finally overcome, and happiness, having been earned, can be legitimately enjoyed.

Though the capacity of film to capture or reflect reality is one of its most valuable attributes, it is equally significant as a popular storytelling medium. Bruno Bettelheim, in *The Uses of Enchantment*, charts the way in which traditional fairy-tales dramatise the transformations children have to undergo before becoming fully adult. These modern, urban fairy-tales are shallower and narrower in their more literal dramatisations of the relationship crises facing young adults, but they fulfil a similar function of guidance and reassurance.

Notes

1. Bruno Bettelheim, *The Uses of Enchantment*, p. 309.
2. Ibid., p. 9.
3. For a more rigorous definition of a fairy-tale, see Vladimir Propp, *Morphology of the Folk Tale*.
4. Bettelheim, *The Uses of Enchantment*, p. 275.
5. The practice of American actresses impersonating Englishwomen continued in 2001 with Renée Zellweger in *Bridget Jones's Diary* and Thora Birch in *The Hole*.
6. Peter Matthews, *Sight and Sound*, June 1998, p. 561.
7. Some critics do pick up on this aspect of the films. The most perceptive are Geoff Brown on *Sliding Doors* (*The Times*, 30 April 1998); Jonathan Romney on *This Year's Love* (*Guardian*, 19 February 1999) and Jason Solomons on *Sliding Doors* and *Martha – Meet Frank, Daniel and Laurence* (*Daily Express*, 1 May 1998) who concludes: 'What comes off best in both films is the resurgence of London as a fairytale location. The city looks superb, bathed in a golden light and shot with great affection and style.'
8. All the locations for the weddings are fictionalised. The first, supposedly at St John's, Stoke Clandon, was shot at St Michael's, Betchworth, near Dorking. The second, which we are told is at St Mary of the Fields, Cripplegate, is actually the chapel of the Royal Naval College at Greenwich. The third, between Hamish and Carrie, isn't in Scotland at all but at Albury Park near Guildford, and the fourth at St Bartholomew's (rather than St Julian's) near Smithfield meat market. See Mark Adams, *Movie Locations: A Guide to Britain and Ireland* (London: Boxtree, 2000), pp. 52–3.
9. In 90s films Albert Bridge, which Helen claims her great-grandfather helped to build, seems to have the iconic status Tower Bridge had in earlier films.
10. *Guardian*, 19 February 1999.
11. Since the early 60s, Notting Hill has been London's most favoured location. Other 60s examples include *Flame in the Streets* (Roy Baker, 1961), *The L-Shaped Room* (Bryan Forbes, 1962), *Leo the Last* (John Boorman, 1969) and *Performance* (Donald Cammell and Nicolas Roeg, 1970); *London Kills Me* (Hanif Kureishi, 1991), *The Punk and the Princess* (Mike Sarne, 1997) and *The Mother* (Roger Michell, 2003) all present a less glamorous view of the area to that seen in *Notting Hill*.
12. *Sight and Sound*, June 1999, p. 50. For a hostile view of life imitating art, with Madonna's marriage to Guy Ritchie involving substantial borrowings from both *Four Weddings* and *Notting Hill*, see Sophie Gilbert, 'All the Fun of the Fair Isle', in *Independent on Sunday*, 'Reality' section, 28 January 2001, pp. 6–7.

Bibliography

Bettelheim, Bruno, *The Uses of Enchantment* (London: Penguin, 1991).

James, Nick, 'Farewell to Napoli', *Sight and Sound*, May 1999.

Propp, Vladimir, *Morphology of the Folk Tale* (Austin: University of Texas Press, 1990).

Roddick, Nick, 'Four Weddings and a Final Reckoning', *Sight and Sound*, January 1995.

40

The More Things Change . . . British Cinema in the 90s

Brian McFarlane

The more things change, the more some things at least stay the same. There are obvious differences in the circumstances of production, distribution and exhibition but from the cultural point of view it is possible to observe continuities which recall the various high spots of British cinema, such as the output of the war years or the 'New Wave' period of the late 50s/early 60s.[1] A relatively relaxed censorship now permits a visual and verbal frankness, as well as the graphic depiction of violent acts, in ways that would have been unthinkable in the early 60s, let alone the 40s; and the once rigidly hierarchical class system as a major determinant of British film narratives is much diminished. But it is still possible to make some of the same sweeping generalisations about British cinema one could have made fifty years ago. It remains a poor cousin in the English-speaking world (like other English-speaking cinemas except the all-powerful one), scoring only the occasional commercial breakthrough at home and abroad. It still has an ongoing need for government support. It is still making a lot of films which no one in their right mind ought to have involved themselves with. But now the huge audiences that once made it possible for British films to recoup their costs at home are only a dim memory.

It is important to ask who still goes to British films. The 90s was the most buoyant film-making decade since the 60s, but it remains a sobering fact that many of the British films made in this decade never saw the light – or dark – of a cinema, and most of those that did brought in only meagre returns. It used to be the case that in Commonwealth countries substantial minority audiences could be relied on for what

was called 'a good British film' (as distinct from Hollywood tinsel): in Australia in 1950, for instance, four British films (plus Disney's British-made *Treasure Island*) were in the top ten box-office films and in the same year ninety-five of the feature films imported were British (compared with 284 US films and twenty-one from 'Other Countries').[2] This kind of audience no longer exists: films such as *Four Weddings and a Funeral* (1994) or *Sense and Sensibility* (1995) or *The Full Monty* (1997) did well in Australia (as elsewhere) but they are the exceptions rather than part of a continuing stream of British films once characteristically shown at certain metropolitan cinemas. Of course not everything was rosy in the past. According to Ronald Neame, producer-director during the prolific days of British film production, the US was, with a few exceptions, not interested in British films. He claims that 'Arthur Rank did everything on God's earth to try to get British films on to the American market and he failed'.[3] Again and again film-makers complained of the difficulties in getting their product screened in the US, where the best that could be hoped for was the art-house circuit in the big cities. But now even that art-house audience has dwindled into insignificance.

Defining Characteristics

Industrial matters have changed enormously, but if one asks 'What is a British film like?', one can still identify some of those same strands that once served to mark off British cinema from the Hollywood competition. There is nothing startlingly original in noticing the persistence of the literary and the realist as the identifying otherness of British cinema; one might just as easily have said this in, say, 1946 or 1960. Where one might have been praising *Great Expectations* (1946) or *Saturday Night and Sunday Morning* (1960) in earlier periods, one can discern the same sorts of impulses at work in *Howards End* (1992) or *Wonderland* (1999). Of course there have been changes in technology and in the prevailing narrative structures, but such films share common concerns with their predecessors.

The literary/theatrical tradition accounts for twenty-odd of the most prestigious films of the last decade of the 90s. Ushered in by Kenneth Branagh's successful re-jigging of *Henry V* (1989) 'for the Batman generation', the decade saw eight more Shakespearean adaptations.[4] Four of Jane Austen's novels were adapted for the big screen (and two for television) and other distinguished authors whose works were filmed, with varying degrees of distinction, include Oscar Wilde (*An Ideal Husband*, 1999, reported to be the only Lottery-funded film to have made a profit), Thomas Hardy (Michael Winterbottom's bleak masterpiece, *Jude*, 1996, Phil Agland's *The Woodlanders*, 1997), Henry James (*The Wings of the Dove*, 1997, arguably the best film yet made from the intractable James), Virginia Woolf (*Orlando*, 1992, and *Mrs Dalloway*, 1997, films about and made by women), E. M. Forster, George Orwell and Graham Greene.[5] All these films are informed by a regard for the verbal, but they are not just photographs of people talking. They are part of a tradition of film-making which helped to account for the post-war prestige of British cinema.

The adaptation was never the only manifestation of the literary in British films. The sheer value set on the verbal, the concern for language to do its part in narrative, could often make British films seem talky, as if they were too little reliant on the imagistic power of *mise en scène*.[6] But in Britain, writers like Wells, Shaw, Greene, Rattigan, Pinter and Christopher Hampton involved themselves far more intimately with the screen than their US counterparts who were more apt to flail in dealings with the new medium and give way to callow venom at their employers' expense.[7] In an essentially realist work like *Naked* (1993), Mike Leigh allows a very long dialogue between his cynical, amoral protagonist (David Thewlis) and a conventional security guard (Peter Wight), ranging eclectically from good and evil to the nature of the universe, taking in Nostradamus and the Book of Revelation. It is as if Leigh is secure in the knowledge that we will be happy to be *auditors*, though he also claims that 'what is going on cinematically and visually is integral to how it works; it's not just a whole lot of talking'.[8] And he would no doubt argue the same case about the famous nine-minute take in *Secrets and Lies* (1996) in which the feckless Cynthia (Brenda Blethyn) and the daughter she had abandoned (Marianne Jean-Baptiste) confront each other with convulsive truths about their pasts. It is hard to think of equivalent US films which place so much reliance on the verbal at the expense of the more obviously 'cinematic' qualities of *mise en scène* and editing.

Another defining factor which spills over into British films of now or of fifty years ago is a preference for the character-driven over the plot-driven. As one watches 'literary' films like *Carrington* (Christopher Hampton, 1995) or *The End of the Affair* (Neil Jordan, 1999) or such 'realist' pieces as *Under the Skin* (Carine Adler, 1997) or *My Name Is Joe* (Ken Loach, 1998), it is less a matter of what happens next than how will he/she react in this situation, given the way he/she is, that compels one's attention. No wonder the British have made cult successes of TV shows like *This Life* (1996–7) and *The Royle Family* (1998–2000), in both of which characters talk their way into our understanding of their lives.

That other source of high 40s prestige, the realist strain, fed by documentary's austere privileging of the 'real' in terms of observation of the physical world, reached its apotheosis in wartime films like *San Demetrio London* (1943) or *The Way Ahead* (1944) and post-war melodramas like *It Always Rains on Sunday* (1947) or *Good Time Girl* (1948), but it is still powerfully present in the work of Ken Loach and Mike Leigh (despite his penchant for Swiftian caricature), and of newer directors such as Michael Winterbottom, Antonia Bird and Coky Giedroyc; and actors Gary Oldman and Tim Roth, who both made excoriating first films in the painful-realist mode, *Nil by Mouth* (1997) and *The War Zone* (1999) respectively. Winterbottom's *Wonderland* dramatises interlocking London lives with a verisimilitude which rivets the attention; Giedroyc's *Stella Does Tricks* (1998), like Gainsborough's *Good Time Girl*, shows some sympathy for a tough but vulnerable young woman enmeshed in dangerous corruptions; Bird's *Priest* (1994) and *Face* (1997) embed melodrama in a realist context, recalling *It Always Rains on Sunday* and *Brief Encounter* (1945), which, though lauded for their surface realism in matters of setting and period mores, both exhibited the boldly structuring oppositions so characteristic of melodramatic narrative.

Enduring Love (Roger Michell, 2004)

Although it falls beyond the period covered by this chapter, *Enduring Love* exemplifies the continuing vitality of the literary adaptation in British cinema; and the career of Ian McEwan is a useful reminder that connections between British film and literature have not been confined to adaptation. Popular writers – poets such as W. H. Auden, playwrights such as Terence Rattigan and Christopher Hampton, and especially novelists such as Graham Greene – have often been drawn to writing for the screen, sometimes in fruitful collaboration with a particular director, as in the cases of Rattigan with Anthony Asquith or Greene with Carol Reed. One result of British cinema's attraction to literary figures may be a cinema more than usually dependent on the verbal.

Ian McEwan, perhaps Britain's most distinguished novelist of the last quarter-century, has not allied himself to a particular film-maker, but his novels *The Comfort of Strangers*, *The Cement Garden* and *Atonement* have been adapted for the screen; and he has written a variety of screenplays, notably for the state-of-the-nation piece *The Ploughman's Lunch* (Richard Eyre, 1983). He has not, except for *The Innocent* (John Schlesinger, 1993), adapted his own novels, and the screenplay for *Enduring Love* is by Joe Penhall; but the film retains that sense of arbitrary and dangerous intervention in the protagonists' lives that is so characteristic of McEwan.[1] He makes for uncomfortable reading and this film leaves one uncheered by human possibilities.

The film opens on a summer day in a vast field in the Chiltern Hills. The picnic idyll, involving Joe (a pre-Bond Daniel Craig), Claire (Samantha Morton) and a bottle of champagne, is interrupted when a hot-air balloon crashes to the ground, and then, as four men rush to the rescue, it lifts up again and all but one man jump safely to the ground. The film's penultimate scene is set in the same field, with Joe and Claire and the champagne again but with no sense that it can ever be as it was. In the time between, Joe has been stalked by the bizarre Jed (Rhys Ifans), claiming to love him and that God has brought them together; Joe has located Mrs Logan, the dead man's widow, bitter at what she perceives as her husband's infidelity; Joe and Claire's relationship has been put under serious strain; and there is a moment of violent blood-letting in their apartment. By the end calmness has returned: there has

Unwelcome shadow: Rhys Ifans stalks Daniel Craig in *Enduring Love*

been clarification about Logan's supposed girlfriend, and Jed is seen in the last moments of the film smiling benignly in an asylum.

There are departures from McEwan's masterly novel, but in the taut direction of Roger Michell and with a uniformly excellent cast, it still challenges Joe's intellectual approach to life – and offers a sustained challenge to the viewer. When Joe tries to explain to Claire that 'it doesn't need to be so complicated', she tells him, 'Don't say anything.' But this is a film, like many a British film, adaptation or not, in which talk matters. There is much talk about the nature of love, about whether the idea of 'love' is, as Joe, an academic instead of McEwan's journalist, suggests to his students, no more than 'a trick played by nature to make us fuck'. The screenplay offers other reflections on this matter, and ironically has Joe promise Jed 'I've always loved you' prior to disarming and stabbing him. It takes ideas seriously and renders them in cinematic terms – and that includes the intelligently verbal as well as the strikingly visual.

NOTE

1. *The Comfort of Strangers* was adapted by Harold Pinter and directed by Paul Schrader in 1990, *The Cement Garden* adapted and directed by Andrew Birkin in 1993, and *Atonement* adapted by Christopher Hampton and directed by Joe Wright in 2007.

FURTHER READING

James Mottram 'Enduring Love', <www.channel4.com/ *film*/reviews>.

Jessica Winter, 'Enduring Love', *Sight and Sound*, November 2004, p. 48.

Comic Traditions

Hollywood's history could largely be written in terms of genres (Westerns, musicals, gangster films, etc.); this was scarcely the case in Britain, where most genres had to be prefixed by a studio name to identify them: Gainsborough melodrama, Ealing comedy, Hammer horror. In any case, the middle-brow, middle-class reviewers rarely found much to say for genre, preferring the modes of the realist and the literary. Nevertheless, over a narrower range, British genres did flourish in the studio years and, despite the inevitable permutations wrought by time, their ancestors are still recognisable in the cinema of the 90s.[9]

Comedy was as important as the two critically approved modes in the earlier decades of British cinema. Ealing, as everyone in the English-speaking world knows, mined a vein of eccentric comedy, ranging from the black (*Kind Hearts and Coronets*, 1949), through the dryly acerbic (*The Man in the White Suit*, 1951) to the cosily reassuring (*Passport to Pimlico*, 1949). Rank made the engaging, sharp-edged comedy of the sexes, *Genevieve* (1953), and the innocuously middle-class *Doctor in the House* (1954) and its successors. They found a vulgar parallel in the *Carry On* series which rang all possible changes on the censor-permitted fun of bodily functions. The exemplars of these sorts of popular comedies have their counterparts in the 90s. A turn of the century fart-fest like *Kevin and Perry Go Large* (2000) which substitutes gauche teenagers for middle-aged comedians makes the *Carry Ons* seem as sophisticated as Congreve and an earlier generation might have found it excessively raunchy, but it maintains the same atmosphere of innocent scurrility. *Shallow Grave* (1994) is not as elegant as *Kind Hearts*, but it is equally black; *Four Weddings and a Funeral* is at best as witty and touching as *Genevieve*; *The Englishman Who Went up a Hill* ... (1995) rehearses the spectacle of the diffident and/or officious outsider being brought to more 'humane' ways of thinking and recalls Paul Douglas's pompous but gullible American in *The Maggie* (1954).[10] The Celtic fringes in which films such as *Another Shore* (1948), *Whisky Galore!* (1949) and *The Maggie* were set have also inspired contemporary whimsical comedies such as *Waking Ned* (1998), where Irish villagers unite to conceal the death of Ned the Lottery winner and claim his prize, and *Saving Grace* (2000), in which the widowed Brenda Blethyn turns her horticultural skills to raising marijuana in her Cornish hothouse. Scotland, Wales and Ireland have also provided the setting for less gentle comedies: the Welsh drug-

and-club scene is humorously but caustically explored in *Twin Town* (1997) and *Human Traffic* (1999); and a blackly Scottish surrealism pervades *Trainspotting* (1996) and *Orphans* (2000). The Roddy Doyle trilogy – *The Commitments* (1991), *The Snapper* (1993) and *The Van* (1996), which are all set in Dublin – offer tougher versions of urban working-class cheerfulness than were found in, say, Ealing's *Hue and Cry* (1947) or *Passport to Pimlico* and 50s working-class comedies like *The Happy Family* (1952) or *Sailor Beware!* (1956), but they share a recognisable populist ethos.

British Genres?

Films like *Billy Liar* (1963) – less amiable and more abrasive – move way beyond Ealing's territory to the industrial North of England. The New Wave filmmakers of the early 60s such as Tony Richardson, Lindsay Anderson, John Schlesinger and Karel Reisz, very consciously chose to draw on areas of Britain which had scarcely been seen on British screens. Richardson claimed that, with location-shooting, 'you get an authenticity that you can never get in a studio' and Anderson had famously characterised British cinema in the mid-50s as 'an English cinema (and Southern English at that), metropolitan in attitude, and entirely middle-class'.[11] The tradition they established of 'scenes from provincial life' was revived in the 90s through films like Peter Chelsom's *Hear My Song* (1991), Mark Herman's *Brassed Off* (1996), Shane Meadows' *TwentyFourSeven* (1997), and Stephen Daldry's *Billy Elliot* (2000). These are films whose reality is rooted in Northern urban settings which are less romanticised than those of the early 60s films, where poetic realism tended to prettify the grim landscape, but their *stories* tend to be more sentimental than those of their predecessors.[12]

The gangster cycle of the late 90s, spawned by Guy Ritchie's visceral, witty *Lock, Stock and Two Smoking Barrels* (1998), and including his own *Snatch* (2000), along with *Dad Savage* (1998), *Gangster No. 1* (2000), *Ordinary Decent Criminals* (2000), *Sexy Beast* (2000) and the appalling, cartoonish *Love, Honour and Obey* (2000), all recall the violence of the post-war gangster cycle which outraged many of the critics of the day.[13] However, it is worth noting some interesting shifts. Caper films such as *Lock, Stock* ... are altogether more bone-crunching than comic crime films of the past like Charles Crichton's *The Lavender Hill Mob* (1951) and Mario Zampi's *Too Many Crooks* (1959) or even Peter Collinson's *The Italian Job* (1969) which played for infinitely more innocent, harmless comic effect. Censorship changes, among other factors, have helped to bring about such shifts in audience responses. In the serious thrillers of the earlier period we were not invited to find the criminals attractive or sympathetic. Pinkie in *Brighton Rock* (1947), Narcy in *They Made Me a Fugitive* (1947) and Slim Grisson in *No Orchids for Miss Blandish* (1948), were no laughing matter and they were made to pay for their crimes. In the late 90s they might have been treated more indulgently.

Costume drama, a 40s staple as both a displacement of and escape from contemporary anxieties and auster-

ities, has surfaced in such tonally diverse 90s entertainments as *Mrs Brown* (1997), *Elizabeth* (1998), *Shakespeare in Love* (1998), *Plunkett & Macleane* (1999), *Onegin* (1999) and *Topsy-Turvy* (2000). There are real distinctions to be drawn between the Gainsborough costume pieces which hindsight has taught us to read as encoding the conflicts and anxieties and aspirations of wartime – wartime *women* in particular – and the often lavish recreation of times past in the 90s costume films. But in its deliberately anachronistic way, *Plunkett & Macleane* echoes Gainsborough's refusal to settle for mere verisimilitude. *Elizabeth* and *Onegin* recall the

Brassed Off (Mark Herman, 1996)

British cinema's dealings with coal mining are no more than a thin tenacious trickle. Cavalcanti's *Coal Face* (1935) made for the GPO Film Unit with distinguished collaborators W. H. Auden and Benjamin Britten, stressed the dangers of the miner's life; but its concern was at least as much poetic as realist. Its celebration of the heroic aspects of 'the basic industry of Britain' left little time for industrial relations or the toll on the health and lives of the miners. Features such as *The Stars Look Down* (Carol Reed, 1939), *The Proud Valley* (Penrose Tennyson, 1940), *Blue Scar* (Jill Craigie, 1949), *The Brave Don't Cry* (Philip Leacock, 1952), *The Big Man* (David Leland, 1990), as well as several documentaries from the likes of Karl Francis and the Amber Film Collective, paid more overt attention to the harsh actualities of the miner's life. And Mark Herman's *Brassed Off* is in that tradition.

Bleakly aware of the legacy of Thatcherite policies, and with the miners' strike of the previous decade still fresh in the mind, *Brassed Off*, set in the small Yorkshire mining town of Grimley, pulls off a tricky balancing act. On the one hand, it doesn't shirk the pain brought on by pit closures – economic stress leading to ruptured domestic and emotional lives. On the other, it still manages to be an exhilarating exercise in human resilience and music-making's power to lift the spirit. In achieving this balance, it never descends to the contemptible level of feel-goodism. It knows that the problems facing Grimley are real and that the Albert Hall triumph, also real, is nevertheless fleeting, that it hasn't changed life back in Grimley.

Critical invocations of Ealing comedy are both understandable and wide of the mark. Yes, the ordinary

folk *are* up against the machinations of the British Coal Board, but, no, there isn't really a sense that they'll succeed against the bureaucrats. The Colliery Brass Band and the demands it makes on its players are complexly rendered: it provides an outlet for a lot of beleaguered men, but it also arouses resentment among some of their wives. Again, the film isn't simple-minded in its gender politics. As well as the exasperated wife who walks out on her husband who'd gone to prison in the 1984 strike, there's the chirpy duo who dye their hair purple as a gesture of solidarity with the purple-jacketed band; and there are those other women manning (as it were) the tents where opposition to the strike is rallied.

There is a not displeasing element of fairy-tale in the way that Gloria (Tara Fitzgerald), returning to her home town to conduct a viability study of the mine, realises the Coal Board has deceived her, and uses her pay-off money to make it possible for the band to appear at the Albert Hall. On the other hand, after the band wins, the bitter speech made by Danny (Pete Postlethwaite), its conductor, is very unfairy-tale-like. Reality reasserts itself, as it does not in an Ealing film like *The Man in the White Suit* (Alexander Mackendrick), when Danny reviles 'this bloody government' which has caused so many to have 'lost the will to win, to live'. Unlike *The Full Monty*, another 'masculinity-in-crisis' comedy-drama, this one ends in irony not liberation.

FURTHER READING

Geoffrey Macnab, 'Brassed Off, *Sight and Sound*, November 1996, p. 44.

'Interview with Stephen Tompkinson', *Film Review*, December 1996, pp. 12–13.

more sombre re-creations of 'quality' costume films such as *Saraband for Dead Lovers* (1948) and *Blanche Fury* (1948); while *Mrs Brown* and *Topsy-Turvy* have obvious ancestors, in subject at least, in the Anna Neagle films, *Victoria the Great* (1937) and *Sixty Glorious Years* (1938) and Launder and Gilliat's version of *The Story of Gilbert and Sullivan* (1953).

This listing is meant not just to draw attention to obvious comparisons, but to suggest that certain genres keep recurring in British cinema, trailing traces of their antecedents. One could make a similar point about the continuities observable in films focusing on social and political problems. Films like *The Gentle Gunman* (Basil Dearden, 1952), with its premise of IRA terrorism, *Yield to the Night* (J. Lee Thompson, 1956), which questions the ethics of capital punishment, *The End of the Road* (Wolf Rilla, 1954), unpretentiously dealing with retirement and old age, and the series of social-problem films made by Basil Dearden and Michael Relph between 1946 and 1962, found worthy successors in the 90s.[14] Violence in Northern Ireland was dealt with in *The Boxer* (1997) and *Some Mother's Son* (1996); unemployment in *Raining Stones* (1993), *Brassed Off*, *The Full Monty* and *Billy Elliot*; and criminal injustice in *'Let Him Have It'* (1991) and *In the Name of the Father* (1993).

Art Cinema

One wouldn't want to push too far the idea that British cinema of the 90s was no more than a recycling of proven paths to critical prestige or commercial success, though the identifiable traces are undeniable. The literary, the realist and the comic: these were essentially what advocates of British cinema admired in the days of its prolificacy and it is instructive to note their persistence. It is just as important, however, to consider the way things have changed. The art cinema created by the likes of Derek Jarman, Terence Davies, Peter Greenaway and Sally Potter in the 80s seemed to indicate a new direction for British cinema, but its progress stalled in the 90s. In Greenaway's case, he may simply have pushed audiences further than they wanted to go, particularly in *The Baby of Mâcon* (1993), which alienated even dedicated Greenaway enthusiasts prepared to collude with his retreat from British cinema's devotion to realism (a rejection recalling that of Michael Powell and Emeric Pressburger in the 40s). It is hard now to imagine Greenaway pulling in the substantial art-house crowd that made *The Draughtsman's Contract* (1982) so commercially viable and *8½ Women* (1999) did little for his reputation or his popularity. It is even harder to imagine Tony Harrison's verse-poem-film *Prometheus* (1998) finding exhibition openings. Derek Jarman died in 1994, though before then he had been prolifically responsible for *The Garden* (1990), *Wittgenstein* (1992), *Edward II* (1993) and *Blue* (1993) a film which testified to the strength of the verbal tradition in British cinema by accompanying its soundtrack with an entirely blank blue screen. Terence Davies meandered into Americana with *The Neon Bible* (1995) and moved nearer the mainstream with *The House of Mirth* (2000). Sally Potter scored a huge critical success with *Orlando* but her next film, *The Tango Lesson* (1999) scarcely made a ripple, and *The Man Who Cried* (2000), with its starry cast (Christina Ricci, Johnny Depp and Cate Blanchett), seemed to presage a move away from the art house. The 80s art-cinema luminaries do not appear to have any clear successors and the audience for art cinema seems increasingly fragile. One might have supposed that the multiplexes, often with cinemas only large enough to hold an extended family, would have provided niches for the art film but so far it seems to have been a casualty rather than a beneficiary of the multiplex revolution.

New Shoots

In other areas British cinema has spawned clusters of films which, though hardly genres, were related either stylistically or thematically, for instance, the male ensemble movie, sparsely if notably exemplified by *Brassed Off*, *The Full Monty* and *Up 'n' Under* (1998), as well as in the caper films, *Lock, Stock . . .* and *Snatch*. The latter two obviously are very different in spirit from the first three, in which men are seen adjusting to situations in which their masculinity has been called into question by economic issues, though they share the subordination of the heterosexual couple to the male group. The idea of the male ensemble film, though it may have echoes in bomber-crew movies like *One of Our Aircraft Is Missing* (1942) or the witty heist film, *The League of Gentlemen* (1960), seems to have been given a distinctly new life in the 90s.

British cinema of the 90s has shown itself responsive to shifts in societal thinking in ways which have produced other such film clusters which may yet coalesce into genres. The ethnic mix which Britain now manifests found representation in *Young Soul Rebels* (1991), with its focus on interracial sexuality, in the genial *Bhaji on the Beach* (1993), the raucous *Babymother* (1998), the comedy-with-dangerous-edge *East Is East* (1999), the multi-storied *Beautiful People* (1999), and such considerations of what it meant to be Jewish in Britain in

Leon the Pig Farmer (1992) and (in period setting) *The Governess* (1999). All these films articulate an awareness that WASP, middle-class, Southern England is not all there is to British life; it never was, but it was many years before British cinema registered the heterogeneity of British society in a sustained, serious way. *East Is East*, though the unexpected crudity of some of its comic effects is disturbing, offers a major breakthrough in its representation of a working-class woman married to a Pakistani husband, who loves – and mistreats – her. There is a taking for granted of the ethnic mix here which is striking and heartening. Other generic categories could be invoked in relation to these films, but their common concern for racial mix suggests another way of looking at them.

A similar point might be made about a batch of films in which alternative sexual preferences have found varied articulation: in the comedy of *Bedrooms and Hallways* (1999), in the wish-fulfilment fantasy of *Beautiful Thing* (1998), in the Basingstoke-set, middle-class version of teenage uncloseting *Like It Is* (1998), in the portraits-of-artists, *Wilde* (1997) and *Love Is the Devil* (1998), in the mildly dopey *Love and Death on Long Island* (1999), the gay melodramas *Hollow Reed* (1996) and *Different for Girls* (1996), and the handful of films which foreground lesbian relationships, such as *Thin Ice* (1994) and *Sister My Sister* (1995). The presence of a gay protagonist is not enough to constitute a genre, but detailed work on how these films construct their narratives might reveal deeper generic congruencies. What happens to the 'couples' in these films? How do the narratives set them up? What sorts of conflicts/comforts do they find in their social contexts?

Stars of Stage and Screen

In further answer to the question of what was a British film in the 90s, it is useful to consider who was making the films. Links between stage and screen, always close in Britain have remained important and directors such as Nicholas Hytner (*The Madness of King George*, 1994), Nick Hamm (*Martha – Meet Frank, Daniel and Laurence*, 1998), Sam Mendes (*American Beauty*, 2000) and Stephen Daldry (*Billy Elliot*) all made their names in the theatre before transferring their skills to the screen. Prominent British stage actors have also successfully crossed over. John Gielgud, who took seriously to the screen later than his famous compeers Laurence Olivier and Ralph Richardson, became a consummate film character actor, filming a dozen times in the 90s. Judi Dench, who claimed in 1994 that she didn't enjoy

filming very much because '[it] is so imperfectly to do with us [as actors]' went on to win an Oscar nomination for *Mrs Brown* and a supporting actress Oscar for *Shakespeare in Love*.[15] Ian McKellen, Brenda Blethyn and Derek Jacobi embraced film with, it seems, conscious determination to forge new careers there. None of this is new, except that, now, actors (Michael Gambon, for example) appear to switch more easily between screen and stage than did some of their great theatrical forebears, and television has superseded both cinema and stage as the medium in which most actors now work. When actors like Jennifer Saunders, Emma Chambers or Hugh Laurie appear in films now, they inevitably come trailing the intertextuality of their TV work.

In looking at stars it is tempting to ask if a national cinema continues to seek out the same sorts of star types and look for parallels between past and present. Robert Carlyle, Ian Hart and Christopher Eccleston bring a whiff of 60s Tom Courtenay, not just in terms of whippet-thin physique, but of hungry discontent with an unjust status quo; Rufus Sewell recalls aspects of the moody James Mason of 40s melodramas; Kenneth Branagh matches Laurence Olivier – at least in his daring – and Hugh Grant seems to combine the silly-ass antics of Ian Carmichael with the light romantic appeal of Dirk Bogarde during his matinée idol phase. Kate Winslet has some of the sensual boldness of the young Googie Withers, Helena Bonham Carter the lady-like determination of Phyllis Calvert and Samantha Morton's wracked intensity evokes Rita Tushingham (whose daughter she plays in *Under the Skin*).

British producers, for reasons both commercial and cultural, have always been tempted to bring American stars across the Atlantic: as far back as 1922 Michael Balcon persuaded the Hollywood actress Betty Compson to star in his first production, *Woman to Woman* to ensure its commercial success. In the 90s Andie MacDowell and Julia Roberts tried to teach Hugh Grant not to be such a floppy-haired diffident in *Four Weddings and a Funeral* and *Notting Hill* (1999). Julianne Moore played Mrs Cheveley in *An Ideal Husband* just as her Hollywood predecessor Paulette Goddard had done in the 1947 version; American women are obviously considered better able to convey the outsider threat Wilde's femme fatale poses to the upper-class English society through which she swishes so dangerously. Gwyneth Paltrow's performances in *Emma* (1996), *Sliding Doors* (1998) and *Shakespeare in*

Paulette Goddard in Alexander Korda's *An Ideal Husband* (1947)

Love almost equalled those of Anne Bancroft in *The Pumpkin Eater* (1964) or Meryl Streep in *The French Lieutenant's Woman* (1981) in her convincing impersonation of Englishwomen. Branagh's casting of *Much Ado about Nothing* (1993) and *Hamlet* (1996), which draws eclectically on both sides of the Atlantic, doesn't betray Shakespeare but suggests instead his universality. Casts which include Denzel Washington, Michael Keaton, Robert Sean Leonard, and Keanu Reeves (*Much Ado*) and Robin Williams, Billy Crystal, Gérard Depardieu (*Hamlet*), alongside the usual British suspects, attest no doubt to box-office solicitation but also to an urge to depict the English playwright as a voice for all times and places. Less in the interests of British cinema, of course, has been the reverse process, by which major talents of every kind are drawn to Hollywood like moths to the flame of serious fame and wealth. But one only has to recall the careers of James Mason, Deborah Kerr, David Niven and Alfred Hitchcock to recognise that there is nothing new here.

One of the great strengths of British cinema at every stage has been its abundance of character-acting talent, and one could be certain in the 50s of at least a few moments of pleasure from, say, Dora Bryan or Maurice Denham or Raymond Huntley, even when the films they appeared in were dire. Today there are hugely enjoyable equivalents such as Linda Bassett (who may turn into Thora Hird as she ages), Philip Davis, a specialist in proletarian bluntness, Richenda Carey, with her magnificent *grandes dames*, and Peter Cellier whose upper-crust urbanities recall his great character-actor father Frank. One might also celebrate the wonderfully civilised Oliver Ford Davies (the Cecil Parker *de nos jours*), Edna Doré (unforgettably singing 'Can't Help Lovin' that Man' in *Nil by Mouth*), and Robert Hardy and Elizabeth Spriggs (outdoing each other in vulgar innuendo in *Sense and Sensibility*). These are the sorts of performers who anchor the star-driven narratives in a recognisable world, who provide in Henry James's famous phrase a sense of 'felt life'.

For those of us to whom British cinema continues to be the most interesting in the world, a powerful sense of optimism is necessary. It might be disingenuous to believe that quirky, small-scale films rooted in British culture can have a wide appeal, but sometimes – whether it's the upper-class froth of *Four Weddings and a Funeral* or the grim industrial life up North seen in *The Full Monty* or *Billy Elliot* – they do. Against the odds, a generation of film-makers – directors, producers, actors, writers – has emerged who persist in making films which, whether or not they see the inside of a multiplex, play against our expectations (even our expectation of being easily entertained), refuse the rewards of

Julianne Moore in Oliver Parker's *An Ideal Husband* (1999)

contemporary Hollywood cinema and continue to pin some sort of faith in people-centred narratives rather than special effects. Notwithstanding the social and film-industrial changes of the last fifty years, many aspects of British cinema, as industry and art form, continue to ring resonant bells. More British films were released in the 90s than at any time since the early 60s, but the number of runaway commercial successes and the number of *succès d'estime* were not notably different. When the 'New Wave' ebbed in the early 60s, there had been the box-office triumph of *Tom Jones* and the critical acclaim afforded *This Sporting Life* (both 1963) to keep the spirits up and persuade the Americans that British film was a good investment opportunity. By the end of the decade that scene had changed and British cinema seemed to be drifting into irreversible decline. In the very different industrial context of the 90s, *Nil by Mouth* has some of the same hard, bashing authority of *This Sporting Life*, and *Shakespeare in Love*, like *Tom Jones*, is a commercially very successful costume romp. Even more remarkable is the record-breaking international box office reaped by *Four Weddings and a Funeral* and *The Full Monty*. But there is no guarantee that British cinema has yet worked out a viable production system that will ensure the perpetuation of this sort of success.

Notes

1. The question of what actually constitutes a British film grows ever more complicated. The *BFI Film and Television Handbook 1999* provided a list of six 'UK Film Categories', from Category A 'where the cultural and financial impetus is from the UK and the majority of the personnel are British' to Category D2, described as 'American films with some UK financial involvement'. *BFI Film and Television Handbook 1999* (London: BFI, 1998), p. 341.

2. *Motion Picture Herald* poll, reported in *The 1951–52 Motion Picture Almanac*, p. 817. *Film Weekly Motion Picture Directory 1950–51* (Sydney, 1952), p. 152.

3. 'Ronald Neame', in Brian McFarlane, *An Autobiography of British Cinema*, p. 434.

4. 'Two Kings', *Film Comment* vol. 25 no. 6, November–December 1989, p. 6

5. Dalya Alberge, 'Ten out of 11 Lottery Films Fail at the Box Office', *The Times*, 3 January 2001 (internet version).

6. Jeremy Paxman writes about 'the moment when the English cultural tradition cut itself off from the rest of Europe': 'you could not find a more striking signal of the new direction in which English creativity was to turn than the tearing-down of altar screens and their replacement in many churches by bare boards listing the Ten Commandments. Here, literally, was the replacement of the visual by the verbal . . . . The English not only came to a new way of appreciating the Word, they came to an appreciation of words.' Jeremy Paxman, *The English: A Portrait of a People* (London: Penguin, 1999), p. 109.

7. See Ian Hamilton, *Writers in Hollywood 1915–1951* (London: William Heinemann, 1990).

8. 'Mike Leigh', in McFarlane, *An Autobiography of British Cinema*, p. 362.

9. See Marcia Landy's *British Genres: Cinema and Society 1930–1960*.

10. Christine Geraghty gives a full account of this phenomenon in *British Cinema in the Fifties: Gender, Genre and the 'New Look'*, pp. 43–6.

11. Tony Richardson, 'The Two Worlds of Cinema', *Films and Filming*, June 1961, p. 41. Lindsay Anderson, 'Get Out and Push', in Tom Maschler (ed.), *Declaration* (London: MacGibbon & Kee, 1957), p. 137.

12. It is curious how little sense, then or now or ever in British cinema, there is of the powerful complex pastoral element Wordsworth celebrates in 'The Prelude'; British cinema rarely gets away from the cities for this sort of purpose.

13. See Brian McFarlane, 'The Critics and Miss Blandish', in Robert Murphy and Steve Chibnall (eds), *British Crime Cinema* (London and New York, Routledge, 1998).

14. See John Hill, *Sex, Class and Realism*; and Alan Burton, Tim O'Sullivan and Paul Wells (eds), *Liberal Directions: Basil Dearden and Postwar British Film Culture*.

15. 'Judi Dench', in McFarlane, *An Autobiography of British Cinema*, p. 162.

Bibliography

Burton, Alan, O'Sullivan, Tim and Wells, Paul (eds), *Liberal Directions: Basil Dearden and Postwar British Film Culture* (Trowbridge: Flicks Books, 1997).

Geraghty, Christine, *British Cinema in the Fifties: Gender, Genre and the 'New Look'* (London and New York: Routledge, 2000).

Hill, John, *Sex, Class and Realism* (London: BFI, 1987).

Landy, Marcia, *British Genres: Cinema and Society 1930–1960* (Princeton, NJ: Princeton University Press, 1991).

McFarlane, Brian, *An Autobiography of British Cinema* (London: Methuen/BFI, 1997).

41

Travels in Ladland:
The British Gangster Film Cycle, 1998–2001

STEVE CHIBNALL

The value of every story depends on it being true.
A story is a picture of either an individual, or of human
nature in general: if it be false it is a picture of nothing.
Samuel Johnson[1]

Over the years, one has become accustomed to critical
protests at films which offend the tenets of good taste.
In 1971 there was an outcry at the upsurge of violence
in films such as *A Clockwork Orange*, *The Devils*, *Straw
Dogs* and *Performance*; ten years earlier there had been
howls of disapproval at Michael Powell's *Peeping Tom*
(1960). But one would have to go back to the Hammer
horror films of the late 1950s and the post-war cycle of
spiv and 'cosh boy' dramas to find such a comprehensive condemnation of a whole genre as met the late
1990s wave of gangster films. When the *Evening
Standard*'s Alexander Walker took up the cudgel against
the 'farrago of brutality' that was the Brighton gangster
movie, *Circus* (2000), he might have been the *Daily
Mirror*'s Reg Whitley laying into the 'false, cheap, nasty
sensationalism' of *Brighton Rock* (1947) more than fifty
years earlier:

> This thuggish mess, along with recent piles of excre-
> ment like *Love, Honour and Obey*, makes it seem as if a
> sizeable section of British Equity has now capitulated
> to East End gangsterism . . . . Its designer violence is a
> rip-off of movies – and novels like *The Big Sleep* –
> that had (sometimes) better motives than simply pan-
> dering to pornographic shock values that very
> quickly become numbingly repetitious . . . Brighton
> Schlock.[2]

In the new millennium, as crime movies jostled the delicate national cinema like muggers in an alley, police
spokesmen came forward to condemn their effects, just
as they had in the new dawn after World War II. John
Abbott, director-general of the National Criminal
Intelligence Service (surely an Orwellian title more
chilling than a brace of sawn-off shotguns) spoke out
against the 'darkly glamorous' image of gangsterism on
screen, the 'concerted attempt to show organised crime
as a "bit of a laugh" carried out by "cheeky chappies" ',
and the portrayal of violence as 'a pretty good way of
doing business'.[3]

The blame for what is seen as the pollution of
British film culture is usually laid at the door of
Guy Ritchie. The unexpected success of Ritchie's
low-budget, privately financed *Lock, Stock and Two
Smoking Barrels* (1998) was responsible, it is assumed,
for the flood of 'imitations' which followed.[4] This is
only partially true. While the verve and vigour of *Lock,
Stock* . . . encouraged a spirit of stylistic innovation,
and its financial returns prompted further excursions
into the crime-comedy genre, the gangster cycle was
already in motion before the release of Ritchie's film.
Some of its cynicism and humour of cruelty was anticipated by J. K. Amalou's more savage and less accomplished *Hard Men* (1996), and the whole gangster
bandwagon could be said to have been set rolling by
Face (1997), Antonia Bird's imperfectly realised attempt
to blend left-wing politics into a professional crime
scenario. However, to understand the impulse which
propelled the bandwagon we first need to appreciate
the longevity of the underworld film in Britain, and

its significance as a covert carrier of unrespectable conceptions of Englishness and unreconstructed definitions of masculinity.[5]

In the early post-war years, spiv films threatened to expose the myth of English respectability by revealing the seamy world of racketeering and vice beneath the surface of metropolitan life. Relegated to supporting-feature status and muffled by censorship throughout the 50s, the crime film was partially liberated by new sensibilities emerging at the end of the decade and began, once again, to explore the realities of professional crime and their relationship to legitimate business practice.[6] Throughout the 60s, however, the social realist aspect of the crime genre remained in creative tension with its melodramatic and comedic elements, finally producing what have turned out to be three of the seminal works not only of the genre, but of British cinema generally, *The Italian Job* (1969), *Performance* (1970) and *Get Carter* (1971). As film began to be superseded by television as the medium of choice for crime dramas, there was time for one last landmark movie, John Mackenzie's droll London thriller, *The Long Good Friday* (1979), proof positive that the crime genre was still capable of offering cogent comment on the state of the nation.[7]

Like so many 70s villains exiled to the Costa del Crime, the British crime film spent the next fifteen years in semi-retirement before receiving a call from 'the boys'.[8] The result was far from being the 'one last job' of gangster lore, however. In the four years between April 1997 and April 2001 at least twenty-four British underworld films were released, more than were released in the twenty years before 1997.[9] Nor was the interest in professional criminals confined to cinema. It was heralded by Duncan Campbell's survey of the contemporary crime scene, *That Was Business, This Is Personal*, in 1990 and followed by two television documentary series, Carlton's *Gangster* and the BBC's *Underworld* in 1993. The cycle of films was paralleled by a stream of memoirs from real-life villains such as 'Mad' Frankie Fraser, Freddie Forman, Billy Webb, Roy Shaw and 'Dodgy' Dave Courtney (the model for Chris in *Lock, Stock . . .*). The fashionability of the genre was confirmed by the success of Jake Arnott's novel, *The Long Firm* (1999), set in the 1960s London underworld, and interest has been further sustained by the deaths and funerals of all three of the Kray brothers and the return from Brazil of train robber Ronnie Biggs.

For the most part, the fascination with underworld activity has been skewed in a very nostalgic direction.

While drug trafficking, money laundering, counterfeiting, forgery, VAT fiddling, vehicle theft and illegal immigration are now the most preferred forms of activity among criminal gangs, British crime films remain preoccupied with protection rackets, armed robbery and unregulated betting and boxing. It does not take Sherlock Holmes to deduce that the gangster cycle might index wider gender anxieties and to relate these anxieties to both changing occupational structures and social expectations and to the demonstrable gains of feminism. There is also evidence of a connection between the gangster craze and the construction of post-feminist versions of masculinity in lifestyle magazines like *Loaded* and *FHM* preoccupied with representations of a time and a setting in which the rules of male association were clear, and the penalties for their infraction draconian.

Many critics see the influence of Tarantino as a crucial factor in turning the more honourable tradition of 'realist' underworld films, exemplified by *Get Carter* and *The Long Good Friday*, into a semi-comedic travesty in which authenticity is replaced by pastiche. As Bryan Appleyard complains:

> There is, in the end, something irredeemably nasty about new British gangster films . . . . The formalism they derive from Tarantino has become, in the hands of these directors, an oppressive wallowing in amorality, as if the only way they can find to entertain their audience is to transport them to a world where nothing matters and anything can be done.[10]

This type of criticism is rooted in a dubiously monolithic notion of the British crime genre in which a handful of classic films supply a template for future film-making. The perception of the classics themselves is equally selective, filtering the texts for those elements that conform most closely to the moral convention of retribution for the wrongdoer and the critically valorised tradition of social realism. For modern audiences, the black humour and triumphant nihilism of *Get Carter* and *The Long Good Friday* are probably more significant than their naturalism or moral appropriateness. In any case they have been used not as templates but as resources to be affectionately rummaged through for inspiration and ironic quotation. The result has been not genre purity but a diversity in which professional crime provides a linking motif for a spectrum of films from those that strive for unvarnished authenticity to those that cheerfully peddle myth. We might call these two ends of the spectrum 'gangster heavy' and 'gangster light'.

'Heavy' films require the suspension of disbelief and work through depth of characterisation, naturalistic dialogue, an emphasis on performances of conviction and power, and close attention to the details of period and place. Their narrative structure is usually one of tragedy in the Shakespearean or Jacobean mode. 'Light' films, by contrast, encourage a more distanced viewing position and an awareness of the artifice of film-making. Characterisations may be thin or even consciously one-dimensional, and performances are stylised and frequently exaggerated for comic effect. Whereas in the 'heavy' mode the textual elements of dialogue, music, performance, cinematography and *mise en scène* operate relatively unobtrusively together to promote audience involvement in the action and identification with the protagonist, in 'light' mode these textual elements are offered as more discrete experiences, attractions which strive to be noticed. Dialogue seeks to be witty and shocking, music blends retro hits with chic club sounds with one eye on the soundtrack album sales. Performance is frequently subordinated to a casting policy that enriches the film's intertextual resonances by using familiar faces from television and pop promos in unexpected ways. Cinematography and *mise en scène* draw attention to themselves by creating striking imagery that employs innovative techniques and hi-tech methods. Narrative structures do not attempt to elicit the depth of feeling that 'gangster heavy' strives to evoke. Instead, by adopting a more fragmented and episodic line of development that is full of complexity and surprise, they opt for the creation of 'cool' moments, offering the audience a rollercoaster ride of plot twists and somersaults that need only a cursory suspension of disbelief for their enjoyment. 'Gangster light' is not for solitary spectators, but invites a more gregarious viewing situation in which comments can be exchanged and excesses of style and performance noted. These are the conditions associated with video rental (and, to a lesser extent, the viewing of sell-through videos) rather than theatrical exhibition. A greater success on video is also suggested by 'gangster light's' lack of cinematic spectacle and elaborate special effects best appreciated on the big screen, and the masculinist subject matter which renders these films problematic as 'date' movies.

However, the most crucial characteristic of 'gangster light' is what we might call its 'faux-ness'. This is not used in the pejorative sense in which 'fake' is used, implying an attempt to fool the viewer with a counterfeit which purports to be authentic, but as a word to describe an idealised pastiche of the real which is willingly, and even enthusiastically, legitimated by the viewer. Faux-ness is a knowing theatrical distortion of real life, a mutually condoned simulacrum that, by a typically post-modern conceit, is something better than the real thing. This quality can most easily be appreciated in the peculiar world evoked in the gangster films of Guy Ritchie where post-modern cinematic techniques meet the sensibilities and concerns of 'New Laddism'.

Gangster Light – Friend or Faux?

> Thank God for Britain's wideboys. We would be lost without them. They will be the saving grace of the British film industry by breathing a waft of fresh air into a business controlled by the Stuffy Luvvy Mob. They seem to only want to churn out frock-perfect period literary adaptations or highbrow intellectual twaddle. It's time for all the old-school tie brigade of Puttnam, Attenborough and Branagh to stand back and let the leary lads have a go.
> Nick Fisher, *Sun*, 29 August 1998

Claire Monk has characterised 'New Laddism' as a 'male backlash against the media – and – female-imposed ideal of the new man' and 'a regressive escape from the demands of maturity – and women'. It is, she argues, reactionary in its attitude to both gender politics and social policy.[11] This idea of 'regressive escape' is clearly evident in Ritchie's and producer Matthew Vaughn's *Lock, Stock and Two Smoking Barrels* and *Snatch* (2000), which both evoke a world of masculine competitive sociability we might call 'ladland'. Ritchie's ladland can be seen as regressive in a number of senses. It is an environment in which conventional paid employment has been largely eliminated, or is confined to repressive jobs such as being a policeman or traffic warden. Sophisticated social organisation has been replaced by a Hobbesian jungle of ruthless competitors, struggling for survival and supremacy. In this picaresque universe, all the world is gangland and the only legitimate occupation is the hustle. Few of Ritchie's wide-boys have reached maturity, a condition largely represented by the coolly violent characters played by Vinnie Jones. Most are struggling to play the roles expected of them, unable to quite fill the clothes they wear no matter how much they puff out their chests. It is the world of the boys' playground where play-acting and bullying are the typical modes of behaviour.[12] Their speech, on the other hand, has achieved a remarkable level of vernacular sophistication, driven by metaphor, coded into colourful rhyming slang and decorated with ironic euphemism and gross obscenities. Ritchie takes great care to ensure that the colour, rhythm and humour of his dialogue suggest a believable milieu.[13]

Moral authority is located not in society's legal apparatus, but in the strict code of the 'straight man' embodied in *Lock, Stock . . .* by Chris (Vinnie Jones), a father whose rule is so powerful that a mother is superfluous. Much criticism has, in fact, been levelled at Ritchie for the invisibility of women in his films. Monk, for example sees this as symptomatic of their underlying misogyny, but the general absence of female characters is less an expression of a hatred of women than the irrelevance of women to the stories Ritchie wants to tell and the concerns he wants to address. Thus, *Lock, Stock . . .*'s scripted romantic subplot featuring Laura Bailey was filmed but dropped in postproduction because it slowed down the action. Or, as Ritchie expressed it: 'Wussy-wushy scenes just bore the hell out of me. I just want them to get on and start bashing people up.'[14] Ryan Gilbey notes that what *Lock, Stock . . .* is really interested in is 'the fabric of male relationships', and draws attention to the way in which the film displays a sentimental 'yearning for the security of family – any family so long as it is exclusively male'.[15] This notion of the male peer group as an alternative family pervades not only Ritchie's films, but also the conditions of their production. As the director says of his casting policies:

> It's about creating a family. That's why casting takes so long – the actors themselves have to be very real and very strong and they also have to gel offscreen. After a long day's shooting, I want to be able to have a pint with the lads.

We can see in this attempt to construct a sustaining single-sex grouping a parallel with feminist imperatives to build a sisterhood, but Ritchie's idea of brotherhood embraces the playful competitiveness which he accepts as vital to male solidarity.

In the same way that Ritchie's films eliminate female characters who might distract from their concern with bonding and competition among male groups, locations are chosen for their generic suggestiveness rather than their specificity of place. This gives the *mise en scène*

'Brick Top' (Alan Ford, centre) and his bad boys in *Snatch* (Guy Ritchie, 2000)

a pared-down, minimalist feel that separates it from most London films and contributes to the sense that we are watching an urban folk tale. Instead of expansive tourist vistas, we are shown the more claustrophobic village London of television's *Minder* (1979–94) – a world of minicabs and sex shops, spielers and lock-ups, pawnbrokers and bookies, and tarted-up pubs with bare brickwork and stripped floors.[16] This is an almost Dickensian vision of a city gone to seed, surviving as a grown-up playground for hustlers adept at 'picking peanuts out of poo'. It is a backstreet London of dodgy deals, risky opportunities and sudden violence. In spite of scrupulously authentic location-filming, there is an inescapable feeling that this is a London of the imagination, floating in time somewhere in the last thirty years without solid temporal or geographical anchors. Outside this metropolitan rookery the country seems to be caught in a time warp – squires in their manor houses and gypsies in the woods.

The fashionable buzz around *Lock, Stock . . .* ensured that the film would be treated not just as a movie but as a cultural event. The clothing industry played a significant role in the financing of the film (French Connection chief executive Stephen Marks was one of its backers, and Ozwald Boateng supplied suits for the characters). Within days of the première, Claudia Croft in the *Evening Standard* was announcing the East End gangster look as 'the biggest thing in menswear since Liam Gallagher's cagoule'.

> The appeal of the film's gangster look is simple. They appear 'ard but are so well dressed that no one in their right mind would want to mess up their suits. The villains look as sharp as Stanley knives, their midnight blue and steel grey tonic suits shine like

knuckle-dusters . . . No gangster wardrobe is complete without a classic piece of English tailoring. A Crombie overcoat is essential, but it must be long enough to hide a shooter . . . . In real life, of course, villains are more likely to wear dodgy tracksuits and prison tattoos.[17]

Like Ritchie's film, Croft's telling of its 'fashion story' erodes the codes of realism, replacing them with the playful codes of faux style. Lifestyle is turned into pose, real life with all the creases ironed out, a masquerade that happily reveals the traces of inauthenticity like the bulge of a shooter under a Crombie.

Ritchie's film-making is an exhilarating extension of the sort of tall storytelling that keeps men in pubs entertained over a few pints.[18] Like the opening lines of *Lock, Stock . . .*, it is the exaggerated spiel of the market trader who assures his incredulous punters that his moody goods are 'not stolen, they just haven't been paid for'. If the British films noirs of the 1940s were spiv films by virtue of their subject matter, Ritchie's are spiv in their style – loud, cheeky, outrageous, quick-witted, seductive and as flashy as a nude on a kipper tie.[19] Rather than trying to hide the faux-ness of his scenarios, Ritchie celebrates them, constantly drawing attention to the false and the masquerade: *Lock, Stock . . .* features a solarium which peddles fake tans, an ostentatious wig on one of its wildly over-drawn scally characters and a Samoan pub in London's East End (a fake without an original?). *Snatch* flaunts a gaggle of men who impersonate Jews ('good for business'), a Russian who dresses like an English country gent and gypsies ('pikeys') who exaggerate their own dialect for commercial advantage. The films' most outrageous use of the fake, however, is reserved for the way in which their anxieties about male potency are signalled. In *Lock, Stock . . .*, porn baron 'Hatchet' Harry (P. H. Moriarty) decorates his desk with dildos that are his weapon of choice when no hatchet is to hand.[20] *Snatch* makes this concern about penis substitutes even more explicit in the sequence where Bullet Tooth Tony (Vinnie Jones) fronts out three would-be hard men, using an elaborate sexual metaphor to contrast their impotence, signalled by their replica guns, with his own virility embodied in his 'Desert Eagle .50' shooter.

Many of Ritchie's thematic concerns can also be found in the 'gangster light' offerings of Dominic Anciano and Ray Burdis, two film-makers who, like Ritchie, cut their teeth on music videos before making their first privately financed feature, *Final Cut* (1999).[21] Although

neither a popular nor a critical success, the film, and the improvisational techniques it employed, were sufficiently impressive for BBC Films to commission *Love, Honour and Obey* (2000). Anciano and Burdis take Ritchie's emphasis on masculine masquerade and the performative pose one stage further by substantially effacing the line between actor and character. Like Mike Leigh, they require their actors to develop their own characters and to improvise scenes within a predetermined narrative structure. Unlike Leigh, however, Anciano and Burdis ask their actors to use their own first names for their characters and use their own personalities as the starting points for their performances. As Jude Law estimates, 'fifty per cent of it is us, fifty per cent is the character'. This is the sort of procedure associated with small experimental theatre troupes of comparatively unknown actors. Anciano and Burdis, on the other hand, attempt it with what the Press Book for *Love, Honour and Obey* calls 'one of the starriest casts in film history', the core of which is a coterie of young London-based actors known in the media as 'The Brit Pack' or 'The Primrose Hill Rat Pack'. *Love, Honour and Obey* provides an opportunity for this group of friends to build on their reputation for heavy-duty partying by constructing an *alter ego* as a criminal gang.

For audiences sufficiently familiar with British films to recognise the actors and attach appropriate star personae, the results of Anciano and Burdis's experiment are a little unnerving. It is not even suggested that viewers suspend their disbelief. Instead, they are invited to consider the ontology of both acting and crime. The concern of Nic Roeg and Donald Cammell's *Performance* with the plasticity of identity and the theatrical aspects of the presentation of self become the vital source of comedy in *Love, Honour and Obey*. When they have exhausted their own personalities as a source, the techniques of improvisation lead the film's actors to base their performances on what they know best – which turns out to be past gangster movies rather than real criminals. The results hover between pastiche and parody, not so much serious performances (or even considered comic performances) as a form of on-screen play that extends the actors' off-screen socialising.

Amid all this self-reflexivity some subtextual space is found for comments on the beleaguered condition of masculinity (the running gag about doorman Ray Burdis's impotence), gangsterism as a state of arrested development ('chased St Trinians out of the playground') and its association with reactionary and militaristic conceptions of Englishness (most obviously in

Jonny's SAS fantasy as he watches videos of the Falklands War beneath the Union Jack pinned to his wall). However, none of this is really allowed to get in the way of the cast enjoying themselves, seen at its most self-indulgent in the protracted karaoke sequences which, by thoroughly obliterating the lines between amateur/professional and actor/character, constitute the film's core metaphor.

Despite being trailed by David Thompson of BBC Films as 'a wickedly funny gangland tale brought to life by some of the most exciting new British screen talent around', the reviews of *Love, Honour and Obey* were contemptuous.[22] Critics were particularly resentful that public money had been spent on such a project. In an *Evening Standard* review with all the hallmarks of Alexander Walker, the cast was described as 'another romper-room assembly of second-and-third-magnitude British talents', and the film as 'a scandalous deployment of public revenues'.[23] So contagious was the gangster bug, it seemed, that 'The Beeb' itself had sacrificed its respectability to join the extortion racket.

The depth of critical hostility towards 'gangster light' revealed in the reviews of *Love, Honour and Obey* was also evident in the response to other films which approached criminal violence with comedic intent. Most of these movies were by first-time directors who saw 'gangster light' as an opportunity to position their film-making in the hip-and-happening section of the market. Some – such as *You're Dead* (1999), director-writer Andy Hurst's embarrassingly unfunny tale of a failed bank heist (Tag line: '*Pulp Fiction* meets Monty Python') – are best left in the oblivion to which they have been consigned, but others call for a little more consideration.

Circus, the directorial début of Rob Walker, was a film that promised much. Written by a new and exciting talent, David Logan, who had been 'discovered' working in a Brighton video-rental shop (after all, Tarantino had followed a similar career path), the script had provoked a bidding war, with Columbia beating off competition from Fox, Polygram and Carlton to secure the $6-million film.[24] Set in Logan's home town, *Circus* might have been the *Brighton Rock* of the new century. Unfortunately, the film owes more to days spent in the video store than in the mean lanes of Brighton. Unlike the Newcastle of *Get Carter* or the London of *The Long Good Friday*, the Brighton of *Circus*, though scenic, never becomes an essential part of the film's action and character. With the exception of the playfully gratuitous scene on the nudist beach (disturbingly moved next to the West Pier), the action might have been set in

any city. The social distinctiveness of cosmopolitan Brighton, its antique dealers, gays, bohemians, tourists and clubland, feature hardly at all.

Like so much of the British gangster cycle, *Circus* is a film based not on life but on other films. When Graham Greene wrote *Brighton Rock*, he drew on first-hand experience of the seaside town's low life. Logan, on the other hand, preferred to base his protagonist, Leo (John Hannah) on Kirk Douglas's character in Billy Wilder's *Ace in the Hole* (1951).[25] Another character, Moose, the love-sick heavy, is lifted straight out of *Farewell My Lovely* (1944). There is a card game from *Lock, Stock* . . ., a torture scene from *Reservoir Dogs* (1992), an accidental shooting from *Pulp Fiction* (1994), a red telephone on the beach from *Local Hero* (1983), a villain who dresses like Dr No, and a running man from *Brighton Rock*. Some scenes, such as the Tarantinoesque stand-off in a diner, seem to have been included for their referential qualities alone. There are some pleasures in this for the genre buff, who might recognise that the film Leo watches in the Duke of York cinema is *The Lady from Shanghai* (1948) and make the connection between the fake blonde hair of its red-headed star, Rita Hayworth, and the disguise adopted by Leo's wife, Lily (Famke Janssen). Ultimately, however, *Circus* encourages the display of cultural capital only to devalue its currency by supplying no satisfactory cause for investment. Whereas the faux characters of *Lock, Stock* . . . are imbued with a psychological realism which gives them both warmth and credibility, expressions of genuine emotion or motivation in *Circus* are as rare as sand on Brighton's pebble beach.

Lack of attention to period and place is a charge that might also be brought against David A. Stewart's *Honest*, which opened in a blaze of publicity on 220 screens over the Whitsun Bank Holiday weekend 2000, but grossed only around £500 from each, leaving the £6-million production severely embarrassed. This tale of fly East End wide-girls meeting draft dodgers and radical toffs evokes the myth rather than the reality of London in the late 1960s. Cosmo Landesman, in an enthusiastic (and thus unrepresentative) review in the *Sunday Times* (28 May 2000), described it as 'a grown-up Austin Powers without the flatulence', a somewhat generous assessment of the film's overdrawn flower-power pastiche, dripping in psychedelic tat and polymorphous perversity. Landesman saw it as a satire of the 60s, lampooning the 'radical postures of the counter-culture', the 'Nell Dunn-Jeremy Sandford-Ken Loach view of working-class life', and 'the cult of the Krays and East End villainy', and deriving its comic appeal from the 'utter sincerity' with which the camp dialogue is delivered. Thus the Poor Cows and tragic Darlings of 60s social realism are replaced by three feisty sisters (played by members of the girl band All Saints) who 'dress up like men and rob from the rich' as if second-wave feminism had already triumphed. The faux treatment ensures that what matters is not social comment but the preservation of media myth, because, as Marvin Gaye and Tammi Terrell sing over the film's closing credits, this 'Ain't nothing like the real thing'.

Honest is a colourful, but ultimately pointless, exercise in filmic dishonesty. The most critically derided film of the gangster cycle, *Rancid Aluminium* (2000), is more effective in putting faux-ness to productive use. Adapted by university lecturer James Hawes from his cult novel, *Rancid Aluminium* manages a provocative subtext that gives some depth to its meretricious surfaces. Beneath its overblown posturing and comic-book capers, it is a film about masculinity and Englishness.

Relieved of the responsibilities of economic survival by the successful business established by his father, Pete Thompson (Rhys Ifans), like the tropical fish he pampers, luxuriates in a slacker's paradise – arranging parties and snorting copious quantities of cocaine. That the film sees this as an erosion of masculine virility is clearly signalled by Pete's problems with a low sperm count which are causing infertility problems in his marriage. 'Western man is dying out,' his doctor tells him. It is no coincidence that the state of decadent decline that Pete symbolises for the nation comes about at the end of the Cold War. Fat and flabby English manhood and business is set in contrast to a lean and hungry Russia, eager to grab a slice of 'the New Europe'. The economic and sexual potency of the emergent nations of the 'Wild East' is embodied in Russian mafioso, Mr Kant (Steven Berkoff) and his femme fatale daughter, Masha (Tara Fitzgerald), to whom Pete turns to solve his apparently deepening business problems. This new Russia of ruthless capitalist enterprise freed from the protectionism of a Communist past is offered as the world we have lost, a world in which a man proclaimed his virility by his readiness for action and his contempt for the constraints of law.

With its melodramatic plot, national stereotypes consciously overplayed in cod-Russian and Irish accents, and lashings of preposterous dialogue, the film announces itself as a tall tale which is interested in the mythic rather than the real, and the symbolic rather than the literal. Why else would Pete meet Mr Kant in a British sports pavilion decorated with Union Jacks and images of Empire and watch the Russian confirm his admiration of the English sea-dog Drake by playing with a set of bowls?[26] Those looking for credibility of characterisation, authenticity of location and directorial lightness of touch were never likely to be charmed by the film's comedy of excess. *Rancid Aluminium*, like other gangster comedies, is keyed not only to particular anxieties in its young, male target audience, but to an appreciation of grossness as a comedic device and 'coolness' as a desired but elusive quality. However unsuccessfully, the film's camped-up, ironic, cine-familiar sensibility aims to match that of a differentiated segment of film-watchers. As Mr Kant puts it: 'Those who should know, know.'

Gangster Heavy – Vanquishing the Faux

> *Gangster No. 1* is not about one Mr Big who controls everything. It's about certain firms being in control of certain areas of London with their own strengths and power bases, which is an authentic perspective. My father was active in this world in the 1960s and I wanted to reflect that authenticity. These people . . . live in a serious world, one of business and power where their life and liberty is on the line. They're shrewd, clever people who live by their own rules. You have to do them justice and I feel we have.
> Jamie Forman[27]

Paul McGuigan's grim tale of cruelty and damnation, *Gangster No. 1* (2000), is almost the only film of the British cycle which can claim to be a classic gangster movie, in the sense that it is a tragedy based on a criminal's rise and fall. Eschewing comedy, it deals with the weighty themes of classical drama: obsession, ruthless ambition, treachery, deception, moral decay and the possibility of redemption. McGuigan has compared the script to Greek tragedy, and its production designer Richard Bridgland has suggested it is like '*The Duchess of Malfi* – but with guns' (Press Book). The film has an epic quality which is conspicuously absent in the rest of the cycle, and clearly signals its intentions to explore the key concerns of the genre and to distance itself from the trivialising treatments of 'gangster light'. In place of the Tarantino conception of crime as work, *Gangster No. 1* reinstates the ancient notion of crime as evil, a product less of social conditions than of individual pathology, particularly the inability to experience love. Great train robber Bruce Reynolds acted as a special consultant, and his influence is evident in the film's faultless recreation of the criminal milieu and subcultural style of 60s London. As McGuigan put it:

> Because it's a simple, character-driven story, we could put a lot of thought into the whole style of the film. It's a big movie that leans on lots of fine details, such as how someone smokes a cigarette or walks down the street.[28]

Richard Bridgland's meticulous design is largely based on Erwin Fieger's photographs from the period and avoids the iconic clichés of *Honest*. It is motivated by a desire to reflect the moral barrenness and superficial glitz of the gangster lifestyle.[29]

The look of *Gangster No. 1*, and its interest in the construction of personal reputation through the performative aspects of style, owe a substantial debt to the first third of *Performance*. *Sexy Beast* (2000) – scripted by Louis Mellis and David Scinto who had written the play on which *Gangster No. 1* was based – is a story of the invasion of domestic space and owes more to the last two-thirds of Cammell and Roeg's film.[30] Both films, however, share the theme of a criminal, who is redeemed by his ability to establish a bond of love with a woman, confronted by a self-obsessed and emotionally autistic psychopath.

Sexy Beast takes the clichéd ingredients of the genre – the *nouveau riche* Cockney wide-boy, the psycho gangster, the Costa del Crime, the one last job (a safety-deposit heist) – and creates something fresh and memorable. Gary 'Gal' Dove (Ray Winstone) is a gangster who has not only gone to seed physically but who (as his name implies) has been feminised and turned against

The face of evil?: Paul Bettany in *Gangster No. 1* (Paul McGuigan, 2000)

violence. Like Pete in *Rancid Aluminium*, he has gone soft. His fish tank is the Spanish swimming pool (tiled with romantically linked hearts) he spends his days sunning himself by. The issue is still one of decadence, but this time it is not associated with England itself, which Gal contemptuously condemns ('what a shit-hole, what a toilet – every cunt with a long face') but a fantasy alternative to England, the idyll of the Essex boy, a hacienda in the sun. The Costa del Crime is pictured as a retirement home for superannuated villains with pot bellies and lobster tans. Gal Dove is happy in his hideaway, now more comfortable with the company of women than men, but the imminent disturbance to his peace is symbolically prefigured by a large boulder splashing into his pool. It is quickly followed by the arrival of boulder-headed Don Logan (Ben Kingsley in a truly demonic performance) a terrifying London hard man entrusted by crime lord Teddy Bass (Ian McShane) with the job of recruiting a team for a lucrative robbery. If Gal is a goldfish, Logan and Bass are definitely piranhas, self-centred, dangerous, unpredictable and utterly ruthless. Logan is not a man who is prepared to take no for an answer, and eventually, goaded into a cold fury by Gal's polite refusal to come out of retirement, he attacks him with a glass. Gal no longer has 'the bottle' to defend himself, but the task is taken up first by his house boy and surrogate son (Alvaro Monje) and then, more decisively, by his devoted ex-porn star wife (Amanda Redman) who empties a shotgun into Logan. Essex girl turns out to be a tougher proposition than Essex boy.

Although the loathsome Logan is safely interred under Gal's freshly tiled pool, that one last job must still be done, if only to dispel suspicion aroused by Logan's disappearance. By his death, Logan forces the peace-loving Dove back into the criminal fraternity, obliging 'Gal' once more to be a 'man', and ensuring that the wannabe Spaniard remains an Englishman. The film's third act sees Gal in a different sort of swimming pool, both literally and metaphorically. He is literally under-water helping to tunnel from a Turkish baths into a safety-deposit vault, but he is also back in the piranha pool of London's gangland, which he is clearly in no shape to inhabit. Forced to witness Teddy's casual murder of the vault's owner (and probably one of Teddy's lovers) Gal is surprised and relieved to leave England alive. He is left in no doubt, however, that the 'big fish' Teddy Bass might splash into his pool some day, or the secret beneath it might return to haunt him.

Like other films in the gangster cycle, *Sexy Beast* is littered with references and allusions to the genre's history: Ian McShane's presence recalls the roles he played in the gangland thrillers *Villain* (1971) and *Sitting Target* (1972), just as James Fox as the raffish vault owner inevitably evokes the memory of *Performance* (although in this instance he is the gangster's decadent host), while the Spanish setting and persecuted gangster-in-retirement are taken from *The Hit* (1984). But *Sexy Beast*, unlike some of the films in its cycle, is much more than the sum of its references. As its director, Jonathan Glazer, put it: 'It's a film for me that happens within the genre rather than about the genre. That's the key.' The faux is vanquished, not by an unswerving commitment to naturalism, but by a sense of dramatic integrity that flows through the dialogue, direction and performances.

Although *Gangster No. 1* and *Sexy Beast* are more impressive pieces of work than any of the non-Ritchie 'gangster lights', they are both backward-looking in their approach to the underworld. Towards the heavier end of the spectrum, only Jim Doyle's low-budget *Going Off Big Time* (2000) and Terry Winsor's factually grounded *Essex Boys* (2000) link professional crime to millennial club and drug culture. Set, for once, in Liverpool rather than London, Doyle's film, like *Twin Town* (1997), *Fast Food* (1999), *The Van Boys* (1999), *The Last Yellow* (1999) and *Small Time Obsession* (2000), offers continuity with the trend of the mid-1990s towards a merger of the underworld film with the drama of underclass life.[31] In *Going Off Big Time*, becoming a gangster is something that literally happens by accident. Criminal motivation is largely contingent on a string of unforeseeable circumstances, and the activities of crime are not so much work as everyday survival. Although the film follows the classic genre template of the rise and fall of a gang leader, its protagonist bears little similarity to the twisted megalomaniac of *Gangster No. 1*. Reluctant gangster Mark Clayton, as played by *Going Off*'s writer Neil Fitzmaurice, is shy and retiring; his ambition not to be number one, but to settle down with the daughter of a local builder; and his tragedy is to be a victim of bad luck and unwise association (as is the ex-con protagonist of *It Was an Accident*, 2000). With the exception of one outburst by Mark's lawyer (Sarah Alexander), dealing in drugs and running protection rackets hardly seem to be reasons for moral censure. After all, what other choice do these scallywag scousers have?

Winsor's film – set in the marshlands and garish seaside fleshpots north of the Thames estuary, where *nouveau riche* East Enders grew fat on the drugs trade – was based on the Rettendon 'Range Rover' murders.[32] Although clearly promoted as a fiction merely inspired by real events, the authenticity of the film's locations and the realistic framework of its story give it a solid grounding. Charlie Creed-Miles, who plays the eager but naive Billy Reynolds, was careful to distance the film from more fanciful examples of the genre: 'At least *Essex Boys* is honest. It may be about an underworld that is nasty and horrible, but it does have a moral base to it . . . I hate the glamorisation of this world. I hate it with a passion.'[33] This does not mean, however, that *Essex Boys* aims for the miserabilist realism of *Nil by Mouth* (1997), in which Creed-Miles had played the drug-dependent brother-in-law of Ray Winstone's hard man. Jeff Pope's script borrows heavily from *Goodfellas* (1990) and the narrative conventions of film noir, but Creed-Miles's fall guy, Sean Bean's psycho-gangster and Alex Kingston's femme fatale are all treated as more than simple stock characters. The film finds space to satirise the aspirations of the post-industrial working class ('S series BMW and a nice little detached house in Billericay'), but it is most interesting for its portrait of gender relations in the county that has given its name to a comic construction of mindless femininity. Although there are numerous examples in this film of 'Essex girls' for whom money has replaced brains and morals, Kingston's beautifully realised Lisa Locke is rather more formidable. After turning her back on a youth spent 'freezing cold under Southend pier with my knickers round my ankles' and a marriage scarred by physical abuse, mental harassment and verbal insult from her 'top boy' husband (Bean), she proves adept at sexual manipulation, deception and planning, to end up 'top girl'. 'Essex boys?', says Creed-Miles with bitterness and irony at the film's close, 'she done the lot of us'.

Conclusion

According to Lord Attenborough, who had shot to fame as the cold-blooded, razor-slashing, boy gangster in *Brighton Rock*, the sort of films made by Guy Ritchie should have no place in British cinema:

> I'll accept *Two Barrels* or whatever it was called, because it was the first – but to do that crap again for purely commercial reasons, to succumb to the pornography of violence because it is a prerequisite for commercial success, that I want no part of.[34]

But, like it or not, Ritchie's films have become more representative of the national cinema than Lord Attenborough's £20 million epic, *Grey Owl* (1999), and commercially much more viable. They are part of what is

British cinema's most significant cycle of films since the New Wave of the early 1960s. The cycle encompasses almost the entire spectrum of quality in British film-making. There have been few better 'Brit-flicks' in the last five years than *Lock, Stock . . .* or *Gangster No. 1*, and few worse than *You're Dead* or *24 Hours in London* (2000), a dumb attempt to set *The Long Good Friday* in the future.

What, finally, can we learn from these films about the state of British cinema? First, they offer proof that Britain's film-makers are not isolated from the aesthetic and narrative trends evident in international cinema. The intertextual referencing, disorienting editing, dynamic cinematography, fractured and elliptical story-telling and sardonic and amoral sensibility of post-modern film style is everywhere on display. Second, however, it is clear that a distinctive national cinema is still identifiable in the way international influences are applied to texts that are decidedly British in their sub-ject matter. But in contrast to the determined efforts of many indigenous films of the last twenty years to pres-ent an inclusive, multi-ethnic portrait of modern Britishness, the gangster cycle indicates a retrenchment and narrowing of view. Though not all the films revert to what Peter Bradshaw has called 'the reactionary nos-talgia of cheeky-Charlie whites-only "firms"', there is a marked tendency to prioritise the concerns of young, white, heterosexual, metropolitan Englishmen.[35] Third, the films of the cycle are representative of the tradition of British popular film-making in the tensions they exhibit between the desire for social realism and needs of melodramatic narrative. There is, however, a disjunc-tion in the prominence given to mock representations, that in some instances, constitute crucial sources of audience pleasure.

Film culture is rarely a simple reflection of prevail-ing politics and, as John Hill has argued of 80s British cinema, may sometimes be at odds with the approved orthodoxies of the age.[36] But if faux-ness has become a significant element in recent British films, part of the explanation may lie in the current state of political rhetoric. In his review of *Rancid Aluminium*, Martin Hoyle called the film 'as slick and shallow and phonily populist as New Labour'.[37] And given that the duration of the gangster cycle coincides exactly with Tony Blair's first term in government, it is perhaps not unreasonable to link the former's faux-ness to the latter's propensity for the politics of spin. Politicians may indeed reap what they sow, especially if what they sow is faux.

Notes

1. Quoted in James Boswell, *Life of Johnson* (Oxford: Oxford University Press, 1980), p. 165.
2. *Evening Standard*, 4 May 2000.
3. *The Times*, 9 September 2000.
4. Cf. Sarah Shannon, 'London's New Stock Market', *Evening Standard*, 18 November 1999. Paradoxically, Ritchie's film was, with a few exceptions, generally admired by the critics, even those working for conservative publications. In the *Daily Telegraph*, for instance, Quentin Curtis (28 August 1998) called it 'a hugely confident début picture', and praised its dialogue, which 'sizzles with a demotic verve rarely found in English movies'.
5. There is a persistent critical view that Britain is intrinsi-cally unsuitable as a location for gangster stories. As Danny Gritten argued, 'Our buildings are too old and stately, our streets too narrow and congested . . . . Add to that the fact that few people carry guns or ever find themselves intimidated or brutalised by violent under-world activities. The reasons that make Britain a relatively pleasant place to live are the same reasons it fails to con-vince as a hotbed of gangsterism.' *Daily Telegraph*, 1 April 2000.
6. For earlier cycles of British gangster films, see Robert Murphy, 'The Spiv Cycle', in *Realism and Tinsel: Cinema and Society in Britain 1939–49* (London: Routledge, 1991), and the essays in Steve Chibnall and Robert Murphy (eds), *British Crime Cinema* (London: Routledge, 2000).
7. See John Hill, 'Allegorising the Nation: British Gangster Films of the 1980s', in Chibnall and Murphy, *British Crime Cinema*, pp. 160–71.
8. There were, however, at least three significant contribu-tions to the genre in this period: *Mona Lisa* (1986), *The Krays* (1990) and, perhaps most appropriately as it was the story of the attempted murder of a retired gangster in Spain, *The Hit* (1984).
9. The films were financed from a wide variety of sources, including American and European partnerships, private backers and television companies such as Granada, BBC and FilmFour. Very few were cinema box-office winners, but they have tended to be more financially successful on video.
10. *Sunday Times*, 11 June 2000. Appleyard complains that the 'New Lad' style is 'sexist and fascist' and links the films to a rise in violent crime.
11. Claire Monk, 'From Underworld to Underclass: Crime and British Cinema in the 1990s', in Chibnall and Murphy, *British Crime Cinema*, pp. 162–3.

12. The arrested development of the male is the main theme of the orally fixated *Fast Food* (1999), Stewart Sugg's bizarre Lynchian take on the gangster genre.

13. As actor Jason Flemyng confirms: 'There was room to improvise with what you were doing, but the dialogue, although it looks very haphazard, is in fact very strictly written, and I've really only worked with one writer who was as strict about what was said – down to inflection and whether you say "and" or "an" – and that was Alan Bennett', in Ian Fortnam 'We Are the Boys', *Neon*, January 1999, p. 49.

14. *Daily Telegraph Magazine*, 20 February 1999.

15. *Independent*, 27 August 1998.

16. *Snatch*'s production designer, Hugo Luczyc-Wyhowski, indicates that considerable research went into making the film's sets 'entirely believable and interesting without being a romanticised version of reality' (www.cinema.com, 13 March 2001).

17. *Evening Standard*, 27 August 1998.

18. What Ritchie is striving for is not so much authenticity as credible mythology. As he admits, 'I'm not at all familiar with the East End . . . . I'm certainly not a villain or anything, but I've heard lots of stories. I know a few lively characters and I've always been interested in listening to their tales,' in Ian Fortnum, 'We Are the Boys', *Neon*, January 1999, p. 46.

19. A nostalgic feel is given to *Lock, Stock* . . . by its washed-out, sepia colour tone, while much of the décor in *Snatch* seems to have been untouched since the 1970s.

20. 'Hatchet' Harry also converts a pair of long-barrelled shot guns and *Lock, Stock* . . . contains two discussions on the size of weapons ('sawn-offs are out, people want a little more range').

21. Anciano and Burdis had previously produced *The Krays* (1990) and *Death Machine* (1994).

22. *Daily Telegraph*, 24 April 1999.

23. *Evening Standard*, 6 April 2000. If Anciano and Burdis hoped for a more sympathetic response from the popular press, they were to be disappointed. In the *Sun*, 8 April 2000, Nick Fisher, who had championed *Lock, Stock* . . . declared: 'There really should be a law against making films like this. If anything is likely to sink the British film industry, it's this sort of self-indulgent twaddle.'

24. Before *Circus* was released Hollywood agency ICM sold Logan's next script *Five Killers Killing* for $200,000 and the wunderkind had been hired to rewrite *The 51st State*. See Akin Ojumu, 'All the Write Moves', *Neon*, January 1999.

25. Caroline Pleic, 'Roll up, Roll up . . . The British Gangster-flick Is Back in Town', *Independent*, 14 April 2000.

26. Peter Bradshaw, like most reviewers, missed the point when he wrote: 'The film-makers clearly have not the slightest interest in how the Russian mafia really look or behave, remaining content with a silly, uninteresting, vodka commercial caricature.' *Guardian*, 21 January 2000.

27. *Gangster No. 1* Press Book. Forman, whose father Freddie was an associate of the Krays, plays the Ronnie-Kray-like Lennie Taylor in the film.

28. *Gangster No. 1* Press Book.

29. In creating his '60s modern' look, Bridgland was aware that, for the aspiring gangster, 'What takes over is the image and the gloss. The gold, mirrors and glitter play a part because it's all empty, like the hollow victory Gangster scores.' *Gangster No. 1* Press Book.

30. Though filmed, like *Gangster No. 1*, in the summer of 1999, *Sexy Beast* had to wait until January 2001 for release. As director Jonathan Glazer remarked to *Empire*'s Tom Doyle (February 2001): 'You can do nothing about the timing of things. The film took so long in post-production and you saw the British public growing progressively more and more bored of British gangster films.'

31. See Monk, 'From Underworld to Underclass'.

32. In December 1995 three drug dealers were shot by rivals in a country lane at Rettendon, Essex. Michael Steel and Jack Whomes were subsequently convicted of the murders.

33. *The Times*, 1 July 2000.

34. *Sunday Telegraph*, 22 October 2000.

35. *Guardian*, 12 January 2001. The ethnically diverse *Small Time Obsession* (2000) and *It Was an Accident* (2000) should be excluded from this generalisation.

36. Hill, 'Allegorising the Nation'.

37. *Financial Times*, 20 January 2000.

Bibliography

Bruzzi, Stella, 'The Instabilities of the Franco-American Gangster', in her *Undressing Cinema: Clothing and Identity in the Movies* (London: Routledge, 1997).

Chibnall, Steve and Murphy, Robert (eds), *British Crime Cinema* (London: Routledge, 1999).

Hill, John, 'Allegorising the Nation: British Gangster Films of the 1980s', in Steve Chibnall and Robert Murphy (eds), *British Crime Cinema* (London: Routledge, 1999).

Hill, John, *British Cinema in the 1980s* (Oxford: Clarendon Press, 1999).

Hutcheon, Linda, *Irony's Edge: The Theory and Politics of Irony* (London: Routledge, 1994).

Leigh, Danny, 'Get Smarter', *Sight and Sound*, July 2000.

Luckett, Moya, 'Image and Nation in 1990s British Cinema', in Robert Murphy (ed.), *British Cinema of the 90s* (London, BFI, 2000).

Monk, Claire, 'From Underworld to Underclass: Crime and British Cinema in the 1990s', in Steve Chibnall and Robert Murphy (eds), *British Crime Cinema* (London: Routledge, 1999).

Monk, Claire, 'Men in the 90s', in Robert Murphy (ed.), *British Cinema of the 90s* (London, BFI, 2000).

Peretti, Jacques, 'Shame of a Nation', *Guardian*, 26 May 2000.

Ritchie, Guy, *Lock, Stock and Two Smoking Barrels* (London: Headline, 1998).

Ritchie, Guy, *Snatch: The Screenplay* (London: Orion, 2000).

Yaquinto, Marilyn, *Pump 'Em Full of Lead: A Look at Gangsters on Film* (New York: Simon and Schuster, 1998).

42
Asian British Cinema since the 1990s

BARBARA KORTE AND CLAUDIA STERNBERG

Asian British cinema has never been a programmatic movement and it eludes clear definition. It is generally understood as involving screenwriters and/or directors of the South Asian diaspora in Britain and as encompassing productions which focus on Asian British life and culture and may be influenced by Asian cinematic traditions. This survey takes the view that a number of thematically distinct and critically and commercially successful films produced since the 1980s warrant a discussion of this body of work as a separate category. It has to be noted, however, that most film-makers with an Asian background have not confined themselves to ethnic minority subject matter, nor are they solely responsible for contemporary representations of British Asianness: some productions are collaborations between Asian and white British writers and directors, and Asian themes have also been taken up by non-Asian film-makers. Any definition of Asian British cinema is complicated further by the fact that 'Asian British' refers to individuals and communities who differ in terms of religion, language and national and geographical background, which is also reflected in the films discussed below.

Perhaps the most striking observation about British Asian cinema is the extent to which it has reached mainstream audiences since the 1990s, both in Britain and abroad. In part, this success coincides with a fascination with popular Asian cinema that has spread over from Bollywood's traditional markets in the East and the various Asian diasporas to non-Asian audiences in the West. Not unexpectedly, Bollywood conventions are now also cited in Asian British productions such as Gurinder Chadha's *Bhaji on the Beach* (1993) and, more

extensively, in her *Bride and Prejudice* (2004), as well as in *Bollywood Queen* (2002), the début feature film of the non-Asian director Jeremy Wooding, and *Nina's Heavenly Delights* (2006), directed by Pratibha Parmar, previously known for her documentary and short films. For Asian British film-makers, Asian cinema not only forms a field of cultural reference, but also provides opportunities to work and to reach spectators outside the British market.

The success of Asian British cinema with national audiences depends primarily on how it crosses over into genres that enjoy general popularity (such as heritage films and comedy), and on its statements about British society and the changes it has undergone as a result of Asian migration. In this respect, recent Asian British films have been influenced by the Hanif Kureishi and Stephen Frears collaborations of the 1980s, *My Beautiful Laundrette* (1985) and *Sammy and Rosie Get Laid* (1987). Set in contemporary multi-ethnic London, these films are peopled by Asian, black and white Britons whose place in society is characteristically unfixed. Kureishi has underlined that he does not consider his stories and characters of the 1980s as representative, since to him essential experiences or identities do not exist: 'Nobody's life can be reduced in that way.'[1] His screenplays purposely undermine binary constructions such as black/white, centre/margin, coloniser/colonised, poor/affluent or male/female. With their interracial relationships, generational clashes and emphases on promiscuity and sexual difference, the Kureishi/Frears films came to signify a subversion appreciated by larger sections of British society during the Thatcher era. They also became internationally known as landmarks of 1980s

British cinema, offering a post-colonial alternative to the historical epics of the decade such as *Gandhi* (1982) and *A Passage to India* (1984).

Kureishi's influence on contemporary Asian British film-makers cannot be underestimated. Gurinder Chadha, the most successful and internationally recognised Asian British director, has pointed out the importance of *My Beautiful Laundrette* for her career, and Meera Syal and Ayub Khan-Din, who both acted in *Sammy and Rosie Get Laid*, later established themselves as actors and writers in their own right.[2] It is notable, however, that most of the 1990s films allegedly inspired by Kureishi toned down his transgressiveness, anarchical humour and ambivalent characterisation. The only Asian British feature to follow directly in the footsteps of the Kureishi/Frears productions failed to make any impact at the box office. *Wild West* (1992), directed by David Attwood and written by Harwant Bains, reflects on issues of misrepresentation and cultural participation of young Asians. Zaf (Naveen Andrews), a young Briton of Pakistani descent, is a picaro whose radical behaviour provokes both Asian and white establishments. The film's main conflict arises from Zaf's desire to succeed with his Asian band, the Honkytonk Cowboys, who specialise in country-and-western music. This demonstrative form of westernisation plays with common constructions of east and west, since Zaf and his band do not stand between white and Asian British culture but beyond any such cultural divides, and thus experience opposition from all sides, including American music producers who tell them that 'Wild West boys is mainstream' and young Asians can only succeed in the business if they exploit their own exoticism.

Most Asian British films of the 1990s and early 2000s were less confrontational than *Wild West*, with more clear-cut characters and strong and conclusive narratives. Two major directions can be distinguished: social realism and dramatic comedy.[3]

Social Realism

A prominent director in this line of Asian British film is Udayan Prasad, also an experienced director of television drama. His two Asian-themed features, *Brothers in Trouble* (1995) and *My Son the Fanatic* (1997), address past and present problems of Asian Muslims. *Brothers in Trouble*, based on a novella by the Pakistani-British author Abdullah Hussein, depicts a group of illegal migrants in a 1960s Northern urban

locale where the principal features are grimy terraced houses and a textile factory. The central character, Amir (Pavan Malhotra), and the other men are exploited both by their white employers and by an Asian landlord who profits from their need to keep a low profile. The illegal workers live in a dark and overcrowded house, which constitutes one of the claustrophobic settings identified by Hamid Naficy as a recurring element in diasporic cinematic narratives.[4] The lives of the men are briefly uplifted when a young pregnant woman moves in, but tragedy evolves when she is urged into a paper marriage to bring another migrant legally into the country. Less restricted than the others, this man goes out, drinks, alienates his Muslim 'brothers' and eventually kills the group's stern father figure. This catastrophe is followed by a coda in which the spectator is confronted with a change of mood and atmosphere. After a lapse of several years, Amir has become a legal resident soon to be joined by his family. The new quality of his life is symbolised by exterior settings and his appreciation of a green and open English landscape that differs markedly from the dreary and confined urban location we have seen before. This is still a space in which the Asian migrant is identified as a trespasser, but Amir's insistence on his right to this space also indicates that he is claiming England as his home.

My Son the Fanatic, which Hanif Kureishi expanded into a screenplay from his own short story, seems to continue the narrative of the migrant generation and characters like Amir in *Brothers in Trouble*, contrasting their desire to belong with the experience of their British-born children. Set in the 1990s, the film shows a generation of young Asian Muslims that feel repulsed by Britain at the very moment when the country's self-image as a culturally diverse society appears to embrace them more fully than ever before.

Despite their focus on migration and Muslim fundamentalism and an emphasis on conflict, Udayan Prasad's films provide audiences of various ethnic backgrounds with many elements for identification and empathy, including family values, gender relationships and generational tensions. Such universal themes are also foregrounded in Asian British dramatic comedies, which – like the working-class comedy dramas *Brassed Off* (1996), *The Full Monty* (1997) and *Billy Elliot* (2000) – offer harmonious solutions to social and familial problems and a good dose of entertainment.

My Son the Fanatic (Udayan Prasad, 1997)

My Son the Fanatic is set in Bradford, the city associated with Islamic fundamentalism since the local burning of Salman Rushdie's *Satanic Verses* in 1989. Less than a decade after this event and four years before 9/11, the film reflects on extremist tendencies among young Muslim men in Britain, depicting generational differences between the taxi driver Parvez (Om Puri) and his son Farid (Akbar Kurtha). Unexpectedly, Farid breaks off his engagement to the daughter of a white police inspector, a match that would have fulfilled his father's dream of complete integration in British society. Instead, Parvez now has to face a son who rigorously rejects the West because 'our cultures cannot be mixed' and who reverts to a way of life which his father deliberately left behind.

Om Puri bemused by fundamentalism in *My Son the Fanatic*

The spectator is invited to share Parvez's perspective visually (through many point-of-view shots) and ideologically, as part of an audience generally uncomfortable in the face of Islamic radicalism. The film's portrayal of Farid's transformation is basically unsympathetic; his reasons for feeling repulsed by Britain are stated rather than shown, his arguments are often reduced to slogans, and the 'holy man' he invites to the house and venerates proves grotesquely unworthy of his disciple's respect. The *maulvi* insists, for instance, that Parvez's wife eat alone in her kitchen in the 'traditional' way. With this detail in particular, the film confirms a common stereotype, and Parvez gains the audience's sympathy when he is adamant that she should eat with the family. At the same time, however, Parvez becomes estranged from his wife. He betrays her with Bettina (Rachel Griffiths), a white sex worker who symbolises the open-mindedness and Western lack of restraint to which Parvez feels attracted. For Farid, by contrast, east and west, *maulvi* and secularised father, prayer and popular music, traditional womanhood and prostitution are irreconcilable opposites.

The film's point of view is biased towards a secular western way of life that, despite its flaws and excesses, appears as the more humane and tolerant option. In the film's climactic scene, fanaticism turns physical: Farid becomes the leader in a raid directed against the neighbourhood's prostitutes and Bettina in particular. When Parvez intervenes and beats his own son, Farid reacts to this outbreak of violence with the question: 'Who is the fanatic now?' This incident finally destroys Parvez's family: His son leaves his home for good, and his wife goes back to Pakistan. Parvez, for whom a return to the East and Eastern values is no option, remains in the now deserted house.

The film's sympathy for the assimilated Asian Briton is constructed not only through the fact that Parvez opposes fundamentalism, but also through his growing aversion to a cynical German businessman who plans to convert a derelict textile factory into a shopping centre. The German stands for European pressure on Britain's traditional economy, and it is significant that in fact he – rather than the first-generation Anglicised migrant – epitomises the decadence against which Muslim fanaticism is directed.

FURTHER READING

Kenneth C. Kaleta, *Hanif Kureishi: Postcolonial Storyteller* (Austin: University of Texas Press, 1998), pp. 156–62 and *passim*.

Hanif Kureishi, *My Son the Fanatic* (London: Faber and Faber, 1997).

Dramatic Comedy

East Is East (1999) was directed by Irishman Damien O'Donnell, from a screenplay by Ayub Khan-Din, which was based on his successful semi-autobiographical stage play. The film centres on conflicts within an Anglo-Pakistani family in Salford in 1971 and became the first big mainstream success of Asian British film. Producer Leslee Udwin described *East Is East* as a film dealing with 'something that every parent and child knows about', and the video release marketed it as 'The Brit hit of the year'.[5]

Backstreets solidarity: Lesley Nicol and Linda Bassett in
East Is East (Damien O'Donnell, 1999)

The 1960s and early 1970s marked a period of particular significance in Asian British history. The first children of the migrant generation were reaching adolescence and early adulthood when the UK government legislated restrictions on immigration which mainly affected migratory groups from the Commonwealth. At the same time, the racist rhetoric of the Conservative politician Enoch Powell and his proposed policy of repatriation received popular support. *East Is East* addresses this racism, but does not make it a central theme. What almost destroys the family in this film is not rejection by a Britain that insists on remaining white, but Muslim patriarchalism. The children of George Khan (Om Puri), an immigrant from pre-partition India, and his white wife Ella (Linda Bassett) all have Asian names, but the family's business is English – a fish-and-chip shop situated in a predominantly white, working-class neighbourhood where the Khans seem well integrated. The film's disputes and clashes are caused by George's determination to enforce Muslim customs on his offspring and his insistence that they marry within the Pakistani-British community. One of the sons is a devout believer, while the others and their sister humour their father as far as possible, but otherwise find their ways of enjoying a Western lifestyle. Eastern customs to them mean masquerade, repression and even physical pain. The eldest son, a homosexual, runs out of his arranged wedding, thus becoming an exile from his father's house. George then tries to marry two of his middle sons into a traditional Muslim family from Bradford. His wife is just as appalled as the intended bridegrooms, one of whom openly declares that he is 'not marrying a fucking Paki'. George refuses to acknowledge that his autocratic traditionalism is seen by his increasingly alienated family as the dis-

avowal of his own marriage and the negation of his children's dual heritage; the more he loses control, the more he resorts to threats and violence against his wife and children.

The conflicts are comically resolved: the future in-laws are driven away by a series of outrageous disasters, George and Ella are reconciled in their chip shop, and the film's last image shows a wide shot of the street in which the Khans will go on living as part of a culturally diverse British society in which they belong. The film's ideology is one of hybridity subordinated to a secular, sexually liberated western lifestyle, which appears to offer the young generation greater freedom. This ideological stance is also suggested by the film's title, which alludes to the first line from Rudyard Kipling's Imperialist 'Ballad of East and West': 'Oh, East is East, and West is West, and never the twain shall meet'. Khan-Din's reference to the verse is ironical in so far as, in his screenplay, a meeting between east and west has taken place right in the heart of the former Empire. But the abridgement of Kipling's original line also suggests that in that meeting and even mixing of cultures problems still exist, and that these problems are caused by an east which remains the east, rather than by the west which remains the west.

It is in these terms that the film was criticised by Asian reviewers for inviting voyeurism and laughter from a white audience and reinforcing stereotypes. To Sanjay Sharma, for instance, *East Is East* fits into a 'hegemonic project of liberal cultural diversity', which criticises traditional Asianness as backwards-oriented while it 'leaves whiteness intact'.[6] Ali Nobil perceives the film as operating

> within the logic of an age-old body of racist
> assumptions and stereotypes about Islam and the
> East . . . *East Is East* invites us to enjoy a film about
> Asians in Britain in terms of what it likes best: arranged
> marriages, domestic violence and oppression.[7]

It is only fair to note that *East Is East* also plays with stereotypical perceptions, for instance in the wedding ceremony where it is not the bride, but the bridegroom who appears as the victim of an arranged marriage, and where the most urgent reason for his escape is the man's homosexuality rather than a reactionary eastern custom *per se*. Nevertheless, such play with expectations of a non-Asian audience appears subordinated to the film's more dominant critique of the rigidity and despotism of Muslim patriarchalism.

A rejection of restrictive traditions, combined with a strong gendered position, also marks the feature films of Gurinder Chadha, a film-maker of Kenyan Asian descent with a Sikh family background. *Bride and Prejudice* takes a global outlook and *What's Cooking?* (2000) was set and shot in Los Angeles; but issues of Asian Britishness are central in the two films that established Chadha's name in British cinema: *Bhaji on the Beach* and *Bend It Like Beckham* (2002). Around the time *Bend It Like Beckham* was released, Chadha declared herself emphatically a British film-maker ('because I have redefined what British means in my work, I'm comfortable with British, because I know British also includes me'), and she is also decidedly committed to making popular films.[8] With *Bend It Like Beckham*, Chadha intended to make 'the most commercial, mainstream, wide-appealing, multiplex movie [she] possibly could — with an Indian girl in the lead.'[9] Such commitment does not mean that Chadha has been unaffected by racial conflict: 'I'm part of a generation that's grown up with racism always around the corner . . . That has really shaped what I do and why I do it.'[10] What marks *Bhaji on the Beach* and *Bend It Like Beckham* most, however, is a reflection about the situation of Asian women in Britain and the way in which these women have been represented.

Bhaji on the Beach was the first mainstream feature written, directed and produced by non-white British women. The film is based on a screenplay by Meera Syal, who developed the story in co-operation with Chadha and who believes that the widest range of people can be reached 'by making them laugh rather than lecturing to them'.[11] In *Bhaji on the Beach*, this strategy is used to show various ways of life in which Asian women of different generations may have been engaged in the early 1990s. The characters go on a day trip from Birmingham to Blackpool during the late summer illuminations. This trip is meant to provide an escape from their everyday lives, and at its end all the women have become more aware of each other and found ways to cope better with their problems — most of which are caused, as in *East Is East*, by traditionalism and ethnic absolutism within the Asian community. The older generations, and also eventually the men, have to learn that their views of femininity are outdated and unsuitable for Asian women in Britain — and would even be seen as such in modern India.

The setting of Blackpool not only serves as a typically English place; it is also significant as a dreamland, a location of façades, make-believe and carnival, where the Asian women test, reconstruct and assert their identities and make plans for the future.[12] The women are Asian, but their experiences have a universal dimension — relating to first love, unwanted pregnancy, motherhood, divorce and misunderstandings between the old and the young — which makes it easy for audiences to find their way into the film. As far as the negotiation of Asianness and Britishness is concerned, the film appears to argue for a creative hybridisation and inversion, which is epitomised in the film's most striking use of off-screen music: the women's trip to Blackpool is accompanied by a bhangrified rendering of the popular Cliff Richard song 'Summer Holiday' with Punjabi lyrics.

Bhaji on the Beach's exploration of the experience of Asian women in a multi-ethnic Britain aroused critical interest; but it was only a modest commercial success and Chadha had difficulty raising finance for subsequent films. She directed *What's Cooking?* in America, but almost a decade elapsed between *Bhaji on the Beach* and her next British feature *Bend It Like Beckham*. The film takes a deliberate cross-ethnic approach and establishes a direct parallel between a white girl and an Asian British girl. Like *East Is East*, it was marketed as a British film with a universal theme, a coming-of-age drama about two young women overcoming bigotry and prejudice to fulfil their refreshingly unexpected potential as footballers.[13] The film's international success was welcomed by Chadha as evidence that films featuring 'people of colour' could reach a wide audience and for the access it allowed her to work in the mainstream with bigger budgets and better distribution.[14]

The marketing strategy of *Bend It Like Beckham* was mimicked in the theatrical and television trailers for *Anita and Me* (2002), the adaptation of Meera Syal's best-selling novel about growing up brown in a former mining village near Birmingham. The screenplay was written by Syal herself, and the film was directed by Metin Hüseyin, who had made his cinema début with the crime comedy drama *It Was an Accident* (2000). *Anita and Me* is set in a similar working-class environment to *East Is East* and is also based on the author's own experiences. The film makes ample use both of 1970s pop music on its soundtrack and the play with Asian and British stereotypes of Syal's popular television comedy, *Goodness Gracious Me*. Meena, the eleven-year-old protagonist, is the daughter of Punjabi parents whose wish to keep in touch with their culture of origin she resists as long as her role model is her precocious blonde friend Anita. Here, the white girl comes from a disrupted and underprivileged family, while the clever Asian girl, with

Bend It Like Beckham (Gurinder Chadha, 2002)

Bend It Like Beckham addresses issues of ethnicity and gender through football. It shows a white girl (Keira Knightley) and an Asian British girl (Parminder Nagra) facing similar problems when they strive for a career in a sport still associated primarily with men. The film starts with a double deconstruction of gender and ethnic stereotypes. In a daydream, the Asian protagonist Jesminder (Jess) scores a winning goal for Manchester United and is hailed as a potential new star for the English national team. To Jess's sari-clad mother, however, she brings shame on the family. Her white friend and counterpart Juliet (Jules) is subject to similar criticism from her mother who wants her to be more 'feminine' and suspects she might be a lesbian.

The girls play in a women's amateur team, but Jess is ordered to give up football when she unintentionally drives away her sister's future in-laws. Jess then accompanies her team to a tournament without her parents' knowledge. This decision proves disastrous both because her parents find out, and because Jess falls in love with the team's Irish coach, Joe (Jonathan Rhys Meyers), who is also worshipped by Jules. Problems escalate but are resolved at the end. The girls are reconciled, and Jess manages to be present at both her sister's traditional wedding and a decisive match. The ceremony and the game are cross-cut, suggesting that a relationship between different cultures and inclinations can be negotiated. At the pivotal moment of the match Jess's initial daydream is repeated as reality, though there is a brief moment of fantasy: before Jess bends the ball into the goal, the wall of players in front of her turns into her mother, sister and aunties, so that her free kick appears as a final liberation from traditional notions of femininity. Jules and Jess are offered a scholarship to study in the United States and play in a women's soccer team.

Bend It Like Beckham is explicit in demonstrating that British Asians interact with all aspects of 'white' Britain, including the national sport. Race relations are not prominent, and Jess and Jules overcome their problems together. Notably, the girls are supported by their fathers, whose appreciation of sport helps to overrule a more restricting view of femininity put forward by both mothers. The lack of understanding between mothers and daughters on the one hand and the celebration of dynamic and assertive 'girl power' on the other have led to the reading of *Bend It Like Beckham* as post-feminist. It is still necessary for Jess and Jules to 'go west' in order to fulfil their potential as women footballers. But back in Britain past injustices are redressed: in Chadha's optimistic final scene, Jess's father, who had given up cricket as a young man because of racist bullying, can be seen playing again – with Joe, his white potential son-in-law.

FURTHER READING

Justine Ashby, 'Postfeminism in the British Frame', *Cinema Journal* vol. 44 no. 2, 2005, pp. 127–32.

Anjali Gera Roy, 'Translating Difference in *Bend It Like Beckham*', *New Cinemas: Journal of Contemporary Film* vol. 4 no. 1, 2006, pp. 55–66.

her cultured and socially ambitious background, will eventually be able to leave behind what she learns to perceive as a dreary and racist environment.

Asian-themed films that followed in the wake of *East Is East* tend to work in established cinematic formats, casting popular actors in roles in which Asian and white British characters interact constructively and often affectionately; they use elements of a cross-ethnic pop culture; they deal with Asianness in terms immediately accessible to diverse audiences; and they show Asian characters who are and see themselves as part of British society. Interracial romance, at the heart of Kureishi's screenplays in the 1980s, is another recurring element, to be found not only in high-profile productions like *Bend It Like Beckham* and *Bride and Prejudice*, and in Ken Loach's *Ae Fond Kiss* (2004), but also in début feature films with limited release. In *Bollywood Queen*, a white country boy meets an Asian city girl; the protagonist of *Halal Harry* (Russell Razzaque, 2006) is a Catholic barman in London who engages with Islam after he has fallen in love with a Muslim woman; *Nina's Heavenly Delights* presents an interracial lesbian love story in a Glasgow setting; a Northern industrial town provides the backdrop for a relationship between a British Asian woman and a white working-class man in *Love + Hate* (Dominic Savage, 2006).

Beyond Comedy and Romance

Two critically successful films of the 2000s take a different approach to those discussed above: *Yasmin* (2004), from the non-Asian director Kenneth Glenaan and screenwriter Simon Beaufoy, is set in the North of England and was originally developed out of research into the Anglo-Pakistani communities in Bradford, Oldham and Burnley after the disturbances which occurred in the summer of 2001.[15] Overtaken by the scale and global impact of 9/11 during the pre-production period, the film-makers modified their narrative, and the final film shows how the terrorist attacks, their media representations, mainstream reactions and radical Islamist responses affect an already marginalised and disadvantaged section of the population. The story concentrates on Yasmin (Archie Panjabi) and her brother Nasir (Syed Ahmed), who lead a double life as dutiful children of a strict Muslim father and as young assimilated Asian Britons. They are forced to reassess their precariously negotiated balance between secular multicultural urbanity and a religious life in an ethnic ghetto in the light of drastic changes in the social and political climate.

Yasmin employs the style of social realism and, both thematically and aesthetically, connects with some of the earlier representations of Muslim life in Britain. Asif Kapadia's first feature film *The Warrior* (2001), deviates radically from such patterns. This visually stunning film is set in rural Rajasthan, in an unspecified mythical past, and presents its sparse dialogue in subtitled Hindi. Its central character, increasingly appalled by his duties as pillager and executioner for the local lord, leaves his master's service. He is vengefully hunted down and his son murdered, but a spiritual journey to the Himalayas leads to his transcendental redemption. Although expressly monocultural in terms of location, characters, language and conflict, Kapadia's film takes its cue from a Japanese folk tale and was inspired by Shekhar Kapur's *Bandit Queen* (1994), East Asian cinema and Sergio Leone's Westerns. The production had an Indian cast, an international crew, an Asian British director, a white English co-writer and was made with British money, but the fact that *The Warrior*'s dialogue was in Hindi led to its rejection as Britain's entry in the Best Foreign Film category at the American Academy Awards. According to Jigna Desai:

> As a testimony to US domination and colonial logic, the judges decreed that it was not eligible because Hindi is not an indigenous language of Britain (though spoken by more than a million people in Britain). They further justified that if the film had been about Hindi speakers in Britain, then the film would have been acceptable.[16]

The problem of *The Warrior*'s Britishness highlights the potential difficulty of discussing Asian British film within the context of a national cinema. Perhaps more than other British productions, British Asian films draw our attention to what Andrew Higson has called the 'instability of the national'.[17] Discussing transnationalism, multiculturalism and 'post-national films', he acknowledges a 'shift from homogeneity to heterogeneity' in response to 'the emergence of new sociocultural . . . communities organised around particular ethnic allegiances'.[18]

Desai goes further, attempting to unhinge Asian British film from its national moorings; she 'interrogates and reformulates the dominant emphasis on the nation and national cinema' and brings together 'films in English from and about the "Brown Atlantic" (South Asian diasporas in the United States, Canada and Britain) as well as India within a transnational comparative framework' under the rubric of South Asian diasporic film.[19] But while most of the films discussed here have redefined, diversified and developed British cinema, few have worked beyond its parameters and opted for an explicitly diasporic and transnational approach. Chadha's *Bride and Prejudice* is a case in point; the film translates the marriage plot of Jane Austen's early nineteenth-century novel *Pride and Prejudice* into the milieu of an Asian and non-Asian global elite, and contributes both to the corpus of Bollywood-style romance, and to British film and television adaptations of literary classics. Furthermore, it ties in with other films celebrating modern middle-class Indianness (such as Mira Nair's *Monsoon Wedding*, 2001) and cinematic adaptations of Western literature produced in India.[20] Thus *Bride and Prejudice* capitalises on two popular 'heritages', Indian musicals and Britain's Jane Austen, while offering a revisionist reading of Austen's novel by scrutinising Eurocentric prejudice as well as social frictions between Asians in India and the western diasporas. The film combines eastern and western storylines, genres, actors and acting styles and contains numerous intertextual references. Consequently, whether the film is received as Asian British, South Asian and/or diasporic depends to a great extent on the decoding position and knowledge base of the individual spectator.

Since the 1990s, the notion of Asian British cinema has expanded as the films considered and traded under this heading reflect the changed political and cultural status of Asians in Britain, explore a wider range of aesthetics and encompass more film-makers of various backgrounds. But even though Asian British film seems even harder to define in the year 2008 than a decade ago, it has established itself as a significant and recognisable part of contemporary British cinema.

Notes

1. Interview with Kureishi in Laurence Chua, 'Double Feature', *Black Film Bulletin*, p. 18.
2. Chadha in Barbara Korte and Claudia Sternberg, *Bidding for the Mainstream?*, p. 250.
3. Social realist films are less influenced by Kureishi's approach than by pioneering productions like *A Private Enterprise* (1974), directed by Peter Smith, co-written by Smith and the Asian British author Dilip Hiro, and *Majdhar* (1984), written and directed by Ahmed Jamal. *A Private Enterprise* portrays Asian entrepreneurship and a migrant's problems of establishing himself in Britain. *Majdhar* was a production of the Retake Film and Video Collective and the first feature film to emerge from the grant-aided workshop sector of the 1980s; it deconstructs stereotypical notions of subdued and passive Asian femininity.
4. Hamid Naficy, *Accented Cinema: Exilic and Diasporic Filmmaking*, p. 191.
5. Sonali Bhattacharyya, 'East Goes West: British Asian Themed Film', p. 6.
6. Sanjay Sharma, '*East Is East*', *Black Media Journal*, pp. 33–4.
7. Ali Nobil, 'Is East . . . East?', *Third Text*, p. 105.
8. Chadha in Korte and Sternberg, *Bidding for the Mainstream?*, p. 245.
9. Ibid.
10. In Chua, 'Double Feature', p. 18.
11. Syal in Shirani Sabratnam, 'Meera Syal: The Fun in Comedy', *Artrage*, p. 6.
12. On this aspect of the film, see Anne Ciecko, 'Representing the Spaces of Diaspora in Contemporary British Films by Women Directors', *Cinema Journal*, pp. 77–8.
13. Monica Baker, '*Bend It Like Beckham*: A Distributor's Dream', *Black Filmmaker*, p. 6.
14. Chadha in Geoffrey Macnab, 'British Directors', *Sight and Sound*, p. 37; Chadha in Korte and Sternberg, *Bidding for the Mainstream?*, p. 252.
15. *Yasmin* was shown at festivals and released internationally, but went straight on to Channel 4 television in the UK.
16. Jigna Desai, *Beyond Bollywood: The Cultural Politics of South Asian Diasporic Film*, p. 51.
17. Andrew Higson, 'The Instability of the National', in Justine Ashby and Andrew Higson (eds), *British Cinema: Past and Present*, p. 35.
18. Ibid. p. 38.
19. Desai, *Beyond Bollywood*, p. ix.
20. For a discussion of hybridity and intertextuality in *Bride and Prejudice* see Christine Geraghty, 'Jane Austen Meets Gurinder Chadha: Hybridity and Intertextuality in *Bride and Prejudice*', *South Asian Popular Culture*.

Bibliography

Baker, Monica, '*Bend It Like Beckham*: A Distributor's Dream', *Black Filmmaker* vol. 5 no. 16, 2000.

Bhattacharyya, Sonali, 'East Goes West: British Asian Themed Film, *East Is East*, Smashes Box Office' (interview with Leslee Udwin), *Black Filmmaker* vol. 3 no. 9, 2000.

Chadha, Gurinder, 'Gurinder Chadha in Interview', in Barbara Korte and Claudia Sternberg, *Bidding for the Mainstream? Black and Asian British Film since the 1990s* (Amsterdam: Rodopi, 2004).

Chua, Laurence, 'Double Feature' (interview with Gurinder Chadha and Hanif Kureishi), *Black Film Bulletin* vol. 2 no. 3, 1994.

Ciecko, Anne, 'Representing the Spaces of Diaspora in Contemporary British Films by Women Directors', *Cinema Journal* vol. 38 no. 3, 1999.

Desai, Jigna, *Beyond Bollywood: The Cultural Politics of South Asian Diasporic Film* (London and New York: Routledge, 2004).

Geraghty, Christine, 'Jane Austen Meets Gurinder Chadha: Hybridity and Intertextuality in *Bride and Prejudice*', *South Asian Popular Culture* vol. 4 no. 2, 2006, pp. 163–8.

Higson, Andrew, 'The Instability of the National', in Justine Ashby and Andrew Higson (eds), *British Cinema: Past and Present* (London and New York: Routledge, 2000), pp. 35–47.

Macnab, Geoffrey, 'British Directors: Gurinder Chadha – Austen Power' (interview with Gurinder Chadha), *Sight and Sound*, October 2004.

Naficy, Hamid, *Accented Cinema: Exilic and Diasporic Filmmaking* (Princeton, NJ: Princeton University Press, 2001).

Nobil, Ali, 'Is East . . . East?', *Third Text* vol. 49, 1999–2000.

Sabratnam, Shirani, 'Meera Syal: The Fun in Comedy', *Artrage*, February–March 1994.

Sharma, Sanjay, '*East Is East*', *Black Media Journal* vol. 2, 2000.

43
Bright Hopes, Dark Dreams: A Guide to New British Cinema

ROBERT MURPHY

Although the international success of films like *Four Weddings and a Funeral*, *Trainspotting*, *The Full Monty*, *Notting Hill*, *Lock, Stock and Two Smoking Barrels*, *Shakespeare in Love*, *Bridget Jones's Diary*, *Billy Elliot*, *Bend It Like Beckham* and *Calendar Girls* has raised the profile of British cinema, only a fraction of British films released every year become box-office hits and the contours of this new British cinema remain vague and ill-defined.

More directors made their débuts between 1994 and 2007 than at any time since the 1930s (when all sorts were roped in to direct the quota quickies called up by the 1927 Cinematograph Films Act). With the exception of Mike Newell (*Four Weddings and a Funeral*, 1994)), Iain Softley (*The Wings of the Dove*, 1997), Gurinder Chadha (*Bend It Like Beckham*, 2002), and Beeban Kidron (*Bridget Jones: The Edge of Reason*, 2004), all the directors of the big British box-office successes are new to the industry. Apart from Guy Ritchie, they have kept a low profile and pursued less familiar paths than one might have expected. Danny Boyle, who came to fame with *Shallow Grave* (1994) and *Trainspotting* (1996), lurched towards Hollywood with *A Life Less Ordinary* (1997) and *The Beach* (2000), but subsequently showed his independence, making the odd and unpredictable *28 Days Later . . .* (2002), *Millions* (2004), *Sunshine* (2007) and *Slumdog Millionaire* (2008). Typically, he backed young Spanish director Juan Carlos Fresnadillo as executive producer rather than directing the sequel *28 Weeks Later* (2007) himself. Roger Michell went on from *Notting Hill* (1999) to three adult, complex and not obviously commercial films, *The Mother* (2003), *Enduring Love* (2004) and *Venus* (2006).

Other directors had problems moving forward, notably Peter Cattaneo who followed *The Full Monty*

(1997) with the lackadaisical *Lucky Break* (2001), the syrupy *Opal Dream* (2006) and the disappointingly trivial *The Rocker* (2008). Peter Howitt, director of *Sliding Doors* (1998), slipped comfortably into the profitable, if anonymous, mainstream with the Rowan Atkinson spy-thriller spoof *Johnny English* (2001), and an American romantic comedy *The Laws of Attraction* (2004) but moved back into riskier territory with *Dangerous Parking* (2007). Kirk Jones took seven years to find the whimsically eccentric *Nanny McPhee* (2005) as a successor to the whimsically eccentric *Waking Ned* (1998); Nigel Cole followed the pleasant but inconsequential *Calendar Girls* (2003) with the pleasant but inconsequential *A Lot Like Love* (2005). By contrast Stephen Daldry moved on from the crowd-pleasing *Billy Elliot* (2000) to an ambitious adaptation of Michael Cunningham's novel *The Hours* (2002), which parallels a day in the life of Virginia Woolf, as she struggles with madness and isolation while beginning to write *Mrs Dalloway*, with that of a suburban 1950s housewife having an existential crisis on her husband's birthday, and an affluent contemporary New Yorker preparing a party for her AIDs-stricken former lover. Even more impressive was Jonathan Glazer's progress from the visually flamboyant *Sexy Beast* (2000) to *Birth* (2004), a complex and original New York mystery thriller as sophisticated and intriguing as Hitchcock's *Vertigo* (1958) and Brian de Palma's *Obsession* (1976).

Guy Ritchie, the only one of these directors to become a household name, paid the price of celebrity: after milking the innovations of *Lock, Stock and Two Smoking Barrels* (1998) for *Snatch* (2000), a film successfully designed to win over the American market, he indulged his wife Madonna in an embarrassing remake of Lina Wertmüller's *Swept Away* (2002), and tied himself in existential knots with the preposterous *Revolver* (2005). *RocknRoller* (2008) returned him to what he does best, but it hardly broke new ground.

Post-Thatcherite Cinema

After Margaret Thatcher resigned in November 1990 there was a move to a more consensual ethos under her successor John Major. In its low-key, disparaging celebration of British values, *Four Weddings* might be seen as an archetypal 'Majorite' film. Hugh Grant's Charles is upper middle class but has none of the obvious accoutrements of wealth and his friends are from a mixed social background. His haphazardly pursued romance with an enigmatic American woman saves him from being absorbed into conventional society. Curtis's vision, subsequently pursued in *Notting Hill*, *Love Actually* (2003) and *The Girl in the Café* (2005) proved more durable than Mr Major's government. *Notting Hill*, despite its trendy location, is peopled by a gallery of endearing inadequates, who nonetheless convince Hollywood's biggest star that their friendly, low-key lifestyle is preferable to the glamorous world she has hitherto inhabited. *Love Actually*, which Curtis directed himself, shows – with unwarranted optimism – the British Prime Minister standing up to a boorish American President, and seeking happiness with his plump and cheery Cockney tea-lady. The naively utopian *The Girl in the Café*, a television film directed by David Yates, features an intrepid young woman whose romantic involvement with a lonely civil servant gives her the opportunity to shame the British Prime Minister and Chancellor of the Exchequer into holding out for humanitarian aid at the G8 Summit Conference.

Contrary to expectations, the success of *Four Weddings* did not release a flood of similar films, only the very modest *Jack & Sarah* (1995), a model Majorite film about an upmarket lawyer who loses his wife in childbirth and – with the help and guidance of lovably eccentric older characters – bonds with his baby daughter and overcomes his snobbery to win the love of the American waitress he has recruited as a nanny. Darker visions of post-Thatcherite society intervened before a proper cycle of romantic comedies got underway. *Shallow Grave*, a culturally sophisticated, visually adventurous thriller from director Danny Boyle, producer Andrew Macdonald and writer John Hodge, was welcomed by critics irritated by the complacent quirkiness of *Four Weddings*. Its trio of sharp, selfish Edinburgh young professionals (Ewan McGregor,

Christopher Eccleston, Kerry Fox), who are easily tipped into madness and murder by the prospect of ill-gotten gains, appeared more representative of contemporary reality than Hugh Grant and his affable chums. *Trainspotting*, which followed two years later – an adaptation of stories by the Scottish writer Irvine Welsh about a group of Edinburgh junkies – was even more unflattering about the state of society and even more popular. By revelling in the pleasures as much as the degradation and perils of a drug-fuelled lifestyle, it seemed to present an exciting alternative to conformity within a cynical, materialist society.

Equally improbable was the box-office success afforded *Brassed Off* (1996) and *The Full Monty*, films set in a post-industrial North of England, where the coal and steel industries had been reduced to unimportant rumps. Both films celebrate resilience and ingenuity in the face of adversity, a theme which would mark later box-office successes such as *Billy Elliot*, *Bend It Like Beckham*, *Calendar Girls*, and even the *Bridget Jones* films. But like the much harsher films of Ken Loach, *Brassed Off* and *The Full Monty* retain an edge of bitterness against a political system which had devastated traditional working-class culture and made men who had earned their living through manual labour redundant.

Despite the eclecticism of most of the new directors, there was an unmistakable move towards genre filmmaking after 1997, with three overlapping waves of romantic comedies, crime films and horror films. The romantic comedies which flowered at the end of the decade looked forward rather than backwards, and might be seen as a manifestation of the optimism around the election of a New Labour government in 1997, but in the best of them at least, doubts surface over the durability of happiness and harmony.

The Revival of Romance

British cinema has proved innovative in its exploration of various forms of romantic comedy. Though many are riddled with hoary clichés and sugary plots, they are balanced by films that are adventurous and original. They can be categorised as:

Sentimental celebrations of eccentricity: *Fever Pitch*, *Shooting Fish*, *House*, *Weak at Denise*, *Janice Beard: 45 WPM*, *Swing*, *Heartlands*, *Strictly Sinatra*, *The One and Only*, *Birthday Girl*, *Girl from Rio*.
Fairy-tales and allegories: *Sliding Doors*, *Notting Hill*, *Martha – Meet Frank, Daniel and Laurence*, *Little Voice*, *About Adam*.

Women's films: Girls' Night, Fanny and Elvis, Mad Cows, the two *Bridget Jones* films, *Crush*.

Films exploring the complicated relationships of young middle-class couples: The Big Swap, Elephant Juice, Emotional Backgammon, Maybe Baby, The Wedding Tackle.

Films charting life and love among young people drifting through the lower reaches of society: This Year's Love, Born Romantic, The Low Down, Late Night Shopping, Peaches, South West 9, Intermission, Once.

Films aspiring to present a vision of contemporary Britain: Wonderland, Love Actually, Chromophobia.

There are of course films which don't fit into any of these categories: Rose Troche's *Bedrooms and Hallways* (1998) has Kevin McKidd exploring his gay sensibilities in a London of nervous men and confident women; Mark Herman's *Hope Springs* (2003) and Clare Kilner's *The Wedding Date* (2005) are icky attempts at transatlantic romance. Irish romantic comedies have tended to go off in different directions. The freshest are Damien O'Donnell's *Inside I'm Dancing* (2004), which has two young paraplegics (Steven Robertson and James McAvoy) in love with their helper (Romola Garai); Liz Gill's *Goldfish Memory* (2003), which interlinks stories in the manner of David Kane's *This Year's Love* (1999) and *Born Romantic* (2000) but in a more upmarket Dublin setting and across a wider range of sexualities. Of films about mismatched couples overcoming their incompatibilities to find romance, Kieron J. Walsh's *When Brendan Met Trudy* (2000) is too smug and knowing (particularly in its film references) though still enjoyable; Karl Golden's *The Honeymooners* (2003) is a little hampered by its non-existent budget but its integrity and commitment shine through; John Carney's *Once* (2007), though it too had a derisively meagre budget, is much more accomplished; a film where the amateurism of the performances is an asset rather than a liability and gives the film the kind of authenticity money can't buy.

Given this wide range, it is dangerous to generalise, though too many of the women's films (especially *Fanny and Elvis* and *Crush*) are irredeemably silly; and too many of the middle-class-couples films (certainly *Elephant Juice* and *Maybe Baby*) are irritatingly smug. With the exception of Nick Grosso's clumsily stage-bound *Peaches* (2000) and Richard Parry's messily amateurish *South West 9* (2001), the low-life films are fresh, original and funny, more than compensating for their low budgets with strong scripts, talented young casts and the enterprising use of unusual locations. The celebra-

tions of eccentricity (admittedly a catch-all category) have attracted abysmal reviews for their rambling stories, patchy acting and uncertain direction, though most of them have redeeming features – an eagerness to please (epitomised by Kelly Macdonald in *House* and *Strictly Sinatra*), unexpectedly powerful performances (Michael Sheen in *Heartlands*, Lisa Stansfield in *Swing*), and a flagrant disregard for the normal standards of glamour and fashion (especially in *Weak at Denise*).

Of the films that cover a cross-section of society, Michael Winterbottom's *Wonderland* (1999) is possibly too grim and Martha Fiennes's *Chromophobia* (2005) too portentous to be classed as romantic comedy. Richard Curtis's *Love Actually* ambitiously weaves together eight romantic stories in which love is the answer not just for the well-heeled, but for misfits, and nondescript low-achievers, But Curtis's striving for social harmony – in this idyllic world everyone from the Prime Minister to his lowly tea-lady send their children to the same school – bleaches out the darkness and uncertainty which give *Notting Hill* and *Four Weddings and a Funeral* their resonance. By contrast all the films that qualify as urban fairy-tales – with the exception of Gerard Stembridge's *About Adam* (2000), which makes too little of Stuart Townsend's capacity to combine malevolence with charm – insist on incorporating sadness and loss into their vision of a world brightened by love.

Crime Wave

A miscellany of gangster films had been made in the 90s – *Under Suspicion, Young Americans, Shopping, Shallow Grave, The Innocent Sleep, Smalltime, Hard Men, Face* – all of some interest, none directly inspiring any successors. Guy Ritchie's *Lock, Stock and Two Smoking Barrels*, with its ethos of irreverent New Laddism, had a resonance that enabled it to transcend its meagre budget and sketchy plot and appeal to a much wider audience. Its success at the box office released the pent-up enthusiasm for British crime films that had been fostered by magazines like *Loaded, Uncut* and *Total Film*, though only a handful of films shared Ritchie's cheery view of the London underworld. Crime films fall roughly into three groups:

Experiments: These are films which depart radically from the usual gangland or crime-thriller formulas; sometimes with annoying indulgence (*Final Cut, Rancid Aluminium, Love, Honour and Obey, Mojo*), sometimes with startling originality (*Lock, Stock, Snatch, Gangster No. 1, Mr In-Between, Croupier*); Marc Munden's *Miranda*

(2002) has a good first half but loses its way trying to incorporate Kyle MacLachlan's psychopathic city slicker and John Hurt's worryingly paedophilic sugar daddy.[1]

Pastiche: Most of these films attempt the jokey tone of the Ritchie films but chain it to lumbering, old-fashioned narratives (*High Heels and Low Lifes*, *American Cousins*); copy genre conventions they don't understand enough to properly parody (*Honest*, *Circus*, *Sorted*, *Fakers*, *You're Dead . . .*, *The Last Yellow*, *Lava*, *New Blood*, *The Baby Juice Express*); or pile up clichés in the forlorn hope that they will add up to something new and interesting (*24 Hours in London*, *Layer Cake*). *The Baby Juice Express* (Mike Hurst, 2004) is at least funny some of the time and boldly if not wisely casts Joe Bugner and Julian Clary among its villains; but the only outstanding film is Jonathan Glazer's *Sexy Beast* (2000).

Underworld films that attempt a degree of realism in dealing with gangland and owe more to Antonia Bird's *Face* (1997) and earlier films like *The Long Good Friday* (John Mackenzie, 1979) and *Get Carter* (Mike Hodges, 1971) than to the Ritchie films. They range from the frothy semi-comedy of *It Was an Accident* to the brutally sardonic *Essex Boys*. Even when deeply flawed (*Out of Depth*, for example), their observations of real-life contemporary crime make them relevant and interesting. Other notable examples are Jim Doyle's *Going Off Big Time* (2000), Colin Teague's *Shooters* (2002) and *Spivs* (2004), and Mike Hodges's *I'll Sleep When I'm Dead* (2003).

Nick Love's *Goodbye Charlie Bright* (2001), *The Football Factory* (2004), *The Business* (2005) and *Outlaw* (2007) share similar casts and milieux, and though their stories are distinctively different, have more in common with each other than with other crime films. They can be grouped with Shane Meadows's *Smalltime* (1996) *Dead Man's Shoes* (2004) and *This Is England* (2006), as films set among the unrespectable working class, though Love's South Londoners are generally more vicious and materialistic than Meadows's Midlanders. Love and Meadows's loyalty to specific communities also links their films to Metin Hüseyin's *It Was an Accident* (2000) and Saul Dibb's *Bullet Boy* (2004), set in Northeast London, Paul Spurrier's *Underground* (1998), which ventures north of the river but is set mainly among the drug-ridden estates of South London; and Piotr Szkopiak's *Small Time Obsession* (2000), whose discontented youths tempted into crime come from London's Polish community. None of these films are as grim as

the underclass films proper – such as Gary Oldman's *Nil by Mouth* (1997), and Ken Loach's *My Name Is Joe* (1998) and *Sweet Sixteen* (2002) – which also incorporate substantial criminal elements. The exception is Paul Andrew Williams's *London to Brighton* (2006), a harrowing tale of a prostitute and a runaway eleven-year-old being hunted down by pimps and gangsters, which makes no concession to delicate sensibilities.

Films which should have been received with interest tended to be dismissed along with the films which gave the genre a bad name – Paul McGuigan's *Gangster No. 1* (2000) and Terry Winsor's *Essex Boys* (2000) were particularly unfairly treated; and Colin Teague's *Shooters* and *Spivs*, with their convincing low-life characters, deserved better than the bemused contempt most reviewers doled out to them.

Several of the weaker films show sparks of vitality in their colourful villains – Samantha Morton's feral council estate-gangster's moll miraculously brings Julian Farino's *The Last Yellow* (1999) back to life; Tim Curry's degenerate club owner in Alex Jovy's *Sorted* (2000), who needs Sienna Guillory to interpret his Shakespeare quotations to less literary-minded associates, alleviates the boredom of a banal plot; Eddie Izzard stands out among the gallery of stereotypes in Rob Walker's *Circus* (2000); Nicholas Ball is chillingly believable as a small-time crook with psychotically grandiose ideas in *Out of Depth*; Art Malik brings much-needed menace to *Fakers* (2004); Michael Gambon's corrupt policeman in *The Innocent Sleep* (1996), a conspiracy thriller set among London's down-and-outs, and his decadent gangster in *High Heels and Low Lifes* (2001), are alternately savage and amusing; though by the time he came to play a gang boss in *Layer Cake* (2004), the mannerisms had turned stale.

Two films that stray from crime to horror also boast frighteningly effective villains, David Calder as the avuncular Tattooed Man in Paul Sarossy's uniquely strange *Mr In-Between* (2001), and Fiona Shaw as the evil-eyed Professor Lebourg in Nick Willing's *Doctor Sleep* (2002). Both films alienated audiences and critics, though they score highly on originality. More straightforward horror films, however, have prompted a popular revival.

Horror

In *A Heritage of Horror*, David Pirie claimed that 'the horror genre, as it has been developed in this country by Hammer and its rivals, remains the only staple cinematic myth which Britain can properly claim as its own'.[2] But that was in 1973, before it became obvious that the British horror film was in terminal decline. A brief revival in the mid-1980s around the talented figure of Clive Barker failed to flourish. George Pavlou's adaptations of Barker's *Underworld* (1985) and *Rawhead Rex* (1986) were amateurish and unconvincing, and though Barker's own début *Hellraiser* (1987) was much more impressive, he was soon snapped up by Hollywood. Another bright hope, Richard Stanley, stalled after two films – *Hardware* (1990) and *Dust Devil* (1992) – and, apart from Kenneth Branagh's *Mary Shelley's Frankenstein* (1994) and Stephen Frears's *Mary Reilly* (1996), British horror films – such as Paul Matthews's *Grim* (1995) and *Deadly Instincts* (1997) – appeared weakly derivative of American models.

A wave of more interesting films began with Julian Richards's *Darklands* (1996), a botched but nonetheless bold attempt to rework Robin Hardy's *The Wicker Man* (1973) in contemporary Wales. Jake West's *Razor Blade Smile* (1998) is equally patchy (not surprising given its shoestring budget), but has the virtue of originality, and achieved minor cult status for its exuberant bad taste and explicit sexuality. It can be grouped with Charly Cantor's intriguing *Blood* (2000), and three more generously funded vampire films: Po-Chih Leong's *The Wisdom of Crocodiles* (1998), an earnest attempt to turn Jude Law into a sympathetic vampire who only wants to drink the blood of women who love him; Elias Merhige's *Shadow of a Vampire* (2000), an ingenious if unconvincing fiction about F. W. Murnau casting a vampire as Count Orlok in his classic horror film *Nosferatu, eine Symphonie des Grauens* (1922); and *Doctor Sleep*, a crime thriller where harassed police detective Shirley Henderson teams up with hypnotist Goran Visnjic to combat ancient evils centred on Fiona Shaw's erudite but evil vampire. All of them are interesting, though none of them enjoyed much commercial success in the UK.

Other horror productions tried to keep costs down by confining most of the action to a single location. Simon Hunter's *Lighthouse* (2000) dumps a ruthless murderer among the luckless shipwreck survivors marooned on a storm-tossed lighthouse. Rob Green's *The Bunker* (2001) confines a platoon of Germans in a haunted network of tunnels, which prove more deadly than the advancing Allied troops. Neil Marshall's *Dog Soldiers* (2002) has not very bright British squaddies take shelter in an isolated farmhouse, which is the home base of the werewolves they're fleeing from; and in *The Descent* (2005) he traps a party of women in caves populated by flesh-eating humanoids.

Nick Hamm's *The Hole* (2001), widened its appeal beyond horror aficionados with an attractive young cast (including Thora Birch and Keira Knightley), and a pleasingly convoluted plot around a group of teenagers who get more than they bargained for when they duck out of a weekend of strenuous exercise by hiding out in a British World War II bunker. Marc Evans's *My Little Eye* (2002), a disturbing study of a reality TV show that becomes a forum for gruesome murder, similarly attracted young UK audiences with his confident manipulation of expectations and witty pastiche of hidden camera techniques. However, the big money came from zombies, creatures with limited power and no personality who are nevertheless effectively deployed by Danny Boyle in his dystopian *28 Days Later . . .*, and disposed of wittily by Edgar Wright in *Shaun of the Dead* (2004).

Most interesting, though more modestly successful, is Christopher Smith's *Creep* (2004), which initially seems to be little more than an updated version of Gary Sherman's *Death Line* (1972). Franka Potenta's overconfident party-girl dozes off and wakes to find herself locked in the London Underground for the night. But she becomes increasingly likeable as she wards off the office Lothario who has followed her down there, and teams up with a bemused sewerman and a young homeless couple to deal with a flesh-eating monster. Smith uses the Underground setting and the mythology around disused tunnels and abandoned branch lines with considerable panache, and Sean Harris's monstrous 'Creep' (unlike the strictly anonymous killer in *Lighthouse*) is humanised enough to inspire pity and admiration as well as horror.[3]

Auteurs

Although genre has become an important channel for British film-makers, few directors beyond the horror specialists chose to confine themselves to a particular type of film. Nick Hamm, for example followed the romantic comedy *Martha – Meet Frank, Daniel and Laurence* (1998) with the horror of *The Hole*; Danny Boyle's range extends from the dodgy characters of *Shallow Grave* and *Trainspotting* to the angels of *A Life Less Ordinary* and the zombies of *28 Days Later. . . .* It is too early to estimate the extent and durability of the talent of many of the new directors, but several have the potential to develop into interesting auteurs.[4]

Michael Winterbottom is the best known and the most prolific. Of his fifteen features the funniest is

A Cock and Bull Story (2005), a chaotic fiction weaved around an attempt to film Laurence Sterne's *Tristram Shandy*, the most moving is *Jude* (1996), his stylish adaptation of Thomas Hardy's gloomiest novel; the most resonant *Wonderland*. Like most of his films it suffers from hasty, semi-improvised construction that leaves too much to chance, but the parts of the film devoted to Gina McKee have a feeling for London and sad romance which links the film back to the modernist city symphonies of the late silent period.

Roger Michell worked in television (notably on the adaptation of Hanif Kureishi's *The Buddha of Suburbia*, 1993), and made his cinema début with *Titanic Town* (1998), set in Belfast in the early 1970s, before directing the hugely successful *Notting Hill*. He was saved from directing *Captain Corelli's Mandolin* (2001) by a heart attack, and turned to smaller-scale projects. English critics and audiences preferred *Enduring Love* and American audiences lapped up Peter O'Toole's performance in *Venus*, but *The Mother*, with a script by Kureishi about a recently bereaved woman having a passionate sexual relationship with a much younger man, is as bold as Fassbinder's *Fear Eats the Soul* (1974), and Michell delights in showing a culturally diverse Notting Hill full of selfish characters who, in marked contrast to Richard Curtis's amiable eccentrics, care only about themselves.

David Mackenzie's low-budget digital feature *The Last Great Wilderness* (2002), part road movie, part revenge film, part psychological thriller, centres on two men (Jonny Phillips and the director's brother Alastair Mackenzie) journeying for different reasons to Scotland, who become trapped among the strange inhabitants of an old, dark house. Though there are deliberate echoes of *Psycho* and *The Wicker Man*, the film is refreshingly original, emulating the Dogme films of Lars Von Trier and Thomas Vinterberg in cinematic inventiveness and adherence to humanist values. Mackenzie's next film, *Young Adam* (2003), is a strikingly austere evocation of life around the Glasgow canals of the 1950s, based on a novel by Alexander Trocchi. Giles Nuttgens's washed-out colour photography and David Byrne's atmospheric score help Mackenzie create a genuinely innovative film that captures the louche amorality of Trocchi's novel, re-assessing rather than nostalgically indulging its bohemian modernism. Despite the film's eroticism and the starring role of Ewan McGregor, *Young Adam* was too gloomy to become a major box-office success, but it consolidated Mackenzie's credentials and led to the more mainstream *Asylum* (2005), with Natasha

Richardson shining as the reluctant wife of a psychiatrist, who starts a passionate affair with a psychotically violent patient when her husband becomes deputy director of an asylum for the criminally insane. With remarkable consistency, Mackenzie continued to explore dangerous male sexual obsessions in *Hallam Foe* (2007), with Jamie Bell as a voyeur who stalks, and intrigues, a woman who resembles his dead mother.

Lynne Ramsay attracted attention with *Ratcatcher* (1999), a sad evocation of Glasgow in the early 1970s and confirmed her talent for making unexpected, unusual films with *Morvern Callar* (2002), a fragmentary tale about a supermarket check-out girl who conceals the suicide of her boyfriend and claims his eagerly snapped-up first novel as her own. Samantha Morton's mask-like face and intense interiority make her ideally fitted to play the troubled, enigmatic heroine.

Marc Evans moved from glum Welsh magic realism in *House of America* (1997) to psychopathic sectarian savagery in *Resurrection Man* (1998), and seemed to be turning into a horror specialist with *My Little Eye* and *Trauma* (2004). But he made an unexpected turn in *Snow Cake* (2006), a sometimes moving, sometimes ludicrous drama centring on a relationship between embittered ex-con Alan Rickman and autistic but vigorous Sigourney Weaver in the snowy Canadian outback. Like Winterbottom, Evans seems to plough through the difficulties involved in getting films into production, but there is a similar downside in terms of hasty construction and uncertain direction (though haste and spontaneity help his 2007 documentary *In Prison My Whole Life* from becoming an indignant rant). His films may be flawed but they are always interesting.

Nick Love made his début in 1999 with the uncomfortably sordid short *Love Story*, a fragment of a tale about a drug-addicted couple (Jamie Forman and Patsy Palmer) bringing a baby into their grotesquely squalid world. The feature film that followed, *Goodbye Charlie Bright*, is more cheerful, a tragi-comedy set on a Bermondsey council estate about a group of lads who zigzag towards their predetermined futures (the army, crime, death, escape) in a tough, claustrophobic, working-class environment. *The Football Factory*, about the perils and pleasures of football hooliganism, and *The Business*, set among British gangsters in the 1980s Costa del Crime, suffer from characters who are too unpleasant to sympathise with and too mundane to thrill. But Love's willingness to show the world from the viewpoint of people generally regarded as beyond the pale make his films both disturbing and interesting. The incipient fascism of Love's milieu is explored more explicitly in *Outlaw* (2007), a lazy daydream of a film about a band of vigilantes, led by Sean Bean, who decide that as the police are corrupt or ineffectual, they must take the law into their own hands to clean up Britain.

Shane Meadows films are all set in the poorest and least fashionable parts of the Midlands. The unpredictable characters in *Where's the Money Ronnie?* (1996) and *Smalltime* (1996) are often appalling but always fascinating to watch. Council-estate life in *A Room for Romeo Brass* (1999) is tough and dangerous with the likes of Paddy Considine's Morrell around, but Meadows's stress is on warmth and absurdity rather than violence and tragedy as it is, for example, in Gary Oldman's *Nil by Mouth*, Lynne Ramsay's *Ratcatcher* or Ken Loach's *My Name Is Joe* and *Sweet Sixteen*. His attempts to introduce outsiders into this authentic, self-contained world – Bob Hoskins in *TwentyFourSeven* (1997), Robert Carlyle, Shirley Henderson, Rhys Ifans, Kathy Burke, Ricky Tomlinson in *Once Upon a Time in the Midlands* (2002) – founder; but his offbeat revenge tragedy *Dead Man's Shoes*, with Considine as a paratrooper who returns home to exact vengeance on the small-time hoodlums who have abused his simple-minded brother, combines deadpan humour with a serious disposition on the futility of violence. *This Is England* (2006), set in the 1980s in the immediate aftermath of the Falklands War, is his most accessible film. The nostalgia for an era when teenage gangs were relatively untroubled by crack and heroin is sharpened by the freshness of Meadows's vision. The skinhead gang who adopt young Shaun (Thomas Turgoose) and brighten up his bullied, lonely life look scary, but they are deferential, kindly and inclusive – at least till the arrival of the National Front-supporting Combo (Stephen Graham). Meadows turns Midlands parochialism to his advantage; this is England, at least to those of us born North of the Watford Gap, but it is an England only occasionally glimpsed in one-off successes like *The Full Monty* and *Brassed Off*. Whereas most provincial film-makers flock to London (or Hollywood), Meadows continues to draw on his Nottingham experiences and presents, with increasing competence and confidence, an England where language, morality, lifestyle, particularly among the working classes, are vigorously different from the metropolitan norm.

Bright Sparks

To this list of promising film-makers I would add another eleven directors, chosen somewhat arbitrarily to represent the diversity of talent currently working in the British film industry. John Maybury and Jonathan Glazer both had long film-making careers before moving into features, Maybury in experimental/avant-garde cinema, Glazer in music videos (among others for Jamiroquai's *Virtual Insanity* and U.N.K.L.E's *Rabbit in Your Headlight*).[5] Glazer made his feature début in 2000 with *Sexy Beast*, which stands out from the pack of British gangster films for its witty script, convincing characters and visually stimulating direction. Its flaw is also its greatest asset: Ben Kingsley's Don Logan is such a mesmerisingly awful villain – made all the more effective by the fact that he is played by an actor best known for his portrayal of Gandhi – that his exit leaves the final third of the film an anti-climax. *Birth* followed in 2004, a much bigger-budgeted film, made in America and with international stars, including Nicole Kidman, Anne Heche and Lauren Bacall. *Sexy Beast* is a witty, intelligent re-working of the old story of the career criminal coerced into doing 'one last job'. *Birth* is a more unusual and complex story about a boy who claims to have inherited the soul of a wealthy New Yorker who drops dead during his early morning run in Central Park. Naturally, his wife (Kidman) is sceptical, but the boy's uncanny knowledge of her dead husband's habits and feelings intrigues her; and in contrast to her husband, who is revealed to have been a less than perfect partner, the boy obviously adores her. Glazer's achievement is to make this seem believable, so that we continue to sympathise with Kidman's desire for the impossible, even when a rational explanation emerges.

Birth leaves cracks through which elements of the supernatural might possibly be squeezed, but like Hitchcock's *Vertigo* (1958), the film is essentially concerned with illusion and obsession. Maybury's *The Jacket* (2005) – a long-delayed successor to his phantasmagorical début feature *Love Is the Devil* (1998) – is more ready to accept elements of the fantastic into its story of a supposedly brain-damaged soldier who (when drugged, wrapped in a straitjacket, and entombed in a cadaver drawer) is able to travel in time. What makes the film so pleasing is its modesty. Jack Starks (Adrien Brody) is concerned less with saving the world than with finding out what is happening to him and avoiding his own death. Travelling to the future (our present), he is reluctantly befriended by a world-weary waitress (Keira Knightley), who turns out to be the child he met, liked and helped before his incarceration. He convinces her that his fantastic story is true and his anguish is lessened by her generosity and unselfishness. In love and gratitude, he does something for her. Returning to the past, he visits her mother, a distracted, unhappy woman who drinks and smokes too much, and, almost incidentally, makes her see the value of her relationship with her daughter. A sort of miracle is effected and the future is changed. The mother doesn't die young, and the waitress, no longer alone in the world, is less sad: hopefully even God wouldn't object to so small a change in the pattern of events.

Birth and *The Jacket* are American-backed films with budgets of over $20 million (far in excess of most British films) but Glazer and Maybury both have a highly personal style and both films can be regarded as personal projects. The success of *Sexy Beast* made it easier for Glazer to find financial backers for *Birth*, but it was a script he developed himself (with the help of Jean-Claude Carrière, a sophisticated and creative writer best known for his collaboration with Luis Buñuel) and was made in America mainly because of the involvement of Nicole Kidman. *The Jacket*, made after a number of aborted projects, including a film based around the brief, colourful and violent life of Christopher Marlowe, was shot in Scotland and Canada and is remarkably successful in integrating its British (Keira Knightley, Daniel Craig and Steven Mackintosh) and American (Adrien Brody, Kris Kristofferson, Jennifer Jason Leigh) casts.

In Asif Kapadia's *The Return* (2006), the transfer of souls posited in *Birth* really does happen, and time travel is one of the facts of life Sarah Michelle Gellar's self-mutilating heroine, plagued by phantoms and dwarfed by big violent men, has to get used to. This is a more thoroughly American project – directed by Kapadia as a fill-in between his more personal films *The Warrior* (2001) and *Far North* (2007). But he imports Australian Peter O'Brien, best known for his appearances in *The Bill* and *Casualty*, to play the grumpy, misanthropic backwoodsman who is the nearest the film comes to a hero; and he makes unusual use of bleak Texan locations whenever he can get out of the studio to present a vision of America as spooky, seedy and desolate.

Kapadia, a British-born Indian, had ignored the conventions of both Bollywood and the heritage film, making *The Warrior*, his feature début, in Hindi rather than English on location in the deserts of Rajasthan and the mountains of Manikaran. His modest budget and a cast made up mainly of non-actors proved to be assets rather than liabilities, resulting in a glow of authenticity and a visual adventurousness to this epic tale of a hired swordsman who tires of bloodshed but finds his master

vengeful when he tries to leave his service, and grounding the hero's mystical quest in a mundane and brutal reality. Kapadia had hoped to make an adaptation of a short story set in the Arctic for his next film, but difficulties in funding and the logistics of shooting in an inaccessible environment with limited daylight delayed the project and he accepted the assignment to direct *The Return*. Modest box-office success would probably have secured him further American assignments; instead he returned to Europe to make *Far North*, a film obviously much closer to his heart.

Saul Metzstein's low-budget slacker comedy *Late Night Shopping* (2001) made up for a desultory plot with unusual and convincing characters and an authentic evocation of the world of the night-worker. Like Maybury, Glazer and Kapadia he strayed into offbeat Americana with his second film *Guy X* (2005) an eccentric comedy set on an army base in Greenland in 1979, though shot in Canada and Iceland. Apart from Jason Biggs, who acquits himself well as the American soldier dumped by administrative error in Greenland when he was expecting to serve out his time in Hawaii, the cast is drawn from British, Canadian and Icelandic rather than American actors, and purists complained about dubious accents and errors in army protocol. But these would hardly be of vital concern to Metzstein, a director more interested in quirky humour than strict realism. The darker aspects of the story – about the sealing away of brain-damaged casualties who, from an administrative point of view, are best considered dead are a little haphazard; and the relationship between Biggs's unwilling recruit and Natascha McElhone's army doctor is not entirely convincing, but there is enough in this rambling but likeable film to confirm Metzstein's qualities as an idiosyncratic and original director.

For the first time in British cinema, a substantial number of women have been able to establish themselves as significant directors, following in the tentative footsteps of Antonia Bird, Gurinder Chadha, Beeban Kidron and Sally Potter. Along with Lynne Ramsay they include Kirsten Sheridan, whose *Disco Pigs* (2001), adapted from a play by Enda Walsh about the passionate but increasingly fraught relationship between two seventeen-year-olds who have been inseparable since birth, is visually flamboyant and disturbingly violent.[6] Andrea Arnold followed her Oscar-winning short *Wasp* (2003) with the austere *Red Road* (2006). Amma Asante made an impressive début with the shockingly realist study of Welsh teenagers *A Way of Life* (2004). Softer,

Far North (Asif Kapadia, 2007)

In *True North*, the very short story by Sarah Maitland from which *Far North* is adapted, two women live an isolated but harmonious existence in the Arctic tundra until their lives are disrupted by the intrusion of a young man. One woman is old and ugly, the other young and beautiful, so the man has no difficulty in choosing between them. In Kapadia's film the older woman is played by Michelle Yeoh and is by no means ugly, and the man is the not so young Sean Bean; consequently the dynamics of the triangular relationship are more complicated.

Kapadia and his scriptwriting partner Tim Miller necessarily flesh out the story, which gives no hint as to who the women are, what the relationship between them is and how they come to be living cut off from the rest of the world. Saiva (Yeoh) is cursed, the tribal shaman forecasting that she will bring death to anyone who loves her. She is driven from her tribe and attracts the comfort of strangers. But the curse remains true and even her kindest act, rescuing a baby who grows into the beautiful young woman Anja (Michelle Krusiec) ends in tragedy. Saiva is a much more active protagonist than the old woman of the story and Kapadia's absence of sentimentality and respect for the cruelty of nature serves his heroine well. The tone is set in an early scene where Saiva fondles one of her sledge dogs, winning its total trust before slitting its throat: she wreaks vengeance on the soldiers who massacre the villagers who have given her shelter; she countermands her instinct to kill Loki (Bean) when she finds him helpless in the snow and nurtures him back to life. Her actions, even at their most horrific, seem a necessary response to the to harshness of the dilemmas she faces.

Far North shares a facility with *The Warrior* for visual storytelling and an evocative use of landscape, but *The Warrior* is an epic eastern tale where the spirits can sometimes be benevolent and redemption is possible; *Far North* is a dark northern fairy-tale where climate and landscape are a constant challenge to survival.

Michelle Krusiec goes hunting with Sean Bean in *Far North*

The relationship between Loki and the two women brings the film to its disturbing climax, but it only occupies the final third of the film. Before that, *Far North* is concerned with the lives of the two women in this strange, forbidding environment (Kapadia used a Russian ice-breaker as his production base and shot the film in the most northerly reaches of Norway). There is a lurking suspicion that clean, lovely Saiva and Anja, with their craft skills and smart coats, might have more sensibly opened a gift shop in Trondheim. But for most of the time Kapadia is able to keep such scepticism at bay. The strength of the film, what lifts it beyond a fanciful tale in a visually splendid setting, is the poignant tragedy of Saiva's fate as a tough, resourceful, resilient woman doomed to isolation in this beautiful but unforgiving landscape.

FURTHER READING

<www.electricsheepmagazine.co.uk/features/2007/10/21/ interview-with-asif-kapadia>.

<www.michelleyeoh.info/Movie/farnorth.html>.

more poetic débuts were made by Emily Young and Shona Auerbach.

Both women attended the Polish National Film School at Lodz and bring a European sensibility to their début films. Auerbach's *Dear Frankie* (2004) tells the story of a fearful, protective mother (Emily Mortimer) who creates a fictional father figure for her deaf son.

This small-scale film made on location in the Clydeside port of Greenock skirts melodrama and avoids the tendency to represent Scotland as the repository of grim realism, Celtic whimsy or drug-fuelled fantasy. Auerbach (who acted as her own cinematographer) creates a vibrant setting for her fable, using a distinctive visual colour scheme and making clever use of voice-over from the otherwise silent Frankie. Though well received at the Edinburgh and Cannes film festivals and snapped up for distribution in America by Miramax, the film has attracted less attention than it deserves and Auerbach is still too little known.

Emily Young beat Auerbach for the 'Carl Foreman Award for the Most Promising Newcomer' with her *Kiss of Life* (2003), but the film failed to gain a release in America and was hardly seen in British cinemas before BBC Films decided it was best fitted for a television audience. It is more difficult to engage with the nebulous and ill-defined dilemmas faced by Helen, *Kiss of Life*'s central female character, particularly as she is only a ghostly presence for much of the film, than it is with Frankie's anguished, poverty-stricken mother. And the complexities of a narrative that not only cuts back and forth between London and Bosnia but shifts backwards and forwards in time are difficult to keep pace with. But it is none the less an impressive début.[7]

If Young and Auerbach are influenced by Kieślowski (and Kapadia cites Polanski's *Knife in the Water* as an influence on *Far North*), Polish-born Pawel Pawlikowski seems to have more in common with their compatriot Jerzy Skolimowski, whose looser, eclectic style of film-making won him few friends at the time but have kept his films fresh and unpredictable. After several notable documentaries and a shaky transition to fiction in *The Stringer* (1998), Pawlikowski established himself with *Last Resort* (2000), a low-budget BBC Television improvised drama, which was well received at film festivals and secured a limited theatrical release. The original idea was to make a modern re-working of the Snow White fairy-tale, with a beautiful, young Russian woman keeping house for seven migrant workers in London. Pawlikowski changed the story shortly before shooting, ditching the seven workers, relocating the action to Margate, and setting the story, now of a young Russian woman (Dina Korzun) who seeks asylum in England after the man she had expected to marry fails to meet her, vaguely in the future. The film's unique vision of a Britain plagued by bureaucracy and pornography, and the odd humour introduced by Paddy Considine's dangerous but finally beneficent bingo-caller, gave the film a resonance and importance which belied its lowly origins.

Considine also appears in Pawlikowski's next film *My Summer of Love* (2004), playing a scarily unpredictable ex-convict who turns the Yorkshire village pub he has inherited into a centre for the evangelical Christianity he has espoused while in prison. But Pawlikowski's main story concerns his sister, a freckled teenager (Nathalie Press), who embarks on a lesbian love affair with a bored rich girl (Emily Blunt). Though the performances are strong and Pawlikowski again makes good use of unusual English locations, the film lacks the unity and significance of *Last Resort*.

Simon Rumley made his first feature *Strong Language* (1998) on a tiny budget raised from friends after failing to get industry or Lottery funding. Sixteen people in their twenties talk about sex, clubbing, debt, politics and the Brit-pop phenomenon, while a more shadowy figure tells a tragic story about love, rape, suicide and murder which finally involves all the other characters. This witty, enlightening and unusual début was followed by *The Truth Game* (2001), which, with its dinner party revelations, almost fits among the romantic comedies exploring the lives of middle-class couples. Rumley is no Chekhov and his characters can seem irritatingly trivial; but he is adept at capturing their uncomfortable interaction through body language and gesture, relying as much on camera movement and framing as on dialogue. *Club Le Monde*, his third film, appeared in 2002, though it is set at the height of the clubbing scene in 1993. Without the macabre undertones of *Strong Language* and *The Truth Game*, the film is curiously sweet and soft-centred. Frothy working-class girls, naive public schoolboys, and comical eccentrics make *Club Le Monde* less innovative than its companions, but Rumley shows considerable aplomb in juggling between his thirty-two characters.

Strong Language, *The Truth Game* and *Club Le Monde* form a trilogy. Rumley's next film *The Living and the Dead* (2006) marked a complete break. A study of madness set in a crumbling stately home, it is less surefooted than Polanski's *Repulsion* (1965) and has nothing to match the performance of Catherine Deneuve, but Rumley's ingenuity and imagination are remarkable.

Penny Woolcock, born in Argentina and brought up in Uruguay, only became involved in film-making in her late thirties, when she joined the Trade Films co-operative in Gateshead. She attracted attention with *Tina Goes Shopping* (1999) and *Tina Takes a Break* (2001), two semi-improvised dramas about the life of a poverty-stricken single mother played with gutsy conviction by Kelly Hollis, made for Channel 4. Her first cinema film, *The Principles of Lust* (2003), a shocking tale about a failed writer who stumbles into a world of orgiastic sex and bare-knuckle fighting just when he is settling into a romantic relationship with a young mother and her child, employed similar filming techniques – hand-held

Control (Anton Corbijn, 2007)

When Ian Curtis committed suicide in May 1980, Joy Division were still struggling for recognition. The release of the single 'Love Will Tear Us Apart' and the album 'Closer' shortly after his death boosted their profile enormously, but the band reformed as New Order and one might have expected memories of Joy Division to slowly fade. Anton Corbijn was an early fan and his photographs of Curtis and the band helped to establish their image. After a twenty-year career as a photographer and music video maker, he chose Curtis as the subject for his début feature.

Samantha Morton and Sam Riley on location for *Control*

Control works because Curtis is a genuinely interesting figure, both as a lyricist and a performer and everyone in the film seems to acknowledge this. Sam Riley is perhaps too robust and sensible to play Curtis; Sean Harris in Michael Winterbottom's *24 Hour Party People* (2002), is better at capturing his strangeness though he has much less to do. What Riley brings is charisma. He sings the well-known Joy Division songs in a way which makes them slightly more Americanised, slightly less anguished, but with an energy and commitment which is entirely convincing. When another singer acts as substitute for Riley's exhausted Curtis, we share the audience's anger and disappointment, although we know one simulacrum is being replaced by another; Riley's performances have become interesting in themselves, not just as an imitation of Curtis.

Corbijn is Dutch but he spent his formative years in England, and he brings the right mix of inside knowledge and outsider's distance. Bernard Sumner and the other members of Joy Division, manager Rob Gretton, impresario Tony Wilson are carefully cast and allowed to develop individual idiosyncrasies; in a surreal time-stopping moment John Cooper Clark appears as himself reciting the inflammatory 'Evidently Chickentown' just as he might have done thirty years earlier. Corbijn is both accurate and fair, even to Annik Honoré, the Belgian woman for whom Curtis wanted to leave his wife. Alexandra Maria Lara might not look capable of inspiring love that could tear you apart, but she has the right quality of quiet Continental exoticism to tempt Curtis, a romantic whose home life has turned into the mundaneness of a wife and a baby in a small house in Macclesfield. Samantha Morton as Deborah Curtis the long-suffering wife assumes the dowdiness one might expect from a Macclesfield girl married in her teens but she endows her with a courage and forcefulness that must have stilled any doubts the real Deborah Curtis had in co-operating with the project. (Her memoir *Touching from a Distance* is the film's main source).

Control is a surprisingly warm film, despite its gloomy subject and black-and-white photography, reminiscent of the Northern realist films of the early 1960s photographed by Walter Lassally. Corbijn had to raise much of the budget from his own resources, as he told his interviewer, 'If I lose my house in England so be it – as an artist it's okay to put money into your art. But for the next film I won't do it again.' Gratifyingly, the film did well at the box office; Corbijn's empathetic, intelligent film-making is an asset to be treasured.

FURTHER READING

Edward Lawrenson, '*Touching the Void* – Interview with Anton Corbijn', *Sight and Sound*, October 2007, p. 31

Jonathan Romney, 'Control', *Sight and Sound*, November 2007, p. 51

cameras, real locations, spontaneous rather than rehearsed performances – though it relied on experienced actors for the main parts and benefits hugely from the performances of Marc Warren and Sienna Guillory. The revelation of an underside of frenzied hedonism in Sheffield is fascinating, but the protagonist's dilemma over whether to sponge off his girlfriend or hang out with sexually deviant petty criminals, strained audience patience.

After an adaptation of John Adams's controversial opera *The Death of Klinghoffer*, about the Palestinian hijacking of the *Achille Lauro* cruise ship, Woolcock returned to Tina's world for *Mischief Night* (2006), slightly bigger budgeted than its television predecessors and a little too sugary and clichéd for its own good. But Woolcock once again reaches a Britain that no other film-maker, even Ken Loach, can reach. Her peripheral characters are cardboard and Tina loses her sharp, tragic edge, but the children are real and the locations too. The overcrowded housing, the brittle friction between the communities has the ring of truth even if the plot does not. One might want Woolcock to be more disciplined and less indulgent but this would probably kill off her strongest asset, a foreigner's fascination, unhampered by guilt and class-consciousness, with the more bizarre aspects of low culture.

Her strengths and faults are even more evident in *Exodus* (2007), a haphazard allegory set in Margate, where the Dreamland amusement park has been turned into a concentration camp and a Fascist demagogue rules the roost. *Exodus* shares apocalyptic concerns (and the actress Clare-Hope Ashitey) with Alfonso Cuarón's *Children of Men* (2006), which sited its camp for those considered unwanted or undesirable further round the coast in Bexhill-on-Sea. *Children of Men*, with its chilling concept of a childless future and its disturbing echoes of the second Iraq war, is an internationally significant film; *Exodus* is more like a village pageant. In terms of script, theme, performances, production values, special effects, Cuarón's film wins hands down (hardly surprising in view of its $76-million budget).[8] But *Exodus* has its own virtues: the people of its ghetto, recruited locally from the Margate area, might not be great actors but they have an aura of authenticity which professional actors cannot manufacture. Peter Watkins used similar techniques in *Culloden* (1964), *The War Game* (1965) and his six-hour *La Commune* (2000) but hitherto he has pursued a solitary furrow. Woolcock's contempt for safe, over-rehearsed methods makes her a welcome antidote to conformity and shallowness in British cinema.

If Pawlikowski has found it difficult to live up to the dazzling achievement of *Last Resort*, Ben Hopkins is still trying to fulfil the promise of his brilliant Royal College of Art student film *National Achievement Day* (1995), at least as far as the film industry is concerned. *Simon Magus* (1999) his ambitious and relatively generously budgeted début feature was a financial disaster, and Hopkins has not been able to work on the same scale since. The fault, however, lies more with the industry than with the film, which intellectually and aesthetically is a considerable achievement. A magic realist

Jewish folk tale set in nineteenth-century Middle Europe and centring on a mad outcast (Noah Taylor) who has regular conversations with the Devil (Ian Holm) was hardly likely to attract big crowds at the multiplex, but fresh performances, inventive cinematography and *mise en scène,* a complex script encompassing anti-Semitism, the coming of the railways, mysticism and the triumph of romantic love, ought to have ensured critical if not commercial success and confirmed Hopkins's reputation as a talented director. The film's final sequence, a series of tracking shots set to the Intermezzo of Dmitri Shostakovich's Piano Quintet, in which Simon (or the spirit of Simon), passes like a wind changing the lives of the other characters − bringing together star-crossed lovers Leah and Dovid, Sarah and Count Albrecht, refilling the landlord's glass of beer, making the very old couple who fear that one of them will die leaving the other alone clasp hands in their sleep, waking the sick child from her fever − is brilliant. A chastened Hopkins called it 'a great ending to a slightly flawed and not really that great film' on his DVD commentary. But looking back at other films from 1999, one is hard-pressed to find many as inventive and original as *Simon Magus*.

His follow-up *The Nine Lives of Tomas Katz* (2000) is odder still, an improvised drama which draws on the solar eclipse of August 1999 for a series of surreal vignettes about a possible apocalypse. A much more low-budget affair, it suffers from the usual *longueurs* and indulgencies of improvised dramas, though its amalgamation of the mystical psycho-geography espoused by Iain Sinclair and Alan Moore with the off-the-cuff film-making style of a director like Aki Kaurismäki would have assured it a cult late-night following if the venues catering for such cults hadn't now disappeared. Hopkins's ethnographic documentary *37 Uses for a Dead Sheep* (2006), like *Simon Magus*, focuses on a remote rural community where ritual, tradition and the temptations of modernisation dominate the lives of the participants, here the Pamir Kirghiz tribe, who after centuries of nomadic life have settled in Eastern Turkey.

The miracle of the ever-full beer mug in *Simon Magus* and Hopkins's proficiency in reproducing the look and feel of silent cinema classics would ensure his future directing sophisticated commercials for Stella Artois, but as with Pawlikowski, his visionary imagination ought to be at the centre, not confined to the periphery, of a vibrant British cinema culture.

Conclusion

It is not my intention to give the impression that all is well with the British film industry. One could write a parallel essay emphasising the waste and extravagance, the bombastic claims and wasted opportunities. But the emergence of a refreshingly cine-literate generation of actors, directors, writers, cinematographers, with a genuine interest in the cinema and a determination to make individual and distinctive films, deserves recognition and support.

Notes

1. Munden's promising talent shone more brightly in *The Mark of Cain* (2007), an uncomfortable story about British soldiers serving in Iraq, with a well-worked-out script by Tony Marchant.

2. David Pirie, *A Heritage of Horror* (London: Gordon Fraser, 1973), p. 9.

3. *Severance* (2006), Smith's next film, is more formulaic, but the director handles comedy-horror conventions with enough wit and originality to win the support of horror fans.

4. This chapter is about post-1990 British directors, but it is worth noting the survival of Ken Loach, Mike Leigh and Stephen Frears who have battled hard to attain the international regard they now enjoy. Less excusably I have omitted undoubtedly talented 'quality' directors Anand Tucker (*Saint-Ex*, *Hilary and Jackie*, *Shopgirl* and *And When Did You Last See Your Father?*), Peter Webber (*Girl with a Pearl Earring*, *Hannibal Rising*), Joe Tucker (*Pride and Prejudice*, *Atonement*) and Kevin Macdonald, whose work includes the brilliant dramatised documentary *Touching the Void* (2003), and an impressive feature début *The Last King of Scotland* (2006). A wider-ranging essay might also have mentioned the achievements of Sam Mendes and Christopher Nolan in America.

5. For Maybury's avant-garde career see Michael O'Pray's ' "New Romanticism" and the British Avant-Garde Film in the Early 80s', Chapter 37 in this volume.

6. Sheridan's reportedly syrupy but accomplished *August Rush* (2007) was released too late to be included here.

7. I have written in more detail about *Kiss of Life* in the Postscript. Young's next project is an adaptation of Paulo Coelho's *Veronika Decides to Die*.

8. Artangel's eighty-foot-high Rubbish Man in *Exodus* is impressive, but it's also an uncomfortable reminder of how much more effectively a similar figure was used in *The Wicker Man*.

Bibliography

For a negative assessment of contemporary British cinema see Alexander Walker, *Icons in the Fire: The Decline and Fall of Almost Everybody in the British Film Industry 1984–2000* (London: Orion, 2004). Walker, who died in 2003, was a caustic critic of the British Film Institute and of the various forms of government-subsidised film-making. He might often have been unfair but his outspoken voice is sorely missed.

For a well-argued, left-wing critique of contemporary British cinema, see Paul Dave, *Visions of England: Class and Culture in Contemporary Cinema* (Oxford and New York: Berg, 2006).

44

Not Flagwaving but Flagdrowning, or Postcards from Post-Britain

WILLIAM BROWN

For some decades now it has been traditional to begin an essay on British cinema with a quotation from François Truffaut, Satyajit Ray or another established *auteur* about how a paradox is created when the word British is used alongside the word cinema. It is then traditional for the essayist in question to refute the comment through the analysis of some of Britain's more canonical films and film-makers. In this chapter, however, I shall work not against but *with* the idea of British cinema being a paradox, through the analysis of various films of the late 1990s and the 2000s that in one way or another are British, but which, whether through their content, their form and/or through their production history, can simultaneously be classified as 'post-British.'

The films that I shall cite both collectively and individually span a range of genres, they come from disparate backgrounds in terms of story, setting and financial backing, and they are not linked by any articulated agenda or manifesto. The 'Britishness' of these films is not always clear-cut, although I shall identify in each case the reasons for their paradoxical status as both British and post-British films. Not all are the result of British funding; not all have British directors. However, each in its own way reaffirms Britain and British cinema as a forerunner in the creation of a post-national (or, particularly and paradoxically, post-British) cinema.

Foremost among these films are *Three Businessmen* (Alex Cox, 1998), *Christie Malry's Own Double Entry* (Paul Tickell, 2000), *Last Resort* (Pawel Pawlikowski, 2000), *In This World* (Michael Winterbottom, 2002), *28 Days Later . . .* (Danny Boyle, 2002), *Millions* (Danny Boyle, 2004), *The Constant Gardener* (Fernando

Meirelles, 2005), *The Road to Guantanamo* (Michael Winterbottom/Mat Whitecross, 2006), *Children of Men* (Alfonso Cuarón, 2006), *V For Vendetta* (James McTeigue, 2005) and *This Is England* (Shane Meadows, 2006) – although I shall make reference to others.

A Cinema of Resistance

Contemporary British cinema seems to be a cinema of resistance. Many films use British money, a British setting or British characters to critique the political and economic status quo both at home and abroad. *Christie Malry's Own Double Entry*, for example, sees its hero form a double-entry ledger in order to balance the books of his life. For every irritation he suffers, Christie (Nick Moran) carries out an act of revenge. These become increasingly extreme as he poisons London's water supply and attempts to destroy the Houses of Parliament in a bid to vent his frustration with the lack of communication and human interaction that life as a bank clerk at the heart of the capital has to offer. *Christie Malry . . .* was overlooked by audiences in spite of promising reviews, partly because the film's release was limited in the aftermath of the destruction of New York's World Trade Center on 11 September 2001. After all, the film does not condemn and perhaps even leads the spectator to approve of Christie's terrorism (vicarious revenge for the ritual humiliation of daily life) – as befits his messianic name and character.

In 2006, however, only a year after the July bombings in London, *V for Vendetta* enjoyed a nationwide release in Britain. Its hero (Hugo Weaving) and heroine (Natalie Portman) succeed where Christie fails: destroying that most potent symbol of Britain's institutional power, the

V for Vendetta (James McTeigue, 2005)

Margaret Dickinson and Sarah Street argue that cultural significance rather than economics should determine the nationality of a film. *V for Vendetta*, an American and German co-production, is a case in point.

Though the film was made with American and German money, and has American and Australian leads and an Australian director, it was adapted from a cult comic book by British writer Alan Moore, features a strong cast of British and Irish actors, and was predominantly shot in the UK with a largely British crew. Its action takes place in a post-apocalyptic London governed by a fascist dictator (played by John Hurt in a curious inversion of his role as Winston Smith in Michael Radford's adaptation of Orwell's *Nineteen Eighty-Four*). Here the Guy Fawkes-masked V (Hugo Weaving) inspires a revolution that culminates in his protégée Evey (Natalie Portman) destroying the Houses of Parliament.

Although Richard Porton views the film as anti-George W. Bush (and therefore anti-American) in sentiment, its message applies equally to a contemporary Britain that is ripe for change. As Patrick Keiller's narrator points out in *London* (1994), it is ironic that Britain should celebrate 5 November, the date of a *failed* revolution – as if the British (compared to, say, the French, who celebrate Bastille Day) were inherently conservative. Rather than being a failure of revolution, however, *V for Vendetta* obviates the bleakness of *Nineteen Eighty-Four* and culminates in the glorious destruction of Parliament.[1]

If the V-sign originated as a sign from English archers to their enemies that they still had fingers to fire their arrows, a sign appropriated and used in Kenneth Branagh's *Henry V* (1989), and if the V-sign has traditionally been used to exclude non-British citizens ('Up Yours, Delors'), then the V-sign is here turned on the British powers that be and, unlike *Christie Malry . . .*'s

Remember, remember: V (Hugo Weaving) proposes a new revolution in *V for Vendetta*

own Guy Fawkes-inspired but failed gunpowder plot, the film ends with revolution and fireworks.

It is noteworthy that the destruction of Parliament takes place on page six in Moore's comic book, but is saved for last here. Unlike *Independence Day* (1996), in which the destruction of the White House takes place early on, allowing for the restitution of order by the end of the film, here the writers (the Wachowski Brothers, who made the similar terrorist fantasy *The Matrix* in 1999) save the cataclysm for last, suggesting open-endedness and hope where in other films there is only the sense of *plus ça change . . . .* Thus *V for Vendetta* marks an important landmark in post-British cinema.

NOTE

1. Another film that features events taking place on and around 5 November is Michael Winterbottom's *Wonderland* (1999), which more subtly uses that date to raise questions about Britain and Britishness.

FURTHER READING

Margaret Dickinson, and Sarah Street, *Cinema and State: The Film Industry and the British Government 1927–1984* (London: BFI, 1985).

Richard Porton, 'Review of *V for Vendetta*', *Cinéaste* vol. 31 no. 3, July 2006, pp. 52–4.

Houses of Parliament. The terrorist fantasy of a post-political Britain has grown from being expressed in a small and rarely seen British independent film into the subject of a big-budget and commercially successful blockbuster.

28 Days Later . . . and *Children of Men* both situate Britain as the locus for change and a new world order in the aftermath of apocalypse. The former sees Britain,

in particular London, depopulated by a viral epidemic. A handful of survivors, two male, two female, fall into the clutches of a sadistic group of male soldiers, whom they defeat before constructing a quarantined micro-commune where Irishman Jim (Cillian Murphy) and black heroine Selena (Naomie Harris) become the surrogate parents of young English girl Hannah (Megan Burns). In other words, the ultimate survivors are not the armed and brutal white British soldiers, but those who belong to minority national and ethnic groups within Britain.[1]

Children of Men involves an even clearer indication of humanity's future lying not in the hands of a white British male, but in those of a black female. Set in 2027, the film tells the story of Theo Faron (Clive Owen), a former activist who finds himself caught up in a plot to save Kee (Clare-Hope Ashitey), the only woman on Earth to have been pregnant since 2009. Although one might criticise the film for sympathising overtly with Theo, a white male (rather than with Kee), the film is ultimately about the necessity for Theo (whose name suggests the previous divine power enjoyed by the white male) to sacrifice himself if humanity is to start over.

Three Businessmen tells the story of Bennie Reyes (Miguel Sandoval) and Frank King (Alex Cox), who embark on a surrealist journey across the globe in search of a suitable meal, finally meeting up with a third businessman, Leroy Jasper (Robert Wisdom), to herald the arrival of a new matriarchal order to which they do not belong.

Three Businessmen (Alex Cox, 1998)

Hailed as a wunderkind of contemporary cinema, Alex Cox was arguably *the* name to watch following the cult successes of *Repo Man* (1984) and *Sid and Nancy* (1986). However, the films that followed (*Straight to Hell, Walker, El Patrullero, Death and the Compass, The Winner*) proved too anarchic and unpredictable for most audiences and critics. *Three Businessmen*, made for Cox's own Exterminating Angel production company and mainly set in his native Liverpool, is more disciplined though equally weird. It tells the story of two businessmen who, in search of food, travel from Liverpool to Rotterdam to Hong Kong to Tokyo and, finally, to Andalusia, where they meet the third of their number. This all takes place in the course of the same evening and without any indication of how they have managed to get from one place to the next.

The dialogue, which involves much improvisation, takes in many topics, including Liverpool, information technology, the Red Flag workers' anthem, and the *Mir* space station. In contrast to the chaos that characterises most of his films, here there is equanimity and calm. The film gently subverts our traditional notions of cinematic space by having the characters believe that they are still in Liverpool, in spite of evidence to the contrary; it seems that, in our globalised world, all space has become homogenised – and the fluid camerawork, which does not mark the transition between places, reinforces this. As Frank (Cox) says: "To me this isn't a foreign country." (Frank also delivers the memorable line: "England, how I hate it.") As a quasi-real-time movie, *Three Businessmen* also subverts the usual notions of cinematic time, with Cox choosing long takes instead of fragmenting experience into the action-filled snippets of narrative cinema.

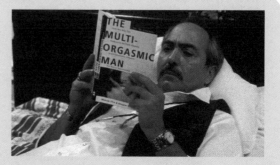

Bennie Reyes (Miguel Sandoval) unwinds in *Three Businessmen*

The film culminates in the three 'kings' (Bennie Reyes, Leroy Jasper, Frank King) seemingly witnessing the birth of a new, female Messiah – the significance of which is entirely lost on them. The scene, set in the Almeria desert, places a globalisation-era socio-economic spin on the film: the businessmen, the 'kings' of the world, are bored with their homogenised space, but they are also blind to the beauty of the desert and its role as the location for the rebirth of humanity.

Jonathan Romney describes the film as 'an object lesson in making the best of being marginal'. Cox uses his 'rootlessness' to tell a story about post-national identity and living in the contemporary world. Vastly underrated, the film might now stand as an important work in the evolution of post-British cinema – and help to reinstate Cox as a director worthy of attention.

FURTHER READING

Maximilien Le Cain, 'Interview with Alex Cox and Tod Davies, *Senses of Cinema*, January 2003, <www.sensesofcinema.com/contents/03/24/cox_davies.html>. Accessed 30 September 2007.

Jonathan Romney, 'Distributor Wanted', *Film Comment* vol. 36 no. 3, May 2000, pp. 18–19.

Tourists, Terrorists and Skinheads

If the above films posit fantasies of a post-national Britain, then other films challenge our notions of 'Britishness' through their apparently realistic portrayal of the present and the recent past. Pawel Pawlikowski's *Last Resort* follows Russian immigrant Tanya (Dina Korzun) and her son Artyom (Artyom Strelnikov) as they struggle to get by in an out-of-season, dead-end seaside town, the concrete barrenness of which provides an apocalyptic backdrop to their plight at the hands of a disinterested and uncaring British government. Tanya meets Alfie (Paddy Considine), a dubious bingo-caller, and a tentative relationship develops between them. But the film ends with Tanya and Artyom returning home, disillusioned with a Britain that is so mistrustful of and abusive towards outsiders.

In This World also deals with immigration. A documentary of sorts, the film follows Afghan refugees Jamal (Jamal Udin Torabi) and Enayat (Enayatullah) from Peshawar and along the 'Silk Road' in a bid to make it to Britain. Like *Last Resort* – as well as Stephen Frears's *Dirty Pretty Things* (2002) and Nick Broomfield's *Ghosts*

(2006) – *In This World* does not leave much space for hope for those seeking refuge in this country, although its use of a commentating voice-over overtly seeks to place responsibility for the plight of refugees like Jamal and Enayat on the shoulders of Britain, which becomes 'fortress-like' in the sense that it is impenetrable and unwelcoming to outsiders.

If foreign citizens seeking asylum in Britain find it inhospitable and intolerant, then *The Road to Guantanamo* and *This Is England* show how Britain has been and continues to treat its own citizens from ethnic minorities as outsiders. *The Road to Guantanamo* charts the plight of the so-called Tipton Three as they are arrested and held in the Guantanamo Bay prison in Cuba under suspicion of involvement in terrorist organisations – seemingly with little help or defence from the British government. *This Is England*, set during the early 1980s, shows a group of young friends of various races torn apart by the return of an overt racist. Twelve-year-old Shaun (Thomas Turgoose) falls in with a group of skinheads who, in spite of their intimidating appearance, are a respectful and loyal group of friends of

Shaun (Thomas Turgoose) flagdrowning in *This Is England* (Shane Meadows, 2006)

different sexes and race. It is only when former convict and outright racist Combo (Stephen Graham) arrives that the group falls apart. Exposed to the radical politics of Britain's neo-fascist movement, Shaun and friends realise that the 'pure' England for which Combo fights, an England that would entail no racial 'combo' (an irony made all the more pointed by Stephen Graham's own mixed race), is not the inclusive and friendly community to which they belonged before Combo's arrival. However, as Combo spirals out of control and out of Shaun's life, the group rehabilitates itself smoothly and quickly, suggesting that an innocent and inclusive society can exist, even after corrupting influences have made their mark. The film ends with a shot of the St George's Cross sinking into the sea: what *This Is England* seems to be saying is that society breaks down when one is forced to live according to an arbitrary notion of 'nationality' defined by flags and other symbols of national identity. Meadows tries to show how the emergence of a multicultural form of expression (in this case, ska music and reggae) can be twisted to nationalist ends, warning us perhaps that a 'national' cinema' might equally become a perversion of more innocent aims.

Millions and *The Constant Gardener* critique a materially wealthy Britain (through very different strategies) for failing to use its economic superiority to help others or to adopt an ethical approach to business abroad. In *Millions*, a fortune lands in the lap of schoolchildren Damian (Alex Etel) and Anthony (Lewis McGibbon) following a bungled train robbery on the eve of Britain's conversion to the euro. The children find themselves the target of a greed-driven robber (Christopher Fulford), who is seeking to regain the stolen money (which is denominated in sterling), before the currency change makes it worthless. *Millions* implicitly criticises the practice of pound-chasing, preferring the prospect of a (post-?) Britain that is more fully integrated into the European Union. Not only this: in *Millions'* final moments, the whole film unexpectedly relocates to Africa, thereby broadening its scope from a British to a European and finally to a global level. Anthony and Damian, having learnt of the corrupting power of money (be it British or European), prefer to use their millions not by investing it, but by giving it to charity and helping needy children in Africa.

In *The Constant Gardener*, Tessa Quayle (Rachel Weisz) dies in her attempts to unmask a corrupt pharmaceutical industry, to which the British government is seen to turn a blind eye. When her widower Justin (Ralph Fiennes) picks up the trail of her investigations, he uncovers her murder and, in a journey that takes him from the Kenyan desert to London, exposes the higher powers that have been involved. *The Constant Gardener* differs subtly from other films concerning British citizens involved in murky African affairs. While *Shooting Dogs* (Michael Caton-Jones, 2005) and *The Last King of Scotland* (Kevin MacDonald, 2006) might also tackle the role of British citizens in Africa (and, in the case of *The Last King of Scotland*, the role of the British in African political affairs), both of those films end with the return of the protagonist to Britain (i.e. they reaffirm the British white male's nationality). In *The Constant Gardener*, however, Tessa and Justin both die, the former in Africa and the latter in an unknown and unknowable location. Their willingness to renounce their 'Britishness' and to sacrifice themselves for Africa rather than to see it as a tourist destination, makes *The Constant Gardener* an exemplar of post-British cinema.

Questions of Style and Questions of Genre

The post-British cinema that I wish to describe takes something from the documentary realist tradition that has been so influential in British cinema, but it also shows awareness of the oneiric fictions of Michael Powell and Emeric Pressburger and the surrealism inherent in the documentaries of Humphrey Jennings and the feature films of Lindsay Anderson.[2] However, perhaps the most important influence on the post-British cinema is Luis Buñuel, whose work similarly straddles documentary (*Las Hurdes*, 1932), politically engaged social realism (*Los Olvidados*, 1950) and surrealism. Paul Tickell cites Buñuel's *The Criminal Life of Archibaldo de la Cruz* (1955) as a key source for *Christie Malry*, where the intermingling of fantasy and reality becomes increasingly difficult to disentangle as Christie's psychosis deepens.[3] Alex Cox named his production company after Buñuel's 1962 film *Exterminating Angel*, where sheep wander freely into the house that has entrapped its dinner guests and the church that has imprisoned its congregation, and a disconsolate but seemingly harmless brown bear makes sporadic appearances. Alfonso Cuarón recalls these surrealist moments in *Children of Men*: a zebra is led through St James's Park, a gazelle trots through a derelict school, a sheepdog drives a flock through the Bexhill-on-Sea refugee camp as Theo and Kee make their escape bid. Buñuel's sheep appear in the house after the dinner guests have begun to turn on each other; in *Children of Men* they presage the vicious fighting that will reduce Bexhill to Fallujah-like devastation.

In addition to Buñuel's influence, various of the films locate their action in liminal spaces such as deserts and coastal areas. *Three Businessmen* ends in Almeria where a Buñuelian donkey and cart transports the besuited businessmen. The switch to a sand-strewn Africa in *Millions* also becomes a surreal (and possibly dreamed) experience through its unannounced abruptness. The desert plays a prominent role in *The Road to Guantanamo* and *In This World*, which could together be seen as an attempt to re-imagine the globe without national borders. *In This World*, shot primarily on Digital Video, is punctuated by narrated segments featuring computerised and aerial views of the route that Jamal and Enayat follow. Boundaries exist in the virtual map that the computer simulation depicts but not in the footage of the 'real' world, emphasising the artificiality of nations and national identity.

Last Resort and *Children of Men* both use international waters to subvert notions of national identity: the scene in which Alfie takes Tanya and Artyom to safety by boat could be seen as the only utopian (from the Greek *ou-topos*, meaning 'no-place') moment in *Last Resort*; whereas, fittingly, it is at sea (and in thick fog) that Theo delivers Kee to the Human Project, a quasi-mythical and a-national group that can ensure the survival of humanity. It is surely no coincidence that Pawlikowski shot his film in Margate; for it is in Margate that Lindsay Anderson filmed his 1953 documentary *O Dreamland*, which investigates this seaside resort in its heyday, before cheap flights dispersed the holidaymakers who had made it prosperous. The very title *Last Resort* evokes the final throes of a place that was once quintessentially British, and which is now populated by refugees and pornographers. The association of Margate with finality can also be found in *Last Orders* (Fred Schepisi, 2001), which similarly involves Margate as the setting for the end of 'good old' British values as friends gather to spread the ashes of deceased British butcher Jack Dodds.

The films not only use deserts and seascapes to give them an a- or trans-national texture, but they also subvert nationality by using recognisable British locations in an unusual and defamiliarising manner. *Last Resort's* depiction of an out-of-season Margate, *28 Days Later . . .'s* eerily deserted London, and the squalid dystopian London and Bexhill-on-Sea of *Children of Men* make us look at these familiar British locations with fresh eyes,

following the surrealist project of showing 'the fantastic at the heart of the natural'.[4]

The way in which the action is framed in these films guides the audience towards a more 'global' or holistic perspective, emphasising a wider, political point of view. *Last Resort*, and *28 Days Later . . .*, for example, both use extreme long-shots rather than character-driven framing. *The Constant Gardener* similarly decentres the human story. A memorable shot involves the orange-red floor of Lake Turkana, with Tessa's overturned car barely in frame (we see a wheel spinning in the top corner. Instead of foregrounding the crashed vehicle, Meirelles makes the action almost invisible (appropriate to a film that deals with the invisible dealings of multinational corporations), leading the spectator to recognise that politics are a human phenomenon made to characterise and divide up an otherwise indifferent earth.

Long shots and continuous takes characterise *Three Businessmen*, *Last Resort* and *Children of Men*, indicating that each film mixes techniques of documentary film-making with more conventional techniques of narrative (montage and human-centred framing). However, nowhere is documentary technique adopted in the services of downplaying narrative more than in the films of Michael Winterbottom. Winterbottom entirely blurs the boundary between documentary and fiction – and not just in his openly politicised films *In This World*, *The Road to Guantanamo* and *A Mighty Heart* (2007), which, with Broomfield's *Ghosts* and Kevin Macdonald's *Touching the Void* (2003), reinvigorated the 're-enactment' film. His playful comedies *24 Hour Party People* (2002) and *A Cock and Bull Story* (2005), together with his music-and-sex film *9 Songs* (2004), become, in effect, documentaries of their own making; the immense amount of footage generated by his digital video cameras creating confusion as to when the acting/fiction begins and ends.

Winterbottom's deliberate confusion of genres is mirrored by other post-British films in their canny use of genre to hide and – paradoxically – to make more subversive their political content. While *The Constant Gardener* might be criticised for being a white couple's love story in Africa, while *Dirty Pretty Things* might be too much of a thriller for its social comment to be foregrounded, and while *Children of Men* and *V For Vendetta* might be deemed too sci-fi- or action-based to merit serious consideration, I would argue that it is precisely through their use of genre that their political content becomes more powerful. If, as experimental film-maker Chris Petit has pointed out, the English establishment has always incorporated the anti-establishment, then it is perhaps by embracing the cinematic 'establishment' that is generic convention that a subversively post-British cinema can take seed.[5] André Breton, the founder of surrealism, argues in the Second Surrealist Manifesto that surrealism must hide itself in order to fulfil its revolutionary potential.[6] Where better to hide than in the mainstream?

Post-cinematic Technology

It is a commonplace to claim that the turn to digital involves cinema without film.[7] However, this does not mean that the role of digital technology, both in terms of the construction and in terms of the content of many 'post-British' films, is not relevant. Information technology, especially its relationship to drug dealing, is discussed at length in *Three Businessmen*; *Last Resort* touches on the lurid world of online pornography; *Millions* marvels at the speed of satellite-enabled telephony; *The Constant Gardener* places emphasis on webcams and electronic communication technology. Each reports how, whether for better or for worse, advances in technology break down national barriers, while imbalances in technological sophistication lead to stratification and the reinforcement of differences.

The use of digital technology to make the films also helps to raise questions of national identity. There are two key ways in which digital technology is used in these films: the first is through the use of image manipulation and digital special effects (seen in *V for Vendetta*, *Children of Men* and *Millions*); the second is through the use of DV rather than film as a means of shooting (as in *28 Days Later . . .*, *In This World*, and other Michael Winterbottom films).

The former category, especially in *V for Vendetta*, sees narrative replaced by spectacle during the moments where the digital special effects become most visible. Given that *V for Vendetta*'s most spectacular moments are those moments where symbols of Britishness are destroyed (St Paul's Cathedral and Parliament), Britishness becomes equated with a virtual (and false) spectacle, while the narrative of 'real life' involves trying to stave off such symbols. The people of Britain themselves adopt a symbol (V's Guy Fawkes mask) to unite in their struggle against the oppressive regime, but at the film's climax they remove their masks and celebrate their diversity. In *Children of Men*'s London of 2027, the city is filled with moving image screens relaying propagandist news: once again, national identity is rendered as a spectacle. However, Cuarón does not allow his

camera to focus too much on these details, thus subverting their status as 'special' effects/spectacles. By relegating the 'special' effects to the background, the national identity with which they are associated (messages to the British people) is downplayed in favour of the film's narrative. Given that the film is also characterised by continuous shots (hand-held and Steadicam), which serve to heighten realism, Cuarón transports us into a simultaneously familiar and unfamiliar London, further subverting the identity of the city within its national context.

Shooting on DV helps to serve a similar defamiliarising function. The graininess of the DV image heightens realism, seeming to lend to the image an aura of authenticity, but it also lessens its 'cinematic' feel (and therefore its 'falseness'). In the case of Winterbottom, his emphasis on post-production (sifting through hundreds of hours of footage shot by multiple cameras) downplays the *mise en scène* that is so overtly fetishised in British heritage cinema and the picture-postcard views of London presented by contemporary romantic comedies.

The use of digital special effects and the decision to shoot on DV create a further condition that enables a post-British cinema. Or, to put it more clearly, they also enable a British post-cinema. Since neither digital special effects nor DV had a place in the lexicon of traditional film-making techniques, both serve to expand cinema beyond its old boundaries. Within the context of a national cinema, such changes in the ways in which films are constructed points to the possibility of a nation that has also expanded beyond its old boundaries, and which deserves to be approached from a post-national (and in this case, a post-British) perspective.

Perhaps it is fitting that, in a post-film world, the emphasis placed on post-production by the likes of Winterbottom means that British film-makers are not producing cinema as it is traditionally understood. Rather, theirs is a 'post-cinematic' cinema that renders the phrase 'British cinema' a contradiction in terms – thus allowing us to turn Truffaut and Ray's own words against them. Digital technologies serve to create a new cinema that, in its mode of production, in its content and in its style, is exciting and original, at once post-cinematic and post-British.[8]

The Naive Mainstream?

If *Three Businessmen* and *Christie Malry* were not commercial successes, several of the other post-British films that I have mentioned have gained both popularity at the box office and won awards at prestigious festivals.[9] As Sarah Street argues, the 'increasing blurring of boundaries between art or oppositional cinema and the mainstream has created opportunities for "other cinemas" which challenge traditional conceptions of British cinema'.[10] However, while these films are popular, several of them, including *Millions, The Constant Gardener, V for Vendetta, In This World* and *The Road to Guantanamo*, have been accused of simplistic politics and/or of failing to engage in an even-handed manner with the political ideas that they present.[11] In other words, their naive and one-sided call for political change renders them films for the impractical idealist.

I would argue, however, that the ways in which these films re-imagine Britain and Britishness are deeply unsettling, not least because they refuse to evoke a mythical and idealised British past. Some of the films depict the end of Britain through an apocalyptic future (*Christie Malry, 28 Days Later . . ., Children of Men, V for Vendetta*). Others filter Britishness through an international perspective (*Three Businessmen, Last Resort, In This World, Millions, The Road to Guantanamo* and *The Constant Gardener*). This international perspective is reinforced when we consider that several of the filmmakers involved are not of British origin: Alfonso Cuarón is Mexican, Fernando Meirelles Brazilian, James McTeigue Australian, Pawel Pawlikowski Polish.[12] When the films do appeal to British traditions, they do so in a problematising manner. For example, *A Cock and Bull Story* refuses to become the adaptation of Laurence Sterne's *Tristram Shandy* that it purports to be (we are far too caught up in the 'real' lives of Steve Coogan and Rob Brydon to follow its hazy plot) while *24 Hour Party People* similarly fails to differentiate myth from fact in its depiction of the 'Madchester' scene of the 1970s onwards. Finally, Shane Meadows's *This Is England* dares to portray skinheads as innocent scamps. This a-historicising tendency contributes to the accusations of naivety, but it also means that these films resist easy definition, both in terms of genre and in terms of established political trends.

If these films feature a white male's privileged and 'naive' vision of the redistribution of wealth and social and racial equality, they do so in such a way as to renounce that privilege – be that through giving up money, literal self-sacrifice, or by exacting a revolution. The seemingly ubiquitous resistance to authority and to the weight of the past with respect to Britain and its national identity is itself subversive and challenges notions of Anglo-centric Britishness. Collectively, the films call not just for the abandonment of British identity as a fixed and definable entity, but for the abandonment *tout court* of Britain and Britishness in a globalised world. Hence the destruction of Parliament in *V for Vendetta* and the desired destruction of Parliament in *Christie Malry*. Hence the fantasy of a post-apocalyptic Britain in *28 Days Later . . .* and *Children of Men*. Hence the desire to criticise a Britain that places too much emphasis on preserving its own national identity in *Last Resort, In This World* and *The Road to Guantanamo*. Hence the desire to leave Britain and to help the Third World in *Millions* and *The Constant Gardener*. Hence the desire to see the St George's Cross not waving but drowning in *This Is England*.

Notes

1. It is noteworthy that the only black soldier is infected with the deadly Rage virus before Jim, Selena and Hannah's arrival. The indication seems clearly to be that he is 'other' to the rest of the all-male and all-white group of soldiers. In fact, it is with his help that Jim, Selena and Hannah manage to escape, suggesting that they too are 'other'; that the real enemy is not the virus but the white patriarchy, and that this patriarchy is ultimately doomed.

2. See Geoffrey Nowell-Smith, 'Humphrey Jennings: Surrealist Observer', in Charles Barr (ed.), *All Our Yesterdays: 90 Years of British Cinema* (London: BFI, 1986) and Lester Friedman and Scott Stewart, 'The Tradition of Independence: An Interview with Lindsay Anderson', in Wheeler Winston Dixon (ed.), *Re-Viewing British Cinema, 1900–1992: Essays and Interviews* (New York: State University of New York Press, 1994).

3. Richard Marshall, 'A Double Entry: Interview with Paul Tickell', *3:AM Magazine*, November 2002, <www.3ammagazine.com/litarchives/2002_nov/interview_paul_tickell.html>. Accessed 30 September 2007.

4. John Orr uses this phrase to describe *Orphans* (Peter Mullan, 1997), *Trainspotting* (Danny Boyle, 1996), *The Butcher Boy* (Neil Jordan, 1997) and *Sexy Beast* (Jonathan Glazer, 2000), themselves arguably post-British films. See Orr, 'New Directions in European Cinema', p. 308.

5. Petit quoted in James Park, *Learning to Dream* (London: Faber and Faber, 1984), p. 19.

6. 'Je demande l'occultation profonde, véritable du surréalisme'. Breton, *Manifestes du surréalisme*, p. 128.

7. See, for example, Matt Hansen, *The End of Celluloid: Film Futures in the Digital Age* (Mies: RotoVision, 2004).

8. We can expand this argument to include not only films shot using digital cameras, but also films that use digital special effects to enhance their look and feel (and which are often not deliberately signalled as 'special' effects).

Examples of these latter include (most obviously) *Children of Men* and *V For Vendetta*.

9. *Last Resort* won thirteen prizes at festivals and award ceremonies. *In This World* won a BAFTA for Best Film Not in the English Language and the Golden Bear at the 2003 Berlin International Film Festival. *28 Days Later . . .* won seven prizes at festivals and award ceremonies. *The Constant Gardener* won an Oscar (Rachel Weisz for Best Supporting Actress) and a BAFTA (Best Editing), as well as being nominated for several more. *The Road to Guantanamo* won a Silver Bear at the 2006 Berlin International Film Festival. *Children of Men* won nineteen awards and was nominated for three Oscars (Best Cinematography, Best Editing, Best Adapted Screenplay). *This Is England* has won four awards, including Best Film at the 2006 British Independent Film Awards.

10. Street, *British National Cinema*, p. 3.

11. Richard Kelly protests that *In This World* is 'no more informative, possibly even less involving, than umpteen pieces of print and reportage', and consequently does not properly get to grips with its topic, '*In This World*', *Sight and Sound*, April 2003, p. 40. Ben Walters describes *Millions* as 'more *Amélie* than *Night of the Hunter*', '*Millions*', *Sight and Sound*, December 2004, p. 58, which suggests that the film does not give full contemplation to its darker, more political elements. Edward Gallafent argues that *The Constant Gardener* 'is a film that does not try to prove that its political insights are true. Rather, it assumes that we accept them, even if we do so with resignation, or anger, or cynicism', i.e. the film does not engage properly with its political content. 'Intuitions in Africa', *CineAction*, November 2006, p. 61. Geoff Andrew believes that *The Road to Guantanamo* is 'predicated on a wholly unquestioning acceptance of the men's own account of why they were in Afghanistan and what befell them', '*The Road to Guantanamo*', *Time Out*, 8–15 March 2006, <www.timeout.com/film/reviews/83540/The_Road_to_Guantanamo.html>. Accessed 10 October 2007. Richard Porton suggests that *V for Vendetta* could be read as 'little more than [a] self-negating manifestation of the "society of the spectacle"', '*V for Vendetta*', *Cinéaste*, July 2006, p. 54.

12. It is also worthy of note that some of the film-makers, while being British, started their careers outside Britain or, more specifically, England. Alex Cox started out in the USA (before spending a long period making films in Mexico). Danny Boyle, who is from Manchester, estab-

lished his reputation through Scottish films *Shallow Grave* (1994) and *Trainspotting* (1996). Other noteworthy Boyle films include *The Beach* (2000), which is about the desire to find an apolitical space in the context of a planet defined by 'nationalised' tourist destinations, and *Sunshine* (2007), which discards all notions of the national as a team of international astronauts travel to the Sun to save humanity not in the name of America (as in *Independence Day*), but in the name of humanity. Carlisle-born Paul Tickell transferred from documentary to fiction through his Irish film *Crush Proof* (1998). Winterbottom's films – which also include *With or without You* (1999), set in Belfast, *Welcome to Sarajevo* (1997), *The Claim* (2000), a transposition of Thomas Hardy's *The Mayor of Casterbridge* to the Klondike gold fields, and *A Mighty Heart* (2007), notable for its location-shooting in the crowded and dangerous streets of Karachi – can be characterised as alternately transnational, a-national or post-national.

This leaves only Meadows, whose regional films (all set in the Midlands) challenge the London-centric view of Britain as put forward by the majority of British films, but which are without doubt English – even if, as in *This Is England*, they challenge conventional interpretations of Englishness.

Bibliography

Breton, André, *Manifestes du surréalisme* (Paris: Gallimard, 2000).

Elsaesser, Thomas, *European Cinema: Face to Face with Hollywood* (Amsterdam: Amsterdam University Press, 2005).

Higson, Andrew, '"Britain's Outstanding Contribution to Film": The Documentary-Realist Tradition', in Charles Barr (ed.), *All Our Yesterdays: 90 Years of British Cinema* (London: BFI, 1986).

Higson, Andrew, *Waving the Flag: Constructing a National Cinema in Britain* (Oxford: Clarendon Press, 1995).

MacCabe, Colin, 'A Post-National European Cinema: A Consideration of Derek Jarman's *The Tempest* and *Edward II*', in Duncan Petrie (ed.), *Screening Europe: Image and Identity in Contemporary European Cinema* (London: BFI, 1992).

Orr, John, 'New Directions in European Cinema', in Elizabeth Ezra (ed.), *European Cinema* (Oxford: Oxford University Press, 2004).

Street, Sarah, *British National Cinema* (London and New York: Routledge, 1997).

Postscript: A Short History of British Cinema

ROBERT MURPHY

1. The Pleasure Garden

Trains rushing by; a wall being knocked down; a kiss; a cameraman being swallowed; a man being run over by a car; firemen putting out a fire; a burglar being chased: simple spectacles, naive tricks. British cinema was good at this sort of thing. Enterprising showmen like Walter Haggar, adaptable magic-lantern men like Cecil Hepworth, ambitious photographers like James Williamson, took to the cinema like ducks to water. Britain had a tradition of optical entertainment, and for a dozen years or so British film-makers were as vigorous and popular and inventive as anyone. Charles Barr demonstrates the narrative sophistication of *Rescued by Rover* (Lewin Fitzhamon, 1905), but also points out that it was a small-scale, family affair.[1] While America created a major industry, Britain remained at the stage of small family businesses.

In the 1920s enterprising young entrepreneurs like Herbert Wilcox and Michael Balcon tried to update British film production by importing American stars for their films and seeking out co-production deals with German companies. The director they most relied on was Jack Graham Cutts, a proficient film-maker but an incessant intriguer who did his best to blight the prospects of two of his rivals, Adrian Brunel and Alfred Hitchcock. Brunel was easily shouldered aside and never did fulfil his early promise, but Hitchcock proved more formidable.

Hitchcock's first film, *The Pleasure Garden* (1926), was made at the Emelka Studio in Munich and, like later Euro-puddings, has a strangely decentred feel about it. It is oddly structured and, as Raymond Durgnat comments, 'It's hard to tell now whether this unusual shape was a product of English primitivism or of Hitchcock's sophistication.'[2] Two sequences attest to Hitchcock's odd sensibility. The first, combining eroticism with comedy, occurs after Patsy (Virginia Valli), the stout-hearted heroine, offers to share her bed with Jill (Carmelita Geraghty), a provincial innocent she has rescued from lecherous stage-door Johnnies. Jill isn't as innocent as she pretends and she later develops into a ruthless femme fatale. As she kneels in her nightdress to say her bedtime prayers, Patsy's dog sniffs her out, distracting her by licking the soles of her feet. The second sequence, demonstrating Hitchcock's penchant for the macabre, comes after Patsy, spurned by Jill, accepts the marriage proposal of a dry, passionless man called Levet (Miles Mander). Her tearful wave to him as he sails off to the tropics to resume his colonial career dissolves into the frantically happy wave of a native girl (Nita Naldi) welcoming him back to a full-blooded, sensual relationship. When Patsy follows him out, Levet discards his lover. Disconsolately she walks into the sea. Levet wades in after her. She turns, smiling, towards him, thinking he wants her after all. But no, he grabs her only to push her head under the waves, making sure she is well and truly drowned.

2. Rich and Strange

The British film industry in the 1930s was a peculiar amalgam – talented refugees from Germany, Austria, Poland, Hungary rubbed shoulders with 'ace' technicians imported from Hollywood, British veterans from the silent period, and ambitious young men determined to grasp the opportunities offered by a new and expanding industry. The chapters in this book by Sarah

Street, Lawrence Napper, Linda Wood, Tom Ryall and Kevin Gough-Yates attest to an interest in the fully fledged industry of the mid-30s, with its flamboyant émigrés, its financial shenanigans and its contrasting modes of production, and Christine Gledhill has restored the reputation of the silent films of the late 1920s. But the British cinema of the early 30s, the period between the coming of sound in 1929 and Korda's success with *The Private Life of Henry VIII* in 1933, remains neglected. Crackly sound, stagy acting, ridiculously plummy accents, make early sound films difficult to take, but once through these off-putting barriers one enters a fascinatingly unfamiliar world.

Hitchcock seemed to make a highly successful transition from silent to sound film, organising the shooting of *Blackmail* (1929) in such a way that it was possible to convert it quickly and release it as Britain's first sound film. His subsequent early sound films, however, share the neglect suffered by the whole of British cinema during this period. Thus a witty, revealing film like *Rich and Strange* (1931) comes as an agreeable surprise.

A huge clock hovers over the heads of serried ranks of clerks as they pack away their adding machines and make for the door. Crowds push and shove their way onto a tube train. Fred (Henry Kendall) stands out from the crowd because his umbrella won't open, his newspaper gets into a tangle and he wrecks a woman's hat. Arriving at his suburban home, he finds his wife busy with her sewing machine and has only an evening listening to the wireless ('Mr Baker will give his twelfth talk on accountancy in three minutes') to look forward to. 'The best place for us is the gas oven,' complains

Innocents fascinated by the oddness of the world. Henry Kendall and Joan Barry begin their journey in *Rich and Strange* (Alfred Hitchcock, 1931)

Fred, but escape from this purgatorial existence comes with the evening post. A rich uncle has decided to grant Fred his wish to see life, providing him with enough money to go on a world cruise.

Amid the sybaritic luxury of a sea cruise, Fred's marriage disintegrates. As he languishes, seasick, below deck, his wife Em (Joan Barry) emerges from under his shadow. She tells a pipe-smoking plantation owner on his way home back east, 'I can talk to you because you're just a man and not my husband.' But she finds she likes being listened to and treated with respect. Fred himself falls prey to an adventuress masquerading as a princess (played by German vamp Betty Amann), and it seems that the couple must part. But when Em learns that the princess is a fraud and that her pompous, gullible, selfish husband will have to learn about life the hard way, she decides she must return to him. Ungracefully, he accepts that he has been a fool and the couple find a bickering but more equal partnership as they make their hazardous way home to the now reassuring comforts of suburbia.

Tom Milne claims that Hitchcock is 'extraordinarily scathing about the timidity and emotional reserve of his central characters: innocence of the most banal and compromised kind confronts experience in the form of exotic strangers and risks, and responds by retreating further into its shell'.[3] But he misreads the tone of the film, which is gently rather than cruelly mocking, and comes from a man himself an innocent fascinated by the oddness of a real world which is unknowably rich and strange.

3. The Common Touch

Although the requisitioning of studios and recruitment into the armed services left the British film industry much depleted during World War II, this is still regarded as a period when British films flowered. Patriotic enthusiasm should not be allowed to obscure the fact that the war years produced nothing to equal the musicals, the comedies, the Hitchcock thrillers of the 30s, not to mention European-inspired experiments like Berthold Viertel's *The Passing of the Third Floor Back* (1935) or Lothar Mendes's *The Man Who Could Work Miracles* (1936). But the war films evoke values – bravery, self-sacrifice, social harmony, unselfish pulling together for the common good – which we have now lost. Documentaries like Harry Watt's *London Can Take It* (1940) and Humphrey Jennings's *Listen to Britain* (1941); feature films like Noël Coward and David Lean's *In Which We Serve* (1942) or the more ruggedly egalitarian *Millions Like Us* (Frank Launder and Sidney Gilliat, 1943) and *The Way Ahead* (Carol Reed, 1944) encapsulate an ethos which is moving and powerful. But the most plangent manifestation of wartime populism resides in the now almost forgotten films of John Baxter.

Baxter made a series of low-budget films in the 30s – *Doss House* (1933), *Say It with Flowers* (1933), *The Song of the Plough* (1933), *Music Hall* (1934), *Song of the Road* (1937) – which dwell uniquely, if sentimentally, on the problems of the poor. When war broke out in 1939, Baxter formed an alliance with Lady Yule, a millionairess determined that her company, British National, should expand rather than abandon production. Baxter's contribution was a series of films (*Love on the Dole*, 1941; *The Common Touch*, 1941; *Let the People Sing*, 1942; *Shipbuilders*, 1943), which pleaded for a post-war society where the evils of the past – unemployment, poverty, class conflict, injustice – would be banished.

If *Love on the Dole* is the most accomplished of these films, *The Common Touch* is the most revealing. It is essentially a bigger-budget version of Baxter's earlier film, *Doss House*, where an undercover journalist investigates what it is like to be down and out in London. In *The Common Touch* a public-schoolboy inherits his father's property company and decides it would be a good wheeze to find out about life in the shelter for down and outs which his managers want to demolish to make way for an ambitious new development. Tony Aldgate and Geoff Brown point out that in *The Common Touch* Baxter restores those elements – cabaret scenes, 'sex appeal' and a romantic subplot – which *Doss House* had won praise from the critics for leaving out.[4] Nonetheless, documentary film-maker Edgar Anstey, who had condemned his colleague Humphrey Jennings's *Listen to Britain* as 'the rarest piece of fiddling since the days of Nero', praised Baxter's 'curious and individual quality of fantasy and of lyricism' and concluded that 'the rich colour of its characterisation and the gusto of its symbolism give the film some of the simple wisdom of a medieval allegory'.[5] Indeed Baxter's utopian populism is a cultural strand which might be traced back to John Ball and the Peasants' Revolt.

4. I Know Where I'm Going

When the war ended in 1945 the British film industry seemed set to conquer the world. British films, once seen as something to be ashamed of, were now lauded by the critics for their realism and maturity. Production,

at last, appeared to be organised on a sound financial basis with a large conglomerate – the Rank Organisation – big and powerful enough to challenge the American majors. And there seemed an abundance of talent – directors, producers, actors, technicians – capable of producing films as good as anything that Hollywood or Europe could offer.

The most successful and inventive of this new talent was distilled into a small company called The Archers, which worked under the umbrella of the Rank-financed Independent Producers. Its two leading lights, Michael Powell and Emeric Pressburger, had made a series of successful films – *The Spy in Black* (1939), *Contraband* (1940), *49th Parallel* (1941), *One of Our Aircraft Is Missing* (1942) – and were given virtual *carte blanche* by Rank to make what they liked. They rewarded Rank's faith with *The Life and Death of Colonel Blimp* (1943), which Churchill did his best to block, and the audaciously eccentric *A Canterbury Tale* (1944).

Their next film, *I Know Where I'm Going* (1945), was quickly written by Emeric Pressburger and has the powerful simplicity of a fairy-story. A bank manager's daughter travels up to Scotland to marry her boss. All her life she has been able to get what she wanted, but at the very last stage of her journey, a short trip across a strait of water to the island where her future husband awaits her, she is held back by the weather. Nonplussed that she cannot control the elements – her wish that the wind blow away the mist is answered by a storm which makes crossing even more hazardous – she is forced to recognise that what the fates have decreed for her is different from what she thought she wanted.

Kevin Gough-Yates stresses the film's concern with exile and cultural bewilderment.[6] But it is also an archetypal tale of love and destiny. The Scottish settings are real enough (much of the film was shot on the island of Mull), but Powell and Pressburger transmute them into a *Brigadoon*-like never-never land. The characters played by Pamela Brown, Captain Knight and Nancy Price, sharing their dim, ruined halls with dogs and eagles, belong as much to Gormenghast as to Scotland, but they are something more than picturesque eccentrics. Their lives, ruled by the elements, rooted in the landscape, represent a reality that is timeless and natural and implicitly more worthwhile than the busy, organised life of the Englishwoman Joan (Wendy Hiller). Catriona (Pamela Brown), from her first appearance as she comes in out of the storm with a pack of huge Irish wolfhounds, haunts the film. With goddess-like dignity she gives up Torquil (Roger Livesey) to Joan and pushes him into the decisive action that will save her from drowning.

Britain's attempt on the world market failed, but *I Know Where I'm Going* and its successors – *A Matter of Life and Death* (1946), *Black Narcissus* (1947), *The Red Shoes* (1948) and *The Small Back Room* (1949) – make up a dazzling sequence of films that any national cinema would be proud of.

5. Reach for the Sky

Respectability, deference, caution, consensus marked the 50s, but beneath the tranquil surface lurked the dreadful memory of the war. World War II, like most wars, was fought by very young men (the average age of Battle of Britain pilots was twenty-one), and for those who survived it was likely to be the most traumatic but also the most exciting period of their lives. War films allowed an opportunity to relive and come to terms with that experience. And for the generation who grew up surrounded by bombed building sites and tales of the war, these films vouchsafed a glimpse into a dangerous world that they had been too young to experience directly.

There is another reason for the popularity of British war films in the 50s. They were something the British film industry did well. Unlike musicals or Westerns or gangster films, war films didn't seem to be the exclusive preserve of Hollywood. Britain's role in winning World War II, though less significant than was believed at the time, was significant enough to fuel a body of often exciting and sometimes serious films. Like the horror films that began to emerge from Hammer studios after 1957, 50s war films constituted a genre. British World War II films were very successful in commercial terms, but their stiff-upper-lip style proved unacceptable to later critics. Neil Rattigan sees them as evidence of a conspiracy: 'a reflection of the last ditch effort by the dominant class to maintain its hegemony by re-writing the history of the celluloid war in its own favour'.[7] And Andy Medhurst claims that:

> In the dominant, common-sense history of British cinema such films are seen as at best worthily dull, at worst the absolute epitome of the cinema of tight-lipped middle-class repression soon to be rightfully swept away by the social realist impetus of the late 1950s.[8]

Medhurst attempts a partial re-evaluation, finding much that is interesting in films like *The Cruel Sea* (Charles Frend, 1953), *Angels One Five* (George More O'Ferrall, 1952), and even *The Dam Busters* (Michael Anderson, 1955), but he draws the line at 'that seminal text of romanticised distortion', *Reach for the Sky* (Lewis Gilbert, 1956).

Reach for the Sky was the top box-office film of 1956, and unlike films such as *Scott of the Antarctic* (Charles Frend, 1948) and *The Magic Box* (John Boulting, 1951), which were devoted to honourable failures, it dealt with a successful British hero. Douglas Bader's brand of cheery, dogged masculinity captured with aplomb by Kenneth More seems unfashionable now, but it caught the public imagination. Never again would Britishness be celebrated on the screen with such uncritical enthusiasm. By the end of 1956 British confidence had been shaken by the Suez débâcle. War films – such as David Lean's *The Bridge on the River Kwai* (1957), Anthony Asquith's *Orders to Kill* (1958) and Val Guest's *Yesterday's Enemy* (1959) – became darker and more unsure of themselves.

The old guard at Pinewood themselves saw their authority and respect eroded as their ebullient certainties crumbled. The other phenomenal successes of 1956 were John Osborne's play, *Look Back in Anger*, Colin Wilson's book, *The Outsider*, and the low-budget American film, *Rock around the Clock*. The Angry Young Men and rock and roll had arrived. Retrospectively, *Reach for the Sky* conjures up images of the band playing on the *Titanic* as the ship slips majestically beneath the water line. It is less for nostalgia (there are more resonant war films than this) than as a record of a set of feelings and beliefs that have now almost completely disappeared that *Reach for the Sky* is invaluable.

6. Hell Is a City

Crime films are an essential element of British cinema – country-house whodunits in the 30s, spiv movies and the huge array of non-generic crime films of the late 40s explored by Raymond Durgnat in this book, police investigation films in the 50s which prepared the way for popular television series like *Dixon of Dock Green*, *Z Cars* and *The Sweeney*. But as television took the middle ground, the cinema began to be more critical and adventurous. A key element in this process was the emergence of Stanley Baker as a major actor.[9] He played numerous minor roles in the late 40s and 50s before finding a satisfying screen persona as a tough but sensitive ex-convict trying to go straight in *Hell Drivers* (Cy Endfield, 1957).

The most significant of Baker's minor roles was in *The Cruel Sea*, as an officer who is not quite a gentleman and is soon removed from Jack Hawkins's efficient ship. Baker had a symbolic revenge by replacing Hawkins as Britain's leading screen detective in the late 50s. In Basil Dearden's *Violent Playground* (1958) he plays a detective unwillingly drafted into service as a community police-man; in Joseph Losey's *Blind Date* (1959) he is an up-from-the-ranks Scotland Yard detective bitterly aware that he has the wrong background and the wrong atti-tude to climb any further up the ladder; and in Val Guest's *Hell Is a City* (1960), made for Hammer (in Hammerscope), he is an overworked policeman with an unhappy home life.

Guest, who had entered the industry in the 30s as a scriptwriter (responsible for films like Will Hay's *Oh, Mr Porter!*), is an uncelebrated director but he is idiosyn-cratic enough to qualify as an auteur. Between 1960 and 1964 he made four films – *Hell Is a City*, *Jigsaw* (1962), *80,000 Suspects* (1963), *The Beauty Jungle* (1964) – shot mainly on location with cinematographer Arthur Grant (who had been John Baxter's camera operator in the 40s). All of them are flawed films in the sense that their elements don't quite gel, but they are also inven-tive, lively and quirky.

The title sequence of *Hell Is a City*, with a police car rushing though night-time streets, seems to promise an American police thriller; the end, with Baker turning away from his chance of a loving relationship and wan-dering off into the rainy night, seems more like an angst-ridden European art movie. What is between is very English. Baker's Inspector Martineau tracks an escaped killer he's known since schooldays and eventu-ally traps him on a roof-top. The chase is dogged and thorough rather than dangerous and exciting, but the incidental detail thrown up – a dodgy pub landlord and his saucy, sensual barmaid; small-time crooks in their billiard halls and backstreet garages; the long-suffering bookie and his flighty wife; a pitch-and-toss game out-side a Lancashire moorland village – jostle for attention in a vividly realised provincial world. Guest is never one to shun a cliché and he is hampered by a maladroitly cast villain, but *Hell Is a City* is a landmark on the road from the staid but visually impressive Scotland Yard films of the 50s to the gritty realism of *Z Cars*.

7. The Reckoning

By the end of the 60s tawdriness and indulgence had infiltrated the British film industry. Some films have acquired a historical fascination as records of unlikely performances: Maureen Lipman as a loud-mouthed Battersea tart in *Up the Junction* (Peter Collinson, 1968),

Joanna Lumley as a revolutionary LSE student in *The Breaking of Bumbo* (Andrew Sinclair, 1970), John Thaw as a Trotskyist activist in *Praise Marx and Pass the Ammunition* (Maurice Hatton, 1970). But what saved the cinema from the bathos of Swinging London was the infusion of talented television directors who brought a fresh infusion of realism to British cinema.

Jack Gold's *The Reckoning* (1969) is a relentlessly flashy film, full of obtrusive camera movements and ugly close-ups, but it has a raw energy that makes it as compelling to watch as a Tarantino film. Nicol Williamson plays a working-class Liverpudlian who has got on in business and acquired a beautiful middle-class wife (Ann Bell) and a house in Virginia Water. The sus-picious death of his father back in Liverpool coincides with marital breakdown and a ruthless boardroom power struggle to throw his life into crisis.

The social rise of a working-class man is a key theme of 60s cinema. In *Room at the Top* (Jack Clayton, 1959), Joe Lampton (Laurence Harvey) finds the path to the top he no longer wants opened by the boss's daughter, whom he has made pregnant; in *Nothing but the Best* (Clive Donner, 1964), Alan Bates murders his aristocratic mentor when he threatens to expose him as a working-class chancer. Six years of a Labour govern-ment changed the ethos of British society. Though classlessness and equality of opportunity were far from fully realised ideals, *The Reckoning* reflects a world where doors to the top could be opened if they were given a sufficiently vigorous kick. This Williamson sup-plies with convincing gusto, employing a Machiavellian energy in using his friends and disposing of his ene-mies.[10] Getting drunk, driving badly, indulging in adul-terous relationships are cathartic releases of energy rather than fatal flaws, and he ends the film exultantly successful. As *The Reckoning* reminds us, the 60s wasn't just about peace and love.

8. Bad Timing

In 1977 the Rank Organisation, in a last-ditch bid to revive its film-making activities, embarked on a £10-million production programme. Unfortunately all but one of the films were marred by 'a fatal sense of unad-venturous orthodoxy'.[11] The exception was *Bad Timing* (1980), the most unlikely Rank film since Powell and Pressburger presented a bemused J. Arthur Rank with *A Canterbury Tale* in 1944. With Art Garfunkel and Theresa Russell as Americans in Vienna, Harvey Keitel as an Austrian policeman and Denholm Elliott convinc-ingly cast as a sad-eyed Czech, one could be forgiven for wondering if this is a British film at all, particularly as it confronts sex with un-English forthrightness. But it bears the unmistakable mark of its director, Nicolas Roeg.

Roeg's first film, *Performance* (1970), had been considered decadent, but it could be blamed on his co-director, Donald Cammell, an unstable figure compared to Roeg, a brilliant cameraman with a long apprenticeship in the industry. The films that followed – *Walkabout* (1971), *Don't Look Now* (1973) and *The Man Who Fell to Earth* (1976) – while quirky and sophisticated, were by no means outrageous. Hence *Bad Timing*, a disturbing tale of passion and sexual violence, with clean-cut Garfunkel as smoothly evil as a concentration-camp commander, shocked critics and audiences as well as Rank executives. Alex (Garfunkel), a professor of psychiatry working in Vienna, has an affair with Milena (Russell), a footloose young cosmopolitan. He is possessive and resentful of her friendships with other men, and when she refuses his offer of marriage he becomes increasingly brutal towards her. Answering her distress call after a drugs overdose, he rapes her while her life ebbs away.

As in *I Know Where I'm Going*, at the film's core there is a clash of values. In Powell and Pressburger's film, Joan has her busy, rational life disrupted, but her awakening to the beauty and terror of the world is untraumatic and she emerges as a more mature and whole person. In *Bad Timing*, Milena is spontaneous, natural, responsive to her environment, and she is destroyed by Alex's insistence on order and convention. His sexual obsession – concealed beneath a veneer of cool rationality – drives him to seek out the dark, unexplored nooks and crannies of her life, making her ever more defenceless and vulnerable.

Such a film was as welcome as a corpse at a children's party and the Rank Organisation refused to show it in its cinemas and abandoned film production for good.

9. High Hopes

The British film industry underwent unpleasant shock therapy under Thatcherism. The quota system ensuring that all cinemas showed a percentage of British films was abandoned in 1982; the Films Act of 1985 abolished the Eady Levy and pulled the plug on the National Film Finance Corporation.[12] British films continued to be made but the infrastructure that ensured they reached an audience was kicked away. In Carlos Castaneda's *Tales of Power*, Don Juan explains that the Spanish invasion of

Mexico was a disaster for the Indians but a marvellous opportunity for the sorcerers. All the energy that had found expression in the culture of Indian society was suppressed and channelled underground into sorcery.[13] Seventeen years of Tory rule were similarly disastrous for the British film industry, but a clutch of films emerged which made a powerful riposte to the Thatcherite ideology of self-interest and materialism.[14] One of the most effective is Mike Leigh's *High Hopes*.

Despite his uniqueness as a perceptive, wryly humorous observer of British society, Leigh's refusal to work with a conventional script (his stories evolve out of extensive improvisation) barred him from most sources of film funding, and between *Bleak Moments* (1971) and *High Hopes* (1988) all his films were made on tiny budgets for television. *High Hopes*, largely funded by Channel 4 but released as a feature film, is not stylistically different from Leigh's television work, though the more generous budget allowed for more extensive location-shooting. The film centres upon three couples – Cyril and Shirley, Laetitia and Rupert, Valerie and Martin, and an old lady, Mrs Bender, who is Cyril and Valerie's mother and Rupert and Laetitia's nextdoor neighbour. Valerie and Martin are familiar Leigh stereotypes: they are vulgar, boorish, offensively loud and have more money than sense. Laetitia and Rupert are Thatcherite yuppies. Cyril and Shirley are gauche, left-wing relics of an earlier era.

In most Mike Leigh films characters are combustible mixtures of the unspeakable and the winsome. Characters who appear as embarrassingly awful eventually reveal some touchingly human trait, and those who start out as sweetly reasonable show unexpected quirks and kinks. In *High Hopes*, Leigh allows a political dimension to creep in, encouraging us to feel unalloyed hostility to Laetitia and Rupert and to develop a close identification with Cyril and Shirley. In the sequence that brings these disparate characters together, Mrs Bender locks herself out and has to rely on the reluctant hospitality of Laetitia and Rupert while she waits for one of her offspring to arrive with a spare key. They make her pay for the privilege of sitting in their kitchen by subjecting her to a barrage of questions about the run-down state of her house and garden, revealing a set of values which exclude compassion, consideration and tolerance. No doubt these are qualities the rich have always lacked, but in British films they tend to be shown as cuddly eccentrics with hearts of gold, and Laetitia and Rupert's callousness comes as a shock.[15]

To balance this, there is a more definite resolution than Leigh normally allows. After a disastrous birthday party, Cyril and Shirley take Mrs Bender home with them. They are all slightly drunk. Cyril gives up his opposition to the idea of having a baby, and in the morning Mrs Bender seems to have emerged from her state of catatonic misery. This is not very high on the scale of human happiness, but it is enough to imbue the film with optimism rather than despair.

10. Riff-Raff

Mrs Thatcher resigned in November 1990. The films released in 1991, though too early to connect with her political demise, nevertheless seemed to signify a new mood. In Alan Parker's adaptation of Roddy Doyle's *The Commitments*, Mike Leigh's *Life Is Sweet*, Hanif Kureishi's *London Kills Me*, there is a new concern with young people, and a feeling of trying to make the best of an absurd, unjust world. Ken Loach's *Riff-Raff* is unusual in that it endorses violent direct action, but it shares the same mood.

Given how much the cause of the working class had been set back by Thatcherism, *Riff-Raff* is remarkably cheerful. An insistence on the need to fight back, and not to be destroyed by the system, unites the two parts of the film: building workers converting what had been a hospital into luxury flats, and a relationship between one of the young workers and a girl whose illusions about life and reliance on drugs ill equip her to survive in the harsh world of the underclass.

Stevie (Robert Carlyle) is sharp, cautious, realistic – the extent of his high hopes is to have a market stall selling boxer shorts – but his decision to ditch his girlfriend, for fear of being dragged into the nightmare world of drug addiction, is shown as sad and painful rather than as a necessary and inevitable step on his path towards success. Her boldness in confronting him at the building site shows her to be something more than a pathetic deadbeat, and the loss of the warmth and sensuality of her company darkens Stevie's world and pushes him towards the cathartic revenge with which the film ends.

Riff-Raff's combination of comedy and tragedy, social criticism and concern for the lives of ordinary people sums up much of what is best in British cinema. There are other things which are absent from Loach's film – sexuality, mysticism, the struggle to uncover a meaningful national identity – and these too are an essential part of British cinema.

11. Kiss of Life

Contemporary British cinema is very different from the tawdry but eclectic cinema of the 1970s or the television-dominated cinema of the 1980s. Changing habits in viewing films presented new problems and opportunities, and from the mid-1990s film production benefited from an unprecedentedly generous level of government support. This has not always been administered wisely; but the emergence of a cine-literate generation of actors, directors, writers, cinematographers with a genuine interest in the cinema and a determination to make individual and distinctive films bodes well for the future. Asif Kapadia, Shona Auerbach, Emily Young, Mark Evans, Amma Asante, Jonathan Glazer, Chris Smith, Paul Spurrier, Marc Munden, Richard Jobson, David Mackenzie, Peter Webber, Joe Wright, Saul Metzstein, Ben Hopkins, Lynne Ramsay, Kirsten Sheridan, Shane Meadows, Simon Rumley, Penny Woolcock, Edgar Wright and Michael Winterbottom, not to mention the American-based Sam Mendes and Christopher Nolan constitute a hitherto unsuspected generation of talented young film-makers around which a viable British cinema might be expected to grow.

Not that the problems that have traditionally plagued British cinema have gone away. If one takes out the American-financed James Bond and Harry Potter films, British films command a smaller share of the box office than at any time since the 1920s, and less than half the films made between 2000 and 2005 were given a limited theatrical release in the UK and Ireland. Consequently film production is precarious and often unprofitable.[16] Channel 4, BBC Films, and the UK Film Council are committed to supporting British films, but generally only as partners in complicated co-production deals that sometimes take years to set up.

Emily Young's *Kiss of Life* (2003) is typical of one strand of this new British cinema. It is an ambitious attempt to imbue an English social realist drama (the original title was *Helen of Peckham*) with the visionary concerns of a director like Krzysztof Kieślowski. The film charts the desperate attempt by aid worker Peter Mullan to get back from the war-torn Balkans to deal with a crisis in his own family life, though its real concern is death and the aura that gathers around those recently deceased. By tragic coincidence Katrin Cartlidge, who was to have played Helen, died suddenly two weeks before shooting began. She was replaced by the Lithuanian actress Ingeborga Dapkunaite, who along with Mullan and the rest of the cast gives an

Kiss of Life: Ingeborga Dapkunaite and Peter Mullan

impressively convincing performance. Helen's death early in the film is disconcerting and the poetic conceit of her ghost returning to reassure and comfort her family risks sentimentality ('never mind, I might be dead but I'm still with you') and obscurity (is she really dead? 'is this a flashback to when she was alive or are we in the realm of the supernatural?). But Young makes it work, and the father's homecoming, when he will discover that despite all the risks he has taken and the hazards he has overcome he is too late to patch things up with his wife, appears not as a tragic denouement but as an affirmation. Unlike the Bosnian woman who befriends him on the bus, he still has a family to return to.

Ben Hopkins and Asif Kapadia both worry about the increasing difficulties faced by film-makers wishing to make unusual, artistically ambitious, not obviously commercial films.[17] Art cinema has always had to struggle for survival in the UK (and to be fair, in most other countries too), but it is something of a paradox that when the UK Film Council is gifted unprecedentedly generous funds from the National Lottery, not only have obviously talented film-makers like Kapadia and Hopkins received little encouragement but there is seemingly no place for the internationally respected Terence Davies, or the invaluable maverick Alex Cox.[18] Several of the films celebrated here (including *Kiss of Life*) did have UK Film Council backing and I have no wish to take on the late Alexander Walker's mantle as the scourge of subsidised film-making. But funding which favours the middle of the road rather than the visionary will surely be the kiss of death to a British film industry that aims to be something more than a poor cousin to Hollywood.

Notes

1. Charles Barr, 'Before *Blackmail*: Silent British Cinema', Chapter 16 in the present volume.
2. Raymond Durgnat, *The Strange Case of Alfred Hitchcock* (London: Faber and Faber, 1974), p. 67.
3. Tom Milne (ed.), *Time Out Film Guide* (Harmondsworth: Penguin, 1989), p. 501.
4. See Anthony Aldgate and Geoff Brown, *John Baxter* (London, BFI, 1989), a modest attempt to rescue Baxter from obscurity.
5. Anstey's opinion of *Listen to Britain* quoted in Elizabeth Sussex, *The Rise and Fall of British Documentary* (Berkeley and London: University of California Press, 1975), p. 144. Anstey's review of *The Common Touch* is quoted in Aldgate and Brown, *John Baxter*, p. 85.
6. Kevin Gough-Yates, 'Exiles and British Cinema', Chapter 14 in the present volume.
7. Neil Rattigan, 'The Last Gasp of the Middle Class: British War Films of the 1950s', in Wheeler Winston Dixon (ed.), *Re-viewing British Cinema, 1990–1992* (New York: State University of New York Press, 1994), p. 150.
8. Andy Medhurst, '1950s War Films', in Geoff Hurd (ed.), *National Fictions* (London: BFI, 1984), p. 35.
9. See Andrew Spicer, 'Male Stars, Masculinity and British Cinema, 1945–60', Chapter 32 in the present volume.
10. For a brief period Nicol Williamson looked to be the best actor of his generation. His Hamlet in Tony Richardson's production at the Roundhouse in London, saved for posterity in Richardson's concise adaptation (1970), stands up well against the performances of Laurence Olivier, Mel Gibson and Kenneth Branagh.
11. The judgment – a fair one – is Alexander Walker's. See his *National Heroes* (London: Harrap, 1985), pp. 204–8, a useful account of the Rank production venture. The films were: *Wombling Free* (Lionel Jeffries, 1977), *The 39 Steps* (Don Sharp, 1978), *The Lady Vanishes* (Anthony Page, 1979), *The Riddle of the Sands* (Tony Maylam, 1979), *Tarka the Otter* (David Cobham, 1979), *Eagle's Wing* (Anthony Harvey, 1979) and *Silver Dream Racer* (David Wickes, 1980).
12. The Eady Levy was, in part, a subsidy for British films calculated in relation to their box-office performance; the NFFC was a government film bank that nursed hundreds of British films into production throughout the 1950s, 60s and 70s.
13. Carlos Castaneda, *Tales of Power* (London: Hodder & Stoughton, 1975), p. 140.
14. See Lester Friedman, 'The Empire Strikes Out', in Friedman (ed.), *Fires Were Started: British Cinema and Thatcherism* (Minneapolis: University of Minnesota Press,

1993), pp. 10–11. 'British films of this period could not help being political (in the broadest sense of the word) as they charted the inexorably downward spiral of their homeland. . . . Though driven by their hatred of the present government, these visual artists still managed to tease the permanent out of the momentary. They instinctively understood that Mrs Thatcher's ideology, her creation and re-creation of past and present history, must be matched by an alternative vision that offered a different version of this era. . . . Their pictures defined a turbulent era, revived the moribund British cinema, and froze a crucial moment in British culture.' See also, in the same book, the essay by Leonard Quart, 'The Religion of the Market: Thatcherite Politics and the British Film of the 1980s', pp. 15–34.

15. Compare, for example, *A Severed Head* (Dick Clements, 1970), where the world is seen from the point of view of a Rupert-like character.

16. 'Out of 871 UK films certified between 2000 and 2005, only 414 (47.5%) had been theatrically released in the UK and the Republic of Ireland by 4 March 2007', <www.ukfilmcouncil.org.uk/information/statistics/yearbook> 2006–7.

17. Hopkins in his director's commentary on the DVD release of *Simon Magus*; Kapadia in his interview with Virginie Sélavy in the electronic journal *Electric Sheep*, <www.electricsheepmagazine.co.uk/features/2007/10/21/interview-with-asif-kapadia>.

18. As a journalist in the early 80s I can remember interviewing Mamoun Hassan, then Head of the National Film Finance Corporation, in a cramped, dowdy office in Holborn, his staff seemed to consist of a kindly secretary who made us both a cup of tea. The UK Film Council occupies a large West End office building, has a staff running into hundreds and maintains an office in Los Angeles. This might all be necessary but it has uncomfortable echoes of the grandiloquent pretensions of London Films, the Rank Organisation, EMI and Goldcrest when they decided to compete in the American market.

Index

Note: page numbers in *italics* indicate illustrations; those in **bold** indicate displayed sections.

List of Illustrations

Whilst considerable effort has been made to correctly identify the copyright holders this has not been possible in all cases. We apologise for any apparent negligence and any omissions or corrections brought to our attention will be remedied in any future editions.

Simon Magius, Film Four Ltd/Arts Council of England/Hollywood Partners; *The Company of Wolves*, © ITC Entertainment; *The Small Back Room*, Archers Film Productions/London Film Productions; *Vera Drake*, © Untitled 03 Limited/Films Alain Sarde/UK Film Council; *Chariots of Fire*, Enigma Productions/Twentieth Century Fox Film Corporation/Allied Stars; *Gregory's Girl*, © National Film Trustee Company Ltd; *The Low Down*, © FilmFour/© Low Down Films Ltd; *Hideous Kinky*, © Film Consortium/© L Films; *The Common Touch*, British National Films; *Poor Cow*, Fenchurch Films Ltd/Vic Films; *Naked*, Thin Man Films/Film Four International/British Screen; *This Sporting Life*, Independent Artists; *O Lucky Man!*, © Warner Bros.; *The Remains of the Day*, Merchant Ivory Productions Ltd; *A Man for All Seasons*, Highland Films; *Anne of the Thousand Days*, Universal Pictures; *Tommy*, © Robert Stigwood Organisation; *Withnail & I*, © HandMade Films; *Jew Süss*, Gaumont-British Picture Corporation; *No Orchids for Miss Blandish*, Tudor Films/Alliance Film Studios Ltd; *The Devils*, © Warner Bros.; *North West Frontier*, © Rank Organisation Film Productions; *Where Eagles Dare*, © Metro-Goldwyn-Mayer; *Casino Royale*, Danjaq LLC/United Artists Corporation/Columbia Pictures Industries, Inc.; *The Ghoul*, Gaumont-British Picture Corporation; *House of Whipcord*, © Peter Walker (Heritage) Ltd; *The Last Great Wilderness*, © Sigma Films; *Somewhere in England*, Blakeley's Productions/Butcher's Film Service; *Passport to Pimlico*, © Ealing Studios; *Funny Bones*, Hollywood Pictures Company; *Men of Two Worlds*, Two Cities Films; *Pressure*, British Film Institute Production Board; *The Marriage of Corbal*, Capitol Film Corporation; *I Know Where I'm Going*, Archers Film Productions/Independent Producers/J. Arthur Rank Film Productions; *Another Country*, Eastern Counties Newspapers Group Ltd; *Sunday Bloody Sunday*, Vectia Films/Vic Films; *Comin' Thro' the Rye*, Hepworth Picture Plays; *The Farmer's Wife*, British International Pictures; *At the Villa Rose*, Stoll Film Company; *The Manxman*, British International Pictures; *A Cottage on Dartmoor*, British Constructional Films/Svensk filmindustri; *Drifters*, New Era Films; *Coal Face*, GPO Film Unit; *The Private Life of Henry VIII*, London Film Productions; *Scrooge*, Twickenham Film Studios Productions; *Music Hall*, Twickenham Film Studios Productions; *The Ghost Camera*, Real Art Productions; *Tangled Evidence*, Twickenham Film Studios Productions; *Piccadilly*, British International Pictures; *The Tunnel*, Gaumont-British Picture Corporation; *The Lodger*, Twickenham Film Studios Productions; *The Love Test*, Fox-British Pictures; *Love on the Dole*, British National Films; *Tawny Pipit*, Two Cities Films; *Madonna of the Seven Moons*, Gainsborough Pictures; *Bedelia*, John Corfield Productions; *The Challenge*, London Film Productions; *The Red Shoes*, © Independent Producers; *Dual Alibi*, British National Films; *The Trojan Brothers*, British National Films; *Cheer Boys Cheer*, Associated Talking Pictures/Ealing; *Saloon Bar*, Ealing Studios; *The Kidnappers*, © Group Film Productions; *No Love for Johnnie*, Five Star Films; *The Card*, British Film Makers Ltd; *A Tale of Two Cities*, Rank Organisation Film Productions; *Rob Roy, the Highland Rogue*, Walt Disney Productions; *Dance Hall*, Ealing Studios; *Woman in a Dressing Gown*, Godwin-Willis Productions/Associated British Picture Corporation; *Corridor of Mirrors*, Cartier-Romney Productions/Apollo Films; *Reach for the Sky*, Pinnacle Productions; *A Taste of Honey*, Woodfall Film Productions; *Beat Girl*, Renown Pictures Corporation; *Hell is a City*, Hammer Film Productions/Associated British Picture Corporation; *Darling*, Vic Films/Appia Films; *Here We Go Round the Mulberry Bush*, Giant Film Productions; *Joanna*, Laughlin Films; *Mademoiselle*, Woodfall Film Productions/Procinex; *Don't Look Now*, © D.L.N. Ventures Partnership; *The Devils*, © Warner Bros.; *Sebastiane*, © Disctac; *The Draughtman's Contract*, British Film Institute Production Board; *Late Night Shopping*, © Film Four Ltd/© Glasgow Film Office/Film Four; *Un Nos Ola' Leuad/ One Full Moon*, Gaucho Cyf; *Gadael Lenin/ Leaving Lenin*, Gaucho Cyf; *Solomon and Gaenor*, APT Film and Television; *Martha, Meet Frank, Daniel and Laurence*, Channel Four Television Corporation/Banshee/Channel 4 Films; *This Year's Love*, Entertainment Film Distributors Ltd/Kismet Film Company/Scottish Arts Council Lottery Fund; *Enduring Love*, © Pathé Fund Ltd; *An Ideal Husband* (1949), London Film Productions; *An Ideal Husband* (1999), Ideal Film Company Ltd/Fragile Films; *Snatch*, © Columbia Pictures Industries, Inc.; *Gangster No. 1*, © No. 1 Films Ltd/© Road Movies Filmproduktion GmbH; *My Son the Fanatic*, © Son of Zephyr Ltd; *East Is East*, © Film Four Ltd; *Far North*, Dreamachine; *Control*, © Northsee Ltd; *V for Vendetta*, © Warner Bros. Entertainment Inc.; *Three Businessmen*, Exterminating Angel Productions/VPRO; *This is England*, © Warp Films/© FilmFour/© UK Film Council/© EM Media/© Screen Yorkshire; *Rich and Strange*, British International Pictures; *Kiss of Life*, © Wild Horses Film Company Ltd/© Haut et Court SARL/© France 3 Cinéma/© Gimages Films.